MARKETING AND ADVERTISING REGULATION
THE FEDERAL TRADE COMMISSION IN THE 1990S

Marketing and Advertising Regulation

THE FEDERAL TRADE COMMISSION IN THE 1990S

Edited by
PATRICK E. MURPHY AND WILLIAM L. WILKIE

UNIVERSITY OF NOTRE DAME
NOTRE DAME   LONDON

© 1990
University of Notre Dame Press
Notre Dame, Indiana 46556
All Rights Reserved

Manufactured in the United States of America

Library of Congress Cataloging-in-Publication Data

Marketing and advertising regulation : the Federal Trade Commission
in the 1990s / edited by Patrick E. Murphy and William L. Wilkie.
   p. cm.
   ISBN 0-268-01382-9 — ISBN 0-268-01383-7 (pbk.)
   1. United States. Federal Trade Commission—Congresses.
2. Trade regulation—United States—Congresses. I. Murphy,
Patrick E., 1948–   II. Wilkie, William L.
KF1611.M37 1990
353.0082'6—dc20   90-34520
                              CIP

To Our Families
Kate, Bobby, Brendan, and Jamie
Barbara, Billy, Allie, and Jimmy

Contents

PART II. THE PAST AS PROLOGUE

The FTC's Recent History

The FTC's First Fifty Years

PART III. THE CONTRIBUTIONS
TO PUBLIC POLICY BY MARKETING ACADEMICS

Marketing Insiders at the Agency

Contents

PART IV. THE 1990S:
POLICY RESEARCH IN MARKETING AND
REGULATION

Acknowledgments

We wish to extend our gratitude to a number of people who helped make this book possible. First and foremost, we want to thank the contributors to the volume. They have demonstrated their commitment to a more effective FTC by first delivering provocative talks to our symposium, then by converting the contents into publishable manuscripts. We have much appreciated their professionalism and conscientiousness throughout this process.

Second, we wish to extend our appreciation to the several sponsors of our symposium and this book. At the University of Notre Dame, Provost Timothy O'Meara, and Deans Yusaku Furuhashi and John Keane offered enthusiastic support for a high-quality forum to investigate public policy research in marketing. Professor David Leege, head of the Hesburgh Program in Public Service at Notre Dame, also provided financial assistance and help in extending our reach into the other departments and colleges of the University. Our Department of Marketing chairman, Joseph Guiltinan, offered departmental financial and administrative support throughout the project. Also, the Aloysius and Eleanor Nathe Chair endowment helped to support the symposium and this volume. Outside of Notre Dame, we wish also to thank Thomas Kinnear, associate dean of the School of Business Administration at the University of Michigan, and the founding editor of the *Journal of Public Policy & Marketing*. Tom arranged for financial support from the University of Michigan for this project and personally provided us with encouragement and ideas from the very start.

Because this book was produced on disk, it required considerable clerical and student support from the able staff at our College of Business Administration. We wish to single out the superb contributions of Dee Sequin, who has served as an administrative assistant and executive secretary for over a year on this project. We also want to recognize the secretarial support provided by Diane Bandurski, Wendy Harmon, Greta Hoisington, Jeanette Phillips, and Madeline Day, who patiently transformed copyedited manuscript into final form. Students from Notre Dame's MBA program assisted us in the research and editing phases of this book. They are Edward Balog, Barbara Chisolm, Greg Pellegrino, Elizabeth Wholihan, and Linda Zucker.

At the University of Notre Dame Press, several people worked to help us turn these papers into the book which you are now holding. We want to thank Jim Langford, director of the Press, for his enthusiasm for this project and his willingness to work with us to create a quality product. Ann Rice, as executive editor, and Gregory Rockwell, as production manager, made significant contributions, as did assistant editor Jeannette Sheerin, who exhibited aplomb while keeping us on schedule and copyediting the entire volume.

To all these people, we offer our heartfelt thanks. Without their support and efforts this book would not have been possible.

PEM
WLW

Contributors

ALAN R. ANDREASEN is professor and chair of the department of marketing at California State University, Long Beach. He has written extensively in public policy issues dealing with nonprofit organizations and social marketing. Alan holds a Ph.D. from Columbia University.

WILLIAM J. BAER is a partner at Arnold & Porter in Washington, D.C., specializing in antitrust and trade regulation matters. He is a former attorney advisor to FTC Chairman Michael Pertschuk and was also FTC assistant general counsel for legislation and congressional relations. Bill received his J.D. from Stanford Law School.

J. HOWARD BEALES, III, is an assistant professor of business administration at George Washington University. Professor Beales held several appointments at the FTC including assistant to the director and associate director for policy and education. He has published numerous articles on the economics of information and consumer protection. Howard received his Ph.D. in economics from the University of Chicago.

KENNETH L. BERNHARDT is Regents Professor of Marketing at Georgia State University. He is a past-president of the Association for Consumer Research and is currently chairman of the board of the American Marketing Association. He served as director of Office of Impact Evaluation in the Bureau of Consumer Protection at the FTC. Ken holds a Ph.D. from the University of Michigan.

PAUL N. BLOOM is professor of marketing at the University of North Carolina at Chapel Hill. Professor Bloom is editor of the JAI Press series *Advances in Marketing and Public Policy*. His research on consumerism, antitrust, consumer education, and consumer protection has been published in a wide variety of journals and monographs. Paul holds a Ph.D. from Northwestern University.

JOHN E. CALFEE is associate professor of marketing at Boston University. He served in the Bureau of Economics at the Federal Trade Commission, where he was the primary economic advisor on the FTC's policy statements on deception (1983) and advertising substantiation (1984). Jack holds a Ph.D. in economics from the University of California at Berkeley.

STEPHEN CALKINS is professor of law at Wayne State University. He is a specialist in antitrust matters and was the major author of the Report of the ABA's Special Committee to Study the Role of the Federal Trade Commission. He served as an attorney advisor at the FTC. Steve holds a J.D. from Harvard Law School.

JOEL B. COHEN is Distinguished Service Professor (Marketing and Anthropology) at the University of Florida. He is a past-president of the Association for Consumer Research and has served as a consultant and expert for the FTC on numerous consumer protection matters. He has written extensively on consumer information processing and other consumer behavior topics. Joel holds a Ph.D. from UCLA.

GARY T. FORD is professor of marketing at American University. He is a former staff member and consultant to the FTC's Bureau of Economics specializing in consumer protection matters. He has written extensively on public policy issues in marketing. Gary holds a Ph.D. from SUNY-Buffalo.

STEPHEN A. GREYSER is professor of marketing at the Harvard Business School. He is a former executive director of the Marketing Science Institute and currently heads the editorial board of the *Harvard*

Business Review. He has served as an expert in FTC's hearings on advertising practices and is widely published in advertising and corporate communications. Steve holds a D.B.A. from Harvard University.

GREGORY T. GUNDLACH is assistant professor of marketing at the University of Notre Dame. He is a former staff member in the FTC's Bureau of Competition and is examining legal issues in marketing in his research on both competitive practices and consumer protection. Greg holds both a J.D. and Ph.D. from the University of Tennessee.

CASWELL O. HOBBS, III, is a partner at Morgan, Lewis & Bockius in Washington, D.C. He is former assistant to the chairman and director, Office of Policy Planning and Evaluation at the FTC. He is a council member for the ABA Section of Antitrust Law and a member of the ABA's Special Committee to Study the Role of the FTC. Cas holds an LL.B. from the University of Pennsylvania.

H. KEITH HUNT is professor of marketing at Brigham Young University. He is a past-president of the Association for Consumer Research and served as an in-house consultant on consumer protection at the FTC and has written extensively on the regulation of advertising. Keith holds a Ph.D. from Northwestern University.

MARY GARDINER JONES is president of the Consumer Interest Research Institute. She is a former FTC commissioner and vice-president of Consumer Affairs at Western Union. Mary holds her law degree from Yale University.

HAROLD H. KASSARJIAN is professor of marketing at UCLA. He is a past-president of the Association for Consumer Research and a former editor of *Journal of Consumer Research*. He served as an in-house consultant on consumer protection at the FTC and is widely published in advertising and consumer behavior. Hal holds a Ph.D. in psychology from UCLA.

JOHN G. KEANE is the Martin J. Gillen Dean of the College of Business Administration at the University of Notre Dame where he also holds the Korth Chair in Strategic Management. He is the immediate past director of the U.S. Bureau of the Census, a past-president of the American Marketing Association and a former president of Managing Change, Inc. Jack holds a Ph.D. in Economics from the University of Pittsburgh.

THOMAS C. KINNEAR is associate dean and professor of marketing at the University of Michigan. He has served as a consultant on consumer protection to the FTC. He is widely published on marketing research issues related to public policy, is the founding editor of the *Journal of Public Policy & Marketing* and is currently the editor of the *Journal of Marketing*. Tom holds a Ph.D. from the University of Michigan.

WILLIAM C. MACLEOD is the director of the Bureau of Consumer Protection of the Federal Trade Commission. He was formerly director of the Chicago regional office of the FTC and an attorney advisor for former Chairman James C. Miller, III, of the Commission. Bill received his law degree from the University of Miami's Law and Economics Center.

THOMAS J. MARONICK is an associate professor of marketing at Towson State University and a current consultant in marketing and advertising research for the FTC. He is a former head of the Office of Impact Evaluation in the Bureau of Consumer Protection. Tom holds a D.B.A. in marketing from the University of Kentucky and a J.D. from the University of Baltimore.

MICHAEL B. MAZIS is professor of marketing at American University. He is a former FTC staff member in the Office of Policy Planning, and has since consulted on numerous matters for the FTC and other federal and state agencies. He has written extensively on consumer behavior, especially in the area of consumer information. Mike holds a Ph.D. from Pennsylvania State University.

PATRICK E. MURPHY is professor of marketing at the University of Notre Dame. He served in the Office of Management Planning in the FTC's Bureau of Consumer Protection. He is widely published in the area of marketing ethics and is the current editor of *Journal of Public Policy & Marketing*. Pat holds a Ph.D. from the University of Houston.

JANIS K. PAPPALARDO is a staff economist at the FTC. She has analyzed consumer protection cases, reviewed empirical studies conducted by outside researchers, and currently is working on an economic analysis of the regulation of health claims for foods. Jan holds a Ph.D. in consumer economics from Cornell University.

LINLEY PEARSON is the attorney general of the State of Indiana. He has been active in the National Association of Attorneys General (NAAG), and served as Prosecutor of Clinton County for ten years. Linley holds a law degree from Indiana University at Indianapolis.

BONNIE B. REECE is associate professor of advertising at Michigan State University. Her research interests include the consumer socialization of children, advertising management, and marketing regulation. Bonnie holds a Ph.D. from the University of Michigan.

ANN R. ROOT is assistant professor of marketing at the University of Notre Dame. Her areas of specialization include the utilization of marketing research, the development of public policy, and the regulation of deceptive advertising. Ann's Ph.D. is from the University of Michigan.

MARK SILBERGELD is director of the Washington office of Consumers Union, the nonprofit publisher of *Consumer Reports*. He is a former staff member of the FTC and also served as an attorney for Ralph Nader's Public Interest Research Group in Washington, D.C. Mark holds the J.D. from the Washington University (St. Louis) Law School.

BRUCE A. SILVERGLADE is legal affairs director of the Center for Science in the Public Interest (CSPI) where he coordinates CSPI's legislative and regulatory activities on food, environment and health matters. Mr. Silverglade has previously served in the Federal Trade Commission's Bureau of Consumer Protection and Office of Policy and Planning. Bruce received his law degree from Boston College.

DARLENE B. SMITH is assistant professor of marketing at Loyola College in Maryland. Her research interests focus on consumer behavior and public policy issues. Her current emphasis is on the economics of information, with implications for advertising regulation. Darlene holds a Ph.D. from the University of Maryland.

WALLACE S. SNYDER is senior vice-president of the American Advertising Federation. He is a former head of the National Advertising Division of the FTC and was lead attorney on the *Listerine* corrective advertising case. Wally holds a J.D. from the University of Iowa.

THOMAS H. STANTON is an attorney with the Washington firm of Olwine, Connelly, Chase, O'Donnell, and Weyher. He is the former acting and deputy director of the Office of Policy Planning at FTC under Chairmen Clanton and Pertschuk. He holds a J.D. degree from Harvard Law School.

LOUIS W. STERN is the John D. Gray Professor of Marketing at Northwestern University. He is a former executive director of the Marketing Science Institute and is widely published in marketing and channels of distribution topics. He has served as a consultant to the FTC's Bureau of Competition and is coauthor of *Legal Aspects of Marketing Strategy*. Lou holds a Ph.D. from Northwestern.

ANDREW J. STRENIO, JR., serves as a commissioner of the Federal Trade Commission. He was previously a member of the Interstate Commerce Commission and earlier served as assistant director for regulatory evaluation in the FTC's Bureau of Consumer Protection, supervising the Commission's intervention program. Andy holds a joint J.D./Master of Public Policy degree from the Law School and the Kennedy School of Government, Harvard University.

JOHN L. SWASY is associate professor of marketing at American University. He specializes in consumer behavior issues within marketing, including the study of how advertising decisions affect consumer behavior. Jack holds a Ph.D. in marketing from UCLA.

CHRISTIAN S. WHITE serves as assistant general counsel at the Federal Trade Commission. His previous FTC positions include assistant to the chairman and assistant director for special statutes in the Bureau of Consumer Protection. Chris holds a J.D. from the University of Pennsylvania Law School.

JOSHUA L. WIENER is associate professor of marketing at Oklahoma State University. He is a former staff economist at the FTC and has written several analyses of the Magnuson Moss/FTC Act. Josh holds a Ph.D. in economics from the University of North Carolina.

WILLIAM L. WILKIE is the Nathe Professor of Marketing at the University of Notre Dame. He is a past-president of the Association for Consumer Research and has written extensively on consumer behavior and public policy issues. He served as an in-house consultant to the Bureau of Consumer Protection at the FTC. Bill holds a Ph.D. from Stanford University.

MARY ELLEN ZUCKERMAN is research fellow at Columbia University's Gannett Center for Media Studies (on leave from the marketing faculty at SUNY Geneseo). She has written numerous articles in the area of business and marketing history. Mary Ellen holds both her doctorate in American History and an M.B.A. from Columbia University.

Prologue

There is an interesting story related to the development of this volume. In 1990, our office addresses read: "Hurley Building, University of Notre Dame." Seventy-five years ago, Edward N. Hurley, the donor of this building, was sworn in as one of the original commissioners and an early chairman of the Federal Trade Commission (FTC). This is one measure of the long-standing interest in public service and public policy on the part of the University of Notre Dame. Presently, three members of our marketing faculty are former staffers at the Federal Trade Commission, including the two editors of this book.

Our Purpose

Our purpose in developing this volume is to contribute to enlightened public policy in the regulation of marketing and advertising practices. Our interest is not limited to the FTC alone: we also wish to see the academic fields of marketing, consumer research, and economics improve their contributions to better public policy decisions. Within these pages, therefore, readers will discover a provocative set of ideas about public policy and business generally, and about the Federal Trade Commission's role in particular.

The volume is based upon a national symposium held at the University of Notre Dame in May 1989. Our purpose was both to commemorate the agency's seventy-fifth anniversary, and to provide a serious forum for assessing its future. A select group of fifty experts, primarily current and former FTC officials and a national roster of marketing academics (most of whom had also worked at the Commission), convened over a three-day period. For the names and backgrounds of the participants, see Contributors.

The symposium was designed to be nonpartisan: past and present government officials joined representatives from the legal, business, consumer, and academic sectors. Individuals holding both conservative and

1

liberal political views participated and offered their insights. As you will find in this volume, debate and discussions ranged from philosophy to politics, and from economic theory to agency operations. The analysis of the past and present creates a basis for informed discussion of the future. It is clear from these discussions that the Federal Trade Commission can be improved, and that public policy research in the future can assist in choosing wise courses and better achieving goals. It is our hope that this volume will contribute to both of these ends.

A Brief Background on the FTC

The Federal Trade Commission is the government agency charged with regulating most of the business marketing activity in our huge and diverse economy. The FTC was created in 1914 as an "independent" regulatory commission, presumably to buffer it from political pressures as administrations changed office (see Appendix I for the text of the original act). It was given only a vague mandate, affording flexibility in dealing with unforseen developments. Essentially, *this mandate requires the agency to provide our nation with a marketplace that is both efficient and fair, for both competitors and consumers*. In so doing, the FTC pursues basically two lines of regulation: (1) competitive structure and practices that involve firms relating to other firms and (2) consumer protection activities that involve firms' relationships with consumers.

Since its inception, however, this broad scope of responsibility, coupled with its vague mandate concerning the specific activities it should undertake, has led to harsh criticisms of the agency, both for being too active and for being too passive. In recent years the controversies have increased to extreme levels. As the FTC has been "captured" by the administrations in power—first the liberal regulators under President Carter, then the conservative deregulators under President Reagan— extreme swings in FTC philosophy and activity have resulted. Very recently, as it had in 1969, the American Bar Association (ABA) appointed a special committee to examine the FTC and recommend new directions for the agency as the Bush administration moves it toward the year 2000.

A Guide to This Volume

The volume is divided into four sections. **Part I, The FTC Today: Evaluations and Prescriptions,** begins with the 1989 ABA report (for interested readers, we have included the entire official report in Appendix II). This blue-ribbon committee of eighteen members was chaired by Miles Kirkpatrick, a former chairman of the FTC and also the chairman of the ABA's 1969 committee, whose report had led to dramatic changes at the agency during the 1970s. The counsel to the ABA committee, Stephen Calkins, leads off this section with a summary and overview of the committee's findings. The remainder of this section documents the positive and negative reactions of nine experts, representing a wide range of institutional vantage points, to the recommendations of the ABA report.

Part II, The Past as Prologue, presents the intimate details of FTC's history and allows the reader to appreciate better why its present status has been reached. This part features four historical overview papers. Three of these special papers focus on distinct periods within the last twenty years. They are written by prominent FTC officials—Mary Gardiner Jones (The FTC in 1968. . .), William Baer (The FTC in 1978), and Andrew Strenio (The FTC in 1988, 1989. . .). Two individuals who served at the Commission during each time period then offer commentaries reflecting their perspectives as attorneys, economists, and marketing academics. Mary Ellen Zuckerman, a marketing professor specializing in business history, contributes the fourth major commissioned paper in the part. She offers an informative overview of the first fifty years of the agency's history, showing why many of the issues faced throughout the early years of the agency have continued to appear in more recent times.

Part III is entitled **The Contributions to Public Policy by Marketing Academics.** For many readers this section will hold some surprises, as it chronicles the scope of expertise and experience marketing academics offer in relevant topic areas. It begins with a paper by Patrick Murphy, listing nearly thirty marketing professors who have worked at the FTC and assessing their impacts. Mary Gardiner Jones, the commissioner who originated the idea of bringing marketing input to the FTC, then comments on how this exchange has evolved over the past twenty years. The remainder of this part then departs from a focus on the FTC itself, to more broadly present a sampling of the current work marketing academics are undertaking on important regulatory problems. Included here are two papers on regulating the advertising and marketing of controversial products (alcohol and cigarettes), three papers evaluating the need for (and some effects of) regulation of advertising in general, and three papers advancing our understanding of how consumer information operates as a marketplace phenomenon and regulatory remedy.

Part IV of the book looks toward **The 1990s: Policy Research in Marketing and Regulation.** It begins with a provocative paper by John Keane on the changing business and social context for regulation, stimulating thoughts about whether some fundamental rethinking might be needed about the goals and methods of public policy in the coming decade and century. The part also includes overviews of the public policy literature in marketing and of the recent research at the FTC. These discussions set the stage for the priority research suggestions of five symposium participants, who reflect their training in marketing, economics, and the law to suggest some interesting and important projects for the future.

Thus this volume presents an opportunity for the interested reader to appreciate the past, present, and future of a key institution within the economic fabric of our society. The roster of concerned experts has put forward a rich compendium of ideas. We hope you will give these thoughts the attention they deserve.

Patrick E. Murphy
William L. Wilkie
South Bend, IN
February, 1990

PART I

The FTC Today:
Evaluations and Prescriptions

In this first part of the volume we examine current issues confronting the Federal Trade Commission. The part opens with a summary of the 1989 report from the special committee appointed by the American Bar Association. Its charge was to examine the performance and potentials of the FTC. Stephen Calkins, counsel to the ABA committee, provides a summary and overview of the committee's findings.

The remainder of the part documents the positive and negative reactions of nine experts to this report. These individuals represent a wide range of institutional vantage points: Caswell Hobbs is a Washington attorney and a member of the ABA special committee; Bruce Silverglade and Mark Silbergeld are consumer advocates with the Center for Science in the Public Interest and Consumers Union, respectively; Linley Pearson is the state attorney general for Indiana; Wallace Snyder is senior vice-president of the American Advertising Federation; Louis Stern and William Wilkie are marketing professors with interests in antitrust and consumer behavior, respectively; and William MacLeod was director of the Bureau of Consumer Protection at the FTC until just recently. Stephen Calkins, a law professor as well as counsel to the ABA Committee, ends the part by responding to the experts' comments about the report.

Counsel's Summary: The ABA Special Committee's Report on the FTC (Kirkpatrick II)

Stephen Calkins

The Report of the ABA Section of Antitrust Law Special Committee to Study the Role of the FTC has now been published.[1] The Committee was appointed in the spring of 1988 by Jim Rill, then the head of the Antitrust Section and currently assistant director in charge of the Justice Department's Antitrust Division. Rill charged the committee with studying the FTC and making recommendations concerning its role in American government. The assignment was to make prospective recommendations, not to prepare a report card on recent administrations. Rill and Miles Kirkpatrick, who had agreed to chair the committee, believed that the latter approach would yield only small dividends while causing deep divisions, given the diversity of political spectrums represented on the eighteen-member panel.[2] This paper will summarize and discuss briefly some of the committee's recommendations.[3]

FTC Structure and Staffing[4]

Leadership. Without first-rate leaders the FTC cannot function effectively. Commissioners should be persons of stature with an expertise that will contribute to the agency's mission.[5] That expertise can be legal, business, governmental, or academic[6]—categories that were drawn broadly (and, it would seem to me, would include marketing). The Commission's mandate and structure make it essential that its leaders enunciate a clear agenda and demonstrate "their belief in the agency and its mission."[7]

Resources. The FTC has 124 lawyers in its Bureau of Competition, 118 in its Bureau of Consumer Protection, and 115 in its regional offices.

This is not enough.[8] FTC workyears, which are only 53 percent of what they were a decade ago, should be increased.[9] At the same time, the FTC should manage its resources better. The management structure has not been adjusted to account for the agency's shrinkage, so as the numbers at lower levels have declined the agency has become top-heavy. The Report also questions a recent shift of resources to the regional offices.

Unity of Functions. The same five FTC commissioners issue and adjudicate complaints. This anomaly, which is at the heart of much administrative structure, has long troubled thoughtful observers.[10] A majority of the committee believes that the FTC has important prosecutorial and adjudicative roles and should retain both functions.[11] These committee members are comforted by the recognition that any perceived unfairness is more imagined than real, given the length of FTC proceedings and the relatively brief tenures of commissioners, and as evidenced by the willingness of the FTC to dismiss administrative complaints.[12]

The conclusion that the unity of functions should be retained was influenced by the dramatic change in the role that the FTC plays.[13] The typical FTC case once was initiated by an administrative complaint and resulted, if successful, in a cease and desist order. This changed somewhat during the 1970s when the agency engaged in a flurry of rulemaking projects, many of which were terminated after President Reagan took office. Today the agency's typical exercise is a lawsuit in federal court: in 1988 more than half of its cases were filed there. The administrative law judge (ALJ) docket has fallen from sixty-three pending cases in 1979 to fifteen in each of 1987 and 1988. Not surprisingly, the number of FTC ALJs has fallen commensurately, from thirteen in 1980 to three today. In 1985 through 1987, FTC professional workyears expended on court and administrative adjudication were close, and in 1988 court workyears were twice as high—and these figures do not include workyears expended on court litigation by the general counsel's office.[14] Since the FTC relies on administrative adjudication much less than it once did, the tensions caused by that process are less severe.

Consumer Protection[15]

Unfairness Cases. Although the FTC's unfairness jurisdiction has and perhaps always will attract attention,[16] there will be few good administrative unfairness cases. If conduct is egregiously unfair a cease and desist order is inadequate and unnecessary: the Commission should proceed directly with a section 13(b) suit for consumer redress. [17] If less egregious conduct is widespread, objections should be communicated widely through guides or rules. If less egregious conduct is only local, state governments will be the best enforcers. Finally, private parties will be the best challengers of some unfair conduct.

Nonetheless, there will be good unfairness cases. [18] Perhaps the best example is *Orkin Exterminating Co. v. FTC.*[19] This was the case in which the FTC challenged the systematic breaking of contractual obligations by the leading termite control company. This unfair practice was widespread, but private litigation was unlikely because the respondent had a colorable justification and individual damages were small. Other examples of good unfairness cases include *Holland Furnace Co. v. FTC.*,[20] in which home furnaces were sold by representatives who dismantled old furnaces and then refused to reassemble them promptly, and *Uncle Ben's Inc.*,[21] in which it was found to be unfair to sell rice with advertisements that appeared to encourage dangerous cooking practices.

Consumer fraud. The FTC's consumer fraud program has skyrocketed during the 1980s. Workyears expended on it have climbed from 13.06 in 1983 to 40.71 in 1988.[22] This troubles some observers, who worry that the FTC is treading where state enforcers, armed with criminal powers, should be in charge. The Report disagrees. The FTC's authority to proceed in federal court to obtain asset freezes and similar equitable relief, although not free from doubt originally, has become well established in recent years.[23] That authority and the easier standard of proof that civil enforcement enjoys give the FTC advantages compared to other enforcers. To be sure, this is an area in which coordination with state enforcers is important, but there is an important role for the FTC.

Advertising. The Report's advertising recommendations were endorsed by *Advertising Age*, which added that the "ideas are basic enough to be embarrassing."[24] Committee members disagreed on whether the FTC has brought enough cases. Advertising workyears are down substantially, from 120 in 1979 to 53 in 1988.[25] Supporters of the current regime point out that between 1984 and 1988 the FTC brought twenty-five cases addressed to advertisements distributed nationally. Critics respond that almost half of these cases concerned dietary supplements, baldness cures, and tanning centers, and only six cases challenged advertisements shown on network television. Supporters and critics on the committee reached agreement on the following propositions: "[T]he FTC can and should do more to articulate its advertising law enforcement agenda. Most of us believe that the FTC properly hesitates before finding implied advertising claims, and is properly concerned about the risk of suppressing truthful advertising. But too rarely has the public received the message that the FTC believes it is important to move aggressively against false and deceptive advertising."[26] The Report also suggests that clearly illegal advertisements should be challenged directly in federal court under section 13(b).[27]

The Report devotes substantial attention to state advertising enforcement.[28] State attorneys general bring many worthwhile advertising cases (indeed, I think that some of the most harmfully misleading advertising occurs at the local level and would not be challenged except by a state attorney general). However, the committee was concerned about the hostility to pricing claims occasionally exhibited by state enforcers. It also was troubled by parts of the National Association of Attorneys General's guidelines on car rental and airline advertising practices.[29] State advertising enforcement, while beneficial in theory and often in practice, can harm the competitive process.

In any event, state enforcement will continue. The sooner the FTC acknowledges this and starts working closely with the states as allies, the better. The states' primary mission should address practices that harm consumers within single states; the FTC's primary mission should address practices that harm consumers in many states. For the system to work well, the FTC should encourage referrals to the preferable enforcement authority. Referrals to the FTC from states should be pursued seriously and expeditiously. In the rare instance when a state challenges an advertisement with substantial interstate effects that is beneficial to consumers and the competitive process—not just neutral, but beneficial—the FTC should consider publicly defending the advertisement, possibly even by amicus participation in the proceeding.

More generally, "the FTC should work with the states to shape a common advertising agenda."[30] Each has much to teach. Whereas the FTC enjoys more sophisticated economics capability, the states are more closely in touch with the actual concerns of consumers. For instance, the increased state activity is "a cry for greater FTC attention to pricing claims."[31] The FTC has come to appreciate perhaps too well that overly aggressive challenges to pricing claims may deter useful advertising. It has tended to forget that "pricing misrepresentations offend and may harm."[32] The FTC should promptly revise and then enforce its pricing guidelines. The larger lesson, however, is that the FTC no longer is the dominant advertising enforcer. It is no longer sufficient, if it ever was, to ask advertisers and the public to trust the FTC to challenge deceptive practices. Now that the FTC is only one player in the advertising game, it is incumbent upon the agency to publicize its thinking, explain its enforcement decisions (including its decisions not to file suits), and, in this way, educate and reassure other enforcers while permitting them to educate the FTC in return.

Antitrust[33]

Nonmerger antitrust. The FTC has an important nonmerger antitrust rule. The prototypical FTC antitrust case would involve an application of uncertain legal principles. Frequently this will require application of the rule of reason, but not exclusively. For instance, questionable conduct might arguably qualify for an antitrust exemption, but, if it did not, it would be per se illegal.[34] The ideal FTC nonmerger antitrust case is addressed to conduct in an industry to which the FTC has used the full panoply of its powers by publishing reports by issuing guides, policy statements, or rules, and by bringing cases. The FTC's efforts in health care are a model. To illustrate the kinds of cases that the FTC should consider bringing, the Report lists other examples of such cases, including the *DuPont* price signaling case, *Detroit Auto Dealers*, the title insurance case, and the taxicab cases.[35] The Report also recommends that the FTC help clarify vertical restraint law by identifying the restraints it considers illegal and filing appropriate challenges.

Dual enforcement. The problems of dual antitrust enforcement (by the FTC and the Antitrust Division) are exaggerated. More than three-quarters of the Antitrust Division's budget is devoted to criminal enforcement and mergers. Criminal enforcement obviously presents little problem.[36] A survey of leading merger practitioners revealed that few if any mergers have been deterred by uncertainty resulting from dual enforcement. The agencies' premerger notification program acts as a form of informal review, with the result that practitioners simply propose profitable mergers, even if of doubtful legality, and learn the governmental reaction.[37]

Moreover, a multiheaded antitrust agency has virtues.[38] For instance, consumers and businesses may be reassured by having the key merger decision—whether there will be a federal complaint—decided by a group of (preferably) experts from diverse backgrounds and different political parties.[39] The committee was also impressed with the benefits of housing antitrust and consumer protection in a single agency, so that each can be informed by the others' particular strengths.[40]

Economics[41]

The Report endorses the important role that economists have at the FTC—including their occasionally controversial research program. However, the Report recommends a modest redirection of that research program to emphasize industry studies and empirical analyses of our antitrust and consumer protection systems rather than to pursue more theoretical research.

Communications with Others[42]

Guidance. Much of the FTC's role is to provide guidance through rules, guides, and cases. (An administrative cease and desist order should be considered and justified as a form of individualized, compulsory guidance.[43] The best guidance is given publicly by the Commission acting as a whole. At one time the FTC provided substantial guidance through administrative adjudication: the agency's views were disseminated through published opinions. Now that the FTC's adjudicative docket has shrunk, it is important for the agency to communicate its collective views in other ways. The Report recommends increased use of guides and policy statements. In addition, existing trade regulation rules should be enforced, and, in spite of the difficulties inherent in trade regulation rulemaking, the Commission should continue a modest rulemaking program, a process that should explicitly consider whether to preempt state regulations.

Advocacy. The Report endorses the FTC's competition and consumer advocacy program.[44] Particularly interesting is the pre-1988 trend toward increased participation at the state level.[45] This is a sensible (if controversial) development, it seems to me, since business interests may be particularly adept at harming consumers through state and local regulation.

Congress. The FTC should move aggressively to shore up relations with congress.[46] Several steps beneficial in themselves, such as clarifying FTC policies, moving expeditiously, and appointing respected leaders (and hoping the president does the same), offer the additional benefit of improving relations with Congress; the FTC can also contribute by taking the initiative to keep Congress informed. However, congressional micromanaging can inflict serious harm and should be resisted within reason. Legislation that treats the FTC differently from other enforcement agencies—for instance, by barring the FTC alone from studying an issue or enforcing a law—is particularly inappropriate. Such legislation and, indeed, much of the FTC's difficulties with Congress result in part from the FTC's unusual attributes and its lack of a natural constituency.[47] It seems to me that this makes programs such as Notre Dame's particularly valuable.

Conclusion

As I have said before, this is a modest Report. Its 135 pages contain a series of small suggestions. Nonetheless, the Report has already received considerable attention. I can only hope that conferences such as this one will help the Report win an audience, that readers will be persuaded by some of its ideas, and that those suggestions that are adopted will prove sound.

Notes

1. 58 *Antitrust L.J.*, 43 (1989) (hereafter "Report").
2. In addition to Kirkpatrick and Rill, the committee included Joan Z. Bernstein, vice-president and general counsel of Chemical Waste Management, Inc.; Michael F. Brockmeyer, assistant attorney general and chief of Maryland's Antitrust Division; Calvin J. Collier, senior vice-president, general counsel, and secretary, Kraft General Foods; Kenneth G. Elzinga, University of Virginia; Alan B. Morrison, director of the Public Citizen Litigation Group; Timothy J. Muris, George Mason University Law School; Robert Pitofsky, dean, Georgetown University Law Center; J. Thomas Rosch, a San Francisco attorney; Alan H. Silberman, a Chicago attorney; Cass R. Sunstein, University

of Chicago; William L. Webster, attorney general of Missouri; and Washington, D.C., attorneys Nancy L. Buc, Ernest Gellhorn, Caswell O. Hobbs, Basil J. Mezines, and Edwin S. Rockefeller. The author was committee counsel.

3. This summary frequently paraphrases the Report and attempts to be faithful to it, although it is not a substitute for the Report itself. For simplicity, except where otherwise indicated, textual language summarizes the Report whereas citations and commentary in the notes are not based on the Report. For additional commentary, see other articles in this volume and "Presentation and Discussion of the Kirkpatrick Committee Report on the Role of the Federal Trade Commission," 58 *Antitrust L.J.*, 1 (1989). Many of the subjects addressed by the Report are also discussed in J. Miller, III, *The Economist as Reformer* (forthcoming, 1989); and T. Muris, "The FTC at 75" (unpublished manuscript, 1989).

4. Report, at 59-60, 104-7, 119-25.

5. For a different formulation, see "Interview with Timothy J. Muris," *Antitrust* No. 2, at 6, 7 (1989) ("The two most important qualifications are that they are smart and they have an open mind").

6. Report, at 53.

7. Report, at 60.

8. For comparison, twenty-three District of Columbia law firms have at least 100 lawyers, and eight have at least 195. "The D.C. 75," *Legal Times*, July 24, 1989, at 29, 33. These figures are understated because they count only locally based lawyers. The top twenty-three D.C. firms do not include such national firms as Baker and McKenzie (1,179 lawyers worldwide, 40 in D.C.); Gibson, Dunn, and Crutcher (680 worldwide, 88 in D.C.); Weil, Gotshal, and Manges (461 worldwide, 34 in D.C.); and Fulbright and Jaworski (453 worldwide, 68 in D.C.). "The NLJ 250," *National L.J.*, Sept. 26, 1988, at S-4.

9. The Report did not measure workyears by marketing specialists. I understand that the FTC currently employs only one.

10. See, e.g., Asimow, "When the Curtain Falls: Separation of Functions in the Federal Administrative Agencies," 81 *Colum. L. Rev.*, 759 (1981).

11. For a recent decision upholding the constitutionality of such unity at a sister agency, see *SEC v. Blinder, Robinson & Co.*, 855 F.2d 677 (10th Cir. 1988), *cert. denied*, 109 S. Ct. 1172 (1989).

12. Indeed, the greater cost associated with the unity of functions may flow from the steps necessary to minimize unfairness to respondents, particularly the inability of commissioners to supervise the prosecution of the administrative cases that they authorize.

That the committee took comfort from delay does not make delay a virtue. Indeed, the Report expresses concern about this continuing, vexing problem, and particularly about the inexcusable length of time that it takes commissioners to write opinions. Report, at 116, n.168 ("Only partly in jest do we suggest that the commissioners announce an official annual period of summer recess, and then, as does the Supreme Court, discipline themselves by delaying its commencement until they have decided that term's cases").

The Report discusses but takes no position on the wisdom of shortening commissioners' terms from the current seven years to five years. This would be sensible, although more for reasons of presidential accountability (it would ensure that a president could quickly select a chair) and commissioner continuity (seven years is so long that few commissioners think seriously of serving full terms) than because of fairness concerns.

13. Changes in the FTC's statutory powers are reviewed in Appendix B to the Report, at 131-35.

14. Report, at 132, 158, 161-62.

15. Report, at 68-82.

16. For recent entries into the debate, see Braucher, "Defining Unfairness: Empathy and Economic Analysis at the Federal Trade Commission," 68 *B.U.L. Rev.*, 349 (1988) (defending paternalism); and Rice, "Toward a Theory and Legal Standard of Consumer Unfairness," 5 *J.L. & Commerce,* 111 (1985) (multifactor test).

17. 15 U.S.C. § 53(b) (1982), quoted in Report, at 131, n.4.

18. FTC administrative enforcement is most important when the following factors are present: (1) a firm engages in a practice in multiple states; (2) the firm has engaged in the practice for a significant period of time without encountering litigated challenges, or litigated challenges are unlikely because individual injuries are small or difficult to quantify; (3) determination of liability will likely turn on a sophisticated application of the FTC's unfairness standards to complicated facts; and (4) absent FTC intervention, the firm is likely to continue engaging in the questioned practice, thereby possibly harming consumers.

19. 849 F.2d 1354 (11th Cir. 1988), cert. *denied*, 109 S. Ct. 865 (1989).

20. 295 F.2d 302 (7th Cir. 1961).

21. 89 F.T.C. 131 (1977).

22. Report graph 18, at 155.

23. See *FTC v. Amy Travel Service, Inc.*, 875 F.2d 64 (7th Cir. 1989), and cases cited therein.

24. "Setting a Course for FTC," *Advertising Age*, Apr. 24, 1989, at 16. The editorial added that "the truth is the FTC has to go back to basics if it hopes to re-establish itself as a serious regulatory force in national advertising."

25. Report, graph 14, at 151.

26. Report, at 71.

27. Report, at 75, n.54. Although the Report did not develop this suggestion at length, it is a potentially important idea. Where an advertisement is patently misleading, it should be halted without delay and possibly lead to consumer redress. This can be accomplished only through court litigation.

28. The Report notes that its suggestions concerning the meshing of state and FTC regulation of advertising "should generally be applicable to other consumer protection (and, indeed, competition) activities." Report, at 73, n.51.

29. For an example included in the Report, the NAAG car rental guideline calls for an end to collision damage waivers. Final Report and Recommendations of the National Association of Attorneys General Task Force on Car Rental Industry Advertising and Practices (adopted Mar. 14, 1989), reprinted in 56 Antitrust & Trade Reg. Rep. (BNA) No. 1407, at S-15-S-16 (Spec. Supp. Mar. 16, 1989) (first of three recommended alternatives). This ill-advised suggestion is likely to lead to price rigidity, to the disadvantage of consumers and small competitors alike. Report, at 73.

30. Report, at 76.

31. Report, at 76.

32. Report, at 76.

33. Report, at 61-68, 113-19.

34. The Report also notes that "FTC action against naked restraints could be more important where problems in showing antitrust standing prevented private enforcement" (Report, at 62, n.10), and this is also true for some other restraints. Standing rules have been employed to cut back substantially on the effective reach of antitrust laws. Page, "The Chicago School and the Evolution of Antitrust: Characterization, Antitrust Injury, and Evidentiary Sufficiency," 75 *Va. L. Rev.*, 1221 (1989). Because of this, one can no longer assume that open restraints will be challenged by private parties. Private enforcement also has been made less certain by the increased regularity with which courts require showings of market power. See Briggs and Calkins, "Antitrust 1986-87: Power and Access (Part I)," 32 *Antitrust Bull.*, 276-301 (1987).

35. *E.I. de Pont de Nemours & Co.*, 727 F.2d 128 (2d Cir. 1984); Detroit Auto Dealers Ass'n., 5 Trade Reg. Rep. (CCH) ¶ 22,653 (FTC Feb. 22, 1989), *appeal docketed* (6th Cir.); Ticor Title Insurance Co., Dkt. No. 9190 [1983-1987 Transfer Binder] Trade Reg. Rep. (CCH) ¶ 22, 419 (FTC initial decision Jan. 6, 1987); *FTC v. Indiana Federation of Dentists,* 476 U.S. 447 (1986); Massachusetts Board of Registration in Optometry, 5 Trade Reg. Rep. (CCH) ¶ 22,555 (FTC June 21, 1988); Michigan State Medical Soc'y., 101 F.T.C. 191 (1983); City of Minneapolis, Dkt. No. 9180 (FTC complaint withdrawn May 7, 1985), reported in [1983-1987 Transfer Binder] Trade Reg. Rep. (CCH) ¶ 22,250; City of New Orleans, Dkt. No. 9179 (FTC complaint withdrawn Jan. 3, 1985), reported in [1983-1985 Transfer Binder] Trade Reg. Rep. (CCH) ¶ 22,223.

36. But cf. *United States v. Price Brothers Co.* (E.D. MI. complaint filed June 22, 1989) (defendants claim that they were prejudiced because the FTC pursued an investigation that should have been referred to DOJ).

37. Ironically, uncertainty flows less from dual federal enforcement than from the supplemental enforcement powers of states—although even here uncertainty is reduced by the likelihood that challenges would be filed in advance of consummation. Cf. *State of California v. American Stores Co.*, 872 F.2d 837 (9th Cir. 1989) (neither private parties nor state entitled to divestiture, so hold separate order should not have been entered), *mandate stayed,* 110 S.Ct. 1, *cert. granted,* 110 S.Ct. 275 (1989).

38. For an interesting discussion, see Jones, "The Federal Trade Commission in 1968: Times of Turmoil and Response," 7 *J. Pub. Policy and Mkting.*, 1, 9 (1988) (describing contributions of commissioners who served with her).

39. It is revealing that many other countries entrust antimerger competition enforcement to collegial bodies. See B. Hawk, *II United States, Common Market, and International Antitrust: A Comparative Guide*, ch. 7A, 7C (2d ed. 1989) (decisions initially made by seventeen-member EEC Commission, subject to review by Court of Justice); H. Iyori and A. Uesugi, *The Antimonopoly Laws of Japan*, ch. II.H, .L (1983) (Japanese merger enforcement by a five-member Fair Trade Commission); Ishikawa, "Antitrust Enforcement by the Japan Fair Trade Commission," 3 *Antitrust* No. 3, at 11, 12 (1989) (absence of private actions leaves antitrust enforcement "nearly exclusively in the hands" of this quasi-judicial agency); cf. Kitchen, "Restrictions on the Acquisition of United Kingdom Corporations by Foreigners," 52 *Antitrust L.J.*, 1035, 1035-36 (1983) (Britain's, Monopolies and Mergers Commission investigates and reports on mergers, although the Secretary of State refers mergers to the Commission and obtains relief). But cf. Goldman, "The New Merger

Provisions of the Competition Act of Canada," in B. Hawk, ed., *Annual Proceedings of the Fordham Corporate Law Institute*, 119, 133-35 (1988) (mergers are reviewed by the Competition Tribunal on the application of the Director of Investigation and Research).

40. The Report notes that consumer protection decisions should be informed by an appreciation of the concern for economic efficiency that is instilled in antitrust experts, and suggests that antitrust decisions can be improved by expertise in consumer protection. As an example (not mentioned in the Report), economists studying consumer protection issues have shown that high search costs can make pricing less competitive. See Ippolito, "The Economics of Information in Consumer Markets: What do We Know? What do We Need to Know?" in E. Scott Maynes, ed., *The Frontier of Research in the Consumer Interest*, 235 (1988). This insight can improve our understanding of the functioning of markets.

41. Report, at 96-104.

42. Report, at 82-96, 107-12.

43. Since orders are a form of guidance, the FTC should limit their duration and avoid imposing unnecessary expenses. Report, at 91-92. "[I]t is generally desirable to treat similarly situated firms alike." Report, at 83.

44. For an unusually strong concurring opinion, see Ginsburg, "The Appropriate Role of the Antitrust Enforcement Agencies," 9 *Cardoza L. Rev.*, 1277, 1277 (1988) (describing DOJ and FTC competition advocacy as "arguably their most important task").

45. Report, graph 23; 58 *Antitrust L.J.*, at 160.

46. See also Report of the American Bar Association Section of Antitrust Law Task Force on the Antitrust Division of the U.S. Department of Justice, 57 Antitrust & Trade Reg. Rep. (BNA) Spec. Supp. S-14 (July 19, 1989) (similar recommendation).

47. The lack of natural constituents has protected the FTC from regulatory capture. R. Harris and S. Milkis, *The Politics of Regulatory Change*, 145 (1989). The agency's challenge has been to minimize the costs and maximize the benefits associated with this exchange.

Kirkpatrick II: Views of a
Member of the Special Committee

Caswell O. Hobbs, III

Stephen Calkins described his role of counsel to the ABA Committee as one that involved listening to the debates and thereafter recording the consensus which resulted from those discussions. I must tell you that frequently his recording was far superior to the debate itself—he was an outstanding general counsel!

I would like to underscore certain findings of the ABA report that I think are particularly significant and worthy of further consideration by policy makers. In addition, I would like to make some personal observations that were not part of the report but that might be of interest. Finally, I will close with a brief comment on the Commission over its seventy-five-year history.

Let me start with what the report did say. In my mind, three points stand out as particularly noteworthy.

First, the report gives clear and explicit recognition of the great influence that the FTC's economic and antitrust bureaus have on its consumer protection mission. The consumer protection programs of the FTC, the ABA committee concluded, compare very favorably to the consumer protection programs of other federal agencies, such as the CPSC, FDA, USDA, NHTSA. And it is clear, at least in the committee's view, that this is the result of the commission's competitive/market-oriented approach to analyzing and addressing consumer protection problems. It is ironic that the FTC's consumer protection mission is now becoming the justification for continuing its antitrust mission, as the latter increasingly comes under attack as being redundant with that of the Department of Justice.

Second, I think the report is significant in its recognition of the important role that the commission plays in the "margins" of antitrust: in considering and, where appropriate, bringing the innovative, complex, or controversial kind of case. There was a period during the early 1970s in which the commission experimented with these kinds of "cutting edge" cases. Those cases, as you would expect, had a much greater rate of dismissal by the commission or in the federal courts than did the mainstream antitrust cases, and this in turn led to a view that the commission should not be doing this kind of enforcement. But the committee—rightfully, in my view—endorsed this important category of FTC activity.

I think our experience has been that those difficult competitive issues do not go away if the FTC does not address them; instead, they get addressed by a state attorney general, or by Congress, or by parties in private litigation. I suggest that, for reasons of comparative advantage, it is important that the FTC be the policy analyst in these kinds of antitrust matters in the first instance. As I indicated, the committee endorsed this proposition, and I think that is a significant endorsement.

The third aspect of the committee report that I think is worth underscoring is the recognition of the importance and potential of rulemaking as an FTC enforcement tool. Everyone is, of course, mindful of the fact that it was rulemaking in the mid- and late 1970s that created many political problems for the FTC. The committee, however, was clearly of the view that these problems were ones of process and approach, rather than fundamental flaws with rulemaking itself. The committee was clear and unanimous in its view that rulemaking ought to be reinvigorated as an enforcement tool by the commission.

Rulemaking has many recognized advantages. In my mind, however, there are two aspects of FTC rulemaking that could make it particularly useful in the upcoming years. First, I believe that rulemaking can provide a vehicle for involving the state attorneys general in policy formulation in appropriate consumer protection and antitrust matters. Commissioner Strenio noted in his paper the growing importance and influence of the state enforcement initiatives, and I believe it is very important to have a coordinated federal-state process to develop and administer policy. FTC rulemaking provides a procedural vehicle for accomplishing this objective. Second, rulemaking can also provide a record and a policy justification for *non*regulation or for a particular form of regulation. The significance of this is that the rulemaking record serves to fill the policy vacuum that otherwise would exist and into which a state attorney general or a private litigant could step without guidance from the federal policy makers. Rulemaking, for these purposes, encompasses any form of prospective, industrywide advice—it could take the form of a policy statement, enforcement policy statement, guidelines, or even formal rules.

In summary, the foregoing are three aspects of the ABA committee report that I think are worth underscoring. Let me now make two comments on subjects that were not covered in the report, but which I think are equally important.

First, in my opinion, the key variable—bar none—in the performance of the FTC in the twenty years that I have been associated with it is the person appointed by the president as chairperson of the agency. Of all of the factors that influence the quantity or quality of the output of the agency (however you measure those), I think the key variable, and by far away the most significant variable, is the quality of the chairperson (by chairperson, I include the bureau directors and general counsel who are appointed by the chairperson).

The report did not cover this aspect of the commission's performance because the charter of the committee specified that it was not to become involved in assessing FTC leadership. I will not try today to identify those criteria that make for a strong chairperson, but I will express my personal view that, if it is possible that a single administrator would attract a higher caliber of person to the chair's job, I would be ready to sacrifice the great advantages of the collegial system to that end. I think Commissioner Jones recognizes in her paper that, of all the commissioners, the role of the chair is special; his or her relationship with the bureau director is special, and his or her relationship to the enforcement agenda is special. I think it is critically important that we attract the highest caliber of person to that position.

Second, I am impressed with the implications of one of the report's key findings that Calkins and I have already mentioned. Recall the report's conclusion that the FTC's consumer protection mission is greatly influenced and benefited by the presence of the antitrust and economic bureaus at the FTC. The point of comparison for this finding, you will recall, was the FDA, the CPSC, the USDA, and NHTSA. Might this not provide a jumping-off point for reexamination of the suggestion that federal consumer programs be consolidated in a single agency? I would personally have no problems with that suggestion as it relates to the CPSC; I think we would lose little, and gain quite a bit, if we were to abolish the CPSC and transfer its programs to the FTC. I pause somewhat longer considering whether I am equally ready to consolidate the FDA, NHTSA, and the USDA, but I do not see any overriding bar to that proposal and I would like to see it studied further. I also note that this concept is closely related to

Commissioner Strenio's support for the FTC's competition advocacy program. I agree that there are great improvements that could be realized in our federal consumer programs if we were able to increase the amount of competition analysis that goes into structuring those programs.

Let me shift gears to a final set of observations. I will not go into all of the detail contained in the paper I have written on this topic (Hobbs 1986), but I suggest that interested parties consult that paper for further detail.

Howard Beales this morning developed a helpful perspective for understanding the commission's evolution over the last twenty years from adjudicator to legislator to prosecutor. I think another perspective is useful: it is my thesis that the FTC, as an antitrust enforcement agency, by and large has not achieved any of the objectives that led Congress to establish it as a second antitrust agency in 1914. I should add that I personally do not attach much significance to that observation in terms of what I think the FTC ought to be doing today but I think that, as we debate where the commission ought to be headed, it provides a useful reference point.

More specifically, the congressional objectives in 1914 in establishing the FTC were to create a politically independent agency, to create a specialized antitrust tribunal that would be superior to the Department of Justice, to provide a means for providing advanced antitrust guidance to business, and to identify and regulate incipient or complex antitrust problems and achieve more efficient and effective antitrust enforcement through the administrative tribunal and process. As I indicated, I do not think any of those ambitions have been recognized in any significant way by the FTC. I think that this point illustrates nicely the evolution of the FTC over the last seventy-five years, and the fact that the commission today is perceived as a valuable federal enforcement agency doing important work and addressing competitive and consumer protection problems in a flexible, competent, and evolving manner. Improvement is clearly possible and needed, but that basic thrust of the agency is sound and needed.

References

Hobbs, Caswell O. (1986). "Antitrust in the Next Decade: A Role for the Federal Trade Commission?" *The Antitrust Bulletin* (Summer), pp. 451-480.

Comments by a Consumer Advocate at the CSPI

Bruce A. Silverglade

I have been asked this afternoon to critique the portions of the American Bar Association report on the FTC that discuss the relationship between the states and the federal government, particularly in the area of deceptive advertising regulation.

On balance, I'm sure that everyone here is somewhat disappointed with the ABA report, because the report fails to make any definitive recommendations in this key area of FTC activity. The authors state that "they are not of one mind on whether the FTC is bringing a sufficient number of advertising cases." Many of the national advertising cases brought by the states in recent years, however, have been predicated on the belief that the FTC has not been doing enough to protect consumers. Thus, because the committee could not agree on the basic question of how many cases should be brought, it, in turn, had difficulty in effectively addressing the broader question concerning the proper federal/state relationship in the area of advertising regulation.

The ABA report contains other statements at the beginning of this chapter that reveal why the committee apparently had great difficulty in agreeing on meaningful recommendations in this area. The authors state: "Rightly or wrongly, the media has conveyed the perception that the FTC has largely abandoned the regulation of advertising, especially national advertising." News reports cited in support for this statement include articles in the *Wall Street Journal*, the *New York Times*, the *National Journal*, and *Business Week*. I would have added articles and editorials in *Advertising Age* as well. Accordingly, the report states, "The attorneys general have responded to the *perceived* slackening of FTC enforcement with vigorous advertising programs of their own."

I read these statements in the ABA report as implying that the controversy over the proper amount of national advertising regulation, as well as the related question of how the states and the federal government should share that function, can simply be blamed on the attorneys general being misled by exaggerated accounts of FTC inaction in such "biased" publications as the *Wall Street Journal* and *Business Week*. With this head-in-the-sand approach to this complex issue, it is little wonder that the committee had such difficulty in arriving at meaningful recommendations for improving FTC performance in the area of consumer protection.

Let us now take a look at some of those recommendations in order to illustrate what I mean. The major recommendation of the committee is that "The states' primary mission should be those practices that harm consumers within a single state; the FTC's special mission should be those practices that harm consumers in many states." This statement, however, ignores the relative resources of the states and the FTC and the incidence of deceptive advertising on an intrastate as compared to interstate level.

As stated elsewhere in the report, the number of FTC workyears devoted to advertising practices has declined over the years to less than fifty today. Although no one to my knowledge has compiled similar figures tracking the increase in workyears devoted to advertising regulation at the state level, one point is nonetheless clear. The states now have more resources to attack deceptive advertising than does the FTC. Thus, the committee's statement that the states' primary mission should be those practices that harm the consumer within a single state would be valid only if it could be demonstrated that the bulk of deceptive advertising problems occurred in the area of intrastate advertising. Since the report does not claim that most advertising problems do in fact occur on a local level, its recommendation that most of the available resources in this country should ideally be devoted to this area is dubious.

The report's recommendation that the states follow the FTC's lead and stay clear of such areas as airline price advertising also seems simplistic. The report chides the attorneys general for issuing airline price advertising guidelines and states that the "net effect" of the guidelines "is to make price advertising more difficult." Indeed, several current FTC officials and representatives of the advertising industry point to the NAAG guidelines as the reason why price advertising in airline ads has supposedly declined over the last year. Those who subscribe to this view, apparently including the authors of the ABA report, ignore the facts that the airline industry has recently become an oligopoly due to lax antitrust enforcement and that the decrease in competition in the industry has probably had much more to do with any reduction in the incidence of price advertising than did the NAAG price advertising guidelines.

One finding in the report that I can certainly agree with is "that the pattern of increased activity by the states will continue." The authors of the report do not explain why they believe that state activity will continue to increase. I have some ideas, however, about why this will almost surely be the case.

First, the FTC's resources over the last eight years have declined greatly and there is little chance, because of the federal budget deficit, that the agency will ever be given enough resources to do the whole job regardless of who is chairing the commission in the 1990s. Thus the states will accurately perceive a need for continued involvement in national advertising regulation, and any chairperson of the FTC who is sincere about enforcing our nation's consumer protection laws will recognize that the agency will need to rely on the states for assistance.

Second, the states have proved themselves to be more efficient law enforcers than the FTC ever was, even during the 1970s when the agency was quite active. For example, the FTC worked unsuccessfully from 1976 to 1982 to develop advertising guidelines for foods. In contrast, the states were able to develop advertising guidelines for the car rental industry in about a year. Since the states have proved that they can do the job and do it more efficiently than the FTC, there will be little support in the consumer protection community for limiting the work of the states to purely intrastate problems.

Third, state as well as local consumer protection agencies are increasingly becoming more sophisticated. By joining together with new affordable technologies such as facsimile machines, electronic mail, and teleconferencing systems, states will continue to wield increasingly larger amounts of enforcement clout that, in some cases, may exceed the resources that can be mustered by the FTC.

Fourth, the Reagan/Bush administration has officially encouraged greater regulatory activity by state and local governments. Executive Order 12,612, often referred to as the "new federalism order," instructs federal agencies to leave regulatory matters to the states whenever possible. The executive order will continue to act as an incentive for greater state activity.

Fifth, state attorneys general have tougher laws at their disposal to prohibit deceptive advertising than does the FTC. Therefore, as long as there is a mandate for consumer protection enforcement, the consumer protection community, including the FTC itself, will need to look toward the states for assistance in prohibiting deceptive national advertising. For example, in contrast to the FTC, which only has authority to force an advertiser to cease and desist from making deceptive claims, many states have authority to assess civil penalties. The state of California, for instance, in an action taken against Procter and Gamble, required the company to pay $350,000 as part of an agreement to cease and desist from making the challenged claims. The FTC could only obtain such sums if an advertiser violated an existing cease and desist order, which does not occur frequently.

Sixth, and perhaps most importantly, state regulation of national advertising will continue to increase because, despite the claims of many FTC officials appointed by the Reagan administration, the public never endorsed abandonment of health and safety regulatory programs, including consumer protection programs. As the ABA report recognizes, state attorneys general are closer to the people and are cognizant of their needs and concerns. For this reason, attorneys general have responded to the demands of the public for a larger government role in this area of regulation and will continue to be major players in the field of consumer protection enforcement.

Remarks by a Consumer Advocate at Consumers Union

Mark Silbergeld

I want to focus on a few limited aspects of the American Bar Association's new report on the FTC. Three aspects of the ABA report are of special interest to me, for I believe that, to a degree, the report has insufficiently addressed these issues: first, FTC leadership; second, the role of economists and economics in the agency's consumer protection function; and third, the FTC's role in producing unique economic information.

Now, I must hasten to state that there is a perfectly obvious and defensible reason why the ABA did not address these issues head on. The criticism of the FTC's leadership, as well as the debate over whose economics to prefer, is too political and in a sense too personal for a body like the ABA committee to take on. Also, the report is the product of a committee that undoubtedly would have experienced a degree of disagreement on these issues directly proportional to the degree of specificity with which they addressed the issues in the report.

And so I will discuss these three issues. I see them as closely interrelated, with the unifying factor being what I will call—for lack of better terms—free market, Friedmanite, or Chicago school economics. But I must put these remarks in the larger context of what I see as a broader application of free market economics to all social welfare and regulatory programs within the federal government for at least the past eight years and more.

In my opinion, decision making in the federal government during the Reagan era and for the few precept years was far too greatly marked by the rise of a very narrow stripe of economics and of economists who practice this particular type of economics. It was evident in—above all places—the Office of Management and Budget (OMB), as well as in the Federal Trade Commission (FTC), the Consumer Product Safety Commission (CPSC), the Food and Drug Administration (FDA), and the Environmental Protection Agency (EPA), to name some of the most important regulatory programs. It applied as well to social welfare programs such as the Women's, Infants', and Children's feeding program (WIC), the federal school lunch appropriation, the food stamp program, and many others.

It is fair, of course, to question whether there is not something seriously amiss with my thesis. There was, after all, an election in 1980 that put into the White House a president who agreed with this school of economics and with its underlying view of society. You may say that President Kennedy, President Johnson, and President Carter all ran administrations peopled by economists and others who agreed with their economic and social views—so why not President Reagan?

My response is that there is something fundamentally wrong with that brand of economics. It is ideological, indeed almost theological, rather than intellectual and analytical. I suspect, although this certainly is not a fact, that if it were to be learned that Milton Friedman has a slight speech impediment and all of this time has been talking about "flea markets," not "free markets," a slew of economists would throw off their econometric models and rush to the library to bone up on barter theory.

This narrow brand of economics disdains any reality that tends to contradict it. It really is libertarianism in economics' clothing. Now, I respect libertarianism's concern for the individual and for individual rights. But I don't think it is a good doctrine for governments to use to make economic decisions that are supposed to be made collectively, decisions that seek to compromise conflicting viewpoints within society, decisions that most people think are appropriately social decisions. Let me illustrate anecdotally some of these points.

A few years ago I attended a conference in San Antonio that was sponsored by the department of economics at Texas A&M University. The topic of the conference was "Product Quality Assurance," a euphemism for product safety regulation and the alternatives to regulation. One of the speakers was a former academician who holds basic libertarian and free market economics viewpoints. Not only was he a former academician, but in his former academic life he had been a colleague of many of those attending the conference. He was on the program because he had just completed a tour of duty with the U.S. Consumer Product Safety Commission in Washington. Early in his remarks he had the audacity to state that after some years at the CPSC and having recently been introduced into parenthood, he had come to believe that some regulations promulgated by the CPSC were indeed cost-effective, especially those aimed at child safety, such as the crib slat width standard. Before he could complete his next sentence, one of his former colleagues shot out of his chair in the audience and bellowed explosively, "Apostasy. Is this the same fellow we used to know and love?" What better indication that free market economics is often mistaken by its adherents for religion?

Also on that conference program was George Douglas, a free market economist and then a commissioner of the Federal Trade Commission. Commissioner Douglas began his presentation with his standard quip—seemingly an essential one in any speech made by an economist who works in the midst of a passel of lawyers—that lawyers consider the plural of "anecdote" to be "data." He then proposed to prove with a single anecdote why federal product safety regulation is a failure. He related quite simply that he had on his Texas farm a power lawnmower that met the CPSC's three-second blade stop safety standard. He could not get it started. End of anecdote. End of proof. Firm conclusion. He didn't even check to see if it was out of gas. Apparently, if you have the right economic credentials, one anecdote is not merely data, it is proof certain.

I would suggest also that many free market economists who have influenced federal thinking during this period are not careful economists. Again, let me illustrate. Last fall I attended a meeting in Washington in which I found myself in the reverse of Commissioner Douglas's situation. I was the only lawyer in a room full of deregulatory economists. One of them I had first met at that San Antonio conference. He has served in important positions in both the CPSC and the FTC, where he has had great influence over caseload screening criteria as well as on case theory. A recent event at the time of this meeting was the proposed Kraft Foods merger. And so I asked this devoted free marketer, now an economics consultant, whether he had taken a look at the merger proposal. He indicated that the only overlapping product line between the two firms was salad dressing. Since, he asserted, there are "very low barriers of entry" in salad dressing, he saw no problem with the merger. And, of course, it is very cheap to make salad dressing. Indeed, in part because of trucking deregulation—a concept with which I wholeheartedly agree and that my own organization supported—salad dressing is not only cheap to deliver f.o.b. plant, but also f.o.b. retailer's warehouse. Salad dressing, however, is not a cheap market to break into, because of the enormous advertising and "slotting allowance" costs associated with marketing it effectively. The latter of these costs imposes an especially high barrier to obtaining premium supermarket shelf space. This incident is but one of numerous examples I could cite that convince me that it may not be possible to be both a devoted, ideologically faithful free marketer and at the same time a pragmatic market analyst.

And so, I contend, the current state of free market economics is associated both with a treatment of its principles as immutable ideology bordering on theology and with a sort of analytical laxness of convenience. This makes it particularly important that the FTC, in heeding the ABA's call for the continued role of economists in various agency functions, to assure that it is deploying an economic discipline—and employing economists—empirical, not ideological, in approaching issues.

What has this to do with FTC leadership? Quite simply put, the two FTC chairmen whose leadership has characterized the agency for most of this decade are rigid devotees of free market economics. Former Chairman Miller was—is—in fact, a practicing free market economist. And while Chairman Oliver is a lawyer by training, he is at least as devoted to the rigid application of free market economic ideology as is any practitioner of the economics profession. Hopefully, the next chairperson of the FTC—while knowing upon entering the office as much about the congressional politics of the job as did Chairman Pertschuk when he departed—will also know what is wrong with the ideological rather than the empirical approach to economics.

Now, the ABA report emphasizes the importance of maintaining the role of economists at the FTC. As I have just suggested, we must ask, What kind of economists and what kind of economics? We should also ask, Why only economists? Perhaps the most important presentation I have heard at this symposium so far, among the many excellent ones, was the paper by Gary Ford and Darlene Smith. Its primary importance would be greatly understated if we said merely that it effectively disputed a long-held economic theorem. Its primary importance, rather, is to show that the discipline of economics is willing to implement without empirical examination theorems that it accepts simply because they comply with the logical precepts of free market theory—even if those theorems may not prove out empirically.

Therefore, I conclude that just as lawyers have benefited from the introduction of economics and economists into their work at the FTC, both lawyers and economists would benefit from working in integrated teams with professionals who are trained and experienced in marketing practices and consumer behavior analysis. The ABA report is deficient in overlooking this issue.

I would add also that these same considerations hold true regarding the ABA's excellent recommendation that the FTC's Bureau of Economics resume its earlier role as the source of excellent, empirical economic studies of industries and marketplace problems relevant to its mission that academic economists otherwise would not produce. That role is very important. But it is important, indeed essential, to emphasize the need for these studies to be empirical. Here, too, economists would benefit from working with those trained in marketing practices and consumer behavior analysis, as well as those trained in studying corporate behavior.

On the whole, I think the ABA Report is important and on target. But in order to get the FTC back on track, we need to look not only at what is—or is not—being done, but also at how, and how well, it is being done.

Comments by a State Attorney General

Linley Pearson

Thank you for inviting me. I am glad to be here. When I arrived today, I saw in my packet an article from *Advertising Age* on April 24, 1989, in which the headline reads: "Industry lauds report on FTC."

The article discusses an American Bar Association report that supports the view that the Federal Trade Commission (FTC)—not the state attorneys general or any other group—is the country's premier regulator of national advertising. Wally Snyder, who is here today, is quoted as saying, "We agree with the general tenor and conclusion that national advertising ought to be regulated by the FTC."

I cannot be too critical of the report because William Webster, attorney general of Missouri, was part of the committee that unanimously adopted the report. But what made it even more difficult for my critique was a comment in the article by New York Attorney General Robert Abrams, president of the National Association of Attorneys General (NAAG) and perhaps the most active state official in challenging national advertising. Abrams said, "The report [is] 'very useful and valuable, and [I] hope the new [FTC] chairman takes its recommendations seriously.'"

I was surprised, but his remark was tempered by his other comments in the article. Mr. Abrams said, "There are some areas in which we differ . . . but what is said about enforcement is enormous support and encouragement to the activism that you've started to see from attorneys general." He also said, "I agree with the report that the attorneys general are not going to cease engaging in [national] ad regulation, so it would be right for them to find ways to improve the liaison from FTC."

The conclusion of the report that the FTC's success depends upon its resources and leadership says it all. Congressional appropriations and executive branch appointments will be the bottom line determinative factors of the future directions for the FTC. With limited resources and an increasing workload at the FTC, the report's questioning of the sound economic policy of regional offices seems warranted. The report's commentary about staff reductions resulting in more generals than privates is interesting, but the report makes no specific recommendations. More effective use of resources results from leadership decisions on how to allocate those resources. But the conclusion of the report did not suggest major structural changes. The report concluded that the current resources are inadequate to perform all the job responsibilities of the agency, including policy statements, advisory opinions, cease and desist orders, and rules.

How does the FTC cope with insufficient resources? Which duties cease to be less important and what are the priorities of the agency? In the antitrust program involving mergers, the report says "The FTC appropriately devotes more resources to merger enforcement than to any other single program" (S-7 in appendix II). The nonmerger cases often involve the health care professions. The cases against dentists, physicians, or optometrists have been successful in court. Where the FTC has engaged in rulemaking, whether in health or nonhealth areas, the nature of the process leaves it open to criticism directed from Congress against the FTC.

When the FTC by rule seeks to occupy the field and preempt all inconsistent state regulation, the FTC risks not only the wrath of a particular profession, but the FTC is striking down state law. However, the FTC seems to recognize this, because only two new trade regulations have been promulgated since 1980.

Consumer protection is an area in which the FTC could look to the states for help with cases that are local in nature. The report suggests, for example, that the FTC should give deference to the states regarding intrastate advertising.

The report does suggest the importance of cooperation between the FTC and NAAG. The Report cites an efficient use of FTC resources— cooperation with the states in the area of telemarketing. Telemarketing is a problem of an interstate nature.

The report suggests that there have been problems of an interstate nature that the FTC until recently has taken little interest in policing. The report mentions "price advertising, which has created a void that the states are filling. The FTC should eliminate this void by bringing meritorious pricing suits, such as the action against Alamo Rent-A-Car" (S14-S15). The report mentions a common agenda. Yet it criticizes in part the adopted airline advertising guidelines and car rental guidelines of NAAG. Although there are criticisms that can be made, the action by NAAG did

help prompt FTC action against Alamo Rent-A-Car. The car rental industry report gives three alternatives as remedies for the collision damage
waiver provision in car rental agreements. As far as I am concerned, they
were given in descending order of importance and workability.

The airline guidelines drafted by the states resulted in clearer and
less misleading newspaper advertisements. Too often fares were not available at the price advertised when they first appeared in the newspaper.
The guidelines definitely improved advertising in the industry. The FTC
should take the lead in reviewing national advertising.

The report notes that as a result of state action on various consumer
protection matters, manufacturers are asking for FTC preemption of state
laws. An example is the auto manufacturers action regarding state lemon
law provisions. Whether it is the airline industry, the auto manufacturers,
or the health professions, each industry will be asserting preemption by
the federal government or advocating state enforcement depending on
which has the least regulation or enforcement activities. Because economic
interests are involved, those most vocal in criticism of regulation or
enforcement efforts will be those protecting economic self-interests.

I agree with the report that economists have a major role to play in
the decisions regarding regulatory and enforcement efforts in an increasingly global economy. Imperfections in the marketplace must be addressed and corrected, if possible. Who attempts the corrections—
industry, state government, or the federal government—will ultimately
depend on the economic climate and political action.

The mood of the nation concerning regulation and enforcement will
determine the scope and allocation of the FTC's resources. More enforcement by the FTC in advertising will mean less need for state activity in
the national marketplace. However, the states will still be active in the
advertising field. The report noted that state action in some areas of the
national arena, such as enforcement of FTC trade regulations, should be
allowed even though the federal government has occupied the field. The
states will hardly agree to give the FTC exclusive jurisdiction in rulemaking.

Congressional action that preempts state law while giving concurrent jurisdiction to the states to enforce a weak federal law is contrary to
the principles of federalism and sound consumer protection policy. States
do not want to be preempted when state law is strong and effective.
However, the states would accept federal action that specifically prevents
preemption.

Better cooperation between the FTC and NAAG is necessary. This means less rhetoric and more action. Joint efforts such as the computer data bank on telemarketing fraud is a step that can make better use of state and FTC resources. More joint enforcement efforts could not only help the FTC and NAAG, but also the consumers of this nation.

The FTC and Advertising Regulation

Wallace S. Snyder

I am honored to join such a distinguished group of FTC alumni and experts to discuss the Federal Trade Commission. I have been asked to provide my reactions to the recent report of the American Bar Association on the Federal Trade Commission.

I am in agreement with the general tenor, conclusions, and recommendations of the report with respect to the regulation of national advertising. In my remarks I will focus on (1) the need for the FTC to articulate better its commitment to national ad regulation, (2) the use of its unfairness authority in advertising regulation, and (3) the problems associated with the dispute between the FTC and the state attorneys general over national ad regulation.

Much of the criticism of the current FTC, which provided the basis for the ABA evaluation of its efforts, is based to a large extent on the perception that the agency is not active enough in national advertising regulation. In my view, there are several actions that a new FTC chairman should undertake to counter this perception.

First, the new FTC administration must articulate that it intends to play the predominate role in national advertising regulation. The new chairman must convince several important constituencies that the commission accepts this responsibility and will devote the necessary resources to the job.

In making the commitment to a national advertising regulation agenda the commission need not—and must not—embrace an activist approach, nor should it rely solely on the number of new cases that it brings. I disagree with the contention of certain state attorneys general and consumer groups that additional national advertising cases need to be brought by the FTC. It must be recognized that the ad industry's successful self-regulation program over the years has obviated much of the need for FTC intervention. Above all, the new FTC administration must not duplicate the type of cases currently being brought by the state attorneys general.

The advertising industry must be assured that the FTC will play the predominant role in national advertising regulation and that there will be uniform standards applied to national ads. The new administration must articulate that it is sensitive to the benefits of truthful advertising and to the harm that can come from overregulation.

Consumer groups must be assured that the agency will devote adequate resources to national ad regulation. The new chairman needs to find a way of convincing the groups of the FTC's commitment. The new administration should not base its commitment on the number of complaints and final consent orders that it obtains.

It should not be assumed that a small number of formal actions indicates that the FTC is not doing its job. Rather, I would be interested in the process being used to monitor national ads and, perhaps, with the number of investigations and voluntary resolutions. Also, consumer groups must be assured that their petitions will be considered expeditiously.

State attorneys general must be assured that the FTC will provide the resources necessary to act in national ad regulation. Also, states must know that they will play a role in helping the FTC to set uniform ad regulations.

A second major responsibility of the chairman will be to establish a productive relationship with one of the FTC's most important constituencies, the United States Congress. The new chairman must establish a positive dialogue with its authorization committees and their respective chairmen, John Dingell and Ernest Hollings. The new chairman must obtain both congressional reauthorization for the FTC and adequate funding for its regulation priorities. This will occur only when better relations are established with the congressional leadership, which must be assured that ad regulation will be pursued appropriately and fairly.

Above all, the new chairman must make reauthorization of the FTC a priority, as did former chairmen Michael Pertschuk and James Miller. The major block in the way of FTC reauthorization is the agency's use of its unfairness authority for advertising regulation. Congress has prohibited the FTC from using unfairness in advertising rulemaking proceedings since 1980. In the last Congress there was a major split between the Senate and the House of Representatives, with the Senate opting for the status quo and the House holding out for the use of unfairness in all advertising matters. If this dispute is not resolved it is unlikely that the FTC will be reauthorized in the current Congress.

I believe that the FTC really has to determine whether it needs this controversial authority. The ABA report on the FTC endorsed very few cases where it has been used, and the report acknowledges that Section 13(b) authority is appropriate for some of these matters.

Yet where unfairness has been tried in advertising matters it has proved burdensome, unwieldy, and unworkable. The advertising industry continues to fear that if the FTC has unfairness authority, a future commission will attempt to use it to ban whole categories of truthful advertising. This was last attempted in the late 1970s when the commission considered a trade regulation rule that would have banned advertising directed to children.

The new FTC administration must work with Congress, industry, and consumer groups to resolve this dispute. Sharper definitions of what constitutes unfair advertising practices are needed, and the first amendment protection articulated by the *Central Hudson* case should be built into those definitions. However, it will be difficult, if not impossible, to provide the necessary framework for how this vague concept will be applied to future advertising. Therefore, I recommend that the FTC work for a resolution along the lines of the Senate bill last year. This would allow the agency to pursue individual unfair advertising cases, but not entire industrywide rules.

The new FTC chairman must respond to the increasing regulation of national advertising by individual state attorneys general. This is one of the major concerns of the advertising industry. The real question is, Who is in charge of national ad regulation? Who sets the standards that advertisers and broadcasters must comply with when they market products nationally?

I certainly agree with the conclusions and suggestions in the ABA report on this important issue. The Federal Trade Commission must play the predominant role in regulating national advertising. But I recognize—as does the report—that the states will stay involved in this area. Iowa State Attorney General Thomas Miller recently reported that the states "will never fully relinquish (this) role unless we're freed of doing so by the Congress."

State attorneys general are involved in national ad regulation because they believe that, as New York Attorney General Bob Abrams states, "The FTC virtually removed itself from the field of policing false advertising." The FTC can help regain control of national regulation by reversing this perception. Also, as the ABA report recommends, the FTC should seek recommendations for cases from the states and in turn should offer its expertise to the states in local matters.

Above all, the new FTC chairman must work for a collegial atmosphere with the state attorneys general instead of the combative and confrontational atmosphere currently surrounding federal-state relations. While it will be difficult to lower the rhetoric, there are useful signs that the FTC and the states are increasingly working together on mutual programs.

The advertising industry urges the FTC to play the predominate role in national regulation because advertisers cannot comply with the rules of fifty different regulators. Currently, there are inconsistencies between the federal government and the states over advertising for the same products and services. This problem is illustrated by the different standards required by the Department of Transportation for airline advertising and the actions taken by the National Association of Attorneys General and individual states in the same domain. There are also inconsistencies between states as basic as the differences in typesize requirements for various affirmative disclosures.

Some suggest that an activist FTC will be necessary to take the ad regulation agenda back from the states. But is this really a solution? The industry does not want over-regulation by either the states or the federal government.

Some believe that federal preemption may be the answer. This certainly is a possibility, especially with respect to specific areas, such as airline advertising, where Congress and federal agencies intend to occupy the whole field. And I think that the states are most concerned about this "remedy." But, before the states are preempted from the national advertising field, perhaps a new FTC administration and the states can work out a uniform program. There have been some encouraging signs, but unfortunately the states are still issuing inconsistent standards. I believe that the federal government must set the standards with which national advertisers are expected to comply. These standards must be fair and effective, and the states must have input into the requirements. But once the requirements are set, I believe that the state attorneys general should abide by them— and, in fact, help enforce them.

At a recent AAF Conference, both Commissioner Terry Calvani and

Attorney General Abrams agreed that "it's a sad day when the principal focus of advertising conferences are shoot-outs between states and federal officials." The advertising industry fully agrees. It's up to the new FTC to take the lead in resolving this controversy.

The Federal Trade Commission: Going, Going, . . .

Louis W. Stern

My comments on the ABA Committee's Report on the FTC are sacrilegious. They may cause my condemnation and even my excommunication (if you'll pardon the pun, given the location of this conference). I have left my academic hat behind and have taken up one similar to those worn by old-time zealots. However, I would prefer you to think of me as Jonathan Edwards instead of Jimmie Swaggart.

While Edwards was not burned at the stake, he could have stood a little toasting (if you've ever read his sermons, you know what I mean). Like him, I shall ramble on, slightly incoherent but strongly evangelical. Unlike him, I shall provide random thoughts rather than a cohesive statement. In other words, I shall comment on issues as they move me and not in any logical manner. All that I can promise is a disjointed polemic, but one that may keep you awake.

First of all, the Federal Trade Commission, is, at present, a travesty. It has been emasculated by others and by itself. It has ended up exactly as Ronald Reagan wished it to end up. Indeed, if its present performance continues along the same trajectory as the past ten years, I would urge that, like a very old dog riddled with an incurable disease, it ought to be put permanently to sleep.

Is travesty too strong a word? I think not, for the following reasons. In the area of antitrust, it has almost totally abrogated its responsibility to challenge horizontal and conglomerate mergers. During an era in our nation's history when the huge are swallowing the colossal, the FTC (and its kin in the Justice Department) have engaged basically in papershuffling mandated by the Hart-Scott-Rodino Act. The entire face of American industry is being restructured, and the FTC has had no comment. It's incomprehensible to me that the major federal agency entrusted with examining mergers and takeovers would have virtually nothing negative to say about what's happening out there. Has the dog become comatose?

As if this were not bad enough, can anyone who views the world of modern packaged goods marketing through anything other than blackened glasses believe what is currently going on in the distribution channel? While I realize that there are serious misgivings about certain aspects of the Robinson-Patman Act, it is still the law of the land, and the FTC is charged to enforce it. Even without it, could anyone really justify either the bribery that is taking place in distribution today under the guise of slotting allowances or the competitive inequity that's happening because major players are able to write calendar marketing agreements with grocery and drug chains and mass merchants? Yes, the FTC is looking at some of these practices, but how much of a look does it take? For instance, isn't it still a per se offense not to offer promotional allowances on a proportionately equal basis to all intermediaries who compete with one another? Isn't it also illegal for buyers to coerce wholesale price discrimination? Or is all of this simply the free market at work? And lest anyone think that my concern is merely old-time rhetoric spawned in the 1960s or earlier, all one needs to do is ask some of the firms producing consumer packaged goods if they believe that the playing field is level. They aren't looking for special favors from the FTC, but they do look to government to regulate some of the rules of the game, especially when the game is being played under strange and wondrous rules.

Antitrust enforcement with regard to vertical restraints is almost a totally dead issue. And yet everybody and his brother can tell you that the trade (wholesalers and retailers) is getting more and more powerful. If this is the case and if already powerful manufacturers can develop alliances with increasingly powerful distributors, isn't it possible that the foreclosure from the market will become a reality for those standing outside the alliances? Isn't this an area worthy of scrutiny? Hasn't it been proved time and again that innovation generally comes from small firms? If access to the market is made increasingly difficult for these firms, what will happen to the robustness of the U.S. economy and to our ability to compete globally? I don't believe that the cavalier attitude of the Chicago School towards vertical restraints should be adopted universally by the agencies entrusted with enforcing antitrust laws.

On the consumer protection side, I have a feeling that the dog was buried a long time ago and that there is a dummy under the oxygen tent in the FTC building on Pennsylvania Avenue. Aside from its efforts with regard to telemarketing, the FTC has basically focused on the warts on the rump of the elephant. The Commission is mesmerized by snake-oil peddlers and swamp deals. It simply doesn't want to mess around with advertising messages and major promotional schemes, because it doesn't want to offend industry. But, interestingly enough, industry is becoming very offended by its lack of activity. The fact that the state attorneys general have had to take on issues that most assuredly belong at the federal level is merely hands-on evidence of the FTC's demise. Anyone who thinks that rental car pricing is an intrastate rather than interstate issue, please raise his or her hand. Now, if your hand is raised, please keep it raised so that the men in the white coats can spot you when they come to collect you.

Second, in their effort to weaken the FTC, both the Reagan and the Bush administrations have appointed some persons with questionable qualifications to the post of commissioner. Without naming names, these people seem to have the responsibility for dismantling the agency, or else they are so underqualified that they couldn't effectively stand in the way of dismantling. Furthermore, the chairperson's position is increasingly being occupied by individuals who are using every opportunity to make political statements about the role of the agency rather than to carry out the agency's enforcement role. Reading the *FTC News Summary* is getting to be like reading the editorials in *The New Republic*.

Third, both the FTC and the ABA report are subject to an identical criticism regarding their tendency to deify economists. There are a number of reasons why both the FTC and the Report should be chastised (or, as Jonathan Edwards would have it, damned) for this mistake beyond the usual reasons—that economists rarely agree on anything and that predictions by economists have limited (to put it kindly) accuracy. To begin with, the field of economics is growing rapidly out of touch with the subjects of its analysis—industrial structure, conduct, and performance. Instead, economics is becoming applied mathematics, and there is limited interest among present-day economists for coming face-to-face with the realities of blood-and-guts competition as it is fought out in the business world. Certainly, there are notable exceptions (such as F. M. Sherer, Oliver Williamson, and Richard Schmalensee), but I believe that these exceptions are more comfortable surrounded by business school professors than they are with the scores of freshly minted Ph.D's with degrees in mathematically oriented economics who issue forth each year from universities around the world. In addition, the FTC must rely on data to challenge structure or conduct, and, frankly, economists by and large, are lousy empiricists. They know something about econometrics, but econometrics is not where the main action is in economics these days. And econometrics (which is primarily correlational) is a rather weak methodology for looking at a number of different kinds of relationships affecting businesses. Further, except for theories about the presence, absence, and economic value of information, economists know precious little, if anything, about consumer behavior. Finally, if we leave the task of antitrust enforcement and consumer protection to attorneys and economists, we are really being very myopic, because those who understand what is likely to be most meaningful for society and who can interpret the consequences of proposals for change are more likely to be trained in psychology, sociology, and political science than in the law or economic theory (which is essentially bloodless).

The upshot of all this is to argue that the FTC should be looking for many of its new recruits from the graduate schools of business or management. Doctoral students coming from those schools are much more eclectic in their training, are more empirically bent, and have a strong, abiding interest in the hands-on functioning of the business world than are doctoral students coming from economics departments. Furthermore, there would be very few obstacles to these individuals finding publication outlets in the learned journals in business academe. Therefore, I suspect that they will be able to find academic positions in business schools after their stays at the FTC are over—which differentiates them from the economists working at the FTC.

Fourth, irrespective of the disciplinary composition of the agency's staff, it is an accepted fact that, without data, antitrust enforcement is impossible. If the FTC is going to have any impact on U.S. industry in the decade of the 1990s and beyond, it should be ordered to start up the *Line of Business* data base again. The industries from whom that data were collected probably have no concept of just how important the analyses of that data were. Bluntly put, the now old *Line of Business* data enabled economists to demonstrate that there is a positive relationship between firm size and efficiency and that high four-firm concentration ratios shouldn't be viewed, on their face, as indicators of monopoly power. These findings, along with others, changed the whole face of antitrust. It is these findings on which the Reagan and the Bush administrations have built their antitrust policies. So business should have a major incentive to continue to provide these data. But in accordance with someone's cost-benefit analysis, the flow of the data has been halted.

Quite frankly, I have a hidden agenda in urging turning on the tap. I believe that, with further analysis, new findings will pour forth that show the deleterious effects on both macro- and microperformance of some of the industrial restructuring that has occurred over the past decade. We need to look at the data for the sake of the U.S.'s economic future. Our competitive posture worldwide may depend on their analysis. Without them, what are economists (or business scholars) going to analyze? The PIMS data, with all its weaknesses? Simulated data?

Finally, it is important to revisit the purpose of section 5. I have an off-beat way of trying to understand what the FTC is all about that I'd like to share with you. It comes from sociology, of all places. I believe that it is the purpose of the FTC, using section 5, to promote competition in the marketplace and to control or mitigate the amount of conflict. Competition is object-centered behavior that is indirect and impersonal and in which the goal or object is held by a third party. In sports, a hundred-yard dash (with lanes clearly marked) is competition. The runners rush toward the finish line in order to win the goal (the gold medal), which is held by the organizers of the track meet. The competitors must stay in their lanes or they are disqualified. In industry, the goal or object is held by potential customers.

On the other hand, conflict is opponent-centered behavior. It is direct and highly personal behavior in which the goal or object is held by the opponent. In sports, football, basketball, hockey, and boxing are examples of conflict. Interference with the opponent is essential to victory. In industrial settings, the means by which rivals can interfere with the progress of opponents are deception, slander, and foreclosures.

Section 5 should be used to make certain that the emphasis is on competition, not conflict. The FTC must always be checking to see that the lanes for the runners are clearly marked and than any interference with their progress is not "unfair." Indeed, in the context of antitrust enforcement and consumer protection, regulating unfair competition really refers to managing and regulating the amount of conflict among industrial rivals. Therefore, section 5 and the Federal Trade Commission still have an extremely important role to play in our society.

Well, I warned you at the outset. The scholars among you are no doubt wincing and cringing over these overstatements and half truths. Puffery is not dead! But, as in the wildest of polemics, there are probably some kernels of truth in what I've said here. I sincerely hope that we can find them and then administer CPR to the FTC before it's too late.

The FTC: An Institution or an Instrument?

William L. Wilkie

The American Bar Association report on the FTC is an impressive document. It represents experts' concern about the role and performance of a key agency in the economic fabric of our society. As with other readers, I see many points in it with which I agree and a few with which I disagree. Rather than delve into those points in detail, however, there are three broad issues I would like to raise from the perspective of a business school academic concerned with the role and performance of the Federal Trade Commission. These are:

1. Better management and strategic planning
2. Respect for organization history and continuity
3. Policy-level integration of the fields of marketing and consumer behavior

Based on the performance of the agency and the contents of the ABA report, it is clear that each of these issues merits considerably more attention from policymakers concerned with the FTC of the future.

Better Management and Strategic Planning

The Federal Trade Commission employs some very talented individuals but needs to examine seriously its strengths and weaknesses in the areas of management and strategic planning. For example, at this symposium we heard of officials' surprise at the strength of the negative reaction to the Trade Regulation Rule (TRR) proceedings during the late 1970s. It is important to realize, however, that some initial elements of that reaction should not have been surprising at all. In fact, the terrible political consequences of the TRR proceedings might have been avoided had some better strategic decisions been made at the start, when FTC had to make a number of decisions about exactly how the TRR development process would proceed.

Many readers will recall that (in reality if not intent) the process the agency chose in essence cast some middle- and lower-level attorneys on the FTC staff as adversarial participants. These staffers would issue an initial report that could call for sweeping changes in current marketing practices within the specific industry, at which point the industry was invited to respond.

This type of process was in keeping with the adversarial model used for cases at the Commission, and this was comfortable in terms of management style. In the instance of TRRs, however, the "opponent" was no longer a single firm but now was the entire set of firms in the relevant set of industries. Further, the basis for acting in each area was not really in response to a narrow practice in which some deception was charged and on which the firm might be understandably on the defensive. Instead, the FTC was cast in the broader role of actively seeking ways to improve the current marketing environment within entire industries or product categories. Given this role, the choice to try to cast parts of the agency as both adversary and judge is a risky one. I am aware, of course, that there were good reasons advanced for this choice. My point is that I am not convinced that *other* alternatives—such as casting the FTC in a more neutral role as information gatherer and expert— were given the weight they deserved, and the consequences were devastating.

This example is admittedly complex and controversial. I raise it to stress that when thinking about better management and strategic planning at the FTC, we are not talking just about program priorities, or budgeting, or other issues of traditional concern. We are also talking about such strategic topics as the posture the agency will adopt in various matters, and such organizational topics as staff morale, the roles to be played by various members and levels of the staff, and other issues that pertain to the effectiveness of the organization both internally and externally. Rather than delve further into this topic here, I would advise interested readers that several authors of later papers in this volume discuss this issue in more detail. I would urge FTC officials to give careful consideration to strategic planning in the future.

Respect for Organizational History and Continuity

In this short section I would like to underscore my belief that the Federal Trade Commission should be seen as an important institution in our society. In organizing this symposium, it became clear that a wide range of persons share this belief, even if at a latent level. That is, we know that what the FTC is intended to do is important in our society, and while we may disagree deeply about how it and the level at which it ought to be done, there is an abiding concern for this Commission.

Two key points follow from this belief in the FTC's role as an important institution. One is that the FTC is not, and should not be seen to be, an instrument of a current administration. It isn't "my Commission" because I'm elected in the current administration. And it doesn't become "someone else's Commission" when the next administration gets elected. It is, instead, "our Commission" as a people.

Let me stress that I attribute this problem equally to the left and the right: this is not a political statement about the Reagan administration alone by any means. I believe this view of the "FTC as instrument" became very strong, if not dominant, in the 1970s and I believe it persisted throughout the 1980s as well. I am speaking of a sense of ownership and exercise of power that is (1) in fact unwarranted, and (2) extremely damaging in the long run to the FTC as an institution. The business community is better served by a commission that knows what it is doing and that offers a general consistency in doing it over time. Consumers are better off when understood and served in a reasonable manner by an agency that retains some powers and uses them wisely and well. Finally, individual commissioners and staff people would also benefit if everyone understood that they are part of a long-standing institution with an important role to play. I hope that we will see this perspective come to characterize the FTC of the 1990s.

The second dimension of the FTC as an enduring institution is that the persons there at any single point in time should recognize the strong need to maintain a sense of continuity and institutional core—a sense that the FTC is *learning* over time. At present, the agency is very weak (some would say terrible) on this dimension, and this weakness strikes at desires to have FTC views and rulings taken seriously by outsiders. For example, some symposium participants from recent FTC years have commented to me how surprised they were to find so many people who are so interested and so knowledgeable about what is going on at the FTC. My response was, Why should you be surprised? Just stop to realize that (in my experience), twenty years ago there were bright people working hard at the FTC, doing very interesting things. This was true fifteen years ago, ten years ago, five years ago, and today. It will also be true five years from now. A repository of knowledge and understanding about the FTC most certainly does exist on the part of many persons who are not presently working with the agency.

The sad aspect of this systematic inattention to the past means that a continuing loss of knowledge has taken place at the FTC. As an educator, I must admit that it is disturbing to appreciate that knowledge can be lost, that it doesn't just accumulate in some natural progression. This realization, in fact, has served as one of the stimulants to holding the symposium and producing this volume. In the event that it is not already clear, let me recommend that FTC officials investigate ways to capture the knowledge that the agency has had in the past so that it can be used today, and to revise its current operations so that it will be able to build upon today's knowledge base in the future.

Policy-level Integration of the Fields of
Marketing and Consumer Behavior

The ABA report contains a special section dealing with the role of economists at the FTC. Clearly this was meant to address a set of internal issues related to the special perspectives embedded in this field of study and was sparked by the key role economists have played in recent years at the agency.

In this regard, I would like to point out strongly that not only was there not a special section, in fact there was *not even any mention* of experts in marketing, business practices, or consumer behavior that I saw in the entire ABA report. I believe that this accurately represents a prevailing view among FTC officials and observers that simply does not include these areas of study as having any expertise relevant to anything the FTC ought to be doing.

However, let's think briefly about what the FTC is supposed to do: Regulate marketing practices as they impact on businesses and as they impact on consumers. Who knows about marketing practices? Who knows about consumer behavior?

There is some general idea in the report that economists should be responsible for these activities. I know some economists. I like some economists. Let me also say sincerely that I respect the intelligence of some economists. But I don't think economists know very much about either marketing practices or consumer behavior. Economists know about aggregate markets, but they generally don't know how managers think or how managers work. They have been trained to take a stilted, incomplete view of consumer behavior. While this view does offer rigor and some useful insights, most economists I have met seem unaware of—and uninterested in—any deficiencies in this view. As we saw at the symposium (and elsewhere in this volume), there are positive developments beginning to occur in meshing economics, marketing practices, and consumer behavior insights. But these developments are still in early stages.

At present, however, there are entire fields of expertise—the study of marketing strategy and practices, the study of consumer behavior—that are being largely ignored by the Federal Trade Commission. My intention is not to use this point as a criticism of the ABA committee. I can appreciate they have significant expertise, and this report reflects their expertise. But the report also supplies, by absence, an accurate current status of my field within the Federal Trade Commission today.

Perhaps it would be useful to point out some aspects of the expertise that is being ignored by the FTC. This symposium heard addresses from two presidents of the American Marketing Association, two former executive-directors of the Marketing Science Institute (a nonprofit center in Cambridge supported by approximately fifty major corporations), four editors of leading journals (*Journal of Marketing, Journal of Advertising, Journal of Consumer Research, Journal of Public Policy and Marketing*) and five presidents of the Association for Consumer Research (an international association of twelve hundred members from twenty-six nations).

Not one of these persons attended this symposium as a representative of these institutions: they spoke here because of their personal interest in the Federal Trade Commission and regulatory issues involving business and consumers. Their papers and talks are included in this volume. I hope that readers from other fields will read them, consider the insights offered, and pass relevant papers on to interested associates. These fields should join law and economics as basic contributors to an improved FTC of the future.

Kirkpatrick II: A View from Inside the Commission

William C. MacLeod

When I heard that the Kirkpatrick Commission was convening to evaluate the FTC I became a little concerned.[1] I remembered that the Nader Report[2] and the first Kirkpatrick Commission Report[3] twenty years ago were quite critical of the management of the FTC. I remembered one example particularly that was raised in the Nader Report. Nader's raiders descended upon the general counsel's office one day and found the assistant general counsel for voluntary compliance in his office, on his sofa, asleep underneath the sports section of the *Washington Post*. When I read that passage, I instituted some reforms myself. From now on, whenever my people take their naps, they lock their doors.

More important to us today is what all the blue-ribbon committees have said about the policy of the FTC. Two issues strike me. First, all of these antitrust lawyers from the antitrust section of the Federal Trade Commission, not only in 1969 but also in 1989, spent more of their effort reporting on the consumer protection activities than the antitrust activities of the FTC. I take this as a sign either that our work in the Bureau of Consumer Protection is far more important, or that our work is just more interesting than antitrust. Maybe it's both.

The second and more serious issue is the influence that those reports had twenty years ago on Commission law enforcement. If you look at the policies that the Federal Trade Commission embraced in the 1970s and the 1980s you will find, I think, a remarkable correlation between the number of recommendations in those reports and the activity that the FTC finally undertook.

A great deal of the 1970s you can see foreshadowed in the Nader Report. Nader's raiders ridiculed advertising. The Commission brought advertising cases that reflected this ridicule, challenging detergent ads (which the Naderites particularly despised) because detergents didn't remove "impossible stains";[4] stopping ads for new chrome razor blades

50

because the blades weren't significantly better than the old blue blades;[5] attacking various food ads because the products didn't deliver all the nutrients essential to healthy growth and development,[6] and, of course, seeking to ban ads for kids' cereals because the products had too much sugar.[7]

Moving into the 1980s you finally can see the emerging influence of the first Kirkpatrick Report. The Kirkpatrick committee urged the Commission to concentrate on real consumer injury: to bring more fraud cases. The fastest growing program of the Reagan FTC was the battle against interstate fraud. The Commission left "ring around the collar" where it belonged—in the laundry room—and started attacking multimillion dollar scams. Of course, there are some overlaps between the two periods, but I will leave the detailed examination of that for later.

With such a track record of influence, the pronouncements and recommendations of any committee should be taken seriously. Today I will focus on three issues that arise in Kirkpatrick II.[8] First is the issue of the perception of FTC activity. The second is the relationship with the states. And the third issue is the Commission's provision of guidance to the community that it governs.

Perception Versus Reality

First of all with regard to perception versus reality in advertising enforcement, there is a quote in the report that runs to the effect, "rightly or wrongly, the media has conveyed the perception that the FTC has largely abandoned the regulation of advertising, especially national advertising."[9] Now I have to say that I am in agreement with a number of findings of the Kirkpatrick Report, and this is one of them. For a while, we didn't see many reporters around the Commission. They were busy covering our critics, who missed the National Nanny. Now reporters have discovered the FTC again, and they cover every move we make. One of the articles in the program materials for this conference was headlined, "FTC, Under Industry Pressure, Shows New Life in Backing Deceptive-Ad Laws."[10] As a matter of fact, when the Kraft decision came down a few weeks ago,[11] one of the questions I got from the press was, "Isn't this case a response to criticism that the Commission isn't doing enough?" I had to remind the reporter that the Kraft complaint actually issued about a year and a half ago, that the case had been in trial for months.

The perception problem is compounded by several factors. First, many of the charts at the end of the Kirkpatrick Report deal with work-years devoted to various activities. There is no question that workyears and budgets have dropped. But these are inputs. It is far more difficult to measure the output of what the Federal Trade Commission does. Some of the crude proxies are noted in the back of the report, and they are revealing. For example, you will note that the number of orders and the number of complaints that the Federal Trade Commission brings have not declined a significant amount. As a matter of fact, they are today about the same as they have been the last ten years.

The Bureau of Consumer Protection has kept track of its total accomplishments for some years now. As you can see, although inputs are falling, output is doing fine.

CONSUMER PROTECTION ACCOMPLISHMENTS
(Approximate Fiscal Year)

	1977	1978	1979	1980	1981	1982	1983	1984	1985	1986	1987	1988
Final Consents*	44	26	40	28	18	14	16	20	21	25	15	7
Complaints**	7	8	5	12	18	9	23	20	16	27	16	26
Civil Penalties	13	12	13	24	26	12	17	10	11	16	22	15
Redress***	10	6	6	10	4	4	2	7	6	5	10	15
Rulemaking	6	18	12	13	11	14	26	30	35	36	20	30
Order Modifications	2	2	1	8	9	7	14	8	2	5	3	3
Contempt Actions:												
Pending****	0	0	0	0	0	0	0	0	0	1	0	0
Completed	0	0	0	0	0	0	0	0	0	2	2	0
Total	82	72	77	95	86	60	98	95	91	117	88	96
Workyears	555	546	545	575	551	505	466	444	440	408	366	359

*   Includes Part II and Part III Consents.
**   Includes Part III Complaints, Civil Actions Filed, and Permanent Injunctions.
***   Does not count Final Consent or Civil Penalty orders that also include redress.
**** Includes actions filed during the fiscal year but not final at the end of the year.

What you don't see on the table is another revealing proxy. Last year the Bureau of Consumer Protection approved more full-phase investigations—these are the conversions of initial inquiries into investigations that are more likely to lead to law enforcement activity—than the Bureau has approved in any year since 1977, when we first started keeping numbers. Reporters don't cover these conversions because we cannot talk about our investigations. Contrast this with the number of investigations that have been carried in the press by state attorneys general. You can pick up your newspaper and read reports about how this investigation is going well, or that a company is resisting an investigation right now.[12] Prosecution by press conference generates news. But it is the kind of news that Commission rules forbid me from generating. I would not change those rules. They are designed to protect the reputations of companies under investigation that may not have violated the law.

Another cause of the perception problem is the FTC's policy of deferring. We may defer to the self-regulatory mechanism, or to other enforcement authorities when someone else has reached a conclusion that results in the same relief that we would have sought ourselves. Does it make sense for us to spend half a million or even twenty thousand dollars of the taxpayers' money to duplicate the kind of relief that the self-regulatory mechanism or another agency has obtained? Perhaps it does, but I think not.

Also contributing to the perception problem is a disagreement over the kind of advertising cases that the Federal Trade Commission ought to be bringing. We have been criticized for failing to bring cases that the states prosecuted. A perfect example is the *Cheez Whiz* case.[13] Kraft, the maker of Cheez Whiz, ran an ad campaign that upset the Center for Science in the Public Interest (CSPI), a public interest group that wants Americans to eat healthy foods. They objected to the claim that Cheez Whiz was "real cheese made easy.... It's a blend of Kraft cheddar and colby cheeses and other wholesome ingredients." The FTC's Bureau of Consumer Protection refused to take action because we didn't see how consumers were being misled.

CSPI had better luck in Texas, which got Kraft to agree to stop running the ads. The attorney general contended that the ads that included the description, "a blend of ... cheeses and other wholesome ingredients," created the perception that the products consisted of "all natural cheese without any other ingredients." I will leave it to you to speculate whether any judge applying federal or state laws of deception would agree that reasonable consumers would be misled by the Cheez Whiz claim. I shudder to speculate on the criticism that the FTC would suffer for spending federal funds to prosecute such a case. Nevertheless, today *Cheez Whiz* contributes to the perception of an inactive FTC. That is a perception that is divorced from fact.

Finally, the perception of inactivity is compounded by the fact that the FTC deals primarily with a "nuclear" deterrent. The FTC, early in the Pertschuk years,[14] decided to abandon the assurances of voluntary compliance —regulatory slaps on the wrist. The only weapon we now use is the cease and desist order, which is generally broad and almost always perpetual. It sometimes involves corrective advertising. Not surprisingly, advertisers are willing to resist it and resist it vigorously. Is it any coincidence that the cases that go into long and complex litigation are at the Federal Trade Commission? Where else can you find cases like *Kraft*, *Campbells*, *Norelco*, and *R.J. Reynolds*, which endure months, sometimes years, of complex and costly litigation? One of the reasons why we have long trials is that companies are willing to fight rather than take the kinds of orders that the Federal Trade Commission delivers.

Consider, on the other hand, some of the advertising that the Kirkpatrick Committee credits the states for enforcing.[15] These typically involve voluntary assurances of the kind the Federal Trade Commission has abandoned. Companies are far more likely to enter into these kinds of agreements than they are to enter into perpetual and multiproduct consent agreements with the Federal Trade Commission. Perhaps it is worthwhile taking a look at whether the FTC ought to be narrowing the scope of its orders and narrowing their duration in order to address this issue.

Federal-State Relations

Nancy Buc of the Kirkpatrick Commission reported last month that the intelligence of the debate between the states and the Federal Trade Commission has sometimes failed to match the rhetoric in that debate. I am sensitive to that. But there is a debate, and it's important. On the airline guidelines, on car rental guidelines, and on a number of other issues, there have been very constructive exchanges between the Commission and the attorneys general. The letters that the Commission has sent to NAAG on car rental and airline guidelines questioned the legal and factual basis for those statements.[16] That criticism was not appreciated by all attorneys general, but I think it's very important for the Commission and the attorneys general to engage in that kind of dialogue. When we are concerned that a state initiative can harm consumers, we would be remiss in our obligations to consumers if we remained silent.

On the other hand, our successful cooperation does not attract much attention. True, the Kirkpatrick Committee does report some of the successes that the states and the Federal Trade Commission have accomplished together. For example, the telemarketing fraud effort was a project begun early on in my tenure at the Bureau of Consumer Protection. Less well known are the efforts in the background. Last year, representatives of the Bureau of Consumer Protection put on a very well-received program at a NAAG meeting on the use of extrinsic evidence and copy tests in consumer protection cases. Also largely unreported is a great deal of daily contact in many cases that we work on together.

I think that it is clearly a mistake to identify the rising activity of the states as a result of the states' perception that the Federal Trade Commission has "abandoned the field." The reality is often to the contrary. I have had advertisers complain to me that they have to deal with the Federal Trade Commission and the states at the same time on the same ads. The states apparently have determined to bring national advertising cases whether we're bringing them or not.

On relations between the Commission and the states, there are three trends that I am fairly confident we will be able to identify in the near future. First, I think that there is going to be an increased effort to emphasize the harmonious and cooperative aspects of the relationship between the FTC and the states. Second, there will be an effort to defuse the rhetoric that has been occasionally bombastic in the past.

Third, I think that we are going to see a little more substantive agreement between the states and the Federal Trade Commission. The time will come when some of the theories over which we have disagreed will be tested in court. You may have heard that some of the airline cases are now in court, where legal theories in the guidelines are going to be tested. We will finally know whether it is legally deceptive when airlines advertise one-way fares based on round-trip purchases. We will have a ruling on whether it is deceptive for airlines to indicate surcharges as part of a footnote, rather than bundled into a total fare. After we have some judicial decrees on some of these issues, there will be less room for disagreement over the FTC's views and the states' views on advertising.

Guidance

There is no question but that some of the traditional sources of guidance from the Federal Trade Commission have declined. Now that we go into federal court, Commission opinions are less frequent. *Southwest Sunsites* and *Amrep*[17] comprised 520 pages in the FTC Reports. Today those cases would be (perhaps unreported) preliminary injunctions providing more relief more quickly than the FTC ever could have provided on its own.[18] Advisory opinions are also down at the FTC. You don't see as many guidelines as you used to see from the Commission, and you certainly don't see the kind of rulemaking that we used to issue.

The Kirkpatrick Report does note that new sources of guidance have emerged—our commentaries, for example, on the Fair Credit Reporting Act and the Fair Debt Collection Practices Act. But there are other sources as well. Occasionally forgotten in this debate is that in the 1980s the Federal Trade Commission issued the Deception Policy Statement,[19] the Substantiation Policy Statement,[20] and the Unfairness Statement.[21]

These statements provide a great deal of guidance to the business community as to what kinds of claims the Commission will pursue and how the Commission will analyze those claims. In fact, these three documents probably lay out more ground rules than you can glean from any number of decisions in any comparable amount of time. What the Commission did in the early 1980s was to distill the best of the precedents and give the business community an idea of how the agency approached its enforcement.

Oddly enough, our most extensive source of guidance was almost entirely ignored in the Kirkpatrick Report. I am speaking of the amicus briefs, statements and testimony, and interventions that the Commission has filed in the last several years. From 1982 to date, we testified, appeared, or filed comments 450 times. Some of these statements simply make the obvious case for competition in a restricted market. But among these documents you will find some of the most thorough arguments and most significant positions that the Commission or the Bureaus have expressed. The Commission's four comments to the National Association of Attorneys General on airline and car rental guidelines,[22] the Bureaus' comment to the FDA on health claims,[23] and my letter to the State of Massachusetts on retail advertising regulations[24] are but a few examples of the more important ones.

Moving From Speculation to Analysis

Let me conclude with what I consider to be the most fundamental issue of all and one that, unfortunately, has hardly been addressed at this conference or in the Kirkpatrick Report. We have been addressing the Federal Trade Commission's efforts to police the marketplace today. We have been debating whether or not the Federal Trade Commission is doing the job that it ought to be doing. Yet we still know very little about the ultimate output of the Federal Trade Commission. The real output is not the cases or rulemakings that the Commission undertakes. The true measure should be compliance with the law.

How should we assess the legitimacy of advertising today versus advertising ten or fifteen years ago? By the number of cases the FTC brings? Do we judge peace by the number of warheads that we maintain in our countries? Do we judge public safety by the number of muggers we arrest? Of course not. We judge peace by the absence of hostilities. We judge safety by the absence of muggings. I often hear complaints that the Commission does not arrest enough advertisers. I seldom hear the complainants describe crimes of deception that merit prosecution. If there is real deception going unprosecuted, I would welcome the evidence. If, on the other hand, the crime wave consists of Cheez Whiz and "impossible stains," then the complainants have lost the debate.

The marketing profession is in a position to contribute to the debate over the Federal Trade Commission's performance. You practice the science that measures the performance of advertising. Yet I have seen nothing in the marketing literature that supports the frequent charge that deception is on the rise. To my knowledge, the only serious study of the trends is the work by Calfee and Ringold, which found that consumer skepticism towards advertising has remained remarkably constant for twenty years, regardless of the regulatory environment.[25] I would like to see more work like this. And I would like to see more marketing experts undertake the kind of study that Murphy and Richards conducted on car rental ads, in which they examined whether consumers were deceived by the kinds of ads that NAAG alleges are deceptive. (The authors found no deception in the ads and no help in NAAG's solutions.)[26] With your help, to paraphrase Nancy Buc, we can elevate the intellectual level of the debate above the rhetorical level. I invite you to join me in making that happen.

Notes

1. The views in these remarks are those of the author and do not necessarily reflect the views of the Commission or any individual commissioner.

2. E. Cox, R. Fellmeth, and J. Schultz, *The Nader Report on the Federal Trade Commission* (1969).

3. Report of the American Bar Association Commission to Study the Federal Trade Commission, Antitrust and Trade Reg. Rep. No. 427 (BNA) (Special Supplement, September 16, 1969).

4. *Lever Brothers Co., Inc., et al.*, 78 F.T.C. 619 (1971); *Colgate Palmolive Co., et al.*, 78 F.T.C. 625 (1971); *The Procter & Gamble Co., et al.*, 78 F.T.C. 631 (1971).

5. *Eversharp, Inc.*, 77 F.T.C. 686 (1970).

6. E.g., *ITT Continental Baking Co., Inc.*, 83 F.T.C. 865 (1973).

7. Notice of Proposed Rulemaking, Children's Advertising, 43 Fed. Reg. 17,967 (1978).

8. Report of the American Bar Association Section on Antitrust Law Special Committee to Study the Role of the Federal Trade Commission, 56 Antitrust and Trade Reg. Rep. (BNA) (Supplement, April 6, 1989) (hereafter "Kirkpatrick II").

9. Kirkpatrick II, at S-11.

10. *Wall Street Journal*, April 17, 1989, at B-4.

11. *Kraft*, Docket No. 9208, slip op. (April 3, 1989).

12. See *Washington Post*, September 21, 1988, at E-1.

13. *In the matter of Kraft, Inc.* consent agreement, Texas Attorney General (February 13, 1986).

14. On August 12, 1977, the Commission repealed the section of its Rules of Practice allowing for Assurances of Voluntary Compliance, § 2.21.

15. See 56 Antitrust and Trade Reg. Rep. No. 1410, at S-11, n.37.

16. Letter from Federal Trade Commission to Christopher Ames, Deputy Attorney General, California (October 1, 1987); letter from Federal Trade Commission to Christopher Ames (March 11, 1988); letter from Federal Trade Commission to Art Weiss, Deputy Attorney General, Kansas (November 4, 1988); letter from Federal Trade Commission to Robert Stephan, Attorney General, Kansas (February 24, 1989).

17. *Southwest Sunsites, Inc.*, 105 F.T.C. 7 (1985), *aff'd*, 785 F.2d 1431 (9th Cir.), *cert. denied*, 479 U.S. 828 (1986); *Amrep Corp.*, 102 F.T.C. 1362 (1983), 768 F.2d 1171 (10th Cir. 1985), *cert. denied*, 475 U.S. 1034 (1986).

18. The reduced size of FTC Reports is occasionally cited as evidence of declining activity. Because so much of the FTC's enforcement now takes place in court, the volume of opinions that the agency issues is a misleading indication of enforcement.

19. Commission Enforcement Policy Statement on Deception, letter from Chairman James C. Miller, III, to Hon. John D. Dingell (October 14, 1983) (Deception Statement), reprinted in *Cliffdale Associates, Inc.*, 103 F.T.C. 110, 174 (1984).

20. Commission Policy Statement Regarding Advertising Substantiation, 49 Fed. Reg. 30,999 (August 2, 1984), reprinted in *Thompson Medical Co., Inc.*, 104 F.T.C. 648, 839 (1984).

21. Commission Enforcement Policy Statement on Unfairness, letter from Federal Trade Commission to Senators Wendell H. Ford and John C. Danforth (December 17, 1980) (Unfairness Statement), reprinted in *International Harvester Co.*, 104 F.T.C. 949, 1070 (1984).

22. See letters cited in note 16, above.

23. Comments of the Bureaus of Competition, Consumer Protection, and Economics of the Federal Trade Commission on Proposal to Amend Governing Health Messages of Food Labels and Labeling, submitted to FDA (January 11, 1988).

24. Letter from William MacLeod, Director, Bureau of Consumer Protection, to Helen Huang, Legal Assistant, Office of the Massachusetts Attorney General (November 18, 1988).

25. J. Calfee and D. Ringold, "Consumer Skepticism and Advertising Regulation: What Do the Polls Show?" 15 *Advances in Consumer Research*, 144 (1988).

26. See J. Murphy and J. Richards, "An Investigation of the Effects of Disclosure Statements in Rental Car Commercials," unpublished paper, University of Texas at Austin (1989).

Kirkpatrick II: Counsel Responds

Stephen Calkins

That a report on which one worked is discussed at an academic conference is occasion for rejoicing. Even if the papers are critical, such attention increases the chance that the report will be read. My principal response is thus one of appreciation. Since the editors presumably desire a more substantive reaction, however, I will address some of the points raised concerning advertising, antitrust, economics, and personnel. Since the Kirkpatrick Committee's work ended with the publication of the Report, obviously I am writing only in a personal capacity.

Advertising

Several speakers focused on the Report's observation that "[r]ightly or wrongly, the media has conveyed the perception that the FTC has largely abandoned the regulation of advertising, especially national advertising."[1] MacLeod agreed with the observation but complained that the media's perception is erroneous; Silverglade read the Report as implicitly agreeing with MacLeod and denounced this as a "head-in-the-sand approach"; Snyder agreed with the observation and expressed hope that the FTC could change the perception without bringing additional cases. It is comforting to have reviewers simultaneously describe a report as both excessively and insufficiently critical. Slightly overlooked in the disagreement, however, are the Report's recommendations.[2]

The Report attempts to strike a balance. The FTC properly worries about driving useful information from the market through overly aggressive enforcement. On the other hand, "the FTC can and should do more to articulate its advertising law-enforcement agenda. . . . [T]oo rarely has the public received the message that the FTC believes it is important to move aggressively against false and deceptive advertising."[3] Accomplishing this assignment will require increased communication of agency concern about advertising[4] and increased or at least more visible enforcement. For instance, the Report expresses concern that the FTC has effectively ceded enforcement of pricing claim advertising to states and calls for the FTC to reclaim leadership of that field by revising its guidelines, making clear its concerns, and "bringing meritorious pricing suits."[5] FTC deference to self-regulatory mechanisms and other enforcement authorities[6] may be false economizing: an enforcement agency should file suits as much for deterrence as for relief.

Much of the dispute about the FTC's advertising program is a disagreement about the kinds of cases that the FTC should bring. Professor Stern accused the FTC of being "mesmerized by snake-oil peddlers and swamp deals."[7] Presumably he was referring to the FTC's consumer fraud program, which challenges telemarketing fraud, land sales fraud, and the like. The program is addressed to the advertising of products that do not function at all. These cases raise few of the subtle issues associated with traditional advertising cases; they do not challenge actions by major advertising agencies; and they are rarely defended by the traditional advertising bar. Much of the story of FTC consumer protection in the 1980s has been the shift to these kinds of cases. Some observers are troubled by this change.[8] However, no one suggests that this kind of fraud is declining, and it is an odd notion to say that the FTC should avoid these cases because the wrongdoing is so obvious.[9] The Report squarely endorses the FTC's consumer fraud program and, by implication, the recasting of the FTC enforcement program that has occurred. The Report merely recommends reemphasizing the FTC's traditional advertising agenda.

The other dispute concerns the role of the states. Virtually all observers at this conference and elsewhere agree that national advertising issues ideally should be resolved at the national level.[10] Not surprisingly, the Report concludes that the FTC is the preferable enforcer for advertising with substantial interstate effects. Bruce Silverglade attacked this conclusion as "dubious." He reasoned that state resources, which he guessed were more abundant than FTC advertising enforcement resources, should be used primarily for intrastate problems only if intrastate advertising problems outnumber interstate ones. He celebrated the states' role in policing national advertising, reasoning that the FTC is unlikely to be given sufficient resources, that the states can act more quickly than the FTC (citing the NAAG car rental guidelines), that the states are more responsive to consumer concerns, and that some states have superior remedies.

I am unpersuaded. Even Silverglade's test for allocating enforcement responsibilities—asking whether most problems are intrastate—would probably have the states concentrate on intrastate issues, since the worst advertising abuses inevitably are local.[11] Nor is the vaunted efficiency of the states necessarily a virtue. One person's efficiency is another person's railroad. Given the flaws in NAAG's car rental guidelines, to use Silverglade's example, the country would have been better served had NAAG proceeded with less dispatch.[12] Moreover, if the FTC lacks sufficient resources, it makes more sense for Congress to allocate increased resources than to approve of the ceding of advertising responsibility to the states. What if, as Silverglade argues, additional resources will not be forthcoming? The Report implicitly recognizes a backup state enforcement role, since it only considers the FTC the *preferable* enforcer of national advertising standards.

Silverglade's most interesting observation was that FTC advertising remedies (typically cease and desist orders) are weaker than the civil penalty authority enjoyed by some states. In contrast, Bill MacLeod described FTC remedies as a "nuclear deterrent" so onerous that firms wage scorched-earth battles to avoid them. Perhaps both are correct. Firms may fear the kind of broad, perpetual orders that the FTC seeks because they impose uncertain compliance burdens, whereas consumers may benefit more from the prompt ending of a deceptive ad and the payment of enough money to serve as a deterrent and enrich the treasury.

If true, what an unfortunate situation! The Report argues that orders should be entered only where likely to yield significant benefits, and rarely for more than ten years.[13] A punitive order is neither lawful nor good policy. Where an advertisement is clearly illegal, the FTC should proceed directly to federal court to halt it and perhaps to obtain consumer redress. Where the issues are more subtle, administrative enforcement is appropriate. Certainly consumers can benefit from corrective advertising orders, which may serve a deterrent purpose as well. If other cease and desist orders fail to provide substantial consumer benefits, perhaps the FTC should request authority to order or seek civil penalties.

Antitrust

Louis Stern won the award for the most colorful paper.[14] The FTC is a "travesty," he asserted, and presumably the Report is flawed for failing to recognize this. There are two responses. First, the committee was not asked to prepare a report card on the FTC's performance or to debate whether the Pertschuk Commission or the Oliver Commission better understood antitrust. Given the diversity of views on the committee and the ink that committee members had already spilled debating such issues, this did not seem the most productive use of time. [15]

Presumably Stern would be unimpressed by this response. For instance, he exclaimed that the FTC "has almost totally abrogated its responsibility" to challenge mergers, and were this true the committee would have been derelict in remaining quiet. But this is not true. The FTC has taken its merger responsibilities seriously. Some responsible observers would have preferred the agency to be a little more aggressive, but the disagreements are one of degree, not kind. [16] Stern protested that "the huge are swallowing the colossal," but size alone is no longer considered the basis of an antitrust objection. [17]

Similarly, Stern lamented the recent paucity of FTC vertical restraint and Robinson-Patman Act cases. Although the Report calls for increased attention to vertical restraints, the mildness of this recommendation and the absence of any call for increased Robinson-Patman enforcement would be serious flaws if respected opinion agreed that the FTC's enforcement program should have been radically different from what it has been. But that is not the case: again, most responsible critics would have increased FTC enforcement only at the margin. The procompetitive potential of vertical restraints is now thoroughly accepted in academia and the courts, and even Stern conceded that "there are serious misgivings" about Robinson-Patman enforcement. [18]

However, there is a kernel of insight in Stern's remarks. He expressed concern about the competitive effects of grocery store slotting allowances and about calendar marketing agreements. He worried that in some industries vertical restraints are becoming so firm and so pervasive that total foreclosure may occur. He is not alone in expressing these concerns. Yet the proper response to the concerns is difficult, not easy— which is why the FTC is ideally suited to address them. The FTC ought to be studying these issues and either explaining why they do not raise competitive concerns or taking action to increase competition. [19]

Economics

Stern faulted the Report for "deifying" economists and suggested that antitrust and consumer protection would be better entrusted to psy-

chologists, sociologists, and political scientists than to lawyers and economists. The economics-oriented nature of recent Supreme Court antitrust
cases would make that a practical impossibility even were it wise.[20] Even
with respect to consumer protection, economists can make important
contributions.[21] Mark Silbergeld reminded us that the best economists
are empiricists.[22] The Committee agrees.[23]

Personnel

"Without naming names" Stern asserted that some commissioners
have had weak qualifications. The Report does not name names either, but
it argues that the quality of leadership is "critical" and that "[a]bove all,
the commissioners should be persons of recognized stature." What would
be gained by debating the qualifications of commissioners whose terms
had expired?

Professor Wilkie also discussed personnel issues. He wondered why
the Report did not call for bolstering the FTC's marketing expertise.[24]
The short answer is that the Committee never considered the question.
Perhaps this is because the Committee's many experts in consumer protection did not include anyone with a marketing background,[25] and no
marketing expert responded to the Committee's public invitation for
suggestions. The FTC's expertise in law and economics ought to be com-
plemented by expertise in marketing, finance, and other business subjects.[26]

Conclusion

The consensus of the conference seemed to be that the second
Kirkpatrick Report has made a significant contribution to our understanding of the FTC and can assist the agency to achieve its potential. This
is gratifying.

The conference also aired a number of interesting issues concerning
the FTC. Two struck me as particularly intriguing. First, it was suggested
that FTC advertising remedies are relatively onerous while simultaneously
being relatively ineffective. If true, improving these remedies—for instance, by proceeding more regularly to federal court—would be an obvious and important change. Second, Stern in particular expressed concern

about certain possible competitive abuses. The Report's analysis suggests that the Commission may be uniquely suited to consider these sorts of practices. This issue is addressed further in a separate paper in this volume.

More generally, the conference revealed a surprisingly amount of affection for the FTC. Notwithstanding all of its difficulties, the agency benefits from a reservoir of goodwill. My hope is that Kirkpatrick II can help the agency replenish and increase that goodwill.

Notes

1. Report of the American Bar Association Section of Antitrust Law Special Committee to Study the Role of the FTC, 58 *Antitrust L.J.*, 43, 70 (1989) (hereafter "Report"); see the papers above, MacLeod, "Kirkpatrick II: A View from Inside the Commission"; Silverglade, "Comments by a Consumer Advocate at the CSPI"; Snyder, "The FTC and Advertising Regulation."

2. Obviously, I have reservations about some of the speakers' positions. MacLeod objected to the Report's statistical analysis of advertising program inputs (workyears) rather than outputs (complaints and orders) and added that FTC consumer protection orders and complaints remained roughly constant during the 1980s. Silverglade was dismayed that the committee was not of one mind on whether the FTC has been filing sufficient advertising cases. I share the regret that the committee was unable to measure advertising enforcement with precision. The difficulty with MacLeod's position is that the number of consumer protection accomplishments tells little about advertising accomplishments. Even advertising accomplishment statistics are ambiguous because they do not distinguish trivial cases from major ones, effective relief from unimportant relief, and a case that stands alone from a case that is part of a group of largely identical cases. With respect to Silverglade's protest, readers of the Report will have to judge for themselves whether the committee's disagreement on the sufficiency of advertising complaints prevented it from saying anything useful.

3. Report, at 71.

4. MacLeod lamented that the Report "almost entirely ignored" the Commission's "most extensive source of guidance," namely, "amicus briefs, statements and testimony, and interventions." In fact, the Report devotes an entire section to the FTC's intervention program and discusses informal guidance in some detail. Report, at 83-84, 93-96. The Report firmly supports the intervention program and expresses appreciation for the value of informal guidance. Unfortunately, much of the guidance to which MacLeod refers comes from staff members, not the Commission, and is nonbinding. Actions by the staff may or may not reflect the views of an agency. See generally Calkins, "Developments in Merger Litigation: The Government Doesn't Always Win," 56 *Antitrust L.J.*, 855, 897-99 (1988) (FTC staff enjoy more autonomy than Antitrust Division staff). Moreover, when reviewing MacLeod's examples, one is struck by the paucity of citations to publications. An unpublished communication is a poor vessel for propagating views.

5. Report, at 76.

6. MacLeod, "Kirkpatrick II." Such enforcement authorities presumably include the states.

7. See above, Stern, "The Federal Trade Commission: Going, Going. . . ."

8. E.g., Baer, "At the Turning Point: The Commission in 1978," *J. Pub. Policy & Mkting.*, 11, 19-20 (1988) (recommending better enforcement of local criminal laws).

9. Even an avowedly liberal transition report endorsed the consumer fraud program. Correia and Rothbard, "Consumer Protection: The Federal Trade Commission," in M. Green and M. Pinsky, eds., *America's Transition: Blueprints for the 1990s*, 248, 260 (1980). The Kirkpatrick Report explains that criminal enforcement may have failed because it faces a higher standard of proof and lacks the FTC's ability to obtain ex parte asset freeze orders and consumer redress. Report, at 81.

10. See above, in this volume, Pearson's "Comments by a State Attorney General" ("The FTC should take the lead in reviewing national advertising"); Snyder, "The FTC and Advertising Regulation"; Stern, "The Federal Trade Commission."

11. Although the Report did not address this issue, the committee reviewed scores of state challenges to advertisements that were false and harmful on their face and far worse than almost any national advertising campaign.

12. See above, Calkins, "Counsel's Summary: The ABA Special Committee's Report on the FTC (Kirkpatrick II)," note 29. See also, Sloane, "Laws Banning Sale of Car Rental Insurance Are Questioned," *New York Times*, Feb. 24, 1990, at 50, col. 1.

13. Report, at 91-92 and n.107.

14. Stern, "The Federal Trade Commission."

15. See also Calkins, "The Kirkpatrick Committee—Objectives and Procedures," 58 *Antitrust L.J.*, 17 (1989).

16. See, e.g., Horizontal Merger Guidelines of the National Association of Attorneys General, Antitrust & Trade Reg. Rep. (BNA), No. 1306, Special Supp. (Mar. 12, 1987) (differing only in degree from DOJ Guidelines); Report of the American Bar Association Section of Antitrust Law Task Force on the Antitrust Division of the U.S. Department of Justice (1989) (endorsing, with one dissent, the 1984 DOJ merger guidelines, but expressing concern that they are not always enforced); Correia and Rothbard, "Consumer Protection," at 263 (generally endorsing DOJ guidelines); Interview with Processor Warren Grimes, 55 Antitrust & Trade Reg. Rep. (BNA) 518, 521 (Sept. 29, 1988) (retiring chief counsel of the House of Judiciary Committee's Monopolies and Commercial Law Subcommittee recommended tightening merger enforcement "incrementally").

17. This is not to deny that some responsible observers are troubled by the perception that firms are seeking to grow for reasons unrelated to economic efficiency. See, e.g., D. Ravenscraft and F. M. Scherer, *Mergers, Sell-Offs, and Economic Efficiency* (1987). The most sensible response to such concerns is to consider changing the tax system by, for instance, removing the disincentive to pay dividends.

18. See above, Stern's "The Federal Trade Commission"; cf. Comanor, "Vertical Arrangements and Antitrust Policy," 62 *N.Y.U.L. Rev.*, 1153 (1987) (critic of DOJ vertical restraint policy merely adds qualifications and conditions); Correia and Rothbard, "Consumer Protection," at 256, 265 (FTC "should not abandon RP enforcement and should enforce rule against resale price maintenance); "Papers Presented at the Airlie

House Conference on the Antitrust Alternative," 62 *N.Y.U.L. Rev.*, 931 (1987) (conference of critics of current policies included no paper advocating vigorous Robinson-Patman enforcement). Elsewhere in his paper Stern expressed his admiration for economists F. M. Scherer, Oliver Williamson, and Richard Schmalensee. It is doubtful that they would share in the harshness of his attack on Commission decisions concerning mergers, vertical restraints, and Robinson-Patman. See, e.g., Scherer, Industrial Market Structure and Economic Performance, 571-82 (critical of Robinson-Patman Act); Scherer, "The Economics of Vertical Restraints," 52 *Antitrust L.J.*, 687 (1983) (vertical restraints usually should be presumptively legal); Schmalensee, "Horizontal Merger Policy: Problems and Changes," 1 *J. Econ. Perspectives* 41 (1987) (current policy could be improved but is not fundamentally flawed); Williamson, *The Economic Institutions of Capitalism*, ch. 14 (1985) (generally supporting enforcement changes since the 1960s).

19. The FTC has stated that slotting allowances may aid competition by compensating retailers for "in-store testing" but the agency "will continue to assess whether slotting allowances may constitute an impediment to new product introductions." Letter to Rep. James J. Florio, quoted in FTC Watch No. 302, at 9 (June 26, 1989).

For additional discussion of how competition can be increased by banning unfair practices, see Calkins, "Antitrust in the 1990s: The Example of Frequent Flyer Program," *infra*. Although the FTC should police competitive practices, Stern's suggested distinction between *competition* and *conflict* may not succeed. He prefers firms to compete in the manner of runners striving toward a goal, rather than in the manner of football players, who engage in "opponent-centered" conflict. This distinction is unclear even in the example. For instance, distance runners routinely engage in psychological gamesmanship in prerace statements, in selecting a pace, and in deciding when to begin sprinting. Does this make them "opponent centered"?

20. See also Areeda, "Introduction to Antitrust Economics," 52 *Antitrust L.J.*, 523 (1983) (law and economics are inseparable in antitrust).

21. See generally P. Ippolito and D. Scheffman, eds., *Empirical Approaches to Consumer Protection Economics* (1986).

22. See above, in this volume, Silbergeld's "Remarks."

23. Report, at 97 (arguing that one of the principal advantages of economic analysis is empiricism); Report, at 101 ("It is important for economists at the FTC to learn how retail markets for consumer goods actually work"). Although Stern exaggerated when he asserted that "economists rarely agree on anything"—the areas of agreement far exceed areas of disagreement—until recently I shared his worry that economists were becoming preoccupied with theory and that industrial organization had fallen in favor. Happily, industrial organization is enjoying a renaissance, and empiricism is not disdained. See, e.g., J. Tirole, *The Theory of Industrial Organization* (1988) (textbook emphasizing the "second wave" of industrial organization); Bresnahan and Schmalensee, "The Empirical Renaissance in Industrial Economics: An Overview," 35 *J. Indus. Econ.*, 371 (1987) (survey article introducing symposium issue devoted to recent empirical IO work); Williamson, "Delimiting Antitrust," 76 *Geo. L.J.*, 271, 303 (1987) (industrial organization, which once languished, today "is alive and well"). The FTC's research mission can make important contributions to this trend.

24. Silbergeld and Stern joined in the call for increased use of experts in marketing and consumer behavior.

25. Bernstein, Buc, Muris, Pitofsky, and Rosch are all former heads of the FTC's Bureau of Consumer Protection, and Webster is chair of NAAG's consumer protection committee. Of course, the committee's membership is fair game for criticism, although I am not in a position to shed much light on the appointment process.

26. Wilkie also emphasized the importance of institutional memory. I agree. Many people interviewed as part of this project stressed the value of those few individuals who understand the FTC's history and care deeply about its future.

PART II

The Past as Prologue

Part II, The Past as Prologue, presents the intimate details of the FTC's history. We believe that this perspective allows the reader to appreciate better the Commission's present status. In this part we feature four historical overview papers. Three of them focus on distinct periods within the last twenty years. They are written by prominent FTC officials—former Commissioner Mary Gardiner Jones ("The FTC in 1968 . . . "), former advisor to Chairman Pertschuk, William Baer ("The FTC in 1978"), and current Commissioner Andrew Strenio ("The FTC in 1988/1989 . . . "). FTC staff members (Christian White, Thomas Stanton, and Howard Beales) as well as marketing professors (Keith Hunt, Kenneth Bernhardt, and John Calfee) who served at the Commission during each time also offer commentaries reflecting their perspectives as attorneys, economists, and marketing academics.

Mary Ellen Zuckerman, a marketing professor specializing in business history, contributes the fourth major commissioned paper, which ends the part. She offers an informative overview of the first fifty years of the agency's history, showing why many of the issues faced throughout the early years of the agency have continued to appear in more recent times.

The Federal Trade Commission in 1968: Times of Turmoil and Response

Mary Gardiner Jones

The decade of the sixties acutely challenged the Federal Trade Commission. Deep-seated changes were occurring in our economy and our political attitudes and sophistication. The strain of this social and political upheaval was also evident at the Federal Trade Commission, then a little-known but important economic enforcement agency.

The marketplace had changed from a relatively simply structured local owner/seller/consumer place of exchange based on personal relationships, to an impersonal marketplace of giant national producer-sellers. By the 1960s most consumer goods were promoted through national advertising and sold by national chains that had few or no ties to the local community. Automation and technology created a raft of new products with unique and unfamiliar properties. These new products made do-it-yourself repairs increasingly difficult and rendered consumers dependent upon third parties, both for information regarding essential characteristics and proper use and for product servicing.

Paralleling these marketplace changes came new political demands and sensitivities growing out of the civil rights movement. The national focus centered on the needs of the disadvantaged and the poor.

In 1962 President Kennedy issued the first consumers' rights charter and created the President's Committee on Consumer Interests. This was followed in 1964 by President Johnson's appointment of Esther Peterson as the first Special Assistant for Consumer Affairs. In 1966 the Freedom of Information Act was passed, opening up much of the federal government's activity to public scrutiny, and the same year also saw the publication of

An earlier version of this paper appeared in the *Journal of Public Policy & Marketing*, Volume 7, 1988, 1-10. Reprinted with permission.

Ralph Nader's first major exposé, *Unsafe at Any Speed*. Nader's book almost single-handedly created a new safety ethic in the marketplace. Nader focused attention on the automobile manufacturers' obligation to produce safe cars rather than on educating the "nut behind the wheel" about accident avoidance.[1]

Thus, consumers began to give voice to their concerns about both the quality and the equality of the marketplace, and to assert their right not to be victimized by the laws and practices of a market that had evolved in a different era, in a different economy, and in a different society. The genius of mass marketing had delivered the goods but not the means for dealing with unhappy consumers. For many, government became as much a part of the problem as it was seen by others as the solution.

The Kerner Commission report concerning the riots following Martin Luther King, Jr.'s assassination in 1968 cited credit and sales practices in the inner cities as one of the inner city residents' twelve most deeply felt grievances, concluding that the rioters appeared to be seeking fuller participation in the social order and the material benefits enjoyed by the majority of American citizens. Rather than rejecting the American system, rioters were anxious to obtain a place for themselves in it.[2]

Also by 1968, the president's recommendations for legislation directed specifically toward consumer problems had become a regular feature of the State of the Union messages. The Congress responded with what was, by 1975, an onslaught of new consumer laws.[3]

Finally, in 1969, Nader unleashed his bitter report criticizing the FTC for its rear-view mirror approach to enforcement, calling the Commission "a self-parody of bureaucracy, fat with cronyism, . . . manipulated by the agents of commercial predators, impervious to governmental and citizen monitoring."[4] Nader's blast was followed by a more temperate but equally critical report on the FTC's performance by a special commission of the American Bar Association that had been created at the request of President Nixon.[5]

We must view the FTC's performance in the sixties against this background of change and turmoil. This paper does not attempt to evaluate the pros and cons of the criticism directed against the FTC.[6] Rather, the paper reviews the FTC's efforts during the 1960s to adapt its powers and its enforcement strategies to deal with the challenges of the new marketplace dynamics and their devastating impact on consumers.

In the decade of the sixties, despite the Commission's slowness and its too frequent distraction by irrelevant issues, it nevertheless was innovative, capable of changing old habits and enforcement patterns, and committed to devising new enforcement strategies and testing new legal interpretations of FTC law in order to deal with the new market conditions confronting consumers. Prior to the Commission's reorganization in 1970 under the aegis of Casper Weinberger and Miles W. Kirkpatrick, the principal author of the 1969 ABA report, the Commission's primary means of adapting to the new marketplace was the product of the commissioners' top-down pressure on the staff.[7]

After 1970, the Commission's more consumer-oriented approach and innovative enforcement strategies were institutionalized and expanded by the new staff brought in by the new chairs. Although popularly held to have begun in 1970, this much-trumpeted revitalization in fact had gathered steam within the Commission during the late 1960s. Nader's and ABA's criticisms of the Commission in large part fueled the revitalization. The FTC's renewed shape and vigor resulted from the imaginative leadership of its new bureau directors, Robert Pitofsky and Alan Ward, and the postreorganization infusion of large numbers of new young attorneys, social scientists, and economists into the agency.[8]

FTC Powers

The Federal Trade Commission (FTC) is a quasi-judicial body charged with enforcing section 5 of the FTC Act. Section 5 is a highly elastic mandate. It prohibits "unfair methods of competition and unfair or deceptive acts or practices in commerce." Under this section the five-member FTC decides in the first instance what conduct is unlawful. The FTC also enforces section 7 of the Clayton Act, which prohibits anticompetitive mergers and price discrimination. The FTC has broad administrative powers that allow it to achieve its statutory goals through litigation, education, advice to business, investigative hearings, and economic reports. The FTC's principal sanction in the early sixties was the power to issue cease and desist orders against businesses operating in interstate commerce that were found to have violated the law.[9]

While recognizing that consumers were an important beneficiary of its actions, the FTC traditionally had regarded its statutory mandate as focused almost exclusively on the conduct of business. Thus, the FTC issued guides and complaints against offending businesses and developed advertising alerts to help business comply with the law. The FTC also issued advisory opinions to businesses which requested the FTC's opinion of the legality of that business's intended actions. The FTC's educational materials centered on helping business executives understand their obligations under the law. The agency's investigative hearings and economic reports dealt primarily with those business community actions that affected other businesses or the market, not with those directly affecting consumers.

FTC Policies and Practices in the 1960s

In the 1960s, the FTC gradually changed this basic approach to its statutory responsibilities. The FTC shifted its enforcement strategies away from simply enjoining violations of law. The Commission began both to develop enforcement programs designed to translate consumer expectations about the marketplace into enforceable business obligations and to redress the imbalance of power that existed between consumers and sellers. These new enforcement programs were reflected in new outreach policies towards consumers, in the exploration of new areas of concern, and in the development of new enforcement strategies and innovative redress mechanisms that were intended to enhance the impact of the Commission's enforcement actions.

Commission Outreach Actions

The Commission had traditionally relied almost solely on its mailbag as its principal source of knowledge about business actions that might violate the FTC Act. In the sixties, the inadequacy of this approach became increasingly apparent. Consumers could not complain unless they knew their rights were being violated. Only a fraction of those consumers who had a complaint would know to write to the tiny Washington agency whose name sounded like the International Trade Commission (ITC), the group handling international commerce issues. The public needed the Commission's guidance as to what practices might be illegal. Essentially the FTC had to find new ways both to publicize its activities and to find out directly from consumers which aspects of the market were giving them the most difficulty.

The Commission compiled its first consumer mailing list for the dissemination of consumer materials and developed new communication vehicles, besides the Federal Register and traditional press release, to inform the public about the Commission's activities. After the Freedom of Information Act became law in 1966, the Commission broadened its disclosure policies to provide the public with increased information about Commission advisory opinions, proposed consent orders, and investigations involving business practices that posed risks to consumer health or safety.[10]

The Commission explored new sources of potential law violations such as the garnishment records of local courts to identify businesses preying on the poor. It began to use its investigative powers much more extensively to detect patterns of potentially abusive practices.

In December 1968, the Commission conducted nine days of hearings to identify public- and private-sector consumer protection and minority business programs. Eighty-seven witnesses testified from consumer groups, businesses, legal assistance centers, and federal, state, and local consumer protection offices. The Commission's goals at the hearings were to identify the most pressing consumer problems, to determine what programs already existed, to determine where the gaps in these programs were, and to determine how the Commission could strengthen its own programs in an effort to close these gaps. The Commission specifically solicited information about the kinds of corrective action required to redress the above problems, including an evaluation of current FTC and other consumer protection and education programs, and the need for linkages between the FTC and private consumer groups, especially concerning low-income consumers' problems.[11]

In its most wide-ranging exploration of national market practices that affect all consumers, the Commission initiated hearings in October 1971 on advertising practices.[12] The Commission's ambitious goal was to enable it to understand better television advertising's impact on consumers and to find ways to provide consumers with more effective relief from damages caused by misleading and deceptive advertisements. Hearings on modern advertising techniques helped to educate both the public and the Commission about the new sophistication of advertisers and their agencies. Here again the technology seemed to have made giant strides forward while the FTC struggled to stay abreast.[13]

The Commission also directly approached consumer groups and state and local consumer protection personnel to learn which types of marketplace deceptions concerned consumers the most. Furthermore, the Commission attempted to ascertain how the marketplace was impacting consumers' ability to choose and to understand the properties of the goods and services being offered to them.

The Commission created a federal-state liaison office in 1966. As a result, the FTC aggressively began to persuade state and local authorities to enact "little FTC acts." By 1969, twenty-eight states had adopted such legislation and the remaining states had some kind of similar legislation on their books. The Commission also worked closely with state and local consumer protection agencies and with local consumer groups in an effort to respond effectively to consumers' problems and needs and to coordinate its enforcement work with the states' attorneys general and consumer protection agency administrators. In 1970, following a pilot program in the District of Columbia, the Commission created both federal- and state-level government and consumer task forces in major U.S. cities. The Commission then worked under the aegis of its regional field offices to better coordinate the efforts of these task forces in combating consumer fraud and deception. [14]

FTC Focus on New Areas of Consumer Concern

In 1965, the Commission launched a concentrated program to elim-inate abuses of retail installment credit that were particularly rampant in inner cities but existed in more affluent areas as well. This effort resulted in a series of complaints that attacked a variety of retail credit practices as deceptive or unfair. [15] These complaints challenged various aspects of the holder-in-due-course doctrine, unfair provisions in retail installment con-tracts, unconscionable pricing, and easy-credit advertising.

In 1968, the Commission developed a special enforcement program that focused exclusively on consumer fraud perpetrated by businesses on inner-city residents. The program was designed to test the Commission's ability to eliminate hard-core fraud. This program followed a 1967 FTC Economic Report on Credit and Retail Sales Practices of DC Retailers. The report compared the access to and cost of credit in the nation's capital for low-income consumers with that of middle-income consumers. [16]

In addition to its concern with credit practices and ghetto frauds, the Commission was also concerned with and reacted to consumer frustra-tion with supermarket games of chance and new car warranties. At public hearings before the Commission both businesses and consumers testified concerning remedies to problems that staff studies had identified. [17] The

FTC enacted a trade regulation rule to address consumer problems with games of chance.[18] The Commission made a comprehensive report to Congress in 1968 concerning new car warranties.[19] That report was one of many factors leading to the Congress's enactment in 1975 of the Magnuson-Moss Warranty Act, a comprehensive scheme to improve consumer protection under consumer product warranties.[20]

Perhaps the Commission's most creative effort to explore the reaches of its Section 5 jurisdiction was its 1968 decision that Sperry Hutchinson's (the marketers of Green Stamps) games of chance were unfair and deceptive. The Commission's unfairness jurisdiction had been largely unused until this time. The Commission's efforts were rewarded by the Supreme Court opinion handed down in 1972 that confirmed the Commission's wide discretion to determine what constitutes a violation of Section 5.[21]

In 1969, the Commission concentrated its efforts in the area of information disclosures. The Commission recognized that the marketplace works properly only when buyers have adequate information about the goods and services they want. With the enactment of trade regulation rules, the Commission began a long series of requirements that sellers provide the information that consumers needed in order to make effective choices in the marketplace.[22] This effort to provide consumers with adequate information both empowered consumers to obtain the products that they wanted and compelled markets to follow the competitive model. Thus the effort marked the FTC's fulfillment of its dual missions of consumer protection and competition.

Another consumer protection innovation was the Commission's development in 1972 of the cooling-off period as a remedy against high-pressure sales. First employed in door-to-door sales cases after the FTC obtained proof that salespeople were delivering deceptive sales pitches and using high-pressure sales techniques against the consumers, the cooling-off remedy was highly effective. By changing the contract rules of the game, the cooling-off remedy allowed consumers to protect themselves while minimizing government involvement.[23]

In 1970, the Commission moved into the field of children's advertising. It filed several complaints that involved advertisements of children's products or advertisements that made special claims about a product's value to children's health. Most importantly, the Commission ruled that children's limited experience and lack of perceptual sophistication called for special scrutiny of advertisements aimed at children. After cases such as Mattel, it was clear to advertisers that children constituted a specially protected group.[24] By 1973, the Commission had tripled the number of lawyers prosecuting false advertising cases.

While concentrating much attention on consumer protection activities during this period, the Commission displayed an equally imaginative approach to its antitrust responsibilities. The Commission initiated major economic and industry studies focusing on industry practices that had a particularly severe impact on consumers.[25] In the early sixties, the Commission established a premerger notification program which required large companies to notify the Commission of any intended mergers.[26] The Federal Trade Commission also led the way in antitrust enforcement involving conglomerate mergers.[27] The FTC conducted studies of marketplace structure and practices that impacted the baking industry, and it issued merger guidelines for the fluid milk industry.[28] The Commission has been uniformly looked to as the chief source of intelligence about industrial concentration.[29]

Enforcement Strategies and Remedies

One of the earliest Commission actions taken to strengthen its enforcement arsenal was its decision to stop accepting companies' "assurances of voluntary compliance" as a means of settling proposed cases. These assurances had had no deterrent effect. In essence, the assurances permitted a company to engage in practices that the Commission regarded as law violations until the Commission challenged the legality of such practices. The Commission also began to shift away from issuing guides to businesses on marketplace standards. Instead, the Commission devoted more enforcement resources to issuing trade regulation rules.[30] These rules established similar standards to those of the marketplace standards guides but carried the same force of law as an FTC complaint.[31]

The Commission also turned its attention to creating more innovative remedies to strengthen the impact of its cease and desist orders. This strength was critically needed if consumers were to realize the benefits of the Commission's actions. Consumer groups aided, and indeed in some cases pushed, the Commission to broaden its arsenal of enforcement tools to encompass requiring the three-day cooling-off periods for door-to-door sales,[32] prohibiting the sale or transfer of installment contracts unless existing consumers' defenses against their original sellers were preserved,[33] and requiring refunds or restitution to consumers misled by the seller's unfair or deceptive practices.[34]

In 1971, the Commission addressed its first request for substantiation of advertising claims to the major domestic automobile manufacturers. This request marked the Commission's opening salvo in the development of its highly successful advertising substantiation program.[35] Under this program, advertisers were required to maintain substantiation of any claims that they made in their advertisements. This program, backed up by a vigorous enforcement effort against false and misleading advertisements, resulted in a significant improvement in television's hourly advertising messages.

Perhaps the most imaginative remedy that the Commission developed in this period was that of corrective advertising. A consumer group that styled itself SOUP (Students Opposed to Unfair Practices) suggested this remedy to the Commission. The Commission first proposed the remedy in 1970.[36] While the Commission declined to order the remedy in the 1970 case, it nevertheless held that in a proper case it could order an advertiser to run corrective advertisements to cure lingering deception caused by claims that the Commission found misleading. One year later, in a complaint brought against the Continental Baking Company, the Commission entered the first corrective advertising order.[37]

Finally, the Commission for the first time permitted a consumer group to intervene and participate formally in a Commission case.[38] The importance of this ruling must not be overlooked. One of the most frequent criticisms leveled at the Commission is that it is overly influenced by industry. No specific evidence has ever been offered to substantiate this criticism against any individual commissioner. Nevertheless, the criticism has some truth in that the Commission tends to pay more attention to questions of whether its complaints in a particular instance were overstated or whether its orders were too strong than whether they were understated or too weak.

This situation has developed not because commissioners are too industry oriented but because of the fact that only respondents can appeal FTC decisions. As a result, the Commission has focused on the arguments that respondents are likely to make in opposition to its complaints or trade regulatory rules, since the respondents are the only parties who can challenge the Commission's actions in court. If those persons injured by the violations alleged in the Commission's complaint were permitted, in proper cases, to intervene as parties, they too would have the right to appeal the Commission's decisions to the courts. Thus, the Commission would be forced to focus its attention on both the strengths and weaknesses of its complaints and orders from the point of view of both the challenged business and the allegedly injured public.

Moreover, if the Commission's actions to dismiss complaints as well as to sustain them could be appealed in Court, the legitimacy of such actions would be substantially increased in the eyes of the public. Unfortunately, the Commission has never pursued its Firestone intervention decision in this direction. I am convinced that this is an important future area for the Commission to explore.

Conclusion

The Commission's actions in 1968, which were implemented, expanded, and institutionalized in the subsequent years, provide a dramatic demonstration of how flexible and responsive the regulatory process is to social, economic, and technological changes in the marketplace. Despite the many valid criticisms of the FTC, the Commission during this period remained able to focus on such significant marketplace practices as health and safety advertising claims, unconscionable credit practices, and warranties that seriously harmed consumers. It proved itself capable both of shifting its priorities and its internal administrative processes and of creating new, innovative remedies. Several key factors enabled the Commission to respond to the challenges that confronted it in the 1960s.

The first of these factors is the multiheaded nature of the Commission's governing body. Much criticism has been leveled at multiheaded agencies because of their alleged diffusion of responsibility and accountability. However, there is disagreement on this point. In the sixties, individual commissioners initially pushed much of the Commission's new enforcement emphases and strategies, frequently over the opposition of the chair. Individual commissioners bring different strengths to their positions and can exercise leadership in different aspects of the Commission's business. Commissioner Elman, for example, lead the way in many pathbreaking, innovative interpretations of the Commission's statutory responsibilities. He wrote the most comprehensive argument justifying the Commission's trade regulation rule authority[39] and was equally critical in focusing the Commission's attention on the anticompetitive aspects of conglomerate mergers.[40]

Much of the Commission's focus on consumers' needs, and particularly on the needs of low-income consumers, resulted from Commissioner Jones's deep concerns in these areas. Ongoing contact with consumer groups through invitations to address them or to participate in various business-consumer panels both informed and enhanced Commissioner Jones's concerns. James Nicholson's interest in the Commission's backlog and case overload was responsible for the development of both important new procedures and a case management system that still plays a vital role in the Commission's management of its business today. Despite whatever one may think about the Commission's Robinson Patman's jurisdiction, it was Commissioner MacIntyre's steadfast championship of this statute that ensured its active enforcement during this period. And it was due to Chairman Dixon's leadership and close congressional relationship that the Commission's budget steadily increased during this period.

The second factor was the Commission's ability to respond to the new needs of consumers in the 1960s. The Commission members' direct and frequent contacts with consumer groups substantially facilitated its ability to respond. In part, contacts during this period depended on the individual commissioners' and bureau directors' personal interests. However, the procedures now in place, plus the traditional regulatory agency enforcement tools such as investigative hearings, limited rights of petition and intervention, and frequent Congress-Commission interchanges, both formal and informal, ensure that the Commission will be forced to confront the various constituencies impacted by its programs or lack thereof.

Finally, the quality of the Commission chair and that of the principal Commission bureau chiefs, is also critical to the Commission's long-term performance. As noted above, individual commissioners can influence the Commission's performance. But it is the day-to-day work of the Commission lawyers, economists, and social scientists, as directed by their bureau chiefs who in turn report to the chair, that will determine the innovativeness, soundness, and relevance of the Commission's programs.

These three factors primarily accounted for the Commission's success in the late sixties and early seventies. They helped the Commission enhance the consumers' awareness of their rights and significantly expanded the deterrent effect of its enforcement strategies. These programs enabled the Commission to raise the standard for acceptable business practice and brought about significant changes in the conduct of the business community. Many of these changes prevail today.

Notes

1. Ralph Nader, *Unsafe at Any Speed*, PB, 1966.

2. Report of the National Advisory Commission on Civil Disorders (Kerner Commission), July, 1968, p. 7.

3. E.g., Fair Packaging and Labelling Act, 80 Stat. 1296, 15 U.S.C. 1451 (1966); and the Consumer Credit Protection Act, 82 Stat. 146, 15 U.S.C. 1601 (1969).

4. E. Cox, R. Fellmeth, and J. Schulz, *The Nader Report on the Federal Trade Commission* (1969), p. vii.

5. Report on the ABA Commission to Study the Federal Trade Commission (September 15, 1969).

6. A rich and lively literature commenting on the FTC has developed. For example, see Ash Council: President's Advisory Council on Executive Organization, A New Regulatory Framework—Report on Selected Independent Regulatory Agencies (Washington, D.C.: GPO, 1971), esp. pp. 1-55 and 87-95.

7. The Commissioners in this period were: Chairman Rand Dixon, Everette MacIntyre, Philip Elman, Leon Higginsbotham, replaced in 1984 by John Reilly, who was succeeded by James Nicholson in 1969, and Mary Gardiner Jones. Casper Weinberger, who was appointed to James Nicholson's seat, was named chair in January 1970 and was succeeded as chair by Miles Kirkpatrick in September 1970.

8. The reorganization also resulted in widespread resignations of many of the older attorneys who had been with the Commission since the 1930s. It also produced extensive changes in the administrative and bureau division directors.

9. Cease and desist orders may be appealed to a U.S. Court of Appeals, which will sustain them if it finds that they are supported by "substantial evidence" and within the broad scope of the powers granted to the Commission.

10. Susan Wagner, *The Federal Trade Commission* (Praeger, 1971), p. 204.

11. FTC Announcement, Antitrust and Trade Reg. Rep. No. 365, p. A15 (7-9-68).

12. FTC Announcement, Antitrust and Trade Reg. Rep. No. 527, p. A14 (8-24-71). The Commission's hearings are summarized and analyzed in A. Howard and C. Hulbert, *Advertising and the Public Interest: A Staff Report to the Federal Trade Commission* (1973).

13. Transcript of Advertising Hearings in FTC Library. This pioneering learning effort has been continued by the Commission to the present day. Advertising technology and the enforcement rules and mechanisms have continued to evolve, if not so rapidly as in 1971.

14. FTC News Release, February 5, 1970.

15. E.g., All-State Industries of North Carolina. FTC Dkt. 8783, 3 Trade Reg. Rep. No. 18,740 (April 1969), aff'd. 1970 Trade Cases, No. 73,112 (4th Cir. 1970); and Leon Tashof t/a New York Jewelry, FTC Dkt. No. 8714, 3 Trade Reg. Rep. No. 18,606 (December, 1968).

16. The Commission's programs to combat inner-city fraud are described in Mary Gardiner Jones, "The Inner-City Marketplace: The Need for Law and Order," *George Washington Law Review*, vol. 37, p. 1051 (1969).

17. Economic Report on the Use of Games of Chance in Food and Gasoline Retailing, 1968; and trade regulation rule proposed 8-16-69, 2 CCH Trade Reg. Rep. No. 7,975; FTC Staff Report on Automobile Warranties, 1968.

18. 16 C.F.R. 419, originally issued in 1969.

19. FTC Report on Automobile Warranties, 1970; Antitrust and Trade Reg. Rep. No. 384, p. A18 (11-19-68).

20. 15 U.S.C. 2301-2312 (1982).

21. *FTC v. Sperry Hutchinson*, 405 U.S. 233 (1972).

22. See, e.g., its trade regulation rules requiring disclosure of the power consumption (in watts), light output (in lumens) and design life (in hours) of electric light bulbs (12 Fed. Reg. 528, July 31, 1969), of the gasoline octane ratings at gasoline pumps (2 CCH Trade Reg. Rep. No. 7969, July 30, 1969), and of permanent care instructions disclosing directions for cleaning and laundering of textiles (2 CCH Trade Reg. Rep. No. 7979, November 4, 1969).

23. 16 C.F.R. 429.

24. *In the Matter of Mattel, Inc.*, 79 F.T.C. 667 (1971). In December 1970 the FTC announced its intention to work with the FCC to explore the possibility of FTC-FCC hearings on children's advertising. Antitrust and Trade Reg. Rep. No. 494, p. A13 (1-5-71).

25. See, e.g., Commission studies conducted of marketplace structures and practices impacting consumers in the bread and fluid milk industries.

26. This was the precursor of the enactment by Congress in 1976 of the Hart-Scott-Rodino Premerger Notification Act to establish the notification requirement for all major mergers. 5 U.S.C. 7A.

27. The first conglomerate merger case, a product extension merger, was brought by the FTC against Procter & Gamble. See *FTC v. Procter & Gamble*, 386 US 568 (1967). In 1969, the FTC sent to the Congress its report on its in-depth investigation of the conglomerate merger movement, analyzing its cases, effects and implications. Wagner, op. cit., p. 124.

28. Economic Report of the Baking Industry, Antitrust and Trade Reg. Rep. No. 369, p. A4 (8-6-68); and Merger Guidelines in the Fluid Milk Industry, Antitrust and Trade Reg. Rep. No. 620, p. A 166 (7-3-73).

29. Louis Kohlmeier, *The Regulators* (New York: Harper & Row, 1969), p. 259.

30. In 1962 the Commission amended its Rules of Practice to provide for issuance of trade regulation rules (TRRs). 27 Fed. Reg. 4636, 4796 (1962). It issued its first TRR in 1964, requiring cigarette companies to disclose the hazardous nature of cigarette smoking. Statement of Basis and Purpose of Trade Regulation Rule, 29 Fed. Reg. 8325, 8369 (1964). The Commission's power to issue such TRRs was finally confirmed in *National Petroleum Refiners Association v. FTC*, 482 F. 2d 672 (DC Cir. 1973), cert. denied, 42 Law Week 3482 (2-26-74).

31. See, e.g., FTC, Trade Regulation Rule Concerning a Cooling-Off Period for Door-to-Door Sales, 36 Fed. Reg. 1211 (1971).

32. First ordered in Household Sewing Machine Co., FTC Dkt. 8671, 3 Trade Reg. Rep. No. 18,822 (August, 1969).

33. See FTC Order in All-State Industries of North Carolina, FTC Dkt. 8783, 3

Trade Reg. Rep. No. 18,740 (April, 1969); and Everette Eugene Miller, FTC Dkt. No. 19,163 (March, 1970), subsequently incorporated into a trade regulation rule.

34. The first complaint containing this remedy was Curtis Publishing Company, FTC Dkt. 8800, 3 Trade Reg. Rep. 18,798 (October, 1969); see also Windsor Distributor, FTC Dkt. 8773, 3 Trade Reg. Rep. No. 19,157; and London Credit and Discount Corp., FTC Dkt. 8812, 3 Trade Reg. Rep. No. 19,195.

35. See Report on the Advertising Substantiation Program of the Federal Trade Commission, April 1972, Antitrust Trade Reg. Rep. No. 574, p. A14 (8-1-72).

36. The Firestone Rubber & Tire Company, FTC Dkt. No. 8818 (October, 1970), Antitrust and Trade Reg. Rep. No. 485, p. A2 (10-27-70).

37. "How Big Does the FTC Want To Be?" *Fortune*, vol. 85, p. 107 (February, 1972).

38. Firestone Rubber & Tire Company, see supra, note 36.

39. See supra, note 30.

40. See supra, note 27.

Reflections of a Commission Staffer

Christian S. White

It was my good fortune that Mary Gardiner Jones lured me to the Federal Trade Commission in 1971. My reaction to her presentation is one of great support. In my opinion, her paper accurately reviews a pivotal period in the modern history of the Federal Trade Commission. Her analysis puts the lie to that story about the acid generation, heavy metal musician who supposedly said, "If you can remember the sixties you probably weren't part of the action." Jones was surely part of the action and she remembers it well.

I cannot resist telling one story about the first time I went to a closed meeting of the commissioners. In the early 1970s it was a privilege for the staff to watch the commissioners' private deliberations. Because I had worked on a matter being discussed, I was invited to attend a certain Commission meeting. I sat in the appointed chair between Jones on my right and Commissioner Paul Rand Dixon immediately to my left. That orientation may not have reflected accurately the political spectrum but the discussion was an eye opener.

I had no experience whatsoever of the tenor and tone of Commission meetings but I knew that advisors to commissioners should speak only when spoken to and then only in a hushed whisper into the ear of your own commissioner. I learned quickly that the debate was spirited, to say the least, when Dixon and Jones began to argue heatedly and at high volume about a particular consumer protection case. I had to duck back out of the way while the shots were fired over my chin. I learned quickly also that the commissioners had passionate and differing views about their responsibilities. To my surprise, the clash of these views did indeed shape the Commission's agenda. It was an exciting time, and Jones's presentation captures the spirit of the Commission during her tenure.

I am grateful to William Wilkie and Patrick Murphy for organizing this conference and for giving me the chance to attend what seems to have become the FTC marketing experts alumni meeting. Virtually all the marketing experts the Commission has been lucky enough to attract over the years are here. Each of them has made a remarkable contribution to the Commission.

It may be said that the FTC is a study in contrast. In my opinion, what is best about the Commission is a product of the contrasts in its roles. From its predecessor, the Bureau of Corporations, the Commission has inherited important research responsibilities. The authority given the agency in section 6 of the Federal Trade Commission Act, 15 U.S.C., section 46, to obtain information about the marketplace and to report on its workings has been critical in the formulation and development of FTC enforcement policies and programs. The combination of research with enforcement has helped the Commission adapt to changing market developments. Both research and enforcement are tempered and improved by the other role.

Another highly productive contrast has flowed from a certain tension between the Commission's two enforcement missions: antitrust and consumer protection. I continue to believe that the FTC is a much better place because the Commission has to wrestle with each of those responsibilities and find a way for them to coalesce effectively. In my opinion, that continues to be a challenge to the Commission.

Later in this program you will hear much more about an important force that has helped the Commission adapt over the past two decades: external oversight. During the years covered by this conference, the Commission has been fortunate to have excellent oversight from the public and private sectors. As Jones has described, private sector oversight goes back to the somewhat acerbic Nader report and to the more polite but nevertheless critical report of the American Bar Association. Later in the conference you will learn in detail about the reprise of the ABA report. I will say only that if the second ABA report has as positive and long-lasting an effect on the Commission as did the first report, the agency easily will reach its one hundredth anniversary and beyond.

William Baer will, I am sure, address the role of congressional oversight of the Commission during his tenure. However, I want to highlight one significant development. When I came to the Commission in 1971, the climate of congressional oversight was quite different from what it is today. A member of Congress who sought to influence a regulatory agency about a specific pending matter ran the risk of adverse publicity. The *Washington Post* had a real interest in such things. It was possible to resist informal congressional inquiries as follows: "You don't really want to interfere in a pending matter, do you?" Not infrequently, the answer was, "Certainly not." Today the relationship between the agencies and Congress is quite different. The unfolding investigation of Speaker Wright's (and other members') contacts with regulators of the thrift industry suggests that the relationship has changed. The nature of the congressional oversight has become much more tightly focused on specific matters. Oversight has occurred almost to the exclusion of the dispassionate analysis of the Commission's mission. I hope the recent ABA report will help the Congress to focus on the Commission's overall performance rather than on specific actions.

In addition to the impact of oversight on the Commission, I want to highlight another issue for you to consider while you review the various periods of Commission history and the critiques of each. That is the role of overstatement. It is the nature of the advocates for and critics of the Commission to focus on the exceptional 5 percent of the agency's activities. There is also a residual core of enforcement activities that the FTC has pursued relatively constantly over the years. This less glamorous work sustains and justifies the agency but does not create much news nor receive much analysis. In the early 1970s, the Commission was said to have brought the advertisers to their knees or to have reformed national advertising in a very dramatic way. One can attribute that notoriety to a very small number of cases, perhaps as few as four or five. It does not take many specific actions for the Commission to get quite a reputation— either for good or ill. Throughout all the changes, the basic work of protecting consumers has been sustained, and fortunately so.

One final point. There have been many major shifts in the public's perception of the Commssion and in the Commission's own view of its missions. For example, consumer protection rulemaking mushroomed dramatically in the late 1970s and receded to a much smaller proportion of the Commission's activity in the late 1980s. Also, since the passage of the FTC Improvements Act in 1975 and the Hart-Scott-Rodino Antitrust Improvement Act of 1976, litigation has been conducted increasingly in federal court rather than in the Commission's administrative process. However, many of the changes in the Commission's activity have concerned process or perception and not the agency's basic missions. During the past twenty years, despite conflict about whether the Commission is doing too much or too little, or whether it is pursuing the right mix of policies, there has been a remarkable consensus on the purpose for which the Commission was created and that purpose continues to be its guide: protecting the welfare of consumers. There is remarkably little current debate about the Commission's ultimate objective. The debate is now about the details and about the application of that basic principle to specific facts. In my opinion, this broad consensus on the Commission's responsibility bodes well for the agency's future.

Second-Order Effects of the FTC Initiatives

H. Keith Hunt

As discussant of Mary Gardiner Jones's paper I would like to focus not on the actions and effects of the proactive FTC of the early seventies but rather on the second-order effects outside the FTC of some of those actions. My point is that the initiatives of the proactive FTC had impacts outside of the FTC sphere that in some cases are as important and interesting as were the internal effects.

Corrective Advertising

Of course I have to start with corrective advertising, because that is what got me into the FTC orbit in the first place. Most of us know of the internal actions based on the corrective advertising initiative. Are you aware that corrective advertising is being used as the legal theory in non-FTC legal disputes? Two quick examples will suffice.

Big O tires, a franchise group of tire dealers, had been using Big Foot as the trade name for its special very wide tires for quite some time, and the name was established in the market. A major tire company, in full knowledge of Big O's ongoing use of the trade name, started using Big Foot as the trade name for one of its tire lines. After the usual amount of court interaction the judge not only required that the major tire company cease using the name but also added a corrective advertising remedy. The major tire company was required to pay Big O 25 percent of the advertising budget spent promoting the major tire company's Big Foot line. Corrective advertising was cited as the legal doctrine on which the award was based.

In a Utah case, Godfathers Pizza opened several company-owned outlets in Utah under the Godfathers name in full knowledge of the existence of a Godfathers Restaurant in Salt Lake City. It was a clear case of name infringement. The restaurant waited until it was obvious that God-fathers Pizza was going to be highly successful and then sued for name infringement. The name infringement decision was clear from the start. The issue was what the penalty should be. In what I have often thought to be a Solomon-like decision, Judge Winder ruled that Godfathers Pizza could continue to use the name even though it was clear name infringement, conditional on Godfathers Pizza paying Godfathers Restaurant 25 percent of Godfathers Pizza's total advertising expenditures in the Utah market each year. That 25 percent could be used by the restaurant for advertising to clarify in people's minds the difference between the two companies. Or the restaurant could pocket the 25 percent (at that time about $50,000 a year). The restaurant hadn't made a profit for several years, so you can guess what course they chose. Judge Winder's decision was based on the legal doctrine of corrective advertising. Both parties were absolutely delighted with the decision, both holding major victory parties. The pizza company was netting over a million dollars a year in profits, so the $50,000 payment was worth it to be able to continue using the name. And the $50,000 made the restaurant profitable for the first time in several years.

Remembering all our concerns with corrective advertising, especially in assessing the "right" percentage to obtain adequate correction, most of us shudder at such cavalier use of the doctrine in nonadvertising cases. Nevertheless, judges are making creative use of the FTC corrective advertising concept.

Consumer Satisfaction and Dissatisfaction

It was during my FTC days that I kept reading your many memos saying that this or that FTC action would increase consumer satisfaction, or decrease consumer dissatisfaction, or both. It all made sense, so it didn't bother me and I kept signing off saying "sure it would." My original academic field is marketing. In marketing we mouth the platitude that the purpose of marketing is to create and maintain consumer satisfaction. All this consumer satisfaction verbiage sounded great to me until one day when I started wondering about how we could actually measure whether consumer satisfaction was increased or maintained or whatever. I started thumbing the marketing research books to find the most common measures of consumer satisfaction/dissatisfaction and I couldn't find any mention of the topic. Undaunted and always looking for an excuse to go to the Library of Congress and bliss out in library heaven, I trundled up the hill. Nothing. After substantial searching I finally uncovered three articles that mentioned the topic. After leaving the FTC I obtained a grant from the National Science Foundation through the Marketing Science Institute to host a conference on the conceptualization and measurement of consumer satisfaction and dissatisfaction. That was in 1975. Today there are upwards of eight hundred articles on the topic and an academic journal is now being published solely on the topic. All of this came from the FTC staff's continual use of the phrase.

Also, those who remember the nightmare days of the budget process when we would use the Better Business Bureau complaint data as a major input for justifying time commitments to projects will also remember how we kept saying that we needed a better way to assess consumer satisfaction. Finally the Office of Policy Planning and Evaluation (OPPE) was charged with doing a national study of consumer satisfaction and consumer complaints for, as I recall it, a budget of about $20,000. I said it couldn't be done for five times that amount and went on to other things. Ralph Day, on the other hand, said, "That's an interesting project. Let's see what can be done with it." Ralph put a lot of work into the project. Then Consumer Affairs got interested in a similar project. Then the FTC project sort of drifted off to Consumer Affairs, and eventually the national study was done by a commercial research firm. But Ralph Day went back to Indiana University and continued developing and field testing his own measurement system. Finally he ran a pilot of the whole system in Bloomington, Indiana, home of Indiana University. The whole system worked fine. Ralph's system was then used by one of his Ph.D.'s to do a truly national study in Canada funded by Consumer and Corporate Affairs Canada that went beyond our wildest imaginings in the U.S. As a result of the FTC initiative, consumer satisfaction/dissatisfaction is now a major topic and an established methodology.

Complaining Behavior

We always worried about the validity of the Better Business Bureau complaint data. We used it extensively at budget time and were grateful for it, but still we recognized that it was probably highly biased due to the characteristics of people willing to call the Better Business Bureau with a complaint and due to the Better Business Bureau's recording of that complaint.

Those of us who were or had been at the FTC and were interested in consumer research kept expressing the need for a better way of obtaining consumer complaints. This expanded to increased attention to how best to handle consumer complaints. All this grew out of our use of the Better Business Bureau complaint data in the budget process. Today there is a substantial body of literature on complaining behavior.

Deception

One of the first FTC initiatives to get academic attention was the issue of deception, especially deceptive advertising. Many of the early initiatives were given life by a different view of unacceptable advertising practice from what had existed until then. And pursuing that different view required a much more extensive understanding of deception. Many of the FTC matters tested the various defining characteristics of deception, trying to find out what the Commission and even the courts would decide was acceptable and unacceptable in various advertisements that some might judge to be deceptive.

This early initiative was one of the first picked up by the academic community and pursued at length. David Gardner, an FTC alumnus, published his outstanding article in 1975, and many articles have been published since then. Ivan Preston's work in the law journals has greatly expanded our understanding of the area.

I also need to mention the research efforts paid for by the advertising community to show that people misperceive all types of information, not just advertisements. The goal of the research is to establish that much misperception occurs in noncommercial communications and that advertising should not be held to any higher standard of correct perception than is evident in other communication perceptions.

All of these are outgrowths of the early FTC initiative to expand the concept of deceptiveness.

Deterrence

One of the magic words at the FTC is *deterrence*. This or that action will deter additional undesirable behavior. As I kept seeing the term over and over, I began wondering exactly what was known about deterrence and whether we really should be expecting our FTC actions to deter anything. This topic is slowly catching on as one of interest in consumer research, public policy, and marketing.

It turns out that deterrence is a major topic in two areas of inquiry: international relations and criminology. What does one nation do to keep another nation from destroying or damaging it? What does society do to keep individuals from initial or repeated criminal behavior? Based on what we know about deterrence from international relations and from criminology, it is easy to see why our FTC actions have had limited if any deterrent effects.

Children and Television Advertising

Our FTC initiatives in the children and television advertising arena has been the major impetus to the expanding knowledge in that topic over the past decade. This is not to take away at all from the exceptional work done by many of the private groups, but it wasn't until the FTC started seriously considering the topic that advertisers got alarmed. Because of this FTC initiative there has been substantial work done on children's interaction with television advertising, research that gives us a better idea of what types of advertising are more and less desirable for children.

Informational Labeling

Finally, the FTC's initiatives in the informational labeling arena have been the foundation for several activities. I will skip over the issue of nutritional information labeling because there are probably no two of us who would totally agree on that issue. But in the more general sense, the FTC's early initiatives led to other groups getting involved.

One example is the work for the Department of Commerce through the National Bureau of Standards, again facilitated by the Marketing Science Institute, which developed prototype information labels for home insulation, smoke detectors, and vacuum cleaners. This all grew out of the FTC's initial work and the key members of the development team were FTC alumni.

Another example was the study for the distilled spirits industry trade association looking at the use of information labels on alcoholic beverages to warn pregnant women that alcohol overdoses could cause birth defects. The study was aborted when the Bureau of Alcohol, Tobacco, and Firearms took off the pressure. When the issue heated up again and moved to its current level, it has been without any input from experts as far as I know.

Conclusion

I have tried to give a short overview of the impacts of the FTC initiatives of the early seventies outside the FTC. Perhaps the second-order effects have had a greater impact than the initial impacts inside the FTC. For those of us involved in the efforts I think we should be pleased that our work was good enough to be picked up and used by others.

And now it is time for a new generation to pick up the pieces and move forward with new and expanded initiatives. As much fun as it would be to reassemble the "old gang," there never really was such a long-term group. Rather, we were individuals moving through a proactive agency, each doing our part to move the programs forward during our time with the agency. For most of us inside and outside of law, it has affected our professional lives since then. I suspect that most of us are too much part of the establishment to move back into that proactive mode. So it falls to new commissioners, new leaders, and new staff to do for the 1990s what we had the fun and professional pleasure of doing in the late sixties and early seventies. And you know what? Many of us aren't going to like what they do any more than the "old dogs" liked what we did.

With all that has happened or not happened at the FTC the past few years, the delight to me is that after all the scourging and holding up to public ridicule and cutting the budget, the FTC we knew has remained unaltered in legislative charge and structure. Through all the designs to emasculate it, it remains virile and ready for new leadership and budget to start forth again in creating proactive initiatives as it did so successfully before.

At the Turning Point: The Commission in 1978

William J. Baer

This article examines the Federal Trade Commission in 1978, at the midpoint of the last twenty years of its history. The Commission was then at the height of its powers and influence. Over the prior ten years a supportive Congress and successive administrations had expanded the FTC's mandate significantly. Its docket of consumer protective initiatives, antitrust actions, and economic studies was full. There seemed little that the Commission was reluctant to challenge or legally unable to accomplish.

The year 1978 was also when the tide turned. Growing dissatisfaction with regulation generally and with a number of specific FTC initiatives produced a strong backlash that tended to overshadow the Commission's many accomplishments and, for a time, imperiled the agency's existence. Congress relieved the crisis in 1980 by passing legislation that preserved the Commission's basic statutory mandate but imposed restrictions on certain rulemaking proceedings and established procedural safeguards on the future exercise of the agency's authority.

Thereafter, and with the advent of the Reagan administration, the Commission began to change direction. Caution and restraint were the new hallmarks as the Commission significantly reduced the number and range of its activities. Thus, 1978 was a critical point for the FTC when compared both to where it had been and to the direction it took later.

The Revitalization of the Commission

To appreciate the Commission in 1978, one must first look to the events of the late 1960s and early 1970s that transformed the "little old

An earlier version of this paper appeared in the *Journal of Public Policy & Marketing*, Volume 7, 1988, 11-20. Reprinted with permission.

lady of Pennsylvania Avenue" into an energized suffragette. In 1969, Ralph Nader and the American Bar Association published separate reports on the Federal Trade Commission.[1] While they differed dramatically in tone, the two studies reached remarkably similar conclusions. Both saw the Commission as an agency with enormous but unused potential, its broad statutory reach over unfair and deceptive acts or practices and unfair methods of competition as well-suited to the demands of a changing, dynamic economy. But the critics also found that inadequate planning, mediocre staffing, suspect economic analysis, and unnecessary restrictions on the Commission's enforcement powers combined to squander the value of that broad mandate. These criticisms, made during a rising tide of consumerism, focused attention on the Commission's potential. The studies served as both catalyst and blueprint for the White House, Congress, consumers, and businesses to insist on the FTC's revitalization.

In 1969, President Nixon chose Caspar Weinberger as the first in a succession of reform-minded chairmen. Although Weinberger remained at the agency for only nine months, he undertook a major housecleaning and reorganization. This basic organizational structure still exists today. The Bureaus of Competition and Consumer Protection serve as the agency's law enforcement arms; the Bureau of Economics provides economic analysis on law enforcement matters and tracks long-term trends in the economy; and the Office of General Counsel advises the Commission and represents the agency in court.

Between 1970 and 1976 three other Republican appointees—Miles Kirkpatrick, Lewis Engman, and Calvin Collier—followed Weinberger. Each was committed to maximizing the Commission's potential as the honest cop on the economic regulatory beat.

Over the same period, Congress aided the agency's revitalization by expanding its jurisdiction and toughening its enforcement powers. Amendments to the FTC Act in 1973 gave the Commission new injunction authority and increased its civil penalty powers.[2] The landmark Magnuson-Moss Warranty/FTC Improvement Act of 1975 empowered the Commission to adopt broad-based consumer protection rules, to sue directly in federal court for FTC Act and FTC rules violations, and to seek both consumer redress and civil penalties.[3] New credit statutes, passed in 1974, 1976, and 1977, mandated equal credit opportunity and provided consumers with protection against unfair debt collection practices.[4] The Energy Policy and Conservation Act of 1975 authorized the Commission to require major consumer appliance manufacturers to disclose their products' relative energy efficiency.[5] And, the Hart-Scott-Rodino Antitrust Improvement Act of 1976[6] enhanced the ability of both the Commission and the Justice Department Antitrust Division to screen, investigate, and block anticompetitive mergers by requiring parties to give the government unprecedented advance notice of large mergers and acquisitions.

The Commission wasted little time in exercising its new authority and breathing new life into its existing statutes. Better planning processes were established. The pre-1970 inclination to let the mailbag of consumer complaints dictate law enforcement priorities was abandoned in favor of more sophisticated case-selection criteria designed to focus the agency's efforts on the most serious and costly market imperfections.

The Commission's Bureau of Competition initiated a series of precedent-setting antitrust activities, for example, challenging the structure of the petroleum and breakfast cereal industries[7] and examining the competitive consequences of self-regulation by the "learned professions," doctors, dentists, accountants, and others.[8]

The Bureau of Consumer Protection also dramatically increased the level and reach of its activities. Advertising by national manufacturers received unprecedented scrutiny. Consumer protection rulemaking, seen as a more efficient and fairer law enforcement tool against widespread misconduct than case-by-case litigation, became a high priority. In the two years following passage of the 1975 Magnuson-Moss Warranty Act, the Bureau of Consumer Protection initiated eighteen major consumer protection rulemakings addressing alleged anticonsumer activity in the sale of hearing aids, used cars, prescription drugs, health spas, funeral services, franchises, nutritional and over-the-counter drug advertising, among others.[9]

The Bureau of Economics increased its staff and its role in Commission priority setting. It also undertook an ambitious new Line of Business program designed to analyze the relationships between industry structure and economic performance. The program sought annual data on sales, costs, profits, and assets from 450 leading manufacturers so that the Commission's economists could track long-range trends in the economy and provide Congress and the Commission with a better understanding of marketplace dynamics.

By 1976, as the Nixon-Ford administration was giving way to Jimmy Carter and the Democrats, the Commission's budget had nearly doubled and its ongoing law enforcement activities contrasted sharply with its 1960s focus on matters of more dubious economic value, such as price discrimination and mislabeling of textiles, wools, and furs. No longer the "little old lady of Pennsylvania Avenue," the Commission was described by one congressional committee as "one of the more effective regulatory agencies."[10]

The Pertschuk Commission

In 1977, Jimmy Carter appointed Michael Pertschuk to serve as Commission chairman, and he served in that capacity until 1981. Pertschuk had been the Senate Commerce Committee's staff director and a key figure in the passage of important proconsumer legislation Congress passed in the late 1960s and early 1970s. He was particularly instrumental in the passage of those laws that strengthened the FTC.

At the Commission, Pertschuk joined one long-time veteran, Democrat Paul Rand Dixon, and Republicans David Clanton, a 1976 appointee who also had served on the Senate Commerce Committee's staff, and Elizabeth Hanford Dole, a former consumer advisor to President Nixon. They were joined a short time later by two additional Carter appointees, Robert Pitofsky, a well-known and widely respected antitrust professor, and Patricia Bailey, a Republican with solid consumer credentials and considerable political savvy.

Pertschuk assembled a talented and diverse group of senior managers from government, the private sector, public interest groups, and academia. They joined an existing staff of young, aggressive lawyers and economists recruited by Pertschuk's activist predecessors. All were committed to maintaining the course the agency had set in the early and mid-1970s and to pursuing additional FTC initiatives consistent with the populist, proconsumer themes sounded during Carter's presidential campaign.

Many of the law enforcement actions Pertschuk and his staff pursued were a continuation of the rulemakings, cases, and investigations that his predecessors had started. Pertschuk and his senior managers also promised to initiate new activities that would test the outer limits of the Commission's authority in such areas as conglomerate mergers[11] and children's advertising.[12]

Easily the most controversial of the Pertschuk Commission's initiatives involved advertising directed to children. Pertschuk's early speeches criticized as commercial exploitation the growing volume of commercials designed to persuade young children to become consumers. These commercials were, in his view, an "unfair act or practice" under the Federal Trade Commission Act.[13] In early 1978, the Commission announced a rulemaking proceeding that would consider the extent of the problem and determine whether it was appropriate to ban television advertising directed to children at times when children comprised a significant percentage of the audience.[14]

Revolt Against Regulation

Also in 1978, the FTC became a principal target of what Pertschuk later termed the "Revolt against Regulation," a fast-spreading view that the expanding federal bureaucracy was overregulating the economy and imposing unnecessary and costly regulatory burdens while failing to appreciate the ability of the market to solve problems for itself. In retrospect, this growing dissatisfaction with federal regulation had been a significant element of Jimmy Carter's popular support. But, at the time, the depth of the antiregulatory sentiment was not apparent, and Carter, who was committed to an activist role for the federal regulatory agencies, installed agency heads, including Pertschuk, who shared his generally proregulation views.

The excruciating details of how the revolt against regulation engulfed the Commission are well documented elsewhere, and I will not repeat them here.[15] In brief, Congress, which had remained strongly supportive of the agency until 1978, began to show increasing hostility towards the Commission's activist agenda and to consider a broad range of proposals to restrict the agency's authority. The proposed restrictions included: (1) limiting the FTC's jurisdiction over unfair, as opposed to deceptive, acts and practices; (2) terminating the FTC's rulemaking proceedings involving children's advertising, used cars, and procedures for private organization standard-setting; (3) allowing one house of Congress to veto any trade regulation rule that the Commission might promulgate; (4) requiring dismissal of pending litigation against the cereal industry and the agricultural cooperatives; and (5) imposing new limits on the FTC's subpoena authority.

Since the Commission's congressional supporters and detractors could not agree on how or even whether to change or restrict the agency's mandate, Congress was stalemated. By 1979 both the debate and resulting frustration spilled over to the Appropriations Committee. The

Committee members, angered by their colleagues' inability to agree on reauthorization legislation, sought to restrict the agency through the power of the purse until substantive legislation could be passed.

The struggle hit a new low in late 1979, when Congress adopted an appropriations measure prohibiting the Federal Trade Commission from engaging in "any new activities" for the next thirty days.[16] An even lower point came six months later in May 1980, when for a brief but traumatic time, funding for the agency ran out and the Commission's staff were obligated to begin shutting down the agency until Congress reopened the tap. Finally, in June 1980, Congress reached an agreement on legislation that reaffirmed the agency's basic statutory mandate, imposed procedural restrictions on its exercise, and gave Congress more control over the agency's actions through a legislative veto mechanism that was later found unconstitutional.[17]

The Causes of the Reaction

How did the Commission find itself at the center of the storm? Some, particularly those Republicans who served on the Commission during the Reagan administration, blamed the Democrats who ran the agency between 1977 and 1980 as regulators who had run amok—oblivious to the cost of regulation, ignorant of marketplace dynamics, and committed to a social agenda that had no place in an economic regulatory agency.[18] However, a closer examination—aided by ten years' hindsight—suggests a somewhat different conclusion.

To be sure, many of the criticisms of the Commission's performance during the mid- and late 1970s were fair. Although the Commission's planning processes and its case selection had been improved, they were far from perfect. While the Commission rigorously identified problem areas in the economy that significantly affected the consumer, it did not always apply the same strict cost-benefit scrutiny when it came time to fashion remedies.

This problem was most evident in the initial trade regulation rules that the agency proposed in the years immediately following Congress's passage of the Magnuson-Moss Act. The Used Car Rule, in its initial form, required dealers but not private sellers to inspect used cars before sale. The FTC seems to have given little thought to the cost of such inspections, the alternative of "as is" sales, or the incentives to sell privately that such a proposal would create. Other rule proposals, such as the Hearing Aid Rule, contained a sensible core idea, for example, a mandatory thirty-day trial period for hearing aids. Too often however, these proposals were encumbered by onerous recordkeeping requirements and other restrictions on conduct that were costly, intrusive, and of questionable value to consumers. While most of these proposals were narrowed and focused by the Commission prior to their adoption, many of the provisions never should have been proposed in the first place.

The agency's initial tendency to overregulate and its seeming insensitivity to the burden of its regulatory proposals made the Commission an easy target. Business interests opposed to an FTC rule found they could take the spotlight off of their alleged anticonsumer conduct by focusing it instead on overly burdensome aspects of the Commission's proposals. Such complaints found a sympathetic audience on Capitol Hill where members of Congress were awakening to the public dissatisfaction with regulation.

Similarly, the Commission could fairly be accused of initiating complicated litigation without adequate preparation. Large structural cases, such as the *Exxon* litigation, were costly, time-consuming, and resource-intensive challenges to well-entrenched industries that were based on untested legal theories. Without the economic data needed to prove the complaint's allegations, the Commission's staff found themselves mired in a litigator's Vietnam.

Critics of the Commission staff's use of compulsory process also had a basis for their complaints. Until the late 1970s, the Commission had not sufficiently monitored ongoing investigations, particularly the staff's use of subpoenas. The staff's tendency to issue overly broad subpoenas needlessly burdened the business community and resulted in unnecessary litigation over subpoena compliance. Moreover, the subpoenas often were counterproductive. When the target of the subpoena actually produced the demanded documents, the Commission staff found itself overwhelmed with paper.[19]

The "Kid Vid" Rule proposal quickly came to symbolize the Commission's problems in 1978. The issue of commercial exploitation of children was important. It merited agency examination. But, as Pertschuk later conceded, the inflammatory rhetoric used to launch the initiative and the focus on a controversial remedy—banning ads at certain times of the day—when the Commission itself was uncertain about the remedy's practicality and its constitutionality, shifted the focus of the debate from a legitimate public policy issue to concern with the Commission's impartiality and judgment. The FTC became, in the words of the *Washington Post*, "the

National Nanny" while advertisers portrayed themselves as the innocent victims of bureaucratic excess.

Thus, the Commission brought on itself much of the controversy that began to engulf it in 1978. But the agency certainly does not deserve all of the blame. Hindsight also teaches us that much of the reaction against an energized Federal Trade Commission was inevitable. It is a lesson not in law or economics, but in political science. The Commission simply took on much more than its political base could support.

Congress contributed to the FTC's problem. Most of the activities that Congress criticized in the late 1970s, including the children's advertising initiative and the *Exxon* case, were actions that the FTC initiated either at Congress's direction or with its encouragement.[20] However, Congress failed to anticipate and brace itself against the reaction from those constituents who would be subject to the FTC's regulations. It was one thing for Congress to support effective consumer protection and vigorous antitrust enforcement. It was quite another to live with the angered reactions of those who became the FTC's targets. The sheer volume of the FTC activity, when coupled with the combined outcry of the affected economic interests and the rapidly shifting attitudes toward regulation, produced a backlash that persuaded Congress that it had to act.

Moreover, Congress and other FTC critics failed to appreciate that controversy is an inevitable cost of the Commission's broad and flexible law enforcement mandate. Congress had broadly empowered the Commission with the responsibility for policing unfair methods of competition and unfair and deceptive acts and practices so that it could respond to the needs of a changing economy by shifting its focus quickly to cope with novel anticonsumer and anticompetitive practices.

But that broad flexibility takes its toll. It means that, unlike such regulatory agencies as the Federal Communications Commission, the Interstate Commerce Commission, or the Food and Drug Administration, the Federal Trade Commission lacks a single industry with a strong, vested interest in its continued vitality. Thus, any significant agency law enforcement activity is likely to receive little support and to generate much controversy and criticism.

Substantive Achievements

A not surprising but more unfortunate effect of the political trauma that consumed the Commission in the late 1970s was that it almost completely obscured the impressive list of accomplishments that the agency achieved in the years following the Nader and ABA Reports. By 1978, years of targeting serious problems in critical areas of the economy had begun to pay off.[21]

The FTC effort to examine critically professional self-regulation and eliminate restrictions on competition was an unqualified success. In the health care area, the Eyeglasses Rule removed restrictions on price advertising and provided consumers with copies of their prescriptions in order to facilitate comparison shopping. Litigated cases against the American Medical Association and the American Dental Association struck down restrictions on advertising by doctors and dentists. The agency entered orders against scores of state and local medical professional associations prohibiting group boycotts and other activities that discouraged price competition and cost-containment programs. The Commission also proposed a model state law that promised significant consumer savings by removing restrictions against pharmacists' substitution of generic drugs for more costly brand-name drugs. Investigations were underway to root out similar forms of anticompetitive self-regulation by lawyers, veterinarians, accountants, real estate brokers, and other professionals.

In addition, FTC merger enforcement was vigilant, particularly in the energy, food, and heavy manufacturing sectors. The FTC removed interlocking directorates among oil and gas producers. The elimination of vertical restraints imposed by clothing, electronic, and other manufacturers of consumer goods resulted in an immediate and measurable increase in price competition between manufacturers of those products.

On the consumer protection side, the Commission zeroed in on high ticket fraud. Challenges to unfair proprietary school tactics, large-scale pyramid schemes, and multistate land development scams prevented significant amounts of consumer injury and secured repayment of millions of dollars to consumers. The Commission promulgated rules requiring insulation and major appliance manufacturers to disclose their products' comparative energy efficiency and the annual cost associated with the products' usage. The Commission's ultimately successful efforts to enact trade regulation rules requiring meaningful disclosure of the costs of funeral services, the condition of used cars, and the merits of franchise opportunities also continued.

National advertisers and their ad agencies were held to a tough standard for truth and honesty. The *Listerine* case, which challenged an advertiser's long-running claim that its product was an effective cold remedy, established the principle that perpetuation of an untruth could create a corresponding obligation to disseminate corrective advertising. The Commission developed a model state life insurance cost disclosure law which for the first time would give consumers the information they needed to compare competing policies.

These initiatives created real and quantifiable dollar savings such that the Commission's 1978 Annual Report pointed to hundreds of millions of dollars in consumer savings resulting from Commission actions in that year alone.

Regulatory Reforms in 1978

Also lost in the controversy swirling around the Commission in 1978 were the initiatives that Pertschuk and his predecessors had taken to reform the Commission's decision-making process and address some of the problems that were the subject of the pending debate over regulation and the need for reform. By the time Congress passed authorization legislation in 1980, it was simply codifying many practices that the agency had adopted on its own.

The Bureaus of Competition and Consumer Protection made improvements in planning and case selection. Each bureau formalized an evaluation process that used experienced attorneys and economists to evaluate projects both at their outset and at regular intervals during their development. This process enabled the Commission's senior management to do a better job of shaping the direction of initiatives, assessing costs and benefits, and making appropriate allocations of resources.

During 1978, the Commission published the rules implementing the Hart-Scott-Rodino Act's premerger notification process. The Bureau of Competition established a sophisticated merger screening process. This screening process allowed the Commission and the staff to make effective and efficient use of the additional time and information that the act provided to the antitrust agencies to aid their evaluation of the competitive impacts of certain mergers and acquisitions.

The Commission also tackled the complaints about its cumbersome rulemaking procedures, which had resulted in seemingly endless days of hearings, voluminous records, and inordinate delay. The Commission adopted experimental rulemaking procedures designed to focus the parties' attention on key factual issues earlier in the process and to set realistic timetables for final agency action on rule proposals. These expedited procedures enabled the Commission to complete hearings on its insulation "R" value disclosure rule within four months, compared to a previous average of eighteen months. In 1978 the Commission also reevaluated 152 trade practice rules it had promulgated prior to the passage of its Magnuson-Moss rulemaking authority and took the unprecedented step of eliminating all but seven. To respond to criticism that its authority over unfair acts and practices was ill-defined and potentially limitless, the Commission in 1980 published a policy statement that outlined the conduct that the FTC potentially would pursue under this authority.

These internal FTC reforms, especially when coupled with the 1980 FTC Improvement Act's restrictions, largely seemed to quell the Commission's congressional and business community critics without hampering the agency's ability to continue to enforce the law effectively. However, significant further changes were in store for the Commission under the Reagan administration. The Reagan administration assumed control of the agency in 1981, pledging to lower the agency's profile, reduce its budget, toughen critical scrutiny of its initiatives, substitute advocacy before legislative bodies and regulatory institutions for traditional law enforcement strategies, and seek further congressional restrictions on its legal authority.

Over the last seven years, under the leadership of two chairmen without prior experience in law enforcement, James Miller, a conservative economist, and Daniel Oliver, a former editor of the *National Review*, the agency has largely achieved the goals that the Reagan administration set for it. The FTC's antitrust enforcement activities have been limited to two principal areas: horizontal mergers and anticompetitive self-regulation by health care professionals. Even in these areas, FTC activity has been sharply reduced. For example, a recent congressional analysis concluded that the rate of Commission's merger enforcement had declined by 75 percent between 1979 and the present.[22]

The Reagan appointees moved quickly to abandon large structural antitrust inquiries. The FTC abandoned the *Exxon* and *Cereal* cases and an auto industry study on the ground that the Commission lacked the economic data necessary to determine the link between industry structure and performance. While discontinuation of those cases may well have been justified due to the data deficiencies, the Commission at the same time inexplicably discontinued the Line of Business reporting program which was designed to provide the information needed to test the premise that structure and performance are related.

In place of successful and high payoff enforcement actions against vertical price fixing, the Commission devoted substantial resources to its Competition Advocacy Program, which provided unsolicited and often unheeded advice to other federal and state agencies, urging them to account better for market forces in their regulatory efforts. While procompetition advocacy is a legitimate Commission function and much of the Commission's advice is undoubtedly sound, the Reagan Commission committed far too much of its scarce resources to the program. Advocacy should complement law enforcement, not supplant it. At times it seems the cop on the economic regulatory beat has been replaced by a little old man on a park bench, dispensing free advice to anyone who will listen.

In the consumer protection area, the scale-back in Commission activity has been even more dramatic. FTC trade regulation rulemaking as well as the enforcement of existing rules have been almost abandoned. No trade regulation rules were proposed in the Reagan administration years. Most rule proposals that were pending in 1981 have been terminated or left half-completed in the depths of the Bureau of Consumer Protection.[23] Advertising enforcement has been reduced significantly on the sometimes questionable premise that the marketplace ultimately will penalize purveyors of false and misleading claims. The Bureau of Consumer Protection's top enforcement priority has been so-called hard-core fraud committed by modern-day snake-oil salesmen engaged in phony investment and real estate speculation schemes. While undeniably a problem, many have questioned whether a more productive approach against these typically underfinanced recidivists is stricter enforcement of local criminal laws.

Contrary to the hopes and expectations of those who engineered this latest Commission transformation, the 1988 model seems to have satisfied almost no one. The reduction in FTC activity has created a vacuum that the states have felt compelled to fill. The state attorneys general, dissatisfied with federal antitrust and consumer protection enforcement, recently developed, over FTC opposition, enforcement guidelines for policing vertical restraints, horizontal mergers, and airline advertising. Investigations into auto rental company advertising, airline systems, and nonprofit vocational schools also are pending.[24] This trend towards state enforcement creates a new and unquantifiable risk that fifty different agencies will be enforcing the law. The business community, the intended beneficiary of the new relaxed atmosphere at the Federal Trade Commission, but which stands to be burdened by this multiplicity of law enforcers, has been vocal in its complaints.

For example, a number of state legislatures have recently adopted "lemon" laws which require auto manufacturers to take back problem cars. This trend has led the auto industry to petition the Commission to issue a trade regulation rule that would impose on the industry a comprehensive federal system of auto warranty regulation and would preempt the states' "lemon" laws. It is ironic that FTC's preemption of state laws is today's medicine of choice, when only ten years ago the business community justified the imposition of further restrictions on FTC authority because it feared that the Commission would assert such authority.

The contrast between 1978 and today is stark. And the present Commission does not fare well by comparison. In its zeal to avoid the "mistakes" of 1978, the present Commission seems to have drifted too far back towards the 1968 model.

Ironically, the American Bar Association has decided that, twenty years after its first report, a major reassessment of the FTC is in order. At its 1988 spring meeting, the Antitrust Section of the ABA appointed a new committee to study the Federal Trade Commission and the role that the Commission should take in the next ten years. Miles W. Kirkpatrick, head of the ABA's last study of the Commission in 1969, will chair the committee.

The timing is right. A candid assessment of the Commission's performance over the last twenty years is needed. The Commission and the public also would benefit from the preparation of a road map charting a course between the activist and the occasionally misguided direction of the FTC in the mid- and the late 1970s and the studied passivity of the Commission today.

Notes

1. E. Cox, R. Fellmeth, and J. Schulz, *The Nader Report on the Federal Trade Commission* (1969); Report of the ABA Commission to Study the Federal Trade Commission (September 15, 1969).

2. Trans-Alaska Pipeline Authorization, Pub. L. No. 93-253, tit. IV., § 408, 87 Stat. 576, 591 (1973).

3. Magnuson-Moss Warranty/FTC Improvement Act, Pub. L. No. 93-637, tit. II, 88 Stat. 2183, 2193 (1975).

4. Equal Credit Opportunity Act, Pub. L. No. 93-495, tit. V, § 503, 88 Stat. 1500, 1521 (1974) and amended, Pub. L. No. 94-239, § 4, 90 Stat. 251, 253 (1976); Fair Debt Collection Practices Act, Pub. L. No. 95-109, 91 Stat. 875 (1977).

5. Energy Policy and Conservation Act, Pub. L. No. 94-163, tit. III, 89 Stat. 871, 901 (1975).

6. Hart-Scott-Rodino Antitrust Improvement Act, Pub. L. No. 94-435, tit. II, 90 Stat. 1383, 1390 (1976).

7. *Exxon Corp.* (Docket No. 8734, July 17, 1973); *Kellogg Co.* (Docket No. 8883, April 26, 1972).

8. Federal Trade Commission, Annual Report 1977, at 6-7.

9. Ibid., at 16-17.

10. See Subcommittee on Oversight and Investigations of the House Committee on Interstate and Foreign Commerce, 94th Cong., 2d Sess., Report on Federal Regulation and Regulatory Reform, at 57.

11. M. Pertschuk, "Remarks before the Eleventh New England Antitrust Conference" (November 18, 1977).

12. Those statements are summarized in *Association of National Advertisers v. FTC*, 627 F.2d 1151 (D.C. Cir. 1979) (reversing the district court finding that Pertschuk had "prejudged" the unfairness of children in advertising).

13. Ibid.

14. See FTC Staff Report on Television Advertising to Children (1978).

15. M. Pertschuk, *Revolt Against Regulation: The Rise and Pause of the Consumer Movement* (1982); S. Tolchin & M. Tolchin, *Dismantling America: The Rush to Deregulate* (1983); B. Hasin, *Consumers, Commissions, and Congress: Law, Theory, and the Federal Trade Commission*, 1968-1985 (1987); John F. Kennedy School of Government, Harvard University, "Michael Pertschuk and the Federal Trade Commission" (1981) (unpublished manuscript).

16. Act of Oct. 12, 1979, § 101(e), Pub. L. No. 96-86, 93 Stat. 656, 658 (the FTC was prohibited from using any appropriated funds to promulgate final trade regulation rules under section 18 of the FTC Act, or to "initiate any new activities").

17. Federal Trade Commission Improvements Act § 21. See *Consumer Union of U.S. Inc. v. FTC*, 691 F.2d 575, 577 (D.C. Cir. 1982), *aff'd*. 463 U.S. 1216 (1983).

18. Report of the Federal Trade Commission Transition Team, [January-June] Antitrust & Trade Reg. Rep. (BNA) No. 997, at G-1 (January 29, 1981).

19. An oft-cited example at the time was a subpoena issued to Brown and Williamson Tobacco Company as part of an investigation of its advertising practices. After protracted litigation, the federal courts ordered Brown & Williamson to comply. The company, ignoring offers from the staff to limit drastically the scope of the subpoena chose to embarrass the Commission by complying literally with the terms of the subpoena by producing over seven tons of documents. Tolchin & Tolchin, supra, note 14 at 292 n. 17.

20. See, e.g., Permanent Subcomm. on Investigations of the Senate Comm. on Government Operations, 93d Cong., 1st Sess., Investigation of the Petroleum Industry (requesting the FTC to investigate the structure of the industry); Senate Comm. on Appropriations, Department of State, Justice, and Commerce, the Judiciary and Related Agencies Appropriation bill for 1978, 95th Cong., 1st Sess., 1977, S. Rept. 95-285, p. 53 (urging additional activities with respect to children's advertising).

21. Federal Trade Commission, Annual Report 1978.

22. 54 Antitrust & Trade Reg. Rep. (BNA) No. 476, 477 (March 17, 1988). (In 1979-1980, the Commission challenged 2.5 percent of transactions reported under the Hart-Scott-Rodino Act; for the period 1982-87, the rate declined to .7 percent.)

23. Rule proposals that have been abandoned since 1981 include over-the-counter

drug advertising, children's advertising, food advertising, health spas, hearing aids, standards and certification and mobile home warranties. D. Pridgen, *Consumer Protection and the Law*, 12-20-12-21 (1986).

24. See "Why the States Are Ganging up on Some Giant Companies," *Business Week*, April 11, 1988, at 62.

Comments on the Commission in 1978

Thomas H. Stanton

Bill Baer has done a marvelous job summarizing the state of the Federal Trade Commission in 1978. As Bill points out, that is approximately the year of the Commission's "turning point" from being an aggressive "cop on the economic regulatory beat" to becoming today's decrepit man sitting "on a park bench, dispensing free advice to anyone who will listen."

Bill's crisp review of events brought back many memories. Perhaps the most important memory from a historical perspective is the enthusiasm so many of us brought to the Federal Trade Commission. One of the FTC's activist leaders said on leaving office, "I came to this job as I left it, fired with enthusiasm," and that summarizes the experience of many others of us as well.

A number of the FTC's new leaders came from the consumer movement. The agency openly advertised for bright activist lawyers by proclaiming itself the country's largest public interest law firm. An important lesson from the first two years of the Pertschuk chairmanship is that those of us with enthusiasm also need especially refined political antennae.

The warning signs of a business backlash were already apparent for those who cared to see them, even before Mike Pertschuk became chairman of the Federal Trade Commission. For example, I have in my files an article from *Business Week* dated December 13, 1976, titled, "The Escalating Struggle Between the FTC and Business: Executives Openly Challenge the Actions and Policies of the Newly Activist Agency."

Yet, as Bill points out, congressional reactions tend to lag behind those of powerful constituents. Well into Mike Pertschuk's tenure, Congress, or at least that part of Congress most supportive of our activist mission, continued to stoke our enthusiasm.

Bill explains the controversy that began to engulf the FTC in 1978 by noting that "much of the reaction against an energized Federal Trade

Commission was inevitable. It is a lesson not in law or economics, but in political science. The Commission simply took on much more than its political base could support." Bill goes on to note the strategic vulnerability of the FTC: Unlike other regulatory agencies, "the Federal Trade Commission lacks an industry with a strong, vested interest in its continued vitality. Thus, any significant law enforcement activity is likely to receive little support and to generate much controversy and criticism."

To me the question of political constituency is the single most important continuing strategic issue for the Federal Trade Commission in its evolution. The Federal Trade Commission has no natural constituent anchor. Over time the agency has simply oscillated according to prevailing political impulses.

Some historical perspective is useful here. Over time the Federal Trade Commission has undergone a series of distinct periods punctuated by turning points such as 1978. From 1914 to 1925, the FTC was a dynamic steward of the antitrust laws; from 1925 to 1933 it swung in the other direction and became a promoter of business interests. After 1933 and President Roosevelt's failure at the hand of the Supreme Court to remove commissioners with whom he disagreed politically, the FTC became a source of patronage appointments from Capitol Hill. With some notable exceptions, the agency was a weak enforcer of the antitrust and consumer protection laws until 1968. From 1968 until perhaps 1981 the Federal Trade Commission again sought to be a dynamic enforcer of the laws. The quality of Federal Trade Commission economic reports can also be divided approximately according to these periods.

These shifts can be seen as the swings of a pendulum between extreme attitudes towards the business community: excessive antagonism or excessive cordiality. I believe that both extremes have serious drawbacks for the economy and for the agency. The problem, of course, is how to achieve a moderate course and adhere to it.

I believe that it would be useful for the FTC to adopt a role as an umpire of the economic game. The baseball metaphor is more appropriate than the cop-on-the-beat role; the FTC may only penalize players within the rules of the game and must leave the punishment of more extreme misbehavior to the criminal authorities. The Federal Trade Commission, with its limited civil penalties and cumbersome procedures, benefits neither from the extent of moral suasion available to the policeman nor from the ability to wield the nightstick; for better or worse, the federal government has largely left the role of policeman to the Department of Justice.

The Realities of the FTC

The question of the FTC's role makes it important to look at some strategic realities. First of all, the Federal Trade Commission is a small institution by Washington standards. In 1981 it had a staff of seventeen hundred including about seven hundred attorneys and one hundred economists. Its budget of $60-$65 million was minuscule compared to the $2.7 trillion economy that year. The Commission is much smaller today. That means that even the umpire role is somewhat overstated; the Federal Trade Commission has the ability to exert leadership in selected areas so long as it does not squander its scarce resources.

Second, the Federal Trade Commission Act represents a classic political compromise. Bill Baer speaks of the "broad flexibility" of that act. Historian George Cullom Davis, Jr., contends that, "in effect, not one but two commissions were established" in 1914 by President Wilson and the Congress. One FTC was the business-oriented commission sympathetic to companies. It was supposed to provide advice about the propriety of intended activities and to resolve doubts and uncertainties that could arise from inconsistent enforcement of the antitrust laws. The other FTC was that sought by progressives. It was supposed to be a powerful regulator that could finally control anticompetitive business combinations. Both President Wilson and members of Congress were ambiguous in describing the purpose of section 5, empowering the FTC to prohibit unfair methods of competition.

Third, this inherent ambiguity in the Federal Trade Commission's mandate, and its structure as an independent agency partially outside the routine political transition from one presidential administration to another, makes it almost inevitable that the Federal Trade Commission has oscillated over time. Indeed, the pendulum swings can be a lot of fun. The agency is always in motion. The agency's leadership is frequently busy turning the FTC around from its past excesses.

Finally, these oscillations are expensive, both for the FTC and in terms of foregone opportunities. Too often the agency has virtually canceled itself out. I share Bill Baer's enthusiasm for the many productive and valuable accomplishments of the Federal Trade Commission between the 1968 ABA report and the coming of the Reagan administration in late 1981. Nevertheless, given that the activist period was so brief, there remain lingering feelings that we could have accomplished even more.

Lessons Learned by the FTC

As Bill concludes, we are apparently heading for another sea-change, in which consumer protection and competitive concerns may well return to prominence. That means it is worth applying some of the lessons that we learned during our past period of strong enforcement activity. The Federal Trade Commission is one agency where hindsight can always be applied again, if only you wait long enough.

The first lesson is to build a strong constituent base among the more responsible members of any particular industry that has attracted Commission concern. In this regard, consider the difference in impact between FTC rulemaking and FTC case-by-case enforcement. Rulemaking is the kind of activity that can have its harshest effects on the most responsible companies in an industry. These are the companies whose performance will not be improved by application of the new rule; nevertheless these companies will bear the full weight of paperwork requirements or other mandated procedures designed to catch the irresponsible firms causing much of the problem.

Case-by-case enforcement is different. It focuses on the malefactors in an industry. Especially if the pattern of abuse is unsavory enough, responsible members of the industry may be quietly pleased about an FTC prosecution. It is much harder for a malefactor to convince a congressional committee that the FTC action is unjust when the facts reveal a clear abuse; by contrast, in a rulemaking the industry has available a range of respectable and genuinely responsible members who can come forth to tell how they are aggrieved by the burdens of a proposed FTC rule.

Second, FTC actions should be based on eliciting a responsible business constituency where it is available. FTC Commissioners and staff should go to trade associations and discuss the difference between the broad range of respectable members of that industry and the minority of malefactors who are unfairly outcompeting those responsible members by cutting costs at the expense of consumers or by engaging in other anti-competitive behavior.

Third, the Federal Trade Commission Act is a broad charter, providing the agency with a variety of sophisticated instruments. FTC staff work to support congressional inquiries, and FTC findings that become the basis for news stories can put pressure on the malefactors in an industry without placing the agency's own political capital squarely on the line. As Bill Baer points out, the FTC was seriously damaged as an effective law enforcement institution when the news stories began focusing on the agency rather than on the abuses the agency was trying to correct.

Leadership at the Commission

Finally, I wish to pay tribute to one of the truly outstanding accomplishments of the Pertschuk chairmanship that unfortunately will have to be reconstructed again. Mike had a strong vision of the need for good management to improve the FTC's effectiveness. He improved the quality of one regional office and FTC division after another by installing capable leaders, managers, and staff. Several of the FTC management team were outstanding managers in their own right. Bureau of Competition workload sessions, FTC budget and policy planning reviews, and other management devices were used well under Mike Pertschuk's leadership. The FTC support offices—personnel, budget, and contracts—were some of the best to be found in government.

Now, unfortunately, many good people at the FTC have endured eight years of incompetent leadership. Federal salaries have dropped dramatically in real terms, compared to what we enjoyed when we were at the Commission. It is not clear how much longer the FTC can retain its necessary core of high-quality attorneys, economists, and other professionals. If the FTC is to end its oscillations, it must maintain a cadre of effective officials who retain an institutional memory and can apply lessons from one industry to another as well as being sensitive to long-term changes in the industries they are overseeing.

The University of Notre Dame, Pat Murphy, and Bill Wilkie should be commended for seizing this opportune moment to examine the Federal Trade Commission and the 1990s. I urge you to provide a copy of proceedings of this conference to each commissioner as he or she is appointed over the coming years.

The FTC in 1978: Some Observations
from a Marketing Academic

Kenneth L. Bernhardt

I have been asked to make some comments on William Baer's fine article, "At the Turning Point: The Commission in 1978." My vantage point is that of a marketing academic who was on the FTC staff from 1978 to 1980. I find Mr. Baer's paper to be extremely insightful in describing the FTC at that time, perhaps the height of the agency's regulatory influence. This is not surprising given his roles as attorney advisor to the chairman and assistant general counsel.

In particular, I find Baer's comments concerning the "Revolt Against Revolution" and its causes to be perceptive. He also documents a number of achievements made by the FTC during the late 1970s, many of which are often overshadowed by the controversies surrounding the agency during that period. Baer concludes by comparing the FTC in the late 1970s with the agency in the late 1980s, calling the contrast "stark." I agree, and I would like to make some observations concerning the earlier period.

The FTC Situation in 1978

First of all, several papers in this book make comments about the FTC budget, and I would like to quantify that. In 1978-79 the FTC budget was $65 million. In 1988, 10 years later, the budget was $66 million, and for 1989 it was again $66 million. The difference is really quite dramatic when you look at it in real dollars: a decline of 41 percent. In case one thinks it is just a function of government as a whole having its budget constrained, the U. S. Government budget in 1978-79 was $369 billion and it went in ten years from $369 billion to $926 billion, in real dollars an increase of 31 percent. So a dramatic change has taken place in

114

the resources available to the FTC, which has had a lot of impact on the things going on at the agency that I want to discuss.

The second point I want to make concerns the business community's revolt against the FTC. In 1978 the FTC was under attack for a number of far-reaching matters. There were seventeen trade regulation rules under various stages of development at the time, but only three of them were initiated by the Pertschuk Commission. Of the other fourteen, one was mandated by Congress and the others were started under the previous two Republican administrations. Of the three that Pertschuk started, only two were really controversial: the kid-vid rule and the standards and certification rule (one that at the time was very controversial and attracted a lot of negative attention). Of all seventeen, only four were highly controversial: children's advertising, standards and certification, funeral homes, and used cars.

Another thing going on at the time that I want to highlight is that in 1978 we were just seeing the beginnings of what was then called regulatory reform. In 1978 rules had just been developed that called for an advance notice of rulemaking. The FTC staff now had to do initial regulatory analyses before starting a rulemaking proceeding. The FTC had to start publishing the semiannual regulatory agenda and the government as a whole, through the Office of Management and Budget, had to start publishing a regulatory calendar. As a result of these regulatory reforms the agency had to disclose what they were up to more openly than had ever been done before, beginning with the initial notices and including the regulatory analyses that the Commission had to publish. Industry could take advantage of this information and could harness their forces much earlier than they had been able to previously.

The political arena was fascinating in 1978. I went to the FTC in February and March of 1978 for a series of interviews. Before I was hired I had some free time between an interview with Al Kramer (director of the Bureau of Consumer Protection) and one with Dick Foster (the bureau's deputy director), so I was able to attend part of the first day of the kid-vid hearings—an interesting way of being introduced to the agency. That trade regulation rule alone managed to draw out forces against it from the cereal industry, sugar industry, toy industry, broadcasting industry, and the advertising industry. Fifteen trade associations including the National Association of Broadcasters, the Grocery Manufacturers' Association, and the Association of National Advertisers testified on various days and used every means available to them to fight that rule. This is an example of the horsepower behind some of those opposed to the FTC rulemakings. Add every used car dealer, funeral home owner, home builder, the whole insurance industry, the American Medical Association, the dentists, every Chamber of Commerce in the U.S., etc. It was fascinating to watch political power in action.

One of the areas where the impact of the budget cuts has been felt the most is the Office of Impact Evaluation, which I headed during 1978-80. Michael Mazis suggested the creation of this office in a planning report on the subject of the FTC evaluating the impact of its actions. My first year at the FTC I had a budget of $1 million for contract research, not counting any expenditures for FTC staff, etc. Close to $1 million was spent that year on some twenty-two research studies. The next year, 1979-80, I had a budget of $853,000 for contract research. Those research studies and other contract research that was done as part of cases and other FTC matters were an important part of the FTC programs at the time.

I began hearing people such as Al Kramer, Dick Foster, and others starting to ask FTC attorneys three very important questions that may have been asked before, but only informally given the lack of resources to answer them. First, what empirical evidence is there that there is a problem here? The mailbag approach had been used until the late 1970s where, for example, programs were initiated based on letters the FTC received (the mailbag). Now, empirical research was done, starting with the housing defects program, in which the research was initiated before any attorneys were even put on to the program. Based on the housing research, the housing defects program was given substantial resources and it became a major FTC program.

The second question being asked was: If you are proposing a remedy, what empirical evidence do you have that the remedy will work? And I think for the first time resources were made available (at a level well beyond William Wilkie's famous $2,000 copy test he managed to do at the FTC in the early 1970s) to do research to test whether some of these remedies would do what they were intended to do. The third question was what empirical evidence are you gathering now that will enable the agency to evaluate whether the regulation will have the intended impact should it be put into effect?

It is sad to see that the Office of Impact Evaluation's budget for contract research is now under $100,000. This is insufficient to do the research to answer the questions that need to be asked. I think that research in the late 1970s had a lot of impact on the management of the

FTC. Had the research program been started earlier it had the potential to help the agency do things more sensibly and maybe avoid some of the attacks that went on.

My Favorite Commission Experiences

I want to tell a couple of my favorite stories about the FTC during the late 1970s. I had read a lot about the agency oversubpoenaing things, and it did not really hit home to me until two of the people who were involved in a detergent industry matter found out that after receiving my MBA I had worked for Lever Brothers as an assistant product manager on ALL detergent. Although this had been several years earlier, I was still somewhat knowledgeable about the detergent industry. So they asked if I could go over to a law firm with them and "spend an hour or two going through the documents and seeing what's there." I said, "Fine, what is it?" And they said, "Well, we subpoenaed the research that they've done over the last few years." I said, "Well, O.K., great. I know what kinds of studies they do." We went into a big room filled with boxes, and started opening some of them. The boxes were filled with research studies that had been done over about a twenty-year period. And I said, "You want me, in an hour or two, to tell you what's here?" We spent a whole day there and obviously touched about one-tenth of one part of the room. Then it hit home to me what really was going on. The staff had all kinds of information that they weren't going to be able to use.

Several of the papers in this book describe the FTC actions in the late 1970s as overzealous. I agree but think the cause was a lack of strategic planning. There were many diverse matters going on, and although there were substantial resources in those days, there was very little direction from the top about what was important. Thus, the resources were spread all over the place. We had major legal initiatives causing lots of turmoil for industry with literally one or two or three attorneys typically working only part-time on the matter. Almost nobody worked full-time on any one matter because there were so many different issues. Hence, the agency encountered some problems.

One of my favorite cases from the late 1970s is the *STP* case which, when I first read about it in early 1978, was a corrective advertising case. STP agreed to a consent order requiring them to pay a $500,000 civil penalty and to run $200,000 worth of corrective advertising. I then saw the media schedule which consisted of such media vehicles as *Advertising Age, Business Week, Barrons* and the *Wall Street Journal*. I thought that doesn't really seem like the target market to me, not that I'm a knowledgeable person about STP users. It just seemed wrong. When I got to the FTC I was asked to work with Mike Mazis to prepare an evaluation of whether or not the STP order did what it was supposed to do. I asked, "Was this really supposed to correct the misperceptions?" I was thinking these people were stupid, which just showed me what I didn't know. It turned out the FTC chairman, Michael Pertschuk, through a friend of his, Tony Schwartz, had gotten the idea that he wanted to tell the business community that things are different at the FTC now. He could not afford to take out $200,000 worth of advertising, but he did get STP to take it out for the agency. They used all those ads in these business publications to reach the advertising community to make the point that enforcement was going to be different, and that there was a Commission in place. According to the research conducted by Thomas Kinnear, the results showed very dramatically that the word had gotten out, that this message did get noticed in the publications, and the message that a change was taking place was clearly communicated.

Additional and Concluding Observations

There are two additional areas that were worked on in the period 1978 to 1980 that I thought had a lot of potential but nothing ever came of them to my knowledge. One is the whole area of performance standards. Instead of trying to dictate what was a corrective message, for example, a lot of people worked on various ways of looking at how performance standards could be developed. Instead of specifying the exact copy, for how many seconds of a TV ad, what size letters, etc., the FTC would specify that a message or disclosure had to be accurately perceived by a set percentage of target market consumers, as determined by a standard copy test. A lot of work was done on that, and unfortunately I don't think it ever amounted to anything in practice. I believe there is still a lot of potential there.

The other matter concerns sunset legislation, where some regulations might go into effect with a "fuse" on them. The regulation would go out of effect if it weren't renewed with a certain period. There was a lot of talk about that during the years 1978-80, and I don't know if any of the regulations enacted ever had a sunset provision built into them. Again, I believe there is a lot of potential in such a program.

A change in the mix of people started at the FTC in the early 1970s when, for the first time, the FTC brought in people like Harold Kassarjian, William Wilkie, David Gardner, Ivan Preston, and a number of others with marketing and consumer behavior backgrounds (see the Murphy paper in part III). Every year there were two or three marketing experts on staff who were available to the FTC attorneys to help in whatever way they could to guide things. It is really a shame that Thomas Maronick, who is there part-time, is the only one at the agency now. There has not been a full-time person serving in this kind of a role for several years. And that is a shame. In addition, in 1978-80 the FTC brought in other experts such as Robert Steiner, a former chairman of the Board of Kenner Toys and George Idleson who had an ad agency background to advise staff in advertising practices and consumer education. Unfortunately, I don't see that continuing.

In the late 1970s the FTC was hiring attorneys who were the "best and the brightest." They had great enthusiasm for what they were doing and had strong academic backgrounds. Unfortunately, they did not get some of the direction and oversight that they should have received. It was a fun time even though some of the things that were done were crazy in retrospect. I could never figure out why nobody could ever stop the things that were crazy. They just seemed to keep going with a life of their own. I enjoyed my time at the FTC and have enjoyed reminiscing about it with you.

The FTC in 1988: Phoenix or Finis?

Andrew J. Strenio, Jr.

The Federal Trade Commission ("Commission," "FTC," or "agency") next year will celebrate the 75th anniversary of its founding. This diamond jubilee undoubtedly will serve as the catalyst for some carousing, but it also calls for sober reflection about the status of the FTC. For, viewed from the perspective of 1988, the agency must make fundamental adjustments if it is to adapt successfully to the challenges of the rest of this century.

The jury is out on whether the FTC will be able to transform itself and rise above its current difficulties, or instead spiral downward with dizzying speed. Although there is a fascinating tale to be told about the impact of the agency's changes during the 1980s, we do not yet have the benefit of the kind of hindsight about this decade that can be applied to the 1960s and 1970s. So, this article does not render verdicts, but instead attempts to use the past and the present to extrapolate the landmarks and landmines ahead for the FTC. If the Commission builds upon the accomplishments of this and earlier decades and learns from contemporary and prior mistakes, then the outlook—while not foreordained—is favorable.

Of course, there is a distinctly cyclical pattern to intensive public analyses of the Commission. In fact, these reviews of the agency have come in roughly twenty-year intervals. If anthropomorphizing the institution is permissible, it can be said that, instead of annual physical exams, the FTC goes in for a checkup once every two decades.

The first serious reexamination of the FTC was begun around 1929, the year of turmoil that witnessed the stock market crash and the

An earlier version of this paper appeared in the *Journal of Policy & Marketing*, Volume 7, 1988, 21-39. Reprinted with permission.

St. Valentine's Day massacre. Chairman William E. Humphrey then led the Commission. Thomas K. McCraw, a winner of the Pulitzer Prize in History, characterized Humphrey as one of the most colorful and least effective commissioners in federal regulatory history. In McCraw's words, Humphrey was a "garrulous and acerbic . . . chairman [who] missed no opportunity to broadcast his own view that the FTC's job was not so much to police business practices as to assist executives in doing what they already wanted to do."[1]

There is a cautionary note for anyone who would follow in Humphrey's footsteps (or pratfalls), for his legacy was very different from what he intended it to be. In the first place, his philosophy and pugnaciousness were instrumental in laying the groundwork for the New Deal era of activism. Even more ironically, President Franklin D. Roosevelt's 1933 firing of Humphrey eventually led to the Supreme Court decision known as *Humphrey's Executor*. That case has provided a bulwark of legal support for the FTC and all other independent agencies.[2] In retrospect, Humphrey would have done well to follow what British politician Denis Healey has labeled the "First Law of Holes," namely, if you are in one, stop digging.

Approximately twenty years after Humphrey's shenanigans caused the public to cast a critical eye on the FTC, the agency underwent another round of criticism. This occurred in 1949, a year of upheaval that saw the fall of China to the communists and the creation of the North Atlantic Treaty Organization (NATO) as a defensive measure in Europe. In addition, this was the time of the first Hoover Commission Report. Former FTC Commissioner James M. Landis wrote the section of that report dealing with regulation. He took the agency to task for a number of failings, including lethargy. A major reorganization followed but, alas, the improvement proved transitory.

Twenty years later a study group sponsored by the omnipresent Ralph Nader and a separate American Bar Association (ABA) panel had some very unpleasant things to say about the Commission.[3] Both the so-called Nader Report and the Kirkpatrick Report, named in honor of the highly regarded Miles W. Kirkpatrick, the ABA group's chairman, were released in 1969. The reports were auspiciously timed, for 1969 was a year of miracles, including the first landing on the moon and the first world championship for the "Amazing" New York Mets.

The Nader and the Kirkpatrick Reports' caustic observations and insightful recommendations led to a revival of the FTC, at least for a while. But the Commission's successes also led to some excesses and, in due course, to its weakened condition today. The agency went from a highly regarded body to a highly derided one, and from the "Consumer Champion" to the "National Nanny." The tide of "Nannyism" ebbed some time ago. Indeed, those taunts have receded so far in memory that today's commissioners freely boast about creating a children's daycare center. That shift in the agency's thinking portends a more activist FTC, although it surely does not foreshadow a new "Kid Vid" rulemaking.

As of the Summer of 1988, the FTC had four sitting commissioners. The fifth seat became vacant on May 15, 1988, when Patricia P. Bailey left the agency. A Republican and a stalwart supporter of FTC authority, Bailey was the last remaining commissioner who had taken office prior to 1980. Chairman Daniel Oliver, a Republican who took office on April 21, 1986, has been dubbed "the last Reagan revolutionary."[4] Commissioner Terry Calvani, a Republican who took office on November 18, 1983, and served as acting chairman from October 1985 through April 1986, has received recognition for his thoughtful and thought-provoking analyses of the agency.[5] Commissioner Mary L. Azcuenaga, an Independent who took office on October 16, 1984, has earned widespread acclaim for her superb legal ability. Last and surely least, the author, a Democrat who took office on March 17, 1986, has embraced modesty out of necessity.

This brings us to the antitrust section of the ABA's recent announcement that it is assembling a committee to review the FTC's operations. Predictably, that committee report is due in 1989. Mr. Kirkpatrick again chairs the group and brings a wealth of experience to the role he is resuming. After all, following the 1969 study, Mr. Kirkpatrick went on to serve as the FTC's chairman from 1970 through 1973. Naturally, there is every hope that 1989 will be a year of good fortune and that "Kirkpatrick II" will prove to be as valuable as "Kirkpatrick I" was.

1988 Needs: Resources and Resolve

For the present, the FTC must come to grips with at least two daunting circumstances. The first involves the severe resource drain afflicting the agency. The second centers upon charges that the Commission no longer has the will to enforce vigorously the antitrust and consumer protection laws.

Regarding resources, the Commission repeatedly has suffered deep cuts from the budget ax. In fiscal year 1979, the FTC had 1,746 work-years available. By fiscal 1987, that number had declined more than 42 percent, to 1,010 workyears. The trend continues. In fiscal 1988, the agency is down to 987 workyears, and this figure will likely be slashed to approximately 900 workyears by the start of fiscal 1989 (see table 1).

Substantial as this drop is, it pales in comparison to the correspond-ing surge in the agency's statutorily required workload, such as that attributable to the upswing in merger activity. For example, in fiscal 1979 the agency received 861 Hart-Scott-Rodino (HSR) Act premerger noti-

Table 1.	Federal Trade Commission Workyear Levels, FY1979 - FY1989

Workyears

Fiscal Year   PROJECTED

fication filings. In contrast, during fiscal 1987, the agency received 2,533 HSR filings, an astonishing increase of nearly 300 percent. Fiscal 1987 was not unique (see table 2). In seven of the past nine fiscal years the Commission has borne the brunt of significant increases in HSR filings. Indeed, if the trend seen so far in 1989 continues, HSR filings for fiscal 1988 will surpass last year's record level.

To put the quandary somewhat differently, consider the following information. In the HSR area, with resources down almost 50 percent in the past eight years while workload has skyrocketed nearly 300 percent, the agency's only hope is to improve productivity. But in order to have increased productivity to compensate adequately for these changes, each staff member in fiscal 1987 was expected to pull six times the weight that an individual staff member pulled in fiscal 1979. This added workload has placed an enormous and increasing strain on the agency staff. After all, how many organizations have increased their productivity 600 percent in the past eight years? How many people can, without lowering quality, finish 240 hours of work in just 40 hours? And how many of those organizations and the people staffing them can sustain this increased rate of productivity indefinitely? The FTC staff is likely to be expected to do so.

These rather grim statistics raise the question of whether the agency continues to have adequate resources to fulfill aggressively its statutory responsibilities. The FTC staff has been stretched to such a point that it cannot pursue expeditiously all worthwhile investigations and cases. Yet, although the agency is short on quantity of staff, it is long on quality of staff. The career staffers struggling under a crushing workload have done a remarkable job given the circumstances. The observation that there is only so much that can be done by so few should not be misinterpreted as criticism of these talented and dedicated individuals.

The FTC of 1988 also has been the target of various criticisms. Such criticisms include assertions that the agency either has not done what it should do to enforce the antitrust and consumer protection laws, or at least it has failed to establish the notion that it is interested in such enforcement.

A related charge is that a reduced level of FTC activity has forced states to spend their scarce resources in order to fill the perceived void. This, in turn, also is said to have engendered confusion for corporations and associations that operate nationwide because, increasingly, they must try to cope with a variety of potentially conflicting state and federal

Table 2.   **Workload and Workyears: The FTC Trying to Do More with Less**

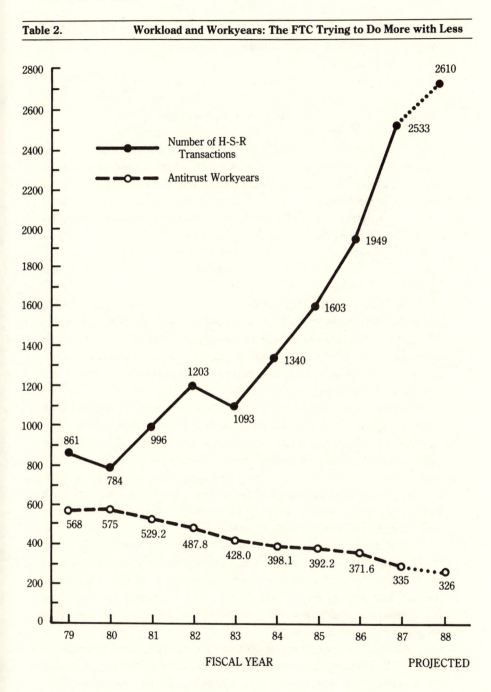

policies. While some of the criticism may be self-serving, misplaced, or overstated, there is too much validity to these critiques overall to justify agency complacency.

Antitrust Concerns

To understand this, let us begin with an in-depth examination of the agency's antitrust mandate, an area in which several troublesome trends have taken place. First, as previously mentioned, the agency has far fewer resources to work with than in days gone by. This agencywide decline in resources is dramatically reflected in the reduced number of staffers assigned to antitrust enforcement duties. In fiscal 1979, the FTC had 568 workyears available to perform its antitrust duties. But by fiscal 1988, the Commission's antitrust resources had shrunk to just 326 workyears (see bottom line in table 2).

The FTC of 1988 unquestionably is more efficient than the FTC of 1979. Improvements in management, analysis, and computerization are substantial. But there is a limit to how much improved efficiency can compensate for such large budget cuts. At some point, the loss of personnel overwhelmed such productivity enhancements and resulted in decreased work quality.

Such a development can be camouflaged, for a while, by "robbing Peter to pay Paul." This entails rejecting resource-intensive cases in favor of simpler cases, relying more heavily upon cases that walk in the door rather than those that are self-generated, reducing the number of these walk-in cases pursued, and even relegating some walk-in cases to the back burner for extended periods in order to free resources for matters with earlier deadlines. Judging from my observations, Peter seems to be getting mugged at least sporadically nowadays.

Also, the precipitous drop in the percentage of transactions in which the Commission issued second requests is disturbing. Second requests are essentially demands for additional information from parties to proposed mergers and acquisitions. The FTC issues such requests to assemble a better basis for deciding whether to mount an antitrust challenge to a proposed merger or acquisition.

Although a second request does not necessarily mean that a transaction will be challenged, it does mean that the agency staff is conducting an especially thorough inquiry. FTC operating procedure empowers the

Bureau of Competition (BC) director to recommend the issuance of a second request to the designated commissioner, usually the chairman, for a decision. To my knowledge, the designated commissioner has agreed with all such BC director recommendations for many years.

To put this issue in context, consider the following trend illustrated in table 3. Beginning in fiscal 1979, second requests, as a percentage of the number of HSR transactions, occurred in the following pattern: 8.4 (1979); 4.5 (1980); 3.8 (1981); 3.7 (1982); 1.3 (1983); 2.7 (1984); 2.0 (1985); 2.2 (1986); 1.1 (1987). While there is some variation in the pattern (the fiscal 1988 estimate is 1.8), there is no denying that FTC staff are subjecting a dwindling percentage of proposed mergers to the highest level of scrutiny. This phenomenon has alarmed the Commission and has only been assuaged partly by the fiscal 1988 "minibounce."

One possible explanation for this serial decline in second requests is

Table 3.   **One Result of Trying to Do More with Less?**

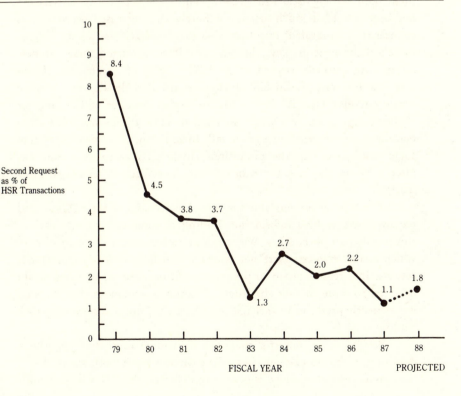

that the staff's review of transactions for potential second requests has become much more efficient. In other words, the hypothesis is that staff has become extraordinarily proficient at recommending second requests only for those proposed acquisitions that are likely to raise competitive problems. This argument is consistent with an analysis of the matters in which second requests were issued. Such analysis shows that virtually all of these matters subsequently involved Commission action in the form of either accepting a consent agreement or authorizing staff to seek a preliminary injunction.

Furthermore, the Commission has been relatively active in challenging acquisitions. In fiscal 1987, the FTC authorized its staff to seek seven preliminary injunctions. This was two more than the highest number issued in any previous fiscal year since the premerger notification program began in 1978. Moreover, the FTC took premerger enforcement action in nine cases in fiscal 1987. This total surpasses the prior record high of eight reached in 1982 and 1984. In fiscal 1988 the FTC is projected to break both of these fiscal 1987 records. The agency's increased activity has not been accorded much attention. Surely this increased activity runs counter to the prevalent misimpression that the FTC has stopped enforcing all of the antitrust laws. Indeed, in a different setting these numbers might have sparked charges that the FTC is being too pugnacious. However, the meteoric rise in HSR filings has dwarfed the increase in these activity levels. That is, even with the higher number of FTC merger challenges in recent years, the increase in HSR filings has caused the percentage of merger challenges to fall. In addition, with the exception of some cases involving the professions, little FTC antitrust action was discernable in the late 1980s other than those actions related to HSR matters.

While it is commendable that a high percentage of the FTC's second requests have yielded information leading to some enforcement action, this is only part of the story. We do not know how many of the matters in which second requests were not issued would have yielded enforcement actions. It is reasonable to suspect that additional second requests would have led to more merger challenges, unless one concludes that the staff was perfectly prescient in anticipating where the Commission would draw the line.

Beyond these concerns, there is a worrisome alternative hypothesis that might fit the existing facts. The alternative hypothesis is that a subconscious kind of triage is occurring. That is, the FTC's lack of sufficient resources may provide a disincentive for staff to seek second requests in all but the strongest cases. Thus, hypothetically, since the FTC staff has more work than it can handle, it concentrates only on the most important matters. However, this type of triage could allow transactions that should at least be investigated microscopically, if not attacked, to slip by. While this alternative hypothesis is unproven, the inability to disprove it readily is discomforting.

Consumer Protection Frustrations

The agency's fight against telemarketing fraud is a key item on the consumer protection side of the FTC's ledger. This problem is appallingly large. According to Chairman Oliver, for instance, telemarketing fraud costs consumers and businesses nearly $1 billion each year.[6] Chairman Oliver is not one to overstate the extent of problems in the private sector. Thus, his estimate is unlikely to be exaggerated. Nor is telemarketing the only boom area for fraudulent operations. Such operations also include health fraud. Published estimates place health fraud costs in the range of $10-25 billion per year.[7]

How has the FTC responded to this situation? The good news is that the Commission has mounted a major attack against swindlers who use telephones to prey upon consumers. The FTC has had some impressive results to show for its efforts. The bad news is that because of limits on the Commission's resources and legal authority, these efforts have not been nearly enough to turn the tide.

The agency's accomplishments deserve recognition. Over the past five years, fighting telemarketing fraud has become a top priority at the Commission. Staff litigating teams have learned effective investigatory tactics and now can operate quickly and aggressively. Further, the staff has clarified successfully the Commission's authority to proceed against these scam artists. Both the staff's track record and dedication have entitled it to high praise.

A look at the record demonstrates what this means in practical terms. Since 1983, the Commission successfully has brought more than twenty-eight federal district court cases against nationwide telemarketing scams with aggregate sales of over $859 million. These actions have put some 165 individual and corporate telemarketers under federal order. In addition, the FTC has obtained judgments for over $91.8 million in redress for scam victims. As a result of Commission actions, more than 6,500 scam victims have received redress checks ranging from $50 to $15,000 to date.

Furthermore, the agency staff regularly monitors compliance with the federal court orders that the Commission obtains. Order violations are prosecuted as civil or criminal contempt of court depending upon the seriousness of the violation. To date, the agency has obtained six criminal convictions for contempt.[8] Several additional criminal contempt actions are pending.

Beyond law enforcement actions, the Commission also has channeled resources into consumer education. Alert and aware consumers are the very best protection against consumer fraud. Consumers are in a better position if they never become victims of fraud than if they fall victim and have to seek agency aid to recover at least a few pennies on the dollar. In light of this truism, the FTC promotes consumer education projects both on its own and in conjunction with a great variety of government agencies and private groups. Still, the agency cannot rely entirely upon such educational efforts. Even the most careful consumers can be duped by a clever and unscrupulous con artist.

Importantly, in January of 1987 the FTC joined with the National Association of Attorneys General (NAAG) to begin a coordinated crackdown on telemarketing fraud. As part of that effort, the two bodies are compiling a nationwide data bank that will consolidate all consumer telemarketing complaints. This nationwide data bank should make it much harder for crooks to hide from the enforcement agencies by simply moving their operations whenever it becomes too hot for them in any locality.

The agency has secured good results from the resources expended in this area, but this is no reason for it to rest on these laurels. Telemarketing fraud still has burgeoned despite the hard work of numerous outstanding individuals. Three factors contribute to this problem.

First, scam artists, in general, speedily and skillfully dissipate their ill-gotten profits. Consequently, even with the authority to obtain asset freezes and other preliminary relief, the Commission typically obtains only cents on the dollar as redress for injured consumers.

In fact, of the $91.8 million in judgments for redress that the agency has secured, only $35 million has been returned to consumers or is available for return to consumers. To make matters worse, in the cases that the Commission has prosecuted, the $91.8 million is but a small percentage of the total consumer injury inflicted. Our inability to obtain a larger percentage of ill-gotten profits is a continuing source of enormous frustration.

Second, the Commission has severely limited resources and a plunging trendline in this area. For example, while the Commission had 530 workyears devoted to its consumer protection mission in fiscal 1981, and 444 workyears in fiscal 1984, there are only 349 workyears in fiscal 1988. Budget projections for fiscal 1989 are more dismal still.

Moreover, the FTC's consumer protection mission includes, but is not limited to, fighting telemarketing fraud. The Commission also must prosecute advertisers who mislead consumers, step in if lenders do not treat loan applicants fairly and without discrimination, challenge debt collectors if they harass or otherwise engage in abusive tactics, enforce the agency trade regulation rules, and so on. Every additional workyear devoted to policing telemarketing fraud is a workyear unavailable for these other critical tasks.

Third, the Commission has considerable existing legal authority with which to strike against telemarketing fraud. Nonetheless, desirable authority has been lacking in a number of respects. The Commission has suggested specific legislative proposals to rectify this situation.[9] Although these proposals have not been enacted into law yet, strong and bipartisan outrage exists on Capitol Hill about the prevalence of telemarketing fraud. Indeed, Congress seems determined to go after these con artists forcefully.

There is nothing irrational, inefficient or partisan about waging a no-holds-barred campaign against hardcore fraud, since fraud clearly hurts consumers. In addition, fraud hurts the vast majority of legitimate businesses. These legitimate businesses either may be directly fooled by con artists or may suffer a consumer backlash as a result of the distrust and fear engendered by the swindlers.

Further, legitimate companies in industries hit hard by fraud may discover that other companies keep their distance as a protective measure. For example, stories have circulated that some banks are not doing business with honest telemarketing travel agencies anymore in order to be absolutely sure they do not get involved mistakenly with the relatively few fraudulent travel hustlers.

This discussion leads to a question posed by Congressman Jim Bates of California. At the House reauthorization hearings for the FTC in June 1987, Congressman Bates asked how effective the Commission is in protecting consumers. That is an excellent question. Unfortunately, the answer leaves something to be desired.

To begin with, the Commission, at best, has an incomplete idea of the amount and the variety of fraud in our economy. This is understandable since the shady nature of consumer fraud makes it hard to develop accurate estimates. But without some coherent view of the extent of the problem, it is extremely difficult to establish objective yardsticks for the fight against fraud. Under these circumstances, the agency is forced to fall back upon "input measures," such as the number of cases brought or amount of redress secured, rather than "output measures," such as how much it has lowered fraud and which of its tactics have been particularly successful.

Accordingly, the Commission would do well to perform a study that estimates, however roughly, the amount of consumer fraud in the American marketplace. Once such a study is completed, the Commission can try to establish some measure of its effectiveness, or lack thereof, rather than having to rely extensively on inference and guesswork.

A study may provide an additional benefit. Specifically, it might reveal that hardcore fraud, which classically is viewed as a type of market failure, exists at an alarmingly high level. Such results would bolster the case for allocating more resources to discover systematically what actions would decrease the level of fraud in the most cost-effective manner. The agency could gain a comprehensive understanding of how much to spend and how best to spend it at the federal, state, and local levels of government. Of course, another benefit of an objective assessment of agency performance is that it would eliminate any possible temptation for insiders to meddle with the measurements to get a more favorable reading.

No discussion of consumer protection issues would be complete without a mention of the FTC's role in the regulation of advertising. In essence, the agency is responsible for prosecuting firms that engage in fraudulent or deceptive advertising practices. Under the current Commission standard, the Commission will find that an advertisement is deceptive if it is likely to mislead materially consumers acting reasonably. In addition, the FTC's advertising substantiation program requires advertisers and advertising agencies alike to have a reasonable basis for advertising claims before they disseminate such claims. The Commission's job is tough, for it must strike ruthlessly against fraudulent or deceptive advertising while simultaneously promoting the dissemination of truthful and nondeceptive information to consumers.

Here, as elsewhere, critics have charged the agency with acquiescing in certain business practices. In particular, during the past year, NAAG has issued guidelines directed at some of the advertising employed in part of the car rental and airline industries and has challenged other companies' advertisements. Although recently the FTC appears to have taken a more aggressive approach toward enforcing the advertising laws, there remains ample room for additional initiatives. Specifically, the Commission needs to take a closer look at fraudulent or deceptive advertising that may threaten public health or safety.

Recurring Concerns

The agency should always take a fair and tough stance in upholding both the antitrust and the consumer protection laws. After all, FTC commissioners have a clear obligation to do so. Moreover, as a general matter, these laws, when intelligently enforced, serve consumers well. Accordingly, there is no incompatibility between honoring the laws and pursuing an economically sound policy that promotes consumer welfare.

Indeed, either a failure to enforce these laws vigorously or a widespread perception of failure to enforce these laws could be disastrous. Such a failure would almost certainly lead to political reactions, in the guise of reregulation or new regulation, to the detriment of consumer interests. Thus, sound economic reasoning compels vigorous law enforcement and is not merely compatible with it.

Some repeated criticisms of the agency's enforcement practices deserve mention. Three such criticisms, in particular, revolve around allegations of procrastination, passivity, and planning deficiencies. The first criticism involves procrastination. The 1969 Kirkpatrick Report complained that "frequently, investigations or studies disappear into the lower levels of the FTC, and reappear only after many years have lapsed."[10] In other words, the agency stood accused of following Mark Twain's dictum: "Never put off until tomorrow what you can do the day after tomorrow." This historical trouble spot still plagues the agency, although some progress has been made.

To put the problem in context, most recent cases have moved comparatively quickly. This is not surprising, since the agency is blessed with a top-notch career staff that uniformly has gone to great lengths to meet deadlines in pressing cases. Commission staff has been exemplary in meet-

ing the tight merger review timetables set out in the Hart-Scott-Rodino
Act. Staff also repeatedly delivered sterling performances in promptly
investigating consumer protection cases, especially those cases involving
fraudulent activities.

Nevertheless, some cases have not reached the Commission until
literally thousands of staff hours had been expended and the evidence had
become so stale that there was no real choice other than to close them.
Other cases have arisen in which the Commission's prerogatives were
seriously limited because of the excessive passage of time. Such cases
constitute institutional mismanagement, for which all commissioners and
bureau directors must take some responsibility. [11]

One partial response to this unacceptable situation is worth highlighting. Earlier this year the FTC implemented a new case management
system. This system enables any single commissioner to place any investigation that has lasted longer than a certain time on a so-called fast track.
Cases on the fast track have to be brought to the Commission for resolution within a specified time. The upshot of this system is that each of the
commissioners now has both the ability and the obligation to ensure that
matters do not get lost or indefinitely put on hold.

But the agency can and should do better. Since a good example can
be the most powerful form of leadership, the Commission should make a
public commitment to expedite its workload. Specifically, the agency
should collegially establish deadlines for making motions in matters assigned to it and for circulating opinions in adjudicatory cases. Establishing such deadlines is the easy part. The hard part then would be putting
into practice a "no exceptions" policy.

A second historical criticism of the Commission involves the allega-
tion of passivity. The Hoover Report of 1949 charged that "the Commission has largely become a passive judicial agency, waiting for cases to come
upon the docket . . . without active responsibilities for achieving [its]
statutory objectives." [12] So, the question is whether the Commission in
1988 largely is a passive judicial agency. The answer is yes, and no. Yes,
because the Commission truly is passive in that it must rely upon staff to
examine the iceberg while often it gets to see only a few ice cubes.
However, the answer also is no, because the commissioners have been
fairly aggressive about demanding staff action in certain areas.

In any large organization, the quality of the product is heavily
dependent upon the performance of the line staff. It not only is impossible
for top management to second-guess all staff actions but, more impor-

tantly, it is counterproductive. The same is true for the FTC. Take mergers as an example. The Commission now receives over 2,500 premerger filings annually under the Hart-Scott-Rodino Act. Staff might seek second requests for information in 2 percent or less of those cases. The Commission subsequently may vote to take enforcement action in twenty cases per year, at most.

Obviously, it is imperative that the staff's approach to the 2,500 potential cases is consistent with the wishes of a Commission majority. But remember that the head of that staff, the bureau director, is appointed by the chairman. Bureau directors also traditionally attend the chairman's personal staff meetings and are generally thought to be closer in outlook, sometimes by a considerable margin, to the chairman than to the other commissioners. How, then, do commissioners ensure that they do not become merely "rubber stamps" or that any chairman so inclined does not "pocket veto" prospective actions?

Commissioners commonly resist passivity by encouraging the career staff to be intellectually independent from bureau management. The staff is called upon to follow bureau management directives but also is expected to express freely any contrary ideas. The agency management is expected to respect dissenting views. It is enormously difficult to create and maintain this proper atmosphere. The managers, staff and commissioners must be constantly on guard against any inclinations to muzzle inconvenient dissent from individuals down the line.

How well does this balancing work in practice now? Although there have been a few dismaying episodes, the agency has not fallen off the high wire. Recently, to give one positive example, a single staff attorney recommended an enforcement action in a particular matter. All other staff members and the management disagreed. Nevertheless, a majority of commissioners concluded that the staff attorney had the better argument. It is to the credit of the lone wolf that he had the courage to howl, and to the credit of bureau management that he was not silenced. It also is to the Commission's credit that it refuses to accept a passive status and that it has communicated that determination to the staff and bureau management.

However, there is another sense in which the Commission, as a whole, is too passive. The commission's passivity involves the case generation process itself. The agency's resource shortage and the explosion in the number of merger filings have made it increasingly rare for the staff to find time to originate matters rather than to simply react to whatever problems have walked in the door. Thus, the Commission properly should be wary about what may be going on in the outside world when it has insufficient resources to send staff on regular scouting missions.

The third historical criticism of the Commission involves its failure to plan and coordinate agency activities effectively. The 1969 Kirkpatrick Report revealed a general agreement among commissioners and senior staff that the agency proceeded on an ad hoc basis. This lack of an overarching direction resulted in a de facto delegation of substantial authority to senior staff. The Commission majority was relegated to the exercise of veto power only.[13] How does the FTC fare on this measure today?

On the plus side, the FTC has advanced remarkably since 1969. In many cases, it now employs more sophisticated legal and economic analyses, yet it has retained the ability to innovate as well. The FTC also has endeavored to focus its efforts upon practices likely to harm competition and consumers most severely. Unfortunately, the Commission lacks a cohesive long-term planning effort. For example, the agency has three separate antitrust units to plan or brainstorm problems in the area. But the relationship among these units is unclear, and the FTC seems to lack sound antitrust case generation projects. Worse, the commissioners have not participated significantly in these planning efforts.

One solution may be to take a page from history. At one time, the Commission frequently held policy review sessions at which general initiatives were discussed with staff. The Commission should consider seriously an immediate return to that practice. But while policy review sessions are a start, more general issues also must be brought to the Commission table for a vote.

In addition, the Commission once again needs to make trade-offs between the various competing demands for staff resources. In the antitrust realm, the agency by default has decided to devote most of its effective strength to reviewing merger applications, preserving the Hart-Scott-Rodino filing requirements, and bringing cases involving the professions.

Is this the best possible use of FTC resources? Maybe. But the distressing reality is that at least for the last two years the Commission really has not addressed the question. Instead, the Commission has relied entirely upon the bureau director's choices. The intent is not to criticize the bureau director's preferences but to note that these decisions should be made by the Commission, in broad outline, rather than by some other FTC official, however sagacious.

Perennial Issues

As the Commission looks to the 1990s and beyond, there are several other issues that are likely to remain part of the landscape. Those issues include: (1) revitalization of the FTC's regional offices; (2) recruitment and retention of capable staff; (3) reauthorization improvements by Congress; and (4) retention of the agency's antitrust jurisdiction.

While the regional office story is complex, the bottom line is that the Commission will maintain all ten regional offices and will increase the resources committed to the regions from 130 workyears, as of early 1987, to at least 190 workyears by the end of fiscal 1989. This represents an increase in the regional staff levels of over 35 percent at a time when the Commission's overall budget is declining in real terms.

In 1987, the Commission concluded that a shift in resources from headquarters to the regions was warranted for three reasons. First, the regional offices were too small to operate effectively. Second, an enhanced regional office presence not only would strengthen the agency's law enforcement program, but also would yield greater dividends by increasing deterrence of future illegal activities. Last, but certainly not least, the regional staff members' closer proximity to both the general public and to state and local officials responsible for consumer protection and competition laws would produce a synergistic effect. The geographic dispersion of the regional offices—located in Boston, New York, Cleveland, Atlanta, Chicago, Dallas, Denver, Los Angeles, San Francisco and Seattle—is consistent with this goal.

The Commission's about-face is a remarkable achievement. To begin with, despite all the talk regarding the benefits of decentralization and federalism, the FTC is the only recent example that comes to mind of a federal agency that has undertaken such a major reallocation of resources from its D.C. headquarters into its regional offices. Given the diversity of backgrounds and philosophies of the five commissioners who made this choice, it is perhaps even more amazing that they adopted the plan unanimously.

The second issue involves both the recruitment of capable new employees and the retention of the agency's highly qualified current staff members. For some time now, the Commission has suffered from an exodus of many of its brightest and most conscientious staff members either to the private sector or to other public agencies.

Obviously, the precise reason for any change in employment varies with the individual. Nonetheless, it has become harder for the agency to compete successfully in the job market. Part of the problem is attributable to the increasingly great disparity between the salary that the FTC can offer and that offered elsewhere. For example, a recent law school graduate may earn $50,000 a year more in a law firm job than that graduate can earn if he or she joins the agency. Moreover, in a number of cities, recent law school graduates earn appreciably more in the private sector than the most senior attorneys earn at the FTC. For law school graduates with extensive loan repayment obligations, it is all the more difficult to elect public sector work and eschew the premium pay available in law firms. Yet, that salary chasm is not the whole story.

Also, presently, there is a lower general appreciation of the contribution that public service makes to our society. These notions come and go in cycles, so it may be that our society already has bottomed out on that score. Moreover, to the extent that staff members or prospective employees respond favorably to a more energetic Commission, some momentum has been generated. Despite these positive notions, there is still much to be done.

Third, in addition to a speedy and sensible reauthorization of the agency, there are a number of very helpful steps that Congress could take. For example, Congress could: (1) repeal the McCarran-Ferguson Act; (2) consider revising similar strictures; (3) empower the agency to bring prosecutions on its own behalf for violations of the HSR Act's reporting requirements; (4) make the availability of a disgorgement-of-profits remedy explicit in the HSR Act rather than limiting penalties to $10,000 per day per violation (a number of entities have made aggregate profits, in violation of the Act, that have exceeded this $10,000 limit); and (5) make certain that the FTC has adequate resources to enforce the laws effectively.

Congressional explosions generated by extremes of agency activity or inactivity frequently have buffeted the FTC. Each Congressional explosion causes extensive reactions at the Commission and moves the FTC toward the opposite extreme. Then the process starts all over again. So, someone interested in maximizing the FTC's contribution to consumer welfare over the long haul should strive for a dynamic equilibrium of steady activism. This would avoid the disruption, demoralization, and disorder caused by alternating "big bangs." Attaining and maintaining a dynamic equilibrium requires that the agency grow and change, neither lagging too far behind nor rushing too far ahead of what the times demand and allow.

The fourth and final issue concerns the dual jurisdiction question of whether to maintain two federal antitrust enforcement agencies despite the continuing federal budget crunch. This issue is sure to be raised again. There are persuasive reasons for retaining the FTC's antitrust jurisdiction.

For one, the FTC has a broader statutory mandate than the Department of Justice. The Justice Department is limited to enforcement of the Sherman and Clayton Acts, which contain narrower statutory language than does the FTC Act. The FTC Act's prohibition against "unfair methods of competition" has been interpreted to encompass not only violations of the Sherman and Clayton Acts, but also incipient violations of those acts[14] and conduct violating the Act's spirit.[15]

In addition, while the Department of Justice may bring criminal as well as civil antitrust actions, the Commission's remedial authority to date has been limited to civil cease and desist orders, except for violations of those orders. Strangely enough, these general limits on the Commission's prospective remedies turn out to be a valuable asset. Specifically, these limits enable the Commission to bring cases that plow new ground without subjecting respondents retroactively to civil or criminal penalties.[16]

Another argument for dual jurisdiction is that the Commission's administrative process is designed to incorporate new economic learning. As a body of experts with a diverse and talented staff of administrative law judges, career economists, accountants, and antitrust attorneys, the Commission utilizes a multidisciplinary array of analyses in reaching its decisions. These decisions, in turn, may provide other bodies with useful insights and may help refine national antitrust policy.

Additional Thoughts

We all know that nature abhors a vacuum. But, while nature abhors vacuums, it is axiomatic that government officials find them positively irresistible. It is moot whether a true or merely a perceived vacuum exists in areas within the FTC's jurisdiction. The consequences are essentially the same. In Washington, D.C., where perceptions often are indistinguishable from reality, the appearance of a vacuum in FTC activity has created a powerful suction that has pulled in other institutions from across the country.[17]

Many states, in particular, have exerted authority in areas previously left largely to the FTC. One such area involves the review of proposed mergers, including those that are national in scope, for possible inconsistency with the antitrust laws. For instance, NAAG recently issued its own set of guidelines for challenging such acquisitions.

In the field of advertising, as noted earlier, NAAG has become very aggressive. For instance, NAAG recently issued a set of guidelines for airline price advertising. *Advertising Age* commented that "the state Attorneys General have definitely moved into the consumer protection vacuum created by the Reagan Administration's 'deregulation' agenda."[18] *Advertising Age* went on to predict that Congress will not stop state regulation of national advertising: "Many on Capitol Hill aren't inclined to protect the prerogatives of Reagan-era federal advertising regulators who, they are convinced, won't act."[19]

It is not this author's purpose now to judge who is right and who is wrong in each of these examples. Certainly, a strong argument can be made that the FTC is more active than it is given credit for. Indeed, because the agency always follows very strict rules which prohibit it from announcing or acknowledging the existence of pending investigations unless and until a legal case is ready, the Commission often is criticized unfairly by people who are unaware that the FTC already is reviewing a particular matter. So, a certain failure to communicate is an element of the problem. Still, suffice it to say that misunderstandings alone do not account for the entire situation.

To date, we have witnessed only the opening act of state activism. Interestingly, these activities may shape decisively the FTC's future profile. That is because the prospect of potentially inconsistent or extremely complex regulation by numerous states could drive national corporations into a virtual frenzy. If so, those corporations will discover that Congress is unwilling to legislate federal preemption in an area in which it perceives little federal presence.

At that point, out of necessity, large corporations likely will join the clamor for a stronger FTC. This is sensible. After all, in most cases, aggressive and consistent federal enforcement of the antitrust and consumer protection laws better serves both the needs of industry and of the public than would the multiplicity of approaches likely to spring up over time in the fifty sovereign states, despite the best efforts of the states to act in unison. Of course, in some cases the states properly should take the lead. In other cases, a combined state and federal effort is best.

The challenge facing the FTC is to counteract the perception of a vacuum. One action the FTC should take in the near future involves using the FTC Act's section 13(b) to disgorge ill-gotten gains or supra-competitive profits from entities who have committed hardcore antitrust law violations, as it already does for egregious violations of the consumer protection laws. In this fashion, the agency can gain redress for victims while deterring violators. Naturally, such actions should be coordinated carefully so that they are a complement to, and not in competition with, any parens patriae suits that state officials may wish to pursue.

Much more needs to be done to refocus agency activities and stream-line agency operations. To assist in refocusing its activities, the agency should hold a series of targeted hearings, such as the one held in March of 1988 on the consumer problems of older Americans. By way of streamlin-ing, the FTC should conduct an intensive, zero-based budget review of all expenditures. The agency has to make absolutely sure that its limited resources are employed to their maximum capacity.

In addition, the agency needs to trim back any overreview within the agency that creates delays, stifles cases, or lowers productivity. Wernher von Braun's observation is apt. When asked about the space program, he said, "We can lick gravity, but sometimes the paperwork is overwhelming." In a like vein, the agency must be more creative both in shifting bureau resources from reviewers to frontline workers and in keeping the staff from disappearing under red tape. Naturally, the Com-mission also should expedite its handling of matters that arrive from the bureaus.

To expand upon these points, look at the agency's present organiza-tional and internal review structure. A Commission with almost twice the resources that we have now originally adopted that structure. Over the years, as the agency contracted, the structure essentially was kept intact. The simplest course was to preserve the framework and to impose propor-tional reductions across all of the operating units. Unfortunately, al-though individually reasonable, these incremental adjustments cumula-tively have resulted in a hodgepodge that is in need of reform.

The FTC needs more resources than the present 987 workyears if it is to fulfill aggressively its statutory responsibilities. But the Commission has a duty to maximize its performance at whatever budget level the executive and legislative branches establish. Since the agency's immediate prospect is for further reductions to about the 900 workyear level, it must overhaul its structure to one which is consistent with this diminished size.

After all, one legacy of the proportional cut system is a relatively top-heavy Commission. When the units are kept intact but the number of people assigned to each unit is reduced, the ratio of generals to privates inevitably grows larger. In response, the agency needs to reassign more of the existing staff to frontline operations and to station fewer behind the lines.

Second, the FTC expends an inordinately high percentage of its resources on review, rereview, and re-rereview of its capable staff. An experienced bureau attorney or economist may have her or his work reviewed by a combination of the shop's deputy assistant director or the assistant director or the associate director. That same work then may run the gauntlet of one or more assistant directors or deputy directors at the bureau level. Then the bureau director becomes involved. Of course, other bureaus or the general counsel may enter the process at any point. Only after these hurdles are surmounted does the work reach the Commission level, where the commissioners and their advisors review the material afresh.

In some cases this system has paid off. But, overall, the FTC's efficiency and morale could be improved by streamlining that part of the review process which is conducted before work gets to the Commission. The agency can save time by trimming back these layers of review, and it can free reviewers for more valuable contributions at the front. The Commission concurrently should shoulder a greater proportion of the review burden of sorting the legal and economic wheat from the chaff.

Future Directions

The commissioners will decide, collegially, which areas of future activity the agency will pursue. Nevertheless, four topics merit consideration:

First, it is time to reassess the FTC's role with an eye to the remainder of the century. The agency should conduct a review of the FTC's existence over the past 75 years, distill what wisdom it can from this accumulated experience and use that wisdom to provide direction for the future.

Second, the FTC could make a major contribution to the resolution of several raging controversies by providing a forum for dispassionate, factual examinations of the premises central to those debates. Take, for example, the controversy over whether the ban against resale price maintenance should be loosened. Proponents contend that if the ban is not loosened, "free-riding" will reach epidemic proportions. Relatively little is known about the incidence of "free-riding." A hearing on this subject, accompanied by objective studies from within the agency, could reveal to what extent, if any, the hypothesized "free-riding" actually has occurred.

Similarly, the agency could try to pinpoint the total amount of consumer fraud present in the economy. Of even greater value, the agency could work in conjunction with NAAG and others to identify not only currently prevalent frauds such as telemarketing scams, but also to spot scams likely to prove troublesome in the future. The advent of new technology often is a good area to explore, since the unscrupulous are adept at exploiting innovations for their own purposes. While the task is difficult, the FTC should look for emerging trends, rather than merely reacting to problems that have grown too large to ignore.

Third, the agency, to its credit, frequently has commented upon government regulation that hurts consumers and competition. However, the FTC has not established as strong a record for its ability or willingness to call attention to market failures that create a need for stronger regulation. So, it would be worth examining this category of activities and reporting to Congress on the agency's findings.

While many areas legitimately fall under this heading, one area that might be particularly worth examining involves the airline industry. The Commission previously has made a number of comments concerning air transportation. But, the agency has remained silent about the specter of increased concentration and fare hikes within the industry. Unfortunately, the benefits of the airline industry's economic deregulation may be jeopardized by a continuing consolidation into fewer and fewer carriers.[20]

It would be a service for the agency to conduct a public review of this issue. If there is no cause for alarm, that would be useful information. But if there are major problems, the airline industry must be held up to public scrutiny. Indeed, the fungibility of airline assets, which was cited as a prime factor in favor of deregulation, also makes it relatively easy to divest a carrier's assets if it behaves in an anticompetitive manner.

Fourth, it is time to reexamine federalism and redefine the relationship between the states and the FTC. Particularly in light of recent developments, such as the larger role of the states in antitrust and consumer protection law enforcement, it is necessary to discuss these issues in a systematic fashion. As an FTC official, my inclination is to support greater economically sound activity at the federal level as an alternative to, and in some instances as a supplement to, continual expansion of the states' role. Without question, the agency also should seize opportunities to work more closely with the states and to increase the states' powers in at least some areas which are now exclusively reserved to the FTC. For example, the state attorneys general may effectively and efficiently enforce some of the FTC's trade regulation rules.

Conclusion

In some regards, the FTC may be likened to a ship. This ship first set sail in 1914 and has weathered fierce storms ever since. Borne along on an uncertain current, the ship also is buffeted by an unpredictable wind. The ship is held together by a courageous, but depleted, crew. At the top, the ship is commanded by as many as five captains at once, all of whom have both hands on the helm, but some of whom may consider scuttling superior to salvaging.

After plowing through these seas for seventy-four years, it is not remarkable that the ship is jury-rigged, hoists patchwork sails aloft, and is encrusted with barnacles. The wonder truly is that this ship remains underway on its mission and retains the ability to give a good account of itself in battle.

The presence of this ship in the waters of the marketplace helps to preserve free and fair commerce. That is in the interest of American consumers. But the ship's crew must be augmented, its operations overhauled, and its course corrected if it is to remain afloat and in fighting trim for another seventy-four years. Decisions to be made shortly will determine if the ship is long to ride the waves or soon to sink beneath them.

Notes

1. Thomas K. McCraw, *Prophets of Regulation* (Cambridge: Harvard University Press, 1984), at 151.

2. *Humphrey's Executor v. United States,* 295 U.S. 602 (1935). The Supreme Court's decision in *Morrison v. Olson,* 56 U.S.L.W. 4835 (U.S. June 29, 1988), appears to reaffirm the constitutionality of independent agencies and refers with approval specifically to the FTC. Perhaps this is the beginning of a fifty-three-year cycle for Supreme Court reviews of the agency's constitutional condition.

3. See E. Cox, R. Fellmeth, and J. Schulz, *The Nader Report on the Federal Trade Commission* (1969); American Bar Association, *Report of the ABA Commission to Study the Federal Trade Commission* (ABA Report) (1969).

4. Paula Dwyer, "Thunder from the Right at the Federal Trade Commission," *Business Week*, January 12, 1987, pp. 139-40. See, also, Paul Harris, "Will the FTC Finally Wake Up?" *Sales & Marketing Management*, January 1988, pp. 57-60.

5. For instance, in a speech delivered on May 6, 1988, Commissioner Calvani proposed reorganizing the FTC by placing all law enforcement decision-making power in the hands of the agency's general counsel. Although I do not endorse this proposal, I agree with Commissioner Calvani's observation in the same speech to the effect that it is extremely difficult for a Commission majority to "impose any enforcement agenda on the agency except with the active consent of the chairman." Of course, the fact that a venture is difficult does not make it unimportant or futile. For a summary, see FTC, "Commissioner Calvani Proposes Reorganization of FTC," *FTC News Notes*, May 16, 1988, p. 1.

6. Daniel Oliver, chairman, Federal Trade Commission, *FTC News*, June 11, 1987.

7. The estimate of $10 billion is from Representative Claude Pepper, Report by the Chairman of the Subcommittee on Health and Long-Term Care, "Quackery: A $10 Billion Scandal" (1984). The estimate of $25 billion is from Sylvia Porter, "Scams' Risk: Your Money and Your Life," *N.Y. Daily News*, August 28, 1987.

8. Five defendants pled guilty; the remaining defendant was convicted following trial. Four of the six defendants were convicted for violating asset freeze orders imposed by the courts to preserve defendants' assets for potential consumer redress. The remaining two were convicted for making misrepresentations to consumers in violation of court orders.

9. Letters to Chairman Luken and Representative Whittaker, Subcommittee on Transportation, Tourism and Hazardous Materials, Committee on Energy and Commerce, U.S. House of Representatives, dated February 11, 1988; Statement of the Federal Trade Commission before the Subcommittee on Transportation, Tourism and Hazardous Materials, Committee on Energy and Commerce, U.S. House of Representatives, dated December 3, 1987.

10. ABA Report, at 15.

11. There may be, of course, mitigating circumstances. Some cases are very complex. Sometimes a new bureau director needs to scrutinize carefully the initiatives of his or her predecessor. Sometimes incumbent bureau directors and commissioners are left holding the bag for delays and indecisiveness properly attributable to those who previously have held office. Indeed, some senior bureau managers deserve credit for attempting to reduce backlogs and shorten the processing time for new cases. For all that, the Commission absolutely must hold itself and bureau directors to the highest standards of punctuality if the agency is to operate efficiently.

12. Committee on Independent Regulatory Commissions, *Report to the Congress by the Commission on Organization of the Executive Branch of the Government* (Hoover Commission), Appendix N, Task Force Report (1949), at 125.

13. ABA Report, at 12 and 13.

14. See, e.g., *FTC v. Brown Shoe Co.*, 384 U.S. 316 (1966); *FTC v. Motion Picture Advertising Serv. Co.*, 344 U.S. 392 (1953); *Fashion Originators' Guild v. FTC*, 312 U.S. 457 (1941).

15. See, generally, Averitt, "The Meaning of 'Unfair Methods of Competition' in Section 5 of the Federal Trade Commission Act," 21 *B.C.L. Rev.*, 227, 251-90 (1980) (author also discusses how section 5 has been interpreted to reach conduct violating

recognized standards of fair business behavior and conduct violating competition policy as framed by the Commission).

16. Of course, this limiting feature of the Commission's remedial authority properly does not hold for cases where the Commission challenges conduct that respondents or defendants knew or should have known was unlawful (e.g., per se offenses).

17. As a few illustrations of the general trend, see, Paul M. Barrett, "Attorneys General Flex Their Muscles," *Wall Street Journal,* July 13, 1988, p. 25; W. John Moore, "Dear Feds—Help!" *National Journal,* July 9, 1988, pp. 1788-92; Irving Scher, "Rising Antitrust, Consumer Protection Activities of State Attorneys General," *New York Law Journal,* June 10, 1988; Daniel Moskowitz, "Why the States Are Ganging Up on Some Giant Companies," *Business Week,* April 11, 1988, p. 62; "A New Federalism?" *National Journal,* May 14, 1988, pp. 1253-54; Jennifer Lawrence, "States Target Campbell Ads," *Advertising Age,* June 27, 1988, p. 107; and Aaron Bernstein, "The New Federalism Hasn't Meant Less Government," *Business Week,* May 2, 1988, p. 110.

18. "Some NAAGing Doubts—and What to Do about Them," *Advertising Age,* February 8, 1988, p. 16.

19. Ibid.

20. See, for instance, Agis Salpukas, "Air Fares Rise for Many Travelers as Big Carriers Dominate Market," the *New York Times,* March 15, 1988, pp. A1, D8; "The Big Trouble with Air Travel," *Consumer Reports,* June 1988, pp. 362-67.

The FTC in 1989: Rising from the Ashes?

Andrew J. Strenio, Jr.

This paper will discuss the shape of things to come at the Federal Trade Commission (FTC, agency, or Commission). Naturally, the views to follow are my own and not necessarily those of the Commission or any other commissioner. That disclaimer serves the purpose of allowing the other commissioners at any point to emulate the Hollywood mogul, Samuel Goldwyn, and exclaim, "Include me out!"

The Proper Role of the Agency

Let me begin with several broad observations about the proper role of the agency. In the first place, I am market oriented. In my view, markets should be allowed to work their magic to the maximum extent possible. The government usually should intervene only to the minimum extent necessary to correct market failures. Even then, the government should intervene only when such intervention is not likely to be counterproductive. This careful approach is consistent with my training and temperament and has been reinforced by the experience of nearly a decade in public service. Ill-advised governmental action in the marketplace can produce unintended adverse consequences and prove terribly resistant to correction.

From that perspective, I am convinced that the analytical methods employed at the Commission are roughly correct. Whether scrutinizing a merger for anticompetitive effects or reviewing an advertisement for false or deceptive content, the FTC properly exercises caution before launching a challenge. Two questions predominate: Is there reason to believe that the proposed respondents violated the law? If so, will FTC action improve conditions for consumers? Unless both questions can be answered in the affirmative, the agency appropriately stays its hand.

147

Consistent with my allegiance to these principles, it is no secret that I have been disappointed during my three years as a commissioner by the FTC's failure to move more aggressively against illegal and inefficient practices that are both harmful to consumers and susceptible to improvement by agency action. The Commission since my arrival in March, 1986, has not been as vigorous in pursuing such actions or in broadcasting an enthusiastic commitment to this pursuit as the public interest has warranted. Not only is this a problem in itself, but public perception of FTC inactivity or disinterest adds momentum to the undesirable imposition of economic reregulation at various levels of government.

To be sure, this disappointment may be overstated. The FTC since 1986 has done many things right. In fact, it has often done so in the face of long odds. But leadership requires a constant push for improvement rather than a smug satisfaction with the status quo. And the fact is that despite the assets of talented personnel and legally and economically sound analytical frameworks, there remains unrealized potential at the Commission. Endorsing the current situation would be akin to applauding Ted Williams for batting .260, or Knute Rockne for finishing a season one game over .500. While others might boast of this level of achievement, it falls far short of the standard of excellence.

Although my support for the FTC's mission and its staff might sound like special interest pleading, it is not. When I was a commissioner at the Interstate Commerce Commission (ICC), I supported budget cuts and the proposal to sunset the ICC. In my judgment, the ICC needlessly hindered the market and thereby hurt the public by way of its price and entry controls. The beneficial portion of ICC activity could have been performed more effectively elsewhere.

The FTC's situation is far different. The agency's antitrust, consumer protection, and advocacy work helps the market operate more efficiently and thereby serves the public. Unfortunately, as resources vanish and agency authority atrophies, the FTC's ability to fulfill that function is impaired. Since the FTC is one of the few government bodies with a mandate to protect all citizens and not just a narrow constituency this trend of decreasing resources and agency authority is disturbing.

Concerns About the Commission

First and foremost of these concerns is the FTC's resource crisis, which is the proximate cause of a number of troubling ripple effects.

To my distress, the severe discrepancy between agency workload and workyears that I cited in my other article (see above), has worsened since 1988.

Indeed, in January, 1989, thirty-four valued agency employees were "RIF'd" (the government euphemism for laid off). The action was taken to reconcile the FTC budget with the appropriation for fiscal year 1989. Although this step was unavoidable after Congress slashed the administration's FTC budget request, it nonetheless was devastating. This involuntary loss of staff has aggravated the resource squeeze and has shaken the morale of the remaining staff members.

The surviving staff members are part of a dwindling band. The FTC now has fewer employees than it has had at any time since fiscal year 1961, when it had 855 employees. Since fiscal year 1961, the gross national product (GNP) has grown from roughly $.5 trillion to $4.5 trillion. When inflation is considered, the economy today is 240 percent of what it was in 1961. Nevertheless, the federal agency with the primary responsibility for policing advertising and a major responsibility for policing the surge in mergers has been left far behind. If FTC staffing had stayed level with GNP growth since 1961, the agency today would have more than 2,050 employees or well over twice the 900 employees supported by the Commission's fiscal year 1989 appropriation.

The latest figures pertinent to some of the comparisons made in my article include the following. From fiscal year 1979 to fiscal year 1989, the number of FTC workyears fell 48 percent from 1,746 to a projected 900. In the same period, the annual number of Hart-Scott-Rodino (HSR) merger filings skyrocketed 334 percent from 861 to a projected 2,878. In other words, with respect to this one measure, half as many staff members are responsible for three times as much work. Such an increased workload creates an enormous strain on the agency staff, even when the appreciable productivity increases that have been realized over those ten years are considered.

The FTC's performance level has suffered under this strain. While many of the effects are difficult to quantify, two illustrative items are worth noting. First, the percentage of HSR filings that are subjected to a second request, that is, to especially close scrutiny, has fallen from 8.2 percent in fiscal year 1979 to a projected 1.4 percent in fiscal year 1989. Second, the workyears devoted to long-term economic research studies capable of illuminating issues central to the FTC's duties have fallen from over 23 in fiscal year 1979 to a projected 8 in fiscal year 1989. It is not an adverse reflection upon the FTC's dedicated and capable staff to acknowledge that there are limits to the amount of work that can be done by so few.

The strain is also beginning to show on the antitrust side. During the past three years, the agency has done little outside the realm of merger reviews and HSR-filing rules enforcement. Nonmerger cases have included only a handful involving small groups of medical professionals and a few multiple-listing-service cases. For example, all fiscal year 1988 final nonmerger part 2 consents involved doctors or real estate. The only nonmerger part 3 consent involved doctors.

In the realm of consumer protection over the past three years, the Commission has exerted only a minor presence with respect to nutritional and health advertising claims for major food products. In 1982, the Commission voted to terminate a rulemaking that considered imposing various mandatory standards on food advertising disclosures. The Commission's rationale for this decision was that the issues were too complex to be solved on an industrywide basis and that case-by-case enforcement was necessary.

The Commission's conclusion was reasonable. Unfortunately, since 1986 the agency's public espousal of case-by-case enforcement has been minimal, although the pace has quickened recently. Even if a generous definition of "food" advertising cases is adopted, there has been a total of only eight public enforcement actions in the last three years. These actions include one initial decision, one administrative complaint, and one consent order in 1989; one consent order and one stipulated injunction in 1988; one consent order in 1987; and one consent order and one permanent injunction in 1986. If one deletes the six food supplement and diet plan cases, then the cupboard is almost bare. Even if additional enforcement actions are not forthcoming, the Commission must at least better explain its positive advertising agenda to the public.

Finally, the agency's economic capacity also is overloaded. This overload may well burn out a number of the agency's most promising economists. For instance, the Bureau of Economics is so busy firefighting mergers that it now regularly raids its "think-tank unit" for resources. As a result, the Commission is unable systematically to:

1. analyze and learn from the cases, whether litigated or not, that come before it;
2. devise measures of the agency's impact on the incidence of illegal

behavior, rather than relying on less direct tests of accomplishment; or

3. devote adequate attention to marketing issues that have clear relevance to its enforcement policy.

In a similar vein, the FTC's recent advocacy comments less frequently possess the value and produce the impact that should accrue to new in-house and in-depth study. Further, as resources dwindle, the entire advocacy program has come under increased attack. These criticisms come from those who, mistakenly, in my estimation, view advocacy comments as a distraction from, rather than an important complement to, the FTC's law enforcement efforts.

Environmental Factors Shaping the FTC

Despite these problems, it soon may figuratively be springtime for the FTC. The combined force of several environmental factors may create a more temperate and favorable climate for the Commission. At least five such environmental factors are at work.

First, the Bush administration has been conducting a review of FTC issues. This new examination may yield insights leading to the agency's reform and renewal that may help the agency meet the challenges of the 1990s.

Second, as a result of the expiration of various terms, as many as three of the five Commission seats could have new occupants by the end of the year. Infusions of fresh blood have been known to stimulate fresh thinking in other settings.

Third, on April 7, 1989, the special committee of the American Bar Association Section of Antitrust Law, known popularly as the Kirkpatrick Committee, released its long-awaited report on the role of the FTC. This 173-page report cogently analyzes the FTC's current problems and provides a supportive and surprisingly harmonious set of proposals for reviving the agency.

Fourth, some recent excesses in the private sector have generated greater appreciation for the notion that a strong FTC is needed as an adjunct to the removal of unnecessarily intrusive regulatory burdens and as a bulwark against their reappearance.

Fifth, congressional bodies with oversight responsibility for the FTC, such as the Senate Consumer Subcommittee under the capable leadership of Chairman Bryan (D-NV) and Ranking Minority Member Gorton (R-WA), both of whom are former state attorneys general, increasingly are expressing a bipartisan sympathy for the agency's enforcement mission.

Getting the FTC into Shape

Where will this lead? It simply is too early to say. Since I have been using a springtime metaphor, I will refer to the words of that renowned philosopher, Yogi Berra. At the start of his first spring training as a player, an equipment manager taking measurements for the team uniforms asked Yogi for his cap size. "How do I know?" replied Yogi, "I'm not in shape yet." Similarly, it is not yet possible to specify precisely how these five factors will interact in the process of getting the FTC into shape.

First, additional resources, as well as better use of its resources, would aid the FTC's mission. This would allow the FTC to undertake new enforcement initiatives. It would permit the FTC to develop and apply better its economics expertise. The Hart-Scott-Rodino process, with its repeated demands for quick legal and economic investigation and judgment (and court challenge, if necessary), has imposed unprecedented burdens on the staff, especially because of the recent increase in merger activity. The staff participants in that process need more relief than is currently available—relief that should come in the form of energetic, entry-level hires.

The Commission needs a stable environment in which to pursue its mission, and the budget problems of recent years, with their resulting reductions in force, have not provided that environment. The decline in real resources should be halted, and an increase in resources provided.

Second, many practices deserve antitrust scrutiny by the FTC. The application of antitrust to deregulated industries continues to be challenging. The scope of numerous antitrust exemptions continues to be undecided, because Congress is considering important legislation and the Commission and the courts are struggling to demark the edges of those exemptions (e.g., *Noerr*, state action, labor). The importance of policing those edges is increasingly recognized. Finally, the expanding importance of the rule of reason and proof of market power emphasizes the importance of the FTC's role.

Third, I believe that the FTC can and should do more to articulate its advertising law enforcement agenda. I believe that the FTC properly hesitates before finding implied advertising claims and is properly concerned about the risk of suppressing truthful advertising. But too rarely has the public received the message that the FTC believes it is important to move aggressively against false and deceptive advertising.

Fourth, economists are now respected, professional colleagues of FTC lawyers. I applaud this development. It must continue if the Commission is to bring important cases that make economic sense. The most important change for the Commission to make concerns its research agenda. To make the FTC the major repository of knowledge about the operation of American industry—including retail markets for consumer goods—and of antitrust and consumer protection enforcement, FTC economists should use their comparative advantage in understanding how industries actually function.

Fifth and finally, the advocacy program is salutary because it allows the FTC to share with other regulators and legislators information that the Commission has gathered through its other activities. Even if the agency's advice were not often accepted, information sharing is valuable. In the whirl of activity that precedes the adoption of federal or state regulations or the enactment of state legislation, the FTC can offer an important, sometimes lonely, voice for the consumer. This should be encouraged, not arbitrarily restricted.

While these five conclusions might sound as if they were extracted from my article or my speeches, they actually were derived from an entirely different source. All five of the conclusions are taken almost verbatim from passages in the Kirkpatrick Committee report. It is mightily encouraging to find such language in the report, and it should be evident that I agree with the preponderance of that document's discussion.

President Bush recently told a French story about two ways to look at the future. The master of a house asked the gardener to plant a particular tree. The gardener objected because the tree would take a hundred years to reach full growth. The master responded, "In that case, there's no time to lose. Plant it today."

Clearly, many of these proposals for the FTC also will require a long time to take root and blossom into maturity. That makes it imperative that the agency loses no time in planting them in the nurturing soil of public discourse. I think that this symposium is a valuable part of that process. In that connection, I also hope that history will credit me with having done some useful tilling and watering, and will not adjudge me guilty of applying excessive amounts of fertilizer.

The FTC in the 1980s

J. Howard Beales, III

Perhaps consistent with its position in the structure of government as an independent regulatory agency, the FTC in the past few decades has experimented with the functions of all three branches of government. Until the 1970s, the agency was probably best described as quasi-judicial. The bulk of its resources were devoted to administrative cases that the Commission ultimately resolved, sitting in essence as a court. During the 1970s, the agency tried out the role of a quasi-legislative body, with a large fraction of staff resources devoted to rulemaking. Unlike a legislature, however, the Commission's rulemaking adventures required both clear legal theories and substantial supporting evidence. Failure to recognize these needs led the Commission into a quagmire from which is has almost, but not yet completely, extricated itself.

During the 1980s, the agency has become primarily a prosecutor, devoting most of its resources to the pursuit of cases in the federal courts. In 1988, the majority of the Commission's complaints were filed in federal district courts, and staff workyears spent on district court litigation exceeded resources devoted to administrative litigation. This change occurred even earlier in the Commission's Bureau of Consumer Protection, which has devoted more staff time to district court litigation than to administrative litigation every year since 1984.[1] In 1980, the Commission had thirteen administrative law judges (ALJs), with a total of fifty cases on their docket. By 1988, it was down to three ALJs with only fifteen cases.[2] Although the total number of law enforcement actions has remained roughly constant, the forum for those actions has shifted dramatically.

On the whole, the shift from administrative to district court litigation has been an extremely positive development. The Commission can seek relief from the courts that it cannot order in administrative litigation, including freezes on assets and preliminary injunctions in fraud

154

cases. District court litigation moves much more quickly than the "leisurely pace typical of FTC proceedings" that a court of appeals once noted. Exploiting the potential of district court litigation has made it possible, for the first time, for the Commission to launch an effective attack on the kinds of frauds that cause really significant consumer losses.

Perhaps the most dramatic, if least recognized, implication of the shift to district court litigation is the change in the role of the commissioners themselves. Because most decisions of administrative law judges are appealed to the Commission, it was the Commission that ultimately resolved most of the fifty cases on the docket in 1980 through a decision and a (usually lengthy) written opinion. Because commissioners cannot discuss matters that are in litigation with the agency's staff, commissioners needed personal staffs to assist in reviewing the record and producing an opinion. Of necessity, a good deal of the Commission's time was devoted to resolving matters in administrative litigation.

As the core of the commissioners' workload declined with the decline of administrative litigation, they had more time to devote to other matters. Indeed, in a classic demonstration of the laws of bureaucratic momentum, they found it necessary to increase their personal staffs. What have the commissioners done with these increased resources? It is perhaps symptomatic of the relative inattention to policy at the Commission level that Commissioner Strenio's paper is about management and resources, not policy.

The decline in administrative litigation has left a gap in the FTC's development of policy. Indeed, the central problem facing the Commission in 1989 is that it has not yet recognized that its role has changed. This comment first discusses the policy-making process at the Federal Trade Commission. It then considers the differences between prosecutorial and judicial policy and their implications for the FTC. Finally, it considers the resource needs of the Commission in light of its changing role.

Policy Decisions at the Federal Trade Commission

Historically, administrative litigation was the central element in the development of Federal Trade Commission policy. Through its opinions, the Commission developed policy in a series of specific examples. It has always been a rare opinion that announced sweeping policy developments.

Indeed, the principles of judicial decision making argue that decisions generally should only resolve the case at hand, after complete development of a full record through administrative litigation. Moreover, anyone who has read any appreciable number of Commission opinions cannot help but notice numerous inconsistencies in approach and rationale from one Commission to the next, and even from one case to the next. Nevertheless, the gradual accretion of specific decisions with specific rationales make it possible to develop a sense of the Commission's policy approaches.

Decisions about broad policy questions are intrinsically difficult in a collegial and highly political body like the Commission. It is always attractive to avoid deciding questions until a decision is unavoidable. Similarly, it is attractive to resolve specific questions that must be answered in ways that avoid resolution of the general policy issue. These temptations are especially great in an agency steeped in the traditions of administrative litigation. Until there is simply no alternative, and sometimes even then, the Commission's persistent tendency is to avoid making choices. A widespread joke among the agency's staff asks, "Given the choice between A and B, which will the Commission choose?" The answer, all too true, is "A and B."

The Commission's tendency to reserve difficult questions for another day is also becoming evident in some of its ever more infrequent administrative opinions. In the recent Removatron case, for example, the question presented to the Commission was whether one or two clinical tests are required to substantiate future advertising claims for electronic tweezers that claimed to remove hair permanently. There were only four sitting commissioners when the decision was rendered, so perhaps it was inevitable that they would split 2-2, develop three rationales for the two results, and reserve for another day the question of whether the claims at issue required one or two substantiating tests.[3]

The tendency to duck is also apparent in another recent administrative opinion, this one involving R. J. Reynolds. The administrative law judge decided that the challenged advertisement, which addressed the relationship between smoking and heart disease, was political speech, fully protected by the first amendment. On appeal, the Commission reversed, holding that a full trial would develop additional information that might possibly bear on the question, and therefore it was premature to decide the issue. The Commission was not specific about what additional evidence was needed, or how it might help answer the question.

Nonetheless, it deferred the question to await the results of further proceedings.[4]

Now, some cases are difficult, and the inability to resolve a particular case is of little consequence when other, similar cases will inevitably arise in the future. But given the shift from administrative litigation, these cases represent a large fraction of the Commission's decision making output. And, one would hope, the agency is not about to launch new waves of litigation to explore either the frontiers of the first amendment or the permissible contours of hair removal claims.

Perhaps the clearest symptom of the Commission's difficulty in making choices is delay. Although the Commission has managed to move quickly in fraud cases that do not raise substantial policy issues, more difficult decisions can remain on hold almost indefinitely. That delay is most visible in the Commission's administrative decisions. In the R. J. Reynolds case, for example, it took the Commission nearly a year to produce a twenty-two-page opinion. The Commission experimented briefly with a system of setting public deadlines for its decisions, but the experiment ended when the first (and only) deadline was missed.

Moreover, delay is not confined to administrative litigation. Anyone who has ever been connected with the agency can point to numerous examples of matters that the Commission "considered" for extended periods of time.

Quasi-judicial versus Prosecutorial Policy

Courts and quasi-judicial agencies develop policy by weighing the evidence and writing opinions to resolve the cases that come before them. Prosecutors, which the Commission has increasingly become, develop policy through resource allocation decisions. Of course, prosecutors still need policies, but the differences have important implications for the nature of the policy process.

First, a court has the luxury of reviewing the parties' substantial investments in explicating the issues before making its decision. All of the evidence that either party believes is likely to assist its case is presented, and the implications of the evidence are spelled out. A prosecutor's decision to launch an investigation is itself a decision that the investigation is a worthwhile use of resources in comparison to the alternatives. Although the decision to prosecute ultimately depends on the facts determined in a thorough investigation, a successful prosecutor cannot spend a large fraction of the available resources exploring blind alleys. Of necessity, a prosecutor's decisions about which policies to pursue are made with incomplete information about the facts. Because the facts are uncertain when an investigation begins, a prosecutor also needs the flexibility to abandon an investigation that no longer appears to be worth pursuing.

Perhaps because a quasi-judicial body like the Commission has a hard time making decisions based on incomplete information, it has historically been the bureau directors who primarily determined prosecutorial policy. The Commission almost never rejects a recommendation for law enforcement action (though it may change the allegations or seek additional relief), and it orders the staff to initiate investigations even less frequently. Bureau directors are of course responsive to the suggestions of individual commissioners, but it is the bureau director who remains the key focus of prosecutorial policy, particularly in consumer protection.

In the last few years and reflected in Commissioner Strenio's paper, the commissioners have grown uncomfortable with this arrangement. Unfortunately, however, they have not addressed the underlying problem, which is the Commission's reluctance as a body to make policy decisions or pursue a consistent policy. Instead, they have tried to view the problem as one of management. As individual commissioners have attempted to second-guess specific management decisions, the result has been to undermine the managers' ability to make decisions as well.

Effective management requires goals that the managers should pursue, flexibility for the managers to pursue those goals in the best possible way, and accountability for failure to achieve those goals. Unfortunately, the Commission has approached the problem backwards. It has, in effect, sought to hold managers accountable for failing to achieve goals that it will not specify and has sought to limit managerial discretion in pursuit of those amorphous objectives.

Consider the management approaches that Commissioner Strenio discusses. For one, he seeks to encourage intellectual independence in the career staff. Independence is obviously critical in evaluating policy issues, including many issues of prosecutorial policy. Vigorous debate is an essential component of intelligent decisions about policy, and the Commission needs to have all points of view presented fully and fairly. The Commission also needs to make choices among those policy views, however. All too often, the debate continues indefinitely because the Commission declines to make a choice.

If independence and debate are essential for policy decisions, they are a sure recipe for no policy at all when applied to resource allocation decisions. A staff attorney who has identified a possible target for investigation has understandable, and generally desirable, incentives to argue for the pursuit of that investigation. Managers, assessing the full range of possible investigations, need the ability to say no.

Unfortunately, the Commission seems to have moved in the direction of encouraging more sources of prosecutorial policy rather than making choices about policy. That is surely the effect, and perhaps the intent, of increased allocation of resources to regional offices. By nearly inviolable tradition, regional offices are free to pursue any matter within the Commission's consumer protection jurisdiction. Whatever the bureau's resource allocations, as reflected in its budget decisions, regional offices have substantial flexibility in making their own resource allocations. The result is an array of semi-independent prosecutors, each potentially with his or her own policy. This generates more choices for the Commission but makes the problem of implementing any one policy much more difficult.

Moreover, despite its professed interest in encouraging intellectual independence, the Commission has exhibited a disappointing reluctance to address inconvenient arguments. This reluctance may have reached its peak when the Commission expressly refused to consider the policy views of a new bureau director in the case against R. J. Reynolds. Despite precedents for considering different policy views of the bureau director and the staff in a litigated case, the Commission simply refused to permit the bureau director to file his views. All too often, the search for intellectual independence is really a search for someone, anyone, who might support a particular commissioner's views. The fact that no such person has come forward is taken as a sign that dissent is suppressed. The alternative hypothesis is simply unacceptable.

Consider the Commission's other "reform": a fast track for cases that have languished too long in the investigation stage. Effective use of prosecutorial resources requires the ability to open an investigation but later shift resources to a more promising target. By far the most common reason that an investigation languishes is that the managers involved have decided it is not the most promising use of resources. It is a strange approach indeed to establish a fast track for the matters that the line managers have decided are the least promising.

Of course, unpromising investigations can and should be closed. Closing a matter that the Commission has ever considered, however, requires almost as much effort as issuing a complaint. Elaborate memoranda must address everything that was learned in the course of the investigation and are subject to careful scrutiny to insure that the staff is not up to something. Unless the investigation establishes that no violation has occurred, the Commission is extremely reluctant to close a matter. Although prosecutors need to be able to close an investigation because there are other, more promising candidates, at the FTC such a decision is enormously costly. The result is a set of perverse incentives to avoid initiating matters that may prove difficult to resolve definitively and to avoid involving the Commission by conducting investigations without the benefit of compulsory process.

A second key difference between courts and prosecutors in policy decisions is that the two have a very different problem in conveying and explaining their policies. When a court dismisses a case, it states its reasons, and the policy is apparent to all. Observers must infer whether a prosecutor fails to act because a practice is legal or because enforcement resources are committed elsewhere. A central institutional problem for the Commission is the search for effective mechanisms for the commissioners to explain their policies to the public.

In the early 1980s, the Commission pursued these goals through a series of policy statements, addressing unfairness, deception, and advertising substantiation. The Commission subsequently adopted each statement in litigated cases, thus giving the principles they set forth the status of legal precedents. Similarly in antitrust, both the Commission and the Department of Justice devoted considerable effort to revising and updating their merger guides. Because these statements articulated the Commission's legal theories and basic policies clearly and concisely, they offered guidance both to the staff about the principles that distinguished good investigations from bad ones and to the public about the principles that distinguished legal from illegal conduct.

Unfortunately, the Commission has not pursued policy statements in other areas. It has not developed any other mechanisms for expressing its views as a body about policy, either in general or in particular areas. And it has not updated ancient policy guides that have not reflected actual Commission policy for at least fifteen years. In too many areas the result has been either a perception of no policy at all or, even worse, a perception of a conscious policy that advertisers could do no wrong.

In the wonderful world of Washington politics, perceptions often matter more than reality. One way to address those perceptions is to bring more cases, whether they fit with a sensible concept of the policy the agency should pursue or not. This approach, often expressed as the notion that the Commission should act because the perception will otherwise lead to even worse regulation in some other fashion, is strangely reminiscent of the Vietnam era report—in order to save the village we had to destroy it. The alternative, at least worth considering, is for the Commission to state and define its policy more clearly as a Commission.

Resource Needs

The FTC's shift to district court litigation has significant implications for the agency's resource requirements. The faster pace of district court litigation makes it possible for a smaller staff to bring more cases. The superior remedies available in district court also produce better results. Adoption of more efficient tools has made it possible for the Commission to achieve more with fewer resources.

Nonetheless, the bulk of Strenio's paper argues that the Commission needs more resources. Perhaps, but only perhaps, he is right. Before it is reasonable to conclude that the agency needs a bigger budget, however, it is essential to inquire what the Commission would do if such a request were granted.

A central problem in prosecutorial decision making is resource allocation. Any prosecutor, at any level, can always point to stones unturned and potential targets not pursued. However large a budget might be, a prosecutor must decide which investigations to pursue and which ones to close. Because they are necessarily made without full knowledge of what an investigation would reveal, such decisions are always difficult. And, for that reason, it is always tempting to seek additional resources to avoid hard choices. Unless we are willing to spend the entire gross national product on prosecutors, however, we have to ask what policy the additional resources would be used to pursue.

Commissioner Strenio's paper does not address that crucial question. Instead, he points to the large number of stones unturned, each with unknown inhabitants lurking underneath. In antitrust, for example, the Commission authorized a record number of preliminary injunction actions and a record number of premerger enforcement actions. Nonetheless, because of the rise in merger activity, those actions constituted a smaller percentage of the mergers that occurred.

The policy implicit in this argument for more resources is that the Commission should investigate and challenge a constant fraction of all mergers. As a policy, such an approach seems indefensible. The nature of merger activity has changed considerably in the past few years, with a vastly larger number of transactions aimed primarily at replacing incumbent management and restructuring corporations. Because they are not aimed at consolidating competing firms, such transactions are less likely to raise antitrust concerns. Moreover, the revisions of the merger guidelines should have defined more clearly which transactions raise antitrust concerns and which do not. With greater clarity in the agency's standards, one would expect fewer transactions that violate those standards. For both reasons, it is no surprise that the fraction of transactions that warrant a second request for information has fallen. Nor is there any evidence that unchallenged mergers have in fact given rise to any appreciable threat to competition. Without such evidence, it is hard to see why the Commission needs more resources to turn more stones.

It is an iron law of bureaucracy that work expands to occupy the available resources. We can always ask more questions, open more investigations, and pursue cases beyond any expectation of real benefits. To avoid simply creating more work, we should ask any agency requesting more resources exactly what it wishes to do but cannot, given the current constraints.

The Commission has a difficult burden in making such a case. After all, this is an agency that still has enough resources to pursue administrative litigation challenging a merger that was called off, to pursue an administrative case after a judge rejected a preliminary injunction because there was no likelihood of success, and to worry about the gory details of reporting requirements whether or not there are potential antitrust problems. Given these choices about how it should spend its resources, it appears that more resources would mean more work but not more results.

Similarly, Commissioner Strenio notes the decline in resources devoted to consumer protection. He does not, however, note the constant or even increasing number of cases addressing consumer protection problems. That increase was possible because the shift to district court litigation and the decline in rulemaking activity enormously enhanced productivity. Again, it is possible that more resources are needed, but the Commission has yet to say what it would like to do but cannot accomplish within current resource constraints.

Perhaps the clearest demonstration that work expands to use the

available resources comes from the offices of the commissioners themselves. The decline of administrative litigation should have freed up the
commissioners' time and reduced their need for personal staffs to do their
jobs. After all, outside of adjudication, commissioners can and do call on
the staff in the bureaus to address and develop the issues that concern
them. Nonetheless, the staffs of commissioners have actually increased
over the past few years. And no doubt each commissioner is fully occupied
and believes that a reduction in his or her personal staff would require a
sacrifice of some valuable activities.

Resource allocation questions are like that. There is always a cost to
shifting resources to some other activity and always more that could be
done with more resources. We can't decide whether additional resources
are needed, however, without careful consideration of the additional benefits those resources are likely to produce.

The role of the Federal Trade Commission is an important one and
one that deserves support. The expanded use of new powers and authorities that the Commission received in the 1970s, however, calls for
some changes in the way the Commission itself approaches its tasks. Only
when the Commission recognizes that it has indeed become a prosecutorial agency can it make the changes that the 1990s will require.

Notes

1. Report of the American Bar Association Section of Antitrust Law Special Committee to Study the Role of the Federal Trade Commission (1989), at 137. The statistics
treat regional offices separately from the Bureaus of Competition and Consumer Protection. Because most regional offices are in fact devoted to consumer protection matters, the
figures for the consumer protection mission would reflect an even earlier shift.

2. Report of the American Bar Association, (see Appendix II).

3. Removatron International Corporation, Docket No. 9200, November 4, 1988.

4. R. J. Reynolds Tobacco Company, Inc., Docket No. 9206, March 4, 1988.

Comments on the FTC in 1988

John E. Calfee

Academic observers of the regulatory process are seldom blessed
with an extended discussion of that process by a sitting member of a major
regulatory agency, in this case the Federal Trade Commission. Commissioner Strenio's paper is therefore most welcome. Perhaps it is best to
begin by recalling that in the early 1980s, before serving as a commissioner of the Interstate Commerce Commission and the FTC, Mr. Strenio
was an assistant director in the FTC's Bureau of Consumer Protection,
where he oversaw the FTC's remarkable regulatory intervention program
that sought to reduce the consumer burden from regulation elsewhere in
the federal or other bureaucracies. The numerous telling comments in his
paper on the accomplishments and frustrations of the FTC staff are rooted
in his own experience as a staffer.

Commissioner Strenio's observations place him squarely in the historical mainstream of FTC regulators. I take the essentials of mainstream
thought to be something along the following. FTC actions have by and
large benefited consumers, especially since the rebirth brought by the
ABA and Nader reports. Occasionally the Commission has fallen asleep or
wandered off the reservation, but it has always recovered its sense of
balance, often with the aid of an outraged Congress or public. The FTC
staff is hardworking and competent—but it is unequal to its relentlessly
increasing workload, and Congress should therefore increase FTC resources. Although the current division of antitrust authority between the
FTC and the Department of Justice is admittedly strange, it is actually a
good thing once you think it through. Also a good thing is the existence
of ten FTC regional offices. On the other hand, the organization of the
Commission itself—with its tenuous relation between FTC staff and commissioners other than the chairman—leaves something to be desired. A
particular problem is how to set overall policy: it is (once again) time for

164

the Commission to conceive a more structured approach to forming and enunciating basic policy.

Commissioner Strenio's voice is therefore a familiar one of moderation and optimism—the kind of voice that has dominated the FTC community through most of its history, excepting only a few brief periods of intense turbulence such as 1969-70 and 1978-83. It is entirely in keeping with this tradition that Mr. Strenio's criticisms of his institution are muted, his bureaucratic self-contemplation anything but soul-searching, his policy proposals moderate and (in a nonpejorative sense) marginal.

A striking characteristic of his paper is the lack both of an explicit view of the intended overall effect of the FTC on consumer markets and of an opinion on the degree to which the FTC's goals (whatever they are) have been met or are likely ever to be met. Were consumer markets improved by the vastly increased scope of advertising regulation that followed upon establishing the ad substantiation program in 1972? Has the substantially reduced scope of such regulation since 1981 harmed markets? Has the past decade of rapidly changing antitrust regulation brought reduced prices and other consumer benefits, in comparison to what would have prevailed with either no antitrust regulation at all or more vigorous antitrust policy? These are the kinds of questions that a more critical analysis might ask when looking toward another decade of FTC presence. Mr. Strenio's emphasis on simple measures of input and output—staff work years, number of merger reviews—appears to stem from simply taking for granted the larger and more difficult matters of market effects from FTC regulation.

Mr. Strenio has surprisingly little to say about the intense debate of the past dozen years over the appropriate role of the FTC. This debate has encompassed the legal, political, and scholarly community and, most remarkably, various past and present FTC commissioners. There is no mention of Chairman Miller's attempts to reformulate policy toward advertising substantiation and deception, the bitter debate over the 1983 policy statement on deception, the tumultuous congressional hearings at about the same time, ex-Chairman Pertschuk's bitter missive to Congress, the strongly worded declarations from many quarters that the Reagan FTC had abandoned consumers, and so on. Even more surprising is the lack of attention to the FTC's much debated regulatory intervention program, where Commissioner Strenio made his mark as a staffer. Perhaps these omissions reflect a feeling that these battles have left no lasting effects. Perhaps these topics will receive consideration in other public forums. At any rate, Commissioner Strenio's views would be most welcome, especially if they appeared in an academic context.

There is also little discussion of specific past successes and failures in FTC policy. For example, the Commission undertook in 1983-84 a systematic review of the advertising substantiation program. The utterly unencouraging results (on overall effects, there is little evidence either favorable or unfavorable to the program) are not mentioned. To cite another example, the late 1970s saw an impressive series of policy review sessions constructed by FTC staff and cooperating academics (some of them in this audience). The existence of these sessions is mentioned but not the crucial question of whether the resulting volumes had any effect either within or beyond the agency's staff. Yet the practical effects of policy review sessions seem an eminently relevant question in view of this commissioner's proposal to resurrect a similar process.

It is only fair to note that this relative indifference to the nuts and bolts of past policy and past results is anything but unique to Mr. Strenio. It is one of the most frustrating aspects of FTC staff work. In my own experience I was amazed that so much excellent work by participants in this very conference (I have in mind, for example, Wilkie's work on mandated disclosure remedies) remained unmentioned in virtually every staff memo I ever saw—and this was even true of memos that dealt with the very problems that FTC-commissioned research was designed to illuminate. Discussion at the Commission table, when it came time to vote on proposed complaints and settlements, similarly ignored this valuable intellectual capital that had been compiled at significant cost. We can therefore welcome Commissioner Strenio's proposal near the end of his paper to revive systematic policy analysis by FTC commissioners and staff—but such an effort is foredoomed to failure if its results are ignored regardless of the magnitude or competence of the effort.

Little attention is paid to the larger intellectual environment in which the FTC operates. Again, Commissioner Strenio may be excused by the simple limitation of length combined with the multitude of possible topics for his review. But the omission of intellectual developments is nonetheless regrettable, given the audience. The deep changes in the past two decades in economic thinking about antitrust are now evident throughout law and regulatory practice. To a lesser extent, a similar change has come in consumer protection as a result of advances in the economics of information, not to mention the entire public choice movement in economics. Much of this thinking has been summarized in FTC conference proceedings.[1]

What of the material that is covered by Commissioner Strenio's paper? One topic assesses current consumer protection activity. What is most remarkable here is the relative lack of attention to advertising and other mainstream marketing practices such as franchising, mail order sales, and so on. This omission should not be interpreted as approval of the more relaxed tempo of regulation associated with the Reagan administration. Rather, Commissioner Strenio in his remarks to the conference made clear his view that more advertising litigation would be appropriate.

In contrast to the lack of focus on advertising, the current attack on hard-core fraud occupies a considerable portion of the attentions of Mr. Strenio's paper and the present FTC staff. It is easy to forget that the FTC has often turned in this direction in the past with indifferent results. One thinks of Judge Posner's dissent to the 1969 ABA report and his later writing on the FTC's mission, where he argued that fraud was one of the few areas in which federal intervention was likely to be beneficial but the benefits could be obtained only by means of criminal penalties unavailable to the FTC.[2] Commissioner Strenio's paper adds something to this long debate. He tackles head-on the matter of whether the FTC can operate effectively without using criminal penalties. His argument is not completely convincing, however. To say that the lower standard of proof associated with civil penalties eases litigation seems to assume away the very reasons for making fraud a criminal offense in the first place: it is in the nature of the crime that offenders usually are incapable of making appropriate compensation and cannot be deterred by anything short of imprisonment. It remains to be seen whether the FTC will meet with success in its latest antifraud campaign, which is founded upon the notion that criminal penalties can come into play when the offender takes a second bite of the apple.

Of special interest is the discussion of the increasing role of the state attorneys general. Of course Mr. Strenio is correct in thinking that the appropriate division between federal and more localized regulation is a complex matter that has thus far resisted quick solution. But what are we to make of the principle, apparently accepted in this paper, that the FTC's reaction should be purely defensive, filling a vacuum more quickly than the state attorneys general can fill it? Is there no room for reasoned policy here? Is it not possible that some voids should be filled by neither the states nor the FTC? After all, the FTC's regulatory intervention program so notably advanced by Mr. Strenio was based upon the idea that regulation is sometimes bad and should therefore be limited.

A former FTC staffer cannot forebear comment on the matter of administrative delay, a problem rightfully condemned by Commissioner Strenio. That matters often move slowly in this particular bureaucracy is no surprise to anyone. But one should remember that the reasons for delay include more than inefficiency. Politics and policy also play a role. Sometimes FTC staffers quietly bide their time and log their hours while awaiting a change in policy or even a change in commissioners. And sometimes commissioners themselves have reasons for keeping matters on hold. Any member of the Bureau of Economics could recount numerous instances in which economic reports were delayed—sometimes for many months—by individual commissioners whose objections seemed to be no more than a desire that certain results not reach the public too quickly. Such examples continue to arise.

Overall, this is a valuable paper, better than these negative comments suggest. This paper is refreshingly informed on the early history of the FTC. It is witty and well written. It is thoughtful, well meaning, and serious. It provides a welcome insight into the much neglected nitty-gritty of the regulatory process. Most importantly, it represents a serious attempt by a sitting commissioner to meet with academics and expose himself to their brand of abstract, hypercritical thinking about regulation. This act of courage is well calculated to improve regulation.

Notes

1. Federal Trade Commission, *Consumer Information Remedies* (1979); Pauline Ippolito and David Scheffman, eds., *Empirical Approaches to Consumer Protection Economics*, Bureau of Economics Report, Federal Trade Commission (1984).

2. R. Posner, "The Federal Trade Commission," *University of Chicago Law Review* 37 (1969): 47-89.

The Federal Trade Commission in Historical Perspective: The First Fifty Years

Mary Ellen Zuckerman

Any analysis of the recent past of the Federal Trade Commission (FTC or Commission), as well as any predictions about its future must be viewed within the historical context of the agency's first fifty years. The FTC's history is a story of cycles and repetitions. The same thorny issues emerge again and again: troubled relations with Congress and the courts; shifting interpretations of the Commission's mandate; swings between action and inaction; and conflicts between advisory and adversarial approaches to regulating business.

Like other regulatory agencies, the FTC's vulnerability to political and marketplace forces often affected its ability to perform. Inevitably, because of the judicial review prescribed in the FTC Act of 1914, much of the history of the FTC revolves around how it has fared in the courts which have granted and withheld powers to the Commission over the decades (see Appendix A of this paper for a chronology of key events in the first fifty years of the FTC). On a more mundane level, the Commission has suffered periodically from poor quality or insufficient personnel, appropriations cuts, and criticism by outsiders. As it evolved, the FTC also confronted new issues. Perhaps the most important change occurred in 1938, when the Wheeler-Lea Act amended the original legislation and gave the Commission a specific mandate to protect consumers from deceptive and unfair practices. This expanded the agency's mission and began its active consumer protection efforts. In fact, the framers of the FTC Act had not envisioned protection of consumers as part of the work of the Commission. Yet consumer protection, an area less ideologically conflicted than regulation of competition, emerged as a key area of FTC enforcement and increased dramatically in importance in the post-World War II period.

169

Despite this expanded focus, overall assessments of the Commission have not been favorable. As historian Thomas McCraw has observed, "Troubled in infancy, awkward in adolescence, clumsy in adulthood, the agency never found a coherent mission for itself. . . . By common agreement of modern scholars, the FTC has been a singularly unsuccessful agency during most of the seventy-odd years since its creation" (McCraw 1984:81; see also Hobbes 1989; and Katzmann 1980). The roots of many of the FTC's difficulties lay in the conflicting ideas about competition, bigness, and regulation of the marketplace that are held by politicians, businessmen, bureaucrats, legal and economic experts, and the American public. An hostility toward bigness and concentration, coupled with a longing for a society of smaller firms engaged in free competition, has persisted in American political thought even as consolidation in the economy continued apace and many secretly admired the very bigness they feared. The political compromise made in 1914 on how to regulate this economic growth, the FTC Act, was necessarily ambiguous in its phraseology, leading ineluctably to the victories and defeats experienced by the agency.

Origins of the Federal Trade Commission

The Federal Trade Commission Act was signed into law by President Woodrow Wilson in September, 1914. In the years preceding this legislation, heated debates had occurred among politicians, businessmen, government bureaucrats, and members of the public concerning the need for oversight of business practices in the marketplace. While conservatives and progressives diverged widely on the means of achieving order in the rapidly expanding economy, surprising agreement existed among these parties about the need for some type of regulation and guidance. Because of the ineffectiveness of state-level regulatory efforts (directed primarily at the railroads), those concerned increasingly looked to the federal government.

Under pressure from the public, Congress had begun addressing the questions of monopoly, competition, and unfair business practices in the late nineteenth century. It devised two solutions: antitrust legislation to prevent the formation and activity of trusts and monopolies; and regulation of business via a commission. Whether to break up large businesses or to allow them to exist under supervision; that was the question Americans would face as economic expansion continued to push up against deeply rooted beliefs about a society of small, independent entrepreneurs.

Early on, the railroads symbolized bigness and the abuses of concentrated power, and they were among the first targets of governmental regulation. The railroads had engaged in a variety of practices called unfair by many, including setting excessively high rates in areas of monopoly and low ones in areas of competition, giving rebates, and eventually forming voluntary pools with one another to reduce competition between lines. Regulation rather than dissolution seemed the best approach for controlling this natural monopoly, but state laws and commissions had generally proved unworkable, in part because railroads usually conducted business across state lines (McCraw 1984). Calls increasingly came for federal supervision of the railroads, using federal power to regulate interstate commerce. This outcry intensified with the Supreme Court's 1886 decision in *Wabash, St. Louis, and Pacific Railroad Company v. Illinois*; here the Court firmly decreed that commerce beginning or ending outside a particular state was not subject to regulation by that state. Clearly a federal solution was needed.

In response Congress passed the Interstate Commerce Act in 1887 that outlawed monopolistic pooling agreements, rebates, and geographical price discrimination and called for "reasonable and just" rates. The Act also set up the five-man Interstate Commerce Commission (ICC) (Garraty 1968). This Commission provided a model for later federal regulatory agencies (including the FTC) in the way members were appointed, the length of time each served, and in its relationship with Congress, the executive branch, and the judiciary (McCraw 1984). Despite the fact that the Supreme Court weakened the ICC in the nineties with several rulings, the precedent of federal regulation and the agency model had been set. The idea of a commission of experts, composed of members of both political parties, appealed to those attempting to impose order and equity on what seemed to be a situation of uncontrollable growth.

Railroads were not the only businesses to enter into agreements with one another to bring order into an industry and end ruinous price wars. Pools (an early form of business agreements used in the 1870s and 1880s) and trusts (where a group of trustees held stock from several different companies in common in exchange for trust certificates) sprang up in a variety of industries, allowing a small group of individuals great control. While the Standard Oil Company led the way, other sectors soon followed, forming trusts in the whiskey, cotton, lead, and sugar industries

(Wagner 1971). The dominance of trusts, holding companies, and large corporations angered smaller businessmen, many of whom were forced to sell out to the larger companies or face ruin as the bigger company cut prices and squeezed suppliers.

All large companies appearing to wield great power came to be called *trusts*, whether or not they actually held that legal form; the term caught the public imagination, signifying *bigness* and all the negative traits associated with that word. Many citizens and politicans alike saw these trusts as a threat to the competitive economic system. Yet as historian John Garraty has noted, "Most Americans objected to trusts in principle, just as they revered competition in the abstract, but few were suffering noticeably or directly. They wanted action but did not know exactly what they wanted done" (Garraty 1968:122).

In response to popular outcry about the trusts and the demand for federal action, Congress passed the Sherman Antitrust Act in 1890. In contrast to a regulatory approach, this law called for breaking up business concentrations harmful to competition. This broad yet ambiguous law made illegal "every contract, combination in the form of trust or otherwise, or conspiracy, in restraint of trade or commerce among the several States, or with foreign nations." Based on common law principles, the Sherman Antitrust Act gave the federal government the power to move against monopolies and restraints of trade.

While hopes for the Sherman Antitrust Act stood high, the reality soon proved otherwise. The Department of Justice (the Sherman Act's enforcer) was slow to act, prosecuting only a small number of cases (twenty-four between 1890 and 1905). Also, the law had left undefined exactly what practices it covered, leaving it to the courts to fill in the meaning (a weakness that would later haunt the FTC). In the 1895 *U.S. v. E.C. Knight Co.* case, for example, the Supreme Court held to a narrow construction of interstate commerce, ruling that the Sherman Act only applied to commerce, not manufacturing. Also, prosecution remained limited in the nineties as firms escaped legal action by switching to the holding company form. Overall, the Sherman Act proved ineffective in its intended goal of slowing down concentration, and merger activity among American producers reached a peak around the turn of the century (Garraty 1968; and Hawley 1966).

Under President Theodore Roosevelt (served 1901-1908), known as an enemy of "the malefactors of wealth," prosecutions of companies impeding competition increased. But Roosevelt, an advocate of expert commissions in government, also tried a different approach to increase government control over business: collecting information about business practices and (reflecting a typical Progressive era belief) publicizing these activities. To carry this out, the Bureau of Corporations was created in 1903, an agency authorized to gather data about firms and to follow economic trends in various industries. Housed in the Department of Labor and Commerce, the Bureau had no powers to compel businesses to provide it with information, and so had to rely on voluntary cooperation. Neither did the Bureau possess any regulatory powers. Nevertheless, the Bureau was well respected by politicians and offered a first step toward the establishment of an agency to monitor business practices, a federal trade commission (Sklar 1988).

Despite calls from politicians and businessmen alike for such an interstate trade commission, the Sherman Act remained the only tool to fight monopolies. Further adding to the uncertainties surrounding this law came the 1911 Supreme Court ruling on the *Standard Oil Company* and *American Tobacco Company* cases, which put forward the "rule of reason," stating that only unreasonable restraints of trade were prohibited by the Sherman Act. The implication was that reasonable restraints of trade were legal, and that it was up to the courts to decide what was reasonable and unreasonable. The effect was to leave companies large and small, as well as the government, in doubt about which business activities were legal. Conservatives feared this ruling, thinking that it made Sherman too broad, while reformers expressed outrage at the weakening of the law. Individuals of a variety of beliefs advocated formation of a bureau or commission with powers to give advice and to rule in advance on business practices constituting unfair competition and monopoly to clarify this hazy arena (Lay 1926; McCraw 1984; and Montague 1927).

These concerns about bigness, trusts, and unfair business practices dominated much of the political debate in the early twentieth century and reached a peak in the presidential election of 1912, where candidates Roosevelt, Taft, and Wilson all called for antitrust legislation to supplement the Sherman Act. By this time, almost no one advocated leaving the market in an unregulated condition. As Wilson's economic advisor Louis Brandeis wrote, "The issue is not . . . Shall we have unrestricted competition or regulated monopoly? It is, Shall we have regulated competition or regulated monopoly?" (quoted in McCraw 1984:110).

Third-party Progressive candidate Theodore Roosevelt had gained a reputation as a trustbuster while in office, but by the time of the 1912

election he believed that concentration in industry was inevitable. Therefore, the federal government should oversee large corporations, treating
them almost as a type of public utility (Sklar 1988). Drawing on the
political philosophy of journalist Herbert Croly, Roosevelt termed this
approach of sweeping social and economic regulation by a strong federal
government "The New Nationalism." As part of this plan, Roosevelt
explicitly called for an interstate trade commission with powers to oversee
and license manufacturing and commerce. Incumbent President William
Taft weakly supported the trade commission idea and early in his term had
called for national incorporation of big businesses. However, he leaned
more strongly to judicial control of the marketplace via decisions in the
courts about unreasonable restraint of trade under the Sherman Act, and
he never favored federal regulation of large businesses as strongly as his
predecessor.

Democratic candidate Woodrow Wilson called for antitrust legislation to protect small businesses, a return to economic democracy, and
limited federal government powers. Unlike Roosevelt, Wilson did not
believe that monopolies were inevitable and therefore should be regulated;
rather, the government should fight them. Wilson labeled his program
"The New Freedom." During his campaign, Wilson only supported the
idea of a commission in a qualified manner, as part of his overall plan to
regulate competition.

Congress had already considered several bills proposing an interstate
trade commission, one as early as 1908. Some plans called for an expanded
Bureau of Corporations; others, introduced by adherents of the Roosevelt
philosophy of allowing cartels and agreements among big businesses,
required large firms to be licensed by a federal government agency. The
commission idea had also gained widespread support from influential
spokesmen outside Congress, including journalists and intellectuals such
as Herbert Croly and Walter Lippmann, and academics such as Charles
Van Hise, president of the University of Wisconsin (McCraw 1984).
Members of the National Civic League and of the Chamber of Commerce
favored the creation of a commission, as did industrial leaders George W.
Perkins and E.H. Gary. However, these groups supported the commission
plan for widely different reasons, a fact that became apparent after the
creation of the FTC.

In this political debate and the many preceding it, significant questions of public policy were raised concerning the extent to which the
federal government should become involved in regulating the market-

place, the rights of consumers and manufacturers (and possible conflict between them), and the direction of the development of the economy (McCraw 1984; and Sklar 1988).

Creation of the Federal Trade Commission

Woodrow Wilson won the 1912 election with 42 percent of the popular vote, and he proceeded to put his version of progressive reform into action. However, by 1914, when Wilson was ready to propose legislation on the trust question, his views had shifted from his election rhetoric; he was now a proponent of some government regulation of business as well as an advocate of antitrust laws. Influenced by future Supreme Court Justice Louis Brandeis, Wilson called for the creation of a federal trade commission, albeit without the significant licensing power proposed by Roosevelt. Wilson favored an agency to investigate, give advice on, and interpret business practices.

In his January 1914 message to Congress, Wilson spoke about measures to address the antitrust problem. He referred to the previous years of debate among the public and congressmen, noting that the proposed legislation "springs out of the experience of a whole generation." That he included the experience of the very businessmen whom the measures were to regulate in this collective generational experience became clear when he declared, "The antagonism between business and government is over. We are now about to give expression to the best business judgment of America" (quoted in Schwartz 1973:1731). Wilson had no desire for legislation antagonistic to business. The prosecutions and the uncertainties existing under the Sherman Act were to end, because "nothing hampers business like uncertainty" (quoted in Schwartz 1973:1732). To eliminate this uncertainty, Wilson proposed first a statute explicitly enumerating practices deemed illegal, along with their penalties (eventually embodied in the 1914 Clayton Antitrust Act).

But Wilson went further, reflecting his observation of the work of the Bureau of Corporations, the ICC, and various state commissions, as well as the urgings of advisors such as Brandeis. He called for a commission, a body to offer advice, guidance, and information to the businesses of the country. Wilson's regulatory agency would be one that collected information and publicized it. He was not calling for an agency that would actively intervene in or attempt to control the marketplace (Sklar

1988:327; see Appendix B of this paper for excerpts from President Wilson's address). Once again, as when Congress had created the ICC twenty-seven years earlier, a regulatory solution was seen as the answer. The commission bill originally backed by Wilson was authored by Democratic Representative James Covington of Maryland. It advocated the formation of a commission with essentially investigative and publicity powers without independent regulatory authority; the commission would be a sort of an expanded Bureau of Corporations. However, as the political process continued and the stringent antitrust law introduced by Democratic Representative Henry Clayton of Alabama (to become the Clayton Act) was eviscerated, Wilson was persuaded to support a stronger commission bill written by Representative Raymond Stevens of New Hampshire with help from lawyer George Rublee (McCraw 1984; and Rublee 1926).

In 1914 two laws resulted from the proposals, arguments, presidential imprecation, and compromise: the Federal Trade Commission Act and the Clayton Act. The Federal Trade Commission Act flatly outlawed "unfair methods of competition in commerce" in its key section 5. The phrase was purposely left broad and undefined so that it could include not only the unfair trade practices of the day but also those to be invented by enterprising businessmen in the future. As Commissioner Abram F. Meyers remembered, "Section 5 was added in the Senate as a sort of complement to the Clayton Act, which was undergoing the legislative process at the same time. It was thought that this catch-all provision would embrace all monopolistic practices not specifically enumerated in the Clayton Act" (quoted in Herring 1934:1017; see also Appendix C of this paper for the reasoning behind the FTC and Wheeler-Lea Acts). This vague phraseology also made the bill acceptable to a greater number of individuals, postponing the problems of definition for the Commission and the courts to resolve (McCraw 1984; Rublee 1926).

The Federal Trade Commission Act created a five-person agency, the Federal Trade Commission, which, it was hoped, would determine just what constituted unfair methods of competition (see Appendix I of the book for the full text of the Act). The commissioners were to be appointed by the president (and confirmed by the Senate) for staggered terms of seven years each, with no more than three commissioners from any one political party. They were to be paid $10,000 (the same salary as ICC commissioners), an amount thought capable of attracting well-qualified individuals. All commerce fell under FTC jurisdiction except common carriers and banking.

The Commission was to incorporate the Bureau of Corporations and continue with that agency's function of data collection. But the Commission also had a quasi-judicial function and could move against firms by ordering cease and desist orders upon discovery of unfair methods of competition. The Commission could require firms to provide it with information to assist in its investigations and was given subpoena power to aid in this. The act called for the Commission to submit annual reports to Congress, as well as special reports, to make recommendations for additional legislation, and to publicize its findings.

The Commission was to inform the attorney general about possible antitrust violations and to help the attorney general and courts decide on terms of dissolution and reorganization of businesses when such action was dictated by the Sherman Act, acting as a master in chancery. In addition to investigating unfair competitive practices, the FTC, as an enforcer of both the Sherman Act and the newly enacted Clayton law, acted against unfair restraints of trade. A crucial piece of the legislation gave the courts the right of judicial review over acts and orders of the Commission (Sklar 1988:329).

In contrast to the ambiguous terms used in the FTC Act concerning unfair competition, the Clayton Act specifically designated certain practices (not, it was feared, covered by the Sherman Act) as illegal: price discrimination, tying and exclusive dealing contracts, and inter-corporate mergers and directorates in certain situations. Even these were not as clearly defined as some had wished; as one observer wrote, the bill shrank "from the long list of highly itemized transactions to the short list of ambiguously described transactions" (Montague 1927:654). Both the FTC and the Justice Department were charged with enforcing the Clayton Act (Sklar 1988; and Wagner 1971). The structuring and provisions of these companion pieces of legislation reflected political expediency.

The FTC emerged as a stronger agency than originally envisioned by President Wilson. However, even firm supporters of the Commission were not united in what function they wanted it to serve. The FTC was a compromise creation, and different adherents looked to it for different things. But the law's very ambiguity allowed it to satisfy the concerns of widely varied parties in the short run. As one observer wrote of the Commission's task, "This administrative agency is expected to interpret, under a vague mandate from Congress, an issue concerning which there is no stable consensus of opinion" (Herring 1934:1022).

Another potential problem arose from the powerful entities (big businesses) to be supervised by the agency (Herring 1935). Unlike other regulatory agencies, such as the later Securities and Exchange Commission and the Federal Communications Commission, the FTC did not have one constituent industry; instead it regulated an entire range of manufacturing and commercial concerns.

Despite its expanded powers, the FTC Act had limitations (as had the Sherman Act). Both the Commission's jurisdictional scope and the power of its rulings remained unclear. The judicial review by the courts of its actions and the poorly defined language of its enabling legislation would pose problems for the Commission. Certain omissions would be remedied in the next seventy-five years, with Congress taking steps to strengthen the power of the Commission and to expand or contract its jurisdiction when dictated by public policy needs.

Early Years and World War I

The early life of the FTC was characterized by a slow beginning, with a spurt of activity during World War I followed by a rebuff. The vagueness concerning both the powers granted the FTC and its exact mission in regulating business made strong leadership crucial to the successful launching of the Commission. Unfortunately, weak appointments plagued the Commission in its first few years, as the agency proved unable to attract the high-caliber individuals hoped for. Wilson asked Brandeis to serve, but he declined, perhaps sensing the troubles inherent in an agency with such a broad and ambiguous mandate (McCraw 1984). The members eventually appointed to the Commission held differing ideas about the role of the FTC, adding to the Commission's slow start.

For the Democratic members of the Commission Wilson chose Joseph E. Davies, the former head of the Bureau of Corporations, Edward N. Hurley, a manufacturer of farm equipment from Illinois, and William J. Harris, an insurance executive from Georgia who had served as director of the Census; the Republican appointees were William H. Parry, an editor and publisher, and George Rublee, the lawyer who had helped write the FTC Act (the Senate eventually refused to confirm Rublee who had run a senatorial campaign in New Hampshire for Ray Stevens; Stevens lost and the winner, Jacob H. Gallinger, blocked Rublee's confirmation). The commissioners elected Davies as head. None of these first commissioners stayed in office more than three years, hindering the development of the agency.

The FTC spent much of its first several years organizing the agency and determining its jurisdiction. Cramped quarters (initially in the old Bureau of Corporation offices in the Department of Commerce and Labor) helped neither morale nor efficient organization (the Commission finally moved into its own building on Pennsylvania Avenue in the 1930s). The economic recession of 1914 and off-year elections caused hesitation in Congress about appearing strongly antibusiness. Consequently, it refused to vote sufficient resources for the newborn Commission. Inadequate appropriations by Congress (a problem recurring throughout the agency's history) led to high turnover of personnel.

The commissioners also did not want to seem antibusiness. To prove this, the Commission sponsored over one hundred informational conferences with industry leaders in the agency's first four months. One question arising at these conferences concerned the possibility of giving "advance advice" to firms about the legal status of practices they were contemplating. In fact, many businessmen had supported the idea of a Commission precisely because they thought this kind of information would lessen their uncertainty. The commissioners held opposing views about the advisability of such a procedure and eventually decided not to offer formal judgments. The Commission staff did offer advice informally about potential practices.

Conflicting ideas among the commissioners about the scope of the agency's jurisdiction over antitrust and unfair practices required time to work out, as did the administrative procedures for acting against prohibited practices (Rublee 1926). The Commission used complaints generated by both outsiders and agency staff to start the process of investigation into unfair practices; however, 95 percent of the cases examined by the Commission derived from complaints by competitors. This opened the Commission up to the charge that it was essentially reactive rather than active in defining policy directions.

In its first year the Commission established the policy of investigating complaints before taking any official action. Three minimal requirements, defined differently in different periods, evolved for case selection. A case must (1) involve interstate commerce, (2) fall under the provisions of one of the acts over which the FTC held jurisdiction, and (3) somehow affect the public interest. If an investigation turned up evidence of a violation, the Commission issued a decree ordering the company to cease and desist from the activity. Initially, the commissioners handed down their decisions without any opinions attached to shed light on their thinking about the case, a procedure frustrating to businesses and their lawyers. (This changed in 1946 when the Administrative Procedure Act required a written reasoning for decisions.)

As the agency began finding its way, U.S. entry into World War I turned public attention away from its concern with the fairness of business practices. President Wilson looked to his new Commission for analyses of the wartime needs of the country. His first request, for a study of the food industry, seemed innocuous enough but proved to be explosive for the FTC. An important part of the food industry was the meat-packing business. After a thorough investigation, involving the commissioners as well as the economic department of the agency, the FTC sent a report to the Senate roundly indicting the meat-packing industry and the major firms within it: Swift, Armour, Wilson, Morris, and Cudahy. The FTC claimed that little real competition existed in the industry, that the big packers colluded to fix prices of their own goods and those of their suppliers, and that the packers' power reached far into other sectors of the food industry. The FTC had also sent its report to the Justice Department, where Attorney General A. Mitchell Palmer decided to bring a criminal suit against the meat packers (Wagner 1971).

The reaction to the FTC's report when it came out in 1919 had profound implications for the financial and psychological well-being of the young agency. The accusations stirred the packers (already nervous from the earlier publication of Upton Sinclair's *The Jungle,* which had brought calls for regulation of the meat-packing industry) into action. Soon several congressmen were calling for an investigation of the FTC itself, rather than of the meat-packers. While some congressmen defended the agency, the end result was to tarnish the new Commission's reputation and to weaken it. The attorney general settled a consent decree with the packers to break up some of their businesses without consulting the Commission (which undoubtedly would have branded the settlement inadequate, as it turned out to be). And Congress passed the Packers and Stockyard Act in 1921, taking authority over the stockyards away from the FTC, giving it to the Department of Agriculture instead. Under threat of investigation, the FTC fired some personnel involved in the study. Funds for other studies were not forthcoming (Wagner 1971). After this traumatic incident, the Commission realized that caution was necessary when fighting entrenched and powerful business interests, a message which shaped future actions.

The Federal Trade Commission in the 1920s

After the war the Commission operated in a different political and social climate, one where people were less interested in trust-busting. The calls for breakups of big businesses receded as Americans gave themselves up to a period of seeming prosperity. During the presidencies of Warren Harding and Calvin Coolidge, businessmen were transformed from economic villains into cultural heroes. The new appointees to the FTC included some liberals anxious to attack monopolies and unfair practices, but neither Congress nor the courts proved supportive. The 1920s also saw the agency's close cooperation with businesses, best exemplified in its trade conference activity.

The courts placed clear limitations on the Commission during the twenties, foiling its attempts to wield its powers in a broad manner. The courts' actions led to a cautious, almost passive attitude on the part of the FTC, and its activities need to be seen in the context of court rulings. This atmosphere produced a reactive and constrained Commission, given the constant threat (and reality) of judicial review. The first case to test the FTC's authority to define "unfair methods of competition," *FTC v. Gratz et al.*, reached the Supreme Court in 1920 (see Appendix D of this paper for full references for all Supreme Court cases mentioned in the text). That tribunal firmly limited the power of the Commission by ruling, "The words 'unfair methods of competition' are not defined by statute and their exact meaning is in dispute. It is for the courts, not the Commission, ultimately to determine as matter of law, what they include" (quoted in McCraw 1984:125). Thus expert analysis, investigation, and judgment by the FTC would not determine unfair methods of competition; that authority inhered in the courts. The Court said further that only those practices defined as unlawful competitive activity prior to 1914 fell in the domain of activities against which the FTC could move.

Justice Brandeis, who had been involved with drafting the legislation for the FTC Act, dissented, contending that the very reason for the Commission's creation was to have an expert body that could be relied upon to move against new practices: "Instead of undertaking to define what practices should be deemed unfair, as had been done in earlier legislation, the Act left the determination to the Commission" (quoted in Wagner 1971:89). But Brandeis's view was in the minority. Eventually the majority of the Court would agree, but efforts of the Commission in the twenties to expand its jurisdiction and powers met with little success in the courts (Montague 1927). This did not shift until 1934 in *FTC v. Keppel & Brothers*, when the Court affirmed the right of the FTC to bring orders against *new* unfair methods of competition.

Cases investigated by the Commission in the twenties covered a variety of practices that it considered unfair methods of competition. These included price discrimination, tying contracts, resale price agreements, selling below cost, deceptive advertising, misbranding, false packaging, trade name copying, and other business activities. In an early ruling, the 1921 *Beech Nut* case, the Supreme Court upheld the Commission's ruling against a plan where the company forced retailers to adhere to their suggested prices, or else be labeled "undesirable" (Lay 1926:350). The Court ruled that this practice interfered with competition among the retailers. But the Commission was not so successful with many of its cases. Its greatest victories lay in bringing actions against companies for false advertising. The courts upheld twenty-two of twenty-nine FTC orders coming before them on this issue through 1931, compared to upholding only a little over half of all orders in the entire period (Montague 1927; and Wagner 1971). Not surprisingly, the Commission gradually focused much of its attention on this type of case, which it had a good chance of winning.

However, experiencing setbacks from the courts and little support from Congress, the FTC generally retreated into a fact-gathering and advisory agency. The Commission turned to sponsoring trade conferences and issuing industry guidelines. This activity reached its zenith in the twenties, with a separate division formed in 1926 to administer the conferences. By 1933, the division had sponsored 131 such conferences (*Columbia Law Review* 1962). At the conferences, industry members met and formulated rules for fair business practices. This type of activity raised the issue of adversarial versus negotiated regulation and reflected the inconsistency in the government's approach between encouraging cooperation between businesses under government sponsorship and the prohibiting of such cooperation under threat of government action. (These conferences were later seen as placing the Commission in too close cooperation with business. The agency shifted to advising industries at a greater distance through booklets containing information about the application of rules to a particular industry.)

The Commission's role in protecting the public interest also was raised. The FTC had long insisted that a case have some effect on the public interest; private parties seeking private justice must go elsewhere. Progress toward a clear definition of the public interest was uneven and would not be clarified until 1938, with the passage of the Wheeler-Lea amendment. But groundwork was laid as early as the 1919 *FTC v. Sears, Roebuck & Co.* case, when the Court upheld the Commission's right to issue a cease and desist order, in part against false advertising, because of its potential to injure competitors indirectly through the deception of consumers (Brown 1947b). And in the 1922 *FTC v. Winsted Hosiery* case, where the Commission had acted against a manufacturer for falsely labeling the underwear materials, the Supreme Court upheld the FTC, stating that such practices hurt competing manufacturers indirectly, but also harmed the consuming public.

The courts vacillated on the public interest point, and varying courts ruled differently. However, first with the *Gratz* case, then the *FTC v. Klesner* case (1929), the Supreme Court ruled that a clear effect on the public interest must be shown; the indirect effect argument, that unfair practices would inevitably hurt consumers who might have purchased a product elsewhere, did not reliably hold up in court as an effect on the public interest. In another twist, in the landmark *Raladam* decision in 1931, the Supreme Court interpreted the jurisdiction of the FTC narrowly, ruling that a clear effect on competitors must be demonstrated. Here the FTC had issued an order against the advertising of a manufacturer of antiobesity remedies, finding them to be false. The Court ruled against the FTC on the grounds that no competitor had been harmed by the admittedly deceptive advertising; the Commission could not require a company to stop running an ad, even if false, unless direct harm to a competitor could be shown. Thus the public interest and consumers alone were not seen to be synonymous.

The Commission found itself in a situation where both damage to competitors and an effect on the public interest must be proved to ensure a foolproof case. As Commissioner Nelson S. Gaskill later noted, "There is no agreement among the several circuit Courts of Appeal in the application of these tests. Some insist upon proof of injury to competitors and disregard injury to purchasers. Some reverse this arrangement. Some require both. Some will assume the one but not the other. There is judicial support for almost any defense of this nature a respondent may bring forward."

The Economic Department of the Commission performed important studies over these years. Building on the base established by the Bureau of Corporations, it collected information on industries and documented trends, mostly at the behest of Congress, other agencies, or the executive branch. One of its early efforts, performed for the Treasury Department, looked into wildcat stocks that competed with the sales of Victory bonds during World War I. In that investigation the Commission discovered important information about the manipulation of stocks on the stock exchange. Eventually Congress would use this documentation to pass the 1934 Securities Exchange Act. A study done in 1928 provided the basis for the Public Utility Act of 1935. Reports on the radio and grain industries provided data used in drafting legislation covering both fields. In fact, a later critique of the FTC, the 1949 Hoover Commission report, singled out the agency's economic studies for praise, stating that they had "the most substantial impact and enduring value" of all the FTC's efforts (quoted in Wagner 1971:76).

Congress expanded the FTC's jurisdiction in one arena, international trade. Using data from a 1916 FTC Report on Cooperation in American Export Trade, Congress passed the 1918 Webb-Pomerone Act, authorizing limited cooperative activity among American firms exporting goods, exempting them from antitrust laws. To ensure that such cooperation did not spill over to the domestic market, these organizations had to submit the details of their associations to the FTC, which was given powers to investigate and suggest changes (Wagner 1971).

That the Commission was still feeling its way administratively as well as jurisdictionally became clear in the mid-twenties. Amid criticisms by scholars and businessmen (for doing both too much and too little, all of it badly), the new Republican majority at the FTC during the Coolidge administration changed several of the Commission's policies to make procedures more efficient. The commissioners hoped this would ease the backlog of cases piling up. They instituted the stipulation procedure, a step short of a consent order. With the stipulation, the party charged agreed to having committed the practices and promised to desist in the future. Since the Commission staff did not have to perform the lengthy investigative work involved in the more formal procedures, stipulation was thought to be quicker and cheaper than, for example, working out a consent order. The FTC also ruled that now, before issuing any complaints, it would allow respondents a hearing at the Commission (Henderson 1924; Moffett 1925; Montague 1926; Redfield 1925; and Stevens 1926).

William E. Humphrey, an outspoken conservative appointed to the Commission by Calvin Coolidge, provided the agency with some color. He served for eight years starting in 1925, attempting, he claimed, to make the Commission a help rather than a hindrance to business. Humphrey's view of the Commission's role did not accord with Franklin D. Roosevelt's, and when Roosevelt came into office in 1933, he decided to replace Humphrey (then chairman of the FTC) with someone who would pursue a stronger antitrust policy. Roosevelt requested Humphrey's resignation. Humphrey refused, accusing the president of trying to make the agency a partisan organization, and asserting that he had done nothing to deserve being removed. When the comptroller general decided that Humphrey could no longer draw his salary as commissioner, Humphrey went to the courts. The Court of Claims ruled against Humphrey, but in 1935 the Supreme Court overturned this judgment in *Humphrey's Executor v. United States*, stating that the president's power to remove officers at his pleasure did not extend to regulatory agencies. Humphrey had died by this time, but the principle of the regulatory agency's independence had been upheld.

Amendment and Expansion:
The Federal Trade Commission in the 1930s

With the crash of the stock market in 1929 followed by the economic depression of the thirties, the previous decade's uncritical approval of business disappeared. Calls were sounded for investigation, prosecution, and explanations. The contradictions in American thinking about the proper way for the marketplace to function in a democracy reemerged, echoing the debates of the first decade of the century. Should the government allow firms to work together in government-sponsored cartels, with firms adhering to price and market guidelines? Even more drastically, should the goverment take over total planning and regulation of all aspects of the economy? Or was more rigorously pursued antitrust action needed to enable small firms and competition to flourish? (Hawley 1966). The fate of the FTC, the regulatory agency charged with enforcing antitrust action and acting against unfair competitive practices, was inextricably tied to the answer to these questions.

Franklin Roosevelt and the New Deal planners believed in strong federal programs to revive the economy; government intervention was necessary to restore order in the marketplace and to protect the public interest. At first, it looked as though the FTC would become obsolete, as early New Deal policy favored cartel-like, yet government-supervised behavior in industries. This approach drew on the experience many business and governmental leaders had had during mobilization of the economy in World War I and on the trade association movement supported by the FTC in the twenties (Benson 1938). With the passage of the National Industrial Recovery Act creating the National Recovery Administration (NRA), industries were permitted to develop codes to regulate aspects of market behavior; usually this meant setting price and production levels. Antitrust laws, the very legislation the FTC was empowered to uphold, were suspended. Thus businessmen were allowed to act in cooperation with one another, in compliance with codes approved by the government.

In some industries, for example steel, adherence to the codes actually resulted in violation of existing FTC cease and desist orders (Wagner 1971). Despite complaints from the FTC, no clarification of the conflict between the NRA and the FTC guidelines was forthcoming, leaving the dilemma unresolved until the Supreme Court ruled the NRA unconstitutional. In the meantime, the FTC was viewed as an agency friendly to business, not susceptible to executive control (especially after Roosevelt lost his battle over Commissioner Humphrey). During these years, the FTC served the patronage needs of those southern Congressmen high up in the Commission's oversight committees (Harris and Milkis 1989).

The Supreme Court invalidated the NRA on May 27, 1935, in *Schechter Poultry Corp. v. U.S.*, ruling that "the code-making authority thus conferred (by the NRA) is an unconstitutional delegation of legislative power." The NRA had already lost support among many groups, and President Roosevelt decided not to try to revitalize the agency. New Deal policy switched to an antitrust approach, placing faith in the restorative powers of the competitive marketplace. The antitrust forces believed that artificially high prices brought about by monopoly power had caused the depression. Their solution, in which the FTC could assist, was to bring back competition to the marketplace through vigorous antitrust prosecution and limits on bigness.

Another area in which the FTC could help was consumer protection. This had not been part of the agency's original mandate. And the work performed by the Commission in protecting consumers, primarily against deceptive advertising and sales practices, had enjoyed only mixed success in the twenties. The 1931 *Raladam* decision had clearly limited the FTC's work in this realm. However, in the thirties, social reformers and economists began paying more attention to consumers, calling on the government to protect individuals from unscrupulous business practices. Also, many consumers were angry about the price-fixing of the NRA. Local and state consumer organizations flourished and, on the national level, the Consumer Advisory Board was established as part of the NRA. While this movement would not blossom fully until the late sixties, the work the FTC had done to assist consumers in receiving honest information in the marketplace suddenly looked very good. The FTC was on the rise.

In the changed environment, the courts became more sympathetic to the work of the FTC. Regarding unfair and fraudulent trade practices, the Supreme Court acted most favorably in those cases of misrepresentation concerning clear-cut falsity about the origin or materials of a product; it proved less supportive in those cases involving exaggerated claims of effectiveness if no harm to competitors could be shown. Initially, when considering the evidence, the courts and the Commission assumed consumers of some hypothetical average intelligence, not those most vulnerable (Brown 1947b). This changed with the 1937 Supreme Court ruling in *FTC v. Standard Education Society*, where the high tribunal ruled that "laws are made to protect the trusting as well as the suspicious" (quoted in Wagner 1971:175). The Commission then proceeded to use lower standards in defining the affected consumers.

Congress, too, became more supportive of the FTC and it increased appropriations; it especially approved of the action of the FTC in protecting the consuming public. However, rulings in several cases revealed the limits of the FTC's powers in consumer protection. To remedy this, in 1938 Congress passed legislation explictly to empower the FTC to continue this work. This legislation, the Wheeler-Lea Act, added to section 5 of the FTC Act, allowing the Commission to move against unfair or deceptive practices in addition to the unfair methods of competition already prohibited. The Commission no longer had to show that an unfair practice had a negative effect on competition; it could move against such an activity if the public was being deceived (see Appendix C of this paper for the reasoning behind the FTC and Wheeler-Lea Acts, and for key sections of the FTC Act). This added to the FTC's power to act against false advertising and overturned the 1931 *FTC v. Raladam Co.* decision.

Some businessmen feared this extension of the FTC's powers, particularly regarding advertising. Others looked at the commissioners and felt reassured; as an analyst in *Advertising and Selling* observed, "They believe regulation should not be severe, that truth should be the basis of advertising, but that a reasonable amount of commercial hyperbole is permissible" (Rippey 1940:20). The author went on to point out that the FTC recommended only three cases to the Justice Department for prosecution in the year following the Wheeler-Lea amendments.

The amendments also expanded the FTC's power over food, drug, and cosmetic advertising (the Food and Drug Administration, FDA, had authority over labeling of these goods and over advertising of prescription drugs). They allowed a court to order a temporary injunction while reviewing an FTC order in food, drug, and cosmetic cases. The amendments also spelled out specific criminal penalties for violations that applied if the FTC took the facts to the attorney general in cases where the product was injurious to the public health or if the advertising was intentionally fraudulent (Brown 1947a).

The FTC's enforcement record proved less than consumer activists would have liked, more than some businesses would have liked, but overall not onerous. (The Carter Little Liver Pills action stood as perhaps the clearest example pointed to by critics as a misallocation of energy and funds; the FTC spent sixteen years, from 1943 through 1959, and great energy to force Carter's to drop the word "Liver" from its name.) Strong consumer advocates had hoped to place authority for the regulation of advertising in the FDA with its stronger enforcement powers, but this movement failed (Harris and Milkis 1989).

The Wheeler-Lea Act also made the cease and desist orders promulgated by the FTC final if the firm did not appeal within sixty days, and ordered a civil penalty for violation of the order of "not more than $5,000 for each violation." Despite these strengthenings of FTC enforcement orders, the Commission's work remained primarily preventive rather than punitive; it could not punish for past violations but only require a firm cease and desist from present activities.

In one sense Wheeler-Lea made explicit what the FTC had been trying to do, giving the agency a clear right to monitor deceptive practices that might harm the consuming public. But in another sense, Wheeler-Lea exacerbated a tension inherent in the mission of the FTC. An important part of the agency's original mandate was to protect small businesses against their larger competitors; yet at times this meant the barring or breakup of bigger firms that, because of higher volume and more efficient methods, might be able to offer consumers lower prices. As analysts have noted, this dual task of protecting both small firms and consumers could create contradictory policies:

> The ambiguous mission that had always hampered the FTC was, if anything, further confused by the Wheeler-Lea amendments. This law enabled the commission to make consumer protection an important new area of concern for public policy; however, the agency's commitment to the consumer was tempered by its continuing responsibility for dealing with the competitive process. (Harris and Milkis 1989:152.)

In 1936 the Robinson-Patman Act amending section 2 of the Clayton Act had increased the FTC's jurisdiction in protecting small businesses. Drawing on material uncovered by the FTC in its investigation of chain store mergers, the Robinson-Patman Act prohibited certain price discrimination tactics harmful to small firms (differential pricing, promotional allowances, brokerage fees). The FTC report had found that chain stores received special discounts and allowances from suppliers because of their size.

Resale price maintenance practices also came under review in the thirties. Previously such actions had been considered unfair methods of competition, violations of the Sherman Act. However, influenced by the NRA and in an attempt to roll back the economic depression, states began passing laws in the early thirties, called *fair trade statutes*, that allowed manufacturers to engage in resale price maintenance practices. Such laws received recognition on the federal level with the passage in 1937 of the Miller-Tydings Act amending the Sherman Act and in 1952 with the McGuire Act amending the FTC Act. These allowed manufacturers to employ a resale price maintenance system if it accorded with the state's fair trade laws. The Commission still acted against this practice in those states without fair trade statutes.

In 1939, Congress expanded both FTC mandates to monitor business and to protect consumers when it passed the Wool Products Labeling Act, authorizing the Commission to develop rules governing this industry, the first instance in which the FTC was given such power. Congress expressed its confidence in the Commission by adding several other industries to the Commission's supervision with the passage of the Fur Products Labeling Act (1951), Flammable Fabrics Act (1953), and Textile Fiber Products Identification Acts (1958).

Cautious Growth: The 1940s, 1950s, and Beyond

Congress, the Supreme Court, and the executive branch continued their willingness to vest authority and power in the FTC during the forties and fifties. The Commission itself began looking more carefully at the economic effects of business practices, extending beyond its mandate to simply ensure equity in the marketplace.

The Supreme Court affirmed expanded investigative powers for the FTC in the areas of visitation and access, requiring special reports from corporations and subpoena. In the 1950 *U.S. v. Morton Salt* case the Supreme Court upheld the Commission's rights to collect information from firms, using the power of subpoena when necessary. While Congress had invested the FTC with broad investigative powers in the 1914 Act, the Supreme Court had subsequently curtailed these. For example, in the 1924 *FTC v. American Tobacco Co.* case, Justice Oliver Wendell Holmes stated that the FTC's right of access pertained only to materials to be placed in evidence, noting:

> Anyone who respects the spirit as well as the letter of the Fourth Amendment would be loath to believe that Congress intended to authorize one of its subordinate agencies to sweep all our traditions into the fire . . . and to direct fishing expeditions into private papers on the possibility that they may disclose evidence of crime. (Quoted in Wagner 1971:60.)

This 1950 decision recognized that at times it was necessary for the FTC to "go fishing."

In the forties the courts also upheld the Commission in its work against the uniform basing point pricing system. Such uniformity was achieved by quoting a delivered price, with all the sellers using the same city or cities as the base from which the delivery started. First employed in the steel industry in the late nineteenth century, other industries had adopted the practice as well. The Commission had moved against the steel industry in the twenties but had failed to monitor its compliance. In the 1940s the Commission issued cease and desist orders against both the cement and steel industries. In 1948 the Supreme Court upheld the Commission's order against the cement industry, calling the basing point system a plan for keeping prices of goods to buyers identical, even when delivered from different geographic areas. A bill passed Congress calling for amendment to the FTC and Clayton Acts to allow for such a delivered pricing system, but President Truman vetoed it and the FTC order stood (Wagner 1971).

The Commission studied the effects of mergers and economic concentration on the American market, producing annual reports on this subject in 1947, 1948, and 1949. This effort indicated the Commission's increasing interest in the economic effect of business actions on markets, as opposed to a simple concern for fairness in the marketplace for all players. The passage of the Celler-Kefauver Antimerger Act in 1950, which amended section 7 of the Clayton Act, marked an achievement for the FTC. This amendment prohibited purchase of assets where such purchases would substantially reduce competition. This legislation, urged by the FTC since 1926, closed a loophole in the Clayton Act. Enforcement by the FTC and the Justice Department of this revised law led to a decline in the number of horizontal mergers by the late 1950s.

The emphasis on economic expertise at the Commission was underlined by new FTC Chairman Edward F. Howrey, appointed in 1953. In an address to the American Bar Association in 1954 Howrey sounded a strongly economic theme, noting that the Commission must

> . . . examine all relevant economic factors, . . . test . . . public interest and competitive injury by such comparative facts as business rivalry, economic usefulness, degree of competition, degree of market control, degree of vertical integration, customer freedom of choice of goods and services, opportunities for small competitiors to engage in business, costs, and prices. (Howrey 1954:114.)

The courts had gradually recognized the Commission's expertise is this area, most notably in the 1952 *FTC v. Rubberoid* case and the 1953 *Motion Pictures Advertising* case. And as early as 1944 Circuit Court Judge Learned Hand had written, "Congress having now created an organ endued with the skill which comes of long experience and penetrating study, its conclusions inevitably supersede those of the courts, which are not similarly endowed" (in *Herzfeld v. FTC* quoted in *Yale Law Journal* 1955:34). Howrey resigned in 1955, but the Commission continued to include economic analysis in its investigations and rulings.

The Commission also responded to the changing nature of advertising and its use by businesses and consumers. Recognizing the increasingly important role played by advertising in determining consumer brand preferences, the Commission issued decrees against acquisitions where the greater advertising power accruing to the merged firms would hurt competition and discourage entry by new firms into that particular industry. The first major case involving this issue came after the acquisition of

Clorox Chemical Company by Procter and Gamble, a product extension merger. Although a fairly small firm, Clorox dominated the household bleach market with 49 percent of all sales. The Commission concluded (in a finding upheld by the Supreme Court in 1967) that combining Clorox's market dominance with Procter and Gamble's resources and advertising discounts would significantly hurt competitors in the field.

Similarly, when General Foods acquired S.O.S. (a major manufacturer of household steel wool) in 1957, the latter gained access to marketing and advertising discounts that helped boost its market share, hurting Brillo, S.O.S.'s chief competitor. The FTC ruled that General Food's advertising accounted for S.O.S's market dominance and created barriers to entry for competitors.

The Commission continued to oversee the ad claims. Sections of the Commission monitored ads in magazine, newspapers, radio, and, eventually, television. Medical experts evaluated the claims of products. The FTC continued its policy of protecting those consumers least able to protect themselves, a position the courts upheld. As the reviewing court stated in the 1944 *Charles of the Ritz Distributors Corp. v. FTC* case, where the Commission had acted against the name Rejuvenescense for a face cream because the ads implied that the complexion of youth could be regained:

> While the wise and worldly may well realize the falsity of any representations that the present product can roll back the years, there remains "that vast multitude" of others who, like Ponce de Leon, still seek a perpetual fountain of youth. . . . It is for this reason that the Commission may "insist upon the most literal truthfulness" in advertisements . . . and should have the discretion, undisturbed by the courts, to insist if it chooses upon a form of advertising clear enough so that, in the words of the prophet Isaiah, "wayfaring men, though fools, shall not err therein." (Quoted in Wagner 1971:175; see also Aaker and Day 1978.)

The Commission also moved against assertions by cigarette companies as early as the 1940s. Ads featuring endorsements by doctors or claiming medicinal qualities (e.g. soothing to the throat, nose, mouth) were carefully scrutinized. Kools and Camels were just two of the brands forced to stop listing false benefits of cigarette smoking. In 1955 the Commission issued its Cigarette Advertising Guides. While never formally endorsed by the Commission, many companies voluntarily complied with these guidelines in their advertising. When the surgeon general established an advisory committee in 1962 to investigate the effects of cigarette smoking, the FTC offered its expertise in this area. Shortly after the committee's report appeared in 1964, the FTC came out with a proposed set of rules for cigarette advertising which would have forced manufacturers to include a strong warning about the dangers of cigarette smoking in ads and on packages. However, politics intruded, and Congress took on the issue (to the relief of the tobacco industry). The law passed by Congress in 1965 called for a relatively mild health warning on cigarette packages, none in advertising. In addition, the law included a three-year moratorium on action by either the FTC or by states. As a student of the agency has written, "Opinion in the FTC was divided as to who 'won' the 1965 battle. Chairman Dixon claimed credit for prodding the government into action while Commissioner Elman considered the moratorium a slap in the face for the Commission" (Wagner 1971:188). Once again, the limits of this regulatory agency were revealed.

In the forties, the Commission used its authority to require disclosure in instances where not to disclose constituted deception (Greig 1947). This principle was upheld in 1951 by the Seventh Circuit Court of Appeals, which reasoned that consumers were being deceived if failure to include certain information (e.g., about country of origin of the product, materials used in manufacturing) affected consumption decisions. In the seventies, the Commission would require manufacturers to have scientific tests to substantiate their claims in ads (Gillmor et al. 1990).

The FTC continued to act against a wide variety of other fraudulent practices to protect the consuming public, including unethical door-to-door sales techniques, fake medical devices, and false bargains. One of the most celebrated cases acted on by the FTC concerned the Holland Furnace company. This firm sought out elderly individuals, used scare tactics to convince them that their furnaces were defective, then sent a salesman in to sell them a new furnace (usually a very old model) at a highly inflated price. The FTC worked out a stipulation with Holland to stop these misleading practices, but the company persisted. The Commission issued a cease and desist order in 1958, which the company appealed. The Supreme Court upheld the order in *Holland Furnace Company v. FTC* (1960), but the company refused to obey it, and in 1965 was fined $100,000. The president of the company was sentenced to six months in jail.

A complaint filed by the Commission in 1960 led to the promulgation of advertising guidelines for mock-ups and gimmicks in television commercials. The case concerned ads for Colgate-Palmolive's Rapid Shave cream. The Ted Bates ad agency had created ads claiming that the "super-moisturizing" power of the cream allowed it to shave sandpaper. The TV ads purported to demonstrate this. In reality, sand was being shaved off plexiglass. Although the agency claimed that it was forced to use a mock-up because sandpaper did not show up well on television, FTC tests revealed that even after immersion for an hour in the shaving cream, sandpaper could not be shaved. The Supreme Court upheld the FTC in 1965, finding mock-ups that misled the public or exaggerated product benefits illegal.

In 1949 the Hoover Commission (chaired by the former president) issued a report suggesting certain changes in the FTC to bring increased efficiency. The Hoover Commission recommended that the chairman of the FTC be appointed by the president and be given increased administrative authority. It also advised that the agency, always organized along functional lines, with a Bureau of Legal Investigation and a Bureau of Litigation, switch to program line organization, with one department focusing on deceptive practices and the other on monopoly. These changes were incorporated in the Reorganization Act of 1950. Although the FTC tried the new organization for several years, in 1954 the bureaus of Legal Investigation and Litigation reappeared. In the 1960s, still another change returned the Commission to a program line organization, featuring the Bureau of Restraint of Trade and the Bureau of Deceptive Practices, as well as departments of Economics, Field Operations, Textiles and Furs, and Industry Guidance (the latter three done away with by Chairman Caspar Weinberger in 1970). In 1947 a Compliance Division was added to ensure that cease and desist orders had been obeyed. This department stepped up its activities in the 1950s.

As consumerism became a more important part of the FTC's mandate, the agency responded. The Commission held a conference on public deception in 1959, when representatives of consumer organizations and public interest groups met and discussed practices harmful to consumers. A series of similar conferences were held on the state and local level. FTC field offices began providing support for consumer protection work. This arena of activity would expand even further with the Commission's assuming responsibility for enforcement of the Truth in Packaging and Truth in Lending laws. The agency also paid attention to especially vulnerable consumers such as the poor, the elderly, and children.

The fifties and sixties saw a renewed emphasis, at least rhetorically, on the need for competition; it was seen as vital to a strong marketplace. In part this reflected the cold war atmosphere pervasive at the time. Paul Rand Dixon, who became commissioner in 1961, talked of the need to maintain vigorous competition and claimed that "the other nations of the world seem to have suddenly seen the folly of their state (and privately-owned) cartels and monopolies, and the merits of the free-enterprise system we in America have enjoyed for so long" (Dixon 1963:408). However, this did not stop businesses from undertaking mergers, pricing agreements, and other noncompetitive practices. The courts strengthened the hand of the agency, making it clear that the Commission should go after noncompetitive practices and, as the Supreme Court ruled in the 1964 *Brown Shoe Company v. FTC* case, "arrest trade restraints in their incipiency." In 1958, the FTC initiated a case, the tetracycline case, which led it into a new area of unfair trade practice, the use of fraudulently obtained patents. Here the FTC claimed that two drug companies, Charles Pfizer and Company and American Cyanamid Company had been deceptive in their application to obtain a patent for tetracycline. These two firms as well as three other major drug manufacturers had negotiated with one another on strategies for obtaining the patents, fixing prices of tetracycline, excluding smaller competitors, and keeping consumer prices unnaturally high. The courts upheld the findings of the FTC in 1968, ten years after the original complaint had been lodged. Prices of tetracycline to the consumers declined. This case allowed the FTC to fulfill its dual missions of protecting small companies in the marketplace and ensuring the free flow of goods at the best price to consumers.

The Commission began issuing trade regulation rules in 1962, continuing the agency's work in offering guidance to businesses, and marking a break with its previous case by case approach. These rules provided information to entire industries about FTC thinking on particular practices. While these industry-wide guidelines are advisory in nature, they can be used in litigation.

Past and Present: Conclusion

The 1949 Hoover Commission report had been generally critical of the FTC, concluding that:

> as the years have progressed, the Commission has become immersed in a multitude of petty problems; it has not probed into new areas of anticom-

petitive practices; it has become increasingly bogged down with cumbersome procedures and inordinate delays in disposition of its cases. Its economic work—instead of being the backbone of its activities—has been allowed to dwindle almost to none. The Commission has largely become a passive judicial agency, waiting for cases to come up on the docket, under routinized procedures, without active responsibility for achieving the statutory objectives. (Quoted in Wagner 1971:221.)

The Hoover Commission was not the first nor the last body to criticize the FTC. Yet given a difficult, unclear, and at times contradictory task, the Commission has struggled, survived, and at times made progress during its first fifty years.

The FTC has been immersed in many of the economic problems facing U.S. society over the twentieth century. Embroiled in public policy issues (from the practices of meatpackers in the teens to Kid Vid in the late seventies) and forced to take stands on widely debated issues, the Commission has inevitably caused controversy and will continue to do so; its position invites it. Several policy issues have continually emerged in the agency's history:

> One important policy question concerns the FTC's role vis-a-vis the businesses it is regulating. The issue of whether to employ an adversarial or a negotiational approach to regulation has been a constant dilemma for the agency. The Commission has resolved it in different ways at various points in its history, coming up in recent years with the trade regulation rules, only to have agency autonomy limited by Congress (McGraw 1984).

> A second constant has been the expansion and contraction of the FTC's powers, which has occurred with regularity throughout its life. Both Congress and the courts have alternately strengthened and weakened the agency. Overall, with its work on consumer protection, the scope of the agency seemed to be enlarging over the years. However, at other times when the agency has moved boldly (as in the late seventies and early twenties), Congress and/or the courts have restricted it. Some FTC watchers believe that the weakening of the Commission's powers that occurred in the eighties with the advent of Reagan appointee James Miller as FTC chairman, and the FTC Improvements Act, is more severe than curtailments of the past.

> Third, the accusation of not being proconsumer enough has been leveled periodically at the FTC, despite the agency's aggressive work in this area, particularly in the seventies. Yet until 1938, protection of the consumer

did not fall clearly within the Commission's mandate. Even after the Wheeler-Lea amendments specifically gave the FTC jurisdiction in the consumer protection area, it retained its mission to fight against unfair trade practices and monopolistic power. At times these separate tasks come into conflict.

Finally, the problem of inadequate resources and staffing surfaces again and again. The resource cuts of the eighties were prefigured by a similar lack of funding in the late teens. The FTC is asked to perform large and various tasks, and is often understaffed or unable to attract qualified individuals. From the very start, the agency had difficulty drawing the caliber of individuals it desired.

Given its structure and vague mandate, the agency may have to live with the perception of never having fulfilled its potential. The Commission has survived over time because it has been resilient enough to cope with these four recurring issues. And the FTC's record during its most recent twenty-five years underscores this resiliency and attempts to respond to political and social trends that have characterized the agency throughout its history. Other papers in this volume discuss this and other events in the life of the FTC in the sixties, seventies, and eighties, when the Commission faced both old and new problems.

APPENDIX A

Chronology of Key Events in the History of the FTC, 1914-1964

1887 Interstate Commerce Commission created
1890 Sherman Antitrust Act passed
1903 Bureau of Corporations created
1914 Federal Trade Commission Act passed
     Clayton Antitrust Act passed
1918 Webb-Pomerone Act passed
1919 *FTC v. Sears, Roebuck & Company*
1920 *FTC v. Gratz*
1921 Packers and Stockyard Act passed
1922 *FTC v. Winsted Hosiery*
1929 *FTC v. Klesner*
1931 *FTC v. Raladam*

1934 *FTC v. Keppel & Brothers*
1935 *Humphrey's Executor v. United States*
1936 Robinson-Patman Act passed
1938 Wheeler-Lea Act passed, amending the 1914 FTC Act
1939 Wool Products Labeling Act passed
1949 Hoover Commission Report
1950 Celler-Kefauver Antimerger Act passed
        Oleomargarine Act passed
1951 Fur Products Labeling Act passed
1952 McGuire Act passed
1953 Flammable Fabrics Act passed
1958 Textile and Fiber Products Act passed

APPENDIX B

Excerpts from President Wilson's Address to the Congress, January 1914: The President's Call for a Federal Trade Commission

. . . The business men of the country desire something more than that the menace of legal process in these matters be made explicit and intelligible. They desire advice, the definite guidance and information which can be supplied by an administrative body, an **interstate trade commission.**

Constructive legislation, when successful, is always the embodiment of **convincing experience,** and of **mature public opinion** which finally springs out of that experience. . . . It is not recent or hasty opinion.

The opinion of the country . . . would not wish to see it [the commission] empowered to make terms with monopoly or in any sort to assume control of business, as if the Government made itself responsible. It demands such a commission only as **an indispensable instrument of information and publicity,** as **a clearing house of the facts** by which both the public mind and the managers of great business undertakings should be guided, and as **an instrumentality for doing justice to business** where the processes of the courts are inadequate to adjust the remedy to wrong in a way that will meet all the equities and circumstances of the case.

APPENDIX C

Reasoning behind the FTC and Wheeler-Lea Acts

FTC Act. The committee gave careful consideration to the question as to whether it would attempt to define the many and variable unfair practices which prevail in commerce and to forbid their continuance or whether it would, by a general declaration condemning unfair practices, leave it to the Commission to determine what practices were unfair. It concluded that the latter course would be the better, for the reason, as stated by one of the representatives of the Illinois Manufacturers' Association, that there were too many unfair practices to define, and after writing 20 of them into the law, it would be quite possible to invent others. (Senate Committee on Interstate Commerce Report, 1914, supporting the trade commission bill.)

Wheeler-Lea. The Commission spent most of its time and most of its money allotted to it by the Congress, in running down the question of whether or not one man has lost some money by reason of unfair trade practices on the part of another. After all, Congress is not interested in whether John Smith lost some money as the result of the advertising complained of, but **the question is whether or not the general public has been deceived or injured by reason of it.** We are here to legislate with respect to that question. (Senator Burton Wheeler in debate on Wheeler-Lea amendments, 1938, quoted in Harris and Milkis, 1989.)

Key Sections of the FTC Act. Section 5. (a) (1) Unfair methods of competition in **or affecting** commerce, *and unfair or deceptive acts or practices in or affecting commerce* and unfair or deceptive acts or practices in **or affecting** commerce are hereby declared unlawful. (Italics show phrase added with Wheeler-Lea amendment; bold shows words added with 1975 FTC Improvement Act.)

Section 5. (b) Whenever the Commission shall have reason to believe that any such person, partnership, or corporation has been or is using any unfair method of competition or unfair or deceptive act or practice in **or affecting** commerce, and if it shall appear to the Commission that a proceeding by it in respect thereof *would be of interest to the public,* it shall issue and serve upon such person, partnership, or corporation a complaint stating its charges. (Italics show passage concerning need for a public interest; bold shows words added with 1975 FTC Improvement Act.)

Section 12. (a) It shall be unlawful for any person, partnership, or corporation to disseminate, or cause to be disseminated, any false advertisement—
    (b) The dissemination or the causing to be disseminated of any false advertisement within the provisions of subsection (a) of this section shall be an unfair or deceptive act or practice in **or affecting** commerce within the meaning of section 5. (This whole section added with Wheeler-Lea amendment; bold words added with 1975 FTC Improvement Act.)

APPENDIX D

References to Court Cases

FTC v. Sears, Roebuck & Company, 258 F.307 (7th Cir. 1919).
FTC v. Gratz et al., 253 U.S. 421 (1920).
FTC v. Beech-Nut, 257 U.S. 441 (1921).
FTC v. Winsted Hosiery Company, 258 U.S. 483 (1922).
FTC v. American Tobacco Company, 264 U.S. 298 (1924).
FTC v. Standard Education Society, 14 F.2d 947 (7th Cir. 1926).
FTC v. Ostermoor & Company, 16 F.2d 962 (2d Cir. 1927).
FTC v. Klesner, 280 U.S. 19 (1929).
FTC v. Raladam Company, 283 U.S. 643 (1931).
FTC v. Keppel & Brother, Inc., 291 U.S. 304 (1934).
Humphrey's Executor v. U.S., 295 U.S. 602 (1935).
Schechter Poultry Corp. v. U.S., 295 U.S. 495 (1935).
Charles of the Ritz Distributors Corp. v. FTC, 143 F.2d 676 (2d Cir. 1944).
Herzfeld v. FTC, 140 F.2d 207 (2d Cir. 1944).
FTC v. Ruberoid Company, 343 U.S. 470 (1952).
FTC v. Carter Products, Inc., 346 U.S. 327 (1953).
FTC v. Motion Picture Advertising Service Company, 344 U.S. 392 (1953).
Holland Furnace Company v. FTC, 269 F.2d 203 (7th Cir. 1959), cert. denied, 361
   U.S. 932 (1960).
FTC v. Colgate-Palmolive Company, 380 U.S. 374 (1965).
FTC v. Brown Shoe Company, 384 U.S. 316 (1966).
FTC v. Sperry & Hutchinson Company, 405 U.S. 233 (1972).

Note

The author would like to thank the following people for their comments on earlier drafts of this article: Mary Carsky, Don Gillmor, Gary Moore, Pat Murphy, Laura Tuchman, and Bill Wilkie.

References

Aaker, David A., and George S. Day (1978). *Consumerism: Search for the Consumer Interest*. New York: The Free Press.

Benson, George (1938). "Has the F.T.C. Become a New NRA?" *Nation's Business* (May), pp. 15, 16, 106.

Brown, William F. (1947a). "The Federal Trade Commission and False Advertising: I." *Journal of Marketing* (July), pp. 38-46.

——— (1947b). "The Federal Trade Commission and False Advertising: II." *Journal of Marketing* (October), pp. 193-201.

Columbia Law Review (1962). "NOTE: The Federal Commission and Reform of the Administrative Process." Vol. 62 (Spring), pp. 671-707.

Dixon, Paul Rand (1963). "Significant New Commission Developments." *Kentucky Law Journal* (Spring), pp. 404-421.

Garraty, John A. (1968). *The New Commonwealth, 1877-1890.* New York: Harper & Row.

Gillmor, Donald, Jerome Barron, Todd Simon, and Herbert Terry (1990). *Mass Communication Law.* St. Paul, MN: West Publishing Company.

Grieg, G.B. (1947). "Some Varieties of Consumer Behavior Described in the Decisions of the Federal Trade Commission." *The Journal of Business,* vol. 20 (October), pp. 191-200.

Harris, Richard A., and Sidney M. Milkis (1989). *The Politics of Regulatory Change: A Tale of Two Agencies.* New York: Oxford University Press.

Hawley, Ellis (1966). *The New Deal and the Problem of Monopoly.* Princeton, NJ: University Press.

Henderson, Gerard (1924). *The Federal Trade Commission: A Study in Administrative Law and Procedure.* New Haven, CT: Yale University Press.

Herring, E. Pendleton (1934). "Politics, Personalities, and the Federal Trade Commission, I." *The American Political Science Review,* vol. 28 (December), pp. 1016-1029.

——— (1935). "Politics, Personalities, and the Federal Trade Commission, II." *The American Political Science Review,* vol. 29 (February), pp. 21-35.

Hobbs, Caswell O. (1989). "Swings of the Pendulum—The FTC's First 75 Years." Remarks before the Section of Antitrust Law, American Bar Association, Washington, D.C., April 7, 1989.

Howrey, Edward F. (1954). "The FTC: A Reevaluation of Its Responsibilities." *American Bar Association Journal,* vol. 40 (February), pp. 113-117.

Katzmann, Robert A. (1980). *Regulatory Bureaucracy: The Federal Trade Commission and Antitrust Policy.* Cambridge, MA: MIT Press.

Kintner, Earl, and Christopher Smith (1975). "The Emergence of the Federal Trade Commission as a Formidable Consumer Protection Agency." *The Mercer Law Review,* vol. 26, pp. 651-688.

Krockman, Arnold (1936). "Newest Bureaucractic Colossus." *Northwestern Miller,* vol. 188 (November 11), pp. 375-390.

Lay, George C. (1926). "The Federal Trade Commission—Its Origin, Operation, and Effect." *American Law Review,* vol. 60 (May), pp. 338-361.

Link, Arthur (1955). *American Epic: A History of the United States Since the 1890s.* New York: Alfred A. Knopf.

McCraw, Thomas (1984). *Prophets of Regulation.* Cambridge, MA: Belknap Press of Harvard University Press.

Moffett, L.W. (1925). "Federal Trade Commission Policy Changed." *Iron Age* (March 26), pp. 919-920.

Montague, Gilbert H. (1927). "Anti-Trust Laws and the Federal Trade Commission, 1914-1927." *Columbia Law Review,* vol. 27 (June), pp. 650-678.

——— (1926). "The New Policy and Procedure of the Federal Trade Commission." *Proceedings of the Academy of Political Science* (January), pp. 684-687.

Rippey, Stephens (1940). "The FTC in Unofficial Profile." *Advertising and Selling* (February), pp. 20-22.

Rublee, George (1926). "The Original Plan and Early History of the Federal Trade Commission." *Proceedings of the Academy of Political Science* (January), pp. 666-672.

Schwartz, Bernard, ed. (1973). *The Economic Regulation of Business and Industry: A Legislative History of U.S. Regulatory Agencies*, vol. III. New York: Chelsea House Publishers in Association with R.R. Bowker Company.

Sklar, Martin (1988). *The Corporate Reconstruction of American Capitalism, 1890-1916.* New York: Cambridge University Press.

Stevens, W.H.S. (1926). "Changes in the Federal Trade Commission's Legal Procedure." *Proceedings of the Academy of Political Science* (January), pp. 688-694.

Yale Law Review (1955). "The 'New' Federal Trade Commission and the Enforcement of the Antitrust Laws." (November), pp. 34-85.

Wagner, Susan (1971). *The Federal Trade Commission.* New York: Praeger Publishers.

PART III

The Contributions to Public Policy by Marketing Academics

For many readers Part III will hold some surprises, as it chronicles the scope of expertise and experience marketing academics offer in relevant topic areas. We begin with a paper by Patrick Murphy, who discusses the experiences of the nearly thirty marketing professors who have worked at the FTC, and assesses their impacts. Mary Gardiner Jones, the FTC commissioner who originated the idea of bringing marketing inputs to the FTC, then comments on how this exchange has evolved over the past twenty years.

In the remainder of this part we turn our attention to a sampling of the current work marketing academics are doing on important regulatory problems. Two papers here discuss regulating the advertising and marketing of controversial products (Michael Mazis on alcohol and Joel Cohen on cigarettes). Given the controversial topics, these papers are not entirely unbiased but do an excellent job of exploring substantive issues as well as regulatory questions.

Our next three papers evaluate aspects of advertising regulation: Bonnie Reece and Stephen Greyser present an interesting survey of business executives' attitudes toward advertising regulation; Harold Kassarjian describes empirical studies of how the advertising substantiation program affected actual ads in four product classes; and Thomas Kinnear and Ann Root provide their assessment of the recent performance of the FTC in regulating deceptive advertising. The last three papers in the part then advance our understanding of how consumer information operates. Paul Bloom describes a new approach for developing consumer information programs; Darlene B. Smith, Gary Ford, and John Swasy present an empirical study of issues in the economics of information; and Joshua Wiener offers insightful comments on both papers.

Past FTC Participation
by Marketing Academics

Patrick E. Murphy

—

This paper examines the participation of marketing academics at the Federal Trade Commission over the past eighteen years. Like the Commission itself, ebbs and flows have occurred in the level of activity by marketing academics. Other authors (Maronick 1983; Preston 1980) have briefly discussed the marketing academics' roles at the FTC over the years. To date, however, no systematic examination has been undertaken of the individual marketing professors and their responsibilities within the Commission.

As an organizing device for discussing the role of marketing academics at the FTC, this paper examines each of the following questions in turn: Who were the participants? When did they start? Where did they work? What roles did they play? Why did they do it? Which outcomes were most significant?

The Participants: When and Where They Worked

The names of those who served at the Commission and the offices in which they worked are listed below. The total of twenty-eight marketing academics includes only those who have worked full time at the FTC and not those who have served as consultants on cases and rulemakings.

The Early Years: 1971-1974

In the early years of marketing academics' participation, 1971 to 1974, thirteen individuals held various positions at the Commission:

Murray Silverman	Assistant to Commissioner Mary Gardiner Jones
William L. Wilkie	Bureau of Consumer Protection (BCP)
David M. Gardner	Office of Policy Planning and Evaluation (OPPE)
Harold H. Kassarjian	BCP
H. Keith Hunt	OPPE
Norman Kangun	BCP, National Advertising
William A. Staples	OPPE
Ralph L. Day	BCP, National Advertising
E. Laird Landon	OPPE
Alan Shocker	OPPE
Neil E. Beckwith	OPPE
John A. Miller	OPPE and BCP, National Advertising
John U. Farley	OPPE

Murray Silverman was the first marketing academic employed at the FTC. Commissioner Mary Gardiner Jones' call to George Day, then at Stanford University, inquiring about his interest in serving as an in-house marketing consultant was the genesis of the marketing field's participation at the Commission. Day was unavailable, but recommended his former student, Silverman, who took the initial position. In turn, Silverman contacted Bill Wilkie about his interest in working there. Wilkie then recruited Hal Kassarjian to take his place, and several additional marketing academics quickly followed. Wilkie and Kassarjian worked in the Bureau of Consumer Protection at the bureau rather than the division level. Six of these marketing academics held positions exclusively in the Office of Policy Planning and Evaluation. This office was not technically associated with any of the three FTC bureaus but provided an overall agency planning an evaluation function. Norm Kangun, Ralph Day and John Miller worked in the Bureau of Consumer Protection's National Advertising Division.

The conclusion that can be drawn about these early days of marketing academics' participation at the FTC is that they played key roles and were engaged in much significant activity. The positive experience of these pioneer marketing academics, in turn, influenced several other of their colleagues to join the Commission later. Specifically, Kangun (my dissertation chairman) and Bill Staples (my roommate during graduate school) influenced me to join the agency. Wilkie was also influential in recruiting several other marketing faculty to work at the Commission.

The Middle Years: 1975-1979

Nine marketing faculty members joined the FTC during these years:

John Eighmey	BCP, National Advertising
Michael B. Mazis	BCP and OPPE
Dennis L. McNeill	BCP, National Advertising
Debra Scammon	BCP, Food and Drug Advertising
Ivan Preston	BCP, National Advertising
Kenneth L. Bernhardt	BCP, Office of Impact Evaluation
Gary T. Ford	Bureau of Economics (BE)
Ronald Stiff	BCP, Office of Impact Evaluation
Richard Mizerski	BCP, National Advertising

Distinct from the earlier group, these academics worked in specific FTC offices, primarily in the Bureau of Consumer Protection. Mike Mazis, who served as advisor within the Bureau of Consumer Protection and the Office of Policy Planning, and Gary Ford, who was an in-house consultant at the Bureau of Economics, were exceptions to this rule. Dennis McNeill and Debra Scammon joined the Commission shortly after finishing their doctoral degrees. Wilkie, McNeill's dissertation chairman, guided him to the Commission. Hal Kassarjian influenced Scammon to take the FTC position. Scammon's dissertation on food and drug issues gave her specific expertise in an area vital to the Commission's work, so they sought her out. Ken Bernhardt initiated the Bureau of Consumer Protection's new Office of Impact Evaluation. He discusses his role elsewhere in this volume (see Part II). Ron Stiff succeeded Bernhardt as director of the Office of Impact Evaluation.

A reasonable assessment of these middle years at the FTC is that although there were still a number of marketing academics joining the Commission, their role had changed from one of providing overall advice to one of performing specific tasks. Thus, the marketing academic's role then became more task-oriented and less policy-oriented.

The Later Years: 1980-1989

Six marketing faculty members worked at the Commission during the decade of the eighties:

Thomas J. Maronick	BCP, Office of Impact Evaluation
Patrick E. Murphy	BCP, Office of Management Planning
Joshua L. Wiener	BE
Edward Popper	BCP, Advertising Practices
Gregory T. Gundlach	Bureau of Competition (BC), Planning Office
John E. Calfee	BE

Two of these academics, Josh Wiener and Jack Calfee, were originally Bureau of Economics' economists and subsequently have taken marketing faculty positions. Tom Maronick succeeded Stiff as director of the Office of Impact Evaluation. He discusses his role at the Commission elsewhere in the volume. Greg Gundlach worked in the Bureau of Competition's planning office for one summer while he was a graduate student. He is the only marketing academic who has been employed by the BC. I joined the Commission in the summer of 1980 and worked in the Bureau of Consumer Protection's Office of Management Planning. This small office employed three professionals who advised the bureau director and worked on projects with the various divisions. I have previously discussed in detail this office's function (Murphy 1984).

One assessment of marketing academics' participation at the FTC in the 1980s is obviously that fewer of them worked at the Commission during this time. Also, the marketing academic's role has been diminished largely to one of advisor on specific projects. This altered role can be starkly contrasted with the role of those marketing specialists at the FTC in the early to mid-1970s.

The average length of time that each marketing academic spent at the Commission is approximately one year, since each of the professors took a leave from his or her university for one academic year. For example, I worked at the Commission from May of 1980 to August of 1981. Two exceptions are John Eighmey, who spent approximately two years at the BCP National Advertising Office, and Tom Maronick, who worked for three years as the full-time director of the Office of Impact Evaluation. Maronick has also served as an in-house, part-time consultant for the past six years. The purpose of marketing academics' participation in the FTC, however, was to keep their tenure relatively short so that others could benefit from the same opportunity. Furthermore, this rotation prevented one individual's views from unduly influencing the Commission over an extended period of time.

Marketing Academics' Roles

The roles that marketing academics have played while at the FTC are these:

1. advising commissioners and bureau directors
2. assisting attorneys with cases
3. administering contract research
4. conducting planning studies
5. participating in policy review sessions
6. providing economic analyses of cases or rules
7. serving as experts in rulemaking

Most of the professors, especially those at the Commission in the later years, served in only one or two of these capacities.

In the early days, the role of advising Commissioners was a key one. In fact, Mary Gardiner Jones envisioned this as the major function of marketing academics at the FTC when she initiated the marketing advisor position. In addition to advising the commissioners, the marketing professors' role of advising the bureau directors was also an important one. Bill Wilkie had entree to Bob Pitofsky, the Bureau of Consumer Protection's director. This was a policy-oriented and policy-making role that marketing academics played, but, as discussed above, it has been diminished over the years of marketing professors' participation at the FTC.

The most prominent role played by marketing academics was that of assisting attorneys with cases. Much time and effort was expended in this endeavor. Attorneys found that marketing research and consumer behavior analysis was rather important. Therefore, they sought the advice of in-house marketing consultants on the cases that they were pursuing. For example, marketing academics contributed significant inputs to the early corrective advertising cases including Wonder Bread, RJR-Hawaiian Punch, and Listerine.

The third role was administering contract research. The Office of Impact Evaluation was specifically chartered to undertake this activity. As mentioned above, Ken Bernhardt, Ron Stiff, and Tom Maronick served as directors of the office. Marketing academics and attorneys also jointly administered contract research relating to specific cases. In fact, while at the FTC, Wilkie persuaded the Commission to spend $200 for a copy test. This was the Commission's first experience in conducting contract research. The amount of contract research grew dramatically, until the late 1970s. Bernhardt's discussion in this volume places the cost of this research at over $1 million.

Another significant role played by marketing academics was that of conducting planning studies. As shown in the lists above, many marketing professors have worked over the years for the Office of Policy Planning and Evaluation. The office under Bob Reich's leadership in the late 1970s dropped the evaluation function. Those marketing academics who worked for OPPE in the early years were actively involved in such evaluation studies. In addition, the Office of Management Planning in BCP undertook a number of planning projects. These studies served as an input to case selection and direction for BCP activities.

The fifth role is participation in policy review sessions. These sessions were used extensively during the Pertschuk Commission. Therefore, marketing academics serving in the late 1970s and early 1980s were involved in such activities. The most influential of these was probably the late 1970s' session that resulted in the Consumer Information Remedies report. Mike Mazis, a major contributor to this report and to subsequent journal articles (Beales et al. 1981; Mazis et al. 1981), has reported the outcome of this policy review session. In addition, both Josh Wiener and I served on the policy review session that resulted in the Comparative Performance Information report which was published in 1981. This is one of the activities that the Commission has eliminated in the resource-poor 1980s.

Another role that a few marketing academics played was that of providing economic analyses for cases or rulemakings. Gary Ford did these types of analyses, first at BE and later as an outside consultant. Jack Calfee also has served in this capacity for several years.

The final marketing academics' role was that of serving as experts in rulemakings. Dennis McNeill was one of the experts in the late 1970s children's advertising rulemaking. Other marketing professors have served as either internal or external experts in rulemaking. Since FTC rulemaking has subsided in the 1980s, this role is one that is not played currently. As discussed earlier, the roles that marketing academics assumed have changed over time. In the early days, their chief roles were those of advising commissioners and bureau directors and conducting planning studies. Today, however, the marketing academics' dominant roles tend to be those of administering contract research and assisting attorneys with cases. This is another example of the marketing academics' diminishing influence at the Commission over the years. In fact, the marketing academics' roles have seemed to evolve from the roles of a generalist to those of a specialist.

Reasons for Working at the FTC

There are a number of reasons why marketing academics decide to work at the Commission. They range from exclusively professional to personal. These reasons are not mutually exclusive and, in fact, most marketing academics have had several reasons for deciding to "stop out" of their academic career and work in government.

From the FTC's perspective, specific marketing faculty members have been sought out because of either their background or their expertise. For example, the FTC contacted Debbie Scammon because of her dissertation on food labeling. The FTC sought Bill Wilkie and others because of their expertise and knowledge about consumer behavior. The Commission attracted still other academics because of their knowledge of marketing research techniques and methodology. These marketing faculty members had skills that the Commission both needed and wanted. From the marketing academics' perspective, the match between their skills and abilities and the Commission's needs was one reason that they decided to work at the FTC.

The quality of the marketing academics' experience at the Commission was efficiently communicated to others via an informal grapevine. Many of them heard about the FTC from other faculty members who had served there previously. Since the experience of those who worked at the FTC in 1971-1974 (see above) was almost uniformly positive, the word-of-mouth information was very favorable. Also, only a small group of academics were interested in public policy issues within the marketing field. The word traveled fast within this group that working at the Commission was not only worthwhile but also very rewarding professionally.

A desire to understand how the public policy process works, at least from one agency's perspective, stimulated some of the marketing professors to take a position at the FTC. Many of the marketing academics wanted to see firsthand how government operates. Working at the FTC offered an opportunity to observe Commission hearings, attend high level staff meetings, and participate in case review and discussion. The interplay between the FTC and other government agencies, including the

Department of Justice and other agencies that were interested in consumer protection matters (e.g., FDA, DOE, and EPA), was best understood by being actively involved at the Commission.

From a career perspective, one reason a faculty member might work at the FTC is to gain both additional experience and credentials. Such experience is viewed as a positive entry on one's resume. For those interested in public policy issues, the match between the FTC and an interest in marketing and advertising issues is a natural one. The experience of working for a federal agency also adds to an individual's expertise.

Faculty members who consider taking a leave or going on sabbatical have a number of options. They range from working in industry, to taking positions in other colleges, and to gaining some international experience. As mentioned above, the public policy group viewed spending time at the FTC as a very desirable option. Working at the Commission combined professional interests with an opportunity to get away from the university's and the students' day-to-day demands on a faculty member's time.

Finally, a drawing card for some of the marketing academics was the excitement of living in the Washington, D.C., area. The city contains a multitude of activities revolving around government and cultural affairs. It provides an interesting counterpoint to the life that most academics lead. In fact, Washington is such a desirable place that one FTC marketing academic and a number of those working at other agencies have decided to relocate there after leaving government service.

Significant Outcomes

The outcomes of the marketing academics' participation in the FTC are somewhat difficult to pinpoint. They appear to be able to be categorized as either within the Commission or external to it. Regarding those outcomes within the FTC, one significant outcome is the access to commissioners and bureau directors that marketing academics enjoyed in the early years. The reason that marketing academics gained a favorable reputation within the FTC is that the roles played by those in the early 1970s were significant in influencing the thinking of top FTC officials.

Another internal outcome revolves around remedy forms that marketing academics suggested. The range of information remedies and disclosure options was one that marketing faculty were particularly prepared to give. For example, marketing academics such as Keith Hunt influenced the FTC's choice of permissible forms of corrective advertising. Furthermore, marketers have had impact on the range of information disclosures that the commission has used over the years (see Wilkie 1982, 1983, 1985, 1986, 1987). Marketers have also influenced the system by helping attorneys select, settle, and specifically litigate cases. Marketing faculty members' expertise can both help attorneys and economists select cases and advise attorneys on settlement issues, such as the remedy and information disclosures discussed previously. Furthermore, marketing professors serving as expert witnesses or evaluators of advertising agencies' or marketing research firms' work have influenced actual case litigation. The final significant outcome that marketing academics have created within the Commission is the Office of Impact Evaluation's evaluation studies. Many of these studies have been conducted over the years. One good example is Dyer and Maronick's recent article (1988) which evaluates the effectiveness of the energy labels placed on major appliances.

Marketing faculty members' participation at the FTC has resulted in a number of external outcomes. Probably the most significant outcome is the amount and type of research that those marketing academics who are interested in public policy issues have conducted. Marketing academics' work at the FTC did lead to substantial research outcomes. The academics published most of this research sometime after leaving the Commission, since the demands of the FTC activities left little time for serious academic research. Within the research area, FTC issues enhanced the theoretical development of information processing in the early years. Some of the work that Bettman (1979) and others undertook on information processing were applied to issues of FTC interest. In addition, the growth in the literature about consumer satisfaction and dissatisfaction was at least in part attributable to marketing academics such as Keith Hunt, who were involved in the FTC's activities in the early years. In addition, marketing faculty members have studied theoretical developments and economics (see Smith, Ford, and Swasy in this section).

The number of journal articles that marketing academics who served at the FTC have published are too numerous to mention. Gundlach and Wilkie's data base documents many of these (see their article which appears later in the book). Work at the FTC did in fact have major impact upon research within the marketing field. The "FTC Alumni" have organized a number of special sessions at AMA, ACR, and other professional association meetings. In fact, one of the most significant of these was a 1981 special session at the ACR conference which was held at the FTC itself. Ken Bernhardt organized this session, at which the then-Chairman Michael Pertchuk gave an interesting discussion of the Federal Trade Commission's consumer research pursuits. These subjects have continued to be issues even into the late 1980s. Conference sessions that deal with public policy issues, including participants from the FTC, were held at both 1989 conferences of ACR and AMA.

The influence that work at the FTC has had on marketing faculty members' teaching is harder to pinpoint. At a minimum, marketing academics have many interesting anecdotes to relay to their students regarding their time at the Commission. On a more substantive level, marketing faculty members who have worked at the FTC can teach students how the public policy process works and how the government operates on a day-to-day basis. This is an area in which most business students do not have much knowledge. In addition, several of the FTC alumni have taught or are teaching public policy issues in marketing courses. For example, Mike Mazis regularly teaches such a seminar at American University.

Conclusion

It is hard to be overly optimistic about marketing academics' participation at the FTC in the 1990s. As mentioned above, the marketing academics' diminished role over the years is well documented. Some marketing analysts would say that we may be in the decline stage of the product life cycle regarding professional influence at FTC. Both the fact that only one part-time marketing academic is employed currently at the FTC and that the agency's budget has declined over the years suggest that there probably will be few marketing academics at the agency in the short term. It may be possible, however, to place marketing academics at the Commission by use of sabbaticals or other mechanisms that would not require the FTC to pay the academic's salary. The AACSB has also halted its program in which many marketing academics participated while at the FTC. Also, conferences and seminars, held at the Commission itself, may stimulate more public policy activity.

The dialogue between FTC commissioners and staff and marketing academics definitely needs to improve. I would not, however, go so far as the title to a significant public policy article, "The Dialogue That Never Happens" (Bauer and Greyser 1967) goes in characterizing the interaction between the Commission and the academic marketing community. We do hope that this conference and subsequent ones will reopen this dialogue so that the marketing academics' influence at the FTC will no longer be on the wane. Many of us have a strong sense of affiliation and commitment to the FTC and want to do whatever we can to insure the agency's long-term viability.

References

Bauer, Raymond A., and Stephen A. Greyser (1967). "The Dialogue that Never Happens." *Harvard Business Review*, November-December, 2-12+.

Beales, Howard, Michael Mazis, Steven Salop, and Richard Staelin (1981). "Consumer Search and Public Policy." *Journal of Consumer Research* 8 (June), 11-22.

Bernhardt, Kenneth L., and Ronald Stiff (1980). "Public Policy Update: Perspectives on the Federal Trade Commission." *Advances in Consumer Research*, Kent B. Moore, ed., 8, 452-454.

Bettman, James R. (1979). *An Information Processing Theory of Consumer Choice*. Reading, Massachusetts: Addison-Wesley Publishing Company.

Dyer, Robert F., and Thomas J. Maronick (1988). "An Evaluation of Consumer Awareness and Use of Energy Labels in the Purchase of Major Appliances—A Longitudinal Analysis." *Journal of Public Policy & Marketing* 7, 83-97.

Maronick, Thomas J. (1983). "Careers 'Enriched' by Spending Sabbatical at FTC." *Marketing News*, August 5, 8-9.

Mazis, Michael B., Richard Staelin, Howard Beales, and Steven Salop (1981). "A Framework for Evaluating Consumer Information Regulation." *Journal of Marketing* 45 (Winter), 11-21.

Murphy, Patrick E. (1984). "Strategic Planning at the FTC." *Journal of Public Policy & Marketing* 3, 56-66.

Preston, Ivan L. (1980). "Researchers at the Federal Trade Commission—Peril and Promise." *Current Issues and Research in Advertising*, 1-15.

Wilkie, William L. (1982). "Affirmative Disclosures: Perspective on FTC Orders." *Journal of Public Policy & Marketing* 1, 95-110.

Wilkie, William L. (1983). "Affirmative Disclosures at the FTC: Theoretical Framework and Typology of Case Selection." *Journal of Public Policy & Marketing* 2, 3-15.

Wilkie, William L. (1985). "Affirmative Disclosures at the FTC: Objectives for the Remedy and Outcomes of Past Orders." *Journal of Public Policy & Marketing* 4, 91-111.

Wilkie, William L. (1986). "Affirmative Disclosures at the FTC: Strategic Dimensions." *Journal of Public Policy & Marketing* 5, 123-45.

Wilkie, William L. (1987). "Affirmative Disclosures at the FTC: Tactical Considerations for Communications." *Journal of Public Policy & Marketing* 6, 33-42.

Marketing Academics at the FTC: Reflections and Recommendations

Mary Gardiner Jones

It is good to be here again among old friends and former colleagues. You have asked me to reminisce a little about the origins of FTC's interest in the fields of marketing and behavior science.

It started back in around 1968 with my desire to learn about what the consumer behaviorists could offer to the work of the Federal Trade Commission. One way to find this out was to add a member of your discipline to my advisory staff. So I hired Murray Silverman on the recommendation of Professor George S. Day (Stanford) to whom I had turned for advice. Murray not only helped me understand how consumers processed information but also how to determine their vulnerabilities to various messages and practices. He also made a lot of contacts with lawyers on the Commission staff and helped them understand the contributions that consumer behaviorists could make to their consumer protection programs.

As a result of Murray's work and my interest, the Bureau of Consumer Protection hired its first consumer behaviorist—Bill Wilkie—the following year. It is important to note that if you want to introduce something new in any bureaucracy—governmental or corporate—you need support from the top. Furthermore, you must also have the cooperation and enthusiasm in the ranks as well. Then change can happen as it did at the Commission.

Opportunities for Early Academic Input

The three areas that I believed offered the most fruitful opportunities for your input were information disclosures, consumer vulnerabilities to

216

deceptions, and effective relief. These are the same areas that you have been talking about at this symposium as still of concern to you. In view of the limited number of complaints that the Commission can bring in any one year, it has become increasingly clear to me that the Commission must focus some of its resources in helping consumers protect themselves against misleading representations. Yet, if the Commission were to develop an effective information disclosure program to achieve this goal, it was essential for us to know what kinds of information consumers need to have disclosed and would be most likely to use. If we understood how consumers process information, we would have a better handle on how such information should or could be communicated to them and what kinds of information we needed to communicate.

In the area of determining what practices and messages are deceptive, your discipline again was invaluable. Your representatives stressed how important it is to know what consumers take away from an advertisement (see ensuing papers in this part). Unless we understand that, our complaints and orders can go easily askew and focus on the wrong aspects of the advertising message.

Devoting valuable resources to developing and trying a complaint can be a vain act unless we can also design effective relief. I saw your research as assisting us in designing effective corrective actions, helping us be imaginative about which kinds of redress—warnings, disclosures, changes in marketing practices, monetary penalties—would be most apt to achieve the kind of honest, fair marketplace we were charged to enforce. We needed to be able to estimate what kinds of impact our relief could have and which types of relief would be likely to be more effective in the particular circumstances involved. In a sense, we were concerned with what today is frequently subsumed under the rubric of cost benefit analysis. But to me your discipline can provide a much richer analysis than the economists, who tend to confine themselves primarily to costs because these are so much easier to quantify than benefits. Typically, the most important variables cannot be precisely quantified, but we still need to try to inform ourselves. Your discipline is much more comfortable handling the less quantifiable variables involved in consumer protection. Hence, it has more potential in my judgment to enhance and enrich the Commission's work.

It is interesting to me when I think back about our expectations in those days that I never conceived of the usefulness of your discipline in competition issues. I was impressed with what Lou Stern said (see his paper in Part I of this volume) about the potential contributions that your discipline can make to our antitrust work since you understand both how managers think and consumers behave. I had thought of it primarily as applicable to consumer protection matters. This is something that needs to be explored and pushed at the Commission, as I believe they are beginning to do.

Lessons Learned from Academics at FTC

You have asked me to touch upon what went wrong in the earlier history that enabled this effort to self-dissipate. I do not believe that we should flagellate ourselves on the disappearance of social scientists at the Commission in recent years. What has happened to the FTC under the Reagan administration I think is quite beyond anything that we did or failed to do. I do not believe that we can say that somehow we did not make an impact, or that people forgot, or that what you all did at the Commission was not valuable. It is simply, I think, that the present administration does not believe in regulating business. Emphasis on enforcement has almost totally disappeared. Advertising no longer plays a central role in what is left at the Commission's investigatory activities. The Commission's case load has plunged to its lowest level in decades. Free market economists seem to dominate the thinking of the Commission to the exclusion of any other discipline. There is little interest in how consumers react and behave. It is these considerations that came into play at the FTC which led to the downgrading of the role of behavioral research.

Proposal for a New Bureau

If and when the Commission should return to a more activist affirmative approach to its statutory responsibilities, it will be very important to institutionalize its consumer behavior research resources. I had always looked forward to establishing a Bureau of Consumer Behavior Research comparable in function, if not in size, to the Bureau of Economics. I realize that the Bureau of Economics might initially oppose such a bureau as irrelevant, redundant, or too competitive. Nevertheless, I am convinced that we must consolidate this resource into an established unit that can build up experience and expertise and maintain some institutional memory.

This avenue is far more preferable in my opinion to contracting consumer behavior research outside or even to bringing people in for short-term consultancies. It is essential that the lawyers and economists have an opportunity over the long term and on a continuing basis to interact with consumer behaviorists and to learn about their skills and resources and ways of thinking. This interaction of the different in-house professional staff—lawyers, economists, and consumer behaviorists—can provide a rich learning experience for all. We will always need short-term consumer behavior consultants (one- or two-year appointments) for special projects and to stimulate the in-house staff. One or two individuals simply cannot make the long-term contribution that is necessary if the Commission's remedial and planning responsibilities are to be most effectively discharged. Moreover, their work would be more productive if a core consumer behavior staff existed at the Commission.

Academics: Market Yourselves

Finally, you have asked me to comment briefly on how I think you might go about reconstituting the consumer behavior input into the Commission's work today. One way of educating people about the contributions that you can make to the Commission's work is to invite commissioners and staff to your meetings so that they will have an opportunity to hear about your work and to converse with you about its applicability to the Commission's responsibilities. Send copies of your articles and papers to commissioners and staff members. Add a cover letter pointing out why you feel that the theories or practices described in the paper would be applicable to the Commission's work; be as specific as you can.

There is an interesting newsletter about the Commission called FTC Watch. It might be possible for you from time to time to get notes into that publication about work that you are doing. You might even get a blurb in about this conference, noting Andy Strenio's participation and some excerpts from his very perceptive and balanced remarks about the Commission.

Another way is for you to participate in national or regional FTC hearings. I recognize that you have funding and timing problems, but it is frequently possible to combine your attendance with some of your other consulting work. The main thing is for you to get out and market your-selves. You never know whom you might spark. I do not really have to tell you how to market yourselves. You know that much better than I. The point I want to make is that you need to educate the commissioners and staff about who you are and what you have to offer. We know you are great. Now you have to get the word out that you are a potentially valuable resource for present and future commissioners and staff.

The Marketing of Alcohol: A Spirited Debate

Michael B. Mazis

In November 1983, the Center for Science in the Public Interest (CSPI), along with twenty-eight other organizations and three individuals, filed a petition with the Federal Trade Commission (FTC) to seek Commission regulation of alcoholic beverage advertising. The petition sought a number of remedies, including a ban on all alcoholic beverage advertising aimed at large numbers of youth or problem drinkers, and rotational warnings in otherwise permissible print ads. In April 1985, the CSPI petition was denied by the FTC, which concluded that any action was unnecessary because there was no proved causal connection between alcohol advertising and alcohol abuse. Since 1985, there has been little FTC attention devoted to regulating alcoholic beverage advertising.

Significant Environmental Changes

However, three significant environmental changes have occurred that have focused attention on alcohol abuse and alcohol advertising. Such changes are causing federal and state officials to reconsider imposing restrictions on alcoholic beverage marketers' promotional practices.

Alcohol Environment

First, there has been a profound change in American drinking habits and attitudes toward drinking. We were recently reminded of this change in the pillorying of Senator John Tower at his confirmation hearing and in the publicizing of the oil spill caused by the tanker *Exxon Valdez* and its allegedly intoxicated captain.

More generally, a great deal has been written about America's new sobriety, a reflection of the aging babyboomers' preoccupation with looking better and living longer. Babyboomers have stopped smoking; they exercise; they are concerned with weight reduction; and they have begun to moderate or stop drinking alcohol.

This change is reflected by the 15 percent annual increase in sales of seltzer and water products such as Perrier and Evian, and the nearly 5 percent annual gain in sales of soft drinks, especially diet products and fruit juice. There has been a tremendous upsurge in the sales of orange juice, which is becoming increasingly segmented into variations, such as more pulp, reduced acid, and not-from-concentrate chilled juice.

These gains are being made at the expense of alcoholic beverage sales. Alcohol consumption has been declining since 1982. In 1978, 71 percent of the American public was classified as drinkers; today, that proportion has fallen to 65 percent.

Especially hard hit has been the market's distilled spirits segment, which declined more than 3 percent last year. Who drinks brands such as Seagrams-7, Jack Daniels, and J & B? People over forty are a major market for these products.

These facts have led to a major conclusion about the change in alcohol beverage consumption: it is not evenly distributed. While 80 percent of those between twenty-five and twenty-nine drink alcoholic beverages, only 58 percent of people over fifty are drinkers. These figures mean that the market has dramatically shifted to younger drinkers. Declines in alcohol consumption, like declines in cigarette use, have occurred most often with older consumers who tend to be more health conscious. Younger consumers, feeling immune from the hazards, continue to drink and to smoke.

Marketing Environment

These societal changes in alcoholic beverage consumption behavior have led to a second change: the development of new marketing strategies to cultivate the major market left to alcohol distributors—the youth market, age twenty-one to twenty-five.

Why else would we have seen the development of products such as wine coolers and Peach Schnapps, which are targeted to the youth market? Why else would we have seen *Moonlighting's* Bruce Willis advertise Seagram's coolers? Why else would we have seen the Coors Light "silver bullet" campaign featuring animated characters?

In addition, we have seen a repositioning of several brands that now cater to the youth market:

-Bud Light was introduced with the theme "bring out your best," an approach that focused on achievement-oriented babyboomers. Recently, the advertising has featured spokesdog Spuds MacKenzie. This campaign has an obvious youth orientation. Some critics claim that Spuds appeals to underage drinkers who buy Spuds's T-shirts and toys.

-Michelob popularized the slogan "weekends are made for Michelob," which appealed to young couples who served the special brew to friends and associates. Now Michelob commercials appeal to the youth market by using rock music and by showing rock stars, e.g., Phil Collins, Eric Clapton, and Steve Winwood.

-Miller Lite continues to use the fifteen-year-old "tastes great, less filling" theme in many of its ads, which feature retired athletes and aging comedians. However, in December 1988, ads that feature clay action figures and are targeted at the youth market began. Such ads will air mostly on late-night and rock programs that are seen by many underage drinkers in high school and college.

This movement toward the youth market is on a collision course with another movement—the consumer movement—that is advocating reduced alcohol use and abuse by youth.

Consumer Movement

The third major change has been the growth of the consumer anti-alcohol movement, which is a grass roots effort considerably broader than many advertisers may realize.

Of course, this movement has been led by Mothers Against Drunk Driving and Students Against Drunk Driving, which have focused on better education about responsible drinking, on training for servers in restaurants and bars, and on stiffer penalties for drunk driving offenses. The antialcohol movement, however, has begun to emphasize the role of advertising in allegedly influencing drinking by youth. For example, the 1988 National Commission Against Drunk Driving report stated that "advertising normalizes alcohol consumption and makes it difficult to raise concern about alcohol abuse." The report goes on to state:

> In the absence of alcohol industry action, legislation should be en-
> acted to regulate alcohol beverage advertising. Repeatedly, testifiers at the
> hearings voiced concern about its detrimental influence on young people;

and with near unanimity, the youths themselves declared that advertising encourages adolescents to drink. (P. 65.)

In addition, women's and medical groups have expressed concern that alcohol advertising may lead pregnant women to drink. Such drinking can lead to fetal alcohol effects and fetal alcohol syndrome in their unborn children.

Representative Conyers and other members of the Congressional Black Caucus have expressed concern about the targeting of minority communities for special alcohol promotion. Representative John Lewis, Democrat of Georgia, plans to introduce legislation aimed at encouraging cities to replace alcohol and cigarette ads (especially in inner-city areas) with public health messages on billboards.

But other groups have also participated in these efforts. The successful drive to place warning labels on alcoholic beverage containers was sponsored by a number of respected groups, including the American Academy of Pediatrics, National Parent Teachers Association, National Council on Alcoholism, Southern Baptist Convention, and Association for Retarded Citizens.

Key Events

These trends are likely to maintain public interest in alcohol beverage regulation over the next few years. Four key events will be the major source of continuing attention to alcohol beverage regulation. These four events—product liability lawsuits, alcohol warning labels, surgeon general's workshop, and voluntary efforts—will be discussed in detail below.

Product Liability

The alcoholic beverage industry is bracing for a series of product liability lawsuits in which it is blamed for causing birth defects. The first such case, which was tried in a Seattle court in May 1989, involved Candace Thorp, a thirty-nine-year-old alcoholic, who sought to recover $4 million in damages to support her four-year-old son. He requires lifetime assistance for problems such as mental retardation and physical deformity, which were attributed to fetal alcohol syndrome. The mother acknowledges drinking as much as half a fifth of Jim Beam bourbon a day while pregnant. But she claimed in court that she would have quit if she had been warned about the risks that drinking posed for her baby.

The case focused on three major issues: whether there is a link between drinking and birth defects; whether fetal alcohol syndrome is sufficiently well-known to relieve the distiller of obligations to issue specific warnings; and whether Mrs. Thorp would have stopped drinking if the warnings had been issued.

Witnesses for Jim Beam Brands testified that Mrs. Thorp was repeatedly warned by relatives and friends about the dangers of drinking alcohol while pregnant and that she and other alcoholics would not have heeded a label warning. Jim Beam also contended that the boy's problems were caused by heredity and neglect, not by his mother's alcohol abuse.

The Seattle jury apparently agreed with the defense attorney's argument that "there is overwhelming evidence that Candace Thorp would not have followed a label." The six-member jury panel deliberated for three and a half days and rejected Mrs. Thorp's lawsuit; jurors interviewed after the verdict was announced indicated that the decision was unanimous.

There are similarities between this case and recent lawsuits against cigarette makers. However, after a number of unsuccessful suits, a Newark man was awarded $400,000 in damages against a tobacco company that was held liable for the death of his wife from lung cancer.

The Thorp case, of course, will not end the issue of negligence by alcoholic beverage manufacturers. Two other federal court suits against the industry have been filed in Washington state. These suits or others may cause changes in promotional practices in the alcoholic beverage industry. Alcoholic beverage distributors may be forced to alter their advertising practices, to increase public service advertising, or to place warnings in their advertisements.

Alcohol Warning Labels

Both public pressure and the fear of product liability lawsuits caused the alcoholic beverage industry in November of 1988 to allow an alcohol warning label bill to pass Congress without a major confrontation. Such warning labels are scheduled to appear in "a conspicuous and prominent place" on every container of beer, wine, and liquor sold in the United States after November, 1989. Under law, the wording of the advisory must read:

GOVERNMENT WARNING: (1) According to the Surgeon General, women should not drink alcoholic beverages during pregnancy because of the risk of birth defects, (2) Consumption of alcoholic beverages impairs your ability to drive a car or operate machinery, and may cause health problems.

However, there is continuing controversy over the size and placement of the warning message. The Treasury Department's Bureau of Alcohol, Tobacco, and Firearms, the agency charged by Congress with the details of implementing the labeling law, has proposed that most containers carry warnings in small type—about two millimeters—and that the alcohol beverage distributors have maximum flexibility in the placement of the warnings. Therefore, the warnings may be placed on the back of the bottle, may be printed vertically, or may appear in any manner that the industry chooses.

This proposal, which has not been finalized, has enraged the sponsors of the law, Senator Strom Thurmond, Republican of South Carolina, and Representative John Conyers, Democrat of Michigan. They want labels to appear in larger print on containers over thirty ounces, in the front of all bottles and cans, and in "easily readable typeface" with dark letters on a white background. Consumer groups that backed the original legislation, including a coalition of churches, health organizations, and antialcohol advocates, can be expected to continue pressure for stronger warning labels. Also, they are expected to push for warning messages in alcohol beverage advertisements.

Surgeon General's Workshop

In addition, the current controversy over the appropriate role of alcohol in society has continued to generate governmental interest. When the 100th Congress asked U.S. Surgeon General C. Everett Koop to declare drunk driving a national crisis, he responded by organizing a workshop on drunk driving in December, 1988. The two-day gathering, which was held in Washington, D.C., consisted of ten panels, including the twelve-person advertising and marketing panel, the workshop's most controversial group.

Before the workshop started, the National Beer Wholesalers Association and the National Association of Broadcasters (NAB) won a court order forcing the advertising and marketing panel to open its meetings to the public and to the press. However, a move to stop or delay the panel's deliberations was unsuccessful. Also, the NAB and the Association of National Advertisers (ANA) turned down invitations to participate, claiming that most of the participants were already on record for supporting alcohol advertising restrictions and that there was insufficient time to prepare for the workshop.

Such actions by the industry were sharply criticized by Dr. Koop, who lambasted these associations for their boycott and for their legal actions. At the close of the workshop, Dr. Koop lashed out against the NAB, ANA, and the American Association of Advertising Agencies (AAAA) for trying to force the workshop's postponement or cancellation. He said that he would await "more helpful" input but indicated that chances of that are "slim" because of the history of smoking and health. Dr. Koop indicated that the behavior of the advertising and broadcasting industries was reminiscent of the fights twenty-five years ago over tobacco advertising and cautioned the groups against repeating past confrontations.

Following the workshop, there was predictable criticism by AAAA president John O'Toole, who described the workshop as "antialcohol," and ANA president DeWitt Helm, who referred to the workshop as a "kangaroo court." On January 31, 1989, the final day on which the surgeon general would accept comments on the workshop recommendations, the NAB, ANA, AAAA, and five other industry associations filed statements and jointly conducted a news conference, expressing their concern about the workshop recommendations.

There were seven major advertising recommendations that emerged from the workshop's advertising and marketing panel. These recommendations can be divided into three categories: unreasonable, questionable, and reasonable.

The two unreasonable recommendations that generated the most debate dealt with removing the tax deductibility of alcohol advertising and with counteradvertising:

1. Elimination of tax deductions for alcohol advertising and promotion other than price and product advertising.
2. A goal of equivalent exposure with the level of alcohol advertising for effective prohealth and safety messages.

These recommendations to restrict and to counter alcoholic beverage advertising are inappropriate because they rely on insufficient research evidence on the association between alcohol advertising and alcohol consumption. A 1985 Federal Trade Commission report concluded that "little, if any, evidence exists" to indicate that alcohol advertising causes alcohol abuse or increased alcohol consumption. In addition, the briefing document prepared for the workshop by Professor Charles Atkin cites equivocal evidence on the relationship between alcohol advertising and alcohol consumption and drunk driving.

The limited body of research is inadequate to justify the panel's recommendation to eliminate the tax deduction for alcohol promotion and advertising. This draconian recommendation is inappropriate because it falsely assumes that the industry's marketing activities encourage drunk driving.

The panel's proposal would mean that any statement, such as "a happy holiday season," would result in elimination of the business expense deduction for that particular advertisement. Only a picture of the product or a statement of its price would be allowed in order to qualify for the deduction. It is simply inappropriate to single out any individual message for adverse tax treatment because of message content. Such discriminatory tax treatment may also be unconstitutional. This action would be a back door approach to an outright ban on alcoholic beverage advertising.

In addition, the advertising and marketing panel recommended that exposure to public service information or counter advertising messages should either be equal to or achieve "parity" with commercial alcoholic beverage messages. Therefore, alcohol advertisers, broadcasters, and the public would be required to pay for these information campaigns in order to expose consumers to an equal number of pro and anti alcohol advertisements. This expensive and impractical proposal is based on the assumption that alcohol information campaigns will deter drunk driving.

However, Professor Atkin's briefing document states: "The research literature evaluating the effects of drunk driving prevention campaigns is quite meager." While public information campaigns represent a promising approach for discouraging drunk driving and alcohol misuse, significant expansion of such campaigns may not change attitudes and behavior. At this time, additional research is needed to evaluate the long-term impact of current efforts.

There are, of course, practical problems related to implementing the requirement of equivalent exposure to prohealth and safety messages. Who would pay for creation of these messages? Would the entire cost of airing such messages fall on broadcasters? What would be the impact on other important information campaigns, such as those for AIDS, drug abuse, and crime prevention? Would similar information campaigns be required to counter products high in cholesterol, fats, sugar, and salt?

The equivalent exposure standard is a radical departure from existing precedent. Even when the Federal Communications Commission's fairness doctrine was in effect, it merely called for reasonable access rather than for equal time for contrasting viewpoints. (A more reasonable goal would be a significant increase in rather than an equal number of pro-health and safety messages.)

Also, a significant increase in counteradvertising may produce unintended negative consequences. The cost of such messages by means of free broadcast time will raise the cost of advertising for all products. Ultimately, these higher advertising costs will be passed on to consumers in the form of higher prices.

These two ill-conceived recommendations should be fought by the advertising community because they could become dangerous precedents. On the other hand, the recommendation to include warning messages in all alcohol beverage advertising, while questionable, should not be totally rejected.

The advertising community understandably views this proposal with suspicion, since it might affect the ability to create effective advertising. However, warning messages have not had a demonstrable impact on cigarette advertising creativity.

Nevertheless, any action to implement this proposal is premature because the warning labels are not scheduled to appear on alcohol beverage containers until November, 1989. The impact of these messages should be evaluated before any extension to another medium is considered.

Finally, the panel's other four major recommendations are reasonable since they are directed at reducing the impact of alcohol beverage appeals to youth. Each of these proposals would require no government regulation but would rely, instead, on voluntary cooperation through revision of broadcast and industry codes. These four recommendations are:

1. elimination of alcohol advertising and promotion on college campuses where a high proportion of the audience reached is under the legal drinking age;
2. elimination of alcohol advertising, promotion, and sponsorship of public events (e.g., musical concerts and athletic contests)

where the majority of the anticipated audience is under the legal
drinking age;

3. elimination in alcohol advertising and promotion of the use of
celebrities who have a strong appeal to youth;

4. elimination of official sponsorship of athletic events (e.g., the
Olympics) by the alcohol beverage industry.

There are obstacles to implementing these recommendations. Many
universities have graduate schools, medical schools, and law schools that
are populated primarily by students above the legal drinking age and that
are in separate locations from undergraduate schools. Exceptions could be
made for these unique situations. Also, communications directed primarily to professors, alumni, and staff could be exempt from the restrictions.

Also, it may be difficult for alcoholic beverage distributors to know
the audience composition before an event is conducted. Determination of
whether a celebrity endorser has "strong appeal to youth" will be difficult
and perhaps arbitrary. However, research can provide guidance, and appropriate guidelines can be established. While these recommendations
may be difficult to implement, they should be strongly considered for
action and should be enacted into voluntary industry and media guidelines.

Voluntary Efforts

In addition to organized action by government agencies and consumer groups, a number of individuals and organizations have taken steps
to restrict alcoholic beverage advertising and marketing. Such actions can
be expected to increase in the future.

For example, the Miller Brewing Company was forced to recall a
March, 1989, advertising supplement entitled "Beachin' Times" that was
designed as a parody of spring break activities by college students. There
were protests by students at several schools, including the University of
Wisconsin and the University of Iowa. The University of Michigan's
Michigan Daily and other college publications refused to run the insert;
students at the University of Wisconsin at Madison passed a resolution
calling for a boycott of Miller products unless the advertising supplement
was withdrawn and the company apologized. Student groups criticized
the insert for depicting women in an insulting way (they were shown as
scantily-dressed "babes") and for including an account of a student vaca-

tioner's day: a twenty-four hour drinking marathon that included only two five-minute breaks for returning empties.

In addition, activities by beer companies, hotels, and restaurants at spring break resorts, such as Daytona Beach, Florida, have been criticized for encouraging irresponsible consumption of alcoholic beverages. Some hotels and restaurants advertise free drinks and two-for-one specials. One hotel sponsors a beer-guzzling contest; students compete to see who can vomit the most.

Moreover, sports teams and stadium operators, who have had a long association with the alcoholic beverage industry, have begun to reconsider this relationship. There has been increasing concern over unruly behavior by drunken fans. As a result, seventeen of the twenty-six major league baseball teams offer family sections where no alcohol is sold. At nine major league stadiums there are no beer vendors in the stands.

Even athletes have begun to speak out against the association between sports and alcohol beverage consumption. Houston Astros' first baseman Glenn Davis has objected to the toast offered by local radio and television broadcasters for one of their sponsors after he or one of his teammates hits a home run: "Glenn Davis, this Bud's for you." Davis, who does not drink and spends a lot of time telling children not to drink, has objected to what he perceives as his implied endorsement of alcoholic beverages. As a result of his protest, Davis's name will no longer be used in the commercials.

Finally, NCAA Executive Director Richard Schultz has proposed the elimination of beer advertising during NCAA championship events. The NCAA's current three-year contract with CBS to broadcast college basketball tournament games calls for no more than ninety seconds per hour of beer commercials. Schultz has argued that such advertising is inconsistent with his association's strong antidrug policy and its anti-alcohol-abuse public service announcements. However, under pressure from beer marketers and college athletic directors, Schultz is likely to drop his proposal.

These efforts suggest that alcoholic beverage advertising is likely to be challenged for many years. Not only will government officials and consumer advocates continue to press for restrictions, but private individuals and associations will seek changes as well. The pattern for alcoholic beverages is similar to the pattern for cigarettes. As consumption declines, the demands for greater restriction on alcohol beverage promotion grows.

Conclusion

There are three major conclusions from this analysis of the new environment facing alcoholic beverage marketers and the advertising community. First, the social and political climates are changing. Fewer consumers are drinking alcoholic beverages, and there is greater concern about the dangers of alcohol abuse. Although the alcohol industry has responded by mounting a series of public service announcements and by training alcoholic beverage servers, the public perceives the need for more responsible alcoholic beverage promotion. Alcohol beverage marketers must recognize that there is growing support of restrictive legislation and voluntary restraints.

Also, advertisers and broadcasters must recognize that the current tactics followed by alcoholic beverage distributors may not serve the long-term interests of the marketing and media communities. As a December 19, 1989, *Advertising Age* editorial observed, the calls for more restraints on beer industry marketing efforts "aren't from prohibitionists, nor are they from the critics who blame advertising for the nation's drinking problems." Complaints are coming from organizations concerned with the "deluge of advertising messages that rain down on young people." The promotional efforts tend to overwhelm public service messages that stress that alcohol is a drug that needs to be consumed responsibly.

Advertisers need to speak out about this problem rather than offer an uncritical defense of alcohol beverage marketing tactics. Currently, Dr. Koop and the public view advertisers in a negative light; a more responsible stance by the industry might help to turn around this unfavorable perception of advertisers.

Second, each proposal to restrict alcoholic beverage advertising and promotional activities must be carefully evaluated. Advertisers and alcoholic beverage distributors reject all proposals that call for restraint, seeing them as infringement on their constitutional freedom to advertise. However, the courts have consistently supported restrictions on the sale and promotion of cigarettes and alcoholic beverages, because they are hazardous products. It is time to stop the "knee-jerk" rejection of every proposal.

On the other hand, neoprohibitionist consumer advocates should refrain from recommending punitive measures, such as banning alcohol advertisements, eliminating tax deductions for alcohol advertising, and requiring "tombstone" messages. Such draconian proposals are quickly rejected as unreasonable and unworkable; these extreme views tend to undermine the efforts of those seeking to curb the most important abuses— youth-oriented alcoholic beverage promotional activity.

Third, there is a need for responsible members of the media, advertising, and alcoholic beverage constituencies to act now to set up a voluntary mechanism to curb youth-oriented alcohol promotion. Perhaps the Children's Advertising Review Unit or some other independent entity could develop workable standards. Unless action is taken soon, intrusive and unwelcome government intervention is a likely outcome.

Charting a Public Policy Agenda for Cigarettes

Joel B. Cohen

This paper examines the public policy and regulatory dilemmas posed by the manufacture, sale, and use of cigarettes.[1] There is general agreement that the health consequences of consumers' use of this product are profound, yet many are troubled by proposals for government action. The overall analysis is not policy-neutral. The author believes it is appropriate for, even incumbent on, government to reduce the magnitude of smoking-induced health consequences.

We first examine the uniqueness of cigarettes as a mass-marketed product, including concerns over the role of marketing and advertising in smoking initiation and reinforcement. We then discuss an array of policy alternatives and appraise their current status.

Cigarettes: A Unique Product

Cigarettes are unique among products marketed in the United States because, when used as intended, they have been determined to reduce life expectancy significantly and to increase the risk of serious illnesses greatly. More than one out of four of all regular cigarette smokers die of smoking-related diseases.

To provide an overall sense of societal impact, we note that while heroin and cocaine together are estimated to kill approximately 5,000 Americans annually, this tragic state of affairs is dwarfed by the surgeon general's conclusion that cigarette smoking is responsible for over 390,000 unnecessary deaths each year in this country alone.[2] That is, approximately 1 out of 6 deaths in the United States is attributable to cigarette smoking. Cigarette smoking has become the single most pre-

234

ventable cause of death and disability in the United States. The human toll from cigarette smoking is staggering:

Surgeon General's Findings: Consequences of Cigarette Smoking

1. responsible for 85-90 percent of the 120,000 annual lung cancer deaths and is a major cause of cancer of the larynx, oral cavity, and esophagus and a contributing factor in cancer of the urinary tract, bladder, kidney, and pancreas
2. the major cause of chronic bronchitis and emphysema and responsible for over 80 percent of deaths from chronic obstructive pulmonary diseases
3. a prime contributor to 21 percent of coronary heart disease deaths and 18 percent of stroke deaths
4. leads to a significantly elevated risk of miscarriage, stillbirth, premature births, and birth-weight deficiencies
5. resulted, in 1985, in the United States health care system spending an estimated $22 billion to treat smoking-related diseases (of which the government paid about $4.2 billion), while lost productivity costs due to smoking-related illnesses and premature deaths were estimated to be upwards of $43 billion
6. leads to the ingestion of hazardous tobacco additives, gases, and other chemical constituents whose identity continues to go undisclosed (Report of the Surgeon General 1989)

Though smoking among adults has dropped from 40 percent in 1965 to 29 percent in 1987, approximately 55 million Americans still smoke. Elsewhere, however, smoking is on the increase. For example, between 1971 and 1981, increases in cigarette consumption exceeded population growth by significant amounts in the developing nations of Africa, Asia, and Latin America, where cigarette marketing and advertising is largely unrestricted.

Finally, despite the fact that nearly half of all living adults who ever smoked have quit, nicotine has been firmly established as a dangerously addictive drug. This gives added meaning to survey evidence indicating that 80 percent of remaining smokers report that they would like to quit and that two-thirds have made at least one serious attempt to quit.

The Controversy over Cigarette Marketing and Advertising

While critics condemn both the amount and types of advertising and promotion used to market cigarettes, cigarette industry officials argue that many products are promoted using similar themes and appeals; many industries utilize sophisticated consumer research to identify segments of consumers for whom particular appeals are likely to enhance sales. In short, the industry position is that they are being assailed for simply being effective. Further, many industry spokespersons advance the view that advertising is highly overrated as a causal factor in smoking initiation, citing peer influence and parental modeling as more important factors.

The Magnitude of Marketing Efforts

In order to understand better some of the public policy proposals (e.g., tombstone advertising), it is useful to present some of the concerns about cigarette marketing and advertising in more depth. First is the concern over the magnitude of these efforts. In 1988 the tobacco industry spent close to $2.5 billion (roughly $6.5 million a day) for advertising and promotion. Commentators add that the purpose and economic justification for such expenditures is to attract new users, retain current users, increase consumption, and generate favorable attitudes and symbolic associations toward smoking and specific brands.

The vast majority of new smokers are teenagers or younger (by one estimate, 60 percent are under fourteen years of age). There is particular concern over the effects of cigarette advertising on children and teenagers. Unless the present rate of initiation into smoking is lowered from its present 29 percent, public health officials expect that of the 70 million children now living in the U.S., over 5 million will die of smoking-related diseases.

There has been a dramatic shift in the allocation of the overall marketing budget, with the result that promotional expenditures now account for over 60 percent of marketing expenditures compared to only 25 percent in 1975. Analysts point out that, increasingly, cigarette companies have promoted their products through sponsorship of sporting events and concerts (thereby appearing to target a youthful segment of the market) and through special promotions. These include the use of logos on nontobacco products having special appeal to teenagers and paying to have cigarettes displayed in youth-oriented movies, including a new James Bond film (for which Philip Morris paid $350,000), *Superman II,* and *Supergirl* (Luken 1989). Promotional expenditures include coupons for price reductions, free product samples, incentives paid to distributors and retailers as well as sponsorship activities.

Assessing Effects of Cigarette Advertising and Promotion

The tobacco industry has argued that advertising informs consumers about brand differences and leads to brand switching rather than to smoking initiation. Critics emphasize advertising's role in glamorizing smoking, attracting new smokers, and impeding the efforts of smokers to quit. Incontrovertible proof of either position would require data that simply do not exist and experiments that cannot be run.

For example, unconfounded large-scale interruptions in cigarette advertising (sufficient to test for long-term changes in smoking behavior) have not occurred in the U.S. As a result, studies are forced to extrapolate from far less meaningful incremental changes in advertising expenditures and sales. In addition, (1) new smokers are a small proportion of total smokers, and (2) the effect of a modest change in advertising is unlikely to alter the amount smoked by those already accustomed to a particular number of cigarettes (e.g., a pack-a-day smoker is unlikely to become a pack-and-a-half-a-day smoker as a result of a small increase in advertising expenditures). Thus, *in the aggregate,* strong advertising effects on smoking initiation may well be swamped by the magnitude of the effects of smoking reinforcement and brand switching.

No statistical analysis can be safely generalized beyond both the sensitivity and scope of the data on which it is based. Critics argue that unless tobacco companies are able and willing to provide data that are capable of isolating advertising and promotion effects on particular segments (e.g., new smokers, those whose incidence of smoking has changed disproportionately over a certain period of time) and for particular cigarette categories (e.g., menthol cigarettes—which have increased substantially in popularity, particularly among black consumers), stronger effects may well be masked. They point to several of the more sophisticated econometric studies that did detect reliable market expansion effects of advertising by disaggregating advertising expenditures for different markets (Report of the Surgeon General 1989, 499-501). For example, Roberts and Samuelson (1988) found that advertising for low-tar cigarettes increased the market demand for cigarettes in general.[3]

The scope of the data is a further concern for those wishing to estimate long-term effects of advertising and promotion or the effects of a ban on such activities. Year-to-year marginal changes in expenditures cannot, of course, capture the broad sweep of advertising effects that critics argue did much to create social acceptability (e.g., the specific targeting of women in this regard is frequently highlighted) as well as to enhance the social and symbolic significance of cigarettes.

Because of the difficulty of extrapolating from U.S. econometric studies to examine more long-term effects, the results of advertising bans in other countries have been scrutinized by those on both sides of the question, and there is a lack of consensus as to the meaning of these results. Unfortunately, such analyses are confounded by circumstances unique to each country. For example, many such bans have been either partial (i.e., allowing tobacco promotion through sponsorship of sporting events or providing few restrictions on package design or other forms of advertising), or they have been poorly enforced, or both.

Also, comparing changes in smoking rates across countries requires the careful consideration of cultural and attitudinal factors. For these reasons, comparisons between individual countries are not likely to be meaningful unless such factors are taken into account. Citing flaws in previous tobacco industry-associated studies, New Zealand commissioned its own thirty-three-country study and concluded: "When countries were grouped according to the degree of governmental restriction of tobacco promotion, the greater the degree of restriction the greater the average annual fall in tobacco consumption. This was also true for the rate of decrease in the percentage of adults and young people who smoke" (New Zealand Toxic Substances Board 1989, 64).

In evaluating aggregate and comparative analyses of advertising's impact, the situation is analogous to estimating the effects of a physical force (e.g., a push) on an object (e.g., a toy car). The same push could be associated with the car moving one foot forward, ten feet forward, or even two feet backward, depending on the slope of the roadway (i.e., flat, downhill, or uphill) and other forces that could act in either direction. With imperfect information as to all the other forces that affect aggregate sales of cigarettes (e.g., changes/differences in demographics, taxes, publicity involving health concerns), it is virtually impossible to isolate the effect of advertising. Thus, in our toy car analogy, if advertising is the push in question, we can see how attempting to isolate its strength based only on the distance the car moves is fraught with difficulty.

Once we move away from large-scale statistical analyses, the debate over advertising and promotion effects centers on three issues:

1. Do these enormous advertising and promotion expenditures make economic sense for cigarette companies if their intention is

merely to retain existing smokers and encourage brand switching?

2. Assuming the above is the intent, How is it possible to spend
such sums without both attracting new smokers and making it
more difficult for existing smokers to quit?

3. Is it plausible that this is the full intent, given the content and
placement of cigarette advertising and promotion?

It is, of course, difficult to know how much advertising and promotion is necessary to retain one's present customers and successfully to
encourage switching from competitors' products. Given the profitability
of cigarettes, substantial expenditures for such purposes may well be
justified on economic grounds. Many, however, are skeptical that the
tobacco industry would be willing to spend $9 per person per year for
advertising and promotion (Warner 1986) simply to chase the approximately 10 percent of smokers who switch brands in an average year
(Report of the Surgeon General 1989, 503). Since most merely switch
among brands of Philip Morris and R.J. Reynolds, who control approximately two-thirds of the U.S. cigarette market, this seems to give added
weight to critics' charges that the goals of advertising and promotion are
somewhat broader.

Also, aggregate analyses and a product life-cycle approach to marketing strategy have led to the "mature market fallacy." This obscures the
fact that even in stable or shrinking markets, customers who leave the
market are being replaced by new users. So, even though the cigarette
industry is referred to by some as a "mature market," it has been estimated
(Myers and Hollar 1989) that some 6,000 new smokers must be recruited
each day just to replace the 1.5 million who quit, the almost 400,000
smokers who die each year from smoking-related diseases, and those who
die of other causes.

Unfortunately, inherent weaknesses in the scope and sensitivity of
the aggregate statistical analyses of U.S. advertising-sales correlations
make it impossible to provide a precise estimate of how much of the
responsibility for smoking initiation has been due to advertising and
promotion. At the individual level, asking people to recall why they
started to smoke, as has been done in some tobacco industry-sponsored
studies, is simply bad science. If this were a valid way to estimate the
impact of advertising, this simple method would be widely used to evaluate both overall expenditure levels and particular campaigns. Such is not

the case. Instead, advertising effects are typically studied by examining variables linked to comprehension, memory, attitudes, behavioral intentions, and sales data, often using sophisticated experimental designs and measurements. It is virtually impossible for a person to be aware of the cumulative effect of persuasive appeals, pictorial images, and subtle associations, not to mention his or her being unwilling to report having been persuaded by advertising.

Accordingly, the debate often centers on the logic of the industry's position regarding the limited brand-switching effects of its expenditures. The industry view places very little weight on the ability of advertising to create or enhance a desire to smoke. Yet one has to wonder whether it is possible to implement advertising and promotion of such magnitude and over many years without making smoking appear to be a desirable and attractive activity for children and teenagers.

This line of argument holds that cigarette advertising and promotion is virtually guaranteed to enhance the attractiveness of smoking because the assortment of brands and the identities they symbolize are designed to create an almost ideal psychosocial fit for the potential smoker. Brands of cigarettes come to have unique drawing powers that extend and modify the act of smoking itself. Considerable time and expense are devoted to consumer research and advertising executions by each competing firm to produce advertising having maximum appeal to particular target segments (e.g., young women, blacks, health-concerned). There has been no convincing defense of a view that would make young nonsmokers immune to the well-established effects of such advertising.

Finally, apart from the magnitude of its effects or its relative weight in converting nonsmokers to smokers, many see any enticement to smoke cigarettes as counter to the public interest (and perhaps morally wrong) in and of itself.

The industry view tends to frame advertising effects in a limited way: Did a certain set of ads in a certain period of time cause a person to smoke? By framing the issue in this way, we assign more responsibility to the decision maker and more weight to precipitating factors in the immediate situation (e.g., peer influence, parental smoking). When our perspective is enlarged to include multiyear campaigns designed to attract particular target segments (e.g., women, blacks, Hispanics) and major promotional programs (e.g., free cigarettes to servicemen in wartime), the more significant effects of tobacco marketing are seen in sharper focus.

Indeed, prior to the time of widespread awareness of cigarette-related illnesses, tobacco and advertising industry representatives took considerable credit for generating social acceptability for cigarettes. Pollay (1988), for example, offers interesting accounts of how compelling brand images were established among present-day smokers' parents and grandparents. Most social scientists would acknowledge that peer influence and social modeling are quite important, but this begs the question of how cigarette smoking came to be part of the behavior that children and adolescents attend to and model. Such indirect effects of advertising complement more direct enticements.

With respect to behavioral targets, critics see advertising and promotion as powerful factors in attracting replacement smokers from among key target groups (e.g., adolescents, minorities, and lower socioeconomic groups). Given the profitability of cigarettes and the economic incentive of attracting new smokers, many have doubted industry assertions that they did not seek to encourage people to smoke. Documents made public in conjunction with product liability actions and the Canadian ban (to be discussed later) have not been helpful to the industry's credibility or their position on this issue.[4] Considered in total, there is considerable evidence of systematic industry attention to factors that motivate people to smoke and to continue smoking in the face of health risks.

Even if critics have misjudged the intent of particular campaigns, young people are particularly vulnerable to many of the themes used in cigarette advertising. Cigarette advertising is rich in imagery and symbolic associations, including exciting lifestyles, masculinity and femininity, and the trappings of success and sophistication. It is not possible to draw a magic curtain around children and teenagers who seek to learn how to fit into the adult world. Further, cigarette advertising messages are more like visually oriented experiences than verifiable propositions. They tend to bypass logical analysis (e.g., Puto and Wells, 1984) and, with constant repetition, produce brand images that help people create and communicate desired self-identities. Their appeal to teenagers and others for whom self-identification and presentation are particular concerns must be matters of particular importance in this public policy domain.

Policy Alternatives

Some of the more noteworthy public policy developments of the past twenty-five years that affect the sale and use of cigarettes are listed in table

1. Currently, a range of further actions are under discussion and will be reviewed in this section. The most extreme restrictions would limit either the sale or use of cigarettes. Other actions would alter the consumer information environment, either by restricting advertising and promotion or by strengthening educational and health warning programs. Additional proposals stress economic disincentives and greater regulatory control over the manufacture and sale of tobacco products. A final issue reflects growing concern over the export of cigarettes to other countries.

Restrictions on Cigarette Sales

The suggestion of an outright ban on the sale of cigarettes often invokes the response that prohibition didn't work and further, that making the sale of cigarettes illegal and thereby branding many millions of people criminals is not in the public interest. Sentiment over freedom of choice runs very deep, especially on matters that appear to involve personal consequences rather than broad societal concerns. However, several types of lesser restrictions are receiving consideration, though the regulatory setting is a stumbling block to action.

TABLE 1

Actions Affecting Cigarette Sales and Use

Year	Action
1965	Congress approved legislation requiring warning labels for cigarette packages.
1970	Congress approved legislation prohibiting cigarette advertising on radio and television and strengthened the cigarette package warning label.
1973	Congress approved legislation to include little cigars in the radio and television broadcast advertising ban.
1982	Congress approved legislation to double the federal excise tax on cigarettes and cigars from $.08 to $.16 per pack.
1984	Congress approved legislation requiring that stronger warning statements appear on labels and in advertisements for cigarettes on a rotating basis.
1986	Congress approved legislation banning smokeless tobacco advertising from radio and television and requiring warning labels on smokeless tobacco product packages and in smokeless tobacco print advertisements.
1987	Congress approved legislation banning smoking on airplane flights of two hours or less.
1988	A jury hearing the *Cipollone* case found that smoking was the cause of death of a woman who had begun smoking in 1941 and died in 1984 from lung cancer. It awarded her husband $400,000 in damages. Further, the jury found that advertising had made express warranties about health aspects of cigarettes.
1973-1988	Beginning with Arizona and supported by the 1975 Minnesota Clean Indoor Air Act, by 1987 84 percent of the states and many governmental agencies and communities had enacted regulations to safeguard workers and occupants of public places from exposure to cigarette smoke.

For example, under the Federal Food, Drug, and Cosmetic Act, a drug is misbranded and can be removed from sale if it is falsely labeled. One might argue that failing to reveal the fact that the product contains nicotine (an addictive drug), the fact that forty-three known carcinogenic agents are contained in tobacco smoke, and the types of additives employed to make low tar cigarettes (Report of the Surgeon General 1989, 79-94) each constitutes mislabeling. The Food and Drug Administration has, however, taken the position that it does not have authority over tobacco products. Also, Congress has apparently exempted tobacco from regulation under the Consumer Products Safety Act, the Toxic Substances Act, the Fair Labeling and Packaging Act, the Controlled Substances Act, and the Federal Hazardous Substances Act.[5] Thus, new legislation seems necessary for any restrictions on the sale of improperly labeled cigarettes.

One recent bill contains provisions that would ban the sale of those cigarettes for which the FDA was not provided with a list of all tobacco additives. Further, the FDA would be required to determine the safety of such additives and other constituents of tobacco smoke. Additives found to be unsafe would be prohibited, and stronger labeling and informational requirements for constituents and risks would be mandated. Finally, a separate nicotine warning would be added to the warning label (on a rotated basis).

A focal point of other proposals is to further reduce sales to children and teenagers. Though forty-three states and the District of Columbia restrict the sale of cigarettes to minors, there are gaps in these laws, and enforcement is bleak.[6] A more uniform and comprehensive bill to ban sales to minors (similar to those enacted by Canada and Great Britain) has been recently introduced. Among its provisions is a ban on sales of tobacco products in any place that people under eighteen years of age may lawfully enter unless the product is sold over-the-counter and by the proprietor or an employee (i.e., hence not by a vending machine).

Restrictions on Cigarette Smoking

Just as the tobacco industry and many smokers proclaim the right to choose to smoke cigarettes (thus providing strong opposition to an outright ban on smoking), so too nonsmokers' rights have become a major issue. There is mounting evidence of health risks to nonsmokers. For example, the risk of lung cancer is 30 percent higher for nonsmoking spouses of smokers (Report of the Surgeon General 1989, 78). Since recent

studies have found that as high as 90 percent of nonsmokers had traces of
cotinine, a breakdown product of nicotine, in their urine—including over
80 percent of those who did not live with a smoker—there is increasing
pressure to ban or restrict smoking in public buildings, work places, and
public transportation.[7] Recently Congress has enacted a ban on smoking
aboard all domestic commercial flights. Such actions appear to reflect
significant underlying support for the rights of nonsmokers and an accompanying drop in the social acceptability of smoking. Survey evidence
indicates that approximately 80 percent believe that tobacco smoke is
harmful for those nearby (Report of the Surgeon General 1989, 200).
With respect to the public's attitudes toward restrictions on smoking,
numerous surveys have documented overwhelming support for some types
of restrictions. For example, even a controversial recent Tobacco Institute
sponsored survey found that 76 percent supported employer-employee
agreements designating places where employees may smoke, and 20 percent supported a total ban on smoking in work places. Further, 74 percent
favored the current policy of restaurants offering smoking and nonsmoking sections, and 24 percent favored prohibiting all smoking in restaurants.

Restrictions on Cigarette Advertising and Promotion

Though legislation to ban all advertising and promotion of tobacco
products has been proposed, it has typically run into strong opposition
along three lines: (1) the claim that an advertising ban is unconstitutional,
(2) the claim that such a ban would be ineffective, and (3) the claim that a
ban would lead to similar restrictions on other consumer products (Myers
and Hollar 1989).

The constitutional issue posed by cigarette advertising involves the
regulation of commercial speech, the substantiality of the public interest,
and whether the remedy is not more extensive than is necessary. A further
analysis of this issue is beyond the scope of this paper. As to a standard of
proof for judging the effectiveness of such a ban, it is difficult to extrapolate from econometric studies of incremental effects or to draw close
parallels with similar bans in other countries.

Experts differ in their assessment of the precise effects of an ad ban
and point out that these would depend on how extensive it was and how
long it was in effect. For example, since many of the important brand and
product symbolic associations are now well established, different types of

promotional activities (e.g., event sponsorship, signs, the use of brand logos on nontobacco products), if unregulated, may be quite effective by themselves, at least in the short run.

A "slippery slope" argument—if advertising for cigarettes is banned, next there will be pressure to ban it for other products demonstrated to be unhealthy in various degrees—seems to assume that responsible government bodies are incapable of making distinctions between acceptable and unacceptable levels of risk in relation to the utility of a product.[8] But protecting the health and safety of its citizens is one of the overriding obligations of government, thus this responsibility should not be so easily evaded.

A final issue raised by proponents of an advertising ban is the possible indirect effect of advertising revenues on the print media's coverage of smoking and health issues. A number of studies report an inverse relationship between a magazine's dependence on tobacco revenue and its coverage of tobacco health and related stories. Warner (1986) cites examples of reported censorship in magazines and newspapers.

The Canadian Initiative. The Tobacco Products Control Act became enforceable in Canada in January, 1989. All Canadian magazine and newspaper advertising of tobacco products ceased, and the voluntary ban on broadcast ads became mandatory. The dollar value of billboard and poster advertising is to be reduced by one-third each year until termination in January, 1991. All on-premise retail signs will be prohibited after January, 1993. In addition, the use of tobacco brand names on nontobacco items (e.g., racing cars, T-shirts) was banned, although brand name sponsorships in place on January, 1988, may continue but at 1987 levels of support.[9] Free distribution of tobacco products as well as the use of rebates, contests, and prizes was also prohibited. The bill contains other provisions that will not be discussed here (e.g., companies must provide information on toxic constituents and have an obligation to warn consumers fully). One interesting provision gives the government the ability to exempt a tobacco product when it is likely to be used as a substitute for other tobacco products and poses less risk to the health of users than those other products.

A series of legal challenges to this Act has been initiated. The courts must now consider important constitutional issues raised by the government's decision to restrict freedom of expression in order to protect the health of its citizens as well as to consider factual evidence regarding the role of advertising and promotion as an inducement to purchase.

Restrictions on Image Advertising. Many in the U.S. consider a Canadian-style ban to be unattainable politically. As a result, they have focused on those aspects of advertising that may play the most significant role in smoking initiation. Among generally similar bills, the Children's Health Protection Act of 1989 would prohibit the use in tobacco advertising of human figures and facsimiles, brand logos and symbols, and pictures other than that of a single package (no larger than actual size) against a neutral white background. Further, the product package must comply with similar restrictions. No tobacco ads would be permitted in stadiums or sports facilities or on sports-related equipment (e.g., racing cars, boats). It would be unlawful to distribute tobacco products as free samples or at reduced cost, or to sponsor any athletic, musical, or similar events in the name of a registered brand name or so that a tobacco product is associated with the event (unless the brand name was also the corporate name prior to January, 1986). Nontobacco products (e.g., clothing, toys) or services could not use a tobacco product brand name or symbol (except as above), nor could a tobacco company pay to have the product or its name and symbol appear in any movie, television show, or other form of entertainment (except as above). Tobacco products advertised or promoted in violation of the above provisions would be a misbranded drug under the Federal Food, Drug, and Cosmetic Act.

Such proposed text only advertising restrictions have come under attack as "tombstone advertising." Its opponents also invoke both first amendment and "slippery slope" arguments (e.g., *Advertising Age,* April 3, 1989). Proponents argue that such bills would allow tobacco companies to communicate product information, hence the bills do not restrict commercial speech more than is necessary to prohibit the images, depictions, and symbolic associations most likely to entice children to begin smoking.

Strengthening Consumer Knowledge and Defenses

Owing to a lack of regulatory agency jurisdiction over the health-related aspects of tobacco, little information has been disseminated regarding the potentially harmful constituents and additives used in tobacco products. Stronger labeling requirements for nicotine and other harmful constituents and additives would close this gap but would require Congress to institute major changes in regulatory authority. However, adding a specific warning that nicotine is an addictive drug has received bipartisan support in Congress following the surgeon general's strong finding in 1988 and has obtained the endorsement of many health organizations and other groups.

There is concern over the visibility and impact of the existing warnings (e.g., moving them to the front of cigarette packages and using eye-catching symbols would certainly increase the attention they received). By itself, however, strengthening the warnings is unlikely to have a pronounced effect on cigarette smoking. Warnings are helpful and signal some level of government concern. However, the dire consequences they present are long-term in nature. Thus a smoker may overweight the absence of short-term symptoms, particularly since the certainty of consequences does not extend to the individual level. Further, some fear that the contradiction between the healthy and vigorous people appearing in the ads and the product warnings may lead people to believe that the warnings are overstated (e.g., that smoking in moderation may be okay) or that the product may not be hazardous to all smokers.

Since our focus is on emerging actions and proposals, we will not review the status of ongoing smoking prevention and cessation activities (such as school-based programs). These important continuing efforts are reviewed in some detail in the 1989 surgeon general's Report (chapter 6).

The Coalition on Smoking OR Health has advocated legislation to mandate a federally funded program of antitobacco public service announcements. Myers and Hollar (1989) note that counteradvertising in the late 1960s (resulting from the application of the fairness doctrine) probably played an important role in reducing tobacco consumption (although it is difficult to estimate the magnitude of this effect in relation to other factors; e.g., McAuliffe 1988).

Those who prefer to focus on informational goals (i.e., taking a neutral view as to normatively "correct" behavior) might wish to emphasize this approach to the smoking and health problem, since information is enhanced rather than restricted. This might also appeal to those who stress improving the ability of consumers to make informed choices.

Others, of course, question whether it is reasonable to adopt a behavior-neutral stance given the magnitude of the health-related consequences of smoking. Further, many of those who generally prefer informed choice solutions have some difficulty with the proposition that providing health-related information by itself is likely to balance the scales relative to extremely sophisticated and powerful enticements to smoke. They note that 25 percent of the smokers-to-be who would be asked to weigh this information will have had their first cigarette by sixth grade, 50 percent by eighth grade (Report of the Surgeon General 1989, 296). One suggestion, then, is that ads making smoking look foolish and "uncool" could comprise an effective counteradvertising program. Financing a counteradvertising program to compete effectively against a $2.5 billion advertising and promotion budget is likely to be a major obstacle, although each penny of additional federal excise tax on cigarettes would generate close to $300 million. A combination of reductions in industry expenditures and industry funding for counteradvertising might be another option (Myers and Hollar 1989).

Economic Disincentives

Direct economic disincentives on the consumer side include excise taxes (which would raise prices) and higher insurance premiums. On the producer/seller side, economic disincentives include lowering tobacco price supports, denying tax deductions for advertising expenses, and product liability suits.

Consumer Disincentives. The federal excise tax (now 16¢ per pack) produces about $5 billion in revenues. It has been increased only once since 1951 and has declined in real terms since 1964. All states, the District of Columbia, and close to four hundred localities impose additional excise taxes ranging from a low of 2¢ per pack to a high of 38¢, with an average of 18¢ per pack (Report of the Surgeon General 1989, 525).

Research on the effect of excise taxes on demand shows that for every 10 percent increase in the price of cigarettes there is a 5 to 7 percent reduction in the quantity of cigarettes sold, with a greater effect on the smoker participation rate than the number of cigarettes smoked (Lewit and Coate 1982). Further, the price elasticity of demand for cigarettes appears to be much higher among teenagers than adults (possibly as a consequence of addiction as well as economic factors), suggesting that increases in excise taxes may have a particular effect on the teenage participation rate. Indeed, one estimate (Harris 1987) is that the 8¢ per pack increase in 1983 has led to 600,000 fewer teenagers smoking and will ultimately result in 100,000 additional persons living to age sixty-five (see Report of the Surgeon General 1989, 529-34). Given these results, there is little wonder that increases in excise taxes are viewed so favorably by those seeking to discourage cigarette smoking. In addition, revenues generated could be used to fund worthy activities in this area, such as consumer education programs or health care.

Insurance premiums present a mixed picture. At present, universal life insurance offers discounts from 12 to 20 percent, leading to annual savings for men on a $50,000 policy of between $48 at age twenty-five and $299 at age fifty-five. However, health insurers tend not to offer discounts to nonsmokers. Since actuarial data documenting differential health care costs are less developed, and widely used group policies typically minimize individual health factors, this situation may not change dramatically (Report of the Surgeon General 1989, 540-49).[10] However, a combination of consumer and manufacturer taxes might be imposed to pay for the otherwise unrecoverable health costs that nonsmokers have to bear as a result of cigarette-induced illness and death. Another alternative would be to alter medicare premiums to cover such overall costs and to provide incentives for smoking cessation treatments.

Producer/Seller Disincentives. Several bills have been introduced that would deny tobacco companies a tax deduction for cigarette advertising expenses, pointing out that, in effect, this is a public subsidy. However, strong objections were raised regarding the discriminatory nature of this legislation (i.e., while almost certainly constitutional, this "backdoor" approach may seem more unfair than a direct challenge to the advertising itself). Thus, at present this approach does not appear to be viable.

Another area of controversy involves the tobacco price support program which cost $280 million in 1987 (Myers and Hollar 1989). The Coalition on Smoking OR Health has been proposing the elimination of this price support program combined with financial assistance (possibly from an increase in the excise tax) to farmers who are willing to stop growing tobacco.

A final economic disincentive is the threat of product liability suits. A recent jury verdict went against tobacco interests (*Cipollone v. Liggett et al.*), producing three major outcomes:

1. the monetary award of $400,000 (which did not cover the costs of prosecuting the case);

2. the release of extensive and previously confidential strategy and research documents from company and Tobacco Institute files, paving the way for future cases; and

3. the willingness of a jury to determine that cigarette advertising has made express warranties about health aspects of cigarettes and that these contributed to the person's smoking and death.

The revelations of industry tactics that resulted from the release of company and Tobacco Institute documents (see note 4) has increased pressure on Congress to clarify the extent and nature of its preemption of state law covering product liability suits. In several cases, including *Cipollone,* courts (backed up by three appellate decisions) did not allow the introduction of evidence of company failure to warn and negligence after 1966 (when the Cigarette Labeling and Advertising Act took effect). Both the likelihood and magnitude of awards in the future will depend on judicial clarification of (1) underlying liability theories (e.g., risk-utility concepts, reliance on implied warranties from advertising); and (2) implications of preemption for the admissability and weight given to the conduct of both the smoker and the cigarette company after 1966.

A number of jurists and legislators have subsequently expressed the conviction that Congress by mandating a particular warning could not possibly have intended to shield tobacco companies from all responsibility to warn consumers or to give companies license to fail intentionally to disclose important health information by mandating a particular warning. "The ultimate irony is: the cigarette companies can now escape liability for their deceptive ads because the federal courts have misinterpreted a law which was intended to impede the use of this death-dealing product by giving consumers more, not less, information" (letter from Representatives Whittaker and Luken urging cosponsorship of the Cigarette Testing and Liability Act, May 11, 1988). However, until Congress acts or the Supreme Court overturns lower court decisions, consumers' injuries resulting primarily from smoking in the post-1966 period may be immune from recovery under product liability theories.

Increased Regulatory Control

We have already discussed the regulatory problems associated with a lack of oversight by any agency specifically charged with protecting the health and safety of the public. There is substantial interest in possible congressional action to declare tobacco products an addictive drug (to be regulated by the Food and Drug Administration). Thus, there is at least the potential for the Food and Drug Administration to acquire broad power to examine tobacco additives and constituents, require appropriate disclosures of potential harm, require reductions or deletion of certain additives, and insure that the information provided in advertising is not in conflict with these determinations.

The recent withdrawal of Premier by R.J. Reynolds, after disappointing consumer acceptance, saved the Food and Drug Administration (and perhaps Congress and the courts) from being forced to decide: (1) whether a product that looked like a cigarette but had very little tobacco (i.e., a heated cylinder delivered tobacco flavor and, of course, nicotine) and (2) that called itself "the cleaner smoke" and was described as "substantially reducing many of the controversial compounds found in the smoke of tobacco-burning cigarettes" was subject to regulation as a drug.

Foreign Trade Policy

The aggressive exporting of tobacco products, particularly to Asia and Third World nations (these have doubled since 1983), and the steep rise in their per capita cigarette consumption has led to the prediction that tobacco will soon become the leading cause of premature, preventable mortality there—ironically, just as major gains are being made to curb deaths from malnutrition and infectious diseases (Aoki et al. 1988; Connelly 1989). To be a leading exporter of nicotine when we condemn other nations for failing to exercise responsible control over their export of other dangerous drugs strikes many as an obvious contradiction. Nevertheless, tobacco exports appear to be given highly favorable treatment by U.S. trade representatives, backed by influential members of Congress (Connelly 1988).

Proposals in this area range widely—from consumer information efforts to prohibitions on promoting tobacco sales abroad. There may be some support for legislation that would require similar health warnings on tobacco products and advertising designed for use in other countries, especially since the level of knowledge concerning tobacco and health is quite variable in many developing nations. In this regard, Connelly (1988) notes that several U.S. companies selling "light" cigarettes abroad had 50 percent higher tar and nicotine yields than the same brands sold here, raising the issue as to whether a disclosure of these levels should be required for exports.

Pressures for Future Action

Though it is difficult to predict the fate of the various public policy options we have discussed, there is increasing pressure on Congress to act in some way. The last several surgeon general's reports have stressed the magnitude of cigarette-related mortality and illness, and the confirmation by the surgeon general that nicotine is a dangerously addictive drug adds another dimension. Further, these reports have led to intensified efforts by health-concerned groups to push Congress to action. One way to summarize the effects of the medical evidence is that cigarettes are now identified as being sufficiently different from any other product so that they can reasonably be singled out for special treatment. This identification of cigarettes as a unique product weakens fears that congressional action in the tobacco arena would serve as a precedent for extensions to other products (i.e., the "slippery slope" argument).

The debate now centers on alternative ways of addressing these serious health problems while at the same time responding appropriately to the rights of private citizens and affected industries. Given the overriding responsibility of government to the health and welfare of its citizens and the knowledge that cigarette smoking is the single most important preventable cause of death in our society, the pressure to take meaningful action may be difficult to ignore.

Notes

1. This paper is based upon a longer paper which also incorporates a consumer behavior analysis. Interested readers may request a copy of Joel B. Cohen, "Public Policy and Regulatory Issues in the Marketing and Advertising of Cigarettes," working paper, Center for Consumer Research, University of Florida, Gainesville, 32611.

2. We are using the latest figures from the surgeon general's report in order to lend greater precision to the discussion and avoid the use of qualitative terminology. Readers who prefer to consider the implications of either higher or lower estimates are free to adjust such figures accordingly.

3. A recent assessment of fourteen econometric studies (which took advertising expenditures, tobacco price, and personal income into account) concluded that in eleven of these, "advertising significantly affected national cigarette sales" (New Zealand Toxic Substances Board 1989, 33).

4. On this point consider the presentation by Judge Sarokin of the factual background introduced by the plaintiff in *Cipollone* as part of his midtrial response to certain motions:

> The jury, based upon the foregoing, may reasonably conclude that (1) defendants negligently failed to conduct research when it was warranted; (2) that they made

affirmative health claims which were untrue; (3) that they failed to warn of risks about which they had knowledge; (4) that they deliberately and intentionally refuted, denied, suppressed and misrepresented facts regarding the dangers of smoking; (5) that they withheld knowledge of and failed to market a safer cigarette in order to avoid any admission of liability; and (6) that they engaged in an industry wide conspiracy to accomplish all of the foregoing in callous, wanton, willful and reckless disregard for the health of consumers in an effort to maintain sales and profits.

5. Federal regulation of tobacco products is largely confined to the Bureau of Alcohol, Tobacco, and Firearms of the Department of the Treasury (regarding taxation) and by a tightly restricted Federal Trade Commission (regarding advertising claims and disclosure of health risks).

6. Prior efforts to restrict children's access to tobacco are reviewed in the Report of the Surgeon General 1989 (591-603).

7. Most earlier smoking restrictions were primarily concerned with fire safety. But, by the end of 1987, 61 percent of the states restricted smoking in public worksites, 25 percent in private worksites, and 45 percent in restaurants. In addition, cities and counties are often given permission to enact more stringent ordinances (see tables 18 and 19 of the Report of the Surgeon General 1989). Through 1988, close to four hundred local ordinances providing significant nonsmoker protection had been enacted. Described as "self-enforcing," such ordinances rely on public awareness (via appropriate placement of signs) and the public's general tendency to comply with restrictions and even to confront violators. In the private sector, worksite smoking policies are more common in larger businesses; however, blue collar workers who are more likely to be exposed to respiratory hazards and are also more likely to smoke are *less* likely to work in industries having restrictive smoking policies (Report of the Surgeon General 1989, 575-590).

8. In this regard, cigarettes are clearly an exceptional product: one out of four persons who use this product for an extended period of time are likely to die of product-related causes.

9. One potential loophole has apparently been uncovered. Because most restrictions apply to brand and not company names, it seems to be possible to reconstitute brands as separate companies. Restrictions on promotional activity may, therefore, not be as effective as intended.

10. Nonsmokers also have fewer fires and, possibly because of less distraction (e.g., finding and lighting cigarettes, locating dropped cigarettes), fewer traffic accidents, thus providing a basis for reduced property and casualty insurance rates.

References

Aoki, M., S. Hisamichi, and S. Tominaga, eds. (1988). *Smoking and Health 1987. Proceedings of the 6th World Conference on Smoking and Health, Tokyo.* New York: Elsevier Science Publishing.

Cipollone v. Liggett Group, Inc. 789 F.2d 181 (3d Cir. 1986), *cert. denied*, 107 S.Ct. 907 (1987).

Connelly, G. N. (1988). "The American Liberation of the Japanese Cigarette Market." *World Smoking and Health* 13:20-25.

———— (1989). "The International Marketing of Tobacco." Final Report, Tobacco Use in America Conference, January, 1989, 49-54. Washington, D.C.: American Medical Association.

Harris, J. E. (1987). "The 1983 Increase in the Federal Cigarette Excise Tax." In L.H. Summers, ed., *Tax Policy and the Economy*, 1:87-111. Cambridge, MA: Massachusetts Institute of Technology Press.

Lewit, E. M., and D. Coate (1982). "The Potential for Using Excise Taxes to Reduce Smoking." *Journal of Health Economics* 1:121-45.

Luken, T. A. Congressional Record, E725-6, March 9, 1989.

McAuliffe, R. (1988). "The FTC and the Effectiveness of Cigarette Advertising Regulations." *Journal of Public Policy and Marketing* 7:49-64.

Myers, M. L., and J. Hollar (1989). "Tobacco Marketing and Promotion." Final Paper, Tobacco Use in America Conference, January, 1989, 29-42. Washington, D.C.: American Medical Association.

New Zealand Toxic Substances Board (1989). "Health or Tobacco: An End to Tobacco Advertising and Promotion." Publications Division, Government Printing Office, Wellington, New Zealand, P.O. Box 12411.

Pollay, R. W. (1988). Promotion and Policy for a Pandemic Product: Notes on the History of Cigarette Advertising. History of Advertising Archives, Working Paper, January, 1988.

Puto, C. P., and W. D. Wells (1984). "Informational and Transformational Advertising: The Differential in Effects of Time." In T.C. Kinnear, ed., *Advances in Consumer Research*, 11:638-43. Provo, UT: Association for Consumer Research.

Report of the Surgeon General (1989). Reducing the Health Consequences of Smoking: 25 Years of Progress. U.S. Department of Health and Human Services.

Roberts, M. J., and L. Samuelson (1988). "An Empirical Analysis of Dynamic, Nonprice Competition in an Oligopolistic Industry." *Rand Journal of Economics* 19,2:200-220.

Warner, K. E. (1986). *Selling Smoke: Cigarette Advertising and Public Health*. Washington, D.C.: American Public Health Association.

Executives' Attitudes toward Advertising Regulation: A Survey

Bonnie B. Reece and Stephen A. Greyser

It seems appropriate in any assessment of the role of the Federal Trade Commission to include the views of those who are subject to the agency's regulatory powers. By considering the views of business, we may be able to learn more about the past successes and failures of the Commission and of regulatory initiatives regarding advertising. Moreover, we may also be able to assess the likelihood of acceptance or resistance to any new initiatives (or lack of them) as we prepare to enter the 1990s.

That business is a consumer of regulation is a self-evident reason for examining what executives themselves think about it. Another reason for doing so now is that the 1980s have seen the regulatory pendulum swing back from the activist-inspired direction of the 1970s. Executives' attitudes today obviously would reflect the recent experiences by business (and consumers) of less vigorous regulation from government.

The Study

The data presented in this paper are preliminary results from a large-scale survey of attitudes toward a wide range of advertising-related issues, among them a number of questions dealing with advertising regulation, part of the FTC's domain. Although the questions do not refer specifically to the FTC, they allow us to describe the general attitudes toward advertising regulation held by business people. From these general attitudes we can draw some conclusions about how they might apply to the Commission's policies and actions.

The authors are grateful for the support of the *Harvard Business Review* in making possible the larger study from which the material reported here is derived.

Our analysis is based on nearly thirteen hundred responses to a survey of subscribers to *Harvard Business Review*. The respondents are primarily middle and top management executives at companies throughout the United States. They represent a variety of areas of functional expertise in a broad range of industries. The study reported here is somewhat longitudinal in nature, in that *Harvard Business Review* has conducted two previous surveys of its readers' attitudes toward advertising (Greyser 1962; Greyser and Reece 1971). The studies are not completely comparable because there have been some changes in the wording of questions. In addition, there has been a change in the respondent profile, which might be responsible for some shifts in attitude. Nonetheless, where appropriate, we make comparisons with the two prior studies.

Before discussing the findings, we want to present one note about the study's methodology. Much of the data that we present in this paper was collected by asking respondents to indicate the extent of their agreement or disagreement, on a five-point scale, with a series of statements about advertising. Because the wording of a question can influence the response, we used both favorable and unfavorable (to advertising) forms of many of the statements in the questionnaire. These alternative wordings were distributed to two versions of the survey so that each version had a balance of statements favorable to advertising and unfavorable to advertising. The two versions of the questionnaire were then mailed to split halves of our sample.

Issues Explored

We asked executives for their reactions on a number of key issues involving advertising regulation. These encompass the desirability of that regulation; its effectiveness (particularly in terms of advertising content); the perceived need for more regulation and if so of what type; and the role of the government in advertising regulation.

Is Regulation Desirable?

It seems clear to us that there is no desire on the part of responding executives to return to those thrilling days of yesteryear when a marketer could make outrageous claims in advertisements with impunity. Our respondents do not subscribe to the doctrine of *caveat emptor*. Instead,

TABLE 1

Summary of Preliminary Results

Form of Statement	AGREE	DISAGREE
Need for Substantiation		
There is no need to force advertisers to substantiate their claims.	6%	92%
Advertisers should be forced to substantiate their claims.	89%	8%
Ads as Accurate Representations		
In general, advertisements present a true picture of the product advertised.	28%	65%
In general, advertisements do not present a true picture of the product advertised.	50%	36%
Need for Content Policing		
Advertising needs stronger policing of its content.	53%	33%
Advertising does not need stronger policing of its content.	32%	56%
Effectiveness of Self-Regulation		
Self-regulation for advertising can be genuinely effective.	37%	50%
Self-regulation for advertising cannot be genuinely effective.	52%	32%
Government Intervention		
If advertising can't keep its own house in order, the government will have to.	42%	49%

there is strong support that it is desirable "to force advertisers to substantiate their claims," and that support is virtually unanimous (see table 1 for a summary of many of these preliminary findings). Moreover, this pattern of response has been consistent over the quarter of a century spanned by the three surveys.

It is also interesting to note that in each of the three studies over the years, there has been slightly stronger disagreement with the laissez faire version of the statement than there has been agreement with the pro-regulation version. It appears that business people are somewhat less willing to force regulation on advertisers than they are to disagree that such regulation is unnecessary. It should also be noted that there is no indication in this particular question as to who should do the forcing.

Is Present Regulation Effective?

If the present forms of advertising regulation are effective, the consequence should be fewer advertisements that misrepresent the products and services of their sponsors. Responses to several questions in this study indicate that business people believe that there may be some deficiencies in the regulatory mechanisms now in place.

Respondents compared the proportion of "ads with invalid and misleading claims" today with the proportion of such ads that they think
existed ten years ago. There is an even split on this question, with 34 percent of the respondents believing that there is a smaller proportion of in-
valid/misleading ads now, 35 percent believing that there is a greater
proportion, and the remainder believing that the proportion has stayed
about the same. Again, there has been little shift in these proportions over
the course of the three survey periods. These data are shown in table 2.

Although this question gives us some idea of business people's perceived trend line with respect to invalid and misleading claims, it does
not tell us what either their baseline or endline positions are. Results from
several other questions offer some insights on their beliefs about the
current situation. In a separate question, respondents disagree by about a
two-to-one margin that "advertisements present a true picture of the
product advertised." The decline in the percentage of respondents who
agreed with the favorable version of this statement ("advertisements present a true picture") represented the biggest change for any statement
between the 1962 and 1971 studies, and there has been little change in
that number in this year's survey.

Further support for the conclusion that things could be better in the
regulatory arena comes from responses to a question in a section of the
survey instrument entitled "Improving Advertising." When asked what
specific forms of self-improvement the advertising industry should undertake, 94 percent of the respondents say the industry should "eliminate
untruthful or misleading ads" and 73 percent say it should "establish and
enforce a code of ethics." It seems unlikely that so many respondents
would suggest that the industry eliminate misleading ads if they perceive
that these ads represent a minuscule proportion of all advertising.

One of the respondents, a project engineer from Indiana, offered a
comment that is representative of the antagonistic attitudes of many

TABLE 2

Ads with Invalid or Misleading Claims Compared with Ten Years Ago

STUDY YEAR	SMALLER PROPORTION	ABOUT THE SAME	GREATER PROPORTION
1962	37%	29%	33%
1971	38%	30%	32%
1989	34%	30%	35%

others toward this particular topic. His key sentence reads: "All untruthful or misleading ads should be pulled from the air, and (1) the company selling the product, (2) the ad agency, and (3) the medium all should be penalized."

In sum, these findings indicate that many business people believe that there are at least as many ads with misleading claims as there were ten years ago, that many ads today do not present a true picture of the products/services advertised, and that it would be highly desirable to eliminate these untruthful or misleading ads.

Is More Regulation Necessary?

If the regulations governing advertising practices are not effective in preventing misleading ads from reaching the marketplace, there may be a need for additional regulation. Thus, we asked respondents whether "advertising needs/does not need stronger policing of its content." There is about a 5:3 split in favor of stronger policing, but this represents a decline from the 7:2 split in favor in 1971. (This statement was not included in the 1962 study.) It is not clear from the responses to these statements, however, whether people are suggesting that there is a need for more rules or for better enforcement of the rules that are already in place. Likewise, it is not clear whether they are reacting solely to their perception of lack of truth in advertising or whether they are also reacting to matters of taste in content.

Additional support for the contention that more regulation may be needed comes from reactions to a series of questions dealing with ethical codes of conduct for advertisers. Nearly two-thirds of the respondents to this study think that a code of conduct or some similar form of self-regulation would be "an excellent idea" for the advertising industry. The percentage of respondents who hold this strong belief is higher now than it was in either 1971 or 1962.

Only 19 percent of the business people in this study claim to be aware of the existence of ethical codes or self-regulation in advertising. This low level of awareness must be somewhat disconcerting for an industry which has had some commitment to codes of conduct since shortly after the turn of the century. Among these early efforts were the vigilance committees of the American Advertising Federation and the model statute proposed by *Printer's Ink* magazine. In addition, the American Association of Advertising Agencies has had a Creative Code since 1962. Finally, an industrywide self-regulatory mechanism was established in 1971 under the auspices of the Council of Better Business Bureaus, including the National Advertising Review Board.

We also asked respondents who should enforce an advertising industry ethical code, assuming one was to be written. The group cited most frequently as the one to be put in charge of enforcement is one composed of "industry executives plus other members of the community." Just under half of the respondents suggest this alternative. Although few respondents are aware of current industry ethical codes and their enforcement mechanisms, it is interesting that the group they would choose to enforce such a code is similar to the actual makeup of the aforementioned CBBB's National Advertising Review Board.

Only 9 percent of the people in our study believe that a government agency should enforce the ethical code of conduct. We are not surprised by this low number. Many observers, ourselves among them, believe that obeying the law is the floor or minimum for ethical behavior. A code of ethics for business ought to go beyond this minimum. Thus, people adhering to this belief could be expected to find it inappropriate to have a government agency enforce a code that transcends the law.

Business people may find self-regulation preferable to government enforcement of a code of conduct; however, they have doubts about its effectiveness. By a margin of about 10:7, respondents state that "self-regulation for advertising cannot be genuinely effective."

As a follow-up, we asked whether "if advertising can't keep its own house in order, the government will have to." Slightly more respondents disagree with this position than agree with it (49 percent vs. 42 percent). The 42 percent agreeing with this statement represents a considerable decline from 1971 (58 percent), and it is also lower than in 1962 (50 percent). This pattern of responses over time may represent a shift in *philosophical* view from one generally favoring government as a regulatory vehicle toward one supporting deregulation. Or it may represent a belief that the government is also incapable of doing the job. Support for the latter position comes from a senior research consultant from Texas who added a note in the margin next to this question: "Big brother—won't work."

What Is the Government's Role?

It is not surprising, given the business community's traditional posture toward government involvement with and intervention in the marketplace, that respondents to this survey see a relatively small role for government with respect to advertising. In a section of the questionnaire entitled "Scoreboard," only 9 percent of the respondents cite the government as a group that should get credit for advertising's achievement. At the same time, nearly as few respondents (15 percent) blame government for advertising's faults.

However, respondents are more likely to say that government has some responsibility for improving advertising. Even here, though, government's rank is low relative to other groups seen as bearing responsibility for improvement. Furthermore, the percentage of business people citing government in this category (29 percent) is much lower than in 1971 (42 percent), although it is somewhat higher than in 1962 (21 percent). The desirability of having other groups shoulder the burden for cleaning up advertising was expressed by a project hydrogeologist from Michigan as follows: "Advertisers need to make sure that they do not push the general public to the point where the public wants additional government intervention."

Responses to another series of questions indicate that responding executives see a rather positive but weak relationship between government leaders and the advertising industry. When compared with other groups, government leaders are not seen as very antagonistic toward advertising. Likewise, respondents view government leaders as having only a modest amount of power to help or hurt advertising. Perhaps because of this, almost no one believes that advertising needs to pay a lot of attention to government leaders' opinions. For each of these categories, the percentage of respondents citing government officials as being antagonistic, powerful, or worthy of attention is lower than in 1971.

Obviously, because these responses are from the executive community, we would expect relatively low importance to be attributed to government. But even if similar data were to emerge from the general public, we would caution the advertising community not to become too complacent. Just because the government is not perceived to be antagonistic toward advertising does not mean that it might not be goaded into action. This view is best summarized by a comment from an Oklahoma respondent who works in accounting:

> In general, I believe the government has little or no role to play in regulating advertising. However, I think there is a high level of unfavorable public opinion of advertising. In addition, many politicians, clergy, and

other "opinion leaders" have highly unfavorable opinions. The media . . . seem to have highly unfavorable editorial opinions of advertising. If advertising cannot reverse this trend, government regulation cannot be avoided—however ineffective it may be!

Conclusion

In general, this study points to strong support for truth in advertising on the part of the business community. Further, responding executives see problems with the current state of advertising content with respect to misleading claims and truthful impressions of the products advertised. While respondents favor stronger policing of advertising content, the proportion in favor is substantially less than that reported in a similar survey at the early stages of the wave of increased regulation of advertising in the 1970s.

Notwithstanding these views, respondents see a relatively modest role for government in the amelioration process. This is true despite their concomitant majority opinion that self-regulation, alone, cannot be genuinely effective. They favor an enforcement mechanism of industry executives plus other members of the community—a vehicle akin to that of the existing National Advertising Review Board.

There appears to be a far greater consensus among business people as to what to achieve by way of regulation than there is about how to achieve it. A strong role for government in the FTC's domain of advertising regulation seems to be characterized by respondents as a last resort. However, many executives look to consumers themselves in the marketplace to play a meaningful role. As the president of a Texas manufacturer's representative firm put it: "The Marketplace regulates advertising. The public will perpetuate quality in the long term. The public is smart; never sell them short."

References

Greyser, Stephen A. (1962). "Business Re Advertising: 'Yes, But . . .'" [Problems in Review]. *Harvard Business Review*, May-June, p. 20.

Greyser, Stephen A., and Bonnie B. Reece (1971). "Businessmen Look Hard at Advertising" [Problems in Review]. *Harvard Business Review*, May-June, p. 18.

Some Effects of Marketing and Advertising Regulation

Harold H. Kassarjian

In this year, the seventy-fifth anniversary of the Federal Trade Commission, it seems appropriate to look at the various programs promulgated by the FTC in the past and to speculate what effects these programs may have had on the advertising industry and the content of advertisements.

If we consider just the past twenty years, we have witnessed massive upheavals in the workings of the Federal Trade Commission. From the benign neglect of the 1950s, an era of stringent regulation of advertising emerged by the mid-1970s with such new concepts as corrective advertising, affirmative disclosure, counteradvertising, and advertising substantiation. At that time, Miles Kirkpatrick, chairman of the Federal Trade Commission, stated, "There is little doubt that the FTC, once known as 'the little old lady of Pennsylvania Avenue,' has now entered a new era. For that 'little old lady' has now put on tennis sneakers with cleats" (Healey 1978; Kassarjian and Kassarjian 1988).

By the late 1970s and the 1980s the political climate again had changed, now from tough enforcement of regulation to an era of deregulation. Advertisers felt that being saddled with the responsibility of having available proof of claims was onerous. The political theorists and conservative economists now in positions of power felt that truth in advertising and appropriate protection of the consumer is best served not by government regulation but by a free market. Firms not providing information

The material in this paper is based in part on works published in the *Journal of Consumer Policy* (Kassarjian and Kassarjian, 1988) and the *Journal of Marketing* (Healey and Kassarjian, 1983). Reprinted by permission. Portions are also from Healey (1978). Details on the data, data analysis, and the methodology can be found in those sources.

desired by the consumer would cease to exist in an unencumbered market-place. Liberal theorists, of course, disagreed and felt that without appropriate and vigorous regulation, many advertisers would revert to their preregulation claims with poorer quality information being presented to the consumer. Nevertheless, under President Reagan's administration, the "little old lady of Pennsylvania Avenue" had not only removed her cleats, but the tennis shoes were traded in for ballet slippers.

The purpose of this paper is to summarize research findings that examine the effect of one of these bold new approaches to advertising regulation—the advertising substantiation program—before, during, and after the spurt of vigorous regulatory activity of the Federal Trade Commission in the 1970s.

The advertising substantiation program, announced in June 1971, demanded that advertisers have available all documentation, proof, and substantiation for claims that purport to be based on objective evidence. And the proof must exist before the claim is advertised. Industry after industry—from air conditioners and television sets to suntan lotions and hair shampoos—were asked to supply the evidence.

Methodology

In the studies examined, the research method chosen was a content analysis of the claims made for four product categories of consumer goods—antiperspirants, skin lotions, prepared foods, and pet foods. The first phase of the study was conducted in 1977 (Healey and Kassarjian 1983; Healey 1978) and focused upon a comparison of the years 1970, almost two years before the advertising substantiation program, and 1976, during its most active enforcement. A second study was conducted in 1985-86 (Kassarjian and Kassarjian 1988). It compares 1984 advertisements with the earlier data—but eight years later and after half a decade of deregulation.

Content analysis is a formal methodology with a respectable history of research findings in communications research, political science, and consumer research. It is a scientific, objective, systematic, quantitative, and generalizable description of communications message or content (Kassarjian 1977). It has been used to study political propaganda; changing values; product and company images in the mass media; the role of minorities and women in radio, television, and print media; the informational content of television advertising; and even a longitudinal analysis of comic strips.

The procedures first require the selection of a reasonable sample from the available population of documents to be studied—in this case print advertisements. The second step is to determine the unit of measurement, whether it be the specific word, an overall theme, the illustration, or simply the existence or nonexistence of some event or claim. Next, judges categorize the advertising content according to predetermined rules, and finally statistical treatment and analysis of the generated data are carried out. The appropriate unit of measurement, sample selection, and data processing, of course, depend upon the hypotheses being tested.

Hypotheses

In the studies reported here, we hypothesized that one way for marketing and advertising management to prevent the expense and the adverse publicity of a governmental investigation during periods of vigorous regulation would be simply to make very few claims. For example, an ad with a completely black background highlighting a bottle of perfume with the words "Chanel No. 5" is unlikely to be challenged as deceptive or to be a candidate for substantiation orders (Healey and Kassarjian 1983). Hence the first hypothesis was that advertising would include fewer claims in 1976, the period of vigorous enforcement, than in 1970 or 1984, periods of neglect and deregulation respectively.

Further, we expected that the type of claim also would be affected. For example, in 1970, a product like Listerine might claim that the use of the mouthwash lessens the severity of colds. During regulatory activity, that sort of claim could be challenged as deceptive. Hence advertising might emphasize that it comes in several flavors or in a large economy size. The latter are claims that are inherently verifiable rather than claims that could have been, but were not, supported with scientific tests. Unsubstantiated verifiable claims was the very stuff of lawsuits in the mid-1970s.

From a slightly different point of view, an advertiser could avoid FTC activity either by making claims about attributes of the product that permit the inclusion of evidence in the ad or by making exaggerated claims for which no verification could be demanded. "Dial soap kills twice as many bacteria" might require verification, but "Dial soap looks as fresh as you feel" would not (Healey 1978). Hence the second hypothesis was that under regulatory siege advertisers would handle verification either by providing inherently verifiable and verifying evidence or by making non-verifiable vague claims (puffery or gross exaggerations). When regulators backed off, advertisers would revert to increased use of unsubstantiated, scientifically unverified assertions.

Finally, if fewer attribute claims are made and if there is an increase in puffery, one would expect that the number of useful information cues would decrease during regulation activity. On the other hand, if advertising were to become more concrete and better verified, one would expect an increase in the number of information cues proffered, such as claims about size, form, color, contents, or other characteristics. Since informed choice is a major tenet of regulators, we wished to see if the number of informational cues increased or decreased during vigorous regulation.

Selection of Advertisements

Every advertisement for every brand of antiperspirants, skin lotions, pet foods, and prepared foods that appeared in randomly selected consumer magazines was included for the years 1970, 1976, and 1984. Antiperspirants and pet foods had been marked by the FTC for substantiation while skin lotions and prepared food (frozen, packaged, or canned people food) had not been so designated and were used as a pseudo-control. The magazines selected were *Better Homes and Gardens, Cosmopolitan, Family Circle, Glamour, Good Housekeeping, Ladies Home Journal, Mademoiselle, McCalls, Newsweek, Parents Magazine, Reader's Digest, Redbook, Seventeen, Sports Illustrated, Vogue,* and *Women's Day.*

Units of Measurement

Judges were first asked to record each claim or assertion about an attribute describing the product or what it does. Second, judges were asked to determine the level of verification of the claim:

1. Evidence presented in the ad or inherently verifiable. These are ads which either present scientific, survey, or laboratory evidence in the ad of claims about size, color, or other characteristics that are inherently clear, e.g., Pepsi-Cola now comes in a two-liter clear plastic container.

2. Sounds verifiable but no evidence. A claim that could have been verified but the evidence is not presented, e.g., Dry Ban keeps you 20 percent drier.
3. Vague, ambiguous, puff, gross exaggeration, e.g., the mile-high ice cream cone, the world's softest mattress.

In all, 662 advertisements were studied over the three separate years. The interjudge reliability ranged from a low of .82 to a high of .97, quite respectable figures.

Results

The Effect of Regulation

With the rampant increase of regulatory activity in the early 1970s it was expected that advertisers would protect themselves from attack by reducing the number of claims made. In other words, advertisements for products targeted for advertising substantiation (antiperspirants and pet foods) would include fewer attributes in 1976 when compared with 1970 than nontarget products.

As can be seen in figure 1a, the nontargeted industries (prepared food and skin lotions) did not change the number of claims per advertisement. Pet food, on the other hand, reduced the number of claims quite significantly (.001 level). Note, however, that the second test product, antiperspirants, did not evidence such a decrease. Since pet foods initially were making so many more attribute claims than the other products perhaps they had more room to maneuver. However, if the substantiation program did have an effect on advertising content, reducing the number of claims made was not the most prominent impact.

When we turn to the verifiability or quality of claims, the results are not as ambiguous (see in figure 1b). We had expected that the number of ads that provided inherent verifiability (e.g., size or shape of container) or verifying scientific evidence within the ad itself (e.g., "according to the latest Gallup poll Brand X is preferred by 30 percent of working women in Chicago") would increase. All four of the products studied increased the number of ads in which the type of claims was inherently verifiable or evidence for the claim was presented in the ad. Both substantiated products as well as skin lotions, but not prepared foods, were significant beyond the .001 level. Our expectation was comfortably confirmed. The

Figure 1a
Mean Number of Attribute Claims Per Ad,
Before and During Regulation

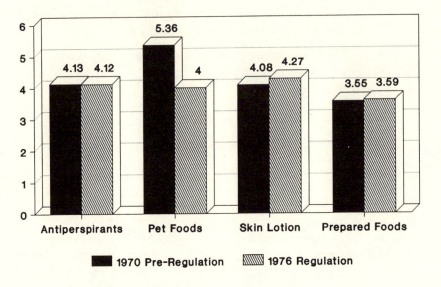

Figure 1b
Percentage of Claims--Evidence
Inherently Verifiable

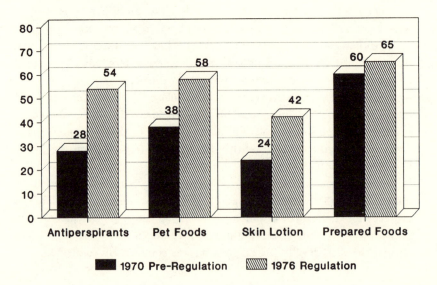

Figure 1c
Percentage of Claims--Sounds
Verifiable But No Evidence

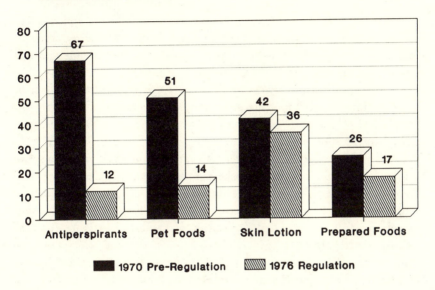

Figure 1d
Percentage of Claims--Vague, Ambiguous,
Puff, Exaggeration

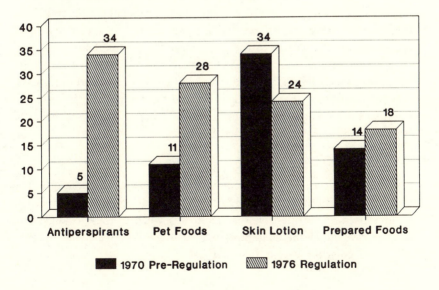

quality of information presented in the ads had improved from 1970 to 1976.

It was expected that advertisers' reaction to vigorous enforcement by the FTC also would reduce the number of claims which implied scientifically verifiable (but unverified) evidence from a laboratory study or survey (e.g., Dry Ban keeps you 20 percent drier or nine out of ten doctors smoke Camel cigarettes). This is the stuff of lawsuits.

Once again this expectation was supported by the data, as can be seen in figure 1c. All four products reduced the number of verifiable but unverified claims quite significantly. The reduction was even more dramatic in the substantiated industries than in the control products.

The results concerning puffery or vague, ambiguous, gross exaggerations were not as clear. We had expected that vigorous FTC activity would lead to increased puffery ("mile-high ice cream cone") since regulators tend not to be excessively concerned with such obvious and gross exaggerations. In some part that expectation was confirmed (figure 1d). The substantiated products (pet foods and antiperspirants) increased the amount of puffery significantly, which was not so for the nonsubstantiated control products. The change in prepared food was slight, and skin lotion actually reduced the amount of puffery. However, note that in 1970, before regulation, 42 percent of skin lotion advertising consisted of gross exaggerations and puffery (compared with an average of 17 percent for the other products). They had a long way to drop and did so.

In summary, we assume that the changes in the content of advertising were at least in part due to the regulatory activity of the Federal Trade Commission rather than to some other causal agent. The major finding of the study was the change in the way product attribute claims were presented after several years of vigorous enforcement. In 1976 claims were either accompanied by more verification in the ad or expressed in a grossly exaggerated fashion that precluded the need for verification. In 1976 the information presented to consumers was of a better quality than it had been six years earlier, the period of benign neglect.

The Effect of Deregulation

By 1984 the deregulation of advertising was rather thorough. The Federal Trade Commission simply stopped monitoring most major national advertisers. The question that arose was whether these changes had become evident in the content of advertising. Did advertisers revert to their preregulation ways of behavior?

First let us turn to the number of claims being made. Since the greater the number of claims the greater the possibility of a lawsuit, we assumed that during regulation advertisers would make fewer claims. Except for pet foods, this was not so in the period 1970 to 1976. Similarly, in the period from 1976 to 1984, we had assumed that the number of claims would increase.

As can be seen in figure 2a, this prediction also was not supported. All four product categories show a reduction in the number of claims being made rather than the expected increase (although the drop in pet food was not significant at the .05 level.) Clearly, the number of claims made in 1984 was less than those made in 1976 and, as indicated earlier, even less than those made in 1970.

The second hypothesis presumed that the number of inherently verifiable claims or ads in which the evidence is presented in the ad would increase during periods of regulation and decrease during deregulation. These are ads reasonably safe from governmental intervention during periods of enforcement, and the evidence is clear that such ads did increase in 1976 when compared to 1970. Figure 2b presents the percent of such claims in the period 1976 to 1984. The two nonsubstantiated industries and pet foods significantly reduced the number of such claims as expected. But turning to antiperspirants, the results are quite the opposite. Antiperspirants actually increased their cautiousness in the claims made under conditions of deregulation. As will be seen again later, this pesky product class simply did not behave as hypothesized.

The stuff of lawsuits under the advertising substantiation program were those ads that made scientifically verifiable claims but for which the verification was missing. As expected in 1976, the period of active regulation, the number of such claims dropped dramatically for all product classes when compared to 1970. As can be seen in figure 2c, by 1984 the percentage of such risky claims increased equally dramatically for all product classes except for the nonconforming antiperspirants. Most advertising had reverted to the preregulation style of making verifiable claims or scientific-sounding assertions for which the evidence was not presented. The quality of information had become much poorer and less reliable.

That brings us to puffery and vague or exaggerated claims. We had expected that puffery would decrease in periods of deregulation. Grossly exaggerated claims such as the "guarantee of the world's softest skin" would be unnecessary if advertisers felt they could present more believable assertions without the need for laboratory or scientific evidence. Figure 2d

Figure 2a
Mean Number Attribute Claims Per Ad,
Before and During Deregulation

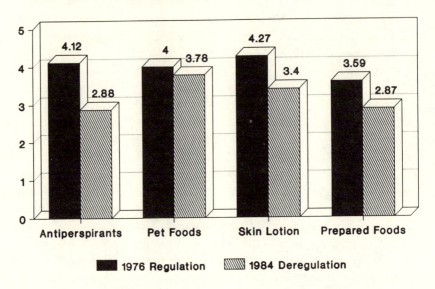

Figure 2b
Percentage of Claims--Evidence
Inherently Verifiable

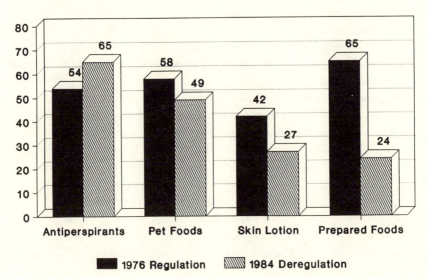

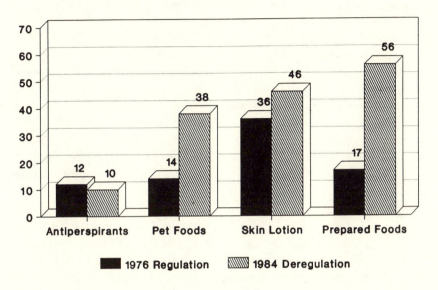

Figure 2c
Percentage of Claims--Sounds Verifiable
But No Evidence

1976 Regulation   1984 Deregulation

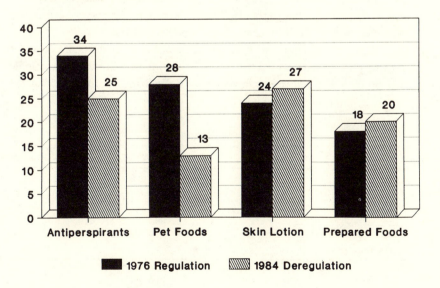

Figure 2d
Percentage of Claims--Vague, Ambiguous,
Puff, Exaggeration

1976 Regulation   1984 Deregulation

indicates that the percent of claims categorized as puffery dropped in 1984 for antiperspirants and pet foods but did not significantly change for skin lotions and prepared foods. We must conclude that neither periods of regulation nor deregulation appear to be uniformly correlated with the degree of puff or grossly exaggerated claims found in consumer advertising. That makes some sense, since regulators have always turned their backs on puff in the belief that such ads are sufficiently incredible to avoid deception.

The final hypothesis examined more directly changes in the number of informational cues provided in the advertisements. These include cues or information about price, quality, warranty, performance, taste, safety, or nutrition. Information level was measured by a method developed for TV advertising by Resnick and Stern (1977). The mean number of informational cues are presented in table 1.

Resnick and Stern (1977), in April 1975, found that 49 percent of television commercials contained at least one informational cue (51 percent contained none at all), with an average number of usable informational cues per commercial less than 0.6. Healey, Fisher and Healey (1986), using the same methodology, point out that the number of cues in television ads had increased to 3.1 and 3.8 (for different sets of ads) during the early 1980s.

The Healey and Kassarjian (1983) results suggest that in the 1970s magazine advertising (for the selected products) contained considerably more informational cues (3.0 to 4.3) than could be found in TV advertising at that time, but by the 1980s that difference seems to have disappeared according to the Healey, Fisher and Healey data.

Turning to hypothesis three, it appears that the effects are opposite of those presumably wanted by the FTC—an increase in the informational cues presented to consumers in advertising. We had hypothesized that the

TABLE 1

Mean Number of Informational Cues

	1970	1976	1984	Total
Targeted Products				
Antiperspirants	4.0	3.7	2.4	3.5
Pet Foods	4.3	4.0	4.3	4.1
Nontargeted Products				
Skin Lotion	3.2	4.1	3.2	3.5
Prepared Foods	3.0	4.1	4.0	3.7

number of cues—the information level of ads—would increase in 1976 and revert back in 1984, for less information and fewer claims might mean less legal liability.

By 1976, the targeted products were giving less information to consumers (although the differences were not significant) while the nontargeted industries were providing significantly more information. By 1984 the number of informational cues available in magazine advertising is mixed. Antiperspirants and skin lotions had significantly fewer informational claims than in 1976, while pet and people food remained more or less the same (differences were not significant). In short, the activists failed in creating advertising with more information either for the long or the short term. If anything, magazine advertising, at least for the targeted products, had become less informative in 1976 and even less so by 1984.

Summary and Conclusions

If one may take a great leap of faith and make generalizations about causality from three data points, some conclusions might be drawn. First, there was a change in the way product attributes were presented in magazine advertisements before and after the advertising substantiation program. By 1976 there were more ads with inherent verification (figure 1b) and more ads that were ambiguous than in 1970 (figure 1d). Fewer ads were of the kind that are scientifically verifiable but without evidence being presented (figure 1c). In general, by 1984 all product classes, except for antiperspirants, had reverted to their earlier types of claims.

Meanwhile the level of informativeness of the ads between 1970 and 1976 dropped for the targeted products, at the time that the nontargeted industries were providing more information. That surely was not what government regulators had in mind. By 1984 antiperspirants and skin lotions continued to drop in the number of informational cues presented, while the remaining products showed minimal variation.

If causality can be claimed, one must conclude that the advertising substantiation program was moderately successful, or at least it seemed to have an impact on the industry as reflected in the content of advertisements. Generally, consumers were provided with less information, but it was of better quality under vigorous enforcement of the program.

The long-run implications seem to point toward increased levels of regulatory activity. By the 1980s deregulation in the United States had freed companies from the fear of governmental lawsuits, and the various trends seem to indicate that, in general, advertisers are slowly returning to their preregulation ways. As advertising becomes less and less informative and less reliable in substance and content, pressure from consumers for the government to do something should increase.

In addition, in the U.S., multimillion dollar civil lawsuits on false advertising have become common in the 1980s. Companies that feel they have been unfairly treated by competitors' advertisements are suing other companies at an alarming rate. For example, cases in which producers of soft drinks and manufacturers of cosmetics have sued their competitors for disparaging claims in advertisements are well known. Recently one manufacturer of vitamins sued a large chain retailer of nutritional foods and vitamins for false advertising because the ads claimed that the retailer carried a wide assortment of the manufacturer's products when they did not. It was asserted that a consumer asking for the branded vitamin was being switched by the sales clerks to the retailer's private label. Fifteen years ago such advertising might have led to a cease and desist order and a slap on the wrist. Today, the settlement was in the millions of dollars.

The fact that civil suits have become far more expensive than litigation involving federal regulators bodes for significantly increased levels of regulatory activity in the coming years. Also more expensive is the emerging vigor of attorneys general of the various states. The enormous void left by the recent apathy of the Federal Trade Commission is being filled in state after state by local officials. Fifty states with fifty different sets of regulations and fifty different attorneys general with varying abilities and varying political aspirations surely must be more expensive that a single strong federal agency regulating advertising and marketing.

The demand for vigorous federal regulation will come not only from the states and the antibusiness and consumerists' sectors, but also even more vigorously from advertisers and the world of business. The FTC and the Nader movement were far less expensive alternatives to the multimillion dollar civil lawsuits and local regulation that are proliferating in this era of deregulation. Whereas a government lawsuit might cost a company some ill will and the cost of litigation, the civil lawsuits filed by competitors are often settled for tens of millions of dollars plus the costs of litigation for both sets of attorneys.

In the 1990s we shall see if our prediction is correct.

References

Healey, John S. (1978). "The Federal Trade Commission Advertising Substantiation Program and Changes in the Content of Advertising in Selected Industries." Unpublished Doctor of Philosophy dissertation, Graduate School of Management, University of California at Los Angeles.

Healey, John S., Melvyn F. Fisher, and Grace F. Healey (1987). "Advertising Screamers versus Hummers." *Journal of Advertising Research*, 26 (December), 43-49.

Healey, John S., and Harold H. Kassarjian (1983). "Advertising Substantiation and Advertiser Response: A Content Analysis of Magazine Advertisements." *Journal of Marketing*, 47 (Winter), 107-117.

Kassarjian, Harold H. (1977). "Content Analysis in Consumer Research." *Journal of Consumer Research*, 4 (June), 8-18.

Kassarjian, Harold H., and Waltraud M. Kassarjian (1988). "The Impact of Regulation on Advertising: A Content Analysis." *Journal of Consumer Policy*, 11 (September), 269-285.

Resnick, Alan, and B. L. Stern (1977). "An Analysis of Information Content in Television Advertising." *Journal of Marketing*, 41 (January), 50-53.

The FTC and Deceptive Advertising: A Performance Assessment

Thomas C. Kinnear and Ann R. Root

If the critics of the Federal Trade Commission were to turn in a grade for the Commission's regulation of deceptive advertising, most would turn in a grade of F. Some, such as these authors, would give the FTC a B, with the encouragement that the Commission has improved lately.

Although there are perhaps as many different opinions about the FTC as there are criteria used to reach those opinions, these authors suggest that the rather harsh view of the FTC is not justified. This paper describes and evaluates some of the criteria used to judge the FTC's performance and then discusses examples that provide support both for and against a grade of B for the FTC. Finally, the future performance of the FTC is projected.

Evaluation Criteria

One of the most prevalent criteria used to assess the FTC's performance has been the number of cases reviewed. Most of the FTC's harshest critics have been counting the number of cases that are brought forth. Michael Pertschuk, a former chairman and commissioner, was convinced that too few cases would result after the 1983 Policy Statement on deceptive advertising was issued (FTC Review 1984). In addition, former chairman James C. Miller once said, "Volume is a sufficient criteria for performance" (FTC Review 1984). Even one of the current commissioners, Andrew Strenio Jr., used number of cases as a criteria for evaluation (*Wall Street Journal* 1989). Strenio compared the 109 commission decisions in a recent six-month period compared to about 1,000 decisions in a comparable period under former chairman Pertschuk. Yet, this bean-counting mentality says nothing about whether important deception issues are being addressed. Furthermore, using volume as a criteria shows that the critics continue to confuse outcome with process.

The second most common criteria for evaluation has been the type of business targeted. In particular, the name and size of company have been mentioned. Pertschuk was concerned with whether the FTC would go after "worthless products from worthless companies" and focus on the "fringes of the marketplace" (FTC Review 1984). Although chasing large companies that advertise nationally can be important as a signal to the marketplace, focusing exclusively on big business may be myopic. Smaller companies may do more deceptive advertising than larger ones because they don't have the resources for pretesting advertisements or substantiating claims. In addition, perhaps the industry structure would be a better criteria than the size or name of the business. For example, those industries where there is little competition would be prime targets for policing deceptive advertising (Best 1985).

The last three criteria described here are perhaps the most important in that they say something about the effect that the FTC has on the marketplace. First, the FTC's effectiveness in using all the remedies that are available for relief from deception should be a criteria for evaluation. Although corrective advertising has not been used for years, cease and desist orders, substantiation, and especially injunctions have been used most recently. Second, the issue or topic that the FTC addresses should be an evaluation criteria; the issue should be of importance to consumers and businesses. For example, health claims have been used with increasing frequency in advertisements, which may be a signal that consumers may be vulnerable to deception. Financial fraud is another important topic, especially for the growing wealthy population of mature adults (over fifty-five years old). Third, the FTC should have an effect on the marketplace, not just on one company. Fourth, this broader effect can be achieved through actions showing initiative rather than lack of planning. For example, targeting a major national advertiser may send a signal to many businesses and therefore create a more wide-spread effect. Fifth, articulating the FTC's agenda and role to businesses may have a strong effect.

These five criteria, whether used together or individually, still do not allow for a fair assessment of the FTC. There are several complementary forums that also police deception as well as administrative constraints such as budgets and policies that affect how the FTC does its job.

Considerations

There are three other forums for relief from deceptive advertising: (1) the National Association of Attorneys General (NAAG), (2) self-regulation through the National Advertising Division of the Bureau of Better Business (NAD) and the National Advertising Review Board (NARB), and (3) the courts. In an earlier paper (Kinnear and Root 1988), the authors suggested that the deception market can be segmented, with each segment being best served by one of the three forums. If one assumes that the FTC has a certain role to play in reducing deceptive advertising, then it would only be fair to judge the FTC on fulfilling that role, not all the other forums' roles. In addition, budget constraints and the current administration's policies regarding regulation must be taken into account when evaluating the FTC. If the FTC is severely constrained by monetary and therefore staff resources, then the commission has a more limited realm from which to regulate. It would be unfair to judge the FTC against the more prosperous period of the Carter years than the budget-con-strained Reagan years. The question must be instead, Is the FTC doing all it can given the resources at its disposal?

The next section describes some of the cases that the FTC has han-dled over the past few years. These examples show that the FTC is polic-ing deception as well as carrying out the commission's other roles.

Examples-Pro

There are perhaps three cases that have been most often reported in the news. The first, Kraft cheese slices, deals with the misrepresentation of the calcium content of the cheese slice (*Advertising Age* April 10, 1989; FTC docket no. 9208). The advertisements ran from early 1985 to mid-1987 and implied that the calcium content of the slices was both equivalent to five ounces of milk and superior to imitation cheese slices. The case has been appealed back to the commission after an administrative law judge ruled in favor of the commission's initial deception complaint. This is an important case for two reasons. First, it addresses a health claim, calcium content, which is an important issue for consumers. Sec-ond, it is a nationally recognized company, which means that the effect of the FTC's ruling may be to send a message back to the food industry, not just to Kraft.

The second case, Campbell Soup and its "soup is good food" campaign, concerns an unsubstantiated claim that soup makes a positive contribution toward reducing heart disease (FTC docket no. 9223). In addition to the unsubstantiation, the ads failed to inform consumers of the sodium content of the soup. The ads ran in the winter of 1988, and the case has been appealed to an administrative law judge. The FTC required Campbell Soup to disclose affirmatively the sodium content of the soup and to cease and desist from making health claims unless they are substantiated. This is an important case for the same two reasons as in the Kraft case: it deals with health claims and concerns a nationally known company.

A third important case, R.J. Reynolds Tobacco Co., pertains to the misrepresentation of a government study in a 1985 "Of Cigarettes and Science" advertorial (FTC docket no. 9206). The FTC considered the advertorial to be commercial speech and therefore under their jurisdiction, while RJR believed the advertorial to be editorial speech and protected under the first amendment to the Constitution. The case is now before the District of Columbia Court of Appeals after the FTC reversed an administrative law judge's ruling that the advertorial was editorial speech. The Supreme Court has given four criteria for determining whether speech is editorial or commercial. Speech is commercial if (1) it refers to a specific product (cigarettes); (2) a specific product attribute is mentioned (health claims); (3) the means used to disseminate the speech is paid for advertisements; and (4) there is an economic motive behind the speech (RJR is in the cigarette business). This case is important because, again, it deals with health claims (an important issue to consumers) and a nationally recognized company. Furthermore, the case addresses the scope of the FTC's jurisdiction and moves the law forward with regard to deceptive advertising and advertorials. In a related matter, the FTC has begun to increasingly focus on infomercials, twenty-to thirty-minute-long programs that advertise products during the program.

The FTC has also been busy targeting companies that are not nationally known but have the potential to cause great economic harm to consumers. Telemarketing fraud (Strenio 1988), mergers, and financial service scams are three such areas in which the FTC has been expending its limited resources.

If businesses in the financial services sector were asked whether the FTC was doing a good job policing deceptive advertising, the answer would be a resounding yes. Over the past two years the FTC has focused on investment, travel, mortgage commitment, and credit repair scams (Noonan 1988). Injunctive relief was sought in most of these cases.

A data base review of what type of news articles have been published in the past year would reveal that antitrust is the hot topic these days at the FTC. Strenio (1988) also points out that antitrust issues take up much of the FTC's resources. The FTC's probe into the takeover of Avon Products Inc. by Amway Corp. is just one such example.

Although antitrust cases are not the same as deceptive advertising, the allocation of resources to each of the FTC's responsibilities must be taken into account when evaluating the FTC. It should also be pointed out that just because the FTC does not seem to be reacting to a case of deception does not mean the commission is not working on the case. Strenio (1988) points out that the FTC does not say anything until the case is prepared. Seeming complacency may just be careful preparation.

The examples above show that the FTC is addressing important deception issues given its limited resources. As to whether the FTC is fulfilling all its responsibilities, the answer cannot be yes. The question of who is responsible for policing national advertisers, the FTC or the NAAG, has been a source of conflict lately.

Examples-Con

The NAAG's activities over the past couple of years have been the most prominent sign that the FTC is not doing its job. The attorneys general have targeted airlines, car companies, Campbell Soup, aspirin manufacturers, and car rental companies. Advertisers and manufacturers alike have been quite displeased with the states' regulation of deceptive advertising. These companies now have to deal with several states and a patchwork of regulations, which increases business costs and general confusion as to what the rule regarding deception is. The activity by the NAAG brings up the questions of whether the states are legally overstepping their jurisdiction (Interstate Commerce Clause) and whether the states should be focusing on their own role in policing deceptive advertising (local advertising) rather than on the FTC's role. Furthermore, although the states have large dollar resources for policing national advertisers, they have little experience.

With regards to airline advertising, more than forty states adopted a national standard for airfare advertising in December of 1987. Recently, however, a U.S. District Judge in Texas enjoined the state from enforcing those guidelines (*Advertising Age* May 1, 1989). Although other states have yet to follow suit, the outcome of appeals in the state of Texas will surely have an effect on other states. The American Bar Association, which just finished an eighteen-month study of the FTC, concluded that the states are not the proper regulator of national advertisers (*Advertising Age* April 10, 1989; April 24, 1989). In addition, the ABA report concluded that the states may have done more harm than good with their regulation of price advertising. Since price is an important attribute for consumers, guidelines that cause companies to be cautious about advertising price may result in price being omitted from advertisements.

With regards to car companies, the states recently settled a case with the American Suzuki Motor Company about the Samurai utility vehicle (*New York Times* March 14, 1989). Seven states complained that advertisements for the vehicle were deceptive. In particular, the advertisements were cited for failing to warn consumers about avoiding sharp turns and abrupt maneuvers. American Suzuki agreed to an affirmative disclosure remedy in future advertisements and to pay $200,000 in investigative costs to the states that brought the complaint.

As previously mentioned, the FTC has issued a complaint against Campbell Soup for unsubstantiated health claims. In addition, nine states also investigated Campbell Soup for deception regarding high fiber claims. Campbell Soup recently settled the issue with the states by agreeing not to make fiber claims and paying the states $315,000 in legal costs. Campbell Soup agreed to settle the dispute since fighting on nine different fronts seemed absurd.

Although this activity by the NAAG clearly sends a signal to the FTC that some national advertisers are not being watched by the Commission, the NAAGs should not necessarily continue to be the major regulator of national advertisers. The FTC needs to send a clear signal to the business community that the Commission is the major regulator of deception.

The activity by the NAAG does not mean that other proper forums should not be involved in regulating national advertisers. In particular, self-regulation, through the NAD and the NARB may be a less costly way to police deception than using the FTC. NAD has been quite active lately with the following advertisements: (1) Pfizer's Plax dental rinse (lacked substantiation); (2) Hilton Hotels (misrepresented savings to the consumer); (3) Kellogg's Mrs. Smith's frozen pumpkin pie (lacked substantiation); (4) Worlds of Wonder Li'l Boppers plush animals (failed to disclose need for batteries); (5) Matchbox Toys' (USA) Pee-Wee's Playhouse and accessories (failed to show that the toys had to be wound) (*Advertising Age* May 15, 1989).

A recent article reviewed the content of advertisements from before 1970 to after 1984 and found that the quality of advertisements was returning to the preregulatory days of verbosity and low quality (Kassarjian 1988). During the regulatory period of the mid-1970s, advertisements were found to be terse but contain high-quality information. These findings suggest that the FTC has been meek in encouraging high-quality information in advertisements. Strenio (see 1988 paper in Part II) has agreed that the FTC seems to have lost its initiative to be a force in the regulation of deceptive advertising.

Conclusion

In balancing the evidence pro and con against the FTC's performance, these authors give the FTC a grade of B, up from a B— a few years ago. The grade is supported by showing the FTC to have been active on important issues, but the commission has room for improvement, especially with national advertisers. Although critics of the FTC would no doubt differ with a grade of B, this paper proposed to show that an evaluation of the FTC must consider which criteria are most important and must take into account complementary forums and budget constraints.

As to the future of the FTC, the ABA report was an important boost to the commission's confidence regarding its role in deceptive advertising. In addition, with President Bush's selection of the next chairperson of the FTC, Janet Steiger, the FTC can hope to begin articulating an agenda. Ms. Steiger, although neither an economist nor a lawyer, is considered to be nonideological and a quick learner.

These authors have a few recommendations for the FTC. A clear articulation of the FTC's mission and objectives would reassure businesses that the NAAG will not be the major regulator of deceptive advertising. In addition, the FTC needs to come to an understanding as to the role that the NAAG should play in regulation. Perhaps that same understanding should be made with the Food and Drug Administration since it seems to have absented itself from all these health claim issues. Finally, although each of the forums that police deceptive advertising should be reviewed for performing its role in regulation, perhaps we would be better off asking the following questions: (1) Is there less or more deception in the marketplace now than ten or fifteen years ago? and (2) Are businesses more or less confused about the rules regarding deceptive advertising?

References

Advertising Age. April 10, 1989. "ABA panel backs FTC over states."

Adverising Age. April 10, 1989. "Kraft Slap. FTC rules against ads."

Advertising Age. April 24, 1989. "Industry lauds report on FTC."

Advertising Age. April 24, 1989. "Setting a course for FTC."

Advertising Age. May 1, 1989. "Judge deals blow to NAAG rules."

Advertising Age. May 15, 1989. "NAD gives Plax claim the brushoff."

Best, Arthur. "Controlling False Advertising: A Comparison Study of Public Regulation, Industry Self-policing, and Private Litigation." *Georgia Law Review*, vol. 20, Fall 1985, pp. 1-72.

FTC docket no. 9206, R. J. Reynolds Tobacco Co.

FTC docket no. 9208, Kraft Inc., April 3, 1989.

FTC docket no. 9223, Campbell Soup Company.

FTC Review (1977-84). "A Report Prepared by a Member of the Federal Trade Commission Together with Comments from Other Members of the Commission for the Use of the Sub-Committee on Oversight and Investigations of the Committee on Energy and Commerce, U.S. House of Representatives," September 1984.

Kassarjian, Harold H., and Waltraud M. Kassarjian. "The Impact of Regulation on Advertising: A Content Analysis." *Journal of Consumer Policy* (Netherlands), vol. 11, issue 3, September 1988, pp. 269-285.

Kinnear, Thomas C., and Ann R. Root. "The FTC and Deceptive Advertising in the 1980's: Are Consumers Being Adequately Protected?" *Journal of Public Policy and Marketing*, vol. 7, 1988, pp. 40-48.

Noonan, Jean. "Federal Trade Commission Activity: Pursuing Unfair and Deceptive Practices in Consumer Financial Services." *Business Lawyer*, vol. 43, issue 3, May 1988, pp. 1069-1079.

New York Times. "Suzuki Will Add Warnings to Samurai Ads in 7 States." Friday March 24, 1989.

Wall Street Journal. "FTC, Under Industry Pressure, Shows New Life in Backing Deceptive-Ad Laws." Monday, April 17, 1989.

Identifying and Resolving Consumer Information Problems: A New Approach

Paul N. Bloom

As a new presidential administration and decade emerge, it seems like an appropriate time to examine ways to refine and improve consumer protection policy. Moreover, with pressure for reduced government spending escalating, the FTC and other consumer protection agencies are in need of ideas to help them become more efficient and effective in their expenditures of public dollars. In this paper, a new approach for developing recommendations about consumer protection policy is suggested. The approach builds on the ideas of a diverse set of researchers and public policy observers, including several of the conservative thinkers who provided guidance to the Reagan administration (Mazis et al. 1981; Beales, Craswell, and Salop 1981; Beales et al. 1981; Ippolito 1985; Ford and Calfee 1986). Specifically, a decision model for prioritizing and addressing consumer information problems is proposed. It is a parsimonious model that public policy makers, managers, and others could use to reach judgments about what markets have the most serious consumer information problems and what policy actions might work best for addressing those problems. The model may be similar to the logic stream that some policy makers have employed (without verbalizing it) in forming judgments about consumer protection priorities and actions.

The consumer protection problems addressed by the proposed model are those which arise from how information is made available to and processed by consumers. A market is viewed as having consumer information

Figure 1, below, reprinted with permission from Paul N. Bloom, "A Decision Model for Prioritizing and Addressing Consumer Information Problems," *Journal of Public Policy and Marketing* 8 (1989), 166.

problems if consumers are making poorer choices for themselves than they would make if they could gain access to the amount and type of information they would like to have to guide their choices. In markets with such problems, desired information is either unavailable or available in inaccurate, misleading, difficult-to-process, or unreasonably expensive forms.

A longer version of this paper has been prepared for volume 8 of the *Journal of Public Policy and Marketing* (Bloom 1989). More extensive definitions and illustration are found in that version. In this version, only a brief description of the decision model can be provided.

A Decision Model

The proposed decision model has two phases. The first phase can be used to diagnose the information problems in a market, helping to point to conditions that contribute to poor consumer choices. The second phase can be used to prescribe solutions to the problems.

Diagnostic Phase

Figure 1 presents a decision tree that can be used to assess the severity and character of the consumer information problems present in a market. A series of questions are posed that a public policy maker could systematically answer to diagnose what seems to be wrong about the way information is provided and utilized in a market. The rationale for including each question is elaborated upon below.

1. Can significant harm come to consumers from making poor choices?

Before investing time and effort diagnosing a market's information problems and prescribing appropriate remedies, it should be established that significant harm can occur to at least some consumers if public policy remains unchanged.

A preliminary assessment of a market's harm potential will involve thinking through a number of worst case scenarios. One should consider the most extensive amount of harm that a consumer could incur from making a single poor choice—as well as the most extensive amount of harm that can be incurred from making repeated poor choices. One should also estimate the probability that consumers would make these extremely harmful choices.

Figure 1. **Diagnostic Phase of the Decision Model**

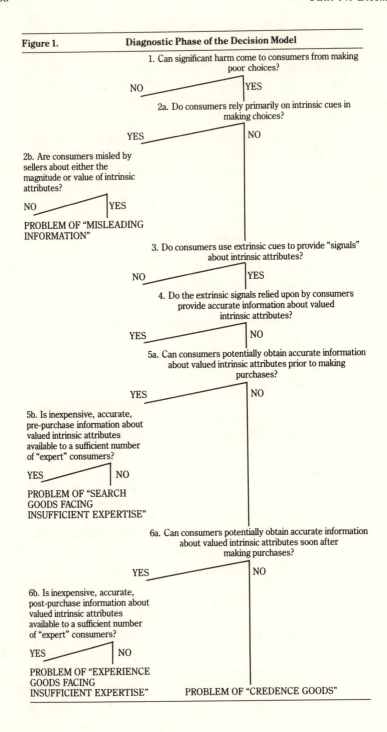

For example, take a product category like mouthwash. A single poor choice seems unlikely to bring significant harm to consumers. However, some consumers may find it difficult to detect that they have made a poor choice in a mouthwash, which could lead them to make repeated poor choices and suffer a significant amount of long-term harm. A consumer might think that the mouthwash protects them from certain illnesses when it does not, and this could lead the consumer to overspend repeatedly on mouthwash (at least until the illnesses are actually contracted, and perhaps longer). Moreover, if many consumers are misled in similar ways, then the company doing the misleading might be able to hurt its competitors badly and take advantage of the situation to get consumers to overpay even more. The case the FTC pursued against Warner-Lambert for its Listerine advertising essentially sought to stop this scenario from developing further (Wilkie, McNeill, and Mazis 1984).

In the opinion of this author, a market must have the potential for producing a level of harm at least as large as the long-term economic harm inflicted in the Listerine situation if a positive answer is to be given to the first question in the decision model. Markets where the potential for greater amounts of short-term or long-term harm exists should clearly be examined further. This would include all markets where consumers can suffer substantial economic losses from even a single poor choice or where the health and safety of consumers can be substantially endangered by such a choice. Thus, most big-ticket items and products that can affect one's health would qualify for further examination. Products that could be excluded from further analysis based on this standard would include deodorants, cosmetics, perfumes, haircuts, and any other products that consumers are unlikely to buy a second time after suffering small levels of harm from an initial purchase.

2a. Do consumers rely primarily on intrinsic cues in making choices?

2b. Are consumers misled by sellers about either the magnitude or value of intrinsic attributes?

Different kinds of problems seem to arise in markets depending on whether consumers rely primarily on intrinsic or extrinsic cues. In general, markets where reliance is primarily on intrinsic cues (i.e., information about a product's intrinsic attributes) should have less frequent and less complicated information problems, although these markets will still require some attention from public policy makers to combat the dissemination of misleading consumer information. Note that markets where neither intrinsic or extrinsic cues are used by consumers are not a concern of this paper, since such lazy or mindless choices are not viewed here as poor choices.

When consumers are focusing primarily on intrinsic cues, a variety of forces should come into play that should limit the incidence of poor consumer choices. Sellers should be motivated to provide offerings with more desirable intrinsic attributes and to invest in providing inexpensive, accurate consumer information (through advertising and other promotional vehicles) about those attributes. Disincentives against providing misleading information should be strong in these markets, as sellers should recognize that many consumers can readily detect and punish (through not repurchasing and spreading bad word-of-mouth) the suppliers of false claims (see Nelson 1970, 1974). In general, consumers and sellers should be able to keep pushing each other to better and better outcomes for consumers. This author suspects that markets for many produce, hardware, and clothing items provide examples of situations where reliance on intrinsic cues is high and the incidence of poor choices is low.

The possibility exists, however, that some sellers will attempt to be deceptive when marketing to consumers who focus on intrinsic cues. If they are selling a search good, then these deceivers will, of course, have trouble taking advantage of the misrepresentation of the magnitude of their product's intrinsic attributes. Consumers can often check the veracity of claims for search goods before buying, using a variety of sources of accurate information such as labels, posted disclosures (e.g., octane ratings), and consumer magazine stories. Moreover, if sellers are selling an experience good, then they will also have trouble misrepresenting the magnitude of intrinsic attributes because consumers tend to ignore or show skepticism toward claims for experience goods (see Nelson 1970, 1974; Ford, Smith, and Swasy 1988).

But some sellers may still be able to deceive by (1) misrepresenting the magnitude of intrinsic attributes that consumers tend to learn about slowly—especially with products that are purchased very infrequently or that are rarely the subject of word-of-mouth discussion—or (2) misleading consumers about the value to them of certain intrinsic attributes. Thus, this author fears deception with, for example, health and nutrition claims for over-the-counter drugs, vitamins, and grocery products. It seems that the magnitude of attributes (e.g., amount of fiber) and the value of attributes (e.g., it prevents cancer) are frequently promoted inaccurately in these markets.

The need for public policy actions against deceivers is mitigated somewhat by the existence of several voluntary labeling programs and the advertising self-regulation program run by the Council of Better Business Bureaus (see Armstrong and Ozanne 1983). Moreover, actions by consumer groups and individual expert consumers (see the discussion under question 5b below) tend to create incentives for sellers to avoid deception. However, there will still be some markets where the answer to question 2b (above) is likely to remain positive for a substantial period of time, suggesting a need for public policy actions. This situation has been labeled the problem of "misleading information." The discussion now turns to examining where problems can arise in markets where consumers rely primarily on extrinsic cues (i.e., information about extrinsic attributes, which are not part of the physical product itself).

3. Do consumers use extrinsic cues to provide signals about intrinsic attributes?

If consumers are relying primarily on extrinsic cues over intrinsic ones, the possibility exists that they are only interested in acquiring the extrinsic attributes themselves and do not really care about intrinsic attributes. They may buy a product to show off its brand name or to brag that they bought the most expensive choice. In these markets, consumer reliance on extrinsic cues would not be a serious problem. Certain types of apparel (e.g., "signature" goods), jewelry, and toiletries may fit this situation.

For reliance on extrinsic cues to create problems in a market, consumers need to care about whether their purchases deliver desired levels of intrinsic attributes, even though they, for one reason or another, tend to use little direct information about those intrinsic attributes. The extrinsic cues must actually be utilized by consumers to provide signals about the extent to which an offering possesses desired intrinsic attributes. Empirical evidence suggests that extrinsic cues are frequently used in this way (e.g., Olson 1977; Griliches 1971; Mazursky and Jacoby 1985; Gardner 1970, 1971; Kirmani and Wright 1988).

4. Do the extrinsic signals relied upon by consumers provide accurate information about valued intrinsic attributes?

Consumer reliance on extrinsic "signals" can be a very positive feature of a market—*if* the signals are accurate reflections of the intrinsic attributes that consumers value. Accurate extrinsic signals can provide a form of quality assurance for consumers, allowing them to save substantial amounts of time, energy, and money in searching for and evaluating market alternatives (Ippolito 1985).

Clearly, sellers frequently have great incentives to police themselves and provide accurate extrinsic signals (Nelson 1970, 1974; Milgrom and Roberts 1986; Schmalensee 1978; Salop 1978). Sellers have often made considerable investments in establishing trusted brand names, highly visible advertising campaigns, or superior warranties, and they do not want to see those investments damaged by having them associated with products that have inferior attributes. Research by Wiener (1985, 1988) suggests that the incentives seem to work for encouraging warranties to be accurate signals of reliability in appliances and automobiles.

Although many self-policing incentives do exist and Wiener's findings about warranties are persuasive, this author still thinks that there are many instances where relied-upon extrinsic signals are inaccurate, providing opportunities for poor consumer choices to be made. This belief is supported by several studies that have shown that price and actual quality, as measured by ratings in *Consumer Reports* or *Consumers' Research Magazine*, are rarely highly positively correlated and are often weakly or even negatively correlated (see Hjorth-Anderson 1984; Sproles 1977; Riesz 1979; Geistfeld 1982; Gerstner 1985).

The effects of having inaccurate extrinsic signals (due to transmission or reception) can be made worse if some sellers are able to transmit inaccurate signals more efficiently and effectively than competing sellers can transmit signals that are processed accurately. Thus, a large firm selling an offering with inferior intrinsic attributes might be able to take advantage of a trademark-protected brand name, quantity discounts offered by the media, or retailer pricing cooperation to send out more attractive signals at a lower cost per consumer reached than smaller competitors could achieve. Without the entrenched position, market power, and financial resources of a large firm, it may be very hard for a smaller firm to establish a trusted brand name, a high level of advertising spending, or an understanding with retailers to maintain high prices. The end result could be a market dominated by a few large firms competing, over which one can provide the most clever and confusing brand names, the largest volume of advertising, and the highest prices—with little effort being placed on providing offerings with more pleasing intrinsic attributes (see Beales, Craswell, and Salop 1981).

5a. Can consumers potentially obtain accurate information about valued intrinsic attributes prior to making purchases?

5b. Is inexpensive, accurate, prepurchase information about valued intrinsic attributes available to a sufficient number of expert consumers?

The existence of heavy consumer reliance on inaccurate extrinsic signals should not automatically suggest that a market requires immediate public policy attention. The market may be able to correct itself within a reasonable period of time, eventually arriving at a situation where accurate extrinsic signals are being transmitted, received, and utilized by consumers. This self-correction can happen in markets where questions 5a and 5b receive positive answers.

If the offerings in a market are essentially search goods (i.e., a positive answer is given to 5a) and if there is some way for at least a significant minority of expert consumers to obtain and utilize accurate information about the intrinsic attributes of the offerings at a low cost (i.e., a positive answer is given to 5b), then incentives can develop for sellers to provide offerings with more pleasing intrinsic attributes and more accurate extrinsic signals.

In essence, it is being argued that expert consumers can potentially police the market for all consumers (Salop 1976; Mazis et al. 1981; Beales et al. 1981; Tellis and Wernerfelt 1987). Their superior skills at interpreting and using consumer information, including extrinsic cues (Rao and Monroe 1988) can help them serve this function—if they exist in sufficient numbers in a market. Unfortunately, determining whether a market has a sufficient number of experts to experience a self-correction promises to be a difficult task. In making this judgment, consideration should be given to whether:

1. sellers seem to recognize the existence of experts by giving special attention to a group of expert consumers in their promotional campaigns, consumer relations programs, or regulatory monitoring activities;

2. word-of-mouth seems to be prevalent between expert consumers and more novice consumers;

3. large numbers of consumers seem to react strongly to either good or bad publicity about sellers.

The more these conditions exist in a market, the more likely it is that a sufficient number of experts exist to allow a self-correction to occur. This author believes that the markets for VCRs, stereos, many major appliances, and microcomputers have tended to experience this type of evolution.

However, there will be markets for search goods where the answer to 5b above has to be negative. There may be an insufficient number of experts and/or an inadequate supply of inexpensive, accurate, prepurchase information to guide the choices of those experts. The latter will tend to happen where significant economies of scale in the production and transmission of consumer information exist and no institution has been willing to make the investment needed to achieve the scale economies (Beales, Craswell, and Salop 1981). Fortunately for consumers, Consumers' Union and others have invested in the production of consumer information on many search goods, allowing consumers to obtain accurate information about valued intrinsic attributes rather inexpensively.

But an investment in the production and transmission of consumer information about many *local* search goods has not been made, and it is in markets like these where many poor outcomes can occur. This author fears that even expert consumers may be making rational choices—in the sense that they are not searching past the point where the marginal benefits and marginal costs of additional search are equal—but choices that are poorer than those they could be making if additional low-cost, accurate, prepurchase information were available.

The situation that arises when 5a is answered positively and 5b must be answered negatively has been labeled the problem of "search goods facing insufficient expertise." As suggested above, this problem can arise in markets for search goods where very few expert consumers exist, where sellers fail to recognize experts, where experts do not provide frequent word-of-mouth advice, where consumers react only mildly to publicity about sellers, or where accurate prepurchase information is too costly for even experts to acquire. In these markets, inaccurate, but relied-upon, extrinsic signals can lead to many poor choices. This author suspects that this problem may exist, for example, in the markets for auto and home-owner's insurance. These seem to be markets where consumers rely heavily on extrinsic signals (e.g., brand name), even though the potential exists for consumers to obtain accurate prepurchase information. Experts may be unable to police these markets effectively because they find state and local consumer information about insurance policies costly to obtain and because word-of-mouth about insurance policies occurs infrequently.

In general, markets for experience and credence goods (i.e., where the answer to 5a is negative) present a somewhat different set of issues. These are addressed below.

    6a. Can consumers potentially obtain accurate information about valued intrinsic attributes soon after making purchases?

    6b. Is inexpensive, accurate, postpurchase information about valued intrinsic attributes available to a sufficient number of expert consumers?

If at least a significant minority of expert consumers are inexpensively able to obtain and utilize accurate information about valued intrinsic attributes shortly after making a purchase (i.e., a positive answer is given to 6b), then the effect should be similar to the situation described above with respect to search goods, where a few expert consumers can police the market and eventually ensure the existence of accurate extrinsic signals about experience goods. For example, restaurant owners and theater managers should want to avoid falling in disfavor with influential restaurant and theater reviewers.

The problem of "experience goods facing insufficient expertise" can emerge if there are an insufficient number of experts in a market or if those experts find accurate information about the intrinsic attributes of experience goods too costly to acquire. The latter can occur if even experts must spend considerable time and money actually purchasing and trying several of the alternative experience goods to conduct sound evaluations. This kind of costly information seems to exist in the markets for many local services, such as auto repairs and home repairs, and it also obviously exists in markets for very infrequently purchased experience goods such as homes and long-distance telephone services. In general, this author sees this problem category occurring more frequently and creating more harm than either of the two types of problems discussed thus far.

Consumer reliance on inaccurate extrinsic signals tends to lead to even greater problems in markets for credence goods (i.e., a negative answer is given to 6a). By definition, a credence good (Darby and Karni 1974) will never (or very late after purchase) have information about valued intrinsic attributes obtainable or usable by consumers. Thus, there is no way for experts or other consumers to have enough information to police the market. Sellers can continue to benefit from the transmission of inaccurate extrinsic signals as long as competitors do not seek to give them bad publicity for doing so (perhaps because they are also transmitting inaccurate signals) and as long as some regulatory body does not try to stop them. Markets that seem to fit this description include those for many professional services, health foods, prescription drugs, and educational programs (e.g., trade schools, MBA programs). Consumers may be making very harmful choices for themselves by relying on extrinsic signals like the size of a company (e.g., a big eight CPA firm), brand name (e.g., affiliation with a major university), or price to guide their decisions. These consumers may never realize that their faith in certain signals caused them, for example, to spend much more money on a product than was required or to ingest substances that could bring them long-term health problems.

Prescriptive Phase

The preceding discussion of the decision tree in figure 1 points to four major types of problem situations that can arise in a market. Table 1 shows these problems along with suggestions of markets that may suffer from each one. A third column of the table proposes public policy actions that might be appropriate for dealing with each problem situation. The rationale for these policy proposals is presented in the longer version of this paper (Bloom 1989).

TABLE 1

Prescriptive Phase of the Model

PROBLEM TYPE	EXAMPLES	POTENTIAL POLICY ACTIONS
Misleading Information	OTC Drugs Vitamins Health Clubs Cigarettes	Better "Metrics" Supporting Comparative Product Information Programs Deceptive Practice Actions Affirmative Disclosures
Search Goods Facing Insufficient Expertise	Insurance	Better "Metrics" Supporting Comparative Product Information Programs
Experience Goods Facing Insufficient Expertise	New Homes Long-Distance Telephone Auto Repair Local Movers	Better "Metrics" Supporting Comparative Product Information Programs "Cooling-Off" Laws
Credence Goods	Professional Services	Minimum Quality Standards Antitrust

Regardless of the problem situation, some type of cost-benefit analysis should be done before adopting any of the policy actions suggested in table 1. The benefits expected from reducing or eliminating consumer harm (partially identified in answering question 1 in the diagnostic phase of the model) must be weighed against the expected costs to society of the proposed remedy. The remedies should be introduced if the expected benefits clearly exceed the expected costs. In addition, those situations where this benefit-cost gap appears the largest should be assigned the highest priority for action.

Concluding Thoughts

Implementation of the model will obviously require the use of consumer research. For a market that is suspected of producing poor outcomes—because of high complaint rates, numerous lawsuits, or other evidence suggesting that consumers have suffered significant harm from making poor choices—research would need to be done on a number of issues (see Bloom 1989). The FTC, FDA, and several other agencies have shown a clear intention to rely more heavily on consumer and market research studies in executing their enforcement duties (Ford and Calfee 1986). Thus, the need to change the mindset of people in these agencies toward research will probably not exist. Instead, a bigger battle will likely be with Congress over obtaining funding to do this kind of research. However, this author feels that the costs of doing the research would be dwarfed by the savings that would accrue to both sellers and the government by reducing the number of ill-advised cases and poorly formulated remedies. Moreover, following this model should permit policy makers to stimulate more competitive vitality and more consumer-responsive behavior in many markets.

References

Armstrong, Gary M., and Julie L. Ozanne (1983). "An Evaluation of the NAD/NARB Purpose and Performance." *Journal of Advertising* 12 (No. 3), 15-26.

Beales, Howard, Richard Craswell, and Stephen Salop (1981). "The Efficient Regulation of Consumer Information." *Journal of Law and Economics* 24 (December), 491-539.

Beales, Howard, Michael Mazis, Steven Salop, and Richard Staelin (1981). "Consumer Search and Public Policy." *Journal of Consumer Research* 8 (June), 11-22.

Bloom, Paul N. (1989). "A Decision Model for Prioritizing and Addressing Consumer Information Problems." *Journal of Public Policy and Marketing* 8, 161-180.

Darby, M., and E. Karni (1973). "Free Competition and the Optimal Amount of Fraud." *Journal of Law and Economics* 16 (April), 67-88.

Ford, Gary T., and John E. Calfee (1986). "Recent Developments in FTC Policy on Deception." *Journal of Marketing* 50 (July), 82-103.

Ford, Gary T., Darlene B. Smith, and John L. Swasy (1988). "Are Consumers More Skeptical of Advertising They Can't Evaluate? Empirical Perspectives on the Economics of Information." Working paper, The American University.

Gardner, David M. (1971). "Is there a Generalized Price-Quality Relationship?" *Journal of Marketing Research* 8 (May), 241-243.

———— (1970). "An Experimental Investigation of the Price-Quality Relationship." *Journal of Retailing* 46 (Fall), 25-41.

Geistfeld, Loren V. (1982). "The Price-Quality Relationship Revisited." *Journal of Consumer Affairs* 16, 334-346.

Gerstner, Eitan (1985). "Do Higher Prices Signal Higher Quality?" *Journal of Marketing Research* 22 (May), 207-215.

Griliches, Zvi (1971). "Introduction: Hedonic Price Indexes Revisited." In *Price Indexes and Quality Change*. Zvi Griliches, ed. Cambridge, MA: Harvard University Press. 3-15.

Hjorth-Anderson, C. (1984). "The Concept of Quality and the Efficiency of Markets for Consumer Products." *Journal of Consumer Research* 11 (No. 2), 708-718.

Ippolito, Pauline (1985). "Consumer Protection Economics: A Selective Survey." In *Empirical Approaches to Consumer Protection Economics*. Pauline Ippolito and D. Scheffman, eds. Washington, DC: Federal Trade Commission.

Kirmani, Amna, and Peter Wright (1988). "Money Talks: Advertising Extravagance and Perceived Product Quality." Working paper, Stanford University.

Mazis, Michael B., Richard Staelin, Howard Beales, and Steven Salop (1981). "A Framework for Evaluating Consumer Information Regulation." *Journal of Marketing* 45 (Winter), 11-21.

Mazursky, David, and Jacob Jacoby (1985). "Forming Impressions of Merchandise and Service Quality." In *Perceived Quality*. Jacob Jacoby and Jerry Olson, eds. Lexington, MA: Lexington Books. 139-154.

Milgrom, Paul, and John Roberts (1986). "Price and Advertising Signals of Product Quality." *Journal of Political Economy* 94 (No. 4), 796-821.

Nelson, Phillip (1970). "Information and Consumer Behavior." *Journal of Political Economy* 78 (No. 2), 311-329.

———— (1974). "Advertising as Information." *Journal of Political Economy* 81 (No. 4), 729-754.

Olson, Jerry G. (1977). "Price as an Informational Cue: Effects in Product Evaluation." In *Consumer and Industrial Buying Behavior*. Arch Woodside, Jagdish Sheth, and Peter Bennett, eds. New York: North Holland. 267-286.

Rao, Akshay, and Kent Monroe (1988). "The Moderating Effect of Prior Knowledge on Cue Utilization in Product Evaluations." *Journal of Consumer Research*, in press.

Riesz, P. (1978). "Price versus Quality in the Marketplace: 1961-1975." *Journal of Retailing* 54 (No. 4), 15-28.

Salop, Steven (1976). "Information and Monopolistic Competition." *American Economic Review* 66, 240-245.

———— (1978). "Parables of Information Transmission in Markets." In *The Effect of Information on Consumer and Market Behavior*. Andrew A. Mitchell, ed. Chicago: American Marketing Association. 3-12.

Schmalensee, Richard (1978). "A Model of Advertising and Product Quality." *Journal of Political Economy* 86 (No. 3), 485-503.

Sproles, George B. (1977). "New Evidence on Price and Quality." *Journal of Consumer Affairs* 11 (Summer), 63-77.

Tellis, Gerard, and Birger Wernerfelt. "Competitive Price and Quality Under Asymmetric Information." *Marketing Science* 6 (Summer), 240-253.

Wiener, Joshua L. (1985). "Are Warranties Accurate Signals of Product Reliability?" *Journal of Consumer Research* 12 (September), 245-250.

———— (1988). "An Evaluation of the Magnuson-Moss and Federal Trade Commission Improvement Act of 1975." *Journal of Public Policy and Marketing* 7, 65-82.

Wilkie, William L., Dennis McNeill, and Michael Mazis (1984). "Marketing's 'Scarlet Letter': The Theory and Practice of Corrective Advertising." *Journal of Marketing* 48 (Spring), 11-31.

The Economics of Information: Research Issues

Darlene B. Smith, Gary T. Ford, and John L. Swasy

The purpose of this paper is to summarize recent research findings and discuss issues for future research in the economics of information (EOI). Our paper first reviews the basics of economics of information theory, then summarizes empirical research and identifies and discusses possible future research.

Basic Tenets of the Economics of Information

Information economists believe that the major role of advertising is to provide information to consumers and that consumers interpret advertising appropriately and use the signals that it provides in their purchase decisions. Policy makers have relied particularly on the theoretical concepts developed by Nelson (1970, 1974) and Darby and Karni (1973) who coined the terms search, experience, and credence properties (SEC) to categorize when, if ever, in the purchase process, consumers can accurately verify a given advertised claim.

The theory predicts that consumers will be most skeptical of advertising claims that cannot be verified even after purchase and use of the product (credence claims) and least skeptical of claims that can be easily and inexpensively verified prior to purchase (search attribute claims). The logic of the SEC framework also implies a difference in levels of skepticism for experience claims about high- and low-priced goods. Specifically, the theory states that since manufacturers know that consumers can inexpensively evaluate the veracity of a claim by purchasing and using the product, there is no incentive to lie in the advertising. Consumers understand advertisers' incentives and thus will be less skeptical of experience claims for low-priced goods more than for experience attribute claims of high-priced goods. Nelson (1974) also predicts that consumers receive more value from objective quality attribute claims than subjective claims and thus will be more skeptical of the latter type of claim.

Research Findings and Future Research

Research testing these basic predictions is quite promising, though equivocal. Ford, Smith, and Swasy (1988) developed operational definitions for SEC attribute claims and tested those definitions by having expert judges classify a randomly drawn sample of actual claims from ads appearing in leading magazines. The results of the coding effort indicated that six out of every seven claims fit into the SEC coding scheme and that operational definitions were achievable. In the sample of 185 prominent claims, 34 percent of the claims were categorized as search claims, 44 percent were experience claims, and 21 percent were credence claims. This coding effort provided an initial description of naturally occurring print ad claims and provided impetus to investigate other aspects of the EOI theory, particularly that dealing with consumers' differential skepticism of SEC claims.

In 1989 Ford, Smith, and Swasy directly examined the influence of SEC claims on consumer skepticism. Three claim characteristics thought to affect skepticism—objective vs. subjective, price of advertised product, and SEC claim type—were manipulated in a repeated measures design using adult consumers. The results provided clear support for Nelson's hypotheses in that consumers were more skeptical of experience claims than search attribute claims and more skeptical of subjective claims than of objective claims. No support was found, however, for the Darby and Karni (1973) hypotheses that consumers would be more skeptical of credence claims than of experience attribute claims or that consumers would be less skeptical of experience claims for low-priced goods. In this study the price of an item did not affect the level of skepticism for experience claims. Possible explanations of this noneffect are discussed later.

A number of additional questions and opportunities are suggested by this initial research into the economics of information. The following discussion focuses on four of these issues: (1) the determinants of consumer skepticism, (2) the completeness of the SEC framework, (3) the signals used by consumers to extract information from advertising, and (4) strategies used by advertisers to bolster nonsearch claims.

The Determinants of Consumer Skepticism

Past research indicates that there is differential skepticism of advertising claims by and large as predicted in the economics of information literature. Consumers are more skeptical of nonsearch claims. Since experience claims for low-priced goods can be easily verified, we might expect consumers to be less skeptical of experience claims for low- than for high-priced goods. On the contrary, however, attributed claims for lower-priced experience products resulted in higher skepticism than with higher-priced products. Several possible explanations and considerations regarding this finding may be offered.

The nature of skepticism toward experience claims for low-priced goods may be different than that for high-priced goods. While the EOI literature assumes that skepticism varies inversely with verifiability (i.e., when in the purchase process an advertised claim may be verified), another determinant of skepticism may be relevant prior knowledge and experience. Certainly, it is not unreasonable to assume that consumers have accumulated more purchase occasions with lower-priced products than with higher-priced products. A rich store of prior knowledge regarding high- and low-priced goods may be developed. This knowledge may include not only product-specific knowledge but perhaps more generalized knowledge about advertisers' influence tactics (e.g., that advertisers frequently employ hyperbole with low-priced goods to induce trial). Using this knowledge, consumers may be able more readily to discern obviously true and obviously false experience claims from those that are of an intermediate uncertain nature. The zone of uncertainty surrounding experience claims for low-priced goods may be narrower than that for high-priced goods. Thus, for frequently purchased (low-price) products, skepticism may be more likely to be rooted in past experiences than when the specific experience claim can be verified.

This heightened skepticism toward experience claims for low-priced products may also be due to the fact that consumers have more purchase occasions with, and search less for, low-priced products. Product experience can and does provide countless opportunities to receive both positive and negative information. Further, with these low-priced products, consumers may substitute purchase for search and thus not evaluate the alternatives carefully. This lack of search for lower-priced goods results in both greater variability in the quality of products purchased and an overall lower mean level in the quality of products purchased. The same may not be true, however, for high-priced products. Since the purchase of a durable good, such as a major home appliance, can potentially take the consumer out of the market for a long time, the amount of search undertaken by a consumer may be greater. This increased search activity results in less variability in the consumer's product-related experiences and raises the mean quality of purchases. This better experience (relative to lower-priced goods as a whole) may reduce skepticism for experience claims for higher-priced goods.

Thus, there may be fundamental differences in the nature of skepticism associated with low-price experience claims and that associated with high-price experience claims. These differences are based not only on the inherent verifiability of claims but prior product experience and knowledge. Future research might attempt to determine whether skepticism is a unidimensional construct and, if not, identify its components and their effects.

The Completeness of the SEC Framework

In evaluating the completeness of the SEC framework, there are a number of issues that need to be considered. The first deals specifically with the SEC trichotomy, which implies a hierarchy of preferred claims, where preference is grounded on verifiability. The issue of interest is whether the three levels of claims (i.e., search, experience, and credence) best capture this underlying construct of claim verifiability or whether a framework based on either more or fewer levels is more appropriate. The second issue pertains to the ability of the framework to code adequately the full range of claims seen in modern advertising.

Previous research by Smith (1986) concluded that it may be more realistic to collapse the experience and credence categories and dichotomize the verification process to "before purchase" and "after purchase" verification. The research by Ford, Smith, and Swasy (1989), however, indicated that four levels may be more appropriate. For the SEC manipulation check in the Ford, Smith, and Swasy (1989) research, subjects were asked to consider when they would be able to tell whether each claim was true or false by responding "before purchase," "after purchase," "only an expert could tell," and "no one could tell, not even an expert." Several of the exemplar credence claims were actually coded by consumers as not verifiable by experts (i.e., no one could tell) even though it was extremely likely that an expert could, in fact, verify the claim. For example, nineteen out of thirty pretest subjects rated the (high-priced product, objective) credence claim, "XX laboratory tests the quality of its recliner by simulating twenty years of actual use" as "no one can tell," and ten rated it as "only an expert can tell." Perhaps there are multiple levels of credence claims based on the perceived availability of expert knowledge or opinion. Future research needs to examine consumers' beliefs about both their ability and the ability of experts to verify claims. It would be interesting to investigate consumers' interpretation of "expert knowledge." Expert knowledge needed for the verification of subjective claims may be meaningfully different from the type of expert knowledge required in the verification of objective claims.

In addition, the concept of verifiability may be directly related to the length of time it takes to prove the claim true. Some experience claims can be evaluated immediately (e.g., car tires handle better in snow), while other experience claims may not be evaluated for years (e.g., mileage claims for tires). For claims that can't be proven true for many years, the line between credence and experience claims often blurs. Consumers may be more skeptical of experience claims that require longer periods of time to evaluate.

Another time aspect likely to be of importance is interpurchase time. Future research might systematically vary this time lag. We would hypothesize that for products with long interpurchase cycles, the potential power that consumers can exert by withholding repeat purchases vanishes, and by inference so may consumers' belief in the veracity of the claims. (The EOI theory asserts that withholding patronage affects future advertising claims. Research has not yet examined whether consumers believe this to be true.) It should be recognized, however, that while repeat purchase behavior does provide a constraint on false claims, that constraint is imperfect, as consumers do not necessarily become well informed by trying a product once. This is particularly evident in markets where products have significant credence or experience attributes.

Regardless of the number of levels of verifiability that are incorporated ultimately into the framework, the future usage and acceptance of this theory will be based on the ability of the framework to capture adequately the dynamics of modern advertising. Some of the factors that could influence the comprehensiveness of the SEC framework are the performance nature of claims (i.e., performance claims, nonperformance claims), and the heightened usage of transformational advertising. Each of these dimensions is discussed below.

The performance nature of the claim may influence perceived verifiability and skepticism. Examination of the experience and credence claims in the Ford, Smith, and Swasy (1989) study showed that each of the twenty experience claims were claims about product performance while fifteen of the twenty credence attribute claims were nonperformance related claims, e.g., claims about ingredients, production processes, etc. (See the appendix for the claims used in the study.) Perhaps consumers are more skeptical of performance claims than nonperformance claims. If so, this may explain the nonsignificant difference in skepticism toward experience and credence claims in the Ford et al. study and, hence, explains the lack of experience-credence differences. Future research needs to control for this possibility since the SEC framework does not include this factor.

It should be noted that while the Ford, Smith, and Swasy (1989) study used only performance-related experience claims, all experience claims may not be of this type. Some experience claims may, in fact, be nonperformance related. It appears to us that all such claims are by definition subjective. In fact, nonperformance experience claims seem to typify the type of claims found in transformational advertising, which sets the experience agenda by showing the consumer how to use and enjoy the product. Clearly, transformational advertising represents an important component in current advertising strategy. But how do consumers view the verifiability of such claims and how do the claims fit within a hierarchy of preferred claims such as the SEC framework?

Consider, for example, the claim "Michelob is made for weekends." It is not immediately clear where in the current SEC framework the claim fits. One could argue that the claim is verifiable by consumers, even though it would be difficult to untangle the effect of the usage occasion from the effect of the brand's advertising. And, assuming the claim is verifiable through experience, is it performance or nonperformance related? The performance characteristics of the claim may not be based on the product but on the performance of the marketer as s/he executes the promotion and advertising campaign (i.e., it is the marketer that defines the experience, not the consumer). Does this make the claim "verifiable" prior to purchase?

In summary, research is needed to gauge better the completeness of the SEC framework. Incorporating the above factors into future research will determine whether the framework will be collapsed ultimately to reflect a more simple ad claim verification process or expanded to reflect more sophisticated consumer decision heuristics.

Signals Used by Consumers to Extract Information

In our research to date, individual subjects were asked to respond to simple, one claim, advertising statements. However, in the real world of advertising, there are multiple bits of information in any ad, including brand names, money back guarantees, other verbal claims, visual cues, etc. It is this real-world phenomenon that brings up a host of interesting issues pertaining to how individuals extract information from advertising.

Research clearly supports the idea that consumers have developed rules for evaluating advertising claims. We do not as yet know the scope of those rules or how they are applied. Hoch and Ha (1986) contend that since consumers have difficulty assessing the value of information, they "consequently rely on a 'more is better' heuristic regardless of the diagnosticity of the decision environment" (p. 230). Certainly, information quantity is one type of signal but more of what type of information? What type of, if any, supporting claims or evidence do consumers prefer? One could speculate that when an experience or credence claim is made, consumers prefer that it be paired with a correlated search claim, e.g., verifiability of a nonsearch claim may be better enhanced by the use of a correlated search claim. For example, the experience claim "Our tent keeps you drier" may be bolstered more by a correlated search claim such as "Our tent is made with material x," than by an uncorrelated search claim such as "Our tent comes in four different colors." It remains to be seen if correlated experience claims bolster the effectiveness of other experience claims. In addition, interaction effects may exist between two correlated claims.

Certainly, research is required to understand the types of signals consumers use to diagnose the veracity of claims, particularly when faced with nonsearch claims. Some signals, such as brand names and money back guarantees, may be viewed as more diagnostic. Other signals may serve as surrogates for firsthand knowledge, and still others may be used simply to reduce risk (warranty). One promising area for research is to examine which types of signals consumers value most highly in advertising; how the utility of signals changes with the price; interpurchase cycles or other characteristics of the item; and how these signals interact to enhance verification and reduce skepticism.

Advertisers' Schemer Schema

The emphasis of the SEC framework is on the verification of performance and quality either before, during, or after purchase. Yet little is known about whether manufacturers actually think about claim verifiability and whether they think consumers are interested in verifying claims. If indeed advertisers are conscious of the ad verification process, research is required to identify the types of strategies used by advertisers to respond to this process.

Advertisers may provide guarantees or warranties in lieu of information to reduce the risks of negative consequences. Ironically, this strategy does not necessarily help consumers verify quality. In fact, it may actually discourage, or at least reduce the need for, claim verification. An alternative strategy is for advertisers to provide information to consumers to simplify the verification process (e.g., Thomas's English Muffins taste better because they have "nooks and crannies"). Or, they may rely on more easily verifiable product attributes. Heinz Ketchup, for example, adopted the easily verified "thickness" claim rather than the more central but less objective "richness" attribute, relying on consumer inference to link viscosity to flavor (see Hoch and Ha 1989). Certainly research is needed to ascertain whether advertisers consciously plan to emphasize search attribute claims or, when products include many credence attributes, whether they intentionally build and maintain reputations. It would be interesting to determine if these or other advertising strategies are common or product category specific.

In addition, we know little about how advertisers bolster nonsearch claims. As mentioned above, advertisers may prefer to emphasize (more believable) search attributes that are less highly correlated with product performance in lieu of (less believable) experience attributes that may be more highly correlated with product performance. Or, perhaps, experience claims are bolstered with ingredient claims and a warranty. This type of research would provide intriguing information about advertisers' schemer schemas.

Conclusion

The purpose of this paper was to summarize some of the promising research that has been completed with the EOI framework and to suggest opportunities for additional research. Clearly, much remains to be done. We hope our discussion will help stimulate research in marketing on the economics of information and eventually expand our understanding of how advertising is used in consumer decision making.

APPENDIX

Stimulus Claims Categorized by Type and Replicate

High, Objective, Search (HOS) Claims

Rep. 1: Portable Microcomputer
"The XX portable computer weighs less than ten pounds."
Rep. 2: Automobile
"XX offers air conditioning, AM stereo/FM stereo, and a leather-wrapped steering wheel as standard features."
Rep. 3: Domestic Truck
"XX trucks are available with V-8 or V-6 engines."
Rep. 4: Automobile
"The back seat of the XX has shoulder harnesses."
Rep. 5: Cedar Chest
"XX has five styles of cedar chests."

High, Objective, Experience (HOE) Claims

Rep. 1: Garden Tiller (mail order)
"After three weeks if you are not completely satisfied with the XX tiller/ cultivator, simply return it for a full refund, including shipping."
Rep. 2: Tent
"XX tent keeps you dry."
Rep. 3: Hot Water Heater
"The XX water heater lasts up to eight years."
Rep. 4: Indoor/Outdoor Carpeting
"XX indoor/outdoor carpeting will not mildew or rot for at least three years."
Rep. 5: Suspended Ceiling Panels
"XX ceiling panels will not sag even after seven years."

High, Objective, Credence (HOC) Claims

Rep. 1: Recliner
"XX laboratory tests the quality of its recliner by simulating twenty years of actual use."

Rep. 2: Automotive Service
"Every XX service center in the United States and Canada carries a full line of genuine XX parts."

Rep. 3: Business Phone System
"The installation of every XX phone system is headed by a crew chief with over seventeen years of experience."

Rep. 4: Electronic Amplifier
"During musical peaks, XX circuitry delivers up to four times the amplifier's rated power."

Rep. 5: Long Distance Phone Service
"XX has invested over $5 billion in their long-distance network."

High, Subjective, Search (HSS) Claims

Rep. 1: Jeweler
"XX has an extraordinary collection of jewelry."

Rep. 2: Microwave Oven
"The XX's size is perfect for smaller kitchens and tight spaces."

Rep. 3: Automobile
"XX has a pleasing contemporary design."

Rep. 4: Radar Detector
"XX is compact and attractively designed."

Rep. 5: Refrigerator
"You're going to like the choice of colors available with the new XX refrigerator."

High, Subjective, Experience (HSE) Claims

Rep. 1: Automotive Repair Service
"XX treats you fairly time after time."

Rep. 2: Automobile Insurance
"XX gives you satisfactory on-the-spot response to claims."

Rep. 3: Recliner
"XX's exclusive Strato-Brace system ensures lasting comfort and support over time."

Rep. 4: Vacation Resort
"The XX resort offers delicious meals in all three of its restaurants."

Rep. 5: Automobile Tire
"The XX tire gives you a comfortable ride."

High, Subjective, Credence (HSC) Claims

Rep. 1: Computer Programs for Small Businesses
"Each of XX's computer programs has been written by the best combination of computer specialists and experts within your industry."

Rep. 2: Domestic Truck
"XX knows more about making trucks than anyone."
Rep. 3: Jeweler
"XX carries the finest quality gems."
Rep. 4: Automobile Tire
"The XX all-terrain tire has been extensively tested."
Rep. 5: Realty Firm
"XX has the most qualified network of agents nationwide."

Low, Objective, Search (LOS) Claims

Rep. 1: Hand Saw
"The XX saw is available in 15", 20", and 24" sizes."
Rep. 2: Margarine
"XX has no cholesterol."
Rep. 3: Soup
"XX offers seventeen different soups."
Rep. 4: Oven Pan
"The XX oven pan comes with a snap-on cover."
Rep. 5: Chocolate Candy
"XX is available in either plain or peanut form."

Low, Objective, Experience (LOE) Claims

Rep. 1: Home Pregnancy Test
"XX gives you results in thirty minutes."
Rep. 2: Athletic Shoe
"The midsole of the XX will not compress even after five hundred miles of running."
Rep. 3: Fertilizer
"Water soluble XX products will not 'burn' plant leaves."
Rep. 4: Pudding
"XX pudding comes out smooth with just three minutes of stirring."
Rep. 5: Exercise Equipment
"Using the XX stomach exerciser for ten minutes a day will give you a flat-as-pancake stomach in thirty days."

Low, Objective, Credence (LOC) Claims

Rep. 1: Ice Chest/Cooler
"Our own ultratherm insulation is everywhere, including the lid."
Rep. 2: Hand Saw
"Three hundred professional carpenters participated in the design and testing of the new XX hand saw."

Rep. 3: Furniture Polish

"XX is used by seventy-seven of the world's one hundred leading galleries and museums."

Rep. 4: Fast Food

"XX's cheese, milk, sundaes, and cones provide up to 90 percent of your recommended daily allowance of calcium."

Rep. 5: Sunglasses

"XX photochromatic copper lenses reduce glare 38 percent more than copper-coated or dyed imitations."

Low, Subjective, Search (LSS) Claims

Rep. 1: Vodka

"XX is affordably priced."

Rep. 2: Pantyhose

"XX comes in exciting spring colors."

Rep. 3: Hair Care

"XX is available at many fine styling salons."

Rep. 4: Athletic Shoe

"XX comes in a variety of attractive styles."

Rep. 5: Clothing Cleaner

"XX gel form comes in convenient sizes."

Low, Subjective, Experience (LSE) Claims

Rep. 1: Instant Soup

"XX's special blend of seasonings makes everything taste especially delicious."

Rep. 2: Golf Video

"XX profoundly simplifies the golf swing."

Rep. 3: Glue

"XX is easy to use with professional results."

Rep. 4: Whiskey

"Coffee and our new blend of whiskey is a delicious warm drink."

Rep. 5: Sexual Videocassettes (mail order)

"The new XX video will make you tingle down to your toes."

Low, Subjective, Credence (LSC) Claims

Rep. 1: Sloppy Joe Mix

"XX is made from only the finest natural ingredients."

Rep. 2: Sparkling Wines

"XX is naturally fermented for better quality."

Rep. 3: Motor Oil
"XX is better for your engine than other brands of motor oil."
Rep. 4: Lotion for Thinning Hair
"XX's double action system strengthens each hair shaft and rejuvenates the follicle."
Rep. 5: Fruit Bar
"The fruit in XX candy bars is picked at the height of ripeness."

References

Darby, M.R., and E. Karni (1973). "Free Competition and the Optimal Amount of Fraud." *Journal of Law and Economics* 16 (April), 67-88.

Ford, Gary T., Darlene B. Smith, and John L. Swasy (1990). "Consumer Skepticism of Advertising Claims: Testing Hypotheses from Economics of Information." *Journal of Consumer Research* 16 (March), 433-441.

———— (1988). "An Empirical Test of the Search, Experience, and Credence Attributes Framework." *Advances in Consumer Research* 15, 234-238.

Hoch, Stephen J., and John Deighton (1989). "Managing What Consumers Learn from Experience." *Journal of Marketing* 53 (April), 1-20.

Hoch, Stephen J., and Young-Won Ha (1986). "Consumer Learning: Advertising and the Ambiguity of Product Experience." *Journal of Consumer Research* 13 (September), 221-233.

Nelson, Philip (1970). "Information and Consumer Behavior." *Journal of Political Economy* 78 (March-April), 311-29.

———— (1974). "Advertising as Information." *Journal of Political Economy* 83 (July-August), 729-754.

Smith, Darlene B. (1986). "An Empirical Examination of the Economics of Information." Unpublished dissertation, University of Maryland at College Park.

Empirical Insights for the FTC: Comments on the Bloom and Smith et al. Papers

Joshua L. Wiener

Frameworks such as that proposed by Bloom (1989) are so valuable because the alternative is that FTC decisions will be influenced by the political (internal marketing) skills of the staff. Screening rules can be identified by drawing upon and integrating marketing, consumer behavior, and economic theories. As prior comments have suggested, the use of economic theory is often framed in ideological terms. This is not helpful. The applicability of economic theories to FTC issues is an empirical question. It is for this reason that research such as that by Smith, Ford, and Swasy (1989) is so needed. Without general screening rules there is no rational way to allocate agency resources; without empirical research there is no rational way to develop screening systems.

Both the Bloom and Smith et al. papers emphasize the importance of self-correcting cues. A cue is self-correcting if market forces will work to insure its accuracy. As Bloom points out, if a cue is self-correcting then there is no need for government intervention.

Economic theory argues that a fundamental difference between a credence and experience attribute (good) is that the experience attribute (good) may be self-correcting, while the credence attribute (good) is not. The core of the argument is that experience attributes (goods) are self-correcting because if a product claim is not delivered the consumer will not buy the product again.

The question raised by Smith, Ford, and Swasy's study is this: Are markets for experience goods self-correcting? It is true that the ability to judge a product's performance is a necessary but insufficient condition for self-correction? A number of other factors may influence whether or not the market will be self-correcting. As Smith et al. point out, the product

313

must be repurchased on a frequent basis. A related timing issue is that the consumer must recall the claim when the product fails to live up to the claim. This is of particular importance when the claim involves how long the product will last.

A second set of issues stems from the interplay of skepticism and satisfaction. If individuals are skeptical of experience goods claims (Smith et al.'s finding) then they will discount the claims made. Dissatisfaction is generally viewed as the discrepancy between expectations and performance. If skepticism reduces the level of expectations then consumers may get what they expect—not what was promised. The result will be a lemons' market for claims—not a self-correcting market. The market will not be self-correcting because consumers will not be motivated to punish the seller for making claims that are not met, i.e., a satisfied consumer is not motivated to punish the seller by not buying the product.

When satisfaction is viewed as the driving force behind self-correcting markets, a number of new issues are raised. These include questions about the array of factors that influence a consumer's expectations. Clearly, product performance expectations will be influenced by nonclaim factors such as product class norms and use circumstances. It raises questions about how a consumer evaluates his or her satisfaction with a product or service. In particular, the commonplace conclusion that satisfaction depends upon far more than instrumental performance takes on added importance.

Finally, even if a consumer is not satisfied s/he might not alter purchase patterns. The attribute that does not meet expectations must be an important attribute. The consumer must think that there is a better alternative. All choices are made relative to the competition—being skeptical of claims, or unhappy with choices may not translate into observable behavior. In all likelihood there are many markets where consumers are not very satisfied with their choices but remain faithful to the "best of the worst."

Although not precisely directed to these papers, I wish also to suggest that researchers attend further to the issue of distributional consequences of consumer protection programs. This is, many consumer protection initiatives provide benefits to some consumers at the expense of others. For example, the promotion of less harmful products, such as ultra low tar cigarettes, might help those who would smoke anyway but harm those who would quit if "safer" alternatives were not available. A second example, is that restricting potentially misleading claims might help those who were deceived by these claims, but harm those who gained valuable information from these claims. Research is needed which will provide some insight into how policy options can be evaluated when there are distributional consequences.

The 1990s: Policy Research in Marketing and Regulation

In Part IV we turn our attention to the role for public policy research in the future. John Keane, dean of Notre Dame's Business School and immediate past director of the U.S. Bureau of the Census, opens this section with a discussion of changes in the business environment with which the FTC must deal. As we consider his points, the shifting challenges confronting the FTC in the future become more apparent.

We then turn our attention to the specific area of public policy research in marketing. Professors Gregory Gundlach and William Wilkie present an overview of the entire literature on public policy compiled in the marketing field since 1970. Here we see the timing of topic coverage as well as gaps in the literature, which provides a basis for considering priority topics for the future. Thomas Maronick next discusses the Federal Trade Commission's own research activity during the decade of the 1980s. From this paper we gain a clearer picture of what has been done and how priorities have shifted during this time.

The final five papers feature researchers from economics, the law, and marketing, each contributing ideas for future academic research projects and/or FTC programs. Janis Pappalardo, an economist on the FTC staff, discusses needs for research knowledge within the agency. It is interesting to compare her list of topics with those provided in the next two papers, by marketing academics Thomas Kinnear and Michael Mazis. Taken together, these three papers suggest a large number of important and potentially researchable projects. Law professor Stephen Calkins next provides an interesting example of a form of analysis infrequently seen by marketing academics but quite important in the public policy sphere: his proposal is that the FTC should move against airlines' use of frequent-flyer programs as representing unfair methods of competition. Our final paper in this part, by marketing professor Alan Andreasen, then offers some broader ideas about how future public policy research can be fostered. His ideas merit consideration by both individuals and institutions interested in improving public policy.

Perspectives on the Future Business Environment and the Federal Trade Commission

John G. Keane

Congratulations to the foresightful sponsors and organizers of this symposium. The University of Notre Dame is pleased to host this timely conclave on an important aspect of an important agency. Ironically, we meet a few blocks from our business school's Hurley Hall, funded by Edward N. Hurley, the first commissioner of the Federal Trade Commission.

On this seventy-fifth anniversary of the founding of the FTC, I heartily agree with current Commissioner Strenio: "It is time to reassess the role of the FTC with an eye to the remainder of the century."[1] From what I've observed you, the assembled, have the experience and motivation to do just that.

Section 5 of the law (Federal Trade Commission Act of 1914) that created the Federal Trade Commission summarized the agency's purpose in the following ten words: "Unfair methods of competition in commerce are hereby declared unlawful."[2] The sixty-third Congress did not define the phrase "unfair methods of competition," leaving that to the FTC and to the courts.

Concern with economic concentrations through business consolidations spawned this legislation. Ironically those feared consolidations of the past now seem the wave of the future.

My perspectives are in the following two categories: business environment considerations; summary observations. Perhaps one or more of the notions conveyed will prod further thinking by interested readers.

319

Business Environment Considerations

The following considerations are indicative business environment shifts of varying relevance to the Federal Trade Commission. They are perceived dimensions of change to factor into "The Federal Trade Commission in the 1990s."

Complexifying Business Environment

It has been anything but "business as usual" during most of this past decade. Consider these occurrences as but a sampling of the turmoil:

- In a cold-war like response, President Carter withdrew the U.S. Olympic team from the 1980 Olympics in Moscow.
- Tylenol tampering set the stage for so-called "crisis management."
- The Three Mile Island scare revamped and reversed nuclear power investment.
- The 1987 stock market crash caught virtually everyone unawares, reminding us anew of the great '29 crash.
- Savings and loan industry difficulties deepen and drain federal resources in unprecedented billions of dollars with no end in sight.
- Devastating oil spill causes mounting damage to Alaska's ecology and economy and some likely damage to Exxon's business.
- Moral and other considerations overpower market considerations in U.S. divestment of South African operations such as Mobil's just-announced sell off.
- On the positive side, each month that our economy remains healthy it sets a record of unprecendented duration.

These developments are barometers of the shifting business environment. Our economy is notably more difficult to forecast accurately because of changes in past patterns and economic relationships. Directly or indirectly these new complexities visit a special challenge to FTC policies and practices.

Mounting Global Competition

Rhetorically, I ask: Does anyone genuinely believe that the United States is not in intense *global* competition? Because the outcome is uncertain, global competition could be unfortunate. As W. Edwards Deming recently observed: "Business practices do not require a visa."[3] The new harmonized trade system and the announced dissolution by 1993 of internal European Economic Community trade barriers are two emerging and particularly significant developments.

At the recent annual American Assembly of Collegiate Schools of Business Deans' meeting, representatives from Yugoslavia, Hungary, and the Soviet Union strongly expressed their needs for business education. The first MBA degree programs are scheduled to be launched in the Soviet Union and Yugoslavia in 1990. Indicative of the times was a lead story in *The Wall Street Journal* earlier this month. Its title, "Global Drug Industry Appears to be Headed for a Big Consolidation,"[4] conveyed a trend. The story describes the planned merger of Philadelphia-based Smith Kline Beckman Corporation and London-based Beecham Group PLC as the largest and most complex drug industry merger ever to occur. It is a part of the consolidation trend necessitated by competition within the $127 billion global drug industry.

Companies and countries are (or they should be) positioning themselves for the 1990s' business environment. Other countries (U.S. competitors) have a basic business-government cooperation that puts U.S. businesses at a disadvantage. The authors of *American Business: A Two-Minute Warning* are among those who believe that there needs to be a reassessment of current approaches. They cast it this way in calling for antitrust reform: "We firmly believe competition is the greatest force for change. But 'competition' is now global. U.S. antitrust laws should reflect this indisputable and inevitable fact."[5] Our checks and balances form of government seemingly needs selectively to relax its traditional resistance to intra- and interindustry cooperation. Otherwise will not the global marketplace escalate the economic penalties that U.S. business incurs? Are such business regulatory bodies as the Justice Department and the Federal Trade Commission truly reflecting current global economic realities?

By not defining "unfair methods of competition" in its 1914 enabling legislation, Congress left it for others to do. What was then essentially a domestic context in which to define and to apply the concept of "unfair methods of competition" is now an international context. Should not the FTC's (and other regulatory bodies') governing concepts reflect the globalized economy?

Credit and Debt Expansions

Consumer credit and consumer debt ever expand, the apparent product of credit card proliferation fueled by intensifying competition and by consumer debt acceptance. Concurrently (and perhaps inevitably), there exists an enlarging debt-collection industry. Characterizing this industry are more companies, larger data banks, and improved systems geared to consumer debt collection. One of the unfortunate results of these developments is overzealous conduct by debt collection organizations. Some of their members resort to fraudulent means to intimidate consumers to pay what they owe. Addressing such deceptions is the responsibility of the Federal Trade Commission. Given the underlying dynamics, such deceptions seem likely to increase. What are the resultant implications for the Federal Trade Commission?

Expanding Negative Advertising

Anyone in doubt about expanding negative advertising need only recall recent election campaigns. The 1988 elections reflected negative advertising in local, state, and presidential contests.

Unfortunately, negative advertising is expanding in the nation's commerce also. An example is in the frenzied competition among national credit card sponsors. A recent MasterCard advertisement presented a mystery entitled "Murder on the American Express."[6] When competitive disparagement reaches such depths and becomes a focal point of marketing strategy, what does it suggest about our competitive propriety? Is there a point where advertising debasement and advertising deception intersect?

Knowledge of Advertising's Effects

How advertising works still defies precise definition and description. Its elusiveness is a function of the complexity of how advertising works. The more we learn about advertising the more we realize (or should realize) just how complex and daunting the understanding of advertising is. An insightful, multidisciplinary exploration of advertising's many dimensions surfaced in a provocative 1986 *Journal of Marketing* article by Richard W. Pollay. His comprehensive study spanned:

> (1) psychologists who view advertising as a source of learning or conditioning, with cognitive and affective results, (2) sociologists who emphasize the role modeling aspects of advertising and its impact on social behaviors, (3) anthropologists who see advertising in terms of rituals and symbols— incantations to give meaning to material affects and artifacts, (4) educators

who question the influence of advertising on child development, and (5) communications specialists who view ads as propaganda and question their role within and influence upon mass media. Also represented is the work of linguists, semanticists, philosophers, theologians, political scientists, economists, and perhaps the most integrative of the social scientists, historians.[7]

Given the Federal Trade Commission's responsibility to assess advertising and to do so in a rigorously scientific way, the FTC needs to encompass a multidisciplinary study approach.

Our Aging Population

Approximately 13 percent of our population is age sixty-five or older. The proportion and the base to which it applies are mounting. They will continue to do so long into the future. Millions more elderly people will be with us during the next decade and the decades beyond. As they have in the past, the elderly pose an inviting and susceptible target for unscrupulous business interests. Are there implications here for the Federal Trade Commission's Consumer Protection Bureau? Need a specially focused unit be formed? If so, what should be its mission, priorities, composition, etc.? Can we afford such a unit? Will the rising political clout of the elderly (who have a higher propensity to vote than any other population age segments) force such regulatory agencies as the FTC to focus on protection of the elderly?

Future FTC developments are currently unclear. What is not unclear is the large and increasing prominence of the elderly in the nation. Already the American Association of Retired Persons boasts a membership of over thirty million people!

Federal Statistical System Updating

Of the major countries of the world, the United States' federal statistical system is the most fragmented. In most nations (such as in neighboring Canada and Mexico), the federal statistical system operates through a single statistical agency. However, in our nation there are numerous statistical agencies of which the United States Census Bureau is the largest. Besides disseminating its own data, the Census Bureau also supplies data to many other statistical agencies.

Inevitably this leads to jurisdictional disputes, overlapping work, miscommunication, etc. Philosophies and practices can and do differ because of underlying differing traditions and conditions. Moreover, laws governing the protection of confidentiality block productive interagency cooperation. This general situation needs to be changed for it inhibits federal regulatory agencies dependent upon various federal statistical agencies for data. An excellent contemporary analysis of the problems and of potential remedial steps appeared in 1988 in *The Brookings Review.*[8] Its knowledgeable author, Sidney L. Jones, is former undersecretary of economic affairs in the Department of Commerce.

Federal Budget Stresses

It would be naive to consider the future of the FTC without considering current stresses on the federal budget. Of immediate and important significance are the so-called twin deficits: the merchandise trade deficit and the federal budget deficit. Both are large. Both seem intractable. Both are constraining influences on the federal budget and on what ultimately gets allocated to executive branch regulatory agencies such as the FTC.

The practical significance of this is that the FTC might well be severely impaired in carrying out its regulatory agenda. Given the current and foreseeable budget situation, this is a likely scenario. This means fewer than desired (and likely needed) resources for the Federal Trade Commission to do its job. Were this likelihood to materialize, the FTC would be consistently forced to establish and to follow enforcement priorities. The likely results seem that (1) less regulation would occur overall, (2) stringent priorities would need to be established and followed, and (3) support activities such as research might well be curtailed, stretched out, phased out, or otherwise negatively modified.

The federal budget situation is a serious and protracted problem. It is of such proportions that it will very likely be an ongoing constraint on the FTC, forcing it to be highly selective in its current and future regulatory agenda.

Government Gridlock Tendencies

From the mid-1980s on, the federal government has been having difficulty operating. Increasingly, deadlines are missed with short-term expediency displacing long-term solutions. The federal budget is a prime example of this where federal agencies are left to operate on a "continuing resolution"[9] basis. This leaves them in limbo as to what their current fiscal year budgets will be and delays final operational planning.

Congress seems to have increasing difficulty getting its work done. More subtle—yet more significant—is the growing tendency for Congress to procrastinate and to defer decisions or to compensate for underlying problems rather than to correct them. Too often expediency instead of effectiveness is the decision rule. Too often a state of uncertainty prevails when issues are overdue for resolution. This trend I term government gridlock. It is a worrisome dilemma.

Summary Observations

The FTC environment is not what it was, nor is it likely to be what it is. As Dorothy in the *Wizard of Oz* said, "Toto, I don't think we're in Kansas any more." Indeed we're not.

I've just identified and described briefly some of the dynamics indicative of the trends and environment challenging the FTC of the future. Consider them as a partial foundation for shaping the FTC and its work in the 1990s.

As further thought starters, I offer the following summary observations:

1. How should our enormous global trade pressures modify what constitutes the FTC's enabling doctrine concerning "unfair methods of competition"? To probe this question with another: Should not our pertinent regulatory agencies seriously consider and perhaps adopt lessened antitrust barriers in order to enhance our competitive capability, for example, in our race with Japan to create and to capture the global market for high density television (HDTV)?

2. The government-business relationship is more adversarial in philosophy and practice in the United States than in most of the rest of the world. Yet global competition demands there be more cooperation. The federal government in general and the Federal Trade Commission in particular need to reflect these new realities in their policies and practices as well as in their organizational structure and composition.

3. Traditionally, FTC policymakers are mostly lawyers and economists. Indeed the recently released American Bar Association

report discussed in the symposium focuses on the Federal Trade Commission's lawyers and economists with virtually no mention of other staff disciplines. Meanwhile the problems confronting the agency are ever more complex, intertwined, and more multidisciplinary in nature. Therefore, a worthwhile response would be to blend in political scientists, marketers, behavioral scientists, technologists, globalists, etc. at various levels but especially at the top echelons.

4. Business seems beset with a bewildering fusillade of national and local laws and regulations administrated by a variety of agencies. Each regulatory body is essentially focused on its own mission without formal coordination regarding any duplication, conflict, or confusion caused a given business or industry. The times call for more coordination among federal regulatory agencies and between federal and state agencies and state attorneys general.

5. Also, is it not time to propound one standard for deceptive advertising and not have each state attorney general pursue and prosecute alleged violators according to individual state statutes?

6. Combining federal statistical agencies on a carefully phased-in basis over time is desirable, however politically difficult. For example, combining the Census Bureau with the Bureau of Economic Analysis would benefit Federal Trade Commission work. Data collection, analysis, and dissemination activities would occur in a single agency. There would not be the current legal block barring data sharing because of confidentiality protection. This could be readily achieved because both agencies reside within the Commerce Department and both report to the undersecretary for economic affairs.

7. Given the business community's stake in this subject matter, its viewpoints should have adequate representation within the policy-setting activities of the FTC. I also note that there is no one from the corporate business community (beyond trade association and law firm representation) as a program participant in this symposium. Because the FTC's mission is to regulate *business*, business ought to have been diligently pursued and induced to participate in this program. In Japan and many other countries, business would be an active participant. Business needs to be a welcomed participant in this kind of conference. Until that occurs, business and government will likely remain in an adver-

sarial relationship that neither should endorse and both can ill afford.

8. My final consideration is to call for formalized strategic planning within the Federal Trade Commission. This would (as this symposium is doing) sensitize the Commission to the future, definitively focusing on obstacles, opportunities, and options. It would thereby help the Commission systematically to shape its future based on the perceived future. This is in contrast to government agencies' inherent predisposition to drift into the future in a change-resistant manner. In assessing this, please remember that it comes from someone who launched and led formal strategic planning in a large and complex federal agency, the United States Census Burea. It can be done. It ought to be done. I urge that it be done.

As the FTC approaches the next century, it seems well for us to reflect on Commissioner Hurley's 1917 observation: "Rivalry without cooperation means reckless, destructive competition; cooperation without rivalry means price fixing—the dry rot of business, deservedly condemned by law."[10] His succinct assertion about the trade-off and balance between business competition and business cooperation merits our continuing study, particularly as the United States becomes increasingly enmeshed with internationalizing economies.

Perhaps these few notions will prod your thinking for the future. I hope so, as I concurrently congratulate those who generated and those who are participating in this symposium. Its premise and promise suggest to me that it ought to become institutionalized.

Notes

1. Andrew J. Strenio, Jr. (1988), "The FTC in 1988: Phoenix or Finis?" *Journal of Public Policy and Marketing,* volume 7, p. 37.

2. Secretary of State (1915), *United States Statutes at Large* (Washington, DC: Government Printing Office), volume 38, part 1, p. 719.

3. Deming made this observation on April 17, 1989, during his speech accepting the Dow Jones Award at the annual meeting of the American Assembly of Collegiate Schools of Business in Montreal, Quebec, Canada.

4. Richard Koenig and Joann S. Lublin (1989), "Global Drug Industry Appears to be Headed for a Big Consolidation," *Wall Street Journal,* April 13, p. 1.

5. C. Jackson Grayson, Jr., and Carla O'Dell (1988), *American Business: A Two-Minute Warning* (New York: Macmillan, Inc.), pp. 262-263.

6. Stuart Elliot (1989), "Credit Card Sharks in a New Feeding Frenzy," *USA Today*, April 18, p. 6B.

7. Richard W. Pollay (1986), "The Distorted Mirror: Reflections on the Unintended Consequences of Advertising," *Journal of Marketing*, April, p. 19.

8. Sidney L. Jones (1988), "Staying on Top of the Numbers," *The Brookings Review*, Spring, p. 37.

9. The term *continuing resolution* refers to spending at the previous fiscal year's budget rate. This creates notable problems for affected agencies. For example, the practice prolongs uncertainty as to what a given budget will be, which impairs programmatic planning. More severe compression occurs when a given agency must cut its budget and has significantly less than a full year's budget span first to plan and then to effect the cut. These examples clue related difficulties.

10. Edward N. Hurley (1917), *Awakening of Business* (New York: Doubleday, Page, and Company), p. 42.

The Marketing Literature in Public Policy: 1970-1988

Gregory T. Gundlach and William L. Wilkie

Nearly two decades have passed since management practices at the Federal Trade Commission (FTC) were severely criticized in separate studies by Ralph Nader and the American Bar Association.[1] These and other criticisms made during a time of increasing consumerism provided the impetus for revitalization and strengthening of the government's role in consumer protection activities during the early 1970s.

Paralleling the strengthening of regulatory activities at the FTC and other governmental agencies during this period was an increase in marketing research on consumer protection issues. Academic researchers and others, through analytical and empirical contributions, began to play a more instrumental role in the regulatory process. Consumer research emerged as a useful mechanism for detecting the incidence and severity of present or potential market failures.

By the early 1980s, however, increasing complaints by businesses affected by enforcement actions, decreasing sentiment towards the effectiveness of regulation, growing foreign competition, and the emergence of a severe recession prompted a reconsideration of the government's role in consumer protection. Congress, acting in response to these occurrences, enacted measures to reduce the effective regulatory power of governmental agencies involved in consumer protection.[2] These measures greatly reduced the regulatory development, enforcement powers, and activities of the FTC and other governmental agencies in favor of a more conservative policy protocol.

During the 1980s, consumer research contributions in the area of public policy and marketing also declined. In contrast to the rigorous governmental research programs of the 1970s, this period emphasized impact evaluation studies directed at the assessment of governmental programs, rules, cases, and enforcement activities. Academic consumer research, while continuing, was de-emphasized in the policy process.

At present, consumer research activity at the FTC has been greatly curtailed. External activity by marketing academics also appears to be declining. On the horizon, continued uncertainty as to the appropriate role of government in consumer protection suggests a questionable future for the FTC and its use of consumer research. Recently, the American Bar Association (ABA) released its study of the role of the FTC. Initial findings indicate a rather lackluster performance over the last eight years. The ABA report suggests the agency redirect its efforts to provide clearer regulatory direction for industry. Disturbingly, however, the report made no mention of a role for marketing and consumer research in FTC decision making.

Given the current political climate and the almost two decades that have passed since policy issues received research prominence in the marketing literature, it should be useful to review the academic marketing literature on public policy. In an effort to provide such a perspective, this paper reports on the contributions of marketing to public policy from 1970 to 1988. As part of a larger project, 673 published marketing contributions to public policy were classified within a framework of key public policy and marketing topics. In this paper we summarize the initial results and implications of this classification process.

Public Policy and Marketing

Policy may be defined as the general principles by which a government is guided in its management of public affairs. Public policy encompasses actions by government in its management of public affairs concerning and affecting the welfare of the general populace (Black 1979). These actions presumably include any and all governmental initiatives. Such activities encompass federal, state, and local efforts in the development and enforcement of regulations and statutes, chosen governmental courses of action, and, as well, the deliberate absence of governmental activity or interference.

Many definitions of marketing are offered in the literature (cf., Kotler 1988; McCarthy and Perreault 1984). Generally these definitions suggest that marketing includes the performance of functions that seek to satisfy human wants by facilitating exchange relationships.

Figure 1
The Conceptual Domain of Public Policy and Marketing

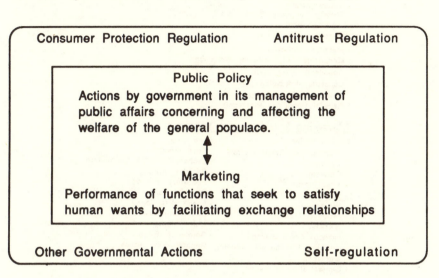

Together, the intersection of these two topical areas provides the domain of public policy and marketing. A comprehensive review of marketing's contribution to public policy research requires an examination of published contributions that appear within this domain. As indicated in figure 1, this encompassing arena includes policy issues that arise in the context of consumer protection, antitrust, and other governmental activities that interface with marketing. In addition, the deliberate absence of governmental action in the form of self-regulation, such as found within some areas of advertising, must also be included.

A Framework for Public Policy and Marketing

Within the general area of public policy and marketing lie many specific topics of interest. In order to classify the work in this area, a comprehensive framework of these topics is needed. Our development of this framework began with the organizational structure employed by Stern and Eovaldi (1986) in their text on the legal aspects of marketing. This structure, centered around the elements of the marketing mix, was then extended into the framework for this study.

Table 1
Framework for Public Policy and Marketing

Consumerism And Consumer Protection Topics
- Consumerism
- Socially Conscious Consumers
- Legal Aspects
- Marketing and Society
- Marketer Behavior
- Management of Consumer Protection
- Consumer Information
- Consumer Education
- Consumer Complaining
- General Consumer Protection

Marketing Management Topics

Product Issues
- Protection Of Trade Secrets
- Patents
- Copyright
- Trademarks
- Certification Marks
- Warranty
- Product Liability
- Safety
- Package And Labeling
- Nutrition Information Labeling
- Services
- General Product Issues

Price Issues
- Price Fixing
- Exchanging Price Information
- Parallel Pricing
- Predatory Pricing
- Discriminatory Pricing
- Credit Practices
- Robinson-patman Act
- Unit Pricing
- Reference Price
- General Price Issues

Place Issues
- Exclusive Dealing
- Tying Contracts
- Territorial And Customer Restrictions
- Resale Price Maintenance
- Reciprocity
- Refusals To Deal
- Functional Discounts
- Vertical Integration
- Gray Markets
- Mergers
- General Place Issues

Promotion Issues
- Deceptive Advertising
- Unfairness In Advertising
- Advertising To Children
- Advertising Substantiation
- Affirmative Disclosure
- Corrective Advertising
- Multiple Product Orders
- Comparative Advertising
- Endorsements
- Price Promotions
- Warranty Promotions
- Credit Promotions
- Sweepstakes And Contests
- Personal Selling Practices
- Mail Order Selling
- Referral Sales
- Brokerage
- Promotional Allowances
- Promotion Of Professional Services
- General Promotion Issues

General Topics

International
- Protectionism
- Corrupt Practices
- General International Issues

Research
- Market Research

Other Governmental Actions
- General Governmental Regulation

Public Policy Participants
- U.S. Supreme Court
- Administrative Agencies
- State And Local Government

General Antitrust
- Antitrust Regulation

Self-regulation
- Self-regulation Issues

As shown in table 1, the extended framework contains three basic subject headings with seventy-four specific topical areas. These areas provide the basis for subject classification in the review. The three basic subject headings are listed below.

Consumerism and Consumer Protection Topics: This heading contains topics related to the more macrodimensions of public policy and marketing. Ten broad subject areas are identified and deal with an array of topics extending from consumerism to general consumer protection issues.

Marketing Management Topics: Under this heading, specific subject areas which address the various elements of the marketing mix are identified. In total, fifty-three issues are listed under the classification of product, price, place, and promotion.

General Topics: A general heading is also specified in the framework and includes international issues, policy implications of marketing research, participants in the policy process, more general antitrust topics, other governmental actions, and self-regulation issues.

Literature Analysis

A modification of the snowball sampling technique in survey research was employed for the gathering of published marketing contributions from 1970 to 1988. The technique requires an initial set of respondents to be identified and then used as a basis for identifying other respondents (Goodman 1961). Initially, journals, major conference proceedings, and monographs containing marketing studies and articles dealing with public policy issues were identified. Figure 2 illustrates the research design and contains a full listing of the sources employed.

Subject indexes and the table of contents within each publication were reviewed for articles that by judgment of both authors addressed topical areas contained in the framework.[3] Additional studies or articles that were cited in these contributions were then examined regardless of their source. In total, 673 articles, studies, and books were included in the review.

Framework Classification

Within the framework, each contribution was classified employing a major and secondary level classification. This allowed for each contribu-

Figure 2

Research Design and Publication Sources

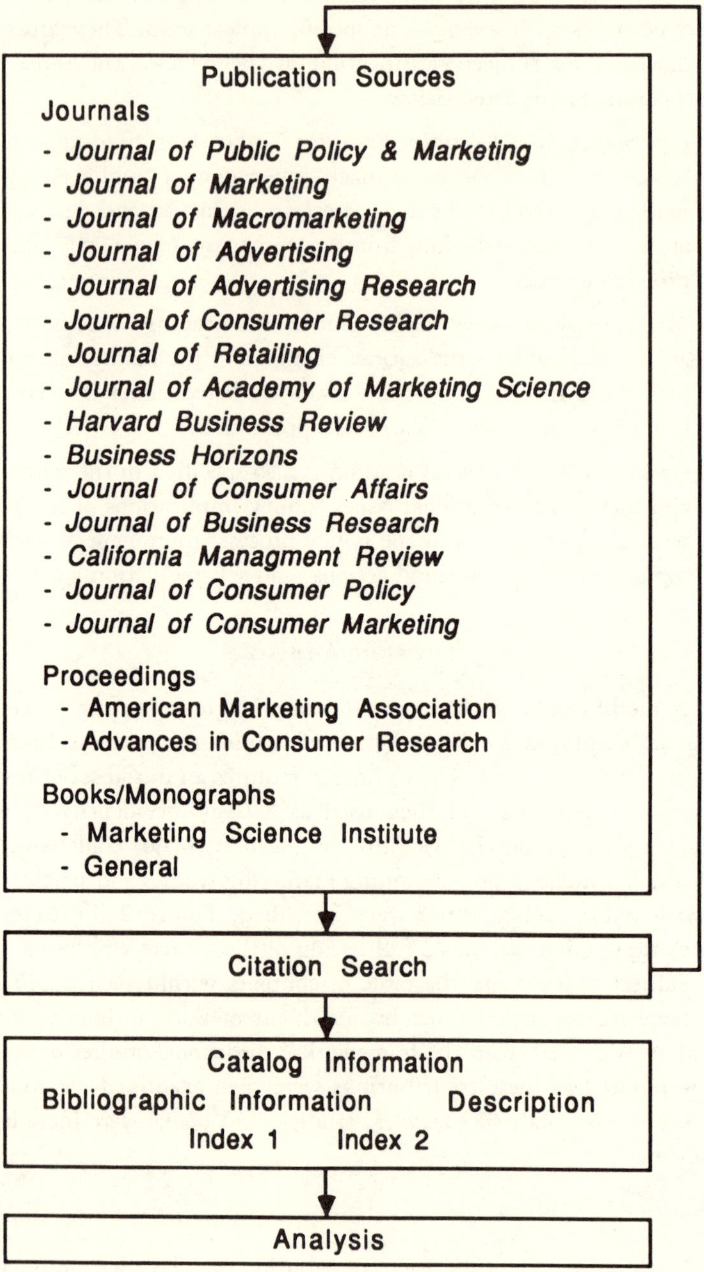

```
┌─────────────────────────────────────────────────────┐
│              Publication  Sources                    │
│  Journals                                            │
│  - Journal of Public Policy & Marketing              │
│  - Journal of Marketing                              │
│  - Journal of Macromarketing                         │
│  - Journal of Advertising                            │
│  - Journal of Advertising Research                   │
│  - Journal of Consumer Research                      │
│  - Journal of Retailing                              │
│  - Journal of Academy of Marketing Science           │
│  - Harvard Business Review                           │
│  - Business Horizons                                 │
│  - Journal of Consumer Affairs                       │
│  - Journal of Business Research                      │
│  - California Managment Review                        │
│  - Journal of Consumer Policy                        │
│  - Journal of Consumer Marketing                     │
│                                                      │
│  Proceedings                                         │
│    - American Marketing Association                   │
│    - Advances in Consumer Research                    │
│                                                      │
│  Books/Monographs                                    │
│    - Marketing Science Institute                      │
│    - General                                         │
└─────────────────────────────────────────────────────┘
                          │
┌─────────────────────────────────────────────────────┐
│                  Citation  Search                     │
└─────────────────────────────────────────────────────┘
                          │
┌─────────────────────────────────────────────────────┐
│                Catalog  Information                   │
│   Bibliographic  Information        Description       │
│          Index 1        Index 2                       │
└─────────────────────────────────────────────────────┘
                          │
┌─────────────────────────────────────────────────────┐
│                     Analysis                          │
└─────────────────────────────────────────────────────┘
```

tion to be classified potentially under two subject areas. For example, an article that dealt mainly with deceptive advertising may also have addressed corrective advertising. Under the major and secondary classification approach, the article would be classified under its major heading—deceptive advertising—and also under corrective advertising as a secondary heading.

Relevant bibliographic and descriptive information for each contribution was cataloged employing a database management system. This approach allowed for organization of the contributions and efficient access to each published contribution.

Publication Frequency Trends: 1970-1988

Figure 3 contains a frequency count of the number of published contributions found each year for the period 1970 to 1988. As can be seen

Figure 3
Publication Frequency 1970-1988
Marketing Contributions to Public Policy

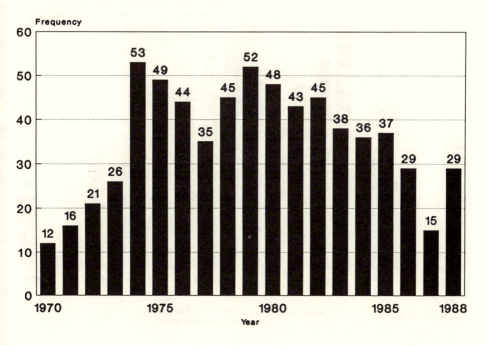

across the yearly frequency counts, marketing contributions to public policy generally increased during the period 1970 to 1980. This trend may be reflective of the revitalized initiative of the Federal Trade Commission during the same period that was highlighted earlier.

In contrast to the period 1970 to 1980, after 1980 a gradual decline in published contributions is evident. Coincidentally, this trend parallels the diminished enforcement activity of the Federal Trade Commission during the same period under the Reagan administration.

The decline in activity during the post-1980 period appears more acute when, as illustrated in figure 4, the contributions that were published in the *Journal of Public Policy & Marketing* are separated. Identifying only those articles and studies appearing within the nonspecialized marketing outlet sources, the frequency of marketing's contribution to public policy appears to have diminished steadily since the mid-1970s.

Trends across the major journals in marketing—*Journal of Marketing*

Figure 4
Publication Frequency 1970-1988
Nonspecialized Marketing Sources•

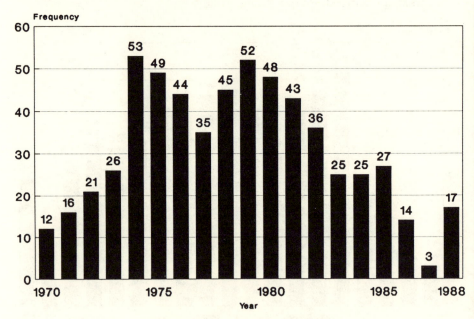

•Journal of Public Policy and Marketing
contributions not included.

Figure 5
Publication Frequency 1970 - 1988
Major Marketing Journals*

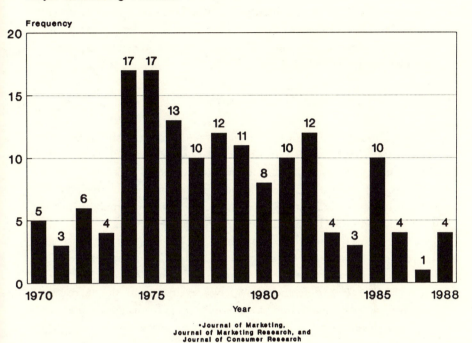

Frequency

Research, Journal of Marketing, and *Journal of Consumer Research*—are shown in figure 5. As illustrated, the frequency counts reveal a similar gradual decline of policy contributions across the major journals from the mid-1970s to 1988.

Topical Classification

Tables 2a-2d contain frequency counts and median year activity for each topical area within the framework. First and second index level frequency counts, their combined total and median year of activity are listed. Bar charts are also included in order to illustrate the first and second index level frequencies. Within the bar charts, second index level frequency counts are shown as additions to each first index level frequency count. For example, under the topic *consumerism*, thirty-three published

contributions were found and indexed under the first level. Two additional contributions were also located and judged to address consumerism
issues as a subtopic. These contributions were classified under the second
index level. In total, thirty-five published contributions were located for
the topic—consumerism issues. For consumerism, the median year of
published activity was found to be 1975.

Consumerism and Consumer Protection Topics

In table 2a, review of the frequency counts of published contributions for each topic under the subject heading—consumerism and consumer protection—indicates the topics: consumerism (33 first index/2
second index), legal (8/22), management of consumer protection (24/6),
and consumer information (42/6) topics received greater emphasis in the
literature than other framework subjects under the heading.

Interestingly, across these categories the median year for contributions addressing management of consumer protection topics was 1982. In
contrast, for the other categories, the median fell earlier, during the mid-
to-late 1970s. This difference may have resulted from the increasing
emphasis by policy makers as to the proper role of consumer protection
regulation during the 1980s under the Reagan administration.

Table 2a

Publication Frequency And Median Year By Topic

Consumerism And Consumer Protection Topics

Framework Topic	Frequency			Median Year Activity	Frequency Index
	First Index	Second Index	Total		0 5 10 15 20 25 30 35 40 45 50 55 60 First Index ▪▪▪ Second Index ▭
- Consumerism	33	2	35	(1975)	
- Socially Conscious Consumers	6		6		
- Legal Aspects	8	22	30		
- Marketing And Society	11	1	12	(1977)	
- Marketer Behavior	9		9		
- Management Of Consumer Protection	24	6	30	(1982)	
- Consumer Information	42	6	48	(1977)	
- Consumer Education	4		4		
- Consumer Complaining	12		12	(1978)	
- General Consumer Protection	14	1	15	(1979)	

Marketing Management Issues

As indicated within tables 2b and 2c, of the marketing mix elements, topics dealing with promotion appear to be represented more often in the review followed by product, price, and place or market channel issues. The apparent emphasis on promotion issues is the result, in part, of the numerous contributions that addressed deceptive and corrective advertising and advertising to children. Surprisingly, in relative comparison, very few contributions were found which addressed market channel issues. One possible explanation may have been the observed emphasis on issues that had a direct impact on the consumer rather than issues which concerned business to business issues. Many of the market channel topics concern this latter category.

Table 2b
Publication Frequency And Median Year By Topic
Marketing Management Topics

Framework Topic	Frequency			Median Year Activty	Frequency Index
	First Index	Second Index	Total		0 5 10 15 20 25 30 35 40 45 50 55 60 First Index ▰ Second Index ▱
Product					
- Trade Secrets					
- Patents		1	1		▫
- Copyright	1		1		▪
- Trademarks	7	2	9		▰▱
- Certification Marks	3		3		▰
- Warranty	19	1	20	(1980)	▰▰▰▱
- Product Liability	19		19	(1982)	▰▰▰
- Safety	10	7	17	(1978)	▰▰▱
- Package And Labeling	18	7	25	(1979)	▰▰▰▱
- Nutrition Information	25		25	(1980)	▰▰▰
- Services	6	3	9		▰▱
- General Product Issues	5	2	7		▰▱
Price					
- Price Fixing	2		2		▪
- Exchanging Price Info					
- Parallel Pricing					
- Predatory Pricing					
- Discriminatory Pricing	9		9		▰
- Credit Practices	14		14	(1976)	▰▰
- Robinson-patman Act	6		6		▰
- Unit Pricing	7	1	8		▰▱
- Reference Price	5		5		▪
- General Price Issues	5	1	6		▰▱

Table 2c
Publication Frequency And Median Year By Topic
Marketing Management Topics

Framework Topic	Frequency			Median Year Activity	Frequency Index
	First Index	Second Index	Total		0 5 10 15 20 25 30 35 40 45 50 55 60 — First Index ▆ Second Index ▭
Place					
- Exclusive Dealing					
- Tying Contracts	2		2		▪
- Territorial / Customer Restrictions	8		8		▭
- Resale Price Maint.	4		4		▪
- Reciprocity	3		3		▪
- Refusals To Deal	1		1		▪
- Functional Discounts					
- Vertical Integration					
- Gray Markets	4		4		▪
- Mergers	1		1		▪
- General Place Issues	6	13	19		▬▭
Promotion					
- Deceptive Advertising	41	15	56	(1978)	▬▬▬▬▬▭
- Unfairness In Adv.	2		2		▪
- Advertising To Children	24	1	25	(1978)	▬▬▭
- Adv. Substantiation	5	1	6		▬▭
- Affirmative Disclosure	7	5	12		▬▭
- Corrective Advertising	26	4	30	(1980)	▬▬▭
- Multiple Product Orders					
- Comparative Adv.	10	1	11	(1975)	▬▭
- Endorsements					
- Price Promotions		1	1		▭
- Warranty Promotions					
- Credit Promotions					
- Sweepstakes / Contests					
- Personal Selling	4	1	5		▬▭
- Mail Order Selling					
- Referral Sales					
- Brokerage					
- Promotional Allowances					
- Promotion Of Professional Services	14		14	(1980)	▬▬
- General Promotion	23	21	44	(1980)	▬▬▭

In addition to the divergence of emphasis in published contributions across the major topical headings representing the marketing mix elements, within each heading are several topics that received only minimal attention or none at all. These topics represent potential areas for future research. The following sections highlight the major contributions within each major topical heading and note those topics receiving minimal attention.

Product Issues. For articles addressing product issues (see table 2b), the topics of nutrition information labeling (25/0), package and labeling (18/7), product liability (19/0), warranty (19/1), and safety (10/7) appear prominently in the literature. Median years of publication for these topics fell in the late 1970s and early 1980s.

As can be seen in the table, several topics contain only a few contributions or none at all. Topics in which fewer than ten publications were found for the first level index include: protection of trade secrets (0/0), patents (0/1), copyright (1/0), trademarks (7/2), certification marks (3/0), package and labeling (8/17), services (6/3), and general product issues (5/2).

Price Issues. For contributions to price-related issues (see table 2b), credit practices (14/0) appear with the greatest frequency. The median year of publication activity for credit practices, the only median calculated, was in 1976.

Several topics, as with the product topics, are represented only minimally in the data base, with several topics containing no contributions. Topics containing fewer than ten published contributions for the first level index include: price fixing (2/0), exchanging price information (0/0), parallel pricing (0/0), predatory pricing (0/0), discriminatory pricing (9/0), Robinson Patman Act (6/0), unit pricing (7/1), reference price (5/0), and general price issues (5/1).

Place Issues. For articles concerning place or market channel issues (see table 2c), very few contributions were identified. Of the topics within the framework, the nongeneral topic appearing with the greatest frequency was territorial and customer restrictions (8/0). Topics containing very few contributions include: exclusive dealing (0/0), tying contracts (2/6), resale price maintenance (4/0), reciprocity (3/0), refusals to deal (1/0), functional discounts (0/0), vertical integration (0/0), mergers (1/0), and gray markets (4/0). The general place category contained a variety of contributions (6/13).

Promotional Issues. Of the contributions to promotional issues (see table 2c), deceptive advertising (41/15), corrective advertising (26/4), advertising to children (24/1), general promotional category (23/21), and promotion of professional services (14/0) appear to have received the majority of attention. The median year of published activity for these categories generally fell in the mid-to-late 1970s or 1980.

Within the review, several topics contained only a few contributions with some topics containing none at all. Topics containing fewer than ten contributions for the first level index heading include: unfairness in advertising (2/0), advertising substantiation (5/1), affirmative disclosure (7/5), multiple product orders (0/0), endorsements (0/0), price promotions (0/1), warranty promotions (0/0), credit promotions (0/0), sweepstakes and contests (0/0), personal selling practices (4/1), mail order selling (0/0), referral sales (0/0), brokerage (0/0), and promotional allowances (0/0).

General Topics

Of the general topical categories contained in table 2d, contributions that deal with administrative agency participants (57/1) in the public policy process contain the highest frequency of contributions. General international issues (33/2) and contributions that address market

Table 2d
Publication Frequency And Median Year By Topic
General Topics

Framework Topic	Frequency			Median Year Activty	Frequency Index 0 5 10 15 20 25 30 35 40 45 50 55 60 (First Index ■ Second Index ▭)
	First Index	Second Index	Total		
International					
- Protectionism	1		1		
- Corrupt Practices		5	5		
- General International	33	1	34	(1981)	
Research					
- Market Research	18	12	30	(1979)	
Public Policy Participants					
- U.S. Supreme Court	4		4		
- Administ. Agencies	57	1	58	(1979)	
- State And Local Gov't	8	1	9		
General Antitrust					
- General Antitrust Issues	18	4	22	(1978)	
Other Gov't Actions					
- General Governmental Regulation	13		13	(1982)	
Self-regulation					
- Self-regulation Issues	12	8	20	(1983)	

research (18/12), general antitrust (18/4), general governmental regulation (13/0), and self-regulation issues (12/8) also contain numerous contributions. The median year of activity for these categories ranged from 1978 to 1983.

Those topics receiving fewer than ten published contributions as identified within the first level index included: protectionism (1/0) and corrupt practices (0/5) under the international issues heading; and U.S. Supreme Court (4/0) and state and local government (8/1) topics under public policy participants.

Implications and Conclusions

This initial analysis of almost twenty years of work in marketing and public policy reveals that a considerable body of work has been done, covering a broad array of topics. At the same time, many topics have as yet received little or no attention from our field. Further, examination of the timing of the research suggests a declining frequency of marketing contributions to public policy since the late 1970s. Notwithstanding contributions appearing within the *Journal of Public Policy & Marketing*, published articles appearing in the major marketing journals have almost steadily declined since the mid-1970s. Such a decline likely suggests diminished interest among academicians towards public policy and marketing topics. This apparent decline, coupled with decreasing interest towards consumer research within the FTC, suggests an uncertain future for public policy and marketing-related research.

In the future, revitalization of public policy and marketing topics may require greater internal initiative within the marketing discipline. Previous reliance on FTC-centered research may have to be shifted in favor of more independently driven research. In this capacity, the *Journal of Public Policy & Marketing* may provide an invaluable outlet for contributions by marketers.

Viewing broadly those topics that have been addressed, many appear to have focused on policy issues originating from consumer-to-organization interaction. These contributions address, largely, consumer protection related issues. Very few marketing contributions were found that addressed business-to-business or antitrust related policy topics (generally, previous research that has addressed this topic has been centered within the economics literature). At present, however, a tradition of social science research on interorganizational relations and competition is developing in marketing, and should provide a foundation for future contributions to antitrust policy issues.

Notes

1. E. Cox, R. Fellmeth, and J. Schulz, *The Nader Report on the Federal Trade Commission VII* (1969). See also, *Report on the American Bar Association Commission to Study the Federal Trade Commission* (September 15, 1969).

2. For a full discussion of these steps see: William J. Baer (1986), "Where to From Here: Reflection of the Recent Saga of the Federal Trade Commission," *Oklahoma Law Review* 39, 51.

3. A modified delphi process was employed for disagreements as to both the determination of inclusion of a contribution in the review and its proper classification. The delphi process is a method of generating and refining group judgment and is based on the premise that several participant inputs are better than a single judgment (Jolson and Rossow 1971). The general approach is to collect individual judgments, summarize individual discrepancies, and return them to the judges for reassessment until a consensus is reached.

References

Baer, William J. (1986). "Where to From Here: Reflection of the Recent Saga of the Federal Trade Commission," *Oklahoma Law Review* 39, 51.

Black, Henry C. (1979). *Black's Law Dictionary*. St. Paul, MN: West Publishing Co.

Cox, E., R. Fellmeth, and J. Schulz (1969). *The Nader Report on the Federal Trade Commission VII*.

Goodman, Leo A. (1961). "Snowball Sampling." *Annals of Mathematical Statistics* 2, 148-170.

Jolson, Marvin A., and Gerald L. Rossow (1971). "The Delphi Process in Marketing Decision Making." *Journal of Marketing Research* (November), 443-448.

Kotler, Phillip (1988). *Marketing Management*. 6th ed. Englewood Cliffs, NJ: Prentice Hall.

McCarthy, Jerome E., and William D. Perreault, Jr. (1990). *Basic Marketing*. 10th ed. Homewood, Ill.: Richard D. Irwin.

Report on the American Bar Association Commission to Study the Federal Trade Commission (September 15, 1969).

Stern, Louis W., and Thomas L. Eovaldi (1986). *Legal Aspects of Marketing Strategy: Antitrust and Consumer Protection Issues*. Englewood Cliffs, NJ: Prentice-Hall, Inc.

Current Role of Research
at the Federal Trade Commission

Thomas J. Maronick

This paper focuses on the current role of research at the Federal Trade Commission and on the historical role that consumer and industrial survey research has played in the formulation and implementation of policy in the Bureau of Consumer Protection at the FTC. It should be noted that the paper does not include any discussion of the theoretical or economic research being done by the Bureau of Economics at the FTC, even though that research may be related to areas of marketing and consumer behavior. Further, the paper focuses primarily on how survey research was used in the Bureau of Consumer Protection during the 1980s to evaluate past FTC activities, specifically Trade Regulation Rules (TRRs), and how it has been used to aid in determining whether to initiate or pursue a case against marketplace participants. Finally, the paper addresses the issue of what role marketing and consumer research, including survey research, is likely to play in the future at the FTC.

A little background is necessary to establish the basis/credibility for the historical perspective. From 1980 until 1987, I was the head of the Office of Impact Evaluation in the Bureau of Consumer Protection at the FTC. Since 1987 I have been a part-time in-house consultant on marketing and advertising research. As head of the Office of Impact Evaluation, I am responsible for the design and implementation of consumer and industry research undertaken by the Bureau of Consumer Protection (BCP) and the Division in BCP.

Impact Evaluation, which was originally established in 1978 in the office of the deputy director of BCP, was envisioned as the institutionalization of the traditional evaluation approach to public policy (Maynard-Moody 1983). In other words, Impact Evaluation was established to undertake baseline and follow-up studies of trade regulation rules such as those identified by Baer (see Part II), with the goal of answering the question: "How well have the activities of the FTC really worked in the marketplace?" The unit was originally seen as a complement to the Office of Policy Planning which was charged with identifying areas where the FTC should have a presence (Jones 1974).

Times Have Changed

In fiscal year (FY) 1980, as noted by Strenio (see 1988 paper in Part II), the FTC had approximately seventeen hundred employees in Washington and the ten regional offices, and an overall agency budget of approximately $60 million. In FY 1980, Impact Evaluation had a staff of seven, including two college professors on leave from their universities, two staff marketing researchers with MBAs, a research assistant, and two secretaries. In addition, the unit had twelve marketing and consumer survey research consultants under contract for ad hoc advice. The budget for contracted survey research in FY 1981 was approximately $1 million. Some of the trade-rule studies contracted in FY 1981 and FY 1982 were:

Vocational Schools Rule	Baseline Study
Mobile Homes Rule	Baseline Study
Mag-Moss Warranty Rule	Follow-up Study
Care Labeling Rule	Follow-up Study
Cooling-Off Rule	Follow-up Study
Franchise Rule	Follow-up Study
Funeral Rule	Baseline Study
Food Rule	Baseline Study
Credit Practices Rule	Baseline Study
Holder-in-Due-Course	Follow-up Study
Used Cars Industry Study	Follow-up Study
R-Value Rule	Baseline Study
Appliance Energy Label Rule	Baseline Study

In addition, consumer survey research was contracted in four major industrywide investigations (advertising by attorneys; truth in lending; volume dentistry; Volkswagen), and one major housing defects case.

By 1984, while the number of employees at the FTC dropped by roughly 30 percent (see Strenio 1988 paper in Part II), the budget for contracted survey research undertaken through Impact Evaluation dropped by over 60 percent, to $325,000. The staff, only slightly reduced at that point, was primarily involved in completing earlier contracted survey research.

And the trend has continued. In FY 1988, as noted by Strenio (1988), the FTC had under one thousand employees and a budget only slightly higher than the 1980 figure ($66 million). Further, the overall budget has remained at the same level for FY 1989 with workyears dropping approximately 10 percent. The consequence of these funding short-falls on contracted research is obvious. When the choice is between retaining legal staff or providing funds for survey research projects, the choice is an easy one.

Impact Evaluation today has one part-time marketing and consumer research consultant and has a budget for contracted research of under $50,000. The funds available to Impact Evaluation support one major case and a number of small-scale studies, now affectionately called ministudies. No rule-related consumer research is currently under way, although a major research effort was recently completed as part of the Funeral Rule evaluation.

The obvious questions are these: Why the drop in funding for consumer research? What impact has it had on the activities of the Bureau of Consumer Protection?

The Changes

Three major policy decisions have had an effect on the role of marketing and consumer research in general and survey research in particular at the FTC. These decisions are: the disbanding of the Office of Policy Planning in BCP, the deemphasis on rule making that followed the Reagan appointees to the FTC, and the increased reliance on the Evaluation Committee in BCP.

Disbanding Office of Policy Planning

The Office of Policy Planning in BCP, which at one time was headed by a deputy director, was responsible for identifying new and emerging areas where the Bureau of Consumer Protection should have a presence. The unit, which in many ways institutionalized the planning function started by Commissioner Mary Gardiner Jones, was also the focal point for the input of marketing and consumer behavior expertise from the academic community into BCP and through the Bureau into the Commission. The distinguished alumni of the planning function in the Bureau of Consumer Protection at the FTC have been identified by Murphy (see his paper in Part III of this volume). The unit served in a capacity of an office of strategic planning for the Bureau.

The impact of disbanding the unit on the role of consumer and industry survey research at the FTC is evidenced by the fact that there have been few new industrywide studies undertaken since 1981. And at least one study (medigap) followed a formal congressional request for the information rather than having been initiated because of a perceived need in the marketplace.

Deemphasis on Rulemaking

The second policy decision which affected the role of consumer and industry research at the FTC was deemphasis of rule-making solutions to marketplace problems, with a shift to a case-by-case approach. As spelled out by Muris (1982) on the Food Rule, the criteria for justifying a trade rule was raised beyond anecdotal evidence to a rigid cost-benefit analysis of both the need for the rule and the remedy proposed. As further articulated by Muris in defining deception (1982), this analysis required reliable consumer and industry research. However, in addition to the cost-benefit standard being used to evaluate the need for trade rules, as budget funds became scarce the same standard was used to decide whether to undertake costly consumer survey research as part of rulemaking efforts.

The application of this new cost-benefit standard in the case of many of the trade rules then under consideration, notably the Vocational Schools, Mobile Homes, Food, Credit Practices, and Used Cars, resulted in decisions that rulemaking was either inappropriate (Vocational Schools, Mobile Homes, and Food Rules) or the rulemaking effort could not support the substantial costs of a consumer survey (Credit Practices).

In times of limited resources such as experienced in the 1980s, consumer research, as might be expected, was particularly vulnerable when the methodological difficulties inherent in studies were likely to result in substantial controversy regarding the results. For example, in the

Vocational Schools rulemaking, a critical element in the success of survey research into experiences of graduates was cooperation from vocational schools in identifying individuals who had enrolled. This meant getting cooperation from individual vocational schools and raised the potential criticism of selection bias in the sampling; schools with questionable practices would self-select out of the study. Further, the real economic issue in a cost-benefit analysis of the rule was whether the vocational school student would be better off in the long run if a rule that required pro rata refunds and disclosures were promulgated. Unfortunately, long-term benefits can only be measured with output measures (income, job security, etc.) at intervals at least five and probably ten years after imposition of the rule on the marketplace. Since the FTC had neither the resources nor the will to undertake such a massive study, it was decided that little valuable information could be generated by a vocational school study, particularly given the selection bias problems. As a result, the study was never undertaken and, ultimately, the rulemaking proceedings were terminated.

Another consequence of the deemphasis on rulemaking, particularly in the cases of the Mobile Homes, Vocational Schools, and Food Rules, was that as rules were terminated, no new baseline studies entered the pipeline for later follow-up evaluation. As a result, as Impact Evaluation undertook and completed studies of rules already promulgated, the demand for contract funds and the need for staff resources declined. Trade rules completed in the years following 1984 were Franchising, Cooling-Off, Care-Labeling, and Funerals. Further, since many of the earlier rules did not have baseline studies, follow-up survey research to assess the impact of the rule in the marketplace could not be justified on either a methodological or a fiscal basis.

Reliance on the Evaluation Committee

The third policy decision made by the FTC which has affected the role of consumer survey research at the FTC was the increased reliance on the Evaluation Committee in BCP. As noted by Baer (see Part II), the Evaluation Committee concept was first developed in 1978 to evaluate projects at their outset and to reassess their value at regular stages in their development. This enabled the Commission's senior management to shape the direction of initiatives, better assess costs and benefits, and make appropriate allocations of resources. The Evaluation Committee, composed of senior staff from BCP and the Bureau of Economics, attempted to assess the likely cost and benefits of any FTC action in any particular investigation. In carrying out its responsibility, in the early 1980s the Evaluation Committee established the 100-Hour Rule whereby investigations required approval by the committee before they could go from "initial phase" to "full phase." This meant that no more than 100 hours of staff time could be committed to a case prior to approval.

The consequence of the reassertion of the role of the Evaluation Committee in BCP and the 100-hour rule, from the perspective of Impact Evaluation and consumer and industry survey research, was a diminution in the magnitude of consumer surveys undertaken. In essence, the target audience for the results of the studies became the Evaluation Committee rather than the public at large or the FTC commissioners. This has led to the use of small-scale/low-budget "snap-shot" studies to justify or support cases brought before the Evaluation Committee. These studies have now evolved into the ministudy concept.

Ministudies

Ministudies typically involve copy tests, in-depth interviews, and occasionally focus groups. The sample sizes are very small, typically twenty to forty consumers, and the studies are usually done in a single mall location. The cost is relatively low, generally under $1,000 per study, and the time frame for the studies is very short, often being completed in two to three weeks.

The ministudy provides the Bureau with data from real consumers gathered by qualified interviewers administering a questionnaire developed by Impact Evaluation, and/or marketing consultants used by the various divisions. The research firms do no analysis but merely provide the Commission with the completed questionnaires. Hence, any tabulation or interpretation is done internally at the FTC.

The objective of the ministudies is to provide a target audience of the Evaluation Committee in general and the director of BCP in particular with some indication of how consumers who are neither lawyers nor economists interpret advertising and other claims in the marketplace. But, since the research effort is part of potential litigation of a case, the research still meets the accepted standards for survey research in general and deceptive advertising research in particular, the latter as spelled out in *Bristol-Myers Co.* (1975)—the Dry Ban standards.

The Kraft *Case*

The *Kraft Singles* case is an example of where the ministudy approach was used by the FTC as part of its decision to recommend litigation against Kraft. The issue was how consumers interpreted ads for Kraft Singles and claims related to milk content in single cheese slices. The initial stage of the investigation into this issue involved two ministudies of twenty and thirty respondents who were shown print ads for Kraft Singles in one mall location. After seeing the ad, respondents were asked questions about the ad. The studies had budgets of under $700 each and were each completed in approximately one month.

Since the *Kraft* case was contested, the FTC subsequently contracted for a full-scale copy test as part of the Bureau's litigation strategy. The full-scale study involved a contract with a major consumer research firm to undertake a print and broadcast copy test in geographically dispersed malls and with a sample of over three hundred. The budget for the contracted consumer research in the Kraft study was $30,000. The results of the large-scale study were introduced as part of the litigation. The ministudy, which was used in the development stages of the full-scale study, was not introduced. Nonetheless, the ministudy was subjected to rigorous scrutiny in the discovery stage of the litigation and tested in terms of the Dry Ban standards.

Benefits of the Ministudy Approach

There are two major benefits to the Bureau from the ministudy approach to litigation. First, the divisions are on firmer ground when they decide to challenge an ad or marketing practice since the decision is based, at least in part, on consumer interpretations of claims gathered by a disinterested party using generally accepted copy test techniques. Further, while recognizing the inherent limitations in the studies because the sample size in each ministudy is small and the research is done at a single mall location, the Evaluation Committee and the Director of BCP have a stronger basis for assessing the probable impact of claims in the marketplace and for their decision to approve or disapprove a particular case. This generally means that resources are used judiciously and frivolous cases are usually avoided.

Second, BCP staff are conceivably on firmer ground when they negotiate with an offending firm. Staff have consumer survey research data which give them a snap-shot of the marketplace and, since the methods used to gather the data are those generally used in advertising research, staff also have an indication of what the results of a larger scale study would likely be. In other words, the ministudy gives staff a reasonable idea what they would find if litigation were to progress and a full scale survey conducted. In addition, if the fact that such a study has been undertaken is divulged by the staff to the opposing counsel, it suggests a willingness on the part of the Bureau to do additional research to support the complaint and the litigation effort. As such, the ministudy conveys the message to the offending firm that the Commission is serious about the case and may stimulate a willingness to negotiate that might not otherwise be there.

Costs of Ministudy Approach

Obviously, while the level of effort necessary to design a ministudy to test a single claim in a single ad is lower than the level of effort involved in a larger scale study, the resulting data are also subject to many more limitations. First, the data are open to criticisms regarding representativeness because of the small sample size and the single mall location. In addition, the studies are open to criticism because they don't always have a control group, or because respondents saw only a single print ad in a forced-exposure setting and frequently without clutter ads. For example, in a recent OTC drug case being considered by the Commission, a ministudy was completed that copy-tested a print ad and package label for a consumer product. The results were criticized because the offending language on a package label had not been modified for any group. Unfortunately, to have modified the package label to address the criticisms would have been a long and costly process—two vices the ministudy seeks to avoid.

Another cost of the shift to the ministudy approach to research, from the perspective of academic researchers, is that the FTC can no longer be viewed as a source of data for academic research. Since the mid-1970s consumer research data from the FTC studies has provided a motherlode for academic research published in most of the major marketing journals. Examples include the professional services area (Eyes II and Lawyers Advertising), warranties (Mag-Moss Warranty Rule), corrective advertising (Listerine), affirmative disclosures, and labeling (R-Value and Appliance Energy Labeling). The consequence of the shift to the ministudy approach is that future FTC-funded consumer research studies will probably not provide the kind of data needed for publishable research in most major marketing journals, both because of the small size of the studies and because of the proprietary nature of the issues involved. In addition, when larger-scale studies are undertaken, they are likely to be industry-specific and not likely to address more global issues important in most reputable marketing journals.

The Future Role of Marketing and Consumer Research at the FTC

There is no question but that the Bureau of Consumer Protection views favorably the benefits it derives from consumer research. The benefits of judicious use of limited resources and better cases are greater than the implicit costs of less rigorous research and data with limited generalizability. Therefore, it is reasonable to expect the use of the ministudy approach to case evaluation to continue over the next few years. Whether the ministudy approach will be used beyond advertising cases is hard to tell. Obviously, cases involving activities outside of advertising are much less conducive of the ministudy approach, if for no other reason than the fact that screening costs tend to be substantially higher when low-incident populations are studied. In addition, mall-intercept studies are generally less appropriate in nonadvertising studies. Nonetheless, it is likely that variations on the ministudy approach will be used in some nonadvertising cases, because the constraints inherent in FTC actions in the 1990s, particularly limited staff and financial resources, make it a necessity.

Second, it is an open question whether the role of marketing and consumer behavior in general and survey research in particular will grow in the near term at the Commission. It is certain that budgets for consumer survey research will never return to the 1980-1981 levels. Budget constraints at the federal level and at the FTC are likely to put severe limits on funds for research activities, particularly for large-scale studies such as those undertaken during the late 1970s and early 1980s. On the other hand, it is likely that there will be a continued need for research for the case-by-case approach to marketplace failures. In short, with budget constraints as they presently exist, the question will always be: "Is the benefit derived from a $30,000 consumer study greater than the injury to consumers and the likely recovery from the offending company?"

Will There Be a Role for Marketing and Consumer Behavior Academics?

Whether academics from marketing and consumer behavior will ever again play as active a role in the planning function of the Bureau of

Consumer Protection and the Commission as they played in the late 1970s is unknown. Similarly, it is unclear what role industry-wide research, which drew heavily on consultants from marketing and consumer behavior, will play in the planning function of the Bureau. Clearly, it is within the mission of the FTC to draw on the expertise of marketing and consumer behavior academics and to undertake studies of the magnitude of Contact Lens, and Lawyers Advertising as a part of the rulemaking and case-selection process. Further, many industrywide issues are clearly beyond the intrastate domain of individual states and can only be effectively addressed at the federal level. However, because of policy shifts and budget constraints, it is doubtful that many industrywide studies will be undertaken in the foreseeable future. In addition, it is doubtful that the planning function using academics from marketing and consumer behavior will be institutionalized in the Bureau of Consumer Protection, partly because of budget constraints and partly because it is inherently inefficient to use academic experts to identify single case failures in the marketplace. It is more efficient to have experts in marketing and consumer behavior help in identifying industrywide problems. Again, as noted above, there is an unwillingness to undertake industrywide remedies to problems once identified.

What is likely to occur in terms of research and planning in the near term at the FTC are industrywide studies undertaken on an ad hoc basis in response to specific inquiries. Unfortunately, these studies are likely to be industry- or activity-specific (e.g., insurance, telemarketing, etc.) and call for very narrowly focused expertise. As for research addressing more fundamental marketing problems of interest to marketing and economic academicians (see Pappalardo's paper in this part), it is highly doubtful that these will be undertaken by the FTC in the foreseeable future. As noted in several papers in this volume, responsibility for research into public policy issues will need to rest with the marketing academic community and shared with the FTC.

References

Bristol-Myers & Co. v. FTC. 85 FTC 688 (1975).

Jones, Mary Gardiner (1974). "Planning the Federal Trade Commission's Consumer Protection Activities." *Journal of Consumer Affairs*, Summer, pp. 8-29.

Maynard-Moody, Steven. "Program Evaluation and Administrative Control." *Policy Studies Review*, vol. 2 (3), pp. 371-390.

Muris, Timothy J. (1982). "Memorandum to the Federal Trade Commission: Food Rule, Phase I." May 17, 1982.

Muris, Timothy J. (1982). "Memorandum for the Chairman of the Federal Trade Commission: Defining Deception." March 25, 1982.

Research Needs of the FTC in the 1990s:
Voice of a Lone FTC Staff Economist

Janis K. Pappalardo

These are the comments of a bureaucrat and a two-handed economist. On one hand, as a bureaucrat, I must warn you that the views
expressed today are my own and are not necessarily shared by any FTC
commissioners or other members of the Commission staff. On the other
hand, to prevent possible deception, I must further disclose that some of
my suggestions are not original but were contributed by my colleagues.

How Strong is the Need for More Research at the FTC?

Professor Wilkie's invitation to discuss the research needs of the FTC
in the 1990s came at a most opportune time. Only a few days earlier, at a
"brown bag" seminar, Commissioner Strenio asked the Bureau of Economics' Division of Consumer Protection for general comments. It wasn't long
before we lamented that the agency is missing the boat on important
policy issues because it is not devoting enough resources to basic research.

Only one week later, the ABA report focused on research (or should I
say the lack of research?) at the FTC. According to the report:

> The most important change for the Commission to make concerns its
> research agenda. FTC economists should use their comparative advantage
> in understanding how industries actually function to make the FTC the
> major repository of knowledge about the operation of American industry—
> including retail markets for consumer goods—and of antitrust and con-
> sumer protection enforcement. (See page S-28 of the ABA report in Appen-
> dix II of this book.)

More specifically, the report recommended that the economists play a larger role in consumer protection activities and that this could best be encouraged "by devoting more resources to basic research on consumer protection issues" (ABA, S-26). Most importantly, the ABA recognized that the expanded research agenda that it recommended "cannot be achieved without an increase in resources devoted to economic research" (ABA, S-28). The first research need in the 1990s—in the language used too often by supercilious professors (but impossible to resist here)—is "trivial" to identify. We need money!

Questions for Marketing Researchers

With the biggest research need identified, I now turn to more specific problems. To prepare for this conference, I informally polled my colleagues about research questions to which they want answers. More specifically, I asked: "What gaps in the marketing literature need to be closed to improve decision-making substantially?"

Improving the FTC's Understanding of Current Marketing Research

A typical response to this question was that gaps per se are hard to identify because nobody really knows where the marketing research frontier is. Given the current lack of manpower at the FTC, this response should not be surprising. Moreover, because the Bureau of Economics is staffed primarily by economists and the Bureau of Consumer Protection is staffed primarily by lawyers, what little time that is available to review academic research tends to be spent on economics or law. The first gap is therefore an admittedly embarrassing ignorance about your discipline.

To close this general ignorance gap, additional resources could be used to support in-house reviews of the marketing literature. An alternative solution is for you to bring your research to us (in economic parlance, you could decrease our costs of search). Conferences such as this one and ACCI's Wingspread conference are also extremely valuable.

I'm not sure whether the more specific research questions that I collected from my colleagues already have answers in the marketing literature. If they have, then let me know the appropriate citation. If they have not been answered, then let's think about ways to work together to get the answers we need. What follows is a grab bag of ideas, in no particular order of importance.

Health Claims

Health claims for foods have been keeping a few economists at the
FTC busy and are likely to continue to be an important area of research.
Jack Calfee and I have been working on a paper—now on about its 100th
rewrite—on how health claims should be regulated in food labeling. Alan
Mathios and Pauline Ippolito have been estimating econometric models to
determine how recent claims about fiber and cancer have affected the
production and consumption of high-fiber cereal and bread.

The FTC has concurrent jurisdiction with the FDA over the advertising and labeling of food. Through a memorandum of understanding,
however, the FTC has primary authority over advertising, and the FDA
has primary authority over labeling. Differences between the agencies'
view of health claims were brought into sharp focus by Kellogg in 1984.
At that time, Kellogg used the NCI's recommendations on fiber consumption and its link with cancer to promote its high-fiber cereal, All-
Bran. FDA staff reportedly responded to the campaign by suggesting that
because Kellogg linked consumption of its cereal with cancer prevention,
Kellogg had turned All-Bran into a drug that was being marketed illegally. In contrast, Carol Crawford, then director of the FTC's Bureau of
Consumer Protection, announced that All-Bran ads had "presented important public health recommendations in an accurate, useful, and substantiated way" (Crawford 1984). A vigorous debate over the appropriate use of
health claims in food marketing soon erupted.

As the health claims debate has evolved, it has occurred to me that
policy makers desperately need more information about how consumers
respond to health information on labels and in ads. One question to which
you might be able to provide an answer is this: "To what extent does the
credibility of health information in advertising differ from health information in labeling?" An answer to this question will help to determine
whether the level of substantiation required for labels should differ from
the level of substantiation required for ads. If consumers rely more on
labels than ads, one might argue that the cost of allowing a claim that
turns out to be false, as scientific understanding improves, is higher in
labeling than in advertising. A study designed to reveal the differential
credibility of information, say, on the front of a cereal box, on the back of
a cereal box, and on the nutrition information panel would be valuable to
policy makers.

I would also like an answer to a more general question. How **do** consumers use specific health information in ads or labels? Do consumers who had never heard about the NCI's findings before the Kellogg campaign began automatically believe the information? Or, do they instead use the information as a catalyst for gathering more information about diet and health from other sources, reserving judgment until verification comes from a less biased source? Surely the net effect of health claims depends on how such information is being processed. An even more general question concerns how to improve consumer understanding about risk trade-offs.

When Is Deceptive Pricing Deceptive?

Colleagues advise me that deceptive pricing is likely to be a hot topic in the future. The FTC's Guides Against Deceptive Pricing have been used to determine when price claims such as "sale," "free," and "below suggested retail price" are deceptive. In recent years, deceptive pricing cases brought on the basis of these guides have fallen into disfavor. At the same time, some states have been enacting rules against deceptive pricing that are similar to the FTC's guides. Possible differences in enforcement postures are likely to trigger a debate on deceptive pricing policy in the near future.

Although I have no special insight on what factors the Commission will consider if such a debate erupts (remember, I am speaking for myself and not for the agency), I can tell you what types of questions economists are likely to ask. The most obvious question is whether claims such as "free" induce people to pay more or buy more than they would have absent the claim. And even if such claims induce consumers to pay more or buy more, are consumers dissatisfied when all is said and done?

There seem to be cases where practices that one might call deceptive are really in the consumer interest. For example, consider the following scenario: If a consumer (1) observes an everyday low price of $2.99 for a product, (2) believes that price signals quality, and (3) observes that $2.99 is a relatively low price, then he might conclude that the $2.99 product is inferior and instead choose a more expensive product of identical quality. In this case, a manufacturer may find it imperative to advertise "buy one for $5.98 and get one free" instead of "every day low price of $2.99," and consumers might be better off if the "buy one get one free" induces them to buy the relatively inexpensive product without sacrificing quality.

Is this scenario a figment of a mad economist's imagination, or is it an outcome observed in the market? Evidence on consumer satisfaction with products for which potentially "deceptive" pricing claims are made vs. consumer satisfaction with products for which no such claims are made would be useful. It might also be useful to find out whether prices for identical products in states that enforce tough deceptive pricing statutes are lower or higher than in states without such enforcement. Finally, a thorough review of the use of such claims across product categories and within product categories for which quality data are available would shed some light on this debate. For example, the above scenario makes more sense for experience or credence goods (goods for which it is difficult for a consumer to evaluate quality prior to purchase and use) than for search goods.

Written Disclosure Statements

Does anybody read before they sign on the dotted line? One question that pops up in case after case is what to do when consumers sign statements indicating, in bold print, that a firm's only promises are those in the written contract. In cases where problems stem from alleged oral misrepresentations it is very hard to figure out what should be done. Economists often wonder whether it could possibly be efficient to run an economy based on the free exchange of property rights if consumers are not held responsible for reading their contracts. On the other hand— there's that second hand again—as a humanitarian one can't help but wonder how to help people who get fooled. Thus, there is a simple question that some of us would like an answer to: "Why do people sign these statements?" If we knew more about what induces people to sign them, we would be better equipped to evaluate possible solutions.

One research project that comes to mind is a comparison of satisfaction rates in states with "plain language" contract laws with satisfaction rates for the same product or service in states without such laws. If one could show that plain language contracts reduce consumer problems, it would be prudent to consider a more widespread application of such laws (assuming that the benefits outweigh the costs).

Resale Price Maintenance

Resale Price Maintenance (RPM) is a hot antitrust issue that would benefit from marketing research. Economists have been arguing for a long time that RPM should not be per se illegal because under certain conditions RPM is efficient. The standard argument is that RPM is sometimes necessary to ensure that retailers provide quality service to consumers. Discounters are likely to skimp on customer services. Consumers searching for good buys are then likely to use the services provided by full-price retailers but purchase from the discounters. If this free-riding is extensive, then the market for goods with high-quality sales services could eventually collapse and consumers would be harmed as a result.

An important question for marketing researchers is : "How extensive is the free-riding problem?" Strong empirical research is especially important on this issue because the argument that restrictions on discounting might actually improve consumer welfare is so counterintuitive.

Wilkie and Dickson's work suggests a basis for believing that standard free-riding stories are plausible (Wilkie 1988; Wilkie and Dickson 1985). In a survey of recent major appliance purchasers they found that "the salesperson" was rated as the "most useful information source." This finding suggests that retailer services of the type often thought to be most affected by free-riding really are important to consumers. The next step in the research is to determine how often consumers actually free-ride on the sales services of high quality stores and whether this type of free-riding is relatively pervasive in industries that have attempted to use RPM.

Consumer Complaint Behavior

The number and type of consumer complaints is considered in most economic analyses of consumer protection cases. Yet we feel that we do not have a very good feel for what the complaint numbers really mean. Andreasen has noted that since 1975 over five hundred papers have been prepared on the topic of consumer satisfaction/dissatisfaction and complaining behavior. Based on this literature he finds that

> as long as we are precise in our definition of the occasion for complaining, we can now conclude that consumers experience problems in about 20 percent of their purchases, complain to the seller (rarely to third parties) 40 percent of this time and perceive that they have received satisfaction from complaining behavior 60 percent of the time. (Andreasen 1988.)

The literature has certainly been helpful, but unfortunately, Andreasen also notes that research in the area has declined considerably. This is unfortunate because there is so much more that we need to know.

Andreasen's summary numbers are helpful because they give us a feel for average complaint rates. Unfortunately, these numbers don't tell us what to do when consumers appear to be satisfied with products that experts swear are worthless. Do we not see complaints in such cases because consumers feel too embarrassed about being duped to complain or because they really are satisfied? And if they are satisfied, what is the appropriate role for the government? What do these consumers think the appropriate role for government is? These are questions that marketing researchers could help answer.

Shopping for Credit

Colleagues who work on credit cases would like to know more about how consumers shop for credit. How much do consumers search for credit? On what basis do they choose a credit source? Do they understand terms such as the APR? How do consumers respond when they are denied credit; do they stop their search or look for another credit source?

Answers to these questions would be helpful for many policy reasons. A better understanding of how consumers shop would give us a basis for estimating the costs and benefits of laws designed to help consumers shop better. An understanding of what consumers do when they are denied credit would be helpful in the estimation of costs associated with violations of the Equal Credit Opportunity Act.

Branding

Another topic that colleagues are interested in is branding. Why do we observe valuable brand names for cheap experience goods that seem easy for competitors to copy? Moreover, why has branding been differentially successful for foods? Are there particular characteristics of foods that makes brand names important for some foods but not for others? This is an issue that comes up in different antitrust cases, and I would be happy to put anyone who is working in this area in contact with economists who also have expertise on this topic.

Relating Consumer Surveys to Actual Purchase Decisions

In many of our advertising cases we rely on copy tests to tell us how consumers interpret ads. Economists are interested in knowing more about how to translate results from such tests into consumer purchase decisions. For example, if we find that an ad might be misleading to some consumers, under what conditions would the misleading statement translate into a detrimental purchase decision? We simply need to know more about the correlation between what people say they will do and what they actually do. In addition, we need to know more about which survey techniques are most suitable for predicting consumer actions under a variety of circumstances.

Conclusion

In conclusion, I have tried to share some research ideas that people have been talking about at the FTC. This list is not definitive, and the ideas were collected on an ad hoc basis. Nevertheless, I hope that I have given you an idea of some topics that I think we should know more about.

One thing that was painfully obvious while preparing for this conference is that I do not know as much as I should about your research. Nor has the FTC set up institutions to make it easy to match up your need (and the needs of your graduate students) for research questions and the FTC's need for answers to these questions. I hope that we can begin a more systematic plan for matching your needs with the FTC's. One possibility is encouraging graduate students to work on topics of interest to the agency. This could be done by sponsoring a contest for the best thesis on a consumer protection question. Another possibility is to arrange a seminar series at the FTC devoted to marketing research similar to the seminar series currently devoted to economics. I am eager to search for better ways of bringing your insight into our analyses. Of course, it would help if we had more research time, which brings me back to my first point: we need money.

References

American Bar Association, Section of Antitrust Law, Special Committee to Study the Role of the Federal Trade Commission (1989). 56 *Antitrust & Trade Regulation Report* (Special Supplement) 1410, 7 April.

Andreasen, A. (1988). "Consumer Complaints and Redress: What We Know and What We Don't Know." *The Frontier of Research in the Consumer Interest*, edited by E. S. Maynes and the ACCI Research Committee, American Council on Consumer Interests, University of Missouri, Columbia, Missouri, 675-722.

Crawford, C. (1984). "Remarks of Carol T. Crawford, Director of the Bureau of Consumer Protection, Federal Trade Commission, before the American Advertising Federation." 4 December.

364 *Janis K. Pappalardo*

Wilkie, W. (1988). "The Marketing Contexts of Consumer Choice." *The Frontier of Research in the Consumer Interest*, edited by E. S. Maynes and the ACCI Research Committee, American Council on Consumer Interests, University of Missouri, Columbia, Missouri, 317-326.

Wilkie, W., and P. Dickson (1985). *Consumer Information Search and Shopping Behavior*. Cambridge, MA: Marketing Science Institute.

Research Priorities for Public Policy and Marketing in the 1990s

Thomas C. Kinnear

The 1990s offer great hope for a resurgence of significant public policy research in marketing. The 1980s have clearly been a time of reduced activity in this area over the level in the 1970s. The coming resurgence will occur as the result of the public's increasing interest in consumer issues, the strong push on the regulation of marketing activity coming from the attorneys general of the states, and from the increasing political interest nationally in these issues.

The purpose of this paper is to present a personal judgment as to those areas of research in the domain of the intersection of public policy and marketing that warrant the serious attention of marketing academics. In summary these areas of research are: (1) impact evaluation studies, (2) the relationship between the regulation of marketing activity by the FTC and by the National Association of Attorneys General (NAAG), (3) the understanding of consumer behavior as it actually occurs and not the economists' model of how it occurs, (4) the true state of channel dynamics especially the issues of slotting allowances and calendar agreements, (5) an understanding of the political process related to the regulation of marketing activity, and (6) the researching of actual marketing managers' behavior. This paper presents a brief personal comment on of each of these research questions.

Major Research Priorities

Impact Evaluation Research. At the very heart of rational decision making by public policy regulators at the FTC and elsewhere should be

365

the impact of their proposed actions on consumers and competition. Narrowly based legal arguments and rationales based on economic theory are unacceptable substitutes for actual impacts in the marketplace.

The FTC budget for impact evaluation studies has fallen from over a million dollars a year in the late 1970s to less than one-tenth of this amount in the late 1980s. Clearly the FTC is not doing the job in this regard. This is then a great opportunity for marketing academics to step forward and fill the void. Competent impact evaluation studies can make a contribution without the massive funding that the FTC previously provided. We need only remember the tremendous research on promotions to children that Terry Shimp did years ago to redirect totally the thinking of the FTC on this issue. It is time for those of us who are interested in a rational set of regulations to apply our research skills to this type of research.

Federal versus State Regulation. The reduced activity of the FTC with regard to consumer protection has resulted in the attorneys' general being much more proactive in the regulation of national marketers, especially national advertisers. NAAG members' approach to this regulation raises potential problems at many levels. First, the theory of regulation, the processes used, the concern for the measurement of the impact of their actions, and the level of legal research undertaken are all inferior to the approach that the FTC staff is capable of implementing. Second, there is a serious risk of the regulation fragmenting the United States economy into a burdensome set of state-specific regulations. The FTC needs to assert its power over the states in this regard. In the interim, there is a great need for research on the impact of NAAG activity on consumers and economic activity as a whole.

Consumer Behavior Research. The 1970s saw the birth of significant consumer research for the benefit of improved FTC actions in the consumer protection area. Unfortunately, budget cuts have greatly reduced the amount and importance of this type of research in FTC deliberations. The attempt truly to understand the real behavior of consumers in the marketplace has been replaced by the naive consumer behavior models of the economists. The regulation of marketing is too important to be abandoned to the economists' models.

Unfortunately, the rush of consumer behavior researchers to study public policy related issues is gone. It went with the lack of funding for this research. Also, it has become a low status type of research for new scholars within consumer behavior research. Those who currently are active as consumer researchers in this area are fundamentally just a subset of those who were active fifteen years ago. There is a tremendous need for this research, and a great opportunity for researchers to fill a void. One hopes that the field of consumer research has not become so insulated from the public policy needs of the day that it is incapable of stepping into this void.

Research on Channel Dynamics. Tremendous changes have taken place in the power relationships and associated behavior of institutions in distribution channels in recent years. A key example of this type of activity is the advent of slotting allowances to assure warehouse stocking and shelf space for consumer packaged goods. Some observers consider this acceptable market dynamics, while others see it as bordering on the extortion of money from the weak by the powerful retailers. The key point here is that the impacts of this and other related channel dynamics have not been studied by the FTC or any academic scholars.

Research on the Political Process of Regulation. It is clear from an examination of the research literature in marketing that there is very little research activity among marketing scholars on the issues surrounding the political process by which regulations are promulgated. It is time for marketing scholars jointly to do research with political scientists and other experts in these dynamics. Otherwise, marketers run the risk of being naive observers of the regulatory process at work.

Research on the Behavior of Marketing Managers. A number of presenters at the FTC Symposium at Notre Dame and at other occasions have made the point that we need to know more about how marketing managers actually think about and behave related to the issues of consumer protection and marketing regulation. I agree totally with this assertion. Indeed, this point is made even more important as one listens to the assumptions that many researchers and regulators make about managerial behavior. Quite frankly, these assumptions about managerial attitudes and behavior bear almost no resemblance to the actual behavior in which I have participated with these managers as a practicing manager, consultant, and board of directors member. Marketing scholars run the risk of doing research and proposing action in the public policy aspect of marketing that have little to do with managerial realities.

Conclusion

There is a great need for marketing scholars to step forward and fill the research void that exists in the six areas of research identified above. Marketing approaches to these issues offer unique insights that are surely needed at this time. Regulatory action will take place in these areas with or without the inputs of marketing scholars. It is just too important for society for marketing's knowledge and skills not to be represented.

Priority Public Policy Research Needs for the 1990s

Michael B. Mazis

There are a number of critical public policy research issues that are emerging in the 1990s. These issues are divided into five major categories and are discussed in detail below.

Advertising Regulation

One of the most important topics faced by the Federal Trade Commission (FTC) is the effectiveness of current efforts to regulate deceptive advertising. Although advertisers, state officials, and consumer advocates have called for more vigorous FTC activity in policing deceptive advertising, the impact of the current depleted regulatory effort has not been studied. Moreover, there have been few previous successful attempts to study the effect of advertising regulation (Healy and Kassarjian 1983; Higgens and McChensney 1984; Kassarjian and Kassarjian 1988; Leffler and Sauer 1984; Peltzman 1981).

Overall, the resources devoted to both public and private advertising regulation have declined substantially. For example, the recent American Bar Association report (1989) lamented the nearly 53 percent decline in FTC workyears over the last decade. Also, the television networks have significantly curtailed their oversight of advertising claims by reducing personnel assigned to standards and practices departments. CBS has cut its staff from eighty to twenty-nine people and NBC has slashed its group from sixty to twenty-nine people. There is also less review of television commercials because cable and independent stations, which devote few resources to advertising monitoring, have increased their share of prime-time TV-viewing audience (*Broadcasting* 1988). Although there have been significant resource declines in advertising regulation, the effect of such cutbacks on advertising claims should be examined. Advertising claims made prior to 1980 should be contrasted with current claims by means of content analyses.

In addition, a careful examination of various advertising guidelines proposed by the National Association of Attorneys General (NAAG) should be undertaken. One such study (Murphy and Richards 1989) investigated the impact of rental car advertising disclosures suggested by NAAG. However, additional research into consumer processing of these reference price advertising guidelines is needed. Also, greater understanding of consumer perception of product prices is needed.

Research into the limits of federal preemption of advertising regulation would be helpful in clarifying the dilemma created by states' efforts to regulate national advertising. Also, there is considerable uncertainty about NAAG's role in regulating national advertising. National advertisers such as Campbell and Kraft have paid fines and have changed their advertising as a result of NAAG complaints. Lawsuits initiated by Texas Attorney General Jim Mattox against TWA, Continental, British Airways, and Pan Am for violating NAAG airline advertising price guidelines currently are before the courts.

Cigarette and Alcoholic Beverage Advertising

There is continuing interest in government-mandated restriction of advertising claims made by cigarette and alcoholic beverage distributors. For example, Rep. Thomas Luken and Rep. Synar introduced legislation in 1989 (H.R. 1250 and H.R. 1493) that prohibits the use of pictures, colors, symbols, and brand-name logos in all tobacco advertisements. Also, the 1988 Surgeon General's Workshop on Drunk Driving (1989) recommended eliminating "youth-oriented" alcoholic beverage promotional activities. However, there is a need for greater research on these issues.

While there has been some recent eye-tracking research on readership of warnings in cigarette advertisements (Fischer, et al. 1989) and on billboards (Davis and Kendrick 1989), additional research is needed because labeling is often recommended as a remedy for providing information to cigarette smokers and to alcoholic beverage drinkers. Since product labels will soon appear on alcoholic beverage containers and warnings have been recommended for all alcoholic beverage advertisements (Surgeon General's Workshop on Drunk Driving 1989), research on health hazard messages for alcoholic beverages should be a high priority. Research on the size and the specific warning message would be useful. Also, the response of high-risk groups, such as pregnant women, should be investigated.

The effectiveness of other proposed regulations also should be studied. For example, although elimination of all models in tobacco and alcoholic beverage ads has been suggested, the role of imagery in processing of these messages has not been carefully examined. The encoding and subsequent retrieval of such images is not fully understood. Moreover, the impact of promotional techniques that may have a strong youth appeal, such as the use of rock-music endorsers, animation, and animals, has not been investigated.

Children's Advertising

While consumer advocates were successful in the 1970s in persuading the FTC and Federal Communications Commission (FCC) to ban practices such as deceptive toy commercials and host selling, the hands off attitude of these regulatory agencies has led to the call by Action for Children's Television (ACT) and others for an end to some current marketing practices. For example, ACT petitioned the FCC to require disclaimers in programs featuring cartoon stars, such as Care Bears, Lazer-Tag Academy, My Little Pony, and G.I. Joe's, who are also toys. Such disclosures would reveal that the programs are essentially advertisements. However, additional research is needed to determine children's processing of these messages and their effectiveness.

Competition

A number of important competitive issues are amenable to research. The FTC has shown some recent interest in studying cooperative advertising and slotting allowances. Such topics reflect the changing nature of retail distribution in the United States; major retailers control supermarket shelf space and they are exerting increasing pressure on manufacturers to pay a premium for this distribution, especially for new products. Economic research currently is needed on the possible disadvantages faced by small distributors and retailers in competing against large chains.

While both horizontal and vertical mergers were rarely challenged in the Reagan era, questions are currently being raised about the wisdom of such a one-sided view of antitrust law enforcement. Examination of the costs and benefits of this policy is needed, especially in industries such as airlines. Mergers have greatly reduced competition in certain airline hubs. A careful economic analysis of the potential anticompetitive effects of this situation should be undertaken. Also, the impact of airline reservation systems that favor major carriers should be studied. Airline agents' processing of computerized reservation information is a fruitful area for research.

In addition, proposals to enact anticompetitive trade bills and to suspend antitrust law enforcement for the purpose of encouraging development of high-technology products should be analyzed carefully. Such proposals have included establishing technical standards for high-definition television (HDTV) that serve as trade barriers to keep out foreign competition. However, these actions may serve to raise the price of HDTV to consumers. The suspension of antitrust laws for the development of HDTV technology and for joint manufacture of HDTV products may raise prices, also. Research is needed on various approaches to establish a U.S. industrial policy.

Information Processing

Research is needed also on the application of recent consumer processing research to public policy issues. For example, further understanding of the framing and representation in memory of risk disclosures is needed. Processing by vulnerable groups such as the elderly and minorities is a neglected research area.

Moreover, greater knowledge of consumers' attributions based on marketplace signals is needed. To what extent do well-known brand names override consumers' inherent skepticism of credence claims? How do consumers use truthful food advertising claims, such as "no cholesterol" or "contains oat bran," to associate healthful qualities with advertised?

Finally, enhanced understanding of marketers' cognitive structures will provide knowledge about "schemer schema." This research would provide needed information about practices that might deter fraudulent or unethical marketing behavior.

References

American Bar Association (1989). Report of the American Bar Association Section of Antitrust Law Special Committee to Study the Role of the Federal Trade Commission. Washington, D.C.

Broadcasting (1988). "Television Network Censured for Censor's Cutback." (September 19), pp. 60-61.

Davis, Ronald M., and Juliette S. Kendrick (1989). "The Surgeon General's Warnings in Outdoor Cigarette Advertising: Are They Readable?" *Journal of the American Medical Association* 261 (January 6), pp. 90-94.

Fischer, Paul M., John W. Richards, Earl J. Berman, and Dean M. Krugman (1989). "Recall and Eye Tracking Study of Adolescents Viewing Tobacco Advertisements." *Journal of the American Medical Association* 261 (January 6), pp. 84-89.

Healy, Jack S., and Harold H. Kassarjian (1983). "Advertising Substantiation and Advertiser Response: A Content Analysis of Magazine Advertisements." *Journal of Marketing* 47 (Winter), pp. 107-117.

Higgins, Richard S., and Fred S. McChesney (1984). "An Economic Analysis of the FTC Ad Substantiation Program." In *Empirical Approaches to Consumer Protection Economics*, Pauline M. Ippolito and David T. Scheffman, eds. Washington, D.C.: Federal Trade Commission. Pp. 197-211.

Kassarjian, Harold H., and Waltraud M. Kassarjian (1988). "The Impact of Regulation on Advertising: A Content Analysis." *Journal of Consumer Policy* 11, pp. 269-285.

Leffler, Keith B., and Raymond Sauer, Jr. (1984). "The Effects of the Advertising Substantiation Program on Advertising Agencies." In *Empirical Approaches to Consumer Protection Economics*, Pauline M. Ippolito and David T. Scheffman, eds. Washington, D.C.: Federal Trade Commission. Pp. 177-195.

Murphy, John H., and Jef I. Richards (1989). "An Investigation of the Effects of Disclosure Statements in Rental Car Commercials." Paper presented to American Advertising Federation Spring Government Affairs Conference.

Peltzman, Samuel (1981). "The Effects of FTC Advertising Regulation." *Journal of Law and Economics* 24 (December), pp. 401-448.

Surgeon General's Workshop on Drunk Driving (1989). *Proceedings.* Washington, D.C.: U.S. Department of Health and Human Services.

"Unfair Methods of Competition" in the 1990s: The Example of Frequent-Flyer Programs

Stephen Calkins

The Federal Trade Commission was once on the periphery of antitrust policy.[1] The Justice Department's Antitrust Division enjoyed the dominant federal role in shaping the law.[2] Even during the antitrust retrenchment of the 1980s the Division's program enjoyed widespread support in part because of the near-uniform approval of criminal sanctions against cartels. Once the FTC's enthusiasm for Robinson-Patman Act enforcement waned, in contrast, the agency became unsure of its mission.

During the past decade the FTC started to identify an important antitrust role. As the Antitrust Division has devoted increasing percentages of its resources to criminal enforcement, the FTC has come to equal or surpass that agency's importance in shaping antitrust law as a litigant.[3] The FTC's most important antitrust assignment is merger enforcement, but there is more[4]. The FTC is well suited to address the antitrust challenge of the 1990s, namely, advancing and drawing upon our knowledge of strategic behavior to reduce harmful conduct without deterring vigorous competition.[5] Analysis of strategic behavior has become a small growth industry.[6] Although there is increasing agreement that such behavior can harm competition, distinguishing harmful from procompetitive behavior is exceedingly difficult.[7] Because antitrust treble damages and suits cannot be based on a finding that a practice is an unfair method of competition under the FTC Act, the Commission could end a harmful practice with minimum risk of chilling competition.

The purpose of this paper is to suggest an example of how competition might be improved by banning an "unfair method of competition":

374

the government should evaluate the competitive effects of airline frequent flyer programs (FFPs) and consider prohibiting them.[8] Although the FTC, which normally enforces the federal rule against unfair methods of competition, lacks jurisdiction over airlines,[9] the Department of Transportation enforces an identical provision.[10] Moreover, Congress could—and probably should—extend the FTC's jurisdiction to include air carriers.

The Features of FFPs

FFPs have two essential features.[11] First, they are designed to benefit the traveler (the "agent") and not necessarily the person or entity who bears the cost of the ticket (the "principal"). The first FFP gave passengers coupons worth 50 percent discounts on future flights. This was quickly abandoned when principals started requiring agents to turn in coupons. Ever since, the programs have been designed to make it difficult for principals to enjoy their benefits.[12]

Second, FFP award structures usually are nonlinear. They thus disproportionately reward repeat business.[13] FFP credits are of little value unless one has been or will be flying regularly on the issuing airline.

FFP's create an agency-cost problem by encouraging agents to act inconsistently with the interests of principals.[14] Even wealthy business travelers were tempted to arrange their schedules to take the then-Eastern Air Shuttle when it was offering $50 personal gift certificates at fashionable stores to anyone traveling round trip (fare: $198).[15] Nonlinearity makes more efficient the exploiting of the principal-agent tension. For instance, a linear award system such as cash payments would be enjoyed by agent and non-agent travelers alike, whereas FFP credits benefit only those who fly regularly, i.e., persons likely to be agents.[16]

There is substantial anecdotal and survey evidence that FFPs work, i.e., they persuade business travelers (agents) to use flights they otherwise would not.[17] This evidence is supported by the programs' proliferation and by the airlines' marketing emphasis on them.[18] Perhaps it is conceivable that principals applaud the rewarding of agents as a means to increase the compensation of those who travel regularly. This seems improbable, however, given the number of firms trying to lessen the programs' distortions.[19] Moreover, FFPs not only harm principals, they also may harm competitors, the competitive process, and nonparticipating consumers.

Impact on Competition

The same two features of FFPs—exploitation of the agency-cost problem, and nonlinear awards—explain their potential for harming competition. First, consider that FFPs rewards the traveler, who is frequently the true customer's agent, for selecting the airline. A market economy seeks to drive price to marginal cost and to achieve the optimal balance of price and quality. This cannot occur, however, if the focus of competition is on something other than price and quality. Rewarding agents normally will increase nominal (gross) prices. This is because rewards, like an excise tax, separate gross and net prices, thereby shifting the supply curve up (or the demand curve down).[20] Moreover, sales will tend to shift to firms rewarding agents, some of which are likely to be relatively inefficient. The genius of the market economy is that it shifts patronage to more efficient firms. Anything that interferes with this harms the competitive process.

Second, FFPs' nonlinear reward structures tend to make entry more difficult and demand less elastic. Again it is helpful to compare FFP credits and cash. FFPs may impede entry and disproportionately benefit leading airlines, whereas cash cannot. Anyone can offer cash, but only an airline operating on a substantial scale—or, which may not be as efficient, a consortium of airlines—can offer an attractive FFP. Perhaps this would not matter were airline gates unlimited, but they are not. FFPs also tend to make demand less elastic for business and personal travel alike. The nonlinearity of rewards means that credits on one's customary airline(s) are worth more than credits on other airlines; a sensible consumer should patronize other airlines only when, ceterus paribus, the savings from a cheaper fare more than outweigh the differential value of credits.

If FFPs influence flight selection—and they appear to—the above factors indicate that FFPs are causing an undetermined amount of harm to competition.[21] FFPs also may benefit airlines and harm consumers by increasing search costs. It is difficult to compare various plans, which, in any event, are subject to change and in fact do change. It is even more daunting for a traveler paying for his or her own ticket to decide how highly to value credits. FFPs make comparison shopping onerous, which is a cost by itself, and they may defeat consumer attempts to select the best value, thus harming the competitive process.[22] For a number of reasons, therefore, FFPs likely are causing significant competitive harm. Certainly they deserve prompt governmental investigation.

An Unfair Method of Competition?

If further investigation confirms that FFPs are competitively harmful, the government should end them by rule, guideline, or litigation under the "unfair method of competition" standard. In making this analysis FFPs can be compared to commercial bribery even though the two practices have quite different criminal and ethical consequences. Bribery has been regarded as an "unfair method of competition" in part because of its competitive distortions.[23] The paucity of recent bribery cases can be attributed less to legal ambivalence than to the factual ambiguity of certain practices and, for clear cases, to the superiority of criminal enforcement.

The only competitively significant difference between bribery and FFPs is that bribery is secret. In theory, openness permits principals to eliminate agency-cost problems and allows competitors to react to programs and eliminate any effect on competition.[24] In practice, however, principals are unable to prevent distortion. Since an essential element of FFPs is exploitation of the agency-cost problem, airlines could be expected to change the programs if this problem was solved.[25] Moreover, openness solves none of the nonlinearity problems (increased difficulty of entry and decreased elasticity of demand) discussed above.

While it would require an extension of existing doctrine to end FFPs, doctrine would not preclude a finding of "unfairness," given the similarity of the effects of FFPs and of commercial bribery. Section 5 of the FTC Act and Section 411 of the Federal Aviation Act reach somewhat beyond the antitrust laws.[26] If strategic behavior such as FFPs in fact harms competition, an agency with authority over unfair methods of competition should be able to end them or lessen their effect.

Ending FFPs would not end principal-agent tensions, of course; presumably airlines would woo business travelers with amenities. However, amenities impede entry and decrease the elasticity of demand less than FFPs, because they are fully consumed when offered; moreover, my guess—and it is only that—is that most feasible amenities would distort competition less than FFPs because travelers do not value them as highly. Finally, even if agency costs lead to excessive amenities, at least the occasional traveler can enjoy amenities, which is more than can be said about frequent flyer credits.

Conclusion

FFPs have existed for over eight years without challenge by the Department of Transportation. This paper recommends that the Department promptly evaluate the competitive consequences of FFPs and take steps to end them if they are harmful. Alternatively, Congress could, and probably should, extend the FTC's authority to reach airlines. In the CAB Sunset Act Congress gave authority over unfair acts and practices to the Department of Transportation rather than the FTC because the FTC was less familiar with airlines, was subject to Magnuson-Moss rulemaking procedures, and to avoid division of responsibility between the two agencies (for instance, with respect to charter flight tariff rules).[27] These reasons are far from compelling. The FTC's economists quickly could master the airline industry if they have not already, classic trade regulation rulemaking has become relatively unimportant, and sensible leadership usually can prevent overlapping authority from presenting serious problems.[28]

A challenge to FFPs, if one is warranted, could contribute to the development of competition law. The law would be particularly likely to benefit from an FTC challenge. The FTC has already developed considerable expertise in analyzing strategic behavior. This expertise would be furthered, and generally applicable legal standards clarified by formal, public evaluation of FFPs.

Concern about strategic behavior is related to a competition-enforcement concern about identifying conduct that should be ended without elaborate proof of market power. For an appellate judge to reverse for failure to prove market power is easy; for a litigant to prove (or disprove) market power is daunting. The current trend toward requiring proof of market power whenever restraints are not as naked as trees in winter[29] threatens antitrust enforcement unless antitrust authorities and courts can develop workable surrogates for market power or can identify restraints that should be ended without proof of market power. The FTC's unusual attributes permit it to make a contribution to this effort.[30] FFPs could be a good example of a practice that should be ended without elaborate proof of an individual firm's market power.

Notes

1. This essay is based on a paper in progress on competition policy. The author acknowledges with gratitude the suggestions of Neil Averitt, Jonathan Baker, Roger Dennis, Kenneth Elzinga, Alan Fisher, Andrew Joskow, Robert Pitofsky, and Frederick Warren-Boulton, none of whom share responsibility.

2. For instance, excluding its Robinson-Patman Act chapter, a leading 1981 anti-

trust casebook contained more than sixty Antitrust Division cases and only eleven FTC cases. P. Areeda, *Antitrust Analysis* (3d ed. 1981).

3. The latest edition of Areeda's casebook added significant excerpts from three FTC cases but no Division cases. P. Areeda and L. Kaplow, *Antitrust Analysis* (4th ed. 1988). An even newer casebook includes seven leading FTC antitrust cases decided in the 1980s, only one of which involved the Robinson-Patman Act, but only one Division case decided in the 1980s. E. Fox and L. Sullivan, *Cases and Materials on Antitrust* (1989). Supplements presumably will add excerpts from *FTC v. Superior Court Trial Lawyers Ass'n.*, 109 S. Ct. 1741 (1989) (granting certiorari). See generally Report of the ABA Section of Antitrust Law Task Force on the Antitrust Division of the U.S. Department of Justice, 57 Antitrust and Trade Reg. Rep. (BNA) S-14 (special supp., July 20, 1989) (troubled by the Division's willingness "to cede its merger authority to the FTC").

Although the FTC may be assuming the leading federal role in developing antitrust jurisprudence though litigation, the Antitrust Division played the critical role in reshaping national antitrust thinking during the 1980s. It accomplished this through speeches, testimony, amicus participation in litigation, and, especially, guidelines. See generally 71 *Calif. L. Rev.*, no. 2 (1983) (symposium on the 1982 merger guidelines).

4. A recommended nonmerger antitrust role is set forth in Report of the American Bar Association Section of Antitrust Law Special Committee to Study the Role of the Federal Trade Commission (Kirkpatrick II), 58 *Antitrust L. J.*, 43 (1989). The Report's recommendations are summarized in Calkins, "Counsel's Summary: The ABA Special Committee's Report on the FTC (Kirkpatrick II)," above. One member of that committee has concluded that the FTC's nonmerger antitrust role should consist principally of challenging horizontal restraints not suitable for criminal enforcement. T. Muris, "The FTC at 75" (unpublished manuscript, 1989). The FTC's nonmerger antitrust agenda should not be limited to such challenges.

5. See, e.g., Williamson, "Delimiting Antitrust," 76 *Geo. L. J.*, 271 (1987). The FTC has already engaged in studying and challenging certain strategic behavior.

6. Consideration of strategic behavior under the rubric of "raising rivals' costs" was popularized by Krattenmaker and Salop, "Anticompetitive Exclusion: Raising Rivals' Costs to Achieve Power over Price," 96 *Yale L. J.*, 209 (1986). Samples of the scholarship are collected in *J. Reprints for Antitrust L. & Econ.*, vol. 16, no. 2, vol. 18, no. 1.

7. Calkins, "Comments on Presentation of Steven Salop," 56 *Antitrust L. J.*, 65 (1987); Holt and Scheffman, "Strategic Business Behavior and Antitrust," in R. Larner and J. Meehan, eds., *Economics and Antitrust Policy*, 39 (1989).

8. FFPs are obviously not the airline industry's only competitive impediment. Indeed, were the industry otherwise perfectly competitive, FFPs would not be a competitive problem. For more general discussions of competition in the airline industry, see Hawk, "Airline Deregulation after Ten Years: The Need for Vigorous Antitrust Enforcement and Intergovernmental Agreements," 34 *Antitrust Bull.*, 267 (1989); Levine, "Airline Competition in Deregulated Markets: Theory, Firm Strategy, and Public Policy," 4 *Yale L. J.*, on Reg. 393 (1987); Bailey and Williams, "Sources of Economic Rent in the Deregulated Airline Industry," 31 *J. L. & Econ.*, 173 (1988); Borenstein, "The Competitive Advantage of a Dominant Airline" (unpublished manuscript, Jan., 1989); Borenstein, "Hubs and High Fares: Airport Dominance and Market Power in the U.S. Airline Industry" (unpublished manuscript, March, 1988, forthcoming in *Q. J. Econ.*). For the debate

about the consequences of increased concentration in airport hubs, compare U.S. GAO, Testimony on Air Fares and Service at Concentrated Airports (June 7, 1989) (concentration has increased prices) with Simat, Helliesen, and Eichner, Inc., "Hub Operations: An Analysis of Airline Hub and Spoke Systems Since Deregulation" (unpublished manuscript prepared for the Air Transport Association, May, 1989) (increased prices explained by other factors).

9. 15 U.S.C.A. § 45(a) (West Supp. 1989) (exempting "air carriers subject to the Federal Aviation Act"). However, the FTC has jurisdiction over hotels and car rental companies, which are initiating frequent user plans. E.g., "Hotels Gamble on 'Frequent-Stay' Plans," *Wall St. J.*, February 27, 1989, at B1. Some of the considerations discussed herein might be applicable to these plans.

10. Federal Aviation Act, 49 U.S.C.A. §§ 1381, 1551(b)(1)(E) (West. Supp. 1989).

11. For additional discussions of FFPs see the papers cited above in note 8, some of which advance positions similar to some positions advanced in this paper.

12. "Frequent Flier Program Facing Hostile Scrutiny," *N. Y. Times*, 22, 1985, at A20, col. 1 (also noting that a few principals attempt to capture FFP benefits); Sherman, "The Airlines' Flying Jackpots," 106 *Fortune*, 103 (November 29, 1982).

13. A few examples from brochures in my files (some of which may be dated): Delta offers one free coach ticket for 40,000 miles, two tickets for 60,000; American offers a free coach ticket for 35,000 miles, two for 50,000; Northwest offers nothing for less than 20,000 miles, a free ticket to Europe for 40,000, and two free tickets for 60,000.

14. Agency-cost problems are not limited to FFPs, of course. Especially before deregulation, airline competition featured amenity wars: airlines charged high prices and offered lavish meals and spacious seating. Agency-cost problems extend well beyond travel. Certain categories of business people regularly receive tangible and intangible inducements such as meals, gifts, and entertainment. It is unclear whether principals approve.

15. Interview with anonymous D.C. lawyer and frequent flyer. Another remarkable promotion was by Continental, which awarded $200 cash to randomly selected passengers with full fare tickets costing $900 or more. "Continental Cash Rebate Draws Fire," 47 *Travel Weekly*, no. 104, at 1 (November 28, 1988).

16. Another disadvantage of cash, at least if it is regularly offered, is that it could easily be recaptured by principals—more easily even than department store gift certificates—thus preventing exploitation of the agent-principal relationship. Paying cash also might have the practical result of making awards taxable, whereas many travelers fail to report FFP awards as income. The distortions caused by frequent-flyer programs would be reduced but not ended were taxes withheld on awards.

It is not surprising that FFP plans are designed to benefit agents. Airlines have largely succeeded in discriminating in price between business and leisure travelers, and probably only for the former are markups consistently high enough to permit such programs. E.g., Kahn, "Lower Fares, More Service—It Works," *N.Y. Times*, August 13, 1989, at F2 (explaining correctly the benefits of discrimination).

17. One survey found that thirty percent of FFP users book circuitous routes to increase their mileage. "What's New in Air Travel," *N.Y. Times*, July 1, 1984, § 3, at 15, col. 1; see also "Frequent-Flier Plans Become Obsessions," *Wall St. J.*, September 6, 1988, at 29; "The Sky's the Limit in Luring the Frequent Flier," *Business Week*, October 18,

1982, at 152 (increased numbers of bizarre routes). Even if a FFP does not induce a traveler to take an extra trip or make an extra stop, it succeeds whenever a participant selects a flight that he or she otherwise would not. This appears to happen regularly.

18. The competitive importance of having an attractive FFP is described in, e.g., "Does the Frequent-Flier Game Pay Off for Airlines?" *Business Week*, August 27, 1984, at 74.

19. Businesses and governments nationwide have become concerned about FFPs and are starting to respond with guidelines, by requiring booking through a controlled travel agent, and by prohibiting the accumulation and personal use of FFP credits. "Frequent Flier Program Facing Hostile Scrutiny," (government requires awards to be used on future government travel); "The Richer Rewards of Frequent Flying," *Money*, April, 1985, at 89; "Flap Over Frequent Fliers," *Dun's Business Month*, January 1985, at 48 (major dilemma for companies).

These measures have had only limited success, however, and only a minority of companies employ them. The techniques are expensive and imperfect. Ordering employees to forego free trips imposes employee relations costs and harms recruiting and retention. Efforts to orchestrate economical travel are expensive, and even the best travel schedulers can be frustrated by enterprising agents with airline guides. Moreover, the true agency-cost tension often is not between top management and employees but, rather, between shareholders and employees—including top management, who are prime beneficiaries of FFPs. Thus the agency-cost problem is not susceptible to easy solution.

20. Cf., e.g., J. Hirshleifer, *Price Theory and Applications*, 3d ed., 35-37 (1984). Since price is determined by the marginal consumer, a few rewards might not affect price, but as rewards become more widespread an effect should be noticed, especially given the airlines' ability to fine-tune pricing. Presumably the same process should cause output to fall, although agents receiving rewards conceivably could increase demand.

21. See also Borenstein, "Competitive Advantage" (he argues that airlines that dominate an airport have disproportionate ability to attract patronage originating there. Since this effect is particularly pronounced for apparent business travelers, it might be explained by exploitation of principal-agent relationships).

The extent and even the existence of competitive harm is somewhat uncertain because FFPs conceivably benefit competition by decreasing price rigidity, thus making pricing coordination more difficult. For instance, for personal travel, FFPs resemble delayed volume discounts. The competitive benefit from this discounting might offset the competitive harm from the nonlinear award function. It also is conceivable that FFPs increase consumer welfare by facilitating the consumption of travel opportunities that otherwise would be wasted. See Borenstein, "Hubs," at 9.

22. See Ippolito, "The Economics of Information in Consumer Markets: What do We Know? What do We Need to Know?" in E.S. Maynes, ed., *The Frontier of Research in the Consumer Interest*, 235 (1988) (high search costs can make pricing less competitive).

23. See Lockheed Corp., 92 F.T.C. 968 (1978) (consent decree against U.S. aerospace companies prohibited them from making illegal foreign payments); cf. *Environmental Tectonics v. W. S. Kirkpatrick, Inc.*, 847 F.2d 1052, 1066 (3d Cir. 1988) (citing cases) (commercial bribery actionable under Robinson-Patman Act), *cert. granted*, 109 S. Ct. 3213 (1989) (Dkt. 87-2066) (limited to different issue). For FTC decisions prohibiting commercial bribery, see 3 Trade Reg. Rep. (CCH) 7903 (1988).

24. *Southmark/Envicon Capital Corp. v. United Airlines, Inc.*, 132 Misc. 2d 586, 505 N.Y.S.2d 491 (Sup. Ct. 1986), held that FFPs were not commercial bribery because they were open and the plaintiff-employer failed to prove that it could not prevent the programs from harming it.

25. This happened when principals solved the agency-cost problems posed by the first FFP. See above, note 12.

26. *United Airlines, Inc. v. CAB*, 766 F. 2d 1111 (7th Cir. 1985); ABA Antitrust Section, Monograph no. 5, *The FTC as an Antitrust Enforcement Agency: The Role of Section 5 of the FTC Act in Antitrust Law*, vol. I (1981); Averitt, "The Meaning of 'Unfair Methods of Competition' in Section 5 of the Federal Trade Commission Act," 21 *B. C. L. Rev.*, 227, 276-84 (1980) (reviewing legislative history of Section 5).

27. See H. Rep. No. 98-763, 98th Cong., 2d Sess., at 6 (1984).

28. See Kirkpatrick II, at 85-93, 113-19.

29. See Briggs and Calkins, "Antitrust 1986-87: Power and Access (Part I)," 32 *Antitrust Bull.*, 275, 276-301 (1987).

30. But cf. *Superior Court Trial Lawyers Ass'n v. FTC*, 856 F.2d 226 (D.C. Cir. 1988), *cert. granted*, 109 S. Ct. 1741 (1989) (discussed in Calkins, "Developments in Antitrust and the First Amendment: The Disaggregation of Noerr," 57 *Antitrust L. J.*, 327 (1988)).

A Public Policy Research Agenda for the 1990s

Alan R. Andreasen

As Commissioner Andrew Strenio has recently demonstrated, the Federal Trade Commission has undergone a significant shrinkage of resources in the past decade (see Strenio's paper in Part II). This shrinkage has been even more dramatic in the area of research, both policy-planning and case-related research. Further, as Beales suggests, the Commission's tactical orientation has shifted from judicial in the 1960s to legislative in the 1970s to prosecutorial in the 1980s (see Beale's paper in Part II). While the current administration and/or new FTC leadership may change or reverse these trends, they are likely to be largely operative for at least the early 1990s.

In the face of these resource constraints, it is unlikely that the Commission will fund a significant level of research, despite the fact that commissioners and staff alike agree such research would significantly improve public policymaking and policy implementation. The question, then, is: can such research be generated by other means?

This paper proposes a deceptively simple solution. It argues that more research can be generated if the *producers* of research can be motivated to increase their output—even in the absence of significant Federal Trade Commission funding. Further, it proposes two broad strategies for achieving this end. These are based on two realities of researcher motivation:

1. researchers will produce more research if they see it as contributing to their personal (e.g., career) objectives;
2. *ceteris paribus*, researchers will research what others will fund.

The solutions to the present dilemma are therefore straightforward. First, we must find ways to make research on public policy *personally* attractive to more scholars. Second, we must find alternatives to the Federal Trade Commission for funding desired research. This paper will offer possible approaches to both strategies.

Making Public Policy Research Attractive

In the 1970s, public policy research on the problems of ghetto consumers was very fashionable. However, as Andreasen (1978) pointed out, research on ghetto marketing went through a life cycle not unlike those exhibited by most new products, ending in a severe decline phase long before many of the key research issues in the area were resolved (or, in some cases, even explored). Recent analysis by Gundlach and Wilkie (see paper in this Part) suggests that the same may be true of public policy research in general between 1970 and 1988.

Andreasen suggests that premature decline in ghetto marketing research could be attributable to three major problems: the lack of scholars, the lack of *repeat* scholars, and changes in the academic/research environment. The first two problems stemmed from a reputation that ghetto marketing research acquired early on that (a) in general, there really wasn't much of fundamental value to be contributed to the basic disciplines from research in the area, and (b) most of the major issues had been addressed and resolved in the field's introductory years. These problems were compounded by the fact that scholarly interest turned out to be faddish. Few of the best scholars in marketing worked in the area of ghetto marketing, and those who did work in the area often generated quick-and-dirty studies that only confirmed the opinions of their peers. Finally, the perceived lack of substance meant that those working in the area would desert it as soon as some other "hot topic" came along to capture their fancy. The spurt of interest in energy issues in the mid-1970s served just this function, offering the coup-de-grace to a dying field.

My sense of the present situation is that the first causal element applies in part: there are too few scholars involved in problems of interest to the Federal Trade Commission. On the other hand, those working in the area, in my judgment, comprise some of the very best consumer behavior and economics scholars in marketing. Further, these researchers are persistent; those who worked in the area ten years ago are still in the trenches.

The problem is how to make public policy research attractive to a much broader range of marketing scholars, most particularly, those who are the intellectual leaders in our field. Part of the problem is that under the Reagan administration research on issues of interest to the Federal Trade Commission has been subject to a certain amount of benign neglect.

Motivating Researchers

In my experience, there are six key personal motivations that individually or collectively can impel a given researcher to tackle a particular subject. These are:

1. the topic fits within and advances an existing line of research, thus achieving *academic synergy*;
2. the topic is *intellectually challenging*;
3. the research process will permit the *learning of new methodologies*;
4. working in the problem domain will lead to personal *networking opportunities*;
5. research will lead to one or more *publications*, preferably in the "better" journals; and
6. research will lead to enhanced *personal recognition*.

I will consider each of these, briefly, in turn.

Promoting Academic Synergy. While the chronology is not always easy to discern, it appears to be the case that a number of scholars in our field have worked on regulation issues as ways of advancing work in which they were already involved. For example, Jack Jacoby's work on miscomprehension (Jacoby and Hoyer 1982) was a natural outgrowth of his earlier work on information processing and information overload (Jacoby, Speller, and Kohn 1974). Valerie Folke's research on consumer satisfaction (Folkes 1984) was a logical extension of her earlier work in psychology on attributional processes (Folkes 1984). In my own case, a study I conducted with Gregory D. Upah of the FTC's proposed Creditors Remedies Rule (Andreasen and Upah 1979) was a conscious extension of my interest in the general problems of disadvantaged consumers (Andreasen 1975).

The "trick" then in promoting new lines of research is to indicate to others the potential for extending current work in an area that would be beneficial to the Federal Trade Commission or to the broader area of public policy. Two areas in which this may be possible are the following:

1. A distressing finding in some of the studies on consumer satisfaction/dissatisfaction and complaining behavior of low income and

less educated consumers is that they are less likely to perceive problems or to complain about them to sellers. We have little understanding of why this is so in the face of considerable anecdotal evidence that they are much more often the victims of deceptive practices (Andreasen 1989). This is a critical public policy issue. However, if we are to study the topic, attention must be paid to my admonition (Andreasen 1976) that disadvantaged consumers are *qualitatively*, not just quantitatively, different from other consumers. This suggests that, in order to understand what is really constraining the disadvantaged's responses to unsatisfactory purchases, we need to understand the role of purchasing and products and services in their lives. For example, do they not complain because, as Caplovitz (1967) suggests, they are afraid to jeopardize their fragile credit ratings? Or is it that they have low self-images and think nothing will come of a complaint action "from people like them"? Such issues seem ready made for some form of naturalistic enquiry. Researchers in this resurgent area (cf. Belk, Sherry, and Wallendorf 1988) could be made to see that their particular methodologies could be advanced by exploring what Magnuson and Carper (1968) once called "the dark side of the marketplace."

2. A second area of consumer protection that can interest researchers from a number of theoretical perspectives is the problem of immigrant consumers in American marketplaces. In other studies (e.g., Caplovitz 1967), we have found that ethnic minorities encounter serious difficulties in urban marketplaces. Researchers who have studied the general process of marketplace socialization (e.g., of children or of American "geographic mobiles") may find interesting possibilities for extending their work by studying how, for example, Guatemalans or Thais learn to be American consumers and whether they face the same kinds of problems as have been documented for American blacks and Hispanics.

Further, as I have noted elsewhere (Andreasen, forthcoming), researchers and scholars should be mindful of the opportunities to explore the power of subtle but elusive theories by studying "extreme consumers." For example, researchers who have difficulty establishing the power of personality (Kassarjian 1973) or information overloading (Jacoby, Speller, and Kohn 1974) as explanatory variables in marketing may find their power revealed in studies of the very old, those with low education, and/or those very new to markets.

Presenting Intellectual Challenges. Researchers frequently seek topics that are new to them because (a) they are intellectually challenged, and/or (b) they see a potential to carve a unique niche for themselves in the difficult world of scholarly competition. I would argue that a research program focusing on the aforementioned problem of recent immigrants would be one that fits both criteria. Clearly, the amount of immigration is growing rapidly as many cities now have large numbers of foreign immigrants, especially from Latin American and Asian countries. Studying their integration processes, either individually or across generations, would add significantly to our understanding of consumer dynamics.

A second fundamental area I believe is insufficiently explored is understanding the nature of the public policymaking process itself as it takes place in the marketing domain. For example, we know relatively little about how the FTC incorporates in its priority setting processes (a) the nature of the problems consumers face and (b) the characteristics of the consumers who face them. It would seem that some of the recent explorations in expert systems models could help us understand the implicit rules used by policymakers. This, in turn, could lead to the development of normative models that could improve the priority-setting processes and their outcomes.

Another issue that researchers may find challenging is: To what extent do consumers engage in conscious "market policing"? Hirschman (1970) sets out a theory that consumers act to regulate markets by their exit and/or voicing behavior. We have studied voicing to business extensively (Andreasen 1988) but with a few exceptions (e.g., Richins 1984) know relatively little about the extent to which consumers talk to others or switch brands or outlets "to teach sellers a lesson." This issue should be of considerable theoretical and empirical interest to consumer researchers. In a time of budget stringency, it should also be of considerable interest to FTC commissioners, who may wish to encourage such behavior or avoid acting themselves when they know such self-policing is taking place.

Creating Opportunities to Develop Methodological Tools. A number of scholars consider their major interest to be studying how to study! There are a number of opportunities for developing new methodologies with respect to problems faced by the Federal Trade Commission. For example, the recent growth in interest in "thick" ethnographic research can certainly be expanded through work on the consumer problems of low income consumers. Further, those with interests in cross-cultural research certainly have ample opportunities on their own doorsteps. By studying the problems of new immigrants, one can explore the methodological problems not only of multilanguage measurements but also how to explore such topics as the information-seeking behavior of new residents from cultures that are notoriously shy, that have different patterns of husband-wife interactions, or that are simply unfamiliar with such techniques as focus group interviews, perceptual mapping, trade-off analysis, and so forth. As immigrant consumers become more dominant in certain markets like Los Angeles or San Antonio, abilities to study these new populations will become extremely valuable to the marketing profession in general.

Building Networks. Many new scholars look to areas of research as opportunities to build networks that can last for a career. There are a number of interesting interaction possibilities that can be promoted in the area of public policymaking. One obvious possibility is the chance to meet and work with those actively engaged in actually setting and implementing public policy. Researchers do not always have the chance to get close to decision makers, even in the private sector, to observe their behavior or to understand firsthand their problems. Such interaction would be rewarding in itself (and would certainly lead to enhanced teaching capabilities). More importantly, it would increase the probability that (a) the research would be directly responsive to the policymakers' real needs and (b) the researcher would have a chance to see the impacts of the research when it is done.

A second inducement would be the possibility of interacting with colleagues overseas. In many respects, scholarly work on the problems of market regulation and consumerism is much more extensive in Europe than in America (Olander 1988). This work has traditionally been more descriptive and theoretical. Thus, there are many opportunities to match American scholars' empirical orientations with the Europeans' theoretical perspective. As I have observed elsewhere (Andreasen and Manning 1980), there is much to be learned just in the process of trying to make such matches work effectively.

Third, there is simply the chance to work with like-minded colleagues who "speak the same language." As Rogers (1976) has pointed out, the way in which much research information gets diffused is through "invisible colleges" within and across formal disciplines. The attendants at this conference form such an invisible college. Unfortunately, it is a relatively small group and, as one participant put it, has not changed much in composition over the last ten years. Clearly, ritualized occasions for this invisible college to meet would help solidify its membership and facilitate its workings. A model of such forced college-building is the series of conferences developed by Keith Hunt and Ralph Day for those working on problems related to consumer satisfaction/dissatisfaction and complaining behavior (Hunt 1988). An alternative vehicle would be the annual conferences of the Association for Consumer Research, the American Marketing Association, or the American Council on Consumer Interest. Each of these associations could be solicited to schedule regularly conference sessions around themes of interest to the FTC. As an incentive to the associations, the FTC might commit itself to making at least one commissioner or staff member available for a major or minor policy statement.

Generating Publications. One considerable advantage that present day public policy researchers have over those involved in earlier work is that the number of journals with explicit interest in publishing material on public policy has grown dramatically. These obviously include the *Journal of Public Policy and Marketing*, the *Journal of Consumer Affairs*, and the *Journal of Consumer Policy*. If the volume of work in the area increases, it would be reasonable to expect the *Journal of Public Policy and Marketing* to increase its publication frequency to twice (or more) yearly.

Creating Opportunities for Personal Recognition. Obviously, scholars, like everyone else, respond to rewards for work well done. One obvious incentive to increased scholarly work with respect to FTC issues would be to create an annual award for superior marketing research and/or theory applied to public policy issues. This could be unconstrained as to publication outlet or time or it could be narrowly constrained to, say, the best article in *Journal of Public Policy and Marketing* each year. The award could be administered by the American Marketing Association, University of Notre Dame, or some private organization or benefactor. Given the importance of bringing new scholars into the area, it would seem desirable to develop a similar award for the best doctoral dissertation in the area of public policy. A model here would be the Ferber awards in the field of consumer behavior.

Who Will Take Responsibility?

A key issue here is: who is going to take the lead in bringing all this about? There are six possible "players" each with distinct roles to play:

The Federal Trade Commission. Given dwindling resources, the FTC is unlikely to provide research incentives in this area. However, they can: (a) more frequently share with scholars their current needs for policy-related research or theory; (b) provide access to scholars wishing to do research on issues involving the Commission; and (c) indicate enthusiasm and moral support for research and writing in this area by actively participating in academic programs and conferences developed by others.

State Attorneys General. To the extent that state attorneys general can be made to see that the pursuit of regulatory issues is in their own immediate political interests (Nadel 1971), they can offer scholars numerous chances to further their work closer to home. In addition, if enterprising research entrepreneurs can put together consortia of state attorneys general, limited local funds can be aggregated to achieve critical mass while at the same time bringing together networks of scholars in different states whose joint contributions can generate significant research synergy.

The Journal of Public Policy and Marketing. The *Journal* can seek to develop an award for superior articles in the area and can consider the possibility of increasing the number of issues per year (e.g., by contracting to publish selected papers from conferences on public policy issues).

Universities (such as Notre Dame). Universities can establish chairs in public policy and marketing, sponsor conferences, encourage faculty to attend conferences in the area sponsored by others, and introduce courses on marketing and public policy.

Corporations and Foundations. A number of corporations and foundations have interests in supporting research and writing on consumer issues and public policy. These corporations include American Express and

Cheseborough-Ponds. Foundations include the Johnson and Shell Oil foundations. (All of these sponsored the recent Wingspread conference on research frontiers in the consumer interest [Maynes 1988].) These sponsors could fund some of the conferences, chairs, and awards noted earlier.

Academic Associations. This is the area of greatest potential for achieving renewed momentum in this domain. While other associations could take the lead, such a role would be most natural for the American Marketing Association. The AMA could, for example, establish a new divisional vice-presidency in the area of public policy. In an era of growing public concern over ethical breaches in the corporate world and a willingness to support responsible self-regulation, it would seem especially timely for the AMA to establish itself as a guiding force in this area. In my judgment, fostering work in this area is central to the profession's long-run interests. This new division could administer the award mentioned above, arrange annual conferences, and, not incidently, create advisory boards to increase the opportunities for national leadership roles for aspiring scholars.

References

Andreasen, Alan R. (1975). *The Disadvantaged Consumer.* New York: The Free Press.
———— (1976). "The Differing Nature of Consumerism in the Ghetto." *Journal of Consumer Affairs* 10 (Winter), 179-190.
———— (1978). "The Ghetto Marketing Life Cycle: A Case of Underachievement." *Journal of Marketing Research* 15 (February), 20-28.
———— (1988). "Consumer Complaints and Redress: What We Know and What We Don't Know." In E. Scott Maynes, ed., *The Frontier of Research in the Consumer Interest*, 675-722. Columbia, MO: American Council on Consumer Interests.
———— (forthcoming). "Consumer Behavior Research and Social Policy." In Harold H. Kassarjian and Thomas S. Robertson, eds., *Handbook of Consumer Behavior: Theoretical and Empirical Constructs.* Englewood Cliffs, NJ: Prentice-Hall, Inc.
Andreasen, Alan R., and Jean Manning (1980). "Conducting Cross-National Consumer Research." In Jerome Olson, ed., *Advances in Consumer Research*, vol. 7, 77-82. State College, PA: Association for Consumer Research.
Andreasen, Alan R., and Gregory D. Upah (1979). "Regulation and the Disadvantaged: The Case of the Creditors' Remedies Rule." *Journal of Marketing* 43/2 (Spring), 75-83.
Belk, Russell W., John F. Sherry, Jr., and Melanie Wallendorf (1988). "A Naturalistic Inquiry into Buyer and Seller Behavior at a Swap Meet." *Journal of Consumer Research* 14/4 (March), 449-470.
Caplovitz, David (1967). *The Poor Pay More.* New York: The Free Press.
Folkes, Valerie (1982). "Communicating the Reason for Social Rejection." *Journal of Experimental Social Psychology* 18, 235-252.

——— (1984). "Consumer Reactions to Product Failure: An Attributional Approach." *Journal of Consumer Research* (March), 398-409.

Hirschman, Albert O. (1970). *Exit, Voice, and Loyalty: Responses to Decline in Firms, Organizations, and States.* Cambridge: Harvard University Press.

Hunt, H. Keith (1988). "Consumer Satisfaction/Dissatisfaction and the Consumer Interest." In E. Scott Maynes, ed., *The Frontier of Research in the Consumer Interest,* 731-749. Columbia, MO: American Council of Consumer Interests.

Jacoby, Jacob, and Wayne D. Hoyer (1982). "On Miscomprehending Televised Communication: A Rejoinder." *Journal of Marketing* (Fall), 35-43.

Jacoby, Jacob, Donald E. Speller, and Carol A. Kohn (1974). "Brand Choice Behavior as a Function of Information Load." *Journal of Marketing Research* 11, 63-69.

Kassarjian, Harold H. (1973). "Personality and Consumer Behavior: A Review." In Harold H. Kassarjian and Thomas Robertson, eds., *Perspectives on Consumer Behavior,* rev. ed., 129-148. Glenview, IL: Scott Foresman.

Magnuson, Warren G., and Jean Carper (1968). *The Dark Side of the Marketplace.* Englewood Cliffs, NJ: Prentice-Hall, Inc.

Nadel, Mark V. (1971). *The Politics of Consumer Protection.* Indianapolis: The Bobbs-Merrill Co., Inc.

Olander, Folke (1988). "Salient Issues in Current European Consumer Policy Research." In E. Scott Maynes, ed., *The Frontier of Research in the Consumer Interest,* 547-584. Columbia, MO: American Council on Consumer Interests.

Richins, Marsha (1983). "Word-of-Mouth as an Expression of Product Dissatisfaction." In Ralph L. Day and H. Keith Hunt, eds., *International Fare in Consumer Satisfaction and Complaining Behavior,* 100-104. Bloomington, IN: Bureau of Business Research, Indiana University.

Rogers, Everett M. (1976). "A Personal History of Research on the Diffusion of Innovations." In Alan R. Andreasen and Seymour Sudman, eds., *Public Policy and Marketing Thought,* 43-64. Chicago: American Marketing Association.

Epilogue

The 1990s represent an especially critical time for the Federal Trade Commission. The decade of the eighties was a period of retrenchment for the agency. It began with a restriction of the agency's power (1980 FTC Improvements Act), then moved to a period of relative inactivity in consumer protection and antitrust matters during the Reagan administration. At this time the states, and particular the attorneys general, became much more activist in FTC matters such as regulation of advertising. The decade closed with the ABA analysis of the agency (covered in depth in Part I of this volume). Although this report was more guarded in its criticism of the FTC than Kirkpatrick I, it is clear that changes must occur during the coming decade to insure the viability and effectiveness of the Commission.

It is interesting to note that serious examinations of the FTC have occurred once every twenty years—1929, 1949, 1969, and 1989 (see the Strenio 1988 paper in Part II). The influential Herbert Hoover Commission of 1949 roundly criticized the agency for its inactivity (see the Zuckerman paper in Part II). In 1969 the expose on the agency by Ralph Nader and his raiders combined with the Kirkpatrick I ABA report to set in motion the changes that propelled the agency into an active (some would say too active) regulator in the 1970s. Once again, following a period of relative inactivity, the agency has received scrutiny by the ABA. It is our hope that this volume and its impressive collection of serious papers will be added to the 1989 evaluations of the agency and contribute to its emergence as a respected and reasoned regulator of marketing and advertising.

We believe that marketing scholars have much to contribute to the Federal Trade Commission. The Commission has long had in place staff members trained in legal and economic analysis of cases and regulatory issues. However, the areas of expertise of many marketing academics— the study of marketing strategy and practices, and consumer behavior— are largely being ignored currently by the FTC (see the Wilkie paper in

393

Part I). If the agency is to be a respected, reasonable, and effective regulator of marketing and advertising practices, expertise in these fields is a necessity. Serious academic research on public policy topics is ongoing by marketing scholars (see Part III and *Journal of Public Policy and Marketing*), but almost entirely without encouragement by the FTC. The active support and encouragement of such research, together with the inclusion of this field in policy-level discussions by Commissioners is clearly needed on the part of key persons at the top of this agency. If this were resumed, we feel that much useful research as well as beneficial information for the Commission policy making would result.

As we have seen, the FTC has been amazingly resilient over the years. The future, however, would benefit from a more steady course. Charting this course in the face of the changing external environment is a worthy challenge in itself, to say nothing of divisions over basic regulatory philosophies. In conclusion, we hope that the analysis and recommendations offered by this volume's expert contributors will be valuable in determining the future of this relatively small, but potentially very influential lady on Pennsylvania Avenue.

Patrick E. Murphy
William L. Wilkie

The Federal Trade Commission Act
as Amended by the Wheeler-Lea Act of 1938

The statutory objectives of the FTC are set forth in the Federal Trade Commission Act, as amended by the Wheeler-Lea Act; the Clayton Act, as amended by the Robinson-Patman Act and the Celler-Kefauver Antimerger Act; the Wool Products Labeling Act; the Fur Products Labeling Act; the Flammable Fabrics Act; and the Textile Fiber Products Identification Act. The Commission also has responsibilities under the Packers and Stockyards Act, the Webb-Pomerene Export Trade Act, the Lanham Trade-Mark Act, the Oleomargarine Act, the Fair Packaging and Labeling Act, and the Consumer Credit Protection Act. Additional statutes and court decisions have further refined the FTC's responsibilities. The text of the FTC Act follows:

Be it enacted by the Senate and House of Representatives of the United States of America in Congress assembled, That a commission is hereby created and established, to be known as the Federal Trade Commission (hereinafter referred to as the commission), which shall be composed of five commissioners, who shall be appointed by the President, by and with the advice and consent of the Senate. Not more than three of the commissioners shall be members of the same political party. The first commissioners appointed shall continue in office for terms of three, four, five, six, and seven years, respectively, from the date of the taking effect of this Act, the term of each to be designated by the President, but their successors shall be appointed for terms of seven years, except that any person chosen to fill a vacancy shall be appointed only for the unexpired term of the commissioner whom he shall succeed: *Provided, however,* That upon the

Reprinted, with permission, from Susan Wagner, *The Federal Trade Commission,* Praeger Library of U. S. Government Departments and Agencies (New York: Praeger Publishers, 1971), pages 233–49.

expiration of his term of office a commissioner shall continue to serve until his successor shall have been appointed and shall have qualified. The commission shall choose a chairman from its own membership. No commissioner shall engage in any other business, vocation, or employment. Any commissioner may be removed by the President for inefficiency, neglect of duty, or malfeasance in office. A vacancy in the commission shall not impair the right of the remaining commissioners to exercise all the powers of the commission.

The commission shall have an official seal, which shall be judicially noticed.

SEC. 2. That each commissioner shall receive a salary of $10,000 a year, payable in the same manner as the salaries of the judges of the courts of the United States. The commission shall appoint a secretary, who shall receive a salary of $5,000 a year, payable in like manner, and it shall have authority to employ and fix the compensation of such attorneys, special experts, examiners, clerks and other employees as it may from time to time find necessary for the proper performance of its duties and as may be from time to time appropriated for by Congress.

With the exception of the secretary, a clerk to each commissioner, the attorneys, and such special experts and examiners as the commission may from time to time find necessary for the conduct of its work, all employees of the commission shall be a part of the classified civil service, and shall enter the service under such rules and regulations as may be prescribed by the commission and by the Civil Service Commission.

All of the expenses of the commission, including all necessary expenses for transportation incurred by the commissioners or by their employees under their orders, in making any investigation, or upon official business in any other places than in the city of Washington, shall be allowed and paid on the presentation of itemized vouchers therefor approved by the commission.

Until otherwise provided by law, the commission may rent suitable offices for its use.

The Auditor for the State and Other Departments shall receive and examine all accounts of expenditures of the commission.

SEC. 3. That upon the organization of the commission and election of its chairman, the Bureau of Corporations and the offices of Commissioner and Deputy Commissioner of Corporations shall cease to exist; and all pending investigations and proceedings of the Bureau of Corporations shall be continued by the commission.

All clerks and employees of the said bureau shall be transferred to and become clerks and employees of the commission at their present grades and salaries. All records, papers, and property of the said bureau shall become records, papers, and property of the commission, and all unexpended funds and appropriations for the use, and maintenance of the said bureau, including any allotment already made to it by the Secretary of Commerce from the contingent appropriation for the Department of Commerce for the fiscal year nineteen hundred and fifteen, or from the departmental printing fund for the fiscal year nineteen hundred and fifteen, shall become funds and appropriations available to be expended by the commission in the exercise of the powers, authority, and duties conferred on it by this Act.

The principal office of the commission shall be in the city of Washington, but it may meet and exercise all its powers at any other place. The commission may, by one or more of its members, or by such examiners as it may designate, prosecute any inquiry necessary to its duties in any part of the United States.

SEC. 4. The words defined in this section shall have the following meaning when found in this Act, to wit:

"Commerce" means commerce among the several States or with foreign nations, or in any Territory of the United States or in the District of Columbia, or between any such Territory and another, or between any such Territory and any State or foreign nation, or between the District of Columbia and any State or Territory or foreign nation.

"Corporation" shall be deemed to include any company, trust, so-called Massachusetts trust, or association, incorporated or unincorporated, which is organized to carry on business for its own profit or that of its members, and has shares of capital or capital stock or certificates of interest, and any company, trust, so-called Massachusetts trust, or association, incorporated or unincorporated, without shares of capital or capital stock or certificates of interest, except partnerships, which is organized to carry on business for its own profit or that of its members.

"Documentary evidence" includes all documents, papers, correspondence, books of account, and financial and corporate records.

"Acts to regulate commerce" means the Act entitled "An Act to regulate commerce," approved February 14, 1887, and all Acts amendatory thereof and supplementary thereto and the Communications Act of 1934 and all Acts amendatory thereof and supplementary thereto.

"Antitrust Acts" means the Act entitled "An Act to protect trade and commerce against unlawful restraints and monopolies," approved July 2, 1890; also sections 73 to 77, inclusive, of an Act entitled "An Act to reduce taxation, to provide revenue for the Government, and for other purposes," approved August 27, 1894; also the Act entitled "An Act to amend sections 73 and 76 of the Act of August 27, 1894, entitled 'An Act to reduce taxation, to provide revenue for the Government, and for other purposes,'" approved February 12, 1913; and also the Act entitled "An Act to supplement existing laws against unlawful restraints and monopolies, and for other purposes," approved October 15, 1914.

SEC. 5. (a) (1) Unfair methods of competition in commerce, and unfair or deceptive acts or practices in commerce, are hereby declared unlawful.

(2) Nothing contained in this Act or in any of the Antitrust Acts shall render unlawful any contracts or agreements prescribing minimum or stipulated prices, or requiring a vendee to enter into contracts or agreements prescribing minimum or stipulated prices, for the resale of a commodity which bears, or the label or container of which bears, the trade-mark, brand, or name of the producer or distributor of such commodity and which is in free and open competition with commodities of the same general class produced or distributed by others, when contracts or agreements of that description are lawful as applied to intrastate transactions under any statute, law, or public policy now or hereafter in effect in any State, Territory, or the District of Columbia in which such resale is to be made, or to which the commodity is to be transported for such resale.

(3) Nothing contained in this Act or in any of the Antitrust Acts shall render unlawful the exercise or the enforcement of any right of action created by any statute, law, or public policy now or hereafter in effect in any State, Territory, or the District of Columbia, which in substance provides that willfully and knowingly advertising, offering for sale, or selling any commodity at less than the price or prices prescribed in such contracts or agreements whether the person so advertising, offering for sale, or selling is or is not a party to such a contract or agreement, is unfair competition and is actionable at the suit of any person damaged thereby.

(4) Neither the making of contracts or agreements as described in paragraph (2) of this subsection, nor the exercise or enforcement of any right or right of action as described in paragraph (3) of this subsection shall constitute an unlawful burden or restraint upon, or interference with, commerce.

(5) Nothing contained in paragraph (2) of this subsection shall make lawful contracts or agreements providing for the establishment or maintenance of minimum or stipulated resale prices on any commodity referred to in paragraph (2) of this subsection, between manufacturers, or between producers, or between wholesalers, or between brokers, or between factors, or between retailers, or between persons, firms, or corporations in competition with each other.

(6) The Commission is hereby empowered and directed to prevent persons, partnerships, or corporations, except banks, common carriers subject to the Acts to regulate commerce, air carriers, and foreign air carriers subject to the Federal Aviation Act of 1958, and persons, partnerships, or corporations insofar as they are subject to the Packers and Stockyards Act, 1921, as amended, except as provided in section 406(b) of said Act, from using unfair methods of competition in commerce and unfair or deceptive acts or practices in commerce.

(b) Whenever the Commission shall have reason to believe that any such person, partnership, or corporation has been or is using any unfair method of competition or unfair or deceptive act or practice in commerce, and if it shall appear to the Commission that a proceeding by it in respect thereof would be to the interest of the public, it shall issue and serve upon such person, partnership, or corporation a complaint stating its charges in that respect and containing a notice of a hearing upon a day and at a place therein fixed at least thirty days after the service of said complaint. The person, partnership, or corporation so complained of shall have the right to appear at the place and time so fixed and show cause why an order should not be entered by the Commission requiring such person, partnership, or corporation to cease and desist from the violation of the law so charged in said complaint. Any person, partnership, or corporation may make application, and upon good cause shown may be allowed by the Commission to intervene and appear in said proceeding by counsel or in person. The testimony in any such proceeding shall be reduced to writing and filed in the office of the Commission. If upon such hearing the Commission shall be of the opinion that the method of competition or the act or practice in question is prohibited by this Act, it shall make a report in writing in which it shall state its findings as to the facts and shall issue and cause to be served on such person, partnership, or corporation an order requiring such person, partnership, or corporation to cease and desist from using such method of competition or such act or practice. Until the expiration of the time allowed for filing a petition for review, if no such petition has been duly filed within such time, or, if a petition for review has been filed within such time then until the record in the proceeding has been filed in a court of appeals of the United States, as hereinafter provided, the Commission may at any time, upon such notice and in such manner as it shall deem proper, modify or set aside, in whole or in part, any report or any order made or issued by it under this section. After the expiration of the time allowed for filing a petition for review, if no such petition has been duly filed within such time, the Commission may at any time, after notice and opportunity for hearing, reopen and alter, modify, or set aside, in whole or in part, any report or order made or issued by it under this section, whenever in the opinion of the Commission conditions of fact or of law have so changed as to require such action or if the public interest shall so require: *Provided, however,* That the said person, partnership, or corporation may, within sixty days after service upon him or it of said report or order entered after such a reopening, obtain a review thereof in the appropriate court of appeals of the United States, in the manner provided in subsection (c) of this section.

(c) Any person, partnership, or corporation required by an order of the Commission to cease and desist from using any method of competition or act or practice may obtain a review of such order in the court of appeals of the United States, within any circuit where the method of competition or the act or practice in question was used or where such person, partnership, or corporation resides or carries on business, by filing in the court, within sixty days from the date of the service of such order, a written petition praying that the order of the Commission be set aside. A copy of such petition shall be forthwith transmitted by the clerk of the court to the Commission, and thereupon the Commission shall file in the court the record in the proceeding, as provided in Section 2112 of Title 28, United States Code. Upon such filing of the petition the court shall have jurisdiction of the proceeding and of the question determined therein concurrently with the Commission until the filing of the record and shall have power to make and enter a decree affirming, modifying, or setting aside the order of the Commission, and enforcing the same to the extent that such order is affirmed, and to issue such writs as are ancillary to its jurisdiction or are necessary in its judgment to prevent injury to the public or to competitors pendente lite. The finding of the Commission as to the facts, if supported by evidence, shall be conclusive. To the extent that the order of the Commission is affirmed, the court shall thereupon issue its own order commanding obedience to the terms of such order of the Commission. If either party shall apply to the court for leave to adduce additional evidence, and shall show to the satisfaction of the court that such additional evidence is material and that there were reasonable grounds for the failure to adduce such evidence in the proceeding before the Commission, the court may order such additional evidence to be taken before the Commission and to be adduced upon the hearing in such manner and upon such terms and conditions as to the court may seem proper. The Commission may modify its findings as to the facts, or make new findings, by reason of the additional evidence so taken, and it shall file such modified or new findings, which, if supported by evidence, shall be conclusive, and its recommendation, if any, for the modification or setting aside of its original order, with the return of such additional evidence. The judgment and decree of the court shall be final, except that the same shall be subjected to review by the Supreme Court upon certiorari, as provided in section 240 of the Judicial Code.

(d) Upon the filing of the record with it the jurisdiction of the court of appeals of the United States to affirm, enforce, modify, or set aside orders of the Commission shall be exclusive.

(e) Such proceedings in the court of appeals shall be given precedence over other cases pending therein, and shall be in every way expedited. No order of the Commission or judgment of court to enforce the same shall in anywise relieve or absolve any person, partnership, or corporation from any liability under the Antitrust Acts.

(f) Complaints, orders, and other processes of the Commission under this section may be served by anyone duly authorized by the Commission, either (a) by delivering a copy thereof to the person to be served, or to a member of the partnership to be served, or the president, secretary, or other executive officer or a director of the corporation to be served; or (b) by leaving a copy thereof at the residence or principal office or place of business of such person, partnership, or corporation; or (c) by mailing a copy thereof by registered mail or by certified mail addressed to such person, partnership, or corporation at his or its residence or principal office or place of business. The verified return by the person so serving said complaint, order, or other process setting forth the manner of said service shall be proof of the same, and the return post office receipt for said complaint, order, or other process mailed by registered mail or by certified mail as aforesaid shall be proof of the service of the same.

(g) An order of the Commission to cease and desist shall become final—

(1) Upon the expiration of the time allowed for filing a petition for review, if no such petition has been duly filed within such time; but the Commission may thereafter modify or set aside its order to the extent provided in the last sentence of subsection (b); or

(2) Upon the expiration of the time allowed for filing a petition for certiorari, the order of the Commission has been affirmed, or the petition for review dismissed by the court of appeals, and no petition for certiorari has been duly filed; or

(3) Upon the denial of a petition for certiorari, if the order of the Commission has been affirmed or the petition for review dismissed by the court of appeals; or

(4) Upon the expiration of thirty days from the date of issuance of the mandate of the Supreme Court, if such Court directs that the order of the Commission be affirmed or the petition for review dismissed.

(h) If the Supreme Court directs that the order of the Commission be modified or set aside, the order of the Commission rendered in accordance with the mandate of the Supreme Court shall become final upon the expiration of thirty days from the time it was rendered, unless within such thirty days either party has instituted proceedings to have such order corrected to accord with the mandate, in which event the order of the Commission shall become final when so corrected.

(i) If the order of the Commission is modified or set aside by the court of appeals, and if (1) the time allowed for filing a petition for certiorari has expired and no such petition has been duly filed, or (2) the petition for certiorari has been denied, or (3) the decision of the court has been affirmed by the Supreme Court, then the order of the Commission rendered in accordance with the mandate of the court of appeals shall become final on the expiration of thirty days from the time such order of the Commission was rendered, unless within such thirty days either party has instituted proceedings to have such order corrected so that it will accord with the mandate, in which event the order of the Commission shall become final when so corrected.

(j) If the Supreme Court orders a rehearing; or if the case is remanded by the court of appeals to the Commission for a rehearing, and if (1) the time allowed for filing a petition for certiorari has expired; and no such petition has been duly filed, or (2) the petition for certiorari has been denied, or (3) the decision of the court has been affirmed by the Supreme Court, then the order of the Commission rendered upon such rehearing shall become final in the same manner as though no prior order of the Commission had been rendered.

(k) As used in this section the term "mandate," in case a mandate has been recalled prior to the expiration of thirty days from the date of issuance thereof, means the final mandate.

(l) Any person, partnership, or corporation who violates an order of the Commission to cease and desist after it has become final, and while such order is in effect, shall forfeit and pay to the United States a civil penalty of not more than $5,000 for each violation, which shall accrue to the United States and may be recovered in a civil action brought by the United States. Each separate violation of such an order shall be a separate offense, except that in the case of a violation through continuing failure or neglect to obey a final order of the commission each day of continuance of such failure or neglect shall be deemed a separate offense.

SEC. 6. That the commission shall also have power—

(a) To gather and compile information concerning, and to investigate from time to time the organization, business, conduct, practices, and management of any corporation engaged in commerce, excepting banks and common carriers subject to the Act to regulate commerce, and its relation to other corporations and to individuals, associations, and partnerships.

(b) To require, by general or special orders, corporations engaged in commerce, excepting banks, and common carriers subject to the Act to regulate commerce, or any class of them, or any of them, respectively, to file with the commission in such form as the commission may prescribe annual or special, or both annual and special reports or answers in writing to specific questions, furnishing to the commission such information as it may require as to the organization, business, conduct, practices, management, and relation to other corporations, partnerships, and individuals of the respective corporations filing such reports or answers in writing. Such reports and answers shall be made under oath, or otherwise, as the commission may prescribe, and shall be filed with the commission within such reasonable period as the commission may prescribe, unless additional time be granted in any case by the commission.

(c) Whenever a final decree has been entered against any defendant corporation in any suit brought by the United States to prevent and restrain any violation of the antitrust Acts, to make investigation, upon its own initiative, of the manner in which the decree has been or is being carried out, and upon the application of the Attorney General it shall be its duty to make such investigation. It shall transmit to the Attorney General a report embodying its findings and recommendations as a result of any such investigation, and the report shall be made public in the discretion of the commission.

(d) Upon the direction of the President or either House of Congress to investigate and report the facts relating to any alleged violations of the antitrust Acts by any corporation.

(e) Upon the application of the Attorney General to investigate and make recommendations for the readjustment of the business of any corporation alleged to be violating the antitrust Acts in order that the corporation may thereafter maintain its organization, management, and conduct of business in accordance with law.

(f) To make public from time to time such portions of the information obtained by it hereunder, except trade secrets and names of customers, as it shall deem expedient in the public interest; and to make annual and special reports to the Congress and to submit therewith recommendations for additional legislation; and to provide for the publication of its reports and decisions in such form and manner as may be best adapted for public information and use.

(g) From time to time to classify corporations and to make rules and regulations for the purpose of carrying out the provisions of this Act.

(h) To investigate, from time to time, trade conditions in and with foreign countries where associations, combinations, or practices of manufacturers, merchants, or traders, or other conditions, may affect the foreign trade of the United States, and to report to Congress thereon with such recommendations as it deems advisable.

Sec. 7. That in any suit in equity brought by or under the direction of the Attorney General as provided in the antitrust Acts, the court may, upon the conclusion of the testimony therein, if it shall be then of opinion that the complainant is entitled to relief, refer said suit to the commission, as a master in chancery, to ascertain and report an appropriate form of decree therein. The commission shall proceed upon such notice to the parties and under such rules of procedure as the court may prescribe, and upon the coming in of such report such exceptions may be filed and such proceedings had in relation thereto as upon the report of a master in other equity causes, but the court may adopt or reject such report, in whole or in part, and enter such decree as the nature of the case may in its judgment require.

Sec. 8. That the several departments and bureaus of the Government when directed by the President shall furnish the commission, upon its request, all records, papers, and information in their possession relating to any corporation subject to any of the provisions of this Act, and shall detail from time to time such officials and employees to the commission as he may direct.

SEC. 9. That for the purposes of this Act the commission, or its duly authorized agent or agents, shall at all reasonable times have access to, for the purpose of examination, and the right to copy any documentary evidence of any corporation being investigated or proceeded against; and the commission shall have power to require by subpoena the attendance and testimony of witnesses and the production of all such documentary evidence relating to any matter under investigation. Any member of the commission may sign subpoenas, and members and examiners of the commission may administer oaths and affirmations, examine witnesses, and receive evidence.

Such attendance of witnesses, and the production of such documentary evidence, may be required from any place in the United States, at any designated place of hearing. And in case of disobedience to a subpoena the commission may invoke the aid of any court of the United States in requiring the attendance and testimony of witnesses and the production of documentary evidence.

Any of the district courts of the United States within the jurisdiction of which such inquiry is carried on may, in case of contumacy or refusal to obey a subpoena issued to any corporation or other person, issue an order requiring such corporation or other person to appear before the commission, or to produce documentary evidence if so ordered, or to give evidence touching the matter in question; and any failure to obey such order of the court may be punished by such court as a contempt thereof.

Upon the application of the Attorney General of the United States, at the request of the commission, the district courts of the United States shall have jurisdiction to issue writs of mandamus commanding any person or corporation to comply with the provisions of this Act or any order of the commission made in pursuance thereof.

The commission may order testimony to be taken by deposition in any proceeding or investigation pending under this Act at any stage of such proceeding or investigation. Such depositions may be taken before any person designated by the commission and having power to administer oaths. Such testimony shall be reduced to writing by the person taking the deposition, or under his direction, and shall then be subscribed by the deponent. Any person may be compelled to appear and depose and to produce documentary evidence in the same manner as witnesses may be compelled to appear and testify and produce documentary evidence before the commission as hereinbefore provided.

Witnesses summoned before the commission shall be paid the same fees and mileage that are paid witnesses in the courts of the United States, and witnesses whose depositions are taken, and the persons taking the same shall severally be entitled to the same fees as are paid for like services in the courts of the United States.

No person shall be excused from attending and testifying or from producing documentary evidence before the commission or in obedience to the subpoena of the commission on the ground or for the reason that the testimony or evidence, documentary or otherwise, required of him may tend to criminate him or subject him to a penalty or forfeiture. But no natural person shall be prosecuted or subjected to any penalty or forfeiture for or on account of any transaction, matter, or thing concerning which he may testify, or produce evidence, documentary or otherwise, before the commission in obedience to a subpoena issued by it: *Provided,* That no natural person so testifying shall be exempt from prosecution and punishment for perjury committed in so testifying.

SEC. 10. That any person who shall neglect or refuse to attend and testify, or to answer any lawful inquiry, or to produce documentary evidence, if in his power to do so, in obedience to the subpoena or lawful requirement of the commission, shall be guilty of an offense and upon conviction thereof by a court of competent jurisdiction shall be punished by a fine of not less than $1,000 nor more than $5,000, or by imprisonment for not more than one year, or by both such fine and imprisonment.

Any person who shall willfully make, or cause to be made, any false entry or statement of fact in any report required to be made under this Act, or who shall willfully make, or cause to be made, any false entry in any account, record, or memorandum kept by any corporation subject to this Act, or who shall willfully neglect or fail to make, or to cause to be made, full, true, and correct entries in such accounts, records, or memoranda of all facts and transactions appertaining to the business of such corporation, or who shall willfully remove out of the jurisdiction of the United States, or willfully mutilate, alter, or by any other means falsify any documentary evidence of such corporation, or who shall willfully refuse to submit to the commission or to any of its authorized agents, for the purpose of inspection and taking copies, any documentary evidence of such corporation in his possession or within his control, shall be deemed guilty of an offense against the United States, and shall be subject, upon conviction in any court of the United States of competent jurisdiction, to a fine of not less than $1,000 nor more than $5,000 or to imprisonment for a term of not more than three years, or both such fine and imprisonment.

If any corporation required by this Act to file any annual or special report shall fail so to do within the time fixed by the commission for filing the same, and such failure shall continue for thirty days after notice of such default, the corporation shall forfeit to the United States the sum of $100 for each and every day of the continuance of such failure which forfeiture shall be payable into the Treasury of the United States, and shall be recoverable in a civil suit in the name of the United States brought in the district where the corporation has its principal office or in any district in which it shall do business. It shall be the duty of the various United States attorneys, under the direction of the Attorney General of the United States, to prosecute for the recovery of forfeitures. The costs and expenses of such prosecution shall be paid out of the appropriation for the expenses of the courts of the United States.

Any officer or employee of the commission who shall make public any information obtained by the commission without its authority, unless directed by a court, shall be deemed guilty of a misdemeanor, and, upon conviction thereof, shall be punished by a fine not exceeding $5,000, or by imprisonment not exceeding one year, or by fine and imprisonment, in the discretion of the court.

SEC. 11. Nothing contained in this Act shall be construed to prevent or interfere with the enforcement of the provisions of the antitrust Acts or the Acts to regulate commerce, nor shall anything contained in the Acts be construed to alter, modify, or repeal the said antitrust Acts or the Acts to regulate commerce or any part or parts thereof.

SEC. 12. (a) It shall be unlawful for any person, partnership, or corporation to disseminate, or cause to be disseminated, any false advertisement—

(1) By United States mails, or in commerce by any means, for the purpose of inducing, or which is likely to induce, directly or indirectly the purchase of food, drugs, devices, or cosmetics; or

(2) By any means, for the purpose of inducing, or which is likely to induce directly or indirectly, the purchase in commerce of food, drugs, devices, or cosmetics.

(b) The dissemination or the causing to be disseminated of any false advertisement within the provisions of subsection (a) of this section shall be an unfair or deceptive act or practice in commerce within the meaning of section 5.

SEC. 13. (a) Whenever the Commission has reason to believe—

(1) that any person, partnership, or corporation is engaged in, or is about to engage in, the dissemination or the causing of the dissemination of any advertisement in violation of section 12, and

(2) that the enjoining thereof pending the issuance of a complaint by the commission under section 5, and until such complaint is dismissed by the Commission or set aside by the court on review, or the order of the Commission to cease and desist made thereon has become final within the meaning of section 5, would be to the interest of the public,

the Commision by any of its attorneys designated by it for such purpose may bring suit in a district court of the United States or in the United States court of any Territory, to enjoin the dissemination or the causing of the dissemination of such advertisement. Upon proper showing a temporary injunction or restraining order shall be granted without bond. Any such suit shall be brought in the district in which such person, partnership, or corporation resides or transacts business

(b) Whenever it appears to the satisfaction of the court in the case of a newspaper, magazine, periodical, or other publication, published at regular intervals—

(1) that restraining the dissemination of a false advertisement in any particular issue of such publication would delay the delivery of such issue after the regular time therefor, and

(2) that such delay would be due to the method by which the manufacture and distribution of such publication is customarily conducted by the publisher in accordance with sound business practice, and not to any method or device adopted for the evasion of this section or to prevent or delay the issuance of an injunction or restraining order with respect to such false advertisement or any other advertisement,

the court shall exclude such issue from the operation of the restraining order or injunction.

SEC. 14. (a) Any person, partnership, or corporation who violates any provision of section 12(a) shall, if the use of the commodity advertised may be injurious to health because of results from such use under the conditions prescribed in the advertisement thereof, or under such conditions as are customary or usual, or if such violation is with intent to defraud or mislead, be guilty of a misdemeanor, and upon conviction shall be punished by a fine of not more than $5,000 or by imprisonment for not more than six months, or by both such fine or imprisonment; except that if the conviction is for a violation committed after a first conviction of such person, partnership, or corporation, for any violation of such section, punishment shall be by a fine of not more than $10,000 or by imprisonment for not more than one year, or by both such fine and imprisonment: *Provided,* That for the purposes of this section meats and meat food products duly inspected, marked, and labeled in accordance with rules and regulations issued under the Meat Inspection Act approved March 4, 1907, as amended, shall be conclusively presumed not injurious to health at the time the same leave official "establishments."

(b) No publisher, radio-broadcast licensee, or agency or medium for the manufacturer, packer, distributor, or seller of the commodity to which the false advertisement relates, shall be liable under this section by reason of the dissemination by him of false advertisement, unless he has refused, on the request of the Commission, to furnish the Commission the name and post-office address of the manufacturer, packer, distributor, or advertising agency, residing in the United States, who caused him to disseminate such advertisement. No advertising agency shall be liable under this section by reason of the causing by it of the dissemination of any false advertisement, unless it has refused, on the request of the Commission, to furnish the Commission the name and post-office address of the manufacturer, packer, distributor, or seller, residing in the United States, who caused it to cause the dissemination of such advertisement.

SEC. 15. For the purposes of sections 12, 13, and 14—

(a) (1) The term "false advertisement" means an advertisement, other than labeling, which is misleading in a material respect; and in determining whether any advertisement is misleading, there shall be taken into account (among other things) not only representations made or suggested by statement, word, design, device, sound, or any combination thereof, but also the extent to which the advertisement fails to reveal facts material in the light of such representations or material with respect to consequences which may result from the use of the commodity to which the advertisement relates under the conditions prescribed in said advertisement, or under such conditions as are customary or usual. No advertisement of a drug shall be deemed to be false if it is disseminated only to members of the medical profession, contains no false representation of a material fact, and includes, or is accompanied in each instance by truthful disclosure of, the formula showing quantitatively each ingredient of such drug.

(2) In the case of oleomargarine or margarine an advertisement shall be deemed misleading in a material respect if in such advertisement representations are made or suggested by statement, word, grade designation, design, device, symbol, sound, or any combination thereof, that such oleomargarine or margarine is a dairy product, except that nothing contained herein shall prevent a truthful, accurate, and full statement in any such advertisement of all the ingredients contained in such oleomargarine or margarine.

(b) The term "food" means (1) articles used for food or drink for man or other animals, (2) chewing gum, and (3) articles used for components of any such article.

(c) The term "drug" means (1) articles recognized in the official United States Pharmacopoeia, official Homoeopathic Pharmacopoeia of the United States, or official National Formulary, or any supplement to any of them; and (2) articles intended for use in the diagnosis, cure, mitigation, treatment, or prevention of disease in man or other animals; and (3) articles (other than food) intended to affect the structure or any function of the body of man or other animals; and (4) articles intended for use as a component of any article specified in clause (1), (2), or (3); but does not include devices or their components, parts, or accessories.

(d) The term "device" (except when used in subsection (a) of this section) means instruments, apparatus, and contrivances, including their parts and accessories, intended (1) for use in the diagnosis, cure, mitigation, treatment, or prevention of disease in man or other animals; or (2) to affect the structure or any function of the body of man or other animals.

(e) The term "cosmetic" means (1) articles to be rubbed, poured, sprinkled, or sprayed on, introduced into, or otherwise applied to the human body or any part thereof intended for cleansing, beautifying, promoting attractiveness, or altering the appearance, and (2) articles intended for use as a component of any such article; except that such term shall not include soap.

(f) For the purposes of this section and section 407 of the Federal Food, Drug, and Cosmetic Act, as amended, the term "oleomargarine" or "margarine" includes—

(1) all substances, mixtures, and compounds known as oleomargarine or margarine;

(2) all substances, mixtures, and compounds which have a consistence similar to that of butter and which contain any edible oils or fats other than milk fat if made in imitation or semblance of butter.

SEC. 16. Whenever the Federal Trade Commission has reason to believe that any person, partnership, or corporation is liable to a penalty under section 14 or under subsection (1) of section 5, it shall certify the facts to the Attorney General, whose duty it shall be to cause appropriate proceedings to be brought for the enforcement of the provisions of such section or subsection.

SEC. 17. If any provision of this Act, or the application thereof to any person, partnership, corporation, or circumstance, is held invalid, the remainder of the Act and the application of such provision to any other person, partnership, corporation, or circumstance, shall not be affected thereby.

SEC. 18. This Act may be cited as the "Federal Trade Commission Act."

Organic Act approved September 26, 1914.

Wheeler-Lea Amendment approved March 21, 1938.

Report of the American Bar Association Section of Antitrust Law Special Committee to Study the Role of the Federal Trade Commission

Reprinted, with permission, from *Antitrust & Trade Regulation Report*, Vol. 56, No. 1410, Special Supplement, pp. S-1 - S-53 (April 6, 1989). Published by the Bureau of National Affairs, Inc.

REPORT OF THE AMERICAN BAR ASSOCIATION
SECTION OF ANTITRUST LAW SPECIAL COMMITTEE
TO STUDY THE ROLE OF THE FEDERAL TRADE
COMMISSION

I. Summary

Twenty years after the 1969 Report of the American Bar Association Commission to Study the Federal Trade Commission, questions about the FTC's role persist. Accordingly, James F. Rill, chairman of the American Bar Association Section of Antitrust Law, with the approval of the ABA Board of Governors, appointed a Special Committee to Study the Role of the Federal Trade Commission. The Committee was not intended to critique the performance of the FTC or its leaders, past or present, or to resolve disputes about various views on legal issues. Rather, the Committee was to consider how the FTC should fit into our system of government regulation.

The FTC today bears little resemblance to the FTC of 1969. Partly in response to the ABA Report, Congress entrusted the FTC with broad authority to petition federal courts for injunctions, civil penalties, and consumer redress, and enhanced the FTC's (and the Antitrust Division's) ability to obtain preliminary injunctions against proposed mergers. Congress also expressly conferred rulemaking authority on the FTC, which the Commission used, primarily in the 1970's, to consider numerous trade regulation rules. More recently, the FTC has devoted an increasing share of its resources to federal court litigation, challenging mergers and consumer fraud, and seeking civil penalties for violations of rules, statutes, and orders.

Leadership: We do not believe it would be productive to attempt to list the ideal credentials of the commissioners. A diversity of background can be a source of strength. Nonetheless, the leadership of the FTC is critical to the effectiveness of its performance. We therefore urge that the President carefully evaluate the qualities and qualifications of the commissioners, and in particular of the chairman. In doing so, the President should consider the legal, business, academic, and governmental experience and knowledge that will enable the appointees to administer the FTC's work in antitrust, consumer protection, and economics. Above all, the commissioners should be persons of recognized stature. This is necessary for the Commission to receive respect in Congress, to attract talented staff, and to enjoy the confidence of the businesses it regulates and the consumers it protects.

Antitrust: Merger enforcement is probably the FTC's most important antitrust assignment. However, we also see an agenda of significant non-merger civil enforcement that the Commission should pursue. It should, consistent with sound economic principles, identify other cases not subject to easy application of the per se rule, and for which criminal penalties or treble damages may be overly severe sanctions because, for instance, the challenged conduct is arguably exempt, the industry is newly exposed to the antitrust laws, or the legal theory is uncertain.

Consumer Protection: FTC administrative adjudication can be useful in resolving factually and legally complex deception cases. Although the Committee is not in agreement on whether the agency is prosecuting its share of advertising cases, we believe that the FTC should do more to articulate its advertising law-enforcement agenda. Most of us agree that the FTC is properly concerned about the risk of suppressing truthful advertising, but the public has not always received the message that the FTC believes it is important to move aggressively against deceptive advertising.

In combatting consumer fraud, the FTC has effectively used its newly established authority under FTC Act Section 13(b) to obtain affirmative relief, including asset freezes and monetary damages. The Commission also has an important consumer protection role to play in enforcing a series of specific statutes and in bringing administrative consumer unfairness cases that involve interstate conduct, less egregious than fraud, that is likely to continue absent FTC challenge.

Guidance: One of the FTC's most important functions is to provide guidance to business. Adjudicated cease-and-desist orders are a form of mandatory, firm-specific guidance. The Commission can also provide guidance informally, and through guides, policy statements, Magnuson-Moss trade regulation rules, and advisory opinions. In choosing among these alternatives, the Commission should, in general, treat similarly situated firms alike. It should regularly speak publicly as a body. The Committee is impressed by the potential significance of guides and policy statements in the FTC's enforcement program. However, the FTC should modify or repeal some existing guides to bring them in line with current policy, and then enforce its guides and rules.

There are few opportunities for broad rulemaking, although the FTC should be able to identify candidates. The FTC should embark on rulemaking only when it is contemplating a particular solution to a widespread problem and when sound legal theory supports its proposed rule. The Committee is particularly impressed with the possibilities for consumer protection rules that are grounded in competition concepts. Finally, the FTC should specifically address the issue of state law preemption whenever it promulgates a trade regulation rule.

Competition and Consumer Advocacy: We believe that the Commission's program to press for competition and consumer interests has been valuable. It should be continued.

Economics: Economists are, and should be, treated as colleagues in the FTC's antitrust, consumer protection, and competition advocacy programs. The Commission should consider the views of economists in deciding whether to initiate action, and should be cautious about proceeding when the economists are opposed. Because of their training and professional incentives, economists are likely to be particularly effective in fashioning and monitoring relief. The Committee also recommends a reorientation of the FTC's economic research mission. The FTC's research should be directly relevant to the agency's agenda of protecting consumers, and the agency should concentrate on becoming the single most important repository of knowledge about the actual operation of major U.S. industries. The FTC also should seek to improve our understanding of the economic consequences of the American antitrust and consumer protection systems.

Resources: FTC workyears are 53 percent of what they were a decade ago. Although the Commission was overstaffed then, and no longer is involved in some of the labor-intensive projects that once consumed it, the current staff level is cause for serious concern. We are also concerned that as the FTC has been reduced in size, it has become top-heavy, both in the operating bureaus and at the Commission level. We urge that the Commission make better use of its resources, that the decline in real resources be halted, and that an increase in resources be provided.

Organization and Structure: The Committee has reviewed the long-standing debate over the wisdom of dividing federal antitrust enforcement between two agencies, and of combining the roles of prosecutor and adjudicator in the FTC. Many of us would favor unitary antitrust enforcement, were we writing on a clean slate, although some would consolidate antitrust in the Justice Department whereas others would consolidate civil antitrust and consumer protection in the FTC. But while dual enforcement imposes some costs, it also provides some benefits. Dual enforcement has wide support and, as a consequence, we believe that any structural change in federal antitrust enforcement is unlikely. A majority of the Committee concludes that the case for proposing abolition of dual enforcement has not been made. Similarly, a majority of the Committee concludes that the current unity of functions, although troubling in concept, in fact provides flexibility and control and is thus superior to the alternatives.

Congress: The Commission should keep Congress fully informed of its programs and plans. Congress should limit its review of such programs and plans to general policies, and, except where it acts through legislation, leave specific case and rule oversight to the courts. The Commission's decisional process must remain confidential while matters are pending. Congress should review or overturn FTC policy only through the responsible substantive committees. Exemptions, if any, should be substantive exemptions, *e.g.*, from the antitrust laws, and not just from FTC supervision.

The States: The Committee considered the relationship between the FTC and state attorneys general as part of its review of advertising and of trade regulation rules, although the principles discussed in these sections have more general applicability. In recent years the states have become more aggressive in antitrust enforcement and consumer protection. Although most of us have some reservations about this trend and concerns about particular actions, we believe that state activity can be beneficial. The states and the FTC have much to learn from each other, and each has an important role to play. The FTC should be the primary enforcement agency with respect to practices and restraints that are regional or national in

scope; the states should have primary responsibility for prosecuting activities that predominantly affect one state. The states and the FTC should work together to aid consumers, in part by referring cases, in the first instance, to the preferable enforcer. The states and the FTC also should attempt to shape a common enforcement agenda, by listening to shared concerns by explaining reasons for actions taken or not taken (where possible), and, when the occasion demands it by engaging in respectful criticism.

II. Introduction

This year marks the twentieth anniversary of the Report of the American Bar Association Commission to Study the Federal Trade Commission ("1969 Report"). During the past two decades, many of its recommendations have been followed, Congress has enacted a number of statutes strengthening the FTC, and the FTC has been led by some individuals of considerable distinction.

Despite these encouraging reforms, questions about the FTC's place in American government persist, and the proper role of the FTC remains ill-defined. Newly appointed antitrust enforcers regularly are asked whether they support the existence of two antitrust agencies (the FTC and the Department of Justice Antitrust Division). Observers continue to be uneasy about the FTC's twin roles as prosecutor and judge and to question whether administrative adjudication superior to adjudication in the federal courts. Tension arise from the overlapping responsibilities of the FTC other federal agencies and, increasingly, state governments. Congress's ambivalence about the agency role is symbolized by its repeated failure to reauthorize the FTC, which has been functioning without formal authorization since 1982. Because these questions persisted as the twentieth anniversary of the 1969 ABA Report approached, and in view of the forthcoming change in Presidential Administration Chairman James F. Rill of the American Bar Association Section of Antitrust Law, with the approval of the ABA Board of Governors, appointed a Special Committee to Study the Role of the Federal Trade Commission.

A. *Purpose of the Study*

The ABA Section of Antitrust Law charged the Committee with considering the appropriate role of the FTC—including whether there is a useful role for such an agency. The Committee was not charged with updating the 1969 Report, or with critiquing the performance of the FTC or its leaders, past or present Nor was the Committee charged with resolving disputes about the legal scope of antitrust and consumer protection law. Instead, the Committee was to consider how the FTC should fit into our system of government regulation.

The FTC possesses an unusual set of attributes. I mandate encompasses both competition policy and consumer protection. It combines, in a single agency

---

[1] See Appendix B.

law enforcement, regulation, and reporting responsibilities. It litigates cases in the federal courts and also internally before administrative law judges and, eventually, the commissioners. It has substantial staffs of lawyers and economists, based in Washington and in regional offices in ten cities. Several statutes give it unusual substantive and procedural authority. Yet, while the FTC is unique in many respects, in many other ways it duplicates or complements the work of other governmental units—most obviously the Antitrust Division of the Department of Justice, but also other federal agencies, state and local enforcement authorities, and private litigants.

The Committee's task was to determine whether the FTC has, or could have, an advantage over alternative enforcement instruments, and—assuming there is a role for the agency—to identify the sort of endeavors in which the FTC is most likely to be effective. The Committee was also charged with asking whether fundamental structural changes would improve the FTC.

B. Committee History and Working Procedures

At the 1988 Spring Meeting of the ABA Section of Antitrust Law, Section Chairman James F. Rill preliminarily announced the Section's intention to form this Committee. He indicated that Committee members would "consist of acknowledged experts in the field who will bring to the work of the task force experience in the management of the Commission, viewpoints from all across the spectrum of the antitrust policy debate, and a diverse orientation including economics and consumer as well as legal backgrounds."[2] After ABA approval was obtained, the Committee and its membership were formally announced on June 29, 1988.

Chairman Rill appointed as head of the Committee Miles Kirkpatrick, who chaired the 1969 ABA Commission and subsequently served as chairman of the FTC. Ten members of the Committee are private lawyers, four are academics, two are lawyers representing states, and one is the director of the Public Citizen Litigation Group. Professor Stephen Calkins was appointed Committee counsel.[3] Kathleen M.H. Wallman and Sandra L. Spear were appointed deputy counsel and assistant counsel, respectively.[4]

---

[2] Rill, Antitrust: Where We Stand Today, 57 Antitrust L.J. 3, 11 (1988).

[3] The Committee is grateful to Wayne State University and Nancy Eisenstein for providing valuable secretarial assistance and support.

[4] The ABA Section of Antitrust Law is grateful to the law firms of Arnold & Porter and Covington & Burling, each of which authorized the participation of one of its associates in this public service project. For the affiliations and background of Committee members and Counsel, see Appendix A. Assistance also was provided by Geoffrey Calkins, Brian Cunningham, Laura S. Fitzgerald, and J. Theodore Gentry, by law students Barbara Heaphy, Kathleen Hunt, and Eric Miller, and by paralegal Jennifer Blum. Special drafting projects were performed by Professor William Kovacic, Phillip A. Proger, Andrew Sandler, Stephen A. Stack, Jr., and Elroy H. Wolff.

The members of the Committee and its staff did not perform their duties as representatives of any organization or other group, but as individuals. The contributions of the members and the staff of the Committee to this Report are reflections of their own independent, personal views. The Report represents a consensus and synthesis of these individual contributions, rather than an expression of each member's individual viewpoint as to each aspect or detail of the Report.

The Committee publicly invited outsiders to offer comments, and it solicited suggestions from former FTC chairmen, selected merger practitioners, and other experts. Representatives of the Committee spoke with sitting commissioners and the heads of the Commission's three Bureaus. The FTC and the Justice Department's Antitrust Division each appointed a liaison to the Committee. At the Committee's request, the FTC provided information about a number of its programs, including computer-readable data files extracted from FTC computer tapes.[5]

The Committee met six times, usually for a day, and attempted to form a consensus on selected issues. Various Committee members prepared papers on assigned topics. Consensus decisions were recorded in Committee drafts, which eventually formed this Report. By design, the Report does not survey and critique the growing literature on the FTC.[6] Rather, it draws upon the diverse expertise of its members and offers their judgment, after careful reflection, on the appropriate role of the FTC.

III. Leadership of the Commission

The Commission functions best when the commissioners as a group bring to the job a mix of legal and economic expertise in government and business. We

---

[5] See Appendix C. The information collection process was coordinated by James M. Giffin, Esq., Associate Executive Director of the FTC. The Committee appreciated his diligence, helpfulness, and good humor.

[6] See, e.g., ABA Antitrust Section, Monograph No. 5, The FTC as an Antitrust Enforcement Agency, Volumes I & II (1981) (hereinafter cited as "Monograph No. 5"); K. Clarkson & T. Muris, eds., The Federal Trade Commission since 1970: Economic Regulation and Bureaucratic Behavior (1981); R. Katzmann, Regulatory Bureaucracy: The Federal Trade Commission and Antitrust Policy (1980); R. MacKay, J. Miller & B. Yandle, Public Choice and Regulation: A View from Inside the Federal Trade Commission (1987); J. Miller, The Economist as Reformer (forthcoming 1989); S. Wagner, The Federal Trade Commission (1971); Braucher, Defining Unfairness: Empathy and Economic Analysis at the Federal Trade Commission, 68 Boston U.L. Rev. 349 (1988); Gellhorn, Regulatory Reform and the Federal Trade Commission's Antitrust Jurisdiction, 49 Tenn. L. Rev. 471 (1982); Hobbs, Antitrust in the Next Decade—A Role for the Federal Trade Commission?, 31 Antitrust Bull. 451 (1986); Pitofsky, Beyond Nader: Consumer Protection and the Regulation of Advertising, 90 Harv. L. Rev. 661 (1977); J. Graham & V. Kramer, Appointments to the Regulatory Agencies: The Federal Communications Commission and the Federal Trade Commission (1949-1974), printed by the Senate Committee on Commerce, 94th Cong., 2d Sess. (Committee Print 1976).

do not attempt, therefore, to list the ideal credentials of a commissioner. The only universal prerequisite is a mind sufficiently keen and open to permit mastery of complicated facts and sophisticated concepts.

The FTC's leadership is critical to the agency's effective performance of its mission, however. The FTC has difficulty giving its staff specific direction, for three reasons. First, its statutory mandate is broad and imprecise. Second, as a collegial body, its views necessarily tend to be amorphous. Third, any time the persons responsible for an agency cannot directly supervise its work, staff uncertainty is likely. The Commission functions well only when commissioners in general, and the chairman in particular, exert strong leadership. Only when the Commission's leaders have enunciated a clear agenda will the staff know what kinds of cases to pursue. Only when its leaders make clear their belief in the agency and its mission can morale be maintained. Commissioners must be free to disagree about policy issues, but they should disagree in ways that engender respect for the seriousness with which they take their responsibilities.

Whenever the President considers the appointment of a commissioner—especially a chairman—he should consider carefully the qualities and qualifications of the candidates, and especially their leadership skills. The determinants of effective leadership are difficult to define, of course, but weight should be given to legal, economics, business, and governmental experience and knowledge that will allow an appointee to administer the FTC effectively and contribute to its work.

Although the commissioners as individuals should be diverse, an ideal Commission, as a group, normally would possess certain attributes. A majority of its members would begin service with specific expertise in some aspect of the Commission's work. At least one of its members would possess expertise in economics, whether or not certified by advanced degrees. A majority of its members would possess the skill in addressing procedural issues that normally is acquired through legal training.

Above all, the commissioners should be persons of recognized stature who will be respected by Congress, the businesses the Commission regulates, and the consumers it protects. With recognized leaders at its helm, the Commission will benefit from improved relations with Congress, increased deference from the courts, and acceptance by, if not cooperation from, the business community. In addition, a Commission composed of individuals of recognized stature will more readily recruit, retain, and motivate talented staff.

During our investigation, we heard complaints about the morale of the Commission staff. Except for considering the obvious problems created by budget reductions and uncertainty, we did not attempt to determine whether these complaints were valid or, if so, to identify their causes. We urge the Commission to look into the question and to deal promptly with any problems that exist.

IV. The Antitrust Program

Questions about the FTC's antitrust role are not new. To overgeneralize only slightly, the FTC's non-

merger antitrust plate was once filled with Robinson Patman enforcement. That era ended around the time of the 1969 Report, and few commentators have lamented its passing. Ever since, observers have debated the FTC's antitrust role. Early in our deliberations we reviewed the long-standing debates over the wisdom of dividing federal antitrust enforcement between two agencies, and of combining the roles of prosecutor and adjudicator. A majority of the Committee concluded that the case for proposing major structural change had not been made. The majority's reasoning is set forth in sections XI and XII. In this section, we assume the continued existence of an FTC antitrust program, and discuss what that program should be.[7]

Federal antitrust enforcement can be divided into three categories: criminal cases, mergers, and all else. The first category traditionally has been reserved to the Department of Justice, and this should not change. The second category is shared by Justice and the FTC; this is healthy and should continue. The recurring question for the FTC is whether, for the third category, the game is worth the candle: Is there a substantial amount of beneficial federal civil antitrust work other than merger enforcement? We believe there is and offer some suggestions for identifying appropriate cases.

The FTC's most important antitrust program is merger enforcement. One can debate which mergers are anticompetitive, and how permanent is their harm, but all agree that anticompetitive mergers inflict serious harm on the economy and on consumers. Moreover, merger enforcement requires substantial resources. Because of the Hart-Scott-Rodino process, an antitrust agency must evaluate proposed mergers under tight time limits. Agency merger lawyers, like private merger lawyers, often have to work "'round the clock" investigating transactions and preparing cases. But unlike some private lawyers, agency lawyers rarely have advance warning. The FTC appropriately devotes more resources to merger enforcement than to any other single program.[8]

However, it is in the "all other" category of noncriminal, non-merger enforcement that the FTC has special role. In part this role has been created by default, since the Antitrust Division devotes more than 75 percent of its resources to criminal and merger enforcement.[9] But this role should also be viewed as creature of the FTC's special attributes: an ability to seek injunctions without establishing antitrust liability

---

[7] Graphs 1 and 2 in Appendix C show that the Bureau of Competition has fairly consistently employed more workyears and professional workyears than the other bureaus.

[8] Graph 3 in Appendix C; see also Federal Trade Commission, Fiscal 1989 Budget Request, at 4 (1988) (workyears for 1988 and requested workyears for 1989) (substantial workyears also devoted to horizontal restaints). For the number of mergers challenged by the FTC each year, see Graph I in Appendix C.

[9] Telephone conversation between Judy L. Whalley, Deputy Assistant Attorney General, Antitrust Division, and Stephen Calkins (Apr. 4, 1989).

for purposes of private damages actions, an ability to devote substantial time to litigating complicated economic questions, and an ability to consider a variety of remedies for competitive harms. The challenge is to identify the kinds of non-merger antitrust cases for which these attributes make the FTC particularly well-suited. In the following discussion, we suggest some principles that may help identify such cases.

A. *Principles of Non-merger Case Selection*

The Commission should file a case only when it can anticipate relief that is practical, likely to remedy the perceived harm, and not unduly burdensome. Cases for which the FTC is particularly well-suited are likely to exhibit several of the following characteristics (which are numbered only for clarity, not to suggest that they are of equal weight or that the majority or any particular number of them must be present):

1. The cases require application of the rule of reason, of a "truncated" rule of reason, or at least of a "thoughtful per se rule." In some of these cases the FTC may eventually condemn the challenged conduct under the per se rule. This would be particularly likely where defendants have engaged in a naked restraint of trade but can assert a colorable claim of immunity from the antitrust laws. The point is not that the FTC should never bring a per se case, but rather that for truly naked restraints not on the periphery of an antitrust exemption, FTC action generally will be inappropriate (because criminal sanctions apply) or unnecessary (because private parties will have sued).[10]

2. The cases may involve development and application of uncertain legal theories. The FTC is a less dangerous forum than the federal courts for testing legal theories and considering their application in difficult cases since the FTC's sanctions are civil and prospective and its decisions cannot be used as prima facie evidence to support treble damages awards.

3. The cases may involve conduct arguably entitled to an antitrust exemption. For instance, a claim that state regulation unduly interferes with competition poses the kind of factually and analytically complex issues for which Commission review can be helpful. Criminal enforcement and treble damages actions may be overly severe sanctions for conduct that is arguably exempt.

4. The cases may involve industries newly exposed to the antitrust laws through deregulation, or in which restraints arguably are justified by the need to further technological innovation or to advance other public purposes. Here, also, criminal enforcement and treble damages actions may be excessively severe. On the other hand, in some instances the Antitrust Division

may have developed superior expertise by participating in regulatory processes.

5. The cases should have a firm foundation in economics. For years, the soul of antitrust has been torn between those preferring an exclusively economic approach and those preferring an approach that considers other values. Even those on the Committee who subscribe to the latter view believe that economics must be antitrust's rudder, and that antitrust enforcement at the FTC should reflect, as a guiding principle, a concern for encouraging and protecting efficiency. At the same time, however, the Committee recognizes that economists do not always agree; by recognizing the vital role of economics we do not mean to endorse any particular economic school.

6. The FTC's strengths are best employed in cases that challenge conduct in an industry in which the FTC has gained experience by using its full panoply of powers, by publishing studies and by giving guidance in various forms. Resources are conserved, quality is improved, and consistency is increased by agency specialization.

7. It may be desirable to investigate practices and industries about which there is substantial public concern. Rather than embarking on exhaustive, unfocused reviews of industries, however, the FTC should search for particular anticompetitive practices. The soundest approach is likely to be incremental, building on past learning. The most dubious cases are those brought to respond to a perceived problem, but which lack a carefully considered theory of violation and remedy.

8. Although the FTC should look for anticompetitive conduct currently unchallenged under the antitrust laws, most cases will not flow from any special breadth of Section 5 as compared to the antitrust laws. Although we have varying views on how far Section 5 extends,[11] we agree that the source and special nature of the FTC's antitrust assignment are derived from its structure and available sanctions, not any special reach of Section 5.

B. *Case Examples*

There are, and will continue to be, a substantial number of cases that satisfy several of these principles. In order to illustrate our views, there follows a group of cases exemplifying the kinds of non-merger antitrust cases that the FTC should at least consider

---

[10] Of course, FTC action against naked restraints could be more important where problems in showing antitrust standing prevented private enforcement. *See generally* Cargill, Inc. v. Monfort of Colo., Inc., 479 U.S. 104 (1986); Associated General Contractors of California v. California State Council of Carpenters, 459 U.S. 519 (1983); Illinois Brick Co. v. Illinois, 431 U.S. 720 (1977).

[11] FTC Act Section 5 provides as follows: "Unfair methods of competition in or affecting commerce, and unfair or deceptive acts or practices in or affecting commerce, are hereby declared unlawful." 15 U.S.C. § 45 (1982). Conduct that violates the Clayton Act or the Sherman Act generally violates Section 5. The FTC also may enforce the Clayton Act directly. *See, e.g.,* FTC v. Cement Inst., 333 U.S. 683, 694 (1948). Although it is well established that Section 5's ban on "unfair methods of competition" permits the FTC to proscribe conduct not reached by prevailing interpretations of the Sherman and Clayton Acts, there is a debate about how far Section 5 reaches beyond those Acts. See ABA Antitrust Section, Antitrust Law Developments 279-83 (2d ed. 1984 & Supp. 1988) (hereinafter cited as "*Antitrust Law Developments*"); Monograph No. 5, supra note 6, Vol. I, at 40-56.

bringing, assuming the FTC would have jurisdiction. By listing the cases, we do not necessarily endorse any particular complaint or the merits of any proceeding.

FTC v. Indiana Federation of Dentists.[12] The FTC found that a collective refusal by dentists to make patients' X- rays freely available to insurance companies violated Section 5. The court upheld the Commission and condemned the dentists' refusal to compete on the available package of goods and services, absent some procompetitive justification. The Court found actual harm to competition, which made unnecessary any finding of market power.

United Air Lines, Inc. v. CAB.[13] This case was brought under Section 411 of the Federal Aviation Act, which parallels Section 5. The court upheld the CAB's regulations forbidding airlines to bias computerized reservation systems, even if this practice would not violate the Sherman Act. The challenged conduct was sufficiently similar to monopolization to withstand claims that the CAB was overreaching.

United States v. American Airlines, Inc.[14] This was the successful Justice Department civil challenge to rather blatant attempted price stabilization by a telephone call between two chief executive officers. The court condemned the request to fix prices as attempted monopolization, finding the required "dangerous probability of success" from the two firms' high combined local market shares. Some of us believe that, with this precedent now established, the next challenge to similar conduct could be criminal.

E.I. du Pont de Nemours & Co. v. FTC.[15] The FTC challenged the use of several "facilitating practice"—exclusive use of delivered prices, advance announcements of price changes, and use of "most favored nations clauses"—by the leading firms in the industry. The Commission found that, under the facts of the case, this violated Section 5.[16] The court of appeals reversed. It ruled that unilateral conduct by members of an oligopoly may be "unfair" only if there is "(1) evidence of anticompetitive intent or purpose on the part of the producer charged, or (2) the absence of an independent legitimate business reason for its conduct." The court also found that no anticompetitive effects had been demonstrated.

Detroit Auto Dealers Ass'n.[17] The FTC condemned a trade association agreement that discouraged auto dealers from being open weekends. It rejected the argument that any such agreement protected by the labor exemption because it resulted

from labor pressure and an interest in avoiding unionization.

Massachusetts Board of Registration in Optometry.[18] The FTC struck down, as violative of the antitrust laws, a state board's ban of even truthful advertising of affiliations and discounts. The Commission ruled that restraints on advertising are inherently suspect and found no plausible efficiency justifications. It held that a state board is a "person" covered by the FTC Act, and it rejected an asserted state-action defense, reasoning that a state board is not sovereign and finding that the state legislature had not clearly intended to displace competition.

Amerco.[19] This complaint challenged U-Haul's allegedly sham litigation designed to interfere with a competitor's reorganization in bankruptcy. The complaint was part of the FTC's efforts to address anticompetitive non-price predation. The consent order prohibits U-Haul and its corporate parent from engaging in litigation intended to harass or injure competitors.

City of Minneapolis and City of New Orleans.[20] The Commission challenged alleged agreements between taxicab companies and these two cities to limit taxicab competition. The FTC withdrew the complaints after Minneapolis increased the number of authorized taxicabs and Louisiana clarified its requirement that municipalities regulate taxicabs.

Michigan State Medical Soc'y.[21] The Commission condemned a physician boycott designed to raise the reimbursement rates of a state medicaid program. It found the boycott illegal under a rule of reason application of Section 5, and not entitled to protection under the *Noerr-Pennington* doctrine.

Ticor Title Insurance Co.[22] ALJ Needelman found that five major title insurance companies had illegally fixed prices by participating in rate bureaus, and that the McCarran- Ferguson exemption did not protect this activity since it was not principally the business of insurance.

Three observations about the cases are worth noting. First, the cases' virtue is also their vulnerability. Some cases were unsuccessful—which is not surprising, since almost by definition the cases are not easy. For several reasons, defeat does not prove that a case should not have been brought: (1) cases can be decided

---

[12] 476 U.S. 447 (1986).

[13] 766 F.2d 1107 (7th Cir. 1985).

[14] 743 F.2d 1114 (5th Cir. 1984), *cert. dismissed*, 474 U.S. 1001 (1985).

[15] 729 F.2d 128 (2d Cir. 1984).

[16] *In re* Ethyl Corp., 101 F.T.C. 425, 598, 601, 606 (1983).

[17] 5 Trade Reg. Rep. (CCH) ¶ 22,653 (FTC Feb. 22, 1989); *see also Cleveland Automobile Dealers' Ass'n*, File No. 851 0162 (FTC consent order announced Dec. 7, 1988), *reported in* 5 Trade Reg. Rep. (CCH) ¶ 22,629 (trade association agreed not to discourage its members from being open weekends and late weeknights). Mr. Rill and Mr. Mezines are counsel in this proceeding and did not participate in any consideration of the inclusion of this case in the Report. They do not share in the views expressed above.

[18] 5 Trade Reg. Rep. (CCH) ¶ 22,555 (FTC June 21, 1988).

[19] [1983-1987 Transfer Binder] Trade Reg. Rep. (CCH) ¶ 22,434 (consent order announced Feb. 26, 1987).

[20] Dkt. 9180 (FTC complaint withdrawn May 7, 1985), *reported in* [1983-1987 Transfer Binder] Trade Reg. Rep. (CCH) ¶ 22,250; Dkt. 9179 (FTC complaint withdrawn Jan. 3, 1985), *reported in* [1983-1987 Transfer Binder] Trade Reg. Rep. (CCH) ¶ 22,223.

[21] 101 F.T.C. 191 (1983) (Clanton, Comm'r); *see also* American Medical Ass'n, 94 F.T.C. 701 (1979) (Clanton, Comm'r) (the original FTC health care case, condemning an AMA ban on advertising and solicitation under Section 5, as a rule of reason violation), *aff'd sub nom.* American Medical Ass'n v. FTC, 638 F.2d 443 (2d Cir. 1980), *aff'd by an equally divided court*, 455 U.S. 676 (1982).

[22] [1983-1987 Transfer Binder] Trade Reg. Rep. (CCH) ¶ 22,419 (FTC initial decision Jan. 6, 1987) (Dkt. 9190).

wrongly; (2) development of facts or advances in economic learning may make appropriate the dismissal of a complaint that was sensible when filed; (3) knowledge is advanced by exploring new theories, although by itself this would not justify litigation; (4) it is preferable for the FTC to explore new theories than for private plaintiffs or state attorneys general to do so, since they may lack the FTC's resources and economic sophistication, and since treble damages may be excessively punitive where the law is unclear; and (5) it also may be preferable for the FTC to address an economic problem or an uncertain theory than for Congress to legislate based on incomplete information.[23] On the other hand, the FTC's involvement in controversial cases leaves it open to criticism from Congress and others.

Second, several of the cases involved the health care industry. This is a critical industry in which antitrust enforcement is relatively new. The FTC's experience illustrates the antitrust role it can play. The Commission has devoted substantial resources to this industry[24] and has not limited its actions to litigation. The Commission also has engaged in rulemaking, through the two "Eyeglasses Rules"[25] which were adopted under the Commission's consumer protection authority but address perceived competitive restraints. In addition, the Commission has studied the industry,[26] engaged in competition advocacy, and regularly given informal advice on antitrust compliance. Without judging the merits of all the positions the FTC has advanced, one can say that this combination of approaches should serve as a model. On the other hand, some health care restraints have predominantly local effects. Before challenging such a restraint, the Commission should conserve its resources by ascertaining the interest of state enforcers in pursuing the matter, where doing so would not compromise an investigation.

Finally, none of the cases involves purely vertical restraints. This is not surprising, given the increased recognition that many vertical restraints are procom-

petitive.[27] Nonetheless, many commentators note that certain vertical restraints lessen competition and should be illegal. Given fewer private challenges to vertical restraints, it would be helpful for the FTC to identify those vertical restraints it considers illegal and, where appropriate, to challenge them.

C. Conclusion

Many practices deserve antitrust scrutiny by the FTC. The application of antitrust to deregulated industries continues to be challenging. The scope of numerous antitrust exemptions continues to be undecided, because Congress is considering important legislation and the Commission and the courts are struggling to demark the edges of exemptions (e.g., *Noerr*, state action, labor). The importance of policing those edges is increasingly recognized. Finally, the expanding importance of the rule of reason and proof of market power emphasizes the importance of the FTC's role and may suggest that the significance of criminal antitrust could decline. Fewer and fewer antitrust cases are decided under easily-adjudicated per se rules. Even when adjudicators apply per se rules, they often do so only after considering competitive consequences.

V. The Consumer Protection Program

The FTC's consumer protection program monitors and regulates a wide range of practices. Most of the Commission's activity is concerned with advertising practices, consumer fraud, and a smorgasbord of specific statutory provisions (equal credit, truth in lending, debt collection). During the 1970's, although less so recently, the Commission devoted substantial resources to rulemaking.[28] Finally, the Commission has brought a few administrative cases under its authority to prohibit unfair acts or practices.

Discussions of the Commission's advertising and consumer fraud programs follow. Rulemaking is discussed as part of the Commission's program for giving guidance to business. Before turning to these topics, however, we want to discuss briefly the Commission's "unfairness" enforcement authority.[29]

Broad authority must be exercised judiciously. The Commission's unfairness authority has long been a source of controversy.[30] Some, but not all, controversy ended with the Commission issuing its policy state-

---

[23] For instance, the country might have been better served by a careful FTC study of the insurance industry, followed by litigation, rulemaking, or a detailed explanation of why action is unnecessary, than by massive litigation by states and private parties. Of course, an FTC proceeding does not absolutely preclude other challenges.

[24] *Cf.* Graph 4 in Appendix C (workyears for health care program). The graph suggests that the health care program has been accounting for increasing percentages of competition workyears, even though, as indicated in the note accompanying Graph 3, the reported numbers may not represent total health care workyears. For health care investigations, see Graph 8.

[25] Trade Regulation Rule on Advertising of Ophthalmic Goods and Services, 43 Fed. Reg. 23,992 (1978), *suspended in part and remanded*, American Optometric Ass'n v. FTC, 626 F.2d 896 (D.C. Cir. 1980), *on remand*, Opthalmic Practice Rules, 54 Fed. Reg. 10,285 (1989). For discussion of these rules, see Section VI.C.3.

[26] Examples of studies include the certificate-of-need regulation study, the hospital competition study, and the dental auxiliary study.

[27] The change in the FTC's enforcement priorities is suggested by Graphs 3-7 and 8-9 in Appendix C, showing workyears and investigations.

[28] For the FTC's allocation of consumer protection resources, see Graphs 14-18 (workyears) and Graph 19 (investigations) in Appendix C.

[29] We have little to say about the Commission's enforcement of specific statutes, although this is an important responsibility.

[30] *See, e.g.,* Gellhorn, *Trading Stamps, S&H, and the FTC's Unfairness Doctrine,* 1983 Duke L.J. 903. For the history of the FTC's enforcement of this authority, see American Fin. Serv. v. FTC, 767 F.2d 957, 965-72 (D.C. Cir. 1985), *cert. denied,* 475 U.S. 1011 (1986).

ment on its consumer unfairness jurisdiction.[31] This policy statement made a major contribution to Commission jurisprudence, but it still must be fleshed out through careful application in cases.

The Commission cannot expect to bring many administrative consumer unfairness cases. When unfairness is so egregious that it borders on fraud, the Commission should challenge it in federal court using its Section 13(b) authority.[32] When other questioned practices are widespread, the Commission should seek to end them through some combination of guides, policy statements, and rulemaking. Some other practices will be best challenged by state attorneys general or private parties.

A case that illustrates the kinds of administrative consumer unfairness cases the Commission should consider bringing is *Orkin Exterminating Co. v. FTC*.[33] (Obviously, we mention this and other cases without necessarily endorsing the Commission's position, in part because we have not read the records and the files in the cases.) Orkin, the world's largest termite and pest control company, had used a standard contract providing lifetime termite protection in return for payment of annual inspection fees of amounts specified in the contract. After inflation made this uneconomic, Orkin, with the tentative blessing of counsel, began to impose substantial, unilateral increases in the annual fees. Orkin's practice had at least a colorable justification, and individual injuries were small, so the practice was an unlikely candidate for private litigation. The Commission challenged the systematic violation of contract provisions as an unfair act or practice, and its order was recently upheld. Although Orkin fits our suggested principles unusually well, there are other examples of the kinds of administrative consumer unfairness cases that the Commission should consider bringing.[34]

A. *Advertising Practices*

The most controversial part of the FTC's consumer protection mission is its advertising practices program. Few doubt the importance of this program. False and deceptive advertisements prevent markets from functioning properly and harm consumers and competitors alike. FTC administrative adjudication can be an advantageous method of resolving factually

and legally complex deception cases. The FTC's advertising program is also symbolically important, as one of the agency's more visible activities. However, there is much debate over the sufficiency of the FTC's activities and the role the FTC should play in the regulation of advertising.

At one time, the FTC was the dominant regulator of advertising. Today, however, the FTC is merely one of several players. A single false advertisement may be challenged by industry self- regulation groups (the National Advertising Review Board ("NARB") and the National Advertising Division of the Council of Better Business Bureaus ("NAD"), by the media in which the advertisement is sought to be placed,[35] by a competitor's Lanham Act suit,[36] or by a state attorney general,[37] as well as by the FTC or another federal regulatory authority.[38]

1. Sufficiency of the FTC's Program

Rightly or wrongly, the media has conveyed the perception that the FTC has largely abandoned the regulation of advertising, especially national advertising.[39] State attorneys general cite this perceived void

---

[31] Letter from Federal Trade Commission to Senators Ford and Danforth (Dec. 17, 1980), *reprinted in* [1969-1983 Transfer Binder] Trade Reg. Rep. (CCH) ¶ 50,421; *see also* Credit Practices Rule; Statement of Basis and Purpose and Regulatory Analysis, 49 Fed. Reg. 7740 (1984).

[32] See *infra* section V.B.

[33] 849 F.2d 1354 (11th Cir. 1988), *cert. denied*, 109 S. Ct. 865 (1989).

[34] See Holland Furnace Co. v. FTC, 295 F.2d 302 (7th Cir. 1961) (unfair to sell home furnaces by dismantling existing furnaces without permission and then refusing to reassemble them promptly, falsely claiming that they were dangerous or not worth repairing); Uncle Ben's, Inc., 89 F.T.C. 131 (1977) (consent order) (allegedly unsafe and unfair to broadcast an advertisement showing an unsupervised young child hovering over a pan cooking on a gas range, and then claiming to have cooked food without assistance).

[35] Although self-regulation continues to be important, there are suggestions that the media are devoting fewer resources to this. *See, e.g., The Media Business: Television; Of Profanity and Profits: A Network's New Focus,* N.Y. Times, Aug. 29, 1988, at D6, col. 5 (city ed.) (NBC's broadcast standards department reduced from 60 to 20 people and consolidated into a "program administration and marketing" unit; CBS and ABC have each reduced employees in program practices from 80 to about 30).

[36] 15 U.S.C. § 1125(a) (1982).

[37] See generally *Kellogg Agrees it Won't Run Some Cereal Ads,* Wall St. J. Aug. 29, 1988, at 14, col. 1 (Rice Krispies promoted vitamin B); *States Assuming a New Role in Consumer Issues,* N.Y. Times, Feb. 8, 1988, at A17, col. 1; *New Cops on the Beat,* 19 Nat'l J. 1338 (May 23, 1987); *Deceptive Ads: The FTC's Laissez-Faire Approach is Backfiring,* Bus. Week, Dec. 2, 1985, at 136 (reviewing increased activity by state and by competitors); *Sponges for Birth Control: A Warning,* N.Y. Times, Mar. 30, 1985, at 48, col. 1 (city ed.) (in consent agreement with New York, contraceptive sponge maker agreed to change national advertising campaign); *Beef Trade Forced to Alter Ads,* N.Y. Times Mar. 2, 1985, at 48, col. 1 (city ed.) ("For the fifth time in less than two years Robert Abrams, the New York State Attorney General, has been responsible for significant changes in a national advertising campaign.") (discussing challenge to beef industry's "Beef Gives Strength" ads, as well as to soft drink advertising of the use of NutraSweet, Campbell Soup's description of soup as "health insurance," and two major snack food companies' use of the term "light").

[38] In addition to the FTC, federal agencies with authority over advertising and labeling include the Food and Drug Administration, the Bureau of Alcohol, Tobacco, and Firearms, the Department of Agriculture, the Environmental Protection Agency, and the Postal Service.

[39] *See, e.g., What Kind of FTC for the '90's?,* Advertising Age, May 2, 1988, at 16; *see also supra* note 5. In addition, Congress has regrettably interfered with the FTC's ability even to study the insurance industry. *See* 15 U.S.C. § 46(h) (1982).

to explain their heightened activities. Much of the dispute concerns two issues: the interpretation of allegedly implied claims, and the seriousness of the risk that overly aggressive enforcement will suppress truthful advertising.

We are not of one mind on whether the FTC is bringing a sufficient number of advertising cases. Those who defend the FTC note that it is currently adjudicating complicated suits against Kraft, R.J. Reynolds, and Campbell Soup,[40] and that during 1984 through 1988 it filed 25 complaints challenging advertisements seen throughout the country. These supporters argue that truthful advertising would have been deterred had the agency found implied claims without evidence of actual consumer perception, and had it pursued the children's advertising and other rulemaking activities that were a prominent part of FTC efforts in the 1970's. Critics respond that the Commission has failed to bring cases of consequence, and that it has devoted insufficient attention and resources to advertising enforcement.[41] They note that of those 25 complaints, 12 involved diet or health supplements, baldness cures, or tanning devices, whereas only six challenged network television advertising (of which four involved air or water cleaners).

Although we have differences on whether the FTC is prosecuting its share of advertising suits, we are united in our belief that the FTC can and should do more to articulate its advertising law- enforcement agenda. Most of us believe that the FTC properly hesitates before finding implied advertising claims, and is properly concerned about the risk of suppressing truthful advertising. But too rarely has the public received the message that the FTC believes it is important to move aggressively against false and deceptive advertising.

2. State Advertising Programs

The state attorneys general have responded to the perceived slackening of FTC enforcement with vigor-

ous advertising programs of their own. Many individual states regularly file suits challenging deceptive and fraudulent practices. A number of states have proposed or enacted special advertising statutes. In 1987 the National Association of Attorneys General ("NAAG") adopted airline advertising and marketing guidelines.[42] More recently, NAAG approved guidelines on advertising and other business practices in the car rental industry.[43]

The states play an essential role in challenging deceptive and fraudulent practices. Frequently, a state attorney general will be the public official best able to end a harmful practice and to redress injury. The attorneys general know local needs and concerns, are experienced in using local court systems, and sometimes enjoy procedural or remedial advantages not shared by the FTC. State officials often will be the best enforcers of laws against consumer fraud.

In addition to their efforts against fraud, state officials bring other important deception cases. Without judging the merits of any particular matter, examples of cases that states should consider filing include the following:

— Illinois won an agreement from a Chicago firm to stop misrepresenting food as kosher, and to refund the money of customers.[44]

— Although not a lawsuit, the Iowa attorney general has criticized car rental price advertisements that exclude mandatory fees.[45]

— Missouri won a consent order against 34 tanning centers that prohibits telling customers that the use of tanning devices is safe, will not cause aging of the skin, will not increase the risk of skin cancer, or is safer than tanning under the sun.[46]

— Ohio sued two firms that mailed advertisements offering a motor cycle or a motor boat to persons who

---

[40] R.J. Reynolds Tobacco Co. v. FTC, Nos. 88-1355, 88-1392 (D.C. Cir. July 1, 1988) (dismissing petitions for stay of FTC Dkt. 9206 and for writ of mandamus), noted in 5 Trade Reg. Rep. (CCH) ¶ 22,565; Campbell Soup Co., Dkt 9223 (FTC complaint filed Jan. 26, 1989), noted in 5 Trade Reg. Rep. (CCH) ¶ 22,641; Kraft, Inc., Dkt. 9208 (FTC complaint announced June 18, 1987), noted in 5 Trade Reg. Rep. (CCH) ¶ 22,454.

[41] The number of work years devoted to "advertising practices" has declined from 98 in fiscal 1978 to 56 in fiscal 1987, and, as a percentage of the FTC's resources devoted to substantive consumer protection work, advertising practices have fallen from 24 percent in fiscal 1978 to 17.3 percent in 1987. Graph 14 in Appendix C. FTC supporters in turn would respond that the agency has conserved resources by refraining from filing ill-advised cases. They also would note that the Commission's numerous consumer fraud suits (see Section V.B), which challenge the advertising and promotion of products that do not work at all, could be considered advertising suits. (The FTC records this activity as part of its "enforcement" program rather than its "advertising practices" program, and resources expended on "enforcement" have been increasing. Graph 14 in Appendix C.)

[42] Report and Recommendations of NAAG Task Force on Air Travel Industry, Antitrust & Trade Reg. Rep. (BNA) No. 1345, at S-1 (Dec. 17, 1987).

[43] National Association of Attorneys General, Final Report and Recommendations of the Task Force on Car Rental Industry Advertising and Practices (adopted March 14, 1989), reprinted in 56 Antitrust & Trade Reg. Rep. (BNA) No. 1407 (special supp.), at S-3 (hereinafter "NAAG Car Rental Guidelines").

[44] Suit Says Shelat Falsely Labeled Foods Kosher, Los Angeles Times, Nov. 6, 1987, part 4, p. 4, col. 3. Similarly, Oregon won a consent order against a grocery store that substituted an inferior grade of salmon for the advertised grade, United Press Int'l Story, Dec. 16, 1986, available on NEXIS, and Missouri won a consent order and consumer redress from a seed purveyor who misrepresented the quality of his seed, News from Attorney General William L. Webster (May 27, 1988).

[45] Regulation by the States is Debated, N.Y. Times, Dec. 15, 1988, at D19, col. 1. The FTC subsequently announced consent orders condemning these practices. Alamo Rent-A-Car, Inc., 5 Trade Reg. Rep. (CCH) ¶ 22,633 (FTC proposed consent order Dec. 29, 1988); Budget Rent-A-Car Corp., 5 Trade Reg. Rep. (CCH) ¶ 22,632 (FTC proposed consent order Dec. 28, 1988).

[46] News from Attorney General William L. Webster (Mar. 10, 1988).

would test the product, failing to mention that the shipping charge often exceeded the product's value.[47]

On the other hand, we are troubled by aspects of some of the states' activity. For instance, one state is considering a legislative rule that would, among other things, limit the use of the term "discount store," ban claims of low prices unless all competitors had been surveyed, and prohibit "sales" where prices are reduced less than 10 percent. Another state has proposed pricing claim regulations that, among other things, would strictly regulate the use of "Buy One—Get One Free" solicitations, and would prohibit reference to "list prices" except where those prices were charged by a significant number of competitors.

Excessive regulation of pricing claims can harm consumers, as experts on advertising have come to appreciate in the past two decades.[48] It is all too easy to drive useful information out of advertisements, and this is likely to happen if compliance with pricing claim regulations becomes onerous. For instance, prohibiting "sales" featuring less than 10 percent price reductions could increase pricing rigidity.

We are also troubled by aspects of the NAAG guidelines on car rental and airline advertising practices. The most disturbing aspect of the former is the recommendation that states adopt statutes ordering car rental firms to provide insurance coverage for all rented cars.[49] Such laws would be likely to encourage price rigidity to the disadvantage of smaller competitors and consumers alike. NAAG's airline advertising guides also may tend to discourage price advertising.[50] But wholly apart from the particulars of the guidelines, car rental companies and airlines typically mount national advertising campaigns, for which a uniform national enforcement policy is desirable. Although NAAG has sought to bring consistency to state enforcement of advertising restrictions—and, commendably, has invited widespread comment on its

proposals—uniform national standards, vigorously enforced and consistently interpreted, would be preferable.

3. The FTC and the States[51]

Although we have reservations about some of the states' advertising practices enforcement, we believe that the pattern of increased activity by the states will continue, and that much state enforcement can be beneficial. In advertising practices — and, indeed, in other consumer protection matters — the states are likely to play active roles and can make important contributions. Accordingly, the FTC should assist the states in better serving consumers. The current liaison arrangement between the FTC and the states should be improved. Where possible, the FTC should share its economic expertise with the states. The FTC should seek to assist the states by, for example, coordinating the states' exchanges with other federal agencies and by performing model evaluations of substantiation evidence and model consumer surveys. The FTC should also recognize that the state attorneys general, being closer to consumers, can be an invaluable resource as a repository of information about issues of consumer concern and as a sounding board for proposed enforcement initiatives.

The states and the FTC each have important roles to play. To overgeneralize, the states' primary mission should be those practices that harm consumers within a single state; the FTC's special mission should be those practices that harm consumers in many states. These are not firm boundaries, of course, but they represent the ideal.[52] Where the FTC is challenging what is essentially a local practice, the enforcement process may be unduly expensive and insufficiently responsive to local concerns. Conversely, where one or more states challenge what are essentially interstate practices, there is a significant risk that the enforcement process will be unnecessarily cumbersome, that inconsistent standards will create uncertainty, and that the interests of consumers nationwide will not be optimally served.

Even local advertising practices often have substantial interstate effects. Many media markets are interstate. Advertisers often use a single advertisement in several states. Yet advertising practices tend to be matters of considerable local concern, and it is unrealistic to expect that the states will refrain from challenging any advertisement with an interstate effect.

---

[47] *Companies Accused of Deceptive Advertising*, United Press Int'l, Oct. 1, 1987, available on NEXIS.

[48] *E.g.*, Pitofsky, *Beyond Nader: Consumer Protection and the Regulation of Advertising*, 90 Harv. L. Rev. 661 (1977).

[49] NAAG Car Rental Guidelines, *supra* note 43, at 45- 46 (first of three alternatives).

[50] For instance, they require that "[a]ny advertised fare must be available in sufficient quantity so as to meet reasonably foreseeable demand on every flight each day for the market in which the advertisement appears, beginning on the day on which the advertisement appears and continuing for at least three days after the advertisement terminates." Section 2.4. The onerousness of this is mitigated by an exception, but the net effect is to make price advertising more difficult.

A deputy attorney general who served on the NAAG airline guide task force suggested that the broadcast media may not be suitable vehicles for price advertising: "There just may be too many limitations in broadcast for fare advertising. Broadcast may be better suited for image rather than price ads.... People either don't hear or don't understand that restrictions apply." *Airlines Lash Out at Guidelines*, Advertising Age, Sept. 28, 1987, at 28. Most of us disagree. Informative advertising should not be discouraged.

---

[51] Although the comments that follow are addressed to the regulation of advertising, the suggestions for harmony among the states and the FTC should generally be applicable to other consumer protection (and, indeed, competition) activities.

[52] For instance, although the FTC's consumer fraud program is generally laudable, see Section IV.B, the FTC should refer complaints about local frauds to state enforcers, in the first instance. Similarly, although the Commission's professions antitrust program has made important contributions, many of these cases are intrastate in principal effect and normally should be brought by state enforcers, assuming they are willing and able.

Overlapping scrutiny of advertisements would not present difficulties if all reviewers used a common standard or if excessive enforcement were benign. However, neither is the case. The FTC's views of appropriate advertising enforcement standards have changed over time, but the views of some state enforcers more closely resemble the FTC's earlier views.[53] Moreover, challenges to certain procompetitive advertisements can harm consumers and the competitive process.

In the first instance, advertising practices should be addressed by the preferable enforcer. When the FTC learns of a questionable advertisement with a principally local effect, the FTC should refer the matter to the appropriate state and offer to help. When a deceptive advertising campaign has substantial interstate effects, the FTC presumptively should be the government enforcement agency.[54] The FTC should encourage states to come forward with advertising concerns: suggestions should be taken seriously and should trigger prompt investigations.[55] The referring state should be consulted actively during the decisionmaking process. If the FTC elects not to challenge the advertisement, the FTC should explain its reasoning to the referring state in as much detail as the confidentiality statutes permit. (For such a referral process to work, of course, the FTC would have to commit itself to making an enforcement decision promptly enough to allow a state to proceed if the FTC does not.)

The FTC and the states will inevitably disagree about the wisdom of challenging certain advertisements. When a state declines to challenge a predominantly intrastate advertisement, federalism requires the FTC normally to defer to the state's decision. Even when states challenge interstate advertisements that the FTC has declined to proceed against, the FTC's usual response should be silence where, for instance, its decision was based on resource allocation or involved a close judgment call about the meaning of an advertisement. Little would be gained and much FTC-state harmony would be jeopardized if the FTC were to participate in such a suit. However, if the FTC decides that a particular advertising practice with substantially interstate effects is beneficial to consumers and to the competitive process — not just

neutral, but positively beneficial — and that a state challenge to it would interfere with the FTC's agenda for improving information dissemination, the FTC should consider taking a public position supporting the challenged advertisement, either through public statements or by *amicus* participation in the lawsuit. This should not be done lightly, but the FTC should not hesitate to make its views known in appropriate cases.[56]

4. Shaping a Common Agenda

The FTC should not routinely criticize the states, which are its allies in protecting consumers. Instead, the FTC should work with the states to shape a common advertising agenda. The FTC will have to take the lead in this, but the relationship between the states and the FTC should not be a one-way street: the states have much to teach the FTC.

The pricing claims cases are an illustration of this. In reviewing reports of state challenges to advertisements, one is struck by the number of suits that involve pricing claims. This was once true of FTC advertising cases, as well.[57] The Commission subsequently came to appreciate the importance of encouraging pricing claims, and to understand that increasing the legal risk of making such claims could deprive consumers of valuable information. Challenges to pricing claims fell into disfavor.

We regard the heightened activity of the states as a cry for greater FTC attention to pricing claims. The FTC's abandonment of this field has created two problems. First, the FTC's 1964 pricing guides, although unenforced for over a decade and not an accurate statement of Commission views, remain as published expressions of national policy, available for citation. Indeed, one can read standard reference works and not begin to appreciate the changes in FTC policy since the 1960's.[58] Second, as the state attorneys general understand, pricing misrepresentations offend and may harm. For instance, some car rental firms have misrepresented prices by advertising rates that failed to include significant mandatory charges.[59] Until recently, the FTC has not prevented this sort of advertising. The FTC appears to have little interest in price advertising, which has created a void that the states are rushing to fill. The FTC should eliminate this void by bringing meritorious pricing suits, such as

---

[53] Compare, for instance, some state enforcement actions with the FTC's 1967 Guides Against Deceptive pricing, 16 C.F.R. part 233, and with FTC v. Mary Carter paint Co., 382 U.S. 46 (1965).

[54] The FTC could file an administrative suit or, where an advertisement's illegality is clear, a suit in federal court seeking an injunction and, possibly, consumer redress. Where a particular state's laws permit it to obtain financial penalties, that suit easily could follow on the FTC action. However, if the success of a state suit to obtain financial penalties would be jeopardized by waiting for FTC action, the state would be more justified in proceeding promptly.

[55] Increased referrals by states, in general, is suggested by FTC data showing that from 1981 to 1988 the number of investigations triggered by state and local referrals increased steadily from 14 to 31. See Graph 20 in Appendix C.

[56] In those cases where a state has worked with the FTC to review the merits of an advertisement, the FTC should participate in a subsequent suit by the state only where FTC is certain of the importance of protecting the challenged advertising. And obviously the FTC should do everything in its power to preserve inviolate the confidentiality of exchanges with state officials.

[57] The FTC devoted considerable effort to adopting and enforcing Guides Against Deceptive pricing, 16 C.F.R. §233 (Nov. 8, 1967); see also proposed Guides Against Deceptive Pricing, 39 Fed. Reg. 21,059 (1974).

[58] See ABA Antitrust Section, Antitrust Law Developments 29091 (2d ed. 1984 & Supp. 1988).

[59] See references in note 45 supra.

Alamo Rent-A-Car,[60] and setting forth more aggressively its advertising enforcement agenda.

The pricing experience teaches a larger lesson. The FTC must not forget that it is only one player in advertising enforcement. perhaps at one time it could leave guidelines unenforced, without rescinding them and without explaining the reasons behind its decision not to bring cases. No longer. The pricing guidelines in their current form are a source of confusion and should be amended immediately to reflect current FTC thinking. When the FTC investigates a significant advertisement, whether or not concerning price, and finds it lawful (not just that the FTC's resources could be better used elsewhere), the FTC should seek, consistent with confidentiality requirements, to make public its decision not to challenge the advertisement, and the reasons for that decision. A skeptical public, including the states and consumer groups, is entitled to an explanation. In addition, the advertising community and other enforcers would be educated and reassured by a better understanding of the FTC's reasoning.

B. *Consumer Fraud*

The 1969 Report criticized the FTC for failing to address retail fraud adequately. The FTC advanced two defenses to its cautious approach, the same arguments that critics of the FTC's current program to prevent consumer fraud advance today: retail fraud frequently is a criminal offense and the Commission's sanctions are a poor substitute for criminal penalties, and retail fraud tends to be a local problem.[61] The Report rejected these justifications, arguing that the FTC's flexible equitable powers could be effective against fraud, and should be used, especially against firms operating across state lines.[62]

The FTC's lack of effective enforcement tools was a more serious deficiency than the Report indicated. The tools available to the FTC today, however, are far superior to those available in 1969. In 1973, Congress added Section 13(b) to the FTC Act,[63] thereby authorizing the Commission to petition district courts for preliminary injunctions to enforce its statutory mandate. Although the Commission's best known use of this authority has been to preserve the premerger status of corporate assets pending Commission review of proposed mergers, Section 13(b) has become the foundation of the Commission's consumer fraud program.

Section 13(b) is an attractive method of winning preliminary and permanent relief. The Commission

has successfully used it to seek *ex parte* asset freezes and asset escrow arrangements.[64] Section 13(b) also permits the Commission in a "proper" case to seek a permanent injunction to enforce any provision of a law within the Commission's jurisdiction. "proper cases" include those in which the FTC relies on established precedent and "does not desire to further expand upon the prohibitions of the Federal Trade Commission Act through the issuance of a cease-and-desist order."[65] With increasing frequency, the Commission has successfully used its authority under Section 13(b) to obtain affirmative relief, including monetary damages, through suits for permanent injunctions. Courts have consistently exercised their equitable authority to award monetary equitable relief in these actions.[66] The affirmative relief granted has included not only restitution to defrauded consumers,[67] but also con-

---

[64] The Commission's authority to seek and the district court's authority to award such relief was sustained in FTC v. Southwest Sunsites, Inc., 665 F.2d 711 (5th Cir.), cert. denied, 456 U.S. 973 (1982); see also, e.g., FTC v. World Travel Vacation Brokers, Inc., 861 F.2d 1020, 1024-26 (7th Cir. 1988) (upholding asset freeze); FTC v. Pannos Mining Co., Civ. No. 88-06453R (C.D. Cal. Nov. 22, 1988) (imposing asset freeze and appointing permanent receiver), noted in 5 Trade Reg. Rep. (CCH) ¶22,631; FTC v. Overseas Unlimited Agency, Inc., Civ. No. 88-2583 (C.D. Cal. June 6, 1988), noted in 5 Trade Reg. Rep. (CCH) ¶22,552.

[65] FTC v. H.N. Singer, Inc., 668 F.2d 1107, 1111 (9th Cir. 1982); see also FTC v. World Travel Vacation Brokers, Inc., 861 F.2d 1020, 1028 (7th Cir. 1988) ("Congress at least expected that the FTC could rely on this proviso when it sought to halt a straightforward violation of section 5 that required no application of the FTC's expertise to a novel regulatory issue through administrative proceedings.").

[66] See FTC v. U.S. Oil & Gas Corp., 748 F.2d 1431 (11th Cir. 1984) (appellate court held that district court has inherent equitable powers to grant ancillary monetary relief incident to its express statutory authority to issue permanent injunctions under the FTC Act); FTC v. H.N. Singer, Inc., 668 F.2d 1107 (9th Cir. 1982) (upholding authority of district court to freeze assets in a Section 13(b) action, but acknowledging authority to order broad ancillary relief); FTC v. Solar Michigan, Inc., 7 Trade Reg. Rep. (CCH) ¶68,339 (E.D. Mich. Sept. 27, 1988) (asset freeze under Section 13(b) was warranted to preserve the possibility of future monetary relief; consumer redress was also appropriate); FTC v. International Diamond Corp., 1983-2 Trade Cas. (CCH) ¶65,506 (N.D. Cal. 1983) (holding that district courts possess ancillary jurisdiction under Section 13(b) to grant consumer redress, including rescission of contracts); see also Paul, The FTC's Increased Reliance on Section 13(b) in Court Litigation, 57 Antitrust L.J. 141, 143-44 & nn. 9-11 (1988) (citing cases).

[67] See, e.g., FTC v. Schoolhouse Coins, Inc., Civ. No 8705415KN (C.D. Cal. announced Sept. 28, 1988), noted in 5 Trade Reg. Rep. (CCH) ¶22,602; FTC v. Rainbow Enzymes, Inc., Civ. No. CIV-87-1522 (D. Ariz. Sept. 2, 1988), noted in 5 Trade Reg. Rep. (CCH) ¶ 22,595; FTC v. Amy Travel Services, Inc., Civ. No. 87C6776 (N.D. Ill. May 4, 1988), noted in 5 Trade Reg. Rep. (CCH) ¶22,546; FTC v. Atlantex Associates, 1987-2 Trade Cas. (CCH) ¶67,788 (S.D. Fla. 1987) ($3.2 million in consumer redress ordered); FTC v. TransAlaska Energy Corp., Civ. No. 84 2001 (C.D. Cal. Apr. 27, 1987) ($2.1

---

[60] 5 Trade Reg. Rep. (CCH) ¶22,633 (FTC proposed consent order Dec. 29, 1988).

[61] 1969 Report at 50-51. The FTC also was uncertain whether it had jurisdiction over local retail fraud.

[62] 1969 Report at 52. The Report also dismissed the FTC's reliance upon a 1941 Supreme Court decision, FTC v. Bunte Bros., 312 U.S. 349 (1941) which found that the FTC did not have jurisdiction to enforce Section 5 against a localized fraud.

[63] 15 U.S.C. §53(b) (1982). The pertinent language is quoted in Appendix B.

tract rescission and permanent asset freezes or receiverships to preserve the possibility of further monetary relief.[68] Largely because Section 13(b) offers a faster and more complete remedy than that available through traditional administrative action, the number of consumer protection cases pursued in federal court has eclipsed the number in administrative adjudication.[69]

1. Development of Program

The 1970's witnessed a large amount of consumer fraud, particularly in land sales and vocational schools. The FTC used its administrative enforcement weapons to combat these types of fraud. The relative slowness of the FTC's administrative procedure was less of a hindrance in these kinds of fraud cases. The Commission saw some success in combatting fraud as it won, at least on paper, significant amounts of consumer redress.

In the 1980's, as the Commission's authority under Section 13(b) became clearer, the FTC's fraud enforcement efforts shifted to federal court, taking advantage of its greater power by expanding the scope of remedies it seeks in consumer fraud cases. While the Commission continues to attack basic consumer fraud, such as in land sales, the Commission has also expanded its use of consumer redress and injunctive remedies to challenge other types of fraud as well, most notably telemarketing fraud.[70] Its new enforcement powers offered the advantages of speed and the ability to tie up assets quickly, making consumer redress a more realistic future possibility. In addition to the consumer redress actually ordered by the courts, the Commission has obtained increasing numbers of consent orders in consumer fraud cases in which the respondent agrees to pay significant amounts of consumer redress.

Land Sales Fraud: The Federal Trade Commission has issued 12 final orders against land developers since 1972. These cases involve charges of misrepresentation that the purchase of land is a sound financial investment, involving little or no monetary risk. Seven of these cases resulted in sizable monetary awards as

well as final Commission orders. These monetary damages included both consumer redress and payment for certain improvements. The potential value of the redress, improvements, and cancelled contracts in all of the land cases since 1972 amount to $147,855,092.

Vocational Schools Fraud: Eleven of the orders issued since 1970 in vocational schools cases provide for a total of $3,691,504 in refunds to 22,341 students. Compliance with these orders, however, has proved to be a serious problem. Of the 84 orders issued since 1959, 16 compliance reports have been rejected or not filed, 25 compliance investigations have been conducted, and three civil penalty actions have been filed (resulting in awards of $113,000).

Telemarketing Fraud: The Commission has prosecuted an increasing number of telemarketing fraud cases in the 1980's, expending greater amounts of shrinking agency resources to combat the problem. In FY 1983, the Commission spent 17,817 hours investigating and prosecuting telemarketing fraud cases. This number increased each year to a high of 55,631 hours in FY 1987 and then dipped slightly to 47,502 in FY 1988. The amount of the Commission's budget devoted to telemarketing fraud cases increased annually from $410,964 in FY 1983 to $2,282,110 in FY 1988.

The Commission typically proceeds against telemarketing fraud through Section 13(b) injunction actions, since they can be initiated *ex parte.* Speed is essential in telemarketing cases because defendants and their assets vanish at the first hint of enforcement activity.

The Commission has enjoyed some success in its attack on telemarketing fraud. Of the 85 investigations of telemarketing fraud initiated by the Commission since June 1, 1983, 17 have resulted in orders requiring consumer redress. The consumer redress ordered in these cases totals $85,632,000, of which $4,337,500 has actually been distributed to consumers, $3,795,000 is on deposit in a bank and $15,228,000 is being held by receivers. Most of the cases have arisen in the areas of investment coins and art (23), mineral leasing (14), consumer goods (11), and travel (11).[71]

The most significant recent development in the FTC telemarketing effort has been the increasing cooperation between FTC and the state attorneys general. In August 1987, the FTC and the NAAG created an automated databank on telemarketing fraud. This databank is intended to pool the information compiled by the participating offices in order to identify and prosecute the most flagrant law violators, and to identify trends in telemarketing that require closer monitoring by enforcement agencies. To date, 22 states have agreed to participate in this databank and two others are in the process of joining.

2. An Appraisal

The current Commission has targeted for special attention cases of outright consumer fraud; the high

---

million in consumer redress ordered); FTC v. TransAlaska Energy Corp., Civ. No. 84 2001 (C.D. Cal. Apr. 27, 1987) ($2.1 million in consumer redress ordered), *noted in* [1983-1987 Transfer Binder] Trade Reg. Rep. (CCH) ¶22,446; FTC v. New England Rare Coin Galleries, Civ. No. 842 3144 (D. Mass. announced Feb. 13, 1987) (restitution payment required), *noted in* [1983-1987 Transfer Binder] Trade Reg. Rep. (CCH) ¶22,431; *Evans Products Co.,* Civ. No. 812 3222 (S.D. Fla. announced June 17, 1986) (bankruptcy court required debtor to pay $2.4 million in consumer redress pursuant to an FTC claim), *noted in* [1983-1987 Transfer Binder] Trade Reg. Rep. (CCH) ¶22,372; FTC v. Leland Industries, Inc., Civ. No. 833589 (C.D. Cal. announced Oct. 11, 1985) (restitution payment required by settlement), *noted in* [1983-1987 Transfer Binder] Trade Reg. Rep. (CCH) ¶22,297; FTC v. Kitco, Inc., 612 F. Supp. 1282 (D. Minn. 1985).

[68] *See, e.g., FTC v. Rare Coin Galleries of Am. Inc.,* 1986-2 Trade Cas. (CCH) ¶ 67,338 (D. Mass. 1986).

[69] *See* Appendix B.

[70] See Table 1 and Graph 18 in Appendix C.

[71] See Table 1 in Appendix C.

level of Commission commitment to combatting telemarketing fraud is the most salient example of this
enforcement focus. Telemarketing schemes are a particularly appropriate enforcement target because they
often involve clever and sophisticated proposals of
"good" deals and "safe" investments. Individual consumers have lost an average of $5,000 to $10,000 in
these schemes, money often taken from savings or
from equity built up in their homes.

Clearly our legal system should provide remedies
for this type of fraud. The question is whether the FTC
is an appropriate body to procure those remedies.
Significant barriers to private causes of action make
individual lawsuits an unrealistic option for most of
these fraud victims. The costs of maintaining a lawsuit can be prohibitively expensive compared to the
potential gains. Each individual loss is likely to be too
small to merit the cost of pursuing it. In addition, the
legal and practical barriers to a class action suit are
often formidable.

State enforcers play a valuable role in attacking
consumer fraud. Frequently a state attorney general
will be the official best situated to bring a suit.
However, fraudulent schemes often operate across
state lines, which can make state enforcement difficult. Optimal enforcement requires a federal presence
to bring certain suits and to help coordinate multistate enforcement efforts. Finally, because the Commission receives complaints from all over the country,
it is in a good position to identify trends and to detect
major fraud schemes.

FTC enforcement also has advantages compared to
criminal prosecution. By using Section 13(b), the Commission is able to go into court ex parte to obtain an
order freezing assets, and is also able to obtain consumer redress. Neither of these remedies is available
through traditional criminal prosecution. In addition,
criminal intent is often difficult to prove to a jury
beyond a reasonable doubt. The FTC's burden is easier: it need only prove a statement's falsity by a
preponderance of the evidence.

These advantages of FTC enforcement suggest that
the FTC should bring cases that cut across state lines
and where criminal prosecution is not a good option,
or where there is reason to supplement criminal prosecution. Optimal use of FTC prosecutorial advantages
requires the FTC to move quickly, however. Currently,
a typical case takes three to six months from the time
the staff hears about the alleged wrongdoing until an
ex parte asset freeze can be ordered. Some cases are
slower, and the Commission should be encouraged to
improve its performance.

Deterring potential consumer fraud is an important
enforcement objective. The supply of fraud is not
perfectly elastic. At the margin, the Commission can
have some deterrent effect by raising the costs of
defrauding consumers. The Commission currently
wields some of the most effective means of raising
these costs: freezing assets, obtaining sizable consumer redress orders quickly, and then collecting them.

Whether the Commission has pursued the optimal
number of consumer fraud cases over the last 20
years is impossible to determine. But by refining the

use of Section 13(b) to move quickly to freeze assets
and impose penalties, the Commission has progressed
well. Further improvement depends on cooperation
with other law enforcement agencies. Given the large
amount of consumer fraud presently practiced, there
is room for improvement in the enforcement effort.
The ongoing cooperative effort between the FTC and
several states to develop a telemarketing data bank is
one example of the future direction of consumer fraud
enforcement.

VI. Providing Guidance

One of the distinguishing features of the FTC is its
array of remedies. Staff members and individual commissioners can offer informal guidance; the Commission can issue guides, policy statements, or advisory
opinions; it can file administrative complaints seeking
cease and desist orders; it can file federal court
actions seeking injunctions and consumer redress; it
can file federal court actions for civil penalties
against those who knowingly engage in an act or
practice previously found to be unfair or deceptive;
and it can promulgate binding trade regulation rules,
enforceable by civil penalty and consumer redress
actions. The Commission's role as a federal court
litigator was discussed above. This section discusses
the Commission's role in providing guidance—including mandatory guidance, through cease and desist
orders and rulemaking.

The various forms of guidance offer different costs
and benefits, and one approach may preclude another.
In choosing among them, the Commission should apply
four principles. The first is simply that the Commission should work aggressively to provide guidance. At
one time, the Commission regularly addressed many
of the issues within its jurisdiction in adjudicative
opinions. The number of opinions issued annually has
fallen sharply, however, in part because the FTC
brings so many of its cases in federal court. Unless
this practice will change, which seems unlikely, the
Commission should pursue other means of disseminating its views.

Second, the best guidance is public. Public pronouncements invite widespread adherence and only
public pronouncements invite widespread evaluation,
which is essential if good policies are to be promoted
and flawed ones reformed.

Third, guidance is best provided by the Commission
acting as a whole, rather than by individual commissioners or staff members. There is always a risk that
the views of a collegial body will be ambiguous. Only
by speaking with one voice (even with dissent) can the
Commission give authoritative guidance to business
and to its own staff. When the Commission speaks
regularly, its staff only fills in the interstices in policy;
when it speaks more rarely, the "interstices" can be
too large.

Fourth, it is generally desirable to treat similarly-
situated firms alike. This is more than a matter of
simple fairness. When only one competitor is handi-
capped, competition is distorted. Unless the market is
perfectly competitive, such distortion also will injure

consumers, who will face less choice, higher prices, or lower quality than they would otherwise.[72]

A. Informal Guidance

FTC employees provide an extraordinary amount of informal guidance, the range and importance of which is underappreciated. One of the major responsibilities of FTC professionals is to give speeches on competition and consumer protection matters. This is valuable, since persons can only comply with what they understand. When education is accompanied by enforcement of enunciated standards, the antitrust and consumer protection systems work well.

Although informal advice is important, it can be overused. Informal advice is frequently rendered by staff members, in private.[73] The advice does not formally bind the Commission. This causes at least two problems. First, businesses cannot completely rely on the advice. Second, the nonbinding nature of the advice creates a risk that it may be given too casually, even though, as a practical matter, the Commission would hesitate before challenging a person who relied on informal advice.

B. Advisory Opinions

Commission advisory opinions do not have the inherent defects in informal advice. Only by public majority vote may the Commission render an advisory opinion, which is the strength but also the weakness of this method of giving guidance.

At one time, the Commission regularly issued advisory opinions. As recently as 1977 and 1978, the Commission issued more than 13 per year.[74] Since then, the Commission has issued a substantial number of advi-

sory opinions in only one year. In the other years, the Commission issued an average of less than one a year, and it has issued only one advisory opinion since 1983.[75]

The recent scarcity of advisory opinions is regrettable. Law enforcement benefits from advisory opinions. They represent the public views of the Commission as a whole and can provide important guidance.[76] For instance, the Commission's health care advisory opinions have become part of the core library of references in that field.[77]

While advisory opinions offer substantial advantages to the legal system as a whole, individual parties no longer see them as a source of effective guidance. There are at least three reasons for this. First, the Commission has frequently issued opinions too slowly.[78] Second, the response to a request for an advisory opinion is uncertain. Antitrust Division business review letters are more predictable, because predictions of how one person will decide are easier than predictions about five. Third, businesses have many alternative sources of guidance, such as informal advice from

---

[72] The presumption against selective enforcement should be as a matter of administrative policy, not law. The Commission is entitled to broad discretion in its choice of remedies. See infra note 81.

[73] In the Hart-Scott-Rodino Act area, for instance, the staff has interpreted the statute and regulations in important ways, but an interpretation is disclosed only to the person who requests it. This has worked to the benefit of merger specialists, who repeatedly consult the premerger office, but to the disadvantage of others—and, perhaps, of the legal system. The problem has been mitigated by publication of a collection of informal interpretations. ABA Antitrust Section, Premerger Notification Practice Manual (1985). In the debt collection and credit practices areas similar problems have been mitigated by publication of staff interpretations. Staff Commentary on the Fair Debt Collection Practices Act, 53 Fed. Reg. 50,097-110 (1988) (consolidating almost 1,000 pages of informal staff interpretations); Fair Credit Reporting Act; Statement of General Policy and Interpretation; Proposed Official Commentary, 53 Fed. Reg. 29,696 (1988).

[74] All figures on advisory opinions are based on reports contained in the CCH Trade Regulations Reporter Service, and exclude advisory opinions that interpreted FTC orders. We included advisory opinions that were issued but later rescinded or amended. (Where an order was rescinded, we counted the issuance of the opinion, only; where an order was amended, we counted the issuance and also the amendment.)

[75] There is one exception to the general decline in the issuance of advisory opinions. Before the FTC and the Division may terminate a waiting period under the Hart-Scott-Rodino Act, they must conclude that neither intends to challenge the transaction during the statutory waiting period. Thus, grants of early termination are a form of quasi-advisory opinion/business review letter. In 1985, the most recent year for which the FTC provided data, early termination was granted in 1,077 proposed acquisitions, and it was denied in 338. Ninth Annual Report to Congress Pursuant to Section 201 of the Hart-Scott-Rodino Antitrust Improvements Act of 1976, at App. A (Nov. 12, 1986).

[76] This guidance can occur through reconsideration of previous opinions. E.g., Advisory Op. No. 147 F.T.C. 1174 (1975) (reconsidering issue of "back-haul" freight allowances under the Robinson-Patman Act); Advisory Op. No. 483, 83 F.T.C. 1843 (1973) (same); see also Advisory Op. No. 198, 73 F.T.C. 1312 (1968) (earlier opinion); Advisory Op. No. 194, 73 F.T.C. 1309 (1968) (same); Advisory Op. No. 147, 72 F.T.C. 1050 (1967) (same).

[77] See ABA Antitrust Section, The Antitrust Health Care Handbook 20, 24, 33 (1988) (citing FTC Advisory Opinion to Health Care Management Associates, [1983-1988 Transfer Binder] Trade Reg. Rep. (CCH) ¶ 22,036 (June 8, 1983); FTC Advisory Opinion to Burnham Hospital, [1979-1983 Transfer Binder] Trade Reg. Rep. (CCH) ¶ 22,005 (Feb. 24, 1983); FTC Advisory Opinion to Iowa Dental Ass'n, [1983-1988 Transfer Binder] Trade Reg. Rep. (CCH) ¶ 22,025 (Apr. 8, 1982)) (volume also cites numerous FTC Staff Advisory Opinions and Antitrust Division Business Review Letters, and the FTC Statement of Enforcement Policy Regarding Physician Agreements to Control Medical Prepayment Plans, 46 Fed. Reg. 48,982 (1981)).

[78] During the ten years ending in 1987 (the last year for which published reports are available), more than half of all advisory opinions were issued more than nine months after a request was filed. Several took more than two years. Many companies will not run the risk of encountering such substantial delays, which makes the advisory opinion process something of a dead letter. We see no reason why the Commission could not issue advisory opinions within a couple of months.

the Commission or its staff, informal advice from the Division, and business review letters. So long as these alternatives are available, there is little reason to subject oneself to the risks and delays of obtaining an advisory opinion.

For these reasons, we understand but nevertheless regret the scarcity of advisory opinions. While we do not anticipate a boom in advisory opinions, the FTC should make the advisory opinion process as attractive as possible, by responding quickly and decisively. The Commission also should consider reminding its staff that requests for advice should be declined sometimes, and, with the questioner's permission, referred to the Commission.

C. *Other Formal Commission Guidance*

The Commission has several choices when it wants to change a practice that is not so clearly illegal as to merit suit in federal court: administrative orders (after trial), guides, policy statements, and trade regulation rules.[79] Each of these is a public declaration by the Commission, acting as a whole. Properly used, the Commission's array of powers should complement each other, each being deployed according to its special attributes. We will briefly describe the nature and current use of each of these powers, and identify the situations in which each should be employed. We then offer some additional comments about cease and desist orders and trade regulation rules.

1. Cease and Desist Orders

Administrative cease and desist orders are the bread and butter of Commission activity outside of federal court litigation. These orders are a form of firm-specific, prospective mandatory guidance or regulation. They are enforceable by civil penalty actions.[80]

The use of cease and desist orders should be informed by the fourth principle discussed above, cautioning against unnecessarily handicapping a competitor. Cease and desist orders are well-suited for four situations: where an unfair or deceptive practice is not common in an industry; where, although the practice is common, a handful of firms account for the bulk of violations or there are one or two leading offenders;[81]

where a practice is common but remedies must be custom-tailored to individual situations; and where the Commission has warned firms that it regards practices as unfair or deceptive, and now seeks to establish this as a matter of law.[82]

2. Guides and Policy Statements

A guide is "an administrative interpretation by the Commission of the laws it administers. . . . [A] guide does not have the force or effect of law and is not legally binding . . . in an enforcement action."[83] Between 1955 and 1980, the Commission issued more than 30 guides. As is true with advisory opinions, however, guides have fallen into disuse.[84] traced in part to the perceived greater attractiveness of rulemaking; both guides and rules are challenging to draft, but only the latter can result in penalties for noncompliance. Existing guides have gone largely unrevised and unenforced.[85] Although rulemaking has recently fallen into disfavor, guides have not regained their former popularity.

In the late 1960's the Commission issued policy statements addressing mergers in several specific industries. All but one have been rescinded.[86] In recent years the FTC has issued important policy statements on consumer unfairness, deception, and merger policy.[87] These are broad, generally applicable declara-

---

[79] Another option, which we do not discuss but which the FTC should occasionally consider, is proposing legislation.

[80] For the possibility that a cease and desist order entered against one person could be used to obtain penalties from certain other persons, see Appendix B.

[81] Ford Motor Co. v. FTC, 673 F.2d 1008 (9th Cir. 1981), *cert. denied*, 459 U.S. 999 (1982), which suggested that principles of general application may be developed only through rulemaking, disregards the basic principle that "the choice between rulemaking and adjudication lies in the first instance within the [agency's] discretion." NLRB v. Bell Aerospace Co., Div. of Textron, Inc., 416 U.S. 267, 294 (1974); *see also* SEC v. Chenery Corp., 332 U.S. 194 (1947). *Ford Motor Co.* generally has not been followed. *See, e.g., Stotler & Co. v. Commodity Futures Trading Comm'n*, 855 F.2d 1288, 1294 (7th Cir. 1988); Colorado Dept. of Social Servs. v. Department of Health and Human Servs., 585 F. Supp. 522, 525 (D. Colo. 1984), *aff'd*, 771 F.2d 1422 (10th Cir. 1985).

[82] There also may be situations when codification of standards is ill-advised because legal standards are changing and economic learning is in flux. For example, it would have been imprudent to promulgate a guide or policy statement on predatory pricing immediately after publication of the seminal Areeda-Turner article.

[83] FTC Operating Manual 8.3.2 (emphasis in original) (adding that "a case brought to enforce a guide, or which embodies the theory of a guide, must plead a violation of the underlying statute on which the guide is based, not a violation of the guide itself").

[84] *See* 6 Trade Reg. Rep. (CCH) ¶¶ 38,006 (Nov. 8, 1988) (listing guides). *But cf.* Proposed Revised Guides for Advertising Allowances and Other Merchandising Payments and Services, 53 Fed. Reg. 43,233 (1988).

[85] *Antitrust Law Developments, supra* note 11, at 328 ("Although there are exceptions, many of the guides that remain in effect appear to carry little or no evidentiary or legal significance.") (noting exceptions).

[86] Resolution Directing Special Report on Mergers and Acquisitions in the Dairy Industry (FTC July 27, 1988), *reprinted in* 4 Trade Reg. Rep. (CCH) ¶ 13,210; *see also* Rescission of Enforcement Policy with Respect to Vertical Mergers in the Cement Industry, 50 Fed. Reg. 21,507 (1985) (rescinding policy issued in 1967); Rescission of Enforcement Policy with Respect to Mergers in the Food Distribution Industries, 50 Fed. Reg. 21,508 (1985) (rescinding policy issued in 1967); Rescission of Enforcement Policy with Respect to [Grocery Products Manufacturing] Product Extension Mergers, 41 Fed. Reg. 51,076 (1976) (rescinding policy issued in 1968); Rescission of Enforcement Policy with Respect to Mergers in the Textile Mill Products Industry, 40 Fed. Reg. 21,078 (1975) (rescinding policy issued in 1968 and clarified in 1969).

[87] Policy Statement on Deceptive Acts and Practices, 4 Trade Reg. Rep. (CCH) ¶ 13,205 (issued in 1983); Commission Statement of Policy on the Scope of Consumer Unfairness

tions of the Commission's approach to recurring, important issues. As with a guide, violation of a policy statement is not a violation of law.

Even though the illegality of conduct violative of a guide or a policy statement must be proven at trial, we believe that guides and policy statements could play an important role in FTC law enforcement. They apply equally to all persons, put all on notice of possible enforcement action, and can contribute to greater public understanding of the Commission's method of analyzing competition and consumer protection issues.[88] Public comment can (and should) be part of the promulgating process, whether or not required by statute.[89]

If guides are to become an important FTC guidance tool, they must be taken seriously. This would require modifying or repealing existing guides to comport with the views of the current Commission, and, once accomplished, a vigorous program of enforcement.[90]

Each guide should be reviewed regularly to see whether it continues to reflect Commission policy.

The Commission's recent use of policy statements is a positive development. They soften the image of an agency with unbridled discretion. The issuance of such statements should be encouraged.[91] The existing statements should be reviewed on a regular schedule and modified if they do not reflect current views; inaccurate statements are worse than none at all.

3. Trade Regulation Rules

The Commission has gone through two phases of activism in trade regulation rulemaking. During the first phase, between 1962 and 1974, the Commission issued a score of trade regulation rules by applying general administrative law principles.[92] In 1975, the Magnuson-Moss amendments authorized the Commission to engage in rulemaking pursuant to that Act's more onerous provisions, but also specified that once a Magnuson-Moss rule was promulgated, violators would be subject to a civil penalty.[93] During the next five years, the Commission initiated more than a dozen Magnuson-Moss rulemaking proceedings.[94] Although the Commission continues to modify, interpret, and review existing rules,[95] in recent years new rulemaking initiatives have dramatically declined. The FTC has promulgated only two new rules since 1980.[96]

Magnuson-Moss rulemaking is a costly and uncertain tool. The ponderous nature of the process has

---

Doctrine, attached to Commission letter to Senators Ford and Danforth (Dec. 17, 1980), *reprinted in* [1969-1983 Transfer Binder] Trade Reg. Rep. (CCH) ¶ 50,421; FTC Statement Concerning Horizontal Mergers, 4 Trade Reg. Rep. (CCH) ¶ 13,200 (issued in 1982). *See generally* Statement of Enforcement Policy Regarding Physician Agreements to Control Medical Prepayment Plans, 46 Fed. Reg. 48,982, *corrected*, 46 Fed. Reg. 51,033 (1981), *reprinted in* 6 Trade Reg Rep. (CCH) ¶ 39,058; Policy Statement Regarding Advertising Substantiation Program, 49 Fed. Reg. 30,999 (1984), *reprinted in* 6 Trade Reg. Rep. (CCH) ¶ 39,060.

[88] The weaknesses of guides have not changed, of course; they still are not legally binding. However, administrative orders can be rejected by courts, as has happened with some of the FTC's more controversial decisions. Were the FTC to use guides or policy statements to signal a change in policy, businesses might adjust their conduct without litigation, and the process of issuing a guide or policy statement might improve the chances that FTC litigation would succeed, by establishing a record supporting change and by eliminating any concern that a particular respondent is being treated unfairly.

[89] The Magnuson-Moss amendments authorized the Commission to issue "interpretive rules and general statements of policy with respect to unfair or deceptive acts or practices." 15 U.S.C. 6 57a(a)(1)(A) (1982). The amendments set forth a notice and comment procedure for promulgating such rules and policy statements. 15 U.S.C. 6 57a(b)(2) (1982). The FTC normally will publish and invite comments on a proposed guide, even though Magnuson-Moss does not specifically require this. FTC Operating Manual 6 8.3.6.4. Because guides have the same effect as Magnuson-Moss "interpretive rules," we do not separately address the desirability of issuing such rules.

[90] One lesson, of course, is that even if the Commission does not issue new guides, it should review its old ones. For example, the potential importance of guides is suggested by the state advertising initiatives that the Commission finds troubling. Some of these are based upon the Commission's old guides concerning pricing claims, bait and switch practices, and use of the word "free"—guides with which the current Commission probably disagrees. Had these guides been updated (and then enforced), there might have been fewer state initiatives of the kind the Commission finds objectionable.

[91] Ideally, when the statement is addressed to an issue for which enforcement responsibility is shared with the Antitrust Division, the Commission should negotiate a joint statement. Industry is more interested in guidance as to what is illegal than as to what a single enforcer will challenge.

[92] 6 Trade Reg. Rep. (CCH) ¶ 38,004 (Mar. 21, 1989) (listing final pre-Magnuson-Moss Trade Regulation Rules).

[93] 15 U.S.C. 6 57a(a)(2) (1982) ("The Commission shall have no authority under [this Act], other than its authority under this section, to prescribe any rule with respect to unfair or deceptive acts or practices . . . . The preceding sentence shall not affect any authority of the Commission to prescribe rules (including interpretive rules), and general statements of policy, with respect to unfair methods of competition . . . ."). Earlier trade regulation rules were "grandfathered in."

[94] 6 Trade Reg. Rep. (CCH) ¶¶ 38,001-03 (Mar. 21, 1989).

[95] For instance, the Commission is considering amending or terminating the Funeral Industry Practices Rule, *see* 53 Fed. Reg. 19,864 (1988), and the Transistor Count of Radio Receiving Sets Rule, *see* 54 Fed. Reg. 5090 (1989), and is considering broadening the Mail Order Rule to cover telemarketing, *see* 53 Fed. Reg. 43,448-49 (Oct. 27, 1988); *see also* Semiannual Regulatory Agenda, 53 Fed. Reg. 42,818 (1988).

[96] *See* 6 Trade Reg. Rep. (CCH) ¶ 38,001-03 (Mar. 21, 1989) (Funeral Industry Practices Rule, issued 1982, first hearing noticed 1976; Sale of Used Motor Vehicles Rule, issued 1985, disputed issues considered starting in 1976); *see also* Opthalmic Practice Rules, *supra* note 25. For the declining workyears devoted to rulemaking, see Graph 17 in Appendix C. The FTC appears unlikely to embark on major new rulemaking initiatives, since recent staff reductions reduced its rulemaking presiding officer staff to a single individual.

been the subject of much comment and criticism.[97] (Indeed, some of us believe that the Magnuson-Moss procedures should be legislatively repealed.[98]) Nothing galvanizes an industry to defend itself like an industry-wide assault such as broad rulemaking. Congress is never more sympathetic than when it is hearing from constituents across the country, as may result from rulemaking. Congress is rarely less deferential than when an agency is engaging in a broad rulemaking process that, unlike law enforcement, resembles activity that is the traditional province of Congress.

Given this, good candidates for broad new rulemaking will be scarce. Rulemaking is not a sensible response to an unfocused belief that the market is working imperfectly. Rather, the FTC should embark on rulemaking only when it is contemplating a particular solution to a widespread problem and where it has a legal theory that supports its proposed rule.[99] Restraint is required in selecting rulemaking targets and in defining a rulemaking's scope. The Commission frequently will find that a mix of guides, policy statements, and administrative proceedings will be superior to Magnuson-Moss rulemaking.

Nonetheless, appropriate targets for rulemaking continue to exist. The Mail Order Rule—a pre-Magnuson-Moss trade regulation rule that was "grandfathered in"—is a good example of a sensible trade regulation rule. There were widespread consumer abuses that were not quickly self-correcting. The FTC was able to craft a remedy that was easy to administer,

not unduly burdensome, and sufficiently precise to justify enforcing with penalties.

The Commission should be able to identify other problems that would benefit from a similar rule. Suitable candidates are industry-wide problems involving perpetrators too numerous to sue individually. Rulemaking also may be appropriate where there is a need to explore complex and confusing issues in hearings.

Consumer protection rules grounded in competition concepts are also promising subjects for rulemaking. The Eyeglasses Rules are good examples of rules intended to benefit consumers by improving market performance. The FTC's first Eyeglasses Rule preempted state laws restricting price advertising of eyeglasses and eye examinations, and proscribed advertising bans adopted by professional and trade associations.[100] The Eyeglasses II Rule removes restraints imposed by state law and bars certain state restrictions on commercial practices.[101] The Funeral Industry Rule, at least in its origins, was designed to address regulatory and industry restrictions on competition in that industry.[102] Given the share of the economy regulated by government bodies (and the accompanying state-action antitrust exemptions), other possibilities for using rules to address competition-oriented consumer protection issues undoubtedly exist.[103]

The FTC periodically reviews trade regulation rules under a plan developed in 1981 pursuant to the Regulatory Flexibility Act.[104] Trade regulation rules, like

---

[97] See Administrative Conference of the United States, Trade Regulation Rulemaking Procedures of the Federal Trade Commission (May 1979) (hereinafter "*1979 Administrative Conference Report*"), which documents the dramatic expansion of rulemaking records associated with the Magnuson-Moss changes. The largest pre-Magnuson-Moss rulemaking record contained 25,285 pages (Franchising Disclosures), whereas the largest Magnuson-Moss record as of that date contained 261,405 pages (Mobile Homes). No Magnuson-Moss rulemaking record contained fewer than 8,000 pages, as of that date. *Id.* at Data Appendix 38, 40, 50.

[98] These Committee members reason that normal Administrative Procedure Act rulemaking provides ample protections for affected interests. Others of us believe that the "judicialization" of the FTC rulemaking process is not necessarily bad. The imposition of an industry-wide rule is a matter of some gravity. If the factual and legal issues are complex, it can be appropriate for the process to resemble adjudication more than legislation, and for the affected parties to have ample opportunity to be heard. Moreover, sharply-focused rulemaking proceedings of the kind that we recommend should be more manageable than some of the rather amorphous attempts that characterized some earlier Magnuson-Moss proceedings. Finally, we note that the Federal Trade Commission Improvements Act, Pub. L. No. 96-252 (1980), addressed some of the important concerns about prior FTC rulemaking, *see 1979 Administrative Conference Report, supra* note 97; Antitrust Section of the American Bar Association, Report Concerning FTC Trade Regulation Rulemaking Procedures Pursuant to the Magnuson-Moss Act (Feb. 1980).

[99] *Accord 1979 Administrative Conference Report, supra* note 97, at 5.

[100] *See supra* note 25.

[101] *See supra* note 25. The rule bars (1) prohibitions on the employment of optometrists by drug stores and optical chains, (2) limitations on the number of branch offices that optometrists may own or operate, (3) prohibitions on the practice of optometry in commercial locations, and (4) prohibitions on the use of trade names by optometrists. The rule also incorporates the prescription release requirement originally promulgated in the Eyeglasses I Rule.

[102] Trade Regulation Rule Relating to Funeral Industry Practices, 16 C.F.R. Part 453 (1988); *see* Ellis, *Legislative Powers: FTC Rule Making*, in K. Clarkson & T. Muris, *supra* note 6, at 166-68 (1981).

[103] Although the Commission retains its pre-Magnuson-Moss authority to engage in competition rulemaking, we are not optimistic about the chances that the FTC could codify antitrust-oriented prohibitions on specific types of business conduct. Only one pre-Magnuson-Moss trade regulation rule expressly addressed antitrust issues. *See* Discriminatory Practices in Men's and Boys' Tailored Clothing Industry, 16 C.F.R. Part 412 (1988). During the 1970's, the FTC's Bureau of Competition searched aggressively but unsuccessfully for candidates for antitrust rules. *See, e.g.*, Lempert, *FTC Rulemaking Not Beginning of Deluge*, Legal Times of Wash., April 30, 1979, at 1, 7; 884 Antitrust & Trade Reg. Rep (BNA) at A-13-15 (Oct. 12, 1978) (reporting that rules were being considered pertaining to delivered pricing in the cement industry, shopping center lease restrictions, physician influence over health insurance payments, and mergers affecting potential competition).

[104] Pub. L. No. 96-354 (*codified at* 5 U.S.C. 66 601-12); *see* 46 Fed. Reg. 35,118 (1981).

like guides, must be enforced. Although we are unable to measure the extent of voluntary compliance with rules, we note that until recently the Commission had filed relatively few enforcement proceedings.[105] The Commission should consider accelerating the review of any rules that have gone unenforced.

4. Additional Observations on Cease and Desist Orders and Trade Regulation Rules

a. Cease and Desist Orders

Cease and desist orders must not be punitive. This is especially true now that the Commission can seek consumer redress in federal court actions. In crafting relief, each provision should be sufficiently beneficial to competition and consumers to offset costs. Unnecessary compliance expenses harm not just a firm but its customers, to whom part of all costs are passed. Similarly, any meaningful limitation on a firm's conduct may impose costs on consumers.[106]

We are troubled by the duration of typical Commission orders, which continue to lack sunset provisions except for specific documentation requirements. Administrative orders should have sunset provisions. If legal standards permit other firms to engage in practices that harm consumers, the standards should be changed—for all firms—through legislation, rulemaking, or guides. A firm-specific order must be justified as removing harm, restoring competition, or preventing likely recidivism; it should last only as long as necessary to prevent the likely resumption of the illegal practices,[107] orders preventing firms from freely participating in acquisitions usually should expire after five years, because most acquisitions of antitrust significance are subject to the Hart-Scott-Rodino reporting requirements. Orders in excess of five years can be justified only when there is a significant chance that the firm would otherwise engage in illegal activity not subject to the Hart-Scott-Rodino reporting requirements.

b. Trade Regulation Rules

Displacing state law enforcement activity through the preemptive effect of trade regulation rules is an issue of continuing controversy in federal-state relations. The Commission's authority to preempt the

states in this area remains unsettled, although the FTC routinely asserts it.[108]

To date, trade regulation rules have preempted only state laws and regulations providing less protection than the FTC rule, but not those providing more.[109] Such one-way preemption can be sound policy, properly recognizing important federalism values. However, whenever the Commission promulgates a final trade regulation rule it should address the preemption issue specifically, and, in doing so, consider whether the rule should preempt all inconsistent state regulations.[110] Whether complete preemption is advisable will depend on the nature of the rule. For example, when the rule merely labels a particular industry practice as unfair, there is no reason to preclude states from identifying other industry practices as unfair as a matter of state law. On the other hand, when the Commission's rule prescribes optimal disclosure guidelines, the benefits of that rule may be undermined by state requirements of additional dis-

---

[108] See, e.g., Advertising of Ophthalmic Goods and Services, 43 Fed. Reg. 23,992, 24,003-04 n.180 & App. (1978) (Statement of Basis and Purpose); Funeral Industry Practices Rule, 16 C.F.R. § 453.9 (1988). Compare Katherine Gibbs School (Inc.) v. FTC, 612 F.2d 658, 666-67 (2d Cir. 1979) (rejecting preemption argument based on theory that Congress intended the FTC's regulation to "occupy the field") with American Fin. Servs. Ass'n v. FTC, 767 F.2d 957, 989-990 (D.C. Cir. 1985) (upholding preemptive effective of Credit Practices Rules where preemption argument not based on "occupying the field" theory), cert. denied, 475 U.S. 1011 (1986).

[109] See, e.g., National Funeral Servs., Inc. v. Rockefeller, 7 Trade Reg. Rep. (CCH) ¶ 68,472, at 60,595 (4th Cir. Mar. 7, 1989) (FTC's funeral rule did not preempt West Virginia code):

[T]here is no language in the Funeral Rule that even alludes to an intent to preempt state regulation in the area it does cover. In fact, the Rule expressly states that where a state law is applicable to any transaction that the Rule covers, and that state law affords at least the same level of protection to consumers that federal law provides, the Rule will not be in effect in that state. 16 C.F.R. § 453.9.

[110] Accord Administrative Conference of the United States, Recommendation No. 84-5, Preemption of State Regulation by Federal Agencies, 1 C.F.R. § 305.84-5 (1988) ("Each Federal agency should establish procedures to ensure consideration of the need to preempt state laws or regulations that harm federally protected interests in the areas of regulatory responsibility . . . , and each agency should clearly and explicitly address preemption issues in the course of regulatory decision-making."). As did the Administrative Conference, we recommend that when the FTC foresees possible conflicts between proposed regulations and state interests, it should consult informally with state authorities, and also should provide them with "an opportunity for appropriate participation" in rulemaking proceedings. See id.

There have been suggestions that state attorneys general should be authorized to enforce the FTC trade regulation rules. Most of us do not support such suggestions. We note, however, that the suggestion would be most persuasive if the FTC in fact "occupied the field" of regulating a particular industry.

---

[105] A review of the FTC's annual reports and of the CCH Trade Regulation Reporter showed that, although the data is not unambiguous, from 1978 through 1986 the FTC appears to have filed, on average, about a half dozen rule enforcement complaints a year. The rate at which complaints were filed increased significantly in 1987 and 1988. Cf. FTC v. Dudley M. Hughes, 7 Trade Reg. Rep. (CCH) ¶ 68,429 (N.D. Tex. Feb. 7, 1989) ($80,000 civil penalty imposed in first litigated case challenging violation of funeral rule).

[106] Crafting relief requires the combined efforts of lawyers and economists. Moreover, evidence of the efficacy and efficiency of various relief alternatives should be developed during any proceedings.

[107] Except in unusual cases this period is unlikely to exceed 10 years. By way of comparison, we understand that state antitrust orders typically are limited to five years.

closures; because information clutter imposes costs and dilutes messages, more is not always better. In this situation, the Commission should consider whether its rule, promulgated with the benefit of a detailed examination of a problem's many facets, should preempt more demanding disclosure requirements as well as more lenient ones.[111]

VII. The Advocacy Program

One of the FTC's more visible roles is that of an advocate for competition and consumers. This activity dates back to the Commission's early years.[112] As early as 1917, the FTC offered comments to the U.S. Fuel Administration on coal pricing policies.[113] During the 1970's and 1980's, under Democratic and then Republican leadership, the FTC began to expand its advocacy program. At first, this program centered on federal regulatory activity. The past several years have seen a trend toward increased state filings and appearances. However, advocacy activity declined sharply in 1988.[114]

The FTC's Competition and Consumer Advocacy Program is one of the most important of the FTC's various projects.[115] Only two other federal government entities, the Antitrust Division and the Council of Economic Advisors, also serve consistently in this capacity. Of these three, the FTC devotes the most intellectual energy and resources to the task. The FTC has consistently, and on the whole correctly, pursued the objective of promoting consumer welfare. It has generally provided quality advice about issues of consequence.

The FTC's competition advocacy program permits it to accomplish for consumers what prohibitive costs prevent them from tackling individually. It is the potential for the FTC to undo governmentally imposed restraints that lessen consumer welfare, and to prevent their imposition, that warrants the program's continuance and expansion. Because ill-advised governmental restraints can impose staggering costs on consumers, the potential benefits from an advocacy program exceed the Commission's entire budget.[116]

The limited available evidence suggests that the FTC's program has generally been successful. In a few instances, decision- makers announcing outcomes have indicated that the FTC's participation was important.[117] Moreover, a recent survey of state and local officials who received Commission comments on regulatory proposals showed that in 39 percent of the decisions, action was generally consistent with at least some of the FTC recommendations, and was taken largely or partly because of those recommendations.[118] In 75 percent of the proceedings, the FTC presented information that the decision-maker had not previously understood well and that was not thoroughly presented by other participants.[119] Despite the difficulty of measuring the effectiveness of FTC participation in a proceeding, these results suggest that the program has substantial value.[120]

The success of the program is especially impressive in light of the modest resources it consumes. The FTC has estimated the cost of the program in recent years to be two to four percent of budget.[121] The resources devoted to the program appear especially modest given the number of times the FTC has participated in proceedings: between 1978 and 1987, the Commission averaged more than 30 filings a year.[122]

---

[111] *Cf.* Advance notice of proposed rulemaking and extension of time, 54 Fed. Reg. 7,041 (Feb. 16, 1989) (FTC is considering broadening the preemptive effect of its trade regulation rule concerning franchising and business opportunity ventures).

[112] Federal Trade Commission, History of Section 6 Report-Writing At The Federal Trade Commission (April 1981). Section 6 of the Federal Trade Commission Act authorizes the Commission to prepare reports and publicize its findings. Other statutory provisions require the FTC to indicate its views. For discussion of the FTC's authority, see B. Yandle, T. Muris, T. Campbell & R. Tollison, Competition and Consumer Advocacy: Policy Review Session 2-7 (May 24, 1982).

[113] Randolph W. Tritell, The Federal Trade Commission's Competition and Consumer Advocacy Program 2 (unpublished manuscript July 20, 1988).

[114] See Graphs 22 and 23 in Appendix C (note that Graph 23 includes data only up to 1987).

[115] As has the Commission, this report will refer variously to this program by its full current title, as "competition advocacy," and as simply "advocacy."

[116] *See* Tritell, *supra* note 113, at 11 (noting that consumers are estimated to have saved $100 million a year when New York eased its milk retailing restrictions, in which decision the FTC played a prominent role).

[117] Memorandum from James M. Giffin to Federal Trade Commission, *Report on Successful Competition Advocacy Efforts* (Jan. 21, 1987).

[118] A. Celnicker, The Federal Trade Commission's Competition and Consumer Advocacy Program 15-16 (unpublished manuscript 1988), forthcoming in St. Louis U.L.J. (sample size: 36).

[119] *Id.* at 16 (sample size: 37).

[120] The survey also found that "47 percent of the respondents gave the comment substantial weight or consideration because it came from the FTC," whereas 20 percent gave the comment only limited weight because of its source. Celnicker, *supra* note 118, at 16-17. Only by maintaining high quality will the Commission be able to preserve and improve its credibility.

[121] Response of Emily Rock, Secretary to the FTC, on behalf of the FTC, to questions posed by Rep. John Dingell dated July 8, 1987, *reprinted in Federal Trade Commission Authorization Hearings Before the Subcomm. on Transportation, Tourism, and Hazardous Materials of the House Comm. on Energy and Commerce*, 100 Cong. 1st Sess. 257, 261 (1987) (estimate for 1987); *see also* Celnicker, supra note 118, at 24-25 (estimating, based on FTC representations, that three to five percent of budget, or $2 to $3 million, was devoted to advocacy "in recent years"). Since some of the best advocacy efforts flow from other Commission activities, any accounting for expenses must be imprecise.

[122] *See* Graph 22 in Appendix C. The Commission's activities during 1985 to 1987 included participation in lawmaking or rulemaking proceedings on a wide variety of issues including metropolitan taxicab licensing, regulations affecting the practice of dental hygienists and other allied profes-

The FTC's advocacy program has elicited criticism from members of Congress and from certain industries.[123] Each house of Congress has passed bills designed to limit the program.[124] Criticism of the program, in general, reflects concern that the Commission is inappropriately spreading a message of economic deregulation at the state and federal levels. Critics also have suggested that the program is draining resources from the FTC's law enforcement mission, although given its modest costs these criticisms seem overstated.

Although competition advocacy is obviously not the FTC's primary mission, the proposed restrictions are ill-advised. The advocacy program is salutary because it allows the FTC to share with other regulators and legislators information that the Commission has gathered through its other activities. Even if its advice were not often accepted, information sharing is valuable. In the whirl of activity that precedes the adoption of federal or state regulations, or the enactment of state legislation, the FTC can offer an important, sometimes lonely, voice for the consumer. This should be encouraged, not arbitrarily restricted. Indeed, the extent to which the program is attacked by those with interests adverse to consumers may best reflect the program's success. Unfortunately, the more successful the program becomes, the more likely it will be subjected to such attacks.

VIII. The Role of Economic Analysis

The founders of the Federal Trade Commission anticipated that it would have economics expertise. There is no hint that the FTC's economic expertise was to be reserved for a few individuals or confined to a separate bureau. Instead, a knowledge of economics was to pervade the organization, from the commissioners' offices on down. This expertise was to inform the FTC in its own decision-making. The FTC was also to educate by offering accurate and objective information about the operation of the United States econo-

my. As the 1969 Report put it, "a principal function of the FTC was to serve as a fact-finding body that would study the economy, investigate industries, and expose corporate practices harmful to the economy."[125] In short, paying attention to the economics of a matter was to be a first principle of FTC behavior. Informing the nation about the operation of the economy was to be a second. These remain worthy operative principles for the agency today.

A. Economic Analysis and the FTC's Enforcement Program

Today, most of the FTC's economic research and analysis is conducted by staff people for whom economic analysis is their primary if not sole responsibility at the agency. In a world increasingly populated by specialists, this is inevitable. Because of this compartmentalization, defining the proper role of economic analysis in the FTC's enforcement activities becomes a problem of defining the proper working relationships between the agency's attorneys and economists. Before the 1970's, FTC economists had relatively little substantive impact. In the years since, their role has been transformed. Rather than simply gathering statistics to support pre-existing positions, economists are increasingly involved in selecting cases, developing theories by which they may be prosecuted, and formulating appropriate remedies.

We applaud this transformation. Economists should be treated as colleagues in the enforcement process. A collegial relationship between attorneys and economists fits the statutory design and, perhaps more significantly, insures that the FTC will benefit from the broader lessons that economic analysis offers.

These lessons are fourfold. First, economists bring an empirical bent to a problem. They can locate and organize data crucial to antitrust and consumer protection enforcement.

Second, economists generally bring a cost-benefit mentality to a problem. In an agency with fixed resources, staff economists can rein in cases and investigations that have little prospect of helping consumers. They can identify and encourage those cases with the greatest potential of generating consumer welfare gains. Some critics of economic analysis contend that a cost-benefit mentality inevitably serves as a brake on the FTC's enforcement program, but this is not necessarily so. To be sure, in some areas—especially concerning vertical restraints and price discrimination—economic input has deterred some antitrust cases. But it can also serve as a throttle. Economic analysis has promoted activity in certain key areas (such as advertising restraints by professions) that the FTC did not address until the lessons of economics were brought to bear. Furthermore, if economists at the FTC assume the more focused research responsibilities proposed below, economists should become more frequent generators of proposed complaints.

Third, economists bring to certain problems an organizing paradigm that might otherwise be absent. This surfaces in broad problem areas, such as compil-

---

sionals, solicitation by lawyers, and motor vehicle dealership franchising. *See* A. Celnicker, *supra* note 118, at 11-12. Of course, some of these filings required substantial time commitments, whereas others were addressed to issues previously mastered and required little more than editorial work.

[123] For example, a witness testifying before a congressional subcommittee on behalf of the National Association of Retail Druggists objected to FTC comments supporting proposals to allow physicians to dispense prescription drugs. *Federal Trade Commission Authorization Hearings Before the Subcomm. on Transportation, Tourism, and Hazardous Materials of the House Comm. on Energy and Commerce*, 100th Cong., 1st Sess. 164 (1987) (Statement of John M. Rector on behalf of the National Association of Retail Druggists). Congressional criticism may be partly responsible for the decline in advocacy activity in 1988.

[124] The FTC Reauthorization bills separately passed by the House (H.R. 2897) and Senate (S. 677) during the 100th Congress would have imposed restrictions on the program. The more stringent restrictions were in the House bill, which, among other things, would have restricted Commission expenditures on the advocacy program to 5 percent of the Commission's budget.

---

[125] 1969 Report at 69.

ing guidelines for merger enforcement, and in narrower problem areas, such as delineating tests for defining markets. The influence of this paradigm is
suggested by a comparison of early predatory pricing
cases with cases brought since publication of the
seminal Areeda-Turner article. While attorneys have
helped formulate merger guidelines, and, obviously,
have contributed to the literature on predatory pricing, their contributions have been made against the
backdrop of economic analysis.

Fourth, economists within the FTC are an important link to the outside world of economic research.
Just as some attorneys contribute to the mission of the
FTC by their link to the organized bar, to Congress, or
to other government attorneys, economists at the FTC
link the agency to the scholarly literature and ongoing research in industrial organization. A government body charged with disseminating accurate and
objective information about the American economy
needs ties to the academy which also generates information of this character.

Just as it would be irresponsible for the Environmental Protection Agency to be unaware of research
on important environmental issues, it would be irresponsible for the FTC to be unaware of important
findings on the state of competition and monopoly.
The FTC should contribute to and monitor these findings. By hiring first-rate economists, the FTC assures
itself of a staff that is informed by and communicates
with the current state of research in industrial organization and related fields.

1. Antitrust Enforcement

Economists play a central role in the FTC's antitrust enforcement mission.[126] They should be involved, as colleagues, in case selection, case prosecution, and remedy formulation and supervision.

a. *Case Selection*

Representatives from the Bureau of Competition
and the Bureau of Economics should work together in
assessing proposed antitrust action. To be sure, attorneys have a comparative advantage in assessing the
legal basis of an action. But it is important to hold
attorneys to a high standard of economic analysis in
case selection. The FTC, like most law enforcement
agencies, exercises prosecutorial discretion. Cases
that can be won should not always be brought. Economic input is important in assessing the actual consequences of a business practice and the benefits to
consumers of bringing it to a halt.

The obligation to justify a proposed action in terms
of its economic consequences strengthens the agency's
case selection process as attorneys seek out and work
with economists in determining the merits of possible
actions. The Commission should consider the views of
economists as well as attorneys in deciding whether to
initiate action, and should be cautious about initiating
action where the economists are opposed.

---

[126] For the distribution of economist workyears by area,
see Table 2 in Appendix C.

A sensible procedure for combining attorneys and
economists in an investigation is for those assigned to
an investigation to write jointly the fact memo based
on their research. If they disagree as to a final recommendation, those conclusions should be separately explained. The FTC's Hart-Scott-Rodino review process
provides a good example of a healthy working relationship between economists and lawyers. Attorneys
and economists both assess possible antitrust consequences. They cooperate in formulating the investigation and in studying the material filed. As a consequence, they virtually can assure that the Commission
will seek to block a merger if both support such
action.

b. *Prosecuting Cases*

After the FTC decides to prosecute a case, economists should not be relegated to a purely supporting
role, but should continue to work alongside attorneys
as colleagues. Of course, economists are needed to
perform such conventional tasks as gathering industry
data, preparing economic affidavits, testifying (or
helping to prepare economic testimony of an outside
expert), and assisting in the investigational hearings of
respondent's economic experts. However, we believe
economists should not be limited to these roles, but
instead should also be involved in framing the overall
theory of a case, drafting interrogatories, helping
ensure that briefs accurately communicate a case's
theory, and formulating a case's remedy.

As colleagues, FTC economists should not be expected to act contrary to their principles. If the Commissioners decide to file a complaint contrary to the
advice of the economists, awkwardness is inevitable.
But while economists should keep their disagreements
confidential and not undermine the Commission, they
should not be expected to endorse an action they
believe to be harmful. If an economic witness is
desired and a private economic consulting firm is
willing to provide such testimony, the Commission
remains free to retain an outside expert.[127] But only
by treating economists as respected, professional colleagues will the FTC continue to be able to recruit and
retain first rate economic talent.

---

[127] The Commission currently retains outside economists
as witnesses, and this is altogether appropriate. In addition,
the Commission should follow more regularly the 1969
Report's recommendation that "advisory panels" be used to
assist the Bureau of Economics. Particularly when the FTC
is mired in a complicated or protracted matter, or where
the legal and economic staff finds itself divided or uncertain, a panel of outside experts may serve to dislodge the
dispute or clarify contending positions. For example, the
panel of outside economists gathered to assess the Exxon
case served not only to guide the FTC in its disposition of
that controversial litigation, but also to explain to Congressional critics the rationale for the action finally taken. Of
course, to the extent that the Federal Advisory Committee
Act applies to such a consultative relationship, certain procedural requirements, such as "Sunshine Act" rules, would
regulate these economists' work. See 5 U.S.C. App. 66 1-15
(1982 & Supp. V 1987).

c. *Formulating and Supervising Remedies*

Both the FTC and the Antitrust Division have been criticized for garnering pyrrhic antitrust victories, where a case is won or a settlement is achieved, but competition is not restored. One of the explanations given for this phenomenon is the inadequacy of incentives for attorneys to be concerned with what happens after a case has been won.

Economists do not face the same set of incentives, in terms of their performance within the agency and their job prospects outside. Because of different professional signals, FTC economists can be invaluable in fashioning and monitoring relief.

First, economists charged with considering relief can insure that the proposed remedy squares with the economic theory of the case. Their knowledge of an industry, and their ability to understand how an industry would be affected by possible changes, should inform the selection of possible remedies.[128] Just as expert economic analysis should support every case brought, so should it support every relief decree.

Second, economists can play key roles in the administration of antitrust remedies. Many lawyers find greater satisfaction in litigating cases than in monitoring compliance with decrees already won. In contrast, an economist's professional instinct is to study resource allocation, and resource allocation can be affected as much by compliance as by litigation. Thus, economists deserve leading roles in monitoring compliance.

2. Consumer Protection

The contribution of economists to the FTC's consumer protection efforts has, over the years, been limited by the relative scarcity of academic research on the economic issues raised by consumer protection. Rationality in the marketplace is closely studied by economists; baseness and mendacity are not.[129]

There are exceptions. Economic analysis has demonstrated the procompetitive potential of advertising. Economic analysis also suggests that consumers are better off if they know a product's qualities before deciding whether to purchase it, and that sellers are less likely to deceive consumers when repeat purchases of a product are common. These illustrations suggest avenues of economic inquiry. But there is relatively little significant economic research on, for example, the costs and benefits of mandated octane posting or mandated cooling-off periods.

As a result, economists have played a modest role in the FTC's consumer protection activities. The FTC can best encourage greater involvement by devoting more resources to basic research on consumer protection issues. (In addition, the reasons why economists should have important roles in fashioning and supervising antitrust decrees also apply to consumer protection decrees.) Much remains to be done. It is important for economists at the FTC to learn how retail markets for consumer goods actually work. It also is important for consumer protection attorneys to learn, or be reminded, how seemingly sensible remedies in these markets may have unexpected costs and drawbacks. Properly harnessed, economic analysis has the potential to shape consumer protection policy in much the same fashion as it influenced antitrust.

B. *Economic Analysis and the Advocacy Program*

Economists have played, and should continue to play, an integral part in the FTC's successful competition and consumer advocacy program. It was economic research in the 1960's and 1970's, originally conducted outside the confines of the FTC, that began documenting and tallying the costs to consumers of many government regulations that hindered or eliminated competition. Economists at the FTC, familiar with this literature and operating in an environment where exposure to these regulations was common, were among those who realized that consumers could benefit more from successful competition advocacy than from some antitrust cases.

In the competition advocacy program, economists should continue to serve as partners with the legal staff. Attorneys generally will know how best to achieve the removal of an anticompetitive regulation, or to prevent its adoption. Attorneys also may have a comparative advantage in sniffing out anticonsumer regulations. But economists generally are better suited to sorting out the economic consequences, direct and secondary, of particular regulations; indeed, because estimating the economic burden of regulations is often difficult, advocacy may require more economic sophistication than litigation. Since advocacy cannot be carried out adequately without substantial economic input, criticism of the FTC's allocation of resources to economists, tied, as it occasionally is, to economists' participation in the advocacy program, is misplaced.[130]

C. *Economic Research*

The FTC has succeeded in attracting some unusually talented economists. Their impact has been evident in the central role played by economic analysis in case selection and prosecution, and competition advocacy. It has not been as evident in improving the FTC's economic research mission, however, largely because staff economists have shortchanged inquiry into the

---

[128] W. Breit & K. Elzinga, Antitrust Penalty Reform: An Economic Analysis (1986).

[129] An FTC conference volume on consumer protection explained that while a substantial body of economics literature "supports the view that information asymmetries can be a substantial force in market performance, it is inconclusive on the appropriate role for consumer protection policy . . . . The literature to date has very little guidance to offer policy makers who ideally seek to implement policy remedies only when they are more efficient than private responses." P. Ippolito & D. Scheffman, eds., Empirical Approaches to Consumer Protection Economics, Bureau of Economics Conference (Mar. 1986).

---

[130] Economist workyears devoted to advocacy are indicated in Table 2 in Appendix C.

structure and conduct of actual industries in favor of more purely academic topics.[131]

The "working papers" of the FTC's Bureau of Economics, along with the publication of research reports, monographs, and conference volumes,[132] represent the pure research contribution of economists at the agency. Scrutiny of the Bureau's working papers, however, reveals that some papers concern topics far removed from actual industry organization and conduct. Further, they have little impact on antitrust scholarship or judicial opinions. A study of 165 numerically-sequenced working papers found that only eighteen had been cited in law reviews, only one in a judicial opinion.[133]

The FTC's research should have a different orientation, one that closely conforms to the agency's mandate "to gather and compile information concerning . . . the organization, business, conduct, practices and management of any person . . . whose business affects commerce."[134] In tune with this mandate, the FTC should not significantly fund research at the frontiers of economic theory, econometrics, or even industrial organization.[135] Instead, the FTC should concentrate on becoming the single most important repository of knowledge about the actual operation of major U.S. industries.[136] Economists at the FTC regularly should

be researching these industries, updating older studies, and publishing their results. As an example, the FTC's influential study of the brewing industry was unlikely to have been done by academic economists.[137] Studies such as this may be a source of antitrust action, or a justification for antitrust inaction, and can increase confidence that correct decisions are being made.

In addition to striving to understand the functioning of American industry, FTC economists, working with lawyers where appropriate, should seek to improve our understanding of the economic consequences of the American antitrust system. For instance, the debate about resale price maintenance has been enriched by an FTC study of all 203 private and public resale price maintenance cases reported during 1976-1982.[138] This kind of study should be the norm, rather than the exception. Too rarely have economists systematically studied the consequences of blocking or permitting controversial mergers. With one major exception,[139] our knowledge of the consequences of private antitrust enforcement—which still constitutes the great bulk of antitrust activity—remains largely anecdotal. Part of the FTC's research mission should be to improve our understanding of the antitrust system, and to identify and learn from its successes and failures. That mission should include improving our understanding of consumer protection enforcement.

A focus on the functioning of various industries, and on America's antitrust system, is simply a matter of good stewardship. Absent FTC support, research at the frontiers of economic theory will continue to flourish in universities across the country. On the other hand, modern academic research in industrial organization rarely undertakes the sort of systematic, institutional study of real-world industries and activities that we are suggesting for the FTC. If FTC economists do not undertake the task, it is difficult to see who else will. Moreover, FTC economists could then use this information, and modern economic theory, to consider and propose new antitrust enforcement directions.

Some argue that the economic outlet for pure research by economists at the FTC is important for recruiting and retaining high quality staff. The case is easily overstated. Some of the best economists at the FTC have not been aggressive in publishing papers for academic consumption. If internal advancement within the Bureau of Economics is seen to come from research that results in solid industry studies, instead of publications on topics outside the scope of antitrust and consumer protection, economists at the FTC will respond.

To be sure, economists who see the Bureau of Economics as a stepping stone to an academic position will be less likely to join the Bureau with such a change in its research focus. Historically, however,

---

[131] We also note the recent decline in economist workyears devoted to research, Table 2 in Appendix C.

[132] Working papers are "preliminary materials circulated to stimulate discussion and critical comment," according to the form description they bear, and usually are drawn from particular FTC projects or an FTC economist's independent research. Monographs and reports typically involve a substantial research effort by more than one staff economist. The published report itself puts forth the Bureau's findings on some topic of direct concern to FTC responsibility. Conference volumes are the result of seminars and conferences the Bureau has convened where a major issue in antitrust economics or consumer protection is studied. These Bureau publications generally contain the invited papers presented at these gatherings.

[133] Citation searches were conducted on the LEXIS legal database and the Social Science Citation Index (which covers most economics journals). The modest number of citations is biased downwards to the extent these papers are cited as papers published elsewhere under different titles (or with a different set of authors). The standard cover for working papers states that references to them "should be cleared with the author."

[134] 15 U.S.C. § 46 (a) (1982) (also noting an exception for certain financial institutions and common carriers).

[135] There will be instances in which an FTC economist's antitrust enforcement responsibilities will require him or her to survey and comment on the literature on a particular issue. Publication of such surveys can be useful. (For a good example, see Pautler, *A Review of the Economic Basis for Broad-Based Horizontal-Merger Policy*, 28 Antitrust Bull. 571 (1983).) Academic economists are unlikely to publish comparable papers, because they lack the exposure to enforcement decision-making, and such papers may earn little academic credit.

[136] *See also* 1969 Report at 71 ("the fundamental economic research falling in the broad field of industrial organization, as well as the study of specific industries and trade practices, is a proper function of the FTC's economic staff").

[137] Bureau of Economics Staff Report to the Federal Trade Commission, The Brewing Industry (1978).

[138] P. Ippolito, Resale Price Maintenance: Economic Evidence from Litigation, an FTC Bureau of Economics Staff Report (1988).

[139] L. White, ed., Private Antitrust Litigation: New Evidence, New Learning (1988).

few economists depart staff positions in economics at the FTC for academic positions. Most who leave enter private sector economic consulting or shift laterally to other government agencies. For these, a reorientation of economic research at the FTC will not pose occupational costs. And for those FTC economists whose professional advancement requires forays into non-antitrust and non-consumer protection research, or who wish to publish articles in mainstream economic journals, the Bureau of Economics could adopt a leave of absence program that would allow them to take visiting appointments at universities or with research organizations. While at the FTC, however, economists engaged in research should endeavor to understand how actual market processes work themselves out in the myriad industries that make up the American commercial landscape, and the role that antitrust litigation plays in influencing these industries.

D. *Conclusion*

Not without some controversy, the role of economists at the FTC has evolved; they are now respected, professional colleagues of FTC lawyers. We applaud this development. It must continue if the Commission is to bring important cases that make economic sense. The most important change for the Commission to make concerns its research agenda. FTC economists should use their comparative advantage in understanding how industries actually function to make the FTC the major repository of knowledge about the operation of American industry—including retail markets for consumer goods—and of antitrust and consumer protection enforcement.

IX. Resources

For fiscal year 1979, which ended September 30, 1979, the Commission employed 1,746 workyears. A decade earlier the FTC had employed 1,311 workyears, but the number of FTC workyears increased steadily during the 1970's. Since 1979, Congress has provided funds for significantly fewer people: 1,719 in 1980, 1,491 in 1982, 1,238 in 1984, 1,107 in 1986, 986 in 1988, and 923 (projected) for 1989.[140] Today there are 124 lawyers in the Bureau of Competition, 118 lawyers in the Bureau of Consumer Protection, and 115 lawyers in the regional offices.[141] Economist workyears fell 21 percent from 1980 to 1989.[142] Of course, many of the tasks on which Commission employees worked 10 years ago, such as large structural antitrust cases and ambitious rulemaking proceedings, are unlikely to be prominent in the future. But even though the Commission could not find useful employment for all of its staff 10 years ago, the current employee level is cause for serious concern.

The Commission's changes in enforcement direction in recent years cannot be attributed solely to declining resources. These changes stem in part from conscious

choices about enforcement policy. But even if one agrees with those choices, additional resources, as well as better use of its resources, would aid the FTC's mission. This would allow the FTC to undertake new enforcement initiatives. It would permit the FTC to better develop and apply its economics expertise.[143] The Hart-Scott-Rodino process, with its repeated demands for quick legal and economic investigation and judgment (and court challenge, if necessary), has imposed unprecedented burdens on the staff, especially because of the recent increase in merger activity. The staff participants in that process need more relief than is currently available—relief that should come in the form of energetic, entry-level hires.

The Commission needs a stable environment in which to pursue its mission, and the budget problems of recent years, with the resulting reductions in force, have not provided that environment.[144] The decline in real resources should be halted, and an increase in resources provided. If Congress does appropriate more resources, the increase should be phased in over a two- or three-year period to allow the Commission to hire attorneys and economists at a junior level.

Although the Commission should not have had such reduced resources in the last few years, we doubt that the FTC has spent its money as wisely as possible. As the Commission has shrunk in size, its staffing patterns have made it top-heavy, both in the operating bureaus and at the Commission level. Moreover, an excessive percentage of supervisors is not just a waste of resources. It also can interfere with an agency's effectiveness by making the decision-making process more cumbersome. Although we did not study this issue in depth, we received enough complaints to persuade us that the Commission should give this problem serious attention.

At least in very recent years, the Commission also appears to have disproportionately allocated resources to the regional offices. Regional office work

---

140 Source: U.S. Government Budget (Office of the President and OMB).

141 Figures provided by FTC. They are current as of January 1989.

142 Table 2 in Appendix C.

143 Resources allocated to the Bureau of Economics have declined fairly steadily since 1982. Table 2 in Appendix C; see also Graph 1 in Appendix C (percentage of FTC's professional workyears). This decline has generally not affected the workyears devoted to antitrust matters, largely because of the urgent need to analyze Hart-Scott-Rodino filings. Because these filings command priority, economic input into consumer protection issues, the competition advocacy program, and research must play second fiddle.

Although economics resources devoted to consumer protection and to competition advocacy have fallen in recent years, the decline in research workyears has been particularly stark: from 22.9 in 1980 and a high of 29.6 in 1983, to 12.1 in 1988 and a projected 7.3 in 1989. Table 2 in Appendix C. While we have recommended a redirection of the FTC's economic research agenda, we have not recommended a reduction. Indeed, we recommend an expanded research agenda. This cannot be achieved without an increase in resources devoted to economic research.

144 In the last few years the FTC has requested more people than Congress eventually funded. For 1988, for example, the budget proposed funding for 1,048 workyears, but Congress funded only 986.

years were about 12% higher in 1988 than in 1987, even though overall Commission workyears declined.[145] This was probably not the most prudent response to budget difficulties. Regional office investigations take longer, and few observers would argue that regional office staffs are superior to those in Washington.[146] Moreover, most of the regional offices are small, and at a certain level of staffing, offices simply are not cost-effective.[147]

Especially in the current resource bind, regional offices should not be operated as independent units providing the full range of Commission activities, and it will rarely make sense to base national programs in those offices. Instead, regional offices should be the Commission's presence in their areas. Their staffs should work closely with headquarters personnel on a specified range of activities, and concentrate on credit, fraud, and other matters for which their greater accessibility to consumers is particularly valuable.[148]

X. The Congress[149]

The 1969 Report recognized that, if its proposals were to be implemented and the FTC were to play the important role that was anticipated, the FTC "must have the continuous vigorous support of the President and the Congress."[150] During much of the 1970's the FTC enjoyed this kind of support. Those days ended, however, and since then the FTC has been criticized for attempting either too much or too little. The brief period of enthusiastic support turns out to have been an exception.[151]

Several factors contributed to the Commission's fall from favor. Legislative preferences changed, in part because of changes in the leadership of the congressional committees responsible for the FTC. Partly in response to the congressional grant of new powers, the Commission had launched a series of litigating and rulemaking initiatives which taxed its resources, raised questions about its judgment, and stirred up a hornet's nest of soft-drink bottlers, funeral directors, used car dealers, and others. As a result, the Senate Commerce Committee concluded oversight hearings by observing that "in many instances the FTC had taken actions beyond the intent of Congress."[152]

The Commission has been unable to ignore this criticism. Moreover, since 1980 Congress has failed to reauthorize the Commission, and has enacted numerous restrictions on the FTC, both in substantive law and in appropriations bills.[153] The FTC's vulnerability to criticism is particularly troubling because of its potential impact on the role of the FTC described above.

---

[145] Graph 1 in Appendix C.

[146] FTC data for 1975-1988 shows the following for headquarters (HQ) and regional office (RO) cases:

Initial Phase Investigation
to Full Phase   6.90 mo HQ, 7.32 mo RO
Full Phase Conversion
to Complaint/Consent   11.05 mo HQ, 16.88 mo RO
Full Phase Opened
to Complaint/Consent   11.00 mo HQ, 16.19 mo RO
Complaint to Final Order   40.55 mo HQ, 35.62 mo RO

Of course, regional office partisans presumably would argue that the lengthier investigative process is partly caused by headquarters' supervisory delays. These partisans also would note that by most statistical measures, regional offices appear to be more productive than headquarters. See FTC Resource Allocation Study 19-21 (Apr. 3, 1987). For instance, FTC data show that regional offices opened 43.16% of all investigations, 1981-88, despite their size. On the other hand, headquarters partisans would dismiss data about investigations and complaints by arguing that headquarters cases tend to be more complicated and offer greater potential consumer benefit per case, and by noting that headquarters staffs assist the regional offices.

[147] The Denver office has employed as few as three attorneys, Memorandum from Claude C. Wild III, Director, FTC Denver Regional Office at 6 (Mar. 13, 1987), reprinted in FTC Resource Allocation Study (Apr. 3, 1987), although it currently employees eight. While we do not advocate the closing of any particular office, it is important for the Commission to have the practical ability to reduce the number of offices so they can be maintained at a reasonable size without unduly draining agency resources.

[148] FTC data show that between 1981 and 1988 regional offices opened 562 investigations triggered by consumer complaints, compared to 570 for headquarters.

[149] This section is in part based upon a paper prepared for the Committee by Professor William E. Kovacic. We gratefully acknowledge his contribution.

[150] 1969 Report at 35.

[151] The FTC's relations with Congress have been uneven, at best. On several occasions, FTC reporting efforts have triggered dramatic political protests. E.g., R. Cushman, The Independent Regulatory Agencies 220 (1941); P. Herring, Public Administration and the Public Interest 116-28 (1936); Stevens, The Federal Trade Commission's Contribution to Industrial and Economic Analysis: The Work of the Economic Division, 8 Geo. Wash. L. Rev. 545, 549-53 (1940). For instance, publication of the 1919 meatpacking report nearly put the FTC out of business, and ultimately cost the FTC its jurisdiction over packing operations and stockyards. P. Herring, supra, at 119.

[152] Senate Commerce Comm. Rep. No. 500, 96th Cong., 2d Sess. 2. For more exhaustive discussion of this saga, M. Pertschuk, Revolt Against Regulation: The Rise and Pause of the Consumer Movement (1982); R. Katzmann, supra note 6; Baer, Where to From Here: Reflection on the Recent Saga of the Federal Trade Commission, 39 Okla. L. Rev. 51 (1986); Gellhorn, The Wages of Zealotry: The FTC Under Siege, Jan./Feb. 1980 AEI J. on Gov't and Soc'y 33; Kovacic, The Federal Trade Commission and Congressional Oversight of Antitrust Enforcement: A Historical Perspective, in MacKay, Miller & Yandle, supra note 6, at 63; Kovacic, The Federal Trade Commission and Congressional Oversight of Antitrust Enforcement, 17 Tulsa L.J. 587 (1982); Debate: The Federal Trade Commission Under Attack: Should the Commission's Role be Changed?, 49 Antitrust L.J. 1481 (1982).

[153] For example, Congress approved an appropriations measure prohibiting the Commission from using its fiscal year 1985 funds to prosecute antitrust cases against cities. CCH Trade Reg. Rep. No. 666, at 7 (Sept. 4, 1984); CCH Trade Reg. Rep. No. 674, at 4 (Oct. 31, 1984) (lifting restriction). The Federal Trade Commission Improvements Act of 1980, Pub. L. No. 96-252, 94 Stat. 374 (1980) (hereinafter "FTC Improvements Act") prohibited the FTC from seeking cancellation of a trademark "on the ground that such mark has become the common descriptive name of an article or

Several of the FTC's characteristics work together to make it unusually vulnerable to congressional criticism. The FTC's broad authority makes it an inviting target. Section 5 is deceptively simple, and its elasticity tempts members of Congress to urge an expansionist enforcement program—a program that may be subsequently attacked. The FTC's array of alternatives for enforcement and guidance makes less compelling a claim of impotence. One of these alternatives, rulemaking, resembles legislative drafting more than law enforcement, and thus is a process that Congress may feel especially qualified to critique. Moreover, the prospect of an industry-wide rule is likely to stimulate an adverse political response.

The Commission has no natural constituency. Few important, organized groups depend on the FTC to provide an essential service. On the other hand, the Commission has selected some politically powerful and motivated targets, such as professionals, funeral directors, used car dealers, and state and local government agencies.

Finally, the FTC's structure handicaps its defenses. Because it is an independent agency, the White House may hesitate to support the Commission. Because they are adjudicators, commissioners must be guarded in discussing particular cases and even legal issues; yet because commissioners also serve as prosecutors, respondents complain of unfair prejudgment. And the Commission's diversity— among commissioners, who are appointed at different times and cannot all be from the same party, and among professionals, who come from varying disciplines—invites internal disagreement and dissent that, although healthy in most respects, may weaken the agency in its dealings with other bodies, including Congress.

For several reasons, therefore, the FTC is unusually vulnerable to congressional criticism. Not all congressional criticism is unhealthy, of course. In the discussion that follows, we discuss appropriate and inappropriate interaction between Congress and the FTC. We also offer some suggestions for promoting beneficial interaction.

A. *Appropriate FTC-Congressional Interaction*

Congress has an important role to play by conducting broad reviews of Commission programs and plans. When Commission enforcement policy has changed in some fundamental way, it is sensible for Congress to request an explanation; this occurred when the FTC curtailed vertical restraint litigation. Such an inquiry could include a discussion of why the agency decided

not to bring a particular case, assuming that a final decision had been made. When the Commission has too little power (or too much), Congress should engage in its traditional role by enacting legislation. Congress made an important contribution, for instance, by expanding the Commission's powers during the 1970's.

Members of Congress, just as other citizens, should be free to call illegal activities to the Commission's attention, and to suggest litigation, rulemaking, and other action. So also, at least before formal proceedings begin, members of Congress should feel free to communicate their opposition to contemplated action. When the FTC has promulgated a trade regulation rule, Congress may consider its desirability and, if Congress and the President think that the rule is harmful, enact substantive legislation undoing it.[154]

Congress should encourage the Commission to undertake important investigative and reporting projects. For instance, we understand that the Commission's useful study of its vertical restraints cases was stimulated by a congressional request. This is a good example of healthy interaction.

B. *Inappropriate Congressional Interference*

In general, Congress should limit its review to general policies and, unless it decides to enact substantive legislation, leave specific case and rule oversight to the courts. Although its discretion is not unlimited, the FTC should discourage improper interference. Excessively detailed review and congressional or other outside intervention increase agency timidity, lessen respect for the agency, encourage circumvention of the agency's procedures, and, in short, undermine the exercise of discretion that is the agency's very rationale.

Certain congressional interference is barred by law: Congress may not investigate "the mental decisional process of a Commission in a case which is pending

---

[154] The current dispute concerning congressional review of trade regulation rules is quite narrow. Although Congress earlier provided for a legislative veto of FTC rules (which was held unconstitutional in Consumers Union of United States v. FTC, 691 F.2d 575 (D.C. Cir. 1982), *aff'd sub nom.* United States House of Representatives v. FTC, 463 U.S. 1216 (1983)), the current issue concerns only whether there should be automatic "fast track" congressional review. The FTC reauthorization bills in the 100th Congress (H.R. 2897, 100th Cong., 1st Sess. § 106(a) (1987) and S. 677, 100th Cong., 1st Sess. (1987) would have required the Commission to submit final rules to Congress for a 90-day review period. A rule would become effective unless a joint resolution disapproving it, passed by Congress and signed by the President, was enacted during this period. Although this procedure would be constitutional, we are not in agreement on whether it would be desirable. Several of us worry that the procedure would politicize FTC rulemaking, but others believe that it is difficult to object in principle to affirmative decisions by the two elected branches of government. In any event, it is clear that fast-track congressional review of proposed rules is preferable to review through avenues such as the appropriations process, in which important policy issues may not receive adequate attention.

---

substance." FTC Improvements Act 6 18, 15 U.S.C. 6 57c note (1982). The Act also imposed a number of limitations upon the FTC's authority in the rulemaking area. The FTC was barred from issuing any rule in its then-pending proceeding on children's advertising or in any new proceeding based on a determination that children's advertising is an "unfair act or practice in or affecting commerce." FTC Improvements Act 6 11, 15 U.S.C. 6 57a (1982). The FTC was also barred from issuing trade regulation rules on private bodies' standards and certifications. FTC Improvements Act 6 7, 15 U.S.C. 6 57a(a)(1)(B) (1982).

before it." *Pillsbury Co. v. FTC.*[155] In *Pillsbury*, the
Senate Judiciary Committee subjected the FTC's
chairman to a "searching examination as to how and
why he reached" an interlocutory decision in a still-
pending case, and criticized him "for reaching the
'wrong' decision."[156] The Fifth Circuit ruled that this
behavior undermined the appearance of Commission
impartiality, and set aside an order subsequently entered against *Pillsbury.*

Although *Pillsbury* was limited to adjudication, the
concern that the Commission's mental decisional process remain inviolate extends further, as a matter of
policy if not law. To the extent possible, the Commission should resist detailed review of specific deliberative decisions concerning possible litigation. More is
at issue than merely a concern with the appearance of
impartiality. Congress entrusted a body of experts
with broad discretion because it believed that this
would accomplish more than legislation could. The
antitrust program that this Report has outlined for the
FTC is risky. When Commission deliberations on particular pending or proposed law enforcement matters
are subjected to detailed, public scrutiny, our recommended program becomes more difficult to achieve
and the Commission's very purpose may be defeated.
Although it is proper for Congress to suggest that the
Commission consider certain kinds of cases, Congress
assumes too much the role of prosecutor when it goes
further by holding hearings, demanding detailed information, and otherwise pressuring the FTC to bring
particular cases.[157]

The legal restraints on congressional participation
in rulemaking are less strict, and appropriately so.
The Commission is required to make copies or sum-
maries of such communications and make them part
of the rulemaking record.[158] Congressional participation in agency rulemaking may lead to the overturning
of a rule only where the participation was "designed
to force [the agency] to decide upon factors not made
relevant by Congress in the applicable statute," and
where the agency's determination was "affected by

---

[155] 354 F.2d 952, 964 (5th Cir. 1966) (original emphasis
deleted).
[156] *Id.*
[157] The Commission also should resist congressional over-
tures during the period that a case is withdrawn from
adjudication for consideration of settlement. Since the case
may be returned to adjudication, it is as inappropriate for
Congress to examine Commission deliberations at that point
as it was in *Pillsbury.* Of course, once a consent order has
been tentatively approved, Congress and others are invited
to comment on the proposed order through normal channels,
and, once a case is finally over, more searching congressional inquiries are appropriate.
[158] 15 U.S.C. § 57a(j) (1982); *see also* 16 C.F.R. § 1.18(c)
(1)(iii) (1988). If the FTC's statutes and rules did not regulate
ex parte contacts during rulemaking, such contacts would
be subject to the normal administrative law limitations.
Compare Home Box Office, Inc. v. FCC, 567 F.2d 9 (D.C.
Cir.), *cert. denied,* 434 U.S. 829 (1977) *with* Action for
Children's Television v. FCC, 564 F.2d 458 (D.C. Cir. 1977)
and Sierra Club v. Costle, 657 F.2d 298 (D.C. Cir. 1981).

those extraneous considerations."[159] Nonetheless, the
concern with protecting the mental deliberative process of the Commission remains, and the kind of
searching predecisional scrutiny that was objectionable in *Pillsbury* would be objectionable in a rulemaking context as well. With rulemaking, too, excessive
interference can defeat the agency's purpose.

Congress should act by passing generally applicable, substantive legislation, with the participation of
the appropriate substantive committees.[160] If part of
the economy should be exempt from antitrust scrutiny, Congress should immunize it from attack by all
government and private litigators. But it makes no
sense, and is harmful to the FTC, to Congress, and to
our system of government, to disable only that agency
from enforcing rules that continue to be generally
applicable. Congress also causes damage whenever it
circumvents the committees responsible for the FTC
by acting through appropriations bills. These committees are the principal repositories of FTC expertise,
and it is with these committees that the Commission
should be regularly consulting. Efforts to achieve
effective oversight are frustrated when these committees do not participate in making important changes.

*C. Suggestions for Improving FTC-Congression-
al Relations*

The Commission should take the following steps to
maintain and improve its relations with Congress:

1. The FTC should take the initiative to keep Congress apprised of its activities and initiatives. It rarely
makes sense to surprise congressional leaders.

2. Conversely, it is important for commissioners to
consider whether congressional inquiries are appropriate. Leadership of the Commission is a trust. When
Congress is intervening in Commission affairs in excessive detail, the leadership must protest, whether or
not a particular matter is of immediate importance.
Even if current Commission leaders are unconcerned
about the matter being addressed, their duty to future
commissioners obligates them to encourage Congress
to limit itself to appropriate oversight. It is important
that harmful requests and actions be identified as such
and brought to Congress's attention.[161]

3. The Commission should make its policies more
clear through increased use of rules, guides, and policy statements, as was recommended in Section VI.

4. Prompt decision-making helps. Long delay,

---

[159] Sierra Club v. Costle, 657 F.2d 298, 409 (D.C. Cir. 1981)
(relying on D.C. Fed'n of Civil Ass'ns v. Volpe, 459 F.2d 1231
(D.C. Cir. 1971), *cert. denied,* 405 U.S. 1030 (1972)).
[160] It also is important for the FTC to remember that it is
obligated to consider the views of Congress as a whole, not
of particular members of Congress.
[161] This could be done by the Commission or, perhaps with
less political risk, by bar associations and other outside
observers. *Cf.* Antitrust & Trade Reg. Rep. (BNA) No. 1380,
at 317, 318 (Aug. 25, 1988); 54 *id.* No. 1354, at 318 (ABA
Sections of Antitrust and Administrative Law responded to
discovery dispute between Congress and an FTC commissioner by urging Congress to use restraint in exercising its
power to compel production of internal agency documents).

whether justified or not, is a source of constant aggravation to respondents, lawyers, and the public. People lose respect for an agency that does not function well, and delay is an easily measurable test of efficiency, if not of ultimate effectiveness. Promptness also reduces the chance that congressional leadership will change during the pendency of a proceeding, and thus lessens the chance of opposition by new congressional leaders.

5. Respect is critical to congressional relations, and avoiding unnecessary delay is only part of the story. Congressional relations are likely to be smoother if Congress respects the agency's leaders.[162]

XI. Dual Federal Antitrust Enforcement

This Committee does not pretend to bring novel insight to the debate about the wisdom of dual enforcement of the antitrust laws. Nonetheless, we considered the issue, and we record here our thinking. We share the common unease about whether the ideal federal antitrust structure would feature two enforcement agencies. But while dual enforcement imposes some costs, it also provides some benefits. It has wide political support and change is unlikely. A majority of us conclude that the case for proposing abolition of dual enforcement has not been made. What follows is an exposition of that majority position.

A. Virtues of Unitary Enforcement

Were we writing on a clean slate, many of us would favor a single federal antitrust enforcer. It would save some resources, since support services could be consolidated and top-level overhead could be reduced. It would eliminate the inherent potential of two federal agencies adopting differing views of antitrust law, thereby holding companies to different standards. Enforcement officials would enjoy easier access to all of the federal antitrust expertise on particular industries. These and other reasons have been developed elsewhere,[163] and need not be discussed in detail here.

Those favoring a single antitrust enforcer note that federal law enforcement generally is under unitary control, and conclude that antitrust is not so exceptional as to justify departing from this model. Dual enforcement may present advantages in specific situations, but these advantages are seen as insufficient to depart from the basic federal model, were the enforcement system being designed anew.

B. Alternative Structures for Unification

Those of us attracted to unitary enforcement are divided on where it should be consolidated. Some Committee members would favor consolidating antitrust and consumer protection in the Justice Department, some would consolidate consumer protection and civil antitrust in the FTC or another separate agency, and some would consolidate antitrust in the Justice Department and establish a federal consumer protection agency.

There is substantial agreement on the value of combining antitrust and consumer protection responsibilities. Both programs are improved by inclusion in a single agency. Occasionally it will be valuable to debate whether a particular problem is better solved by antitrust or consumer protection tools.[164] More routinely, the quality of decision-making about one kind of issue will be increased by a sensitivity to the concerns and approaches of the other program. It is particularly beneficial for consumer protection decisions to be informed by an understanding of antitrust's concerns with economic efficiency.[165] Benefits also occur from the exchange of personnel between programs. Economists attracted by an interest in antitrust can teach valuable consumer protection lessons; lawyers can benefit from litigating a variety of cases, some of which require lengthy development of facts and analysis, some of which require regular appearances in court. Antitrust and consumer protection complement each other; indeed, antitrust is a particularly potent form of consumer protection.

Some Committee members would have combined antitrust and consumer protection in the Justice Department. These members argue that it would be a mistake to separate civil enforcement from criminal enforcement, which must remain at Justice. They note that criminal and civil experience develop complementary skills, and that the path an investigation will take is not always obvious at the beginning. These Committee members also value presidential accountability. They argue that the FTC's vaunted independence has been bought at a steep price. Rather than

---

[162] This issue was discussed in Section III. Congress obviously is more likely to have confidence in and to defer to persons of stature. For instance, respect for SEC personnel regularly is cited as an important factor in that agency's relatively harmonious relations with Congress. E.g., National Academy of Public Administration Panel on Congressional Oversight, Congressional Oversight of Regulatory Agencies: The Need to Strike a Balance and Focus on Performance 35 (1988).

[163] E.g., Pogue, Gellhorn & Sims, Has Antitrust Outgrown Dual Enforcement: A Rationalization Proposal, 33 Antitrust Bull. No. — — (forthcoming 1989).

---

[164] For example, the FTC recently took action to prohibit as unfair acts or practices certain restraints imposed by state law on ophthalmic practice. See supra note 25. The FTC also might have challenged these restraints as unfair methods of competition. However, because the restraints were imposed by state law, the FTC would have confronted a defense based on the state ¶action doctrine established in Parker v. Brown, 317 U.S. 341 (1943). Without prejudging any challenge to this trade regulation rule, one can say that the Commission's consumer protection powers may have permitted it to improve competition in ways normally unavailable to antitrust enforcers.

[165] The FTC's combination of antitrust and consumer protection expertise is perhaps indispensible to promulgating consumer protection rules grounded in competition concepts, as we recommend below. Moreover, agencies that lack antitrust sophistication, such as the Consumer Product Safety Commission or the Food and Drug Administration, lack an appreciation of the efficacy of market-oriented rules and may tend to over-regulate.

being liberating, the absence of direct presidential accountability has made the FTC unduly subject to pressure from Congress and from competitors and other special interests.

Other Committee members would have separated criminal from civil antitrust, and given the latter responsibility to a separate agency also charged with consumer protection. They note that the Antitrust Division's director of Operations primarily handles criminal matters, while his deputy primarily handles civil matters. Over time the criminal efforts of the Division have come to resemble those of other criminal prosecuting teams.[166] Civil and criminal enforcement differ markedly in their procedures (CID's and the like instead of grand juries) and their inquiry (economic consequences instead of the existence of an agreement). Although combining civil and criminal antitrust has advantages, it is not nearly as essential as combining antitrust and consumer protection.

These Committee members also are impressed by the possible advantages offered by administrative adjudication (see discussion below), and accordingly continue to believe that the ideal structure would offer an alternative to federal court adjudication. For some, the preferred model would be a multi- member special trade court. For others, the ideal would be a single administrator, similar in function to the head of the Environmental Protection Agency. Whatever the exact structure preferred, these members agree that antitrust adjudication before economically sophisticated experts—assuming such individuals could be appointed—would be superior to adjudication in the federal courts.

Thus, various Committee members would have preferred a number of different structures as the ideal. Most members are impressed by the virtues of entrusting federal consumer protection, civil antitrust enforcement, and perhaps criminal antitrust enforcement to a single division or agency—if the question were being decided for the first time.

C. Virtues of Dual Enforcement

The benefits or possible benefits of the existing system concern resources, reassurance, and expertise. There is some risk that abolishing an antitrust agency would reduce antitrust enforcement resources, either because only part of the formerly available resources would be shifted or because, if the Division were the surviving entity, resources might subsequently be redirected to other enforcement priorities. The availability of adequate resources is especially critical

[166] *See, e.g.,* C.F. Rule, *Antitrust Agenda for the New Administration: Pressures for New Perspectives* (remarks before New England Antitrust Conference Oct. 28, 1988) (First of five recommendations for successor is to pursue the "abundance of good" criminal investigations, and "to improve the Division's relationships with federal investigators and U.S. attorneys." Second recommendation is to expand the use of criminal investigative techniques and to charge antitrust defendants with other criminal violations.), *as reprinted in part in* CCH Trade Reg. Rep. No. 23, at 11-12 (Nov. 2, 1988).

given the many major mergers currently proposed. The Hart-Scott-Rodino merger review process does not permit delay. Dual enforcement offers flexibility because both agencies engage in merger enforcement; if one agency is unable to shift adequate resources into merger enforcement, the other may be able to do so.

The second benefit is reassurance. Antitrust enforcement is important, and many of us see value in having one federal antitrust agency backstop another. Substantial harm could occur were antitrust consolidated into a single agency that then failed to function effectively.

There also may be value in reassuring Congress. The antitrust statutes and the FTC Act are unusually broad. Congress has trusted the courts and the FTC to provide detailed guidance. Congress may have done this in part because it expected a special relationship with the FTC. Were it not for that relationship, and the outlet for congressional concerns that it provides, Congress might feel compelled to legislate in the antitrust area with greater specificity—which would generally be unfortunate.

The third possible benefit of dual enforcement is expertise in judging and prosecuting. Although the FTC's record as an adjudicator is mixed,[167] many Committee members believe that the FTC continues to have the potential to conduct economically sophisticated adjudication, or at least to serve as an alternative adjudicatory forum that can function as satisfactorily as federal courts. In part because of the decline of per se rules, an understanding of economics is becoming essential to sound antitrust adjudication. Even an economically sophisticated jurist has trouble applying the rule of reason well without the luxury of time. Yet all too often federal judges lack both economic expertise and time.

[167] It is disappointing that the Commission, which ought to offer the potential for innovation and flexibility, and for custom-tailoring trial procedures, historically has lagged behind the federal courts in developing techniques for complex cases. It also is disappointing that the Commission continues to have problems of delay. The 1969 Report found that "[p]roblems of delay have vexed the FTC ever since it was established." 1969 Report at 28-32. External exigencies have prodded the Commission to move quickly in its prosecutorial role on Hart-Scott-Rodino matters and, with some exceptions, on proposed federal court consumer fraud challenges. The Commission also has improved the speed with which it disposes of discovery disputes. For most other matters, however, delay continues to be a problem at the FTC. *See* Table 3 in Appendix C.

Particularly troubling is the length of time between oral argument and issuance of an opinion. Data provided to us by the FTC show that between 1975 and 1988 the Commission took an average of 15.1 months from oral argument to issuance of an FTC final order (not counting subsequent appeals). This period was 13.5 months for consumer protection cases, 15.9 months for competition cases. There is no excuse for taking more than a year to write an opinion. Only partly in jest do we suggest that the commissioners announce an official annual period of summer recess, and then, as does the Supreme Court, discipline themselves by delaying its commencement until they have decided that term's cases.

There also are advantages in having antitrust enforcement decisions made by a multi-member agency. The best example is provided by merger enforcement. Frequently, the critical question in merger litigation is whether a complaint will be filed. Time and again, parties abandon or restructure proposed transactions in the face of a federal complaint; when they proceed, they often lose in court, at least when the FTC sues. Our system of government traditionally has entrusted many critical legal decisions to multi-member panels (e.g., three-member courts of appeals panels, the nine-member Supreme Court, and multi-member independent agencies). Multiple voices may improve quality and increase public trust. With the critical merger enforcement decision having moved from the courts to the prosecutors, there is virtue in preserving a multi-member prosecuting agency.[168]

In addition to the benefits and possible benefits of dual enforcement, those Committee members favoring its retention are impressed by the apparent absence of real harm. Critics of dual enforcement usually point to the waste that stems from having two federal agencies, to increased uncertainty, to questionable case selection, to flawed adjudication processes, and to the lack of any genuine expertise. These points are worth considering briefly.

Most Committee members doubt that dual enforcement wastes substantial resources. Consolidation of support services such as libraries could save only a little. Even if there is a minimum efficient size for antitrust enforcement agencies, below which agency leadership resources would inevitably be used inefficiently, many Committee members doubt the FTC and the Antitrust Division have shrunk below this threshold.

Many Committee members also doubt that dual enforcement presents substantial problems of uncertainty. Although Section 5's wording differs from that of the antitrust laws, the FTC has interpreted them as being the same or very similar, and recent court decisions have rebuffed the FTC when it interpreted Section 5 expansively.[169] The area of greatest interagency overlap is merger enforcement, but a Committee survey of leading merger lawyers found almost unanimous agreement that dual enforcement has created little uncertainty and has prevented very few transactions. Most lawyers surveyed perceive that the two agencies evaluate mergers by similar standards. Moreover, the Hart-Scott-Rodino process permits relatively quick, inexpensive government merger reviews, and this clients are undeterred by uncertainty. Of course, uncertainty costs would rise were the areas

of overlap between the agencies to increase, and the agencies to adopt significantly different antitrust policies. In part because the agencies are aware of this risk, most Committee members are not persuaded that the uncertainty cost of dual enforcement is high.[170] Moreover, if the agencies adopted substantially different policies, the President might be able to use his supervisory authority to encourage greater consistency.[171]

There is general agreement that the FTC has engaged in some questionable case selection over its history. Some on the Committee believe that this has been caused in part by the agency's rather amorphous mandate and by its vulnerability to congressional pressure. Others point to the cases that were brought by the Antitrust Division that have now fallen from favor,[172] noting that the FTC has not had any monopoly on prosecutorial misjudgment. The Committee is not persuaded that the likely costs from future questionable case selection are sufficiently great to justify abolishing the FTC's antitrust role.

FTC adjudication is considered above as a possible strength, but the agency's perceived lack of expertise is a greater concern. The agency is at the mercy of the presidential appointment process, and without first-rate commissioners the agency cannot serve its intended role.[173] Although the Committee is troubled by the uneven quality of FTC appointments, our concern is insufficient to persuade a majority of us that FTC's role in antitrust enforcement should be ended.

A majority of the Committee have concluded that, on balance, it should not recommend consolidating antitrust enforcement in a single agency. Dual enforcement has certain benefits and imposes only limited costs. Moreover, antitrust enforcement is less "dual" than sometimes thought. The Antitrust Division generally limits its activities to criminal antitrust enforcement and merger enforcement, and ever

---

[168] This argument counsels in favor of shifting all civil antitrust enforcement to the FTC. This seems unlikely to occur, and the Committee did not discuss the possibility at any length.

[169] See E.I. du Pont de Nemours & Co. v. FTC, 729 F.2d 128 (2d Cir. 1984); Official Airline Guides, Inc. v. FTC, 630 F.2d 920 (2d Cir. 1980), cert. denied, 450 U.S. 917 (1981). But cf. United Air Lines, Inc. v. CAB, 766 F.2d 1107 (7th Cir. 1985) (interpreting Section 411 of Federal Aviation Act, which parallels Section 5).

[170] Other Committee members are more concerned about possible uncertainty, for the reasons stated earlier. The Committee is in agreement that, assuming dual enforcement will continue, both agencies should strive to adopt consistent enforcement policies.

[171] See generally American Bar Association Recommendation, reprinted in 38 Admin. L. Rev. 206 (1986) (supporting executive oversight of agency rulemaking); Strauss & Sunstein, The Role of the President and OMB in Informal Rulemaking, 38 Admin. L. Rev. 181, 200-201 (1986) (arguing that the President "may consult with and demand answers from" independent agencies, and exercise supervisory authority, although the "ultimate power to decide rests with the relevant agency").

[172] E.g., United States v. Arnold, Schwinn & Co., 388 U.S. 365 (1967); United States v. Von's Grocery Co., 384 U.S. 270 (1966); United States v. International Business Machines Corp., Civ. No. 69 Civ. 200 (S.D.N.Y. 1982) (dismissed by stipulation); United States v. Cuisinarts, Inc., Crim. No. H-80-49 (D. Conn. Dec. 19, 1980) (nolo contendere plea accepted and $250,000 fine ordered in criminal resale price maintenance case).

[173] It is trite but true that the Commission can be no better than its leaders. The importance of strong leadership is addressed above at Section III.

greater percentages of federal merger cases are brought by the FTC, not Justice. To a large extent, therefore, the United States has shared, not dual, antitrust enforcement. Perhaps this trend should continue; in any event, a majority of the Committee believe that the case for ending the FTC's role has not been made.

XII. Unity of Functions

The debate about the merits and problems of the FTC's dual roles as prosecutor and adjudicator has raged for years.[174] Nothing would be served by repeating the standard arguments at great length. Instead, we set out briefly the considerations that motivate a majority of us to conclude that the current unity of functions, although troubling, is superior to the alternatives and, indeed, flows logically from our conception of the Commission as an adjudicator of difficult antitrust issues. No thoughtful observer is entirely comfortable with the FTC's (or other agencies') combining of prosecutory and adjudicatory functions. Whenever the same people who issued a complaint later decide whether it should be dismissed, concern about at least the appearance of fairness is inevitable. The distinction between deciding whether a complaint should be issued and whether it should be dismissed, even if real, is subtle. The slenderness of this distinction is made more acute by the FTC's annual obligation to justify its expenditures. Tension may arise when an agency that has cited an important proceeding as part of its budget requests is asked to dismiss that proceeding as unwarranted. Finally, commissioners who have recruited and promoted lawyers and other professionals, and who encounter these professionals daily, may be uncomfortable ruling against them.

Those who argue that the Commission's unity of functions should be ended suggest two principal alternatives. One would direct the Commission to bring all of its cases in federal court;[175] the other would remove the prosecutorial function from the control of the Commission. The 1969 Report urged that the Commission staff be given the authority to file complaints;[176] others have advocated assigning the role of prosecutor to a Commission lawyer, who would be appointed by the President. This is the NLRB model, which was recently endorsed by Commissioner Terry Calvani. Rulemaking authority could lie with the prosecutor, with the commissioners, or with the prosecutor subject to Commission review. Another alternative would involve reconstituting the Commission as a special trade court, perhaps to hear cases brought by the Antitrust Division or even private litigants, as well

as by the FTC prosecutor.[177] Combinations of thes models and other alternatives also are possible.

A. *The Adjudicative Role*

Those who favor requiring the Commission to fil its cases in federal court—and there is little suppor on the Committee for this position—argue that court are specialists in adjudication, whereas the Commis sion specializes in the kind of policy balancing ident fied with rulemaking and prosecutorial discretio Those who favor this model point to the examples c merger enforcement and consumer fraud, where th Commission operates principally as a prosecutor: de ciding which cases to bring, settling cases, and litiga ing cases before federal judges. The process work well. In each instance the decision of which cases bring is important and often outcome-determinativ since the FTC settles many cases and loses relative few. Moreover, the Commission is free to issue guid lines and policy statements and to intervene befor various governmental bodies. If anything, its ability do so would be enhanced by abandoning its adjudica tive function. Finally, federal courts have talente judges with impressive credentials, who know th rules of procedure, enforce discipline, and resolv cases with some dispatch.

Nonetheless, most Committee members do not fa vor ending the FTC's adjudicative role. This conclu sion stems from our conception of the Commission antitrust role and, in part, its consumer protectic role. As discussed in Section IV, FTC administrativ adjudication is well suited to pursuing challengir cases, usually applying the rule of reason, or, for p se rule cases, requiring the initial resolution of diff cult legal issues. These cases often require the caref development of a factual record and a sensitive appl cation of difficult legal principles. This takes time ar expertise. It cannot be done at the preliminary stag when one is deciding whether to issue a complaint; can only be done through adjudication. Accordingly, strip the Commission of its adjudicative role wou frustrate one of its principal functions. Similarly, a ministrative adjudication can be an effective metho of addressing complicated consumer protection issue such as may be present in deception or unfairne cases. Particularly for these rather vague legal sta

---

[177] This is the model suggested in the 1971 Ash Counc Report. It proposed that the FTC's antitrust enforceme function be transferred to a newly constituted federal ant trust board that would (1) provide research and analysis ar economic advice to the Department of Justice and affecte industries; (2) merge considerations of economics and law establishing policy and deciding particular cases; and (assure that antitrust enforcement policies are consiste with the broad and long-range economic interests of th nation. The Board was to consist of a chairman and tw economic administrators, one responsible for research ar analysis and the other a member of the Council of Econom Advisors ("CEA") whose function would be to provide ec nomic advice. The President's Advisory Council on Exec tive Organization, *Report on Selected Independent Reg latory Agencies*, at 93-95 (January 1971).

---

[174] For review of the debate see *Monograph No. 5, supra* note 6, Vol. II, at 67-71.
[175] For suggestions to this effect, see S. 1980, 96th Cong., 1st Sess. (1979); H.R. 6589, 96th Cong., 2d Sess. (1980); White, *FTC: Wrong Agency for the Job of Adjudication*, 61 A.B.A. J. 1242 (1975).
[176] 1969 Report at 82-83.

dards, there can be virtue in the consistency that can be generated by administrative adjudication.

B. *The Prosecutorial Role*

Several members of the Committee favor eliminating the commissioners' prosecutorial role through one of the approaches noted above. They argue that the commissioners' most important role is as adjudicators, and this should be preserved at the cost of delegating their prosecutorial responsibilities. They reject the suggestion that federal courts are superior adjudicators, arguing that district judges lack the time, temperament, and expertise to learn the kind of sophisticated economics that ought to be considered in many FTC cases. Indeed, these Committee members hope that limiting the Commission to an adjudicative role might further enhance its expertise by attracting commissioners with judicial dispositions and by encouraging them to help shape and manage litigation. They also argue that the Commission's trial staff is entitled to the full support of (and supervision by) top management, which is impossible today but which could occur if the staff were headed by a presidentially-appointed prosecutor. These Committee members argue that the current unity of functions creates an unacceptable perception of unfairness that taints the agency's decisions; they would solve this by eliminating the agency's prosecutorial function.

A majority of Committee members are unpersuaded. In 1988, the FTC filed more than half its complaints in federal court.[178] Shifting to an exclusively adjudicatory model would eliminate the commissioners' role in these cases—typically merger, fraud, and credit practices cases, and cases challenging violations of rules—which are among the most important cases brought by the Commission. Merger cases, especially, call for the kind of expertise and balanced reflection that the Commission is supposed to bring to its work. Relinquishing this responsibility would be too large a price to pay.

Shifting to an exclusively adjudicatory model would also hamper the varied and creative use of the broad range of tools that characterizes the Commission's work at its best. A trade court would presumably not issue guidelines or policy statements. Further, the impact on the Commission's rulemaking function is unclear: it might shift to the prosecutor, thus following the OSHA model, or it might remain with the commissioners. Either way, each decision-making person or body would have fewer remedies from which to choose. Also, some members of the Committee worry that limiting the Commission to adjudication might make it more difficult to attract talented, experienced commissioners.

C. *Unity of Functions*

Largely for the reasons suggested above, a majority of Committee members believe that the current unity

of functions should continue. This conclusion is not reached without some uneasiness. In reaching it, however, the Committee is comforted by several factors:

1. FTC administrative adjudication inevitably takes time.[179] Indeed, simple matters are inappropriate for FTC administrative adjudication. Given this, and the regular turnover of commissioners, the unfairness argument is often only theoretical; it would be even more theoretical were terms shortened, as some suggest.

2. Given the length of time that adjudication takes, it would be quite plausible for a commissioner who voted for a complaint to conclude that changes in market conditions, in the law, or in economic learning make ill-advised what once seemed sound.

3. The Commission has not hesitated to dismiss its complaints. During the 1980's, for instance, the Commission dismissed 45 percent of its complaints, including approximately 60 percent of its antitrust complaints, partly because of changing views about antitrust policy.[180]

4. The argument that commissioners will worry about budgetary implications when deciding cases is unpersuasive.[181] The increasing predominance of federal court cases lessens its force. Moreover, the argument is remotely plausible only for very large, complex cases, yet it is these cases that are most likely to take sufficiently long for turnover to reduce the appearance of bias.

Accordingly, a majority of the Committee's members believe that the FTC should retain its unity of functions. All of us recognize that this is awkward, and the Commission should continue to be sensitive to the awkwardness. When a commissioner has unduly prejudged an issue, he or she should consider recusing him or herself, as a matter of discretion. With sensitivity, however, the problems can be made manageable, and the substantial benefits of a unity of functions can be preserved.

D. *Possible Structural Changes*

The Committee considered two minor structural changes that might improve the functioning of the FTC: changing the length and timing of commissioner terms to coincide with those of SEC commissioners, thereby reducing FTC commissioner terms from seven to five years, and reducing the number of commissioners from five to three. The Committee was unable to achieve consensus on these changes. The reasoning of supporters and opponents is noted here.

1. Commissioner Terms

Some Committee members believe that the agency would function better if the length and timing of its

---

[178] Appendix B; *see also* Graphs 24 and 25 in Appendix C (more 1988 workyears expended on court litigation than on administrative litigation).

[179] *See* Table 3 in Appendix C.

[180] Source: Computed from FTC Reports. Some complaints were dismissed because of changed circumstances, but more than 40 percent of the antitrust complaints appear to have been dismissed on the merits.

[181] To be sure, Congress and the White House should understand that the Commission is *supposed* to dismiss some cases, and that there is cause for concern if it does not.

members' terms were patterned after those of SEC commissioners. Each of the SEC's five commissioners has a five-year term, so a term expires every June. FTC commissioners are authorized to serve seven-year terms, so for five years a term expires each autumn, and then for two years no term expires. In actual practice, however, most commissioners have served less than seven years.

Committee members favoring the SEC model cite four advantages. First, it assures that shortly after his inauguration a new President will be able to appoint a commissioner who may be designated chairman. In contrast, a President may not be able to name even a single FTC commissioner until the autumn of his second or even third year in office. A presidential election should result in the possibility of prompt new FTC leadership. Second, the SEC model guarantees that each president will have appointed a majority of commissioners shortly after his term is half over. In contrast, a President can leave office without appointing a majority of FTC commissioners, which can hinder the gradual evolution of FTC policy.

Third, seven-year terms are so long that no one expects commissioners to serve them. If terms were shorter that expectation might change, which might improve the Commission by lengthening the average period of service. Fourth, the frequent availability of partially expired terms means that many commissioners are appointed to truncated terms. For instance, only one of the five current commissioners began with a guarantee of a seven-year term.[182] Commissioners appointed to very short terms inevitably begin their service by contemplating renomination and confirmation, which threatens the FTC's independence. If shorter terms resulted in a higher percentage of commissioners serving them out, this problem would be reduced.

On the other hand, some Committee members prefer the existing seven-year terms. They observe that because so many commissioners resign without serving full terms, Presidents are virtually assured of the opportunity to appoint a commissioner during their first year in office. These Committee members doubt that shortening the length of terms would induce commissioners who otherwise would have served less than five years to serve full terms. They also note that the change would shorten the length of service of those commissioners who do serve full terms. Finally, they worry that the change might reduce the independence of commissioners interested in long tenures, by requiring more frequent renomination.

---

[182] The exception was Commissioner Calvani. Commissioner Azcuenaga took office November 1984, by recess appointment, and was confirmed in March 1985 for a seat whose term expires in September 1991. Commissioner Machol was nominated by recess appointment in November 1988. If she is confirmed during the current session of Congress, her term will expire in 1994. Chairman Oliver was confirmed in 1986 for a term that expired in 1988. Commissioner Strenio was confirmed in 1986 for a term that expires in 1989.

2. Number of Commissioners

Some Committee members would prefer to have only three commissioners. This reduction would increase each commissioner's responsibility, which might make the positions more attractive and probably would increase the seriousness with which appointments are made and accepted. It would permit the agency to reverse the gradual increase in the percentage of its resources (and of its more talented personnel) devoted to management and supervision. It might increase accountability. Presidential accountability would be especially increased if, as these members prefer, the reduction in numbers were accompanied by a change in the chairman's conditions of service, so that he or she served at the pleasure of the President and could be removed from the Commission without cause.

Other Committee members prefer five commissioners. The larger size permits greater diversity. It also may enhance collegiality since commissioners can form shifting coalitions. These Committee members also worry about recusal problems with a three-member FTC, especially in an era with so many dual-career couples. They fear that between recusals and delays in nominations and confirmations, a three-member FTC frequently could result in two-member deadlocks. Finally, they prefer that the FTC chairman be removable from the Commission only for cause. This poses little problem with a five-member Commission, since terms regularly expire and the President can choose any commissioner to serve as chairman, but, as advocates of a three-member Commission concede, would be difficult with fewer commissioners.

XIII. Conclusion

Our study of the FTC has not generated recommendations for major structural changes. We declined to endorse suggestions that the FTC relinquish its antitrust enforcement mission to the Antitrust Division. A majority of us concluded that, on balance, the antitrust enforcement efforts of the FTC are a worthwhile complement to those of the Division, and that the administrative procedures available within the FTC provide valuable opportunities for the Commission to bring cases founded on new and emerging theories of antitrust.

We also declined to propose severing the agency's prosecutorial and adjudicative functions. Most of us did not feel that the union of these functions seriously impedes the FTC's work or deprives respondents of fair adjudication of complaints brought against them. The majority did not deem it necessary, therefore, to propose the creation of a trade court to adjudicate antitrust and consumer protection cases.

In the consumer protection area, we focused our attention on two generic issues: the relationship between FTC enforcement and state enforcement, and the manner in which the agency should divide its enforcement efforts between administrative action and those brought directly in federal court. We ventured some observations on these subjects and attempted to provide advice as to how the FTC should allocate its resources and assist the states. In addition, we voiced our strong support for the Competition and Consumer Advocacy Program.

We also emphasized that it is important to both the public and the agency that the FTC provide guidance as to its current thinking on antitrust and consumer protection. "Guidance," as we defined it, includes a range of activities, cease and desist orders, guides, policy statements, advisory opinions, and Magnuson-Moss rules.

We urged that economists continue to participate in all aspects of the Commission's work—not only in deciding the cases or projects to be undertaken, but throughout the proceedings. We recommended that studies by FTC economists should focus on the operation of U.S. industries and the U.S. antitrust and consumer protection systems, rather than on abstract economic research.

The Report also examined two other topics essential to the FTC's success: obtaining adequate resources and ensuring that Congress exercises a proper role with respect to the FTC's work. On the former topic, without selecting specific budget figures or personnel numbers, we expressed our belief that current resources are insufficient and should be gradually increased. On the latter, while we recognize Congress's obligation to oversee FTC activities, we expressed concern that Congress may have unduly interfered with the details of FTC proceedings, particularly in pending matters. Congress should continue to review the general policies of the FTC, but it should not become involved in pending proceedings, nor alter the outcome of specific decisions except by substantive legislation.

Respectfully submitted,

Miles W. Kirkpatrick *Chairman*	Basil J. Mezines Alan B. Morrison Timothy J. Muris
Joan Z. Bernstein Michael F. Brockmeyer Nancy L. Buc Calvin J. Collier Kenneth G. Elzinga Ernest Gellhorn Caswell O. Hobbs, III	Robert Pitofsky James F. Rill Edwin S. Rockefeller* J. Thomas Rosch Alan H. Silberman* Cass R. Sunstein William L. Webster

---

* See separate statements by Mr. Rockefeller and Mr. Silberman.

APPENDIX A:

MEMBERS OF THE AMERICAN BAR ASSOCIATION SECTION OF ANTITRUST LAW SPECIAL COMMITTEE TO STUDY THE ROLE OF THE FEDERAL TRADE COMMISSION

Miles W. Kirkpatrick (chairman), a Philadelphia, Pa., attorney and a member of the Advisory Board to BNA's Antitrust and Trade Regulation Report, and formerly chairman of the ABA Antitrust Section, chairman of the 1969 ABA Commission to Study the Federal Trade Commission, and chairman of the FTC

Joan Z. Bernstein, vice president and general counsel of Chemical Waste Management, Inc., and formerly a Washington, D.C., attorney who served as general counsel to the Environmental Protection Administration and to the Department of Health, Education, and Welfare, and as director of the FTC's Bureau of Consumer Protection

Michael F. Brockmeyer, assistant attorney general and chief of Maryland's Antitrust Division, and chairman of the Multistate Antitrust Task Force of the National Association of Attorneys General

Nancy L. Buc, a Washington, D.C., attorney and a fellow of Brown University, who has served as chief counsel to the Food and Drug Administration and as assistant director of the FTC's Bureau of Consumer Protection

Calvin J. Collier, Senior Vice President, General Counsel and Secretary, Kraft General Foods, who has been chairman and general counsel of the FTC, associate director of the Office of Management and Budget, and deputy under secretary of the Commerce Department

Dr. Kenneth G. Elzinga, professor of economics at the University of Virginia, co-author of *The Antitrust Penalties: A Study in Law and Economics*, co-editor of *The Antitrust Casebook: Milestones in Economic Regulation* and *The Morality of the Market: Religious and Economic Implications*, and a member of the Board of Trustees of Hope College

Ernest Gellhorn, a Washington, D.C., attorney, co-author of *The Administative Process* (1st, 2d, & 3d eds.), a public member and chair of the Rulemaking Committee of the Administrative Conference of the United States, and a member of the American Law Institute, who has served as a professor of administrative law and antitrust law at Duke University and the University of Virginia, and as dean of the law schools at Arizona State University, Case Western Reserve University, and the University of Washington

Caswell O. Hobbs, a Washington, D.C., attorney, author of articles on antitrust and trade regulation, and a member of the Council (and formerly an officer) of the ABA Antitrust Section, who has served as director of the FTC's Office of Policy, Planning, and Evaluation

Basil J. Mezines, a Washington, D.C., attorney, author of *Administrative Law* and *Trade Associations and the Antitrust Laws*, and a member of the Advisory Board to the BNA Antitrust and Trade Regulation Report, who has served as executive director of the FTC and as director of its Bureau of Competition

Alan B. Morrison, director of the Public Citizen Litigation Group and a member of the Administrative Conference of the United States, and formerly a visiting professor at Harvard Law School and a member of the Board of Governors of the District of Columbia Bar

Timothy J. Muris, George Mason University Foundation Professor of Law at George Mason University Law School, co-editor of *The Federal Trade Com-*

mission Since 1970: Economic Regulation and Bureaucratic Behavior, and formerly executive associate director of the Office of Management and Budget and director of the FTC's Bureaus of Competition and of Consumer Protection

Robert Pitofsky, dean and executive vice president for Law Center Affairs, Georgetown University Law Center, co-author of *Cases and Materials on Trade Regulation*, a member of the Council of the ABA Antitrust Section, and a member of the Advisory Board to BNA's Antitrust and Trade Regulation Report, and formerly an FTC commissioner and director of its Bureau of Consumer Protection

James F. Rill, a Washington, D.C., attorney, immediate past chairman of the ABA Antitrust Section, author of articles on antitrust and trade regulation, and a member of the Advisory Board to BNA's Antitrust and Trade Regulation Report

Edwin S. Rockefeller, a Washington, D.C., attorney and chairman of the Advisory Board to BNA's Antitrust and Trade Regulation Report, author of *Antitrust Counseling for the 1980's* and *Desk Book of FTC Practice and Procedure*, and formerly chairman of the ABA Antitrust Section and an FTC staff member

J. Thomas Rosch, a San Francisco attorney who is vice-chair of the ABA Antitrust Section, a fellow of the American College of Trial Lawyers, a member of the Advisory Board to BNA's Antitrust and Trade Regulation Report, and author of *Manual of Federal Trade Commission Practice*, and who formerly served as director of the FTC's Bureau of Consumer Protection

Alan H. Silberman, a Chicago attorney who is finance officer of the ABA Antitrust Section and a member of the Advisory Board to BNA's Antitrust and Trade Regulation Report, and who was editorial chairman of *The FTC as an Antitrust Enforcement Agency: The Role of Section 5 of the FTC Act in Antitrust Law* and coordinating editor of *The FTC as an Antitrust Enforcement Agency: Its Structure, Powers and Procedures*

Cass R. Sunstein, a professor of administrative law and constitutional law at the University of Chicago Law School and the University of Chicago's Department of Political Science, co-author of *Constitutional Law*, and a member of the council of the ABA Section of Administrative Law

William L. Webster, attorney general of Missouri and chairman of the consumer protection committee of the National Association of Attorneys General

COMMITTEE COUNSEL: Stephen Calkins, Professor of Law at Wayne State University Law School, a member of the American Law Institute and of the Council of the ABA Antitrust Section, co-editor of *Antitrust Law Developments* (2d ed.), secretary to the Antitrust Section of the American Association of Law Schools, and formerly an attorney advisor to FTC Commissioner Stephen Nye

COMMITTEE DEPUTY COUNSEL: Kathleen M.H. Wallman, a Washington, D.C., attorney, and formerly

a law clerk to Judges Laurence Silberman and Edward Tamm of the District of Columbia Circuit, and Judge Pauline Newman of the Federal Circuit.

COMMITTEE ASSISTANT COUNSEL: Sandra L Spear, a Washington, D.C., attorney.

APPENDIX B:
CHANGES IN PTC'S STATUTORY POWERS
SINCE THE 1969 REPORT[1]

The two decades since the 1969 Report have witnesse a number of changes in the Commission's statutory pow ers. Most of these changes have resulted from fou statutes.[2] Three of these statutes generally broadened th Commission's power. However, in reaction to the Com mission's use of many of these powers, the 1980 Ac amendments imposed several significant substantive an procedural restrictions. The four statutes changed th Commission's remedies, rulemaking authority, investiga tional powers, ability to challenge mergers before con summation, and jurisdiction.

A. *Remedies*

1. Injunction Relief

In 1973, the Commission was empowered to obtai preliminary injunctions in federal district court to pre vent violations of FTCenforced statutes pending disposi tion of the Commission's administrative proceedings One of the more striking developments of the past twent years has been the FTC's increasing reliance on Sectio 13(b)'s second proviso, which states that "in proper case the Commission may seek, and after proper proof, th court may issue, a permanent injunction."[4] The FTC ha

---

[1]This section was in part based upon or taken from paper prepared for the Committee by Stephen Stack, Jr. W are grateful for his contribution.

[2]The Trans-Alaska Pipeline Authorization Act of 197: Pub. L. No. 93-153 (1973); the Magnuson-Moss Warranty Federal Trade Commission Improvements Act of 1975, Pub L. No. 93-837 (1975); the Hart-Scott-Rodino Antitrust Im provements Act of 1978, Pub. L. No. 94-435 (1978); and th Federal Trade Commission Improvements Act of 1980, Pub L. No. 98-252 (1980).

[3]Pub. L. No. 93-153, §408; 15 U.S.C. §53(b) (1982). Previous ly, the FTC could obtain a preliminary injunction only fror a court of appeals under the All Writs Act — a powe limited to where an injunction was necessary to protect th court's jurisdiction. *See* FTC v. Dean Foods Co., 384 U.S. 59 (1968).

[4]15 U.S.C. §53(b) (1982):
Whenever the Commission has reason to believe—
(1) that any person ... is violating, or is about to violate any provision of law enforced by the Federal Trade Com mission, and
(2) that the enjoining thereof pending the issuance of complaint by the Commission and until such complaint dismissed by the Commission or set aside by the court c review, or until the order of the Commission made therec has become final, would be in the interest of the public— the Commission by any of its attorneys designated by it fc such purpose may bring suit in a district court of the Unite States to enjoin any such act or practice. Upon a prope showing that, weighing the equities and considering th

persuaded the courts to order, pursuant to Section 13(b), not only permanent injunctions, but also to enter other remedial equitable relief, including consumer redress.[5]

Since 1980, the FTC has invoked Section 13(b) with increasing frequency. The result has been a transformation of the FTC's practice, particularly for consumer protection.[6] From 1981 through 1986, FTC complaints in federal court represented about 30 percent of all FTC complaints. In 1987, court complaints represented approximately 40 percent of the total; in 1988, more than half.[7] FTC workyears spent on court and administrative litigation have been comparable since 1985, and in 1988 court workyears were greater.[8] In the Bureau of Consumer Protection, workyears spent on court litigation have exceeded workyears spent on administrative litigation in every year, 1984 to 1988.[9] Not surprisingly, the number of cases pending before FTC ALJ's has been declined sharply during the past decade, and the number of FTC ALJ's has also been declining steadily, from 13 in 1980 to three today.[10]

2. Consumer Redress

The 1975 Magnuson-Moss amendments gave the Commission the power to obtain consumer redress from federal or state courts in cases involving unfair or deceptive acts or practices. Redress may include (but is not limited to) rescission or reformation of contracts, restitution, return of property, payment of damages, and "public notification" of the violation.[11] The amendments authorize redress when the Commission proves a violation of a trade regulation rule. They also authorize court-ordered redress after an administrative proceeding has been successfully completed, but only if the challenged practice was one "a reasonable man would have known under the circumstances was dishonest or fraudulent."[12]

As described immediately above and in Section V.B, the FTC has increasingly used Section 13(b) to obtain

consumer redress in cases involving unfair or deceptive acts or practices. Given the much greater speed of Section 13(b) litigation, it is not surprising that in recent years the Commission has relied on its authority to seek redress following an administrative case in only a handful of reported cases.[13] Since 1976, the FTC has won consumer redress valued at hundreds of millions of dollars in dozens of cases.[14]

3. Civil Penalties

The Commission's civil penalty sanction has been augmented in three respects since 1969.[15] In 1973 the maximum penalty was increased from $5,000 to $10,000 per violation ($10,000 a day for continuing violations).[16] In 1975 the Commission was authorized to seek civil penalties for violations of trade regulation rules.[17] Also in 1975 the Commission was given the controversial power to request a court to order the payment of a civil penalty by a person engaging in conduct the Commission has previously determined to be unfair or deceptive and has prohibited in a final cease-and-desist order entered against someone else, provided that the person had actual knowledge that the conduct is unfair or deceptive and is unlawful.[18] The Commission has invoked this power in only a few cases.[19]

B. *Rulemaking*

In 1975 the Commission gained explicit authority to issue substantive rules defining specific conduct constituting "unfair or deceptive acts or practices" under Section 5. Congress detailed the rulemaking procedures to be followed, including requirements for published notice, submission of written comments, an informal hearing, cross-examination of witnesses, scope of review and reimbursement of expenses for certain participants.[20]

The Commission's rulemaking authorization proved a mixed blessing, however.[21] In 1980 Congress erected additional procedural safeguards for rulemaking. Congress called for more detailed advance notice and for meetings between Commissioners and outside parties concerning proposed rules, and it limited compensation for outside participants.[22] In reaction to particularly

---

Commission's likelihood of ultimate success, such action would be in the public interest, and after notice to the defendant, a temporary restraining order or a preliminary injunction may be granted without bond: *Provided, however,* ... That in proper cases the Commission may seek, and after proper proof, the court may issue, a permanent injunction....

[5]*See* authorities cited *supra* notes 84-88.

[6]The FTC has not invoked Section 13(b)'s permanent injunction powers in its antitrust mission, in part because litigated antitrust cases tend to present more difficult legal issues. Paul, *supra* note 88, at 142. Graphs 24 and 25 in Appendix C also show that regional offices have devoted most of their litigation resources to federal court proceedings.

[7]These figures were derived by examining the FTC's annual reports and the CCH Trade Regulation Reporter.

[8]See Graphs 24 and 25 in Appendix C.

[9]See Graphs 24 and 25 in Appendix C; *see also* Paul, *supra* note 66 (In 1988, the Bureau of Consumer Protection had more enforcement actions in progress in federal courts than in Part III before ALJ's.).

[10]Graph 21 in Appendix C; number of ALJ's provided by FTC.

[11]Pub. L. 93-837 §208; 15 U.S.C. §57b (1982).

[12]*Id.*

---

[13]*Cf.* Carley, *FTC Muscle Evident in Its Settlements,* Legal Times, Nov. 7, 1983, at 11 (FTC had filed three to date) (also arguing that Section 19(a)(2), with Section 13(b), helped the FTC win settlements).

[14]*See* Table 4 in Appendix C (also noting that not all amounts awarded have been collected).

[15]For civil penalties awarded during the past decade, see Table 4 in Appendix C.

[16]Pub. L. No. 93-153, §408(c); 15 U.S.C. §45(1) (1982).

[17]Pub. L. No. 93-637, §205; 15 U.S.C. §45(m)(1)(A) (1982).

[18]Pub. L. No. 93-837, §205(a); 15 U.S.C. §45(m)(1)(B) (1982).

[19]*Cf., e.g.,* United States v. Hopkins Dodge, Inc., 849 F.2d 311 (8th Cir. 1988); United States v. Allied Publishers, Inc., 1982-83 Trade Cas. (CCH) ¶84,983 (E.D. Cal. 1982); *Audobon Life Insurance Co. v. FTC,* 543 F. Supp. 1382 (M.D. La. 1982).

[20]Pub. L. No. 93-837, §202 (codified as amended at 15 U.S.C. §57a (1982)).

[21]*See supra* Section X.

[22]Pub. L. No. 98-252, §§8, 9, 10, 12, 15; 15 U.S.C. §57a (1982).

controversial rulemaking proceedings, Congress prohibited the FTC from continuing its children's advertising and its standards and certification rulemakings, and it limited the content of the Commission's funeral industry rule.[23] Finally, Congress enacted a legislative veto,[24] which was later held unconstitutional under the separation of powers doctrine.[25]

C. *Investigational Powers and Procedures*

The scope of the Commission's investigative authority has been expanded in several respects since 1969, but it has also been narrowed in one respect. In 1973 the Commission gained the power to extract information from banks and common carriers in connection with investigations of other firms.[26] In 1975 the Commission's general investigative authority was enlarged beyond "corporations" to include partnerships and other legal entities as well.[27] In 1980, however, Congress revoked the Commission's power to investigate the insurance industry.[28]

Procedurally, in 1980 the Commission was authorized to issue civil investigative demands to compel oral testimony and production of documents in consumer protection ("unfair or deceptive acts or practices") investigations.[29] The 1980 Improvements Act imposed stringent requirements to protect the confidentiality of investigational materials.[30]

D. *Premerger Notification*

One of the most significant powers conferred on the Commission has been the premerger review procedure enacted in the Hart-ScottRodino Antitrust Improvements Act of 1976.[31] The Act requires parties to substantial transactions to notify the Commission and the Justice Department about the transaction, provide further information if requested, and observe a specified waiting period before consummating the transaction. The program has fundamentally changed the nature of merger enforcement by giving the antitrust agencies the necessary information to seek a preliminary injunction before most acquisitions are consummated.

E. *Jurisdiction*

The principal change in the Commission's jurisdiction was in 1975, to expand the scope of its subject matter

---

[23]Pub. L. No. 98-252, §§7, 11, 19; 15 U.S.C. 57a (1982); *id.* 57a note.

[24]Pub. L. No. 98-252 sec. 21; 15 U.S.C. §57a-1 (1982).

[25]Consumers Union of United States v. FTC, 891 F.2d 575 (D.C. Cir. 1982), *aff'd sub. nom.* United States House of Representatives v. FTC, 483 U.S. 1218 (1983); *see also* INS v. Chadha, 482 U.S. 919 (1983).

[26]Pub. L. No. 93-153, §403(e); 15 U.S.C. §48(h) (1982). The Commission does not have substantive jurisdiction over banks or common carriers. 15 U.S.C.A. §45(a)(2) (West Supp. 1988).

[27]Pub. L. No. 93-637, §203(a)(3); (codified as amended at 15 U.S.C. §46(a) (1982)).

[28]Pub. L. No. 96-252, §5; 15 U.S.C. §46(h) (1982).

[29]Pub. L. No. 96-252, §13; 15 U.S.C. §57b-1 (1982). Congress has not authorized this form of compulsory process in competition investigations.

[30]Pub. L. No. 96-252 §§3 14; 15 U.S.C. §57b-2 (1982).

[31]Pub. L. No. 94-435, §201; 15 U.S.C. §18a (1982).

jurisdiction and investigational powers from matters "in commerce" to matters "in or affecting commerce."[32] The amendments also authorized the Commission to regulate warranties.[33] Congress also narrowed the Commission's jurisdiction in one minor area.[34]

APPENDIX C

The graphs and tables included in Appendix C were developed from data provided by the Federal Trade Commission in response to a Freedom of Information Act request. The notes at the end of the graphs are an integral part of the graphs themselves. Three points deserve special mention.

First, except for 1988 data, the data for the competition mission do not reliably depict competition mission resource allocation because until 1988, workyears were kept either according to industry (e.g., Health Care) or according to kind of violation (e.g., horizontal). *See* Note 3. We are told that the trends in the data are accurate, however.

Second, in designing the graphs, we have used differing scales in order to increase legibility. In reading the graphs, pay particular attention to the Y-axis scale.

Third, the time period covered by the individual graph was determined by the availability of data. When data sources reporting comparable data for different missions or bureaus were not available for the same period of time, graphs comparing the two missions only addressed the common time period.

GRAPH 1
NOTE 1
% OF PROFESSIONAL WORKYEARS PER BUREAU
FTC TOTAL

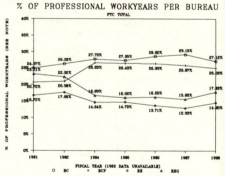

---

[32] Pub. L. No. 93-637 §201 (codified as amended at 15 U.S.C. §45(a)(1) (1982)).

[33]15 U.S.C. §§2302, 2310 (1982). Subsequent legislation also expanded the FTC's jurisdiction in other areas. *See, e.g.,* 15 U.S.C. §4404 (Supp. IV 1986) (smokeless tobacco).

[34]In response to an FTC director interlock complaint against a savings and loan, Congress exempted savings and loan associations from FTC jurisdiction. Pub. L. No. 96-37 (codified at 15 U.S.C. §45(a)(2) (1982)).

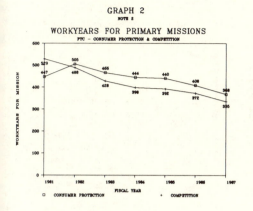

GRAPH 2
NOTE 2

WORKYEARS FOR PRIMARY MISSIONS
FTC – CONSUMER PROTECTION & COMPETITION

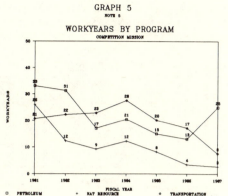

GRAPH 5
NOTE 5

WORKYEARS BY PROGRAM
COMPETITION MISSION

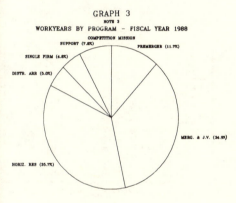

GRAPH 3
NOTE 3

WORKYEARS BY PROGRAM – FISCAL YEAR 1988
COMPETITION MISSION

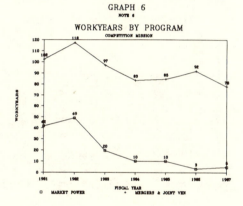

GRAPH 6
NOTE 6

WORKYEARS BY PROGRAM
COMPETITION MISSION

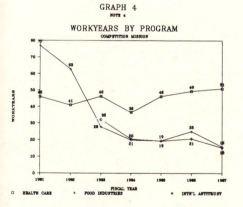

GRAPH 4
NOTE 4

WORKYEARS BY PROGRAM
COMPETITION MISSION

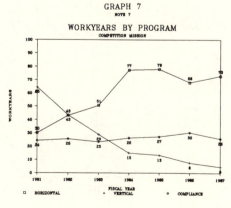

GRAPH 7
NOTE 7

WORKYEARS BY PROGRAM
COMPETITION MISSION

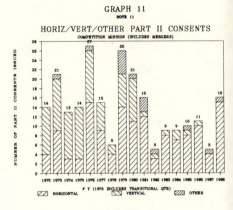

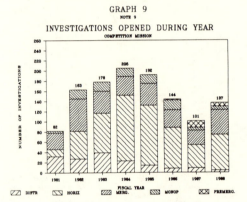

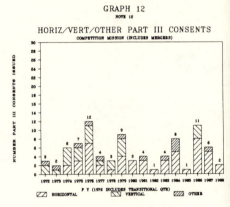

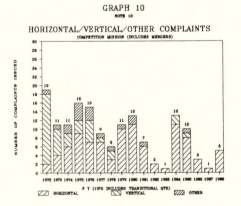

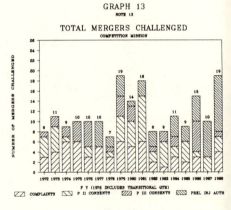

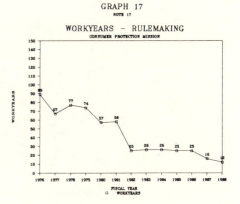

GRAPH 14
NOTE 14
WORKYEARS – ADVERTISING & ENFORCEMENT
CONSUMER PROTECTION MISSION

(SEE NOTES: WORKYEARS FOR ADVERTISING, SERVICES, MARKETING AND
CREDIT INCLUDE TIME SPENT IN RULEMAKING FOR THOSE PROGRAMS.)

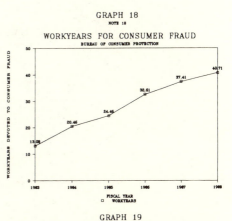

GRAPH 17
NOTE 17
WORKYEARS – RULEMAKING
CONSUMER PROTECTION MISSION

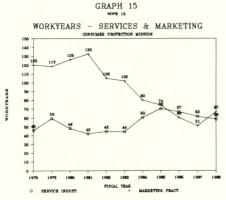

GRAPH 15
NOTE 15
WORKYEARS – SERVICES & MARKETING
CONSUMER PROTECTION MISSION

GRAPH 18
NOTE 18
WORKYEARS FOR CONSUMER FRAUD
BUREAU OF CONSUMER PROTECTION

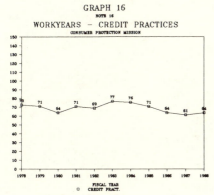

GRAPH 16
NOTE 16
WORKYEARS – CREDIT PRACTICES
CONSUMER PROTECTION MISSION

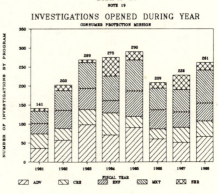

GRAPH 19
NOTE 19
INVESTIGATIONS OPENED DURING YEAR
CONSUMER PROTECTION MISSION

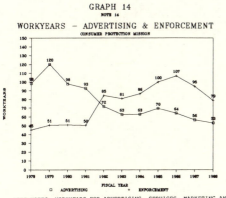

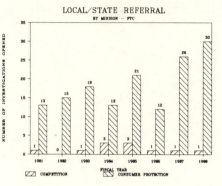

GRAPH 20
NOTE 20

LOCAL/STATE REFERRAL
BY MISSION — FTC

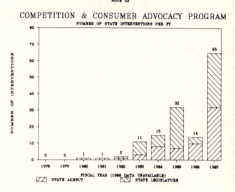

GRAPH 23
NOTE 23

COMPETITION & CONSUMER ADVOCACY PROGRAM
NUMBER OF STATE INTERVENTIONS PER FY

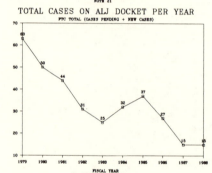

GRAPH 21
NOTE 21

TOTAL CASES ON ALJ DOCKET PER YEAR
FTC TOTAL (CASES PENDING + NEW CASES)

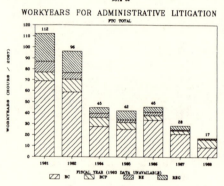

GRAPH 24
NOTE 24

WORKYEARS FOR ADMINISTRATIVE LITIGATION
FTC TOTAL

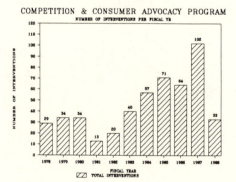

GRAPH 22
NOTE 22

COMPETITION & CONSUMER ADVOCACY PROGRAM
NUMBER OF INTERVENTIONS PER FISCAL YR

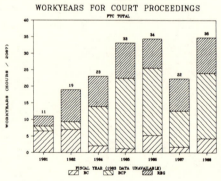

GRAPH 25
NOTE 25

WORKYEARS FOR COURT PROCEEDINGS
FTC TOTAL

NOTES TO GRAPHS

NOTE 1: Source: Time By Activity Reports, run by FTC in December 1988 from archive tapes. Tape for 1983 was missing. Report lists hours reported by professional staff, excluding clerical and senior management staff, spent in various activities. Also, certain support offices do not report time through this system. Graph 1 shows the percentage of total Commission non-support-function professional workyears represented by each bureau and the regional offices. The legend abbreviations, from left to right, are Bureau of Competition, Bureau of Consumer Protection, Bureau of Economics and Regional Offices.

NOTE 2: Source: Program Status Summary Reports based on FTC time sheets. Data for each mission include workyears from Regional Office and Headquarters personnel. Graph includes only 1981 through 1987 data. Competition data were available from 1981 through 1988, but the FTC changed its reporting system for Competition workyears effective fiscal year 1988 to program codes that are incompatible with previous years' codes.

NOTE 3: Source: Program Status Summary Report for FY88 based on FTC time sheets. Data include workyears from Regional Office and Headquarters personnel. Incompatible program codes for the competiton mission preclude comparison of 1988 data with that from prior years. Before 1988, the FTC tracked Competition resources through 12 different programs: 6 industry-specific programs (Health Care, Food Industries, Petroleum, Non-petroleum Energy, Transportation, International Antitrust (beginning in 1983)), 5 violation-specific programs (Market Power, Mergers & Joint Ventures, Horizontal Restraints, Vertical Restraints and Compliance) and Support Functions. Commission policy preferred tracking, for example, all activity related to health care under that program, irrespective of the alleged violation. However, personnel working on matters involving one of the six industries above occasionally reported their time under violation-specific programs. Therefore, no individual program figure accurately reports all time for that activity.

Beginning in 1988, the FTC changed to six programs, with industry-specific subcategories in each. Those programs are: Pre-Merger Notification, Mergers & Joint Ventures, Horizontal Restraints, Distribu-tional Arrangements, Single-Firm Violations (Monopoly and Predation) and Support Functions.

NOTE 4: Source: See Note 3. Graph 4 + Graph 5 + Graph 6 + Graph 7 + Support Functions = Total Competition Workyears. International Antitrust was added as an industry category in 1983.

NOTE 5: Source: See Notes 3 & 4. Natural Resources includes non-petroleum energy and other natural resources.

NOTE 6: Source: See Notes 3 & 4. Many workyears spent on market power, mergers or joint ventures in one of the six industries (see Note 3) will not appear in these numbers.

NOTE 7: Source: See Notes 3 & 4. Many workyears spent on horizontal and vertical restraints or compliance in one of the six industries (see Note 3) will not appear in these numbers.

NOTE 8: Source: Data file provided by FTC, listing all investigations opened, the date opened, the source of the investigation, the violation, program code and organization code. Graph 8 tallies all investigations opened under program codes corresponding to the industries the FTC tracks. includes investigations opened at headquarters and in regional offices. Investigations under each are understated to the extent they appear under a violation grouping in Graph 9. To arrive at total investigations for the Competition mission, add the numbers from Graphs 8 and 9. Energy includes non-energy natural resources.

NOTE 9: Source: See Note 8. Graph 9 tallies investigations opened under non-industry-specific program codes. Legend abbreviations, from left to right, are: Distributional Restraints, Horizontal Restraints, Mergers & Joint Ventures, Monopoly or Predation, and Premerger. Investigations under each may be understated to the extent they appear under an industry grouping in Graph 8.

NOTE 10: Source: List of Competition Mission Accomplishments, 1972 to 1988. Report lists violation code. From violation codes, Complaints were categorized as horizontal, vertical and other (monopoly, etc.). Fiscal Year 1976 data include the transitional quarter, July 1 to September 30, 1976, between the June 30 fiscal year end and the October 1 fiscal year beginning.

NOTE 11: Source: See Note 10. Graph 11 tallies the number of Part II Consents entered per fiscal year.

NOTE 12: Source: See Note 10. Graph 12 tallies the number of Part III Consents entered per fiscal year.

NOTE 13: Source: See Note 10. Graph 13 tallies the Complaints, Parts II Consents, Part III Consents, and Preliminary Injunctions Authorized against mergers, both horizontal and vertical.

NOTE 14: Source: Program Status Summary Reports based on FTC time sheets. Data for each mission include workyears from Regional Office and Headquarters personnel. Graph 14 + Graph 15 + Graph 16 + Program Management = Total Consumer Protection Mission Workyears. Advertising Practices includes general advertising, food and drug, cigarette and energy advertising. Advertising workyears also includes time spent on rulemaking for advertising. Enforcement includes rule and statute enforcement and compliance.

NOTE 15: Source: See Note 14. Service Industries Practices includes credence goods & services, professional services and standards and certification. Marketing Practices includes product information, deceptive sales practices and warranties and reliability. Both include workyears for rulemaking in their totals.

NOTE 16: Source: See Note 14. Credit Practices includes general credit, Equal Credit Opportunity Act, credit information and Fair Credit Reporting Act issues. It also includes workyears for rulemaking in the totals.

NOTE 17: Source: Rulemaking Resource History Estimates (Report prepared by FTC). Report lists workyears, by Fiscal Year, spent on each Consumer Protection Rule. This graph tallies those workyears by Fiscal Year. These figures do not include enforcement of rules. They are the combined rulemaking workyears from Advertising, Service Industries, Marketing and Credit reported in Graphs 14 through 16.

NOTE 18: Source: Report prepared by FTC. Tallies staff time devoted to consumer fraud investigation and compliance. These numbers are included in graphs 14, 15 and 16.

NOTE 19: Source: Data file provided by FTC, listing all investigations opened, the date opened, the source of the investigation, the violation, program code and organization code.

Graph 19 tallies all investigations opened under Consumer Protection program codes. It includes investigations opened at Headquarters and in Regional Offices. Legend abbreviations are, from left to right, Advertising, Credit Practices, Enforcement, Marketing Practices and Service Industry Practices.

NOTE 20: Source: Data file provided by FTC, listing all investigations opened, the date opened, the source of the investigation, the violation, program code and organization code. Graph 20 tallies the number of investigations prompted by referrals from local or state governments.

NOTE 21: Source: ALJ Caseload Summary, 1979-1988, prepared by FTC. Graph shows the total number of FTC cases on the OALJ docket each fiscal year. Total = number of cases pending at the beginning of the fiscal year, plus the number of cases added to the docket during the fiscal year.

NOTE 22: Source: Internally-prepared FTC report. Graph 22 tallies total interventions per year in all non-FTC initiated proceedings.

NOTE 23: Source: See Note 22. Graph 23 tallies all interventions in state proceedings. Data for FY88 were not available.

NOTE 24: Source: Time By Activity Reports, run by FTC in December 1988 from archive tapes. Tape for 1983 was missing. Report lists hours reported by professional staff, excluding clerical and senior management staff, spent in various activities. Also, certain support offices do not report time through this system. Graph 24 tallies professional time spent in Administrative Litigation by the Bureau of Competition, the Bureau of Consumer Protection, the Bureau of Economics and Regional Offices. It excludes time spent by the General Counsel's Office.

NOTE 25: Source: See Note 24. Graph 25 tallies professional time spent in Court Proceedings by the Bureau of Competition, the Bureau of Consumer Protection, and Regional Offices. It excludes all time reported by the General Counsel's Office. Bureau of Economics personnel spent less than one-half workyear per year in this activity, so their time is excluded from the graph.

TABLE 1

FTC - BUREAU OF CONSUMER PROTECTION

TELEMARKETING CASES - PRELIMINARY INVESTIGATIONS BROUGHT
JUNE 1, 1983 TO PRESENT

	TRAVEL	PROMOTIONAL MERCHANDISE	MINERAL LEASING	OFFICE SUPPLIES	CONSUMER GOODS	INVESTMENT COINS & ART	CONSUMER SERVICES	NON-MINERAL BUS. OPPORT.	TOTAL
				TYPE OF PRODUCT OR SERVICE BEING SOLD					
NUMBER OF PI	11	5	14	9	11	23	5	7	85
STAFF HOURS	12052	6617	61564	13864	3526	111799	4364	23082	236,868
WORKYEARS 1/	7.73	4.24	39.46	8.89	2.26	71.67	2.80	14.80	151.85
FTC RESOURCES	$607,727	$256,711	$2,180,667	$404,867	$112,401	$3,613,781	$150,505	$775,399	8,102,058.
SALES 2/	49,280	2,500	136,500	32,000	5,600	266,410	15,850	18,000	548,640,000.
SALES UNKNOWN #	6	2	4	5	8	9	3	3	40
REDRESS ORD. 2/	$6,600	$75	$70,881	$610		$6,366		$1,100	85,632,000.
PI W/ REDRESS	1	1	7	3	0	3	0	4	19
INVEST. ONGOING	5	1	4	1	4	11	4	3	33
CASE CLOSED, NO REDRESS	2	2	2	5	7	3	0	0	21
IN LITIGATION	3	1	1	0	0	4	1	2	12
AMT DISTRIB 2/	0	0	$2,671.5	$300	0	$266	0	$1,100	4,337,500.
DISTRIB #	0	0	2	1	0	1	0	2	6
ON DEPOSIT 2/	0	0	$2,065	0	0	0	0	$1,730	3,795,000.
ON DEPOSIT #	0	0	1	0	0	0	0	2	3
HELD BY RECEIVER 2/	0	0	$15,028	0	0	$200	0	0	15,228,000.
HELD BY RECEIVER #	0	0	2	0	0	1	0	0	3

1/ Workyears = Staff hours ' 1560 (unofficial conversion factor, per Exec. Dir. Office).

2/ Dollar amounts for annual sales of business investigated, redress ordered and redress paid are in thousands.

TABLE 2

**Distribution of Total Economist[1]
Workyears by Area**

Fiscal Year	1980	1981	1982	1983	1984	1985	1986	1987	1988	1989[2]	Percent Change 1980-89
					(Workyears)						
Antitrust	33.1	30.6	37.0	33.4	31.8	32.0	35.7	31.6	35.9	39.0	+18
Consumer Protection	12.6	16.4	14.3	13.3	13.4	16.3	15.2	12.2	12.4	10.7	-15
Research	22.9	22.2	25.9	29.6	25.8	24.3	18.1	15.7	12.1	7.3	-68
Advocacy	3.8	4.2	6.1	7.4	5.4	6.1	8.1	6.0	5.2	3.0	-21
Part III	.6	.6	.6	.3	.6	1.3	.5	.2	0.0	0.0	-100
Statistical Reporting	3.0	4.0	0.0	0.0	0.0	0.0	0.0	0.0	0.0	0.0	-100
Total Workyears	76	86	84	84	77	80	78	66	66	60	-21

Source: Data provided by the FTC.

[1] Excludes Office of the Director. The sum of the rows for each year may not add to the total workyears because of rounding.

[2] Planned for FY 89

TABLE 3

AVERAGE MONTHS BETWEEN EVENTS 1975-1988

EVENT PAIRS		CONSUMER PROTECTION		COMPETITION	
SOURCE EVENT	TARGET EVENT	AVG. MONTHS	NUM	AVG. MONTHS	NUM
(A) Initial Phase Invest.	Converted to Full Phase	10	841	7	536
(B) Initial Phase Invest. Converted to Full Phase.	Part III Compl. or Part II Consent	15	185	12	159
(C) Full Phase Invest. Opened.	Part III Compl. or Part II Consent	13	295	12	244
(D) Part III Compl.	Final Order	28	175	34	171
(E) Oral Argument	Final Order	13	22	16	45
TOTAL (A + B + D)		53		53	
TOTAL (C + D)		41		46	

TABLE 4
CONSUMER PROTECTION AWARDS

FISCAL YEAR	CONSUMER REDREST[1]/	CIVIL PENALTIES
1977	$ 51,790,431	$ 515,000
1978	1,524,203	1,108,000
1979	49,403,236	576,000
1980	113,122,854	2,743,000
1981	15,274,492	1,391,500
1982	58,370,305	537,000
1983	30,375,000	1,209,200
1984	7,282,000	709,800
1985	7,248,000	2,999,300
1986	6,035,000	1,267,000
1987 [2]	16,584,400	3,788,000
1988	33,838,500	1,040,000

---

[1]The listed amounts represent the sum of redress dollars ordered during a fiscal year. Redress may actually be paid out over several years, and may be in the form of goods or services for which estimated values may vary. Some redress was never paid; the amount actually paid is unavailable. This does not include redress ordered through arbitration or through fulfillment of warranty claims.

[2]FY 1987 Consumer Redress total includes $4,400,000 in accounts receivable that will not be collected as part of redress orders.

SEPARATE STATEMENT OF EDWIN S. ROCKEFELLER

I agree with the Committee's basic recommendation to leave things pretty much as they are, so my disagreement with many opinions contained in the Report is of no consequence. There is one point, however, on which it would be irresponsible to remain silent - the matter of "resources." The Report recommends an increase but does not explain why, for what, or from where the money is to come (the Justice Department? Social Security? new taxes?). The Report contains no basis for evaluating whether the present spending level is too low, too high, or just right, except for the pronouncements that the staff is "top-heavy" and money is being "disproportionately allocated" to regional offices.

The Committee was appointed to consider how the FTC should fit into our system of government, not how much money to spend on it. The recommendation for a spending increase is without foundation, illogical, and beyond the Committee's reason for existence.

SEPARATE STATEMENT OF ALAN H. SILBERMAN

The separate statement which follows is submitted with extreme reluctance. The work of the Special Committee has been accomplished with extraordinary collegiality, with a sense of respect for divergent views and the fullest possible exposition and debate of issues. It has been a signal privilege to participate in that process. In addition, the Report fairly reflects positions which were advanced but did not attain majority support, and I do not hesitate to concede that

at the moment of decision the comments set forth below were supported by the very-smallest of minorities (albeit a passionate few). Nonetheless, I believe it is useful to detail a separate position on the issue of whether the FTC should continue to combine prosecutorial and adjudicative functions so that the record will continue to reflect the fact that (at least in the view of a few Committee members) this question continues to be one which merits detailed consideration.

The Committee majority notes that "[n]o thoughtful observer is entirely comfortable" with an agency which combines prosecutorial and adjudicative functions. Indeed, the FTC's current "unity of functions" is characterized as "troubling". Despite these doubts, and a debate which has "raged for years", the majority opts for a continuation of the *status quo*.

The majority acts in the belief that the dual prosecutorial-adjudicative function (1) is superior and (2) flows logically from a conception of the Federal Trade Commission as an agency which will, in the future, deal with challenging antitrust issues. I share those objectives: the FTC should have an organizational structure which can fairly be called "superior" and it should be one which is particularly appropriate to an agency dealing with antitrust and consumer protection issues of major significance. However, I believe that the pursuit of those objectives points toward a different conclusion; *viz.*, the development of separate, specialized prosecutorial and adjudicative units within the present agency.

Appearance of impropriety and the possibility of unfairness which attends the dual role arrangement are the concerns most commonly voiced, and for good reason. As the Antitrust Section noted long ago, an organizational structure of this type is "conceptually wrong".[1] More importantly, I believe it limits the Commission's ability to act more efficiently.

The Committee correctly notes that the FTC can have a special role in complex antitrust and consumer

---

[1] Would we accept trial before a federal district judge who had already announced that he or she had "reason to believe" that the law had been violated, directed the United States Attorney to proceed with prosecution and then controlled the expenditure of funds — determining what resources will be put behind the effort? We disqualify judges for far less. If we take the FTC's adjudicative role seriously (and if we see it as an increasingly serious function in the future) we should not accept that arrangement at the FTC. Of course, the principle that it is possible for a dual functioning prosecutor-adjudicator to navigate the waters without going aground on the shoals of due process is established by precedent. One must also acknowledge, at the outset, that despite comments which surface from time to time concerning the unseemliness of the dual prosecutor-adjudicator role there is no basis for asserting that it has led to actual demonstrable due process violations in the course of the Commission's work. But successful navigations of a rock-strewn course do not make the route "superior", especially when it is relatively easy to chart a different course which avoids any perception of impropriety and which hold the promise for improved performance.

protection issues if we expect the FTC to function as an adjudicator of serious (and hotly debated) issues; if we expect it to function by using expertise to focus and guide adversary inquiry; and if we expect the FTC to carefully articulate the scope and rationale of its decisions, we should give those who carry out these functions an organizational structure which confers the same degree of status and respect as is accorded others who discharge similar functions. The principle that "form follows function" applies beyond architecture. It is a salutary rule for organizing government.

The focus of those who see no need for a change is that the FTC's past performance in a dual role has been acceptable — that given delay, turnover in personnel and the fact that a significant percentage of the fully- adjudicated antitrust complaints are dismissed at the Commission level, the dual role has not been a problem. But this fails to address what ought to be a far more crucial issue; *viz.*, is the dual role the best model for the future performance which we expect from the FTC?

The issue is not the "appearance of unfairness" or the "possibility of impropriety". It is the prospect of achieving enhanced expertise and more focused public policy development appropriate to an agency which we expect to address issues on the "cutting edge" of antitrust and consumer protection. We want a future FTC to specialize in applying the Rule of Reason in cases where the analysis is less than certain; we want it to become involved in matters which require detailed understanding of industry segments or where the focus may be on balancing of competing public policy concerns; and we expect the caseload to involve evaluation of novel legal theory. These goals can best be achieved by establishing a new organizational format: a "Court of the Federal Trade Commission" consisting of three FTC judges who will serve for set terms (staggered to maintain continuity) and a separate Federal Trade Commission Directorate, consisting of an overall Director and Deputy Directors for Competition Policy and Consumer Affairs, serving as Presidential appointees in the same manner as the leadership of the Department of Justice.

A. *The FTC Directorate*

Case selection and refinement (at both the investigation and the complaint stage); analysis of advocacy options (including studies, promulgations of guides and rulemaking) and management of an investigative and prosecutorial staff each involve significant public policy issues calling for high-level personnel. The men and women charged with this responsibility ought to be selected for their abilities in these specific areas. Thereafter, their exclusive focus should be toward doing the best possible job in these tasks. They should know that they will be judged by their successes (or failures) in these responsibilities.

Moreover, unlike those who judge, they are entitled to be (indeed, obligated to be) advocates for the public policy positions of the then-incumbent Administration. The public debate on matters such as the contours of resale price maintenance; the competitive effects of certain types of price discrimination; or the actual impact of advertising restrictions on provision of consumer information and price levels should be vigorous, open and intense. These are not functions which are properly discharged by those who will sit in judgment in adversary proceedings.

Once an adjudicative proceeding is going to commence (if not before), the prosecutorial staff is entitled to full support of (and control from) its own top management — an objective which can hardly be enhanced when, *e.g.*, the staff must proceed with an action in the face of a 3-2 vote in which the FTC Chairman and an influential commissioner are opposed to prosecution. There are also key judgments to be made as an adjudicative proceeding develops — not the least of which is the refinement or dismissal of all or part of the complaint. Again, these are policy judgments which ought to be made by top management on an ongoing basis, before a "big" case becomes unmanageable or unduly protracted. The dual prosecutor-adjudicator role does not lend itself to this kind of detailed ongoing supervision.

A position as "Director of the Federal Trade Commission" will be undeniably attractive to a senior-level practitioner. The deputy appointments ("Deputy Director for Competition Policy" and "Deputy Director for Consumer Affairs") would also be attractive high-profile leadership positions. The net result should be an investigative/prosecutorial organization that attracts talent at high levels and can attract and maintain talent at lower levels; investigatory and prosecutorial leadership that will be judged by the nature, quality and efficiency of its actions and policies in those areas; and an agency which is capable of maintaining that role on an ongoing basis.

B. *The Court of the Federal Trade Commission*

The case for judges of a "Court of the Federal Trade Commission" is similar. If the adjudicative docket of the FTC is composed of significant matters such as those recommended by the Commission (and described above), we should seek out economically sophisticated and procedurally sophisticated adjudicators equal to the task. Those who are charged with deciding those kinds of issues ought to be selected because they have those abilities and because they are willing to devote their full efforts toward developing and improving a decision-making process appropriate to the blend of law and economics which is involved. That, to my mind, is the expertise which we seek.

Historically, the dual-function Commission has lagged *behind* the federal courts in developing techniques for complex cases. One thinks it should be the other way 'round, particularly when it comes to adjudicative proceedings involving economic and legal issues which are intellectually complex and precedentially significant. There should be a substantial opportunity for FTC judges to develop procedural techniques which will avoid protracted litigation and channel adversary inquiry so that it focuses on evidence which is truly probative. Indeed it would seem that the potential for innovation and flexibility should be greater in FTC adjudication than in federal district courts where certain procedural devices may not be appropriate given the variety of types of general civil litigation and where many adjudicators do not have a specialized background in economically-linked questions.

Today, however, examples of innovation and flexibility are more often found in federal district court litigation: e.g., elimination in certain cases of the answer and interrogatory process as a means of framing issues; early summary disposition on issues framed by the Court; quick-look analysis; or the framing of a specific issue for a mini-trial leading to a factual/legal finding that serves as a foundation for further proceedings. One can see FTC Court adjudicators whose job is to focus on the adjudicative process fashioning novel procedures specifically appropriate to a particular case.[2]

In addition, the FTC today spends a substantial amount of time in federal district courts securing temporary restraining orders and other preliminary

relief pursuant to FTCA § 13(b). Of course, the Commission could hardly be permitted to authorize a complaint and then be authorized to give itself preliminary relief! Judges of a separate adjudicative unit, on the other hand, could hear and decide such questions (and possibly others).

Judges of a Court of the Federal Trade Commission, like other judges, will be looked to solely for *judicial* performance; the reasoned explication of principle and precedent, its application to facts and the development of procedures which appropriately lead to such determinations. The position would be particularly attractive to persons whose skills and interests are focused on the adjudicative process. The FTC Court might also be assigned a validation role in the rule-making process, hearing argument on the issue (if presented) of whether a rule provisionally adopted by the FTC Director after notice and hearing correctly states applicable law or meets due process requirements, and ruling accordingly.

If, on the other hand, the judges of the Court of the Federal Trade Commission do not enhance the agency's adjudicative process and do not reflect subject matter expertise beyond that achieved in federal district courts, then the adjudicative function at the Commission should be studied further. While I do not think that will be the case, if, after seeking out and gaining the full-time efforts persons who wish to focus on the judicial function in matters coming before the FTC, it appears that there is no differentiatable judicial function to be performed (i.e., if FTC adjudication offers no benefit which cannot be achieved through federal district court litigation), it is appropriate to consider whether the organizational form ought to be adjusted further. We should not avoid the obligation to consider whether change is desirable, then or now.

---

[2] For example, it is possible for an adjudicator who has not previously considered issue a complaint and has no responsibility to the staff initiating it to review a complaint, to hear the theoretical bases for the allegations on a preliminary basis and suggest that the legal sufficiency of the theory should be tested (and resolved) preliminarily or that specific factual issues should be severed and made the subject of a focused evidentiary hearing before an Administrative Law Judge who would report to the Court (as opposed to authorizing plenary ALJ proceedings) or that a procedure for a "quick look" at key questions should be employed. There may be (indeed, I suspect, there are) cases in which certain issues are best probed in a manner other than the traditional "witness-opposing witness: direct examination/cross examination" process. Judges can introduce these procedures; dual prosecutor-adjudicators do not (and, in light of due process considerations, most likely cannot).

About the Editors

Patrick E. Murphy is professor of marketing in the College of Business Administration at the University of Notre Dame. Dr. Murphy currently serves as editor of the *Journal of Public Policy & Marketing,* a scholarly journal devoted to examining public policy issues in marketing. He is a former vice-president of Marketing Education and president of the Milwaukee chapter of the American Marketing Association. He also is a member of the editorial boards of the *Journal of Marketing* and *Journal of Macromarketing.* His research interests center on ethical, societal, public policy, and managerial issues facing corporations and nonprofit organizations. He is a coauthor (with Gene R. Laczniak) of a forthcoming book— *The Higher Road: A Path to Ethical Marketing Decisions* (Allyn & Bacon, 1992).

Dr. Murphy received his B.B.A. from the University of Notre Dame, an M.B.A. from Bradley University, and Ph.D. from the University of Houston. His previous faculty appointment was at Marquette University, where he also served as chairman of the Marketing Department. While at the Federal Trade Commission, he was a member of the Office of Management Planning in the Bureau of Consumer Protection. He now resides in Granger, Indiana, with his wife Kate and three sons (Bobby, Brendan, and Jamie).

William L. Wilkie is the Aloysius and Eleanor Nathe Professor of Marketing at the University of Notre Dame. Dr. Wilkie has served as president of the Association for Consumer Research, an international professional group with members in twenty-six nations around the world. He has also served as a member of the editorial boards of the *Journal of Consumer Research, Journal of Marketing, Journal of Marketing Research, Journal of Public Policy & Marketing,* and the *Journal of International Consumer Marketing.* Dr. Wilkie's research in marketing and consumer behavior has received a number of awards and recognitions. He is listed in *Who's Who in America.* He has been recognized as one of the most-cited authors in the field of marketing; one of his articles has been named a "Citation Classic in the Social Sciences" by the Institute for Scientific Information.

Dr. Wilkie received his undergraduate degree from the University of Notre Dame, and his M.B.A. and Ph.D. degrees from Stanford University. Prior to joining Notre Dame's faculty, he served as an in-house consultant to the FTC, as a research professor at the Marketing Science Institute in Cambridge, Massachusetts, and as a faculty member at Purdue University, Harvard University, and the University of Florida. He now lives in South Bend with his wife, Barbara; three children, Billy, Allie, and Jimmy; and dog, Blaze.

Index of Authors Cited

Index